Taxonomies of Human Performance
THE DESCRIPTION OF HUMAN TASKS

TAXONOMIES OF HUMAN PERFORMANCE

PERFORMANCE

THE DESCRIPTION OF HUMAN TASKS

EDWIN A. FLEISHMAN

Advanced Research Resources Organization
Washington, D.C.

MARILYN K. QUAINTANCE

Advanced Research Resources Organization
Washington, D.C.

with the assistance of
LAURIE A. BROEDLING

United States Navy Personnel Research and Development Center
San Diego, California

1984

ACADEMIC PRESS, INC.
Harcourt Brace Jovanovich, Publishers
Orlando   San Diego   New York
Austin   Boston   London   Sydney
Tokyo   Toronto

ACADEMIC PRESS, INC.
Orlando, Florida 32887

United Kingdom Edition published by
ACADEMIC PRESS, INC. (LONDON) LTD.
24/28 Oval Road, London NW1 7DX

LIBRARY OF CONGRESS CATALOG CARD NUMBER: 84-70594
ISBN 0-12-260450-4

PRINTED IN THE UNITED STATES OF AMERICA

87   9 8 7 6 5 4 3 2

Contents

Preface

For many years, my colleagues and I have been concerned with taxonomic issues in psychology. In particular, we have been interested in methods of classifying tasks that people perform in ways that might tie together several areas of basic and applied psychology. Thus, we study the effects on task performance of different training methods, environments, conditions of work, attitudinal factors, and individual differences in abilities. Vast quantities of data have been accumulated from these studies. However, it has been difficult to apply the accumulated data and experience of the past to new situations and tasks in the absence of a taxonomy of human performance. It is indeed surprising that more attempts have not been made to conceptualize and classify the variables associated with the kinds of *tasks* that people perform.

There is a problem not only with generalizing principles from one area of application to another, but also with generalizing findings from laboratory tasks to operational tasks. Tasks selected in laboratory research are rarely based on any clear rationale about the class of task or skill represented. One reason why much current research on learning in the experimental laboratory is difficult to apply to real-life training situations is the absence of information on the relevant common task dimensions. This is also true, of course, for laboratory studies of the effects of environmental factors, drugs, and other variables.

This book reviews recent efforts to grapple with taxonomic issues. Some of the material is based on a research program at the American Institutes for Research, for which I was Principal Investigator. The book updates the work carried out in this program and integrates it with recent related research. The program attempted to develop and evaluate systems for describing and classifying tasks that could improve generalization of research results about human performance.

The objective was to develop theoretically based language systems (*taxonomies*) that, when merged with appropriate sets of decision logic and appropriate sets of quantitative data, might be used to improve predictions about human performance. We believed that progress toward a common task-descriptive language would help to integrate the human-performance research literature. This effort also represents one of the few attempts to bridge the gap between basic research on human performance and the applications of this research to the real world of decisions. The assumption was that the world of human tasks is not impossibly diverse and that common task dimensions that allow improved predictions of human performance on these tasks can be identified.

To provide a foundation for the program, considerable conceptual and methodological development was necessary, bringing together ideas from such diverse fields as job and task analysis, experimental psychology, human factors technology, and differential psychology. All these, in one form or another, are concerned with the specification of performance functions required in human tasks. However, lack of communication across these fields has caused problems in generalizing results. One of the first steps in our project was to bring together staff representing diverse fields of interest to assist in resolving differences in approaches, methods, and terminology. Because each field has developed a specialized vocabulary, severe problems of communication were encountered during the early phases of the project. However, with continued participation, discussion, and common review of salient reports and articles, many communications problems were resolved and many differences turned out to be more apparent than real.

Some of the results of this program have appeared in technical reports and in journal articles. However, prior to this book, much of the work has not been available to a wider audience. In addition, some of the thinking generated in this work would be lost unless integrated in the context of the total program. The nature of the program made for some unevenness in the development of different avenues and approaches. Funding curtailments and some redirection of priorities by sponsors also caused certain shifts in emphasis. In this book professionals and students in the field will see the false leads and aborted efforts, as well as the efforts that received further development. We hope that some of the ideas not fully developed can be picked up later, and that the book will help other researchers avoid treacherous paths in the future.

Acknowledgments

The book updates and extends earlier work initiated as a basic research effort under a contract funded by the Advanced Research Projects Agency of the Department of Defense. The program, called the Taxonomy Project, was originally to be a 5-year developmental effort, but funding constraints limited it, as originally conceived, to 3 years. During this time, the Air Force Office of Scientific Research was the cognizant agency. An additional period, sponsored by the U.S. Army Research Institute for the Behavioral and Social Sciences, allowed certain major threads of the program to be brought to some conclusion.

During the Taxonomy Project there was also considerable consultation with prominent investigators and experts in different fields, who in one way or another had been involved in work relevant to taxonomic issues. I am grateful to the following individuals for the time taken to discuss these issues with us:

Dr. Earl A. Alluisi, now at the Air Force Human Resources Laboratory, who is identified with one of the major attempts to develop analytical measures of component human performances and has developed a battery of tasks around this classification.

Dr. Robert M. Gagné, at Florida State University, who has long been associated with attempts to cast information about tasks into a limited number of human functions and who, in his book, *The Conditions of Learning*, discusses "general" categories based on a hierarchical classification system.

Dr. Robert B. Miller, of IBM, who is known for this pioneering work in the development of task analysis and classification methods and the analysis and specification of performance requirements for training. Dr. Miller later became a participant in the project.

Dr. Warren Teichner, who, under a NASA project, was concerned with the classification of environmental variables in terms of physiological and performance effects. Dr. Teichner later became a member of the project staff.

Drs. John E. Taylor, Wayne Fox, and Ernest Montague, then at HumRRO, Monterey, who have developed experimental tasks utilizing Gagné's categories for testing the interaction of learning methods and ability level for Army personnel.

Drs. Robert White, Ruth Ginsberg, and Calvin W. Thomson, San Jose State University, who were involved in an Air Force sponsored project attempting to classify the results of learning studies in order to derive generalized principles.

Drs. Donald F. Haggard and Elmo E. Miller, then at HumRRO, Fort Knox, Kentucky, who worked on taxonomic models of skilled performance, the former emphasizing structural issues and the latter concentrating on response processes as a basis for classification.

Drs. J. P. Guilford and Ralph Hoepfner, then at the University of Southern California, who have long been recognized for their pioneering and extensive factor-analytic research on intellectual abilities.

Dr. Lois L. Elliott, now at Northwestern University, who has carried out research on the dimensions of perceptual performance.

Dr. Sidney A. Fine, now at Advanced Research Resources Organization, who was largely responsible for the trait rating system used at the United States Employment Service, and for the development of "Functional Job Analysis."

Dr. Raymond E. Christal, Air Force Human Resources Laboratory, an innovator of the job analysis system used in the Air Force providing a task-level, computer-compatible system.

Dr. James W. Altman, now at Synectics Corporation, who has worked extensively on problems of task and training analysis, systems design, and the dimensional problems of vocational job performance.

Dr. Kasten Talmadge, now at RMC Research Corporation, who has directed projects under Navy sponsorship concerned with classifying learning styles and task design factors relating to learning effectiveness.

Dr. Lawrence E. Reed, Air Force Human Resources Laboratory, who has been involved in extensive work on the computerization of task analysis data.

These consultations reinforced the view of a need for a human performance taxonomy linking basic and applied areas. Different investigators had approached the problem from different angles, often tangentially and frequently with the narrow focus of a specific substantive area of interest. There was evident dissatisfaction with current progress and with the limited scope of previous efforts. It was also apparent that previous attempts at developing classificatory schemes had not reached the stage at which their utility could be tested; quite often they had even failed to produce systems that would lend themselves to such testing. These discussions were extremely useful in pointing up the difficulties that would have to be faced in developing a taxonomy.

Grateful acknowledgment is made for the contributions of individuals who were members of the project staff during some phase of the project's existence: William J. Baker, Armand N. Chambers, Charles A. Darby, Alfred J. Farina, Jr., Robert G. Kinkade, Arthur L. Korotkin, Marjorie J. Krebs, Jerrold M. Levine, Robert M. Miller, Tania Romashko, Robert W. Stephenson, Warren H. Teichner, George C. Theologus, Harold P. Van Cott, and George R. Wheaton. This book would not have been possible without them. Additional specific acknowledgments of their contributions are made in the following pages and in the references to the original reports.

I am particularly indebted to Dr. W. Cody Wilson, who was director of the Behavioral Science Division of the Advanced Research Projects Agency at the time the project was initiated, as well as to Dr. George H. Lawrence, who succeeded him, and to Dr. Glen Finch in the Air Force Office of Scientific Research, who provided valuable support. Special appreciation is given to Dr. Julius G. Uhlaner, then Technical Director of the Army Research Institute for the Behavioral and Social Sciences, for his continued support throughout the project.

This book integrates considerable work carried out by my colleagues and me under various sponsors over many years. In addition to the foregoing agencies, these include the National Science Foundation, the National Aeronautics and Space Agency, the Army Surgeon General's Office, the National Institutes of Health, a number of state and local governmental agencies, and several industrial organizations.

This volume would not have existed without the encouragement and assistance of a number of individuals and agencies. The book was prepared under Contract N0014-76-C-0285 from the Office of Naval Research (ONR). Contributing sponsors also included the Army Research Institute (ARI) and the Air Force Office of Scientific Research (AFOSR). Thanks are due Dr. Glenn L. Bryan, then head of the Psychological Sciences Division; Dr. Marshall J. Farr, director, and Dr. Joseph L. Young, then assistant director, of the Personnel and Training Research Programs at ONR; Dr. Uhlaner, Dr. Joseph Zeidner, and Dr. Robert M. Sasmor at ARI; and Dr. Charles Hutchinson, former director of the Behavioral Sciences Directorate, AFOSR, and Dr. Alfred R. Fregly, the current director.

I also thank Dr. Lyman W. Porter, Dean of the Graduate School of Administration, for providing a congenial atmosphere for writing the first draft of the book during my appointment as Visiting Professor at the University of California, Irvine. The completion of this book was made possible by the support received from the Advanced Research Resources Organization (ARRO), a division of Response Analysis Corporation. At ARRO, Dr. Michael Mumford made valuable contributions to sections of Chapters 4 and 14, and Rick Sample provided essential literature search and retrieval assistance. Nancy Wertheimer and Ruth Bruns at ARRO were particularly helpful in getting the final manuscript in shape, while mastering the mysteries of the word processor.

I am pleased to acknowledge the contributions of Dr. Laurie A. Broedling, who provided valuable assistance in an early draft of the book and was the primary author of the chapter on Data Bases and Taxonomic Development. I am particularly grateful to Dr. Marilyn K. Quaintance for the scholarship and dedication that helped bring this effort to fruition.

Edwin A. Fleishman

Note on JSAS References

Throughout this volume references are made to the *JSAS Catalog of Selected Documents in Psychology*. The citation includes the year, inclusive pages of the abstract of the report, and the number for retrieval of the complete report (Ms. No.). These references allow the reader to obtain copies of reports that may no longer be available in the original technical report series. Reports thus cited may be obtained from the American Psychological Association, 1200 Seventeenth Street, Washington, D.C. 20036

Taxonomies of Human Performance
THE DESCRIPTION OF HUMAN TASKS

CHAPTER 1

The Need for Taxonomic Development in the Field of Human Performance

Tasks are pervasive in everyday life, representing the context and focus of much of human behavior. Factors affecting individual performance on tasks are the subject of study in the psychological laboratory, in educational settings, and in the work place. In particular, much of our research in the behavioral sciences is concerned with factors affecting human performance. For example, we may study the effects on task performance of different learning conditions or training methods, different physical and social environments, different motivational and attitudinal factors, or individual differences in abilities.

There is a need to conceptualize tasks and their characteristics to resolve central problems in the study of human behavior. If we are going to generalize about conditions affecting human performance, it is necessary to consider the properties of tasks as important constructs in psychological research and theory as well as in our conceptions of human work and achievement. Such constructs may help to address many common concerns in basic and applied psychology and to integrate concepts and research in a number of seemingly diverse fields.

Surprisingly, there have not been many attempts to conceptualize and classify the variables associated with the kinds of tasks that people perform. This book is an attempt to do so. Specifically, the book describes and evaluates some taxonomic efforts to develop classificatory systems for describing human task performance. The objectives of such systems, their role in scientific development, and their practical implications are discussed. Emphasis is on the conceptual and methodological issues in taxonomic development and on the cri-

1

teria for the evaluation of classificatory systems. Recent taxonomic efforts in other areas of psychology (e.g., personality, conditioning, team and organizational behavior) are discussed; however, the emphasis throughout the book is on the description of classificatory systems involving the behavior of individuals performing human tasks.

Problems in Human Performance Research and Application

The lack of effort in developing uniform conceptions, definitions, and categories of different human performances is surprising in view of the need to make more effective use of behavioral data generated by human performance research. This need is intensified as more research is conducted and the available body of information on factors affecting human performance grows. In particular, better ways are needed to generalize research findings from laboratory studies to operational settings, from one experimental study to another, and from one operational situation to another. There are serious limitations on the extent to which we have been able to do this in the human performance area. Tasks selected in laboratory research often are not based on any clear rationale about the class of task or skill represented. This absence of information on the relevant common task dimensions is one reason why much current laboratory research on factors affecting human performance (e.g., stress, noise) has resulted in vast amounts of data with few principles extrapolated from such research to human performance in real-world tasks. Research on learning, conducted in the experimental laboratory, is difficult to apply to real-life training situations. This is also true for laboratory studies of the effects of environmental factors, drugs, and other variables. As a result, it is difficult for those in operational settings to make predictions about factors affecting human performance from knowledge of the performance research literature. Similarly, it has been difficult for behavioral scientists to develop general principles about factors affecting human performance that can serve as a basis for further theoretical and scientific development.

The absence of a generally accepted set of unifying concepts for the systematic description and prediction of human behavior is a major problem confronting behavioral scientists in basic and applied fields. Lacking an organizing framework, experimentalist and technologist alike find generalization, communication, and application of research findings to be difficult. The behavioral scientist sifts through seemingly unrelated masses of data in search of even a rudimentary theory of behavior. The behavioral technologist struggles with the application of an ostensibly unlimited number of principles. Thus, neither the scientist nor the technologist is able consistently and systematically to relate his or her results to those from previous studies, to "similar" situations with which he or she has yet to deal, or to the findings of researchers and technologists working on allied problems. The state of affairs argues strongly for a mechanism to provide the needed structuring. More specifically, psychologists must provide organization by coming to grips with the complex taxonomic problems of their discipline.

A number of psychologists have recognized the need for development of a set of concepts that might help us make more dependable generalizations of research results to new tasks (e.g., Fleishman, 1967b; Gagné, 1965; Melton, 1964). The essential problem is the need to generalize the effect of some training, environmental, or procedural condition, from the knowledge of its effect on one task to its probable effect on some other task. What has been lacking, it is felt, is a system for classifying such tasks that would lead to improved generalizations and predictions about how such factors affect human performance (Fleishman, 1982). In essence, what is needed is a learning and performance theory that ascribes a central role to task dimensions.

A major problem that limits generalization of research results has been the absence of a unifying set of dimensions that could relate the human performance observed in one task situation to new situations. Many categories in common use (e.g., "cognitive," "motor," "perceptual," "problem solving," "information processing") turn out to be too general, whereas the detailed job elements derived from task analysis (e.g., "rotates knob control") seem too specific. We need a more useful taxonomy of human performance to serve as a basis for describing human tasks.

Although many of these issues are as old as psychology itself, they have been especially disconcerting since World War II, the time when engineering psychology began to emerge as a discipline (see Grether, 1968). The engineering psychologist views human performance within a "human–machine system" context. The goal is to optimize system performance through careful allocation of functions to humans and to machines. This goal is achieved through the design of equipment compatible with human capacities and limitations, the selection of personnel to match human abilities with task requirements, and the training of personnel in task performance. As new systems have been developed, vast amounts of descriptive material about human performance in these systems have been generated. However, past experience has provided few rigorous guidelines for determining the applicability of previously acquired data to new systems. In other words, both the principles of human–machine system design and the rules for their application are lacking. Without an adequate system for the classification of human task performance, it is especially difficult to organize and apply the results of behavioral research to the solution of applied problems.

A taxonomic system for classifying task variables could aid in bridging the gap between basic research and applications by (1) eliminating redundant terms, (2) disclosing similarities and differences between "operations" in the laboratory and the applied world as well as between various subject matter areas within research (Verplanck, 1968), and (3) alerting behavioral scientists to possible sources of variance that may contaminate or even negate their research findings in the operational setting.

Earlier, a number of prominent behavioral scientists in basic as well as applied fields have recognized these problems. For example, Melton and Briggs (1960) were prompted to write in the *Annual Review of Psychology:*

> It is clear to those working in the area of engineering psychology, and it should become clear to others, that this vigorous and expanding universe of knowledge has semantic and taxonomic problems which have not been overcome. Nor can they be overcome in any stable way by the ingenuity of organizers of its literature. The roots of these difficulties are many, not the least being the semantic and taxonomic problems of experimental psychology. Foremost among deficiencies of this type is the lack of taxonomies of tasks or skills [p. 89].

Paul Fitts (1962), writing in the book *Training Research and Education* (Glaser, 1962), stated the issue in a learning context:

> The importance of an adequate taxonomy for skilled tasks is widely recognized in all areas of psychological theorizing today. A taxonomy should identify important correlates of learning rates, performance level, and individual differences. It should be equally applicable to laboratory tasks and to tasks encountered in industry and in military service [p. 178].

And Robert B. Miller (1962), in the same volume, writes:

> It is unfortunate that psychologists lack a behavioral taxonomy which is related to the generalization of characteristics of task performance. Such a taxonomy would enable the task analyst and training designer to find a common ground in the psychological research literature [p. 57].

Similar points have been made in a variety of contexts by others, such as Altman (1964); Cotterman (1959); Eckstrand (1964); Fleishman (1962, 1967a, 1975); Gagné (1965); Ginsberg, McCullers, Merryman, Thomson, and Whitte (1966); Hackman (1968); Haggard (1963); Sells (1963); Silverman (1967); and Stolurow (1964). Implicit in these earlier calls for taxonomic systems were requirements for statements of their purpose, operational utility, and criteria for their evaluation. In spite of these earlier expressions of concern, until recently few systematic attempts at taxonomic development have been undertaken.

Usefulness of a Human Performance Taxonomy

A taxonomy of human performance has important practical and scientific implications in a variety of fields of interest as well as to state-of-the-art questions. In fact, a number of ostensibly disparate problems are drawn together and can be viewed in a new light by the application of such a taxonomy. These can be divided into the scientific–theoretical benefits and the applied–practical benefits. These will be elaborated upon in later chapters, but an overview is provided here.

SCIENTIFIC–THEORETICAL BENEFITS

Among the most important scientific areas of usefulness are the following:

1. *Conducting literature reviews.* Psychologists' first encounters with classification take place when they try to locate literature relevant to their research problems. They are then faced with the difficulty of locating and matching descriptors of human task performance in the literature with their own particular terminology. Are their variables the same ones that other scientists have employed? Do they represent the same class of human performances? After completing their research, the experimenters will again confront the same problems of semantics and measurement in relating the results of their experiments back to a body of experimental or theoretical knowledge.

2. *Establishing better bases for conducting and reporting research studies to facilitate their comparison.* A comprehensive classificatory system should aid in disclosing the reasons why studies can or cannot

be compared. Although it may be quite some time before such a perfected system is available, in the interim, a taxonomic system could at least provide some guidelines for improving the conduct and reporting of research.

3. *Standardizing laboratory methods for studying human performance.* A critical problem in the experimental study of factors affecting human performance is the lack of standard tasks and measures that make it possible to compare results from various laboratories. The experimenter often selects a laboratory task without a clear rationale regarding the category of human performance and associated skills represented. One spinoff from research on taxonomic questions can be the specification of standardized tasks that are diagnostic and reliable measures of defined human functions (e.g., Fleishman, 1960).

4. *Generalizing research to new tasks.* A human performance taxonomy should assist in extrapolating from previously attained research results to new tasks. For example, the effect of a given environmental factor, such as high temperature, on performance of Task A may be known, but will this hold for Task B or Task C? A useful taxonomy would tell us if these tasks are in the same or different categories, as a basis for generalizing from Task A to the other tasks in the same category.

5. *Exposing gaps in knowledge.* At the general scientific level, a taxonomy can help expose gaps in the body of knowledge regarding human performance. By delineating categories and subcategories of human performance, a taxonomy makes much more evident where extensive research has been done, and conversely, where it has not been done.

6. *Assisting in theory development.* There are many points at which taxonomic development supports theory development. The success of a theory primarily depends upon how satisfactorily the theory can organize the observational data of the science. Although theories have various classification requirements depending on their type and stage of development, an adequate classificatory system seems a prerequisite to the ultimate establishment of quantitative relationships. In developing theories about human performance, we need concepts that will help us to classify these performances.

More recent efforts, notably those by Glass (1976, 1977; Glass, McGraw, & Smith, 1981), Schmidt (1980), Hunter (1979) and Hunter and Schmidt (1978), attempt to deal with some of the quantitative issues involved in cumulating findings across research studies. Similarly, cognitive psychologists such as Sternberg (1977), Carroll

(1980), Hunt (1976), and others have become increasingly aware of the need for attention to methods of categorizing human performances. Stevenson (1972) has also highlighted a number of these scientific issues working in the context of social–genetic influences on child development. Stevenson reviews some typical experiments in developmental psychology, and gives examples of tasks selected to study the influence of (1) preschool attendance on intellectual functioning; (2) verbalization on learning; and (3) anxiety on performance. The leaps from the tasks examined to the generalizations and theoretical positions taken are enormous, as are the difficulties in reconciling discrepant results across studies. Stevenson documents the need for a taxonomy of tasks in this area, indicating the need to be at least as attentive to the sampling of tasks as we are to the sampling of subjects.

APPLIED–PRACTICAL BENEFITS

The ways in which a taxonomy would be useful in applied and practical areas of human performance include the following:

1. *Job definition and job analysis.* In our rapidly changing society, jobs are continually being eliminated or altered, and new ones generated. To make a determination regarding the training and/or selection requirements needed to produce effective job incumbents, one could use a taxonomy to analyze the task performances involved in a new (or altered) job. A taxonomic system utilizing appropriate general descriptors can help establish the similarity of new and different jobs and can group jobs into families having similar personnel requirements. Pearlman's (1980) review of the development of job families came to this conclusion and offers some useful guidelines.

2. *Human–machine system design.* The planning and allocation of functions to people and machines requires the making of decisions about human performance. An important input to such decisions should be the category of performance with which one is dealing, and the categories of the various factors that can affect that performance. This information requires translation from human performance terms (e.g., "visual acuity") to design-relevant terms (e.g., "size of characters on display").

3. *Personnel selection, placement, and human resource planning.* When system design has progressed to the point at which the human resource requirements have been reasonably well established, the need arises for locating and assigning personnel to the new system. In order to effect the most suitable match of people to jobs, data about

the task dimensions of the job and about the characteristics of personnel must be available. A useful taxonomic system would include concepts linking the characteristics of job tasks, their performance requirements, and the capacities measured by selection tests. The need for such linkages has been recognized by Dunnette (1966; see Campbell, Dunnette, Lawler, & Weick, 1970) who incorporated them into a model for test validation and selection research. Some attempts to develop task and job classificatory systems for the purpose of supporting organizational human-resources planning systems have been reviewed by Milkovich and Mahoney (1978) and Dunnette, Hough, and Rosse (1979).

4. *Training.* The first problem that training specialists face is obtaining sufficient task-descriptive data in a form that will permit them to design and conduct their training courses. They must know the procedures the person is expected to follow, the equipment and tools required, and the conditions of the job. Additionally, they must know what constitutes an acceptable level of job performance. These data may be system specific. Application of the principles of learning to training would appear desirable, for example, but it is quite difficult in practice because there is insufficient information about the categories of human task performance within which different training methods are effective. The problem is one of developing a classificatory system that will match those training techniques found effective with particular categories of tasks and associated skills. The work of Gagné (1965) and Miller (1962) is particularly relevant here.

5. *Performance measurement and enhancement.* Many investigators have recognized the need for standards of human performance that can serve as points of reference for the effects of experimental variables and program interventions. Such standards can serve as an indication of performance enhancement as a function of the interventions. Measurement of human performance also enters into such inadequately solved problems as the assessment of training outcomes, the evaluation of human–machine system performance, and the appraisal of job performance. For all these purposes, the development of a taxonomy of human task performance would provide the foundation for new, valuable measurement techniques.

6. *Development of retrieval systems and data bases.* An entire field of information science has been developed, with associated computer systems for the storage and rapid search and retrieval of scientific information. The efficiency and utility of such systems could be enhanced if the information about factors affecting human performance

were indexed according to the class of human performance involved. A taxonomic system for doing this would aid not only in the efficient retrieval of documents, but also in the development of systems for integrating, updating, and summarizing data about classes of human performance. Modern computer technology and information science, merged with newer taxonomic concepts, has tremendous potential.

These various possible uses for taxonomies of human task performance are not mutually exclusive, of course, and the reader will think of others. The distinctions between the basic and applied uses are artificial, and they overlap as well. However, having presented these uses we can see the diverse implications of scientific development in this area, as well as the potential contributions to theoretical and applied problems. The applications described for taxonomic systems provide a set of objectives to guide future taxonomic development and offer a set of criteria against which the utility of future taxonomic development can be assessed.

Objectives of the Book

It is only recently that concerted efforts have been made to explore more intensively some of the issues and alternatives in taxonomic development in psychology and to proceed on an empirical basis in the evaluation of these alternatives. This book describes some of these recent attempts along these lines and evaluates their contributions to the taxonomic state of the art in different areas of human performance research.

Although a number of developments are reviewed, considerable attention is given to a research program conducted by Edwin A. Fleishman and his colleagues, referred to throughout this book as the *Taxonomy Project*. This program attempted to develop and evaluate systems for describing and classifying tasks to improve generalization of research results about human performance. The objective was to develop theoretically based language systems (taxonomies) that, when merged with appropriate sets of decision logic and appropriate sets of quantitative data, might be used to improve predictions and generalizations about human performance. It was hoped that progress toward a common task-descriptive language would help to integrate the human performance research literature and allow better communication between researchers and individuals who need to apply research to practical problems. The assumption was that the world of human tasks is not impossibly diverse, thus enabling the identification of common task dimensions that would allow improved predictions of human performance on these tasks. The effort represents one of the few attempts to find ways to bridge the gap between basic research on human performance and the applications of that research to the real world of human decisions.

OVERVIEW OF THE TAXONOMY PROJECT

To provide a conceptual and methodological foundation for the Taxonomy Project, colleagues and ideas were brought together from diverse fields of interest, such as experimental psychology, differential psychology, industrial psychology (specifically job and task analysis), and human factors. All these disciplines are concerned in one form or another with the specification of performance functions required in human tasks. However, little communication has occurred across these fields, presenting one of the problems of generalizing results from one area to another. Because each field has developed a specialized vocabulary, severe problems of communication were encountered during the early phases of the work. However, with continued participation, discussion, and common review of salient reports and articles, many communications problems were resolved and many differences turned out to be more apparent than real.

Early stages of the research program involved considerable conceptual work regarding the bases, purposes, and methods of classification in other sciences, as well as in behavioral science. Reviews of earlier related work indicated a variety of task-descriptive systems varying from highly detailed and specific task descriptors to the general categories frequently seen in the experimental literature (e.g., motor vs. cognitive skills). It was concluded that neither highly specific nor highly general categories are likely to be the most useful in generalizing principles across tasks.

There was also considerable consultation with prominent investigators and experts in these different fields who had been involved in work relevant to taxonomic issues. The literature reviews and consultations reinforced the need for a human performance taxonomy linking basic and applied areas. Different investigators have approached the problem from different angles, often tangentially and frequently with the narrow focus of a specific substantive area of interest. It also appeared evident that previous attempts at developing classificatory schemes did not reach the stage of testing their utility, nor, quite often, of producing a system that lends itself to such testing. In fact, it was found that no empirical evaluations had been made of the extent to which these various descriptive systems could improve prediction and generalization about factors affecting human performance. The early sections of this book draw on these reviews.

Next, the decision was made to develop a number of alternative taxonomic systems based upon different rationales about common factors in task performance. These approaches eventually developed into the Ability Requirements Approach, the Task Characteristics Approach, the Criterion Measures Approach, the Information–Theoretic Approach, and the Task Strategies Approach. Some of these approaches are essentially empirically inductive, whereas others involve testing of a priori theoretical formulations. The arguments for and against these various approaches, the initial literature integrations and consultations, and the preliminary conceptual development gradually convinced the program staff that more than one provisional approach was needed. The decision to set up more than one system may in retrospect appear obvious, but at the time it was an insight that provided a major advance toward the solution of some taxonomic problems. The book describes these different approaches and the status of taxonomic development using these and other methodologies.

In the development of all of the alternative classificatory systems, there were several primary considerations that were kept in mind; these were intended to enhance the quality of the resulting taxonomic systems and to correct the deficiencies in some of the taxonomic work done prior to this project. One such consideration was the need to translate some of these approaches into usable *measurement systems*. Some approaches did not reach this stage of development, but for at least one approach some relatively sophisticated measurement methods are described.

Major attention was also given to the development of *criteria* and *evaluative systems* for testing the reliability, validity, and utility of these approaches. For example, observer ratings, using scales based on the abilities taxonomy, have had some success in predicting empirical factor loadings as well as in predicting performance levels on tasks in various categories. In addition, the task characteristics approach has had some success in predicting performance levels on a variety of tasks.

A third consideration included defining the requirements for *data bases* to be used in evaluating the capabilities of the various taxonomic systems to integrate the experimental literature. The basic notion here was that a taxonomic system should be translatable into an indexing system that allows entry into the available literature so that the tasks used in a large variety of studies can be classified. The data contained within these task categories could then be examined for consistencies within classes and consistencies and inconsistencies between classes. To what extent do the various systems improve the kinds of generalizations that can be made about the performance effects of certain variables of interest? If such taxonomies could be developed, especially if they are made computer compatible, the possibilities for deriving principles of human performance would be greatly enhanced.

Considerable progress was made with respect to a number of these important taxonomic issues and some successful applications of classificatory systems to the human performance literature were achieved. This book describes the Taxonomy Project and integrates this work with other related developments in the field of human performance.

ORGANIZATION OF THE TEXT

Chapter 2 is an intensive look at the role of taxonomies in scientific development. The reader is given a review of the issues in the science of classification, including a discussion of the objectives, processes, and subject matter of classification. The role of classification in the development of other sciences is described, and the status of taxonomic development in biology is used as a prototype for comparison to highlight the issues faced in psychology. Early taxonomic efforts in psychology are described, with emphasis on concepts developed in the field of learning. The changing nature of categories used in the field of learning is instructive and has implications for general human performance taxonomies.

Chapters 3 and 4 deal with specific issues in classifying human performance. Past efforts are reviewed and the "state of the art" is assessed to provide procedural guidelines for future taxonomic efforts. Approaches to and dilemmas encountered in developing systems of classifying human task performance are discussed. Chapter 3 emphasizes conceptual issues of purpose and descriptive bases in terms of available alternatives. Different ways of defining and conceptualizing human tasks are described, with each way leading to different models and rationales for describing and classifying tasks. Chapter 4 emphasizes methodological issues in developing classificatory systems and presents criteria for evaluating the utility and validity of such systems.

Chapters 5 through 7 examine specific task or job descriptive systems developed by earlier investigators. Included in these reviews are schemes that employed such conceptual units as overt behaviors, functions, abilities, and task characteristics. These schemes are evaluated in terms of the criteria specified in earlier parts of the book.

Chapter 8 is concerned with both the role and the use of human performance data bases in taxonomic development. Such problems as indexing and classifying, formatting, search vocabulary, cross-referencing, and the needed technology are discussed. A prototype attempt to build a data base of previous research findings in several areas of human performance is described. The use of the data base for evaluating taxonomic systems is illustrated by such questions as: Are generalizations improved when the data on factors affecting human performance are reorganized according to different classes of tasks? Are new relations uncovered? Are better descriptions of functional relations provided?

The next several chapters describe some newer attempts at developing taxonomic systems for describing tasks.

Chapter 9 briefly describes a *criterion measures approach* that categorizes tasks in terms of dependent operator response measures. For example, one class of task performance called *switching* is defined by measures indicating the latency (or reaction time) of the operator's responses; another called *coding* is defined by the percentage of correct responses made; and a *searching* category is defined by probability of detection. There are subcategories for these types of broader categories.

Chapter 10 describes an *information–theoretic approach* based on a theoretical model that provides for a systems language common to tasks. Information processing is seen as the common denominator, in which a task is defined in terms of types of information transferred between sources and receivers. The types of descriptors used include classes of constraints on stimulus and response events, amount of redundancy, and types of relations between input and output.

Chapter 11 describes a *task strategies approach* that characterizes tasks in terms of discriminable task functions, task context, task environment, and level of learning. The approach lays out the terminology needed to interrelate these activities in accomplishing task goals. The emphasis is on categories that characterize the sequence of goal-directed transactions between the operator and the task environment. The types of terms used include *search, interpret, transmit, plan,* and *test.*

Chapter 12 describes the approach that has received the most development and most extensive evaluation. This is the *ability require-ments approach*, in which tasks are described in terms of the human capacities required to perform them effectively. The abilities on which the system is based were derived from empirical studies on the interrelationships among performances on a wide variety of tasks, including those in the sensory, cognitive, perceptual, motor, and physical performance areas.

Chapter 13 describes the *task characteristics approach*. The ap-proach classifies tasks in terms of descriptors that are independent of the characteristics of the human operator. The model developed characterizes tasks in terms of general components of goal, stimuli, responses, and their relations. Within these components, major com-ponents of a task are identified and treated as categories within which to devise task characteristic descriptors.

Chapter 14 provides a brief review of recent efforts at taxonomic development in other fields of psychology, including personality, so-cial, clinical, and educational psychology. Chapter 15 concludes with an overview and some implications for future research.

References

Altman, J. W. Improvements needed in a central store of human performance data. *Human Factors*, 1964, *6*(6), 681–686.

Campbell, J. P., Dunnette, M. D., Lawler, E. E., & Weick, K. E. *Managerial behavior, performance and effectiveness.* New York: McGraw-Hill, 1970.

Carroll, J. B. *Individual difference relations in psychometric and experimental cognitive tasks* (Rep. 163). Chapel Hill, NC: L.L. Thurstone Psychometric Laboratory, Uni-versity of North Carolina, April 1980.

Cotterman, T. E. *Task classification: An approach to partially ordering information on human learning* (WADC TN 58-374). Wright Patterson Air Force Base, OH: Wright Patterson Air Development Center, 1959.

Dunnette, M. D. *Personnel selection and placement.* Belmont, CA: Wadsworth, 1966.

Dunnette, M. D., Hough, L. M., & Rosse, R. L. Task and job taxonomies as a basis for identifying labor supply sources and evaluating employment qualifications. *Human Resource Planning*, 1979, *2*, 37–54.

Eckstrand, G. A. *Current status of the technology of training* (AMRL-TR64-86). Wright Patterson Air Force Base, OH: Aerospace Medical Division, September 1964.

Fitts, P. M. Factors in complex skill training. In R. Glaser (Ed.), *Training research and education.* Pittsburgh: University of Pittsburgh Press, 1962.

Fleishman, E. A. Psychomotor tests in drug research. In J. A. Miller & L. Uhr (Eds.), *Drugs and behavior.* New York: Wiley, 1960.

Fleishman, E. A. The description and prediction of perceptual-motor skill learning. In R. Glaser (Ed.), *Training research and education.* Pittsburgh: University of Pitts-burgh Press, 1962.

Fleishman, E. A. Development of a behavior taxonomy for describing human tasks: A correlation– experimental approach. *Journal of Applied Psychology*, 1967, *51*, 1–10. (a)

Fleishman, E. A. Performance assessment based on an empirically derived task taxonomy. *Human Factors*, 1967, *9*, 349–366. (b)

Fleishman, E. A. Toward a taxonomy of human performance. *American Psychologist*, 1975, *30*, 1127–1149.

Fleishman, E. A. Systems for describing human tasks. *American Psychologist*, 1982, *37*, 821–834.

Gagné, R. M. *The conditions of learning* (1st ed.). New York: Holt, Rinehart, & Winston, 1965.

Ginsburg, R., McCullers, J. C., Merryman, J. J., Thomson, C. W., & Whitte, R. S. *A review of efforts to organize information about human learning, transfer, and retention.* San Jose, CA: San Jose State College, 1966.

Glaser, R. (Ed.). *Training research and education.* Pittsburgh: University of Pittsburgh Press, 1962.

Glass, G. V. Primary, secondary and meta-analysis of research. *Educational Researcher*, 1976, *5*, 3–8.

Glass, G. V. Integrating findings: The meta-analysis of research. *Review of Research in Education*, 1977, *5*, 351–379.

Glass, G. V., McGraw, B., and Smith, M. L. *Meta-analysis in social research.* Beverly Hills, CA: Sage, 1981.

Grether, W. F. Engineering psychology in the United States. *American Psychologist*, 1968, *23*, 743–751.

Hackman, J. R. Tasks and task performance in research on stress. In J. E. McGrath (Ed.), *Social and psychological factors in stress.* New York: Holt, Rinehart, & Winston, 1968.

Haggard, D. F. *The feasibility of developing a task classification structure for ordering training principles and training content* (Research Memorandum). Fort Knox, KY: Human Resources Research Organization, 1963.

Hunt, E. B. Varieties of cognitive power. In L. B. Resnick (Ed.), *The nature of intelligence.* Hillsdale, NJ: Lawrence Erlbaum, 1976.

Hunter, J. E. *Cumulating results across studies: A critique of factor analysis, canonical correlation, MANOVA, and statistical significance testing.* Presented at the 86th Annual Convention of the American Psychological Association, New York, September 1979.

Hunter, J. E., & Schmidt, F. L. Differential and single group validity of employment tests by race: A critical analysis of three recent studies. *Journal of Applied Psychology*, 1978, *63*, 1–11.

Melton, A. W. The taxonomy of human learning: Overview. In A. W. Melton (Ed.), *Categories of human learning.* New York: Academic Press, 1964.

Melton, A. W., & Briggs, G. E. Engineering psychology. *Annual Review of Psychology*, 1960, *11*, 71–98.

Milkovich, G. T., & Mahoney, T. A. Human resource planning models: A perspective. *Human Resource Planning*, 1978, *1*, 19–30.

Miller, R. B. Analysis and specification of behavior for training. In R. Glaser (Ed.), *Training research and education.* Pittsburgh: University of Pittsburgh Press, 1962.

Pearlman, K. Job families: A review and discussion of their implications for personnel selection. *Psychological Bulletin*, 1980, *87*, 1–27.

Schmidt, F. L. *The research tasks of the 1980s: Integrating research findings across studies to produce cumulative knowledge.* Paper presented at the 87th Annual Convention of the American Psychological Association, Montreal, August 1980.

Sells, S. B. (Ed.). *Stimulus determinants of behavior.* New York: Ronald Press, 1963.

Silverman, J. *New techniques in task analysis* (SRM 68-12). San Diego, CA: U.S. Naval Personnel Research Activity, 1967.

Sternberg, R. J. *Intelligence, information-processing, and analogical reasoning: The componential analysis of human abilities.* Hillsdale, NJ: Erlbaum, 1977.

Stevenson, W. H. Taxonomy of tasks. In F. J. Monks, W. W. Hartop, & J. DeWit (Eds.), *Determinants of behavioral development.* New York: Academic Press, 1972.

Stolurow, L. *A taxonomy of learning task characteristics* (AMRL-TD 12-74-2). Wright Patterson Air Force Base, OH: Aerospace Medical Research Laboratories, January 1964.

Verplanck, W. S. *Operational analysis of behavioral situations* (AF-AFOSR-1269-69-67). Knoxville, TN: University of Tennessee, 1968.

CHAPTER 2

Role of Taxonomies in Scientific Development

This chapter deals with the role of taxonomies in science and discusses some of the general issues of classification. Specifically, our purpose is to introduce some taxonomic concepts by examining the experience of other sciences where taxonomic development has had a longer history. This should help us to understand the relevance of these issues to taxonomic development in the behavioral sciences.

The recognition of similarities and differences of things and events is the first step in organizing knowledge about nature. These observations are then the basis for classifications of things and events and for the formulations of criteria of category inclusion or exclusion. Classification is necessary for drawing generalizations across events, one of the important goals of science, and for establishing efficient communication among scientists (see Melton, 1964b).

Here a distinction must be made. On the one hand, there is the science of classification itself, and, on the other, there is the role of classification in the development of particular sciences and scientific areas. This chapter explores classification as a science in its own right, and then discusses the role of classification in science with particular reference to experiences in biology. Finally, this chapter examines some recent taxonomic developments in psychological science, particularly in the field of human learning, and describes implications for taxonomic development in the field of human performance.

The Science of Classification

BEGINNINGS OF CLASSIFICATION PROCESSES

The process of classification—the recognition of similarities and the grouping of objects based on those similarities—dates back to

17

primitive man (see Raven, Berlin, & Breedlove, 1971; Sarton, 1952). It is inconceivable that primitive people (see Boring, 1942) did not have some classificatory system for organizing objects in their environments along certain dimensions, such as long–short, heavy–light, hot–cold, rough–smooth, and dangerous–safe. Perhaps early enemies forced humans to become sensitive to some of these dimensions.

In these primitive systems, self-reference appeared to be the criterion by which the classification was made; that is, the basis for the class was how an object felt or what it did to or for the observer. Durkheim and Mauss (1901–1902) suggested, however, that the classification systems of primitive peoples reflected not the qualities and properties of objects, but the social organization of the tribe, with the first observed classes being classes of people. Among the very earliest dimensions for such classifications were probably male–female, young–old, kinship, owner–slave, and tribe membership. Zubin (1968a) noted that such classifications are the forerunners of later logical classifications. The hierarchies and subgroups established in the classification of people may represent the beginning of the search for the essence of objects, later illustrated by the theories of classification developed by Plato and Aristotle.

Boring (1942) suggested that distinguishing between invariant and variant aspects of the environment may have been the first classificatory act. It is this singling out of the "invariances or permanencies," as Neyman (1950) calls them, that may constitute the first step in scientific observation.

Why did such observation arise in the first place? Perhaps observation and categorization led to certain expectancies and in that way simplified the environment of primitive people. Thus, future or past events could be rated as probable or improbable. Perception of tallness brought with it the expectation of strength and possible danger, whereas shortness in stature suggested the opposite. Further, by distinguishing sheep as a collective class, differing from goats in another collective class, certain expectancies could be attached to the sheep object (wool, meat) and certain others to the goat object (butting, milk). The creation of such collectives simplified primitive herding considerably. It became possible to count the objects in each collective. In addition to enumeration, the singling out of certain classes of objects could lead to prediction or explanation of behavior. In this way, the perception of invariances served primitive people in a utilitarian fashion. These perceived permanencies may constitute the lowly beginnings of classification and science (see Zubin, 1968b).

Scientific Beginnings

The origin of the science of classification goes back to the writings of the ancient Greeks (see, for example, the reviews of Crowson [1970] and Mayr [1969]). The theory of classification propounded by Plato and developed by Aristotle depended on the following assumptions: (1) a universal order exists in nature; (2) this order, when discovered, will permit carving nature into natural classes to yield a permanent conceptual framework that consists of a hierarchy of genus, species, and subspecies progressing downward from general to specific; (3) the principle of differentiation that operates throughout the hierarchy is derived from the similarities of the attributes or components (likeness or unlikeness) of the classified objects; and (4) the properties concerned partake of the substantive nature of the units being classified (or of their physical properties) and are not fortuitous.

Plato divided classificatory systems into two types: (1) classifications based upon visible things or their images, and (2) classifications based on concepts or ideas. His student, Aristotle, began to classify all objects and organisms on the basis of what he called their *essence*. For a given group one could abstract the essence from the definition of the group through logical procedures.

In modern times, however, beginning with William James, the question of the existence of an essence for classification purposes began to be brought into doubt. For example, a tree could be classified by the botanist as an organism, by the landscape architect as an aesthetic entity, and by the lumberjack as a potential source of income. All of these are equally good bases for describing and classifying trees and the relative merits of different trees in accordance with the way in which they satisfy a variety of criteria. Thus, the red twig dogwood tree is a beautiful object for the landscape architect, but merely a weed for the forester (Zubin, 1968b). By the same token, books could be classified either by weight and size from the point of view of the shipper, by color and geometric proportion from the point of view of the interior designer, or by content from the point of view of the scholar or educator. Thus, there is no single criterion for classifying in any field and we need not be sensitive about attaining a single criterion in the field of human behavior. Even the chemical structure of objects, which seems to be so fundamental an essence, is not satisfactory when it comes to classifying the taste of substances because there is little connection between chemical structure and taste. As a further example, the search for tranquilizing drugs has revealed thus far that there is no way of telling the characteristics of a drug from its structure; consequently, there is currently no way to develop better tranquilizers from a mere knowledge of the structure of the substance (Zubin, 1968b).

Before dismissing the early attempts at classification, we should point out some contributions relevant to today's issues. Aristotle's great attempt to build a system for seeing order in our world, the emphasis on taxonomy and types based on essence, led to a system of explanation fitting the syllogistic form that is now referred to as *Aristotelian*. For example, "All mammals are warm-blooded (major premise); whales are mammals (minor premise); therefore, whales are warm-blooded (conclusion) [see Guralnik, 1978]."

One places objects in a class in order to "explain" why they have certain properties. "McKeever is a dog;" therefore, you may anticipate that McKeever will bark. The gain in prediction comes from the act of first recognizing to what type (class) the given animal, object, individual, etc., belongs.

An objection to the all-or-nothing typing approach of Aristotle is that few objects individually fit a type, and that additional functional relations, involving attributes, can be discovered that may allow more precise predictions. The evolution of science, following Galileo, involved the analysis and explanation of observable phenomena in terms of measurable degrees of attributes. Yet one of the common sense reasons for the Aristotelian approach is that in many areas it enables us to make predictions and scientific generalizations that cannot be made without it. By assigning objects or individuals to a class, our decisions are enriched because we draw on all the information that exists about the class. Such systems have been useful in biology, in a form extended in the eighteenth century by Linnaeus.

The issues of type taxonomies and attribute measurement have had their day in psychology. For example, classifying a person as schizophrenic may or may not lead to improved predictions about likely behavior. Thus, Kraepelin (1895), like Linnaeus in biology, undertook the search for logical treatments of the scientific problems of type taxonomies in mental illness. The problems, of course, are in the original specifications of the classes and in the subjectivity inherent in many such classifications (see Michner & Sokal, 1957). Elsewhere, Cattell (1968) has discussed the issues of type taxonomies and attribute measurement.

Some Basic Concepts

The *subject matter of classification* arises from questions regarding the nature of similarity (Sokal, 1974). How do we recognize similarity? What are the criteria by which we group objects and events into classificatory systems? How do individual differences in the perception of similarity and in the ability to classify affect scientific and everyday communication? Can one derive principles of classification? Are some principles and procedures of classification better than others? Such questions are critical to the *science of classification.*

Classification is defined as the ordering or arrangement of entities into groups or sets on the basis of their relationships (Simpson, 1961). These relationships can be based on observable or inferred properties. In later chapters, we shall see examples of taxonomic approaches, based on either inferred or observed properties, applied to the behavioral sciences.

Some philosophers, mathematicians, and statisticians also employ the term *classification* for what is here called *identification*, the term being defined as the allocation or assignment of additional, unidentified objects to the correct class, once such classes have been established by prior classification. Thus, we "identify" a table as being a piece of furniture, or a rose as being a flower. In addition to indicating a process, the term classification is frequently employed to denote the end product of this process. Thus, the result of the process of classification is a set of categories or "a classification." It seems better to term such an end result a *classificatory system* (Sokal, 1974).

The term *taxonomy* is used here to mean the theoretical study of systematic classifications including their bases, principles, procedures, and rules. This would include classification as well as identification. It is the science of how to classify and to identify. The term *taxon* is defined as any taxonomic grouping that occurs as the result of a particular technique of classifying; it is used to designate a set of objects recognized as a group in a classificatory system. A taxon has, therefore, been arrived at by some classificatory procedure, often as the result of an explicit methodology. The search for these taxonomic categories or taxa represents one of the basic features of work in this area. *Units* are identified as objects or entities belonging to one or more taxa constituting a classificatory system based upon some explicit methodology, generally focusing upon the similarities/dissimilarities of the units. Table 2.1 summarizes the hierarchy of terms described in this section.

TABLE 2.1

Hierarchy of Taxonomic Terms

Taxonomy: The theoretical study of systematic classifications including their bases, principles, procedures, and rules. The science of how to classify and identify.

Classificatory system: The end result of the process of classification, generally, a set of categories or taxa.

Classification: The ordering or arrangement of entities into groups or sets on the basis of their relationships, based on observable or inferred properties.

Identification: The allocation or assignment of additional, unidentified objects to the correct class, once such classes have been established by prior classification.

Taxon (plural: *taxa*): A group or category in a classificatory system resulting from some explicit methodology.

Units: Objects and entities that are identified as belonging to one or more taxa constituting a classificatory system. Identification is based on an explicit methodology usually focusing on the similarities/dissimilarities of the units.

Theories of taxonomy have frequently followed the development of classificatory systems and have attempted to formalize this methodological activity. In other instances, classificatory systems have been set up on an a priori, logical basis, with the methodology tailored subsequently to fit the principles involved. Both approaches have their advantages and drawbacks, but recent work tends to reflect an interactive approach in which neither "methodology" nor "principles" dominates. There is certainly room for both strategies in the behavioral sciences (see Chapter 3).

For our purposes, a taxonomy is more than a mere classification. Rather, it is the study of systematic classifications, each with some reference to one or more theoretical models that embrace the domain to which the taxonomy is to be applied (see Miller, 1975). The application of a taxonomy to a set of facts or observations results in adding more information to those facts or observations by revealing patterns, enabling predictions, and by giving guidance to various kinds of future actions. The taxonomic system also operates as a code for accessing organized information.

The periodic table in chemistry, arranging chemical elements according to their atomic numbers, is a classic example. The table demonstrates the occurrence of similar properties in elements occupying similar positions in the periodic table. Another example exists in physical medicine. Its applied taxonomy is based on disease entities. Thus, the taxonomic characterization of chicken pox points to diagnostic descriptors for identifying the entity, for distinguishing it from a similar entity (say, smallpox), and for selecting from alternative treatments. Correctly naming the entity also enables prediction of what is likely to happen to the patient who takes the therapy and what is likely to happen to the patient who does not.

OBJECTIVES OF CLASSIFICATION IN SCIENCE

It follows that there are general objectives of classification in science. The primary purpose of a classification is to *describe the structure and relationships of the constituent objects* in regard to each other and to similar objects, and to simplify these relationships in such a way that general statements can be made about classes of objects. The definition, description, and simplification of taxonomic structure is a challenging task. It is easy to perceive structure when it is obvious and discontinuous. Thus, as Sokal (1974) pointed out, horseshoe crabs and ginkgo trees are unique species, quite different from their nearest relatives. And a language such as Basque, the language of a certain people living in the western Pyrenees, is similarly unique, being unrelated to any other known language. But these situations are not typical. Much of what we observe in nature varies continuously on one or another characteristic. Where should boundaries be drawn in such cases? Most classifications require a drawing of boundaries. Would an adequate description and summarization of the continuity of the objects be preferable to artificially erected boundaries? Taxonomists need to be concerned with such issues, including the relative importance of the size of "clusters" representing categories, the number of objects in the clusters, and the gaps between or among the clusters.

Classificatory systems that describe relationships among objects in nature should *generate hypotheses*. In fact, the principal scientific justification for establishing classifications is that they are heuristic; they lead to the stating of hypotheses for further investigation. A classification also raises the question of the derivation of the perceived order. Moreover, in cases in which forces and relationships among the objects are transitory, one may conjecture about the maintenance of the taxonomic structure. Examples include inferences about the evolutionary lineages obtained from biological classifications, based on morphological or biochemical characteristics. Other examples include the inferences about population structure in sociology and anthropology that result from patterns of geographic variation, and inferences about acculturation in anthropology that are engendered by evolving models of language and material artifacts.

All classificatory systems aim to *achieve economy of memory* and to *facilitate communication*. The world is full of single cases: single entities of animal or plant species, single case histories of disease, single books or rocks. By grouping numerous individual objects into a taxon, the description of the taxon subsumes the individual descriptions of the objects contained within it. By saying that someone speaks Spanish, we imply that the individual's linguistic inventory resembles that of millions of other people in the taxon "Spanish-speaking people," and we save ourselves a whole catalog of statements about the particular word lists and sentence structures familiar to the individual. Unless we qualify our statement further, we are aggregating varieties of thought, speech, and writing patterns collectively known as the Spanish language. Without a clearer definition of boundaries, we cannot be certain whether local dialects are included. Yet without the ability to summarize information and attach a convenient label to it, we would be unable to communicate.

Another purpose of classification is *ease of manipulation of observations*. Ideally, the classificatory system should consist of taxa that can easily be named and related to each other. However, if the relationships are very complex, as are the functional roles of individuals in certain societies, for example, no easy labeling or handling of the taxa will be possible. *Ease of retrieval of information* from a classificatory system is, therefore, another criterion frequently considered desirable.

In addition to those objectives derived from the search for structure and relationships in nature, there are some utilitarian objectives of classification. For example, what is the most useful way to classify objects at hand—into two, three, or k classes? Sokal (1974) describes two general approaches to such problems: (1) the imposition of an external constraint by fitting the data to a fixed number of classes, and (2) the search for natural structure, which will dictate the number of classes. These two approaches are not necessarily completely distinct. The first approach is most frequently used in applied or practical fields. Thus, in regionalization studies, a given political area is to be divided into a fixed number of districts given some optimal criterion. For example, what is the best way to subdivide a country into five voting districts to achieve maximal, or in some recent redistricting problems, minimal, intraclass homogeneity? Many "routing problems" can be considered classification problems in this sense. Thus, if a bakery possesses four trucks, how can it best route these through the city to cover the set of n grocery stores in the city at minimal cost and/or in minimal time?

As an example of the second approach, many biological taxonomists, without explicitly saying so, assume that they already know the major natural subdivisions of the organisms they study and only need to allocate properly the finer taxonomic units to these major natural subdivisions.

In biological and some other classifications, it is sometimes stated that the number of major subdivisions should be partly a function of the number of included taxonomic units. Such a scheme is not really based on fundamental scientific principles but largely on considerations of practicality. The number of major subdivisions may also be related to the number of names human beings are able to handle or to recall from some data base.

The Role of Taxonomies in the Biological Sciences

The biological sciences have devoted more effort to taxonomic issues and methodology than any of the other sciences. Consequently, within the Taxonomy Project, a major review of the taxonomic efforts of the biologists was undertaken in order to gain some lessons relevant for the classification of human performance (Theologus, 1973). The focus in this review was on the concepts, principles, and procedures that the biologists employ in classifying, rather than on the content of their classifications.

PRIORITIES IN CLASSIFICATION

The review by Theologus (1973), which forms the primary basis for this section, demonstrated that there are some priorities and an order that must be established in beginning a classificatory effort. First, one must state the *purpose* or the *why* of classification. At the most basic level, biologists classify in an attempt to supply some order and organization to the vast number of living organisms that they observe. Within this general goal, there are three specific purposes for which biologists classify: (1) to relate living organisms to some external variable of interest (ecological classification), (2) to show the usefulness of organisms to human beings (teleological classification), or (3) to reveal the interrelationships among the organisms themselves in terms of their attributes or characteristics (theoretical classification).

Once a purpose for classification has been established, the *attributes* of the organisms or relationships to be classified can be specified. In other words, this step constitutes the subject matter or the *what* of classification. Thus, if the purpose of the classification is ecological, then the organisms' relationships with environmental variables constitute the basis for the classification system (e.g., freshwater fish or forest plants). If the purpose is teleological, then the usefulness of the objects to human beings is classified (e.g., animals that provide food for people). Finally, if the purpose is theoretical, then organisms are classified in terms of their inherent characteristics (e.g., blood chemistry).

The third step in classifying involves the question of *how* one should classify: how and where to seek the relationships, by similarity and contiguity, necessary for classification. The examination of biological classification revealed that there had been no explicit taxonomy developed in biology for the "how" of ecological and teleological classifications. For the most part, these classifications have been ad hoc efforts.

THEORETICAL CLASSIFICATIONS IN BIOLOGY

Modern taxonomic thought in biology appears to be dominated by three types of theoretical classifications. The first is *Linnaean taxonomy,* which, as was noted earlier in the chapter, is based upon Aristotelian logic. Linnaean taxonomy reduces the "how" of classification to an attempt to define the "essence" or "essential nature" of groups of organisms. Some unique set of characteristics is deemed necessary and sufficient (e.g., "breasts characterize mammals") for classification.

The major criticism of this approach is that it involves a large amount of a priori, subjective judgment. The subjectivity arises from the fact that the taxonomist must critically examine the organism and extract only those features of the organism that, in the professional's opinion, comprise its essential nature. Such subjectivity can never serve as the basis for a scientific classification, mainly because of its inherent lack of empirical verification. Another difficulty that Linnaean taxonomists encounter is that in some instances, when essences are used to define a group, the resulting group is monothetic. In a monothetic group, each member possesses all of a unique, but limited, set of features. In many instances, the features must all be possessed to the same degree. "The ruling idea of monothetic groups is that they are formed by rigid and successive logical divisions so that possession of a unique set of features is both sufficient and necessary for membership in the group thus defined [Sokal & Sneath, 1963, p. 13]." The greatest danger in the use of monothetic groups is that an organism, which is aberrant in but one of the features employed to make the primary division for a given group, will inevitably be classified in a category far removed from that group.

A second type of theoretical classification is represented by *Darwinian taxonomy*, which holds that the theory of evolution that revolutionized biology when introduced by Darwin in 1859 constitutes the only valid taxonomic basis for classification. Simpson stated, "Species exist because they evolved. That, in briefest form, is the natural reason for the existence of species and is therefore also the truly natural basis for classification [1961, p. 57]."

The major criticism of Darwinian taxonomy is that Darwinian theory, due to the small amount of data available (e.g., the fragmentary nature of the fossil record), is largely deductive. Consequently, the argument goes, Darwinian theory cannot provide a sufficient basis for classification. For the most part, the criticisms that have been directed at Darwinian taxonomy have been quite valid. These criticisms point out an essential and basically insurmountable difficulty in the Darwinian approach that should be noted with respect to human performance taxonomy. In order to constitute a useful tool, a scientific classification must be founded inductively upon relationships that have a factual basis; that is, the relationships must have been derived directly from data. A scientific classification should not be founded upon hypothesized relationships or speculations that merely reflect the subjective opinions of some taxonomist. If subjective opinions or theories solely deductive in nature are permitted as the bases for classification, there could well be as many classifications as there are theorists, with the resulting classifications being only as stable as the speculations upon which they are founded.

The third school of thought in biology is *numerical taxonomy*, which holds that the relationships of contiguity and similarity should be sought by a quantitative analysis of the overall similarity of the organisms, based upon the widest possible range of physical and functional characteristics of the organisms themselves (e.g., morphological, genotypical, cytological). This involves empirical deter-

to psychologists if they would but apply them to the relevant taxonomic questions.

The Role of Classification in Psychological Science

The general taxonomic issues described in biology and other sciences
extend to the behavioral sciences. As Melton (1964b) has pointed out,
all areas of psychological science have a taxonomic problem. Moreover, classification efforts in those areas concerned with such human
functions as learning and performance receive little guidance from
the physical structure of the organism. They have had as their main
source the ingenuity of the scientist in discovering commonalities
between apparently different phenomena and differences between
apparently identical phenomena.

   Like biologists, psychologists interested in making their discipline
more systematic have displayed more interest in actually classifying
than they have in the scientific issues pertaining to taxonomy. Chapters 5–7 will show that one inevitable result of ignoring the logic
underlying taxonomies is the generally unsatisfactory nature of the
various human performance classificatory systems that have been
developed. Logical and empirical bases for classification should be
carefully developed before classification is attempted. Failure to take
this necessary step minimizes any chance for the development of a
successful and useful classificatory system.

   Most of the human performance classificatory systems that have
been developed in psychology appear to be essentially Linnaean. For
the most part, as we shall see in later chapters, the existing task
classifications have been developed by an examination of a set of
tasks, followed by the creation of a word or phrase that supposedly
describes their essential nature. Some would argue that the relatively
rudimentary stage of psychology as a science permits psychologists
to employ rudimentary methods in developing human performance
classifications. On the other hand, it makes sense to use the most
sophisticated taxonomic techniques available and to learn from the
experiences in other disciplines. Linnaean taxonomy has decreased
in popularity in biology over the past 100 years to a point where
today it seems to be disappearing. There is a lesson in this trend for
those concerned with the development of taxonomies in the behavioral sciences.

   Melton (1964b) has noted that an important development in the behavioral sciences related to taxonomic issues was the recognition of the need to limit the generalization of empirical findings to a category, or even to a subclass of a category, until there was evidence to support a wider generalization. Thus, approximately 50 years ago, Carr (1933) felt compelled to caution investigators about the pitfalls in the "quest for constants." He not only warned against generalization of findings across categories, but also within categories, and even within specific experimental procedures when some critical aspect of the procedure was permitted to vary. Carr's implication was that the relationships between variables that are observed in some experimental context, as defined by the task, procedures, and measures, should not be assumed to be true for other tasks, procedures, or measures until shown to be so. Although some recent research efforts by Schmidt, Hunter, and their colleagues (Pearlman, Schmidt, & Hunter, 1980; Schmidt, Gast-Rosenberg, & Hunter, 1980; Schmidt & Hunter, 1977; Schmidt, Hunter, & Pearlman, 1981; Schmidt, Hunter, Pearlman, & Shane, 1979) suggest that relationships between variables can be generalized to a greater extent than previously believed (i.e., across situations and jobs), other research by Fleishman and his associates (see summaries in Fleishman, 1975, 1978) has supported Carr's proposition. Fleishman found that variations in task requirements make significant differences in terms of which ability tests are predictive of criterion performances, and in terms of the magnitude of predictions by individual tests. The essential finding by Fleishman is that when one has better control over the measurement of the criterion performances, it is possible to show that different task requirements moderate test validities. Thus, Fleishman (1978) concluded that systems for classifying human tasks will lead to improved generalizations and predictions of human performance, and he has repeatedly called for the development of a taxonomy of human performance.

TAXONOMIC DEVELOPMENT IN THE FIELD OF HUMAN LEARNING

A good example of the taxonomic state of the art in psychology can be given by describing taxonomic development in a field closely related to human performance, namely, the field of human learning. Melton (1941) was among the first of today's generation of experimental psychologists to express the need for the development of a taxonomy of human learning. Moreover, Melton (1964b) has noted that over the past 40 years governmental and industrial organizations have recognized the need for fundamental knowledge about human learning and the consequent need to organize and apply such knowledge effectively. The tasks of concern to these organizations have been varied, including those involving simple or discriminative reactions as well as problem-solving tasks, such as diagnosing a malfunction in complex electronic equipment. These needs for a technology of human learning highlighted the issues surrounding the need for a taxonomy of learning processes (e.g., Cotterman, 1959). When one is confronted with a decision to use massed or distributed practice, for instance, taxonomic issues become critical. The ability to relate relevant findings of the effects of such differing practice techniques from the experimental laboratory to the real world of tasks may be difficult indeed without the assistance of a classificatory system (see Chapanis, 1967; Fleishman, 1967, 1972a).

In 1964, Melton brought together a number of prominent psychologists from different areas to examine the internal structure of the traditional categories of human learning (Melton, 1964a). The objective of this landmark effort was to give impetus to consideration of taxonomic problems by those in the field of human learning. As incisive as the papers prepared by these psychologists were, they revealed that learning theories were still, for the most part, theories about: (1) conditioning, (2) rote learning, (3) short-term and long-term memory, (4) concept learning, (5) probability learning, (6) skill learning, and (7) problem solving. As such, they were closely tied to a limited set of experimental investigations within each category. Parallel, systematic empirical investigations across categories of learning were found to be rare and still are rare today.

For our present purposes, the major contribution of that volume was Melton's (1964b) overview paper that drew together the taxonomic implications of the individual papers. As Melton pointed out, a science cannot tolerate the limitation of the generality of an experimental phenomenon to the particular context in which the phenomenon is observed. Levels of generality, both within and between categories, must be achieved through systematic empirical investigations that bridge the boundaries between postulated categories. There is a need for hypothetical constructs and intervening variables that reveal the presence of similarities and differences that are more fundamental than those obtained at the observational level.

Early learning theorists postulated a variety of categories of human learning. Thorndike (1933) contended that all learning is basically the same: *operant conditioning.* Thorndike, a reinforcement theorist, offered the law of effect. The "stamping in" of stimulus–

response connections depended not simply on the fact that the stimulus and response occurred together, but on the effects that followed the response. Reward (or a satisfier) strengthens connections, but punishment (or an annoyer) does not directly weaken them (see Hill, 1963).

Skinner (1938, 1953) recognized two different kinds of learning: one, *respondent behavior*, in which behavior is elicited by specific stimuli either by reflex or through conditioning (labeled classical conditioning by others), and the other, *operant behavior*, in which behavior is demonstrated without a particular stimulus (i.e., behavior operates on the environment). Skinner noted that if an operant response were followed by a reinforcement (the occurrence of a positive reinforcer or the termination of a negative reinforcer), the response's probability of occurring would increase. Whereas reinforcement increases the probability of a response, punishment does not necessarily reduce the probability. Later, Hull (1943, 1952) proposed a formal theory that rejected Skinner's distinction between respondent and operant behavior and stated that all behavior involves stimulus–response connections, with intervening variables influencing the connections. In spite of their differences, Skinner (1938, 1953) and Hull (1943, 1952) in their treatment of habit-family hierarchies seemed to accept a case of learning now called *chaining* (see Gagné, 1977).

Thus, Tolman (1949) distinguished six kinds of distinctive learning classes including cathexes, equivalence beliefs, field expectancies, field cognition modes, drive discrimination, and motor patterns, whereas Woodworth (1958) discussed five. Mowrer (1947) recognized discrimination or sign learning and concept or solution learning, in addition to the simpler types, although he later replaced his two-factor theory with a new, cognitive-sounding one-factor theory in which all learning was *sign learning* (Mowrer, 1960; see also Hill, 1963). Harlow (1949) distinguished the acquisition of concepts as *learning sets* from simpler discrimination learning.

In the field of human learning, the original categories, such as *conditioning, rote learning*, and *insight*, were primitive ones based on sorting learning processes into classes that have obvious differences at some descriptive level. These primitive categories then underwent a variety of changes as psychologists gained a greater understanding of learning phenomena. For example, *probability learning* and *operant conditioning of autonomic responses* represent relatively recent additional learning categories, and *short-term memory* has become distinguished from *long-term retention* (see Hilgard & Bower, 1975). *Motor skill* has been replaced by a number of subcategories, and there is increasing information about the boundaries of these subcategories, their limits, and the possibilities for generalizations across their boundaries (Fleishman, 1972b).

Melton (1964b) described some of the ways in which such primitive learning categories have been changed over time, some having been absorbed into others, whereas some have been split into subcategories. An example of the consolidation of categories is the encompassing of the category *memory span* ("immediate memory" or "short-term memory") under the category of *rote learning* (Adams, 1976; Underwood, 1964). *Insight learning* as a category now seems to be properly encompassed by the category *problem solving* (Gagné, 1962). On the other hand, the fission of categories is well represented by the now-traditional separation of classical and instrumental conditioning (see Grant, 1964; Kimble, 1964). In a similar vein, Fitts (1964) suggested radical revision of the category of *skill learning*. In his view, the learning processes usually subsumed under this category show such strong similarities to the processes of language learning, concept learning, and problem solving that he questioned whether skill learning should be retained as a major primitive category.

Gagné (1964, 1970, 1972, 1975, 1977) is one experimental psychologist who continues to examine the processes involved in various categories of learning. In his earlier work, Gagné identified eight different classes of situations in which human beings learn. He referred to the eight *types* as signal learning, stimulus–response learning, chaining, verbal association, multiple discrimination, concept learning, rule learning, and problem solving. Gagné felt that each type is related to a different state of the organism and with a different capability for performance. Gagné orders these into a hierarchical system in which each type of learning is a prerequisite for the next, as one goes from signal learning or identification toward problem solving. On the basis of his later research, Gagné further separated and collapsed some of these categories. The new categories are presented in Chapter 6 in conjunction with our description of Gagné's classificatory system.

In addition to such revision in the major categories of learning, there have been some important taxonomic changes within categories. Melton (1964b) noted that subcategories have been invented or discovered, and the distinctions between old subcategories have been refined. Thus, Grant (1964) discussed four subcategories of classical conditioning and eight subcategories of instrumental conditioning, whereas Hilgard and Marquis (1940) had one and four subcategories, respectively. A recent attempt to handle taxonomic issues within the area of instrumental conditioning has been provided by Wood (1974). In the case of subcategories of rote verbal learning, Underwood (1964) identified and differentiated five, and Postman (1964) discussed at least four subcategories of short-term memory tasks (memory span, running memory span, continuous paired–associative memory, and memory for single items) that may be considered as belonging to the rote learning category. More recently, Underwood, Borush, and Malmi (1978) have applied factor analytic methods to the identification and definition of processes common to a variety of memorization tasks.

Melton (1964b) concluded that, in much the same way, probability learning, concept learning, skill learning, and problem solving have had their subcategories increased and the distinctions between them refined. Much research effort, analytical ingenuity, and theoretical sophistication have been devoted to make distinctions where none existed before, or to adding varieties that were not known 10 or 20 years ago.

Although the original, primitive categories of learning may persist in the language of psychology, they now serve mainly to denote the general categories of tasks engaged in rather than the subdomains within which empirical findings can be generalized. The conclusion reached by Melton (1964b) about the original categories is that they are *not* the proper categories for use in understanding human learning, even though they may serve a useful, denotative function.

We need to look beyond the verbal labels used by different investigators. Are decision making and problem solving the same process? Some authors use one term or the other, some use both as two distinct descriptors, others use the terms interchangeably, and still others combine the two terms into the broader category of *cognition*. How does one relate experimental data obtained with a task described by one term to those from a task described by a different, although related, term. Obviously we must answer this question before we can generalize performance data across tasks or predict performance on new tasks. A classificatory system should reduce the probability that psychologists, or the users of psychological knowledge, will be "tricked" by names (Meister, 1976; Melton, 1964b).

Different experimenters in the field of human learning have operational definitions, implicit or explicit, for these categories. If we examine these operational definitions, we find three potentially useful criteria for classifying human task performance. These are task dimensions, behavior (response) requirements, and inferred processes or intervening variables. We see in later chapters that these form the basis for several alternative systems developed to categorize human task performance.

IMPLICATIONS FOR TAXONOMIC DEVELOPMENT IN THE FIELD OF HUMAN PERFORMANCE

The previous section described taxonomic issues relevant to categories of human learning; however, the relationship of learning taxonomic issues to human performance classification should be obvious. Such categories as *perceptual–motor* and *problem solving* have been used to describe areas of human capacity and performance. Furthermore, there is a need in human learning theory for an adequate taxonomy of human performance measures. All measures of human learning are measures of performance at a given stage of practice or experience. These linkages between performance capacities, learning, and performance measurement represent other implications for taxonomic development and are amplified in later sections of this book and elsewhere (Fleishman, 1972a, 1975, 1978).

It is clear from the preceding discussion that critical questions must be answered pertaining to the types of predictions about human performance that will be improved by each kind of taxonomy of human learning. Proof of the utility of the various learning category and subcategory revisions described will come from the achievement of greater predictive power for a variety of scientific and practical purposes. Predictive ability should be increased as our data and theory permit us to move from a phenotypical taxonomy to a genotypical taxonomy, from one based on observables to one based on constructs, and from a variety of specific theories to a more general theory (Melton, 1964b).

From this review we conclude that work on taxonomies to synthesize research information has a long history in the natural sciences, but only a short one in the behavioral sciences. This chapter has described some historical trends in the role of taxonomic development in science and in the biological and behavioral sciences in particular. Some general principles, assumptions, and goals of taxonomic development were discussed. The aim was to show relations between the evolution of taxonomies in other sciences and the needs in the present stage of taxonomic development in psychology, particularly in the areas of human learning and performance.

Taxonomic development typically has occurred in heavily re-searched fields in which impetus has come from an overwhelming cascade of unorganized facts. With the mushrooming of research in the behavioral sciences, the need for some organizing systems simi-larly becomes more critical. Taxonomic efforts make it easier to be comprehensive, to track development of the field, and to contribute to its growth.

Further taxonomic research in the behavioral sciences will facili-tate the development of a standard metalanguage to describe con-cepts in a field. Translation into the language of taxonomy should facilitate comparisons of findings across investigations. One can also determine areas of well-established findings; areas of confused, un-certain, or conflicting results; and neglected areas of study. More-over, if the taxonomy has underlying ordering principles, it can be used to predict new relationships. If such predictions are upheld, the classificatory system and its underlying structure are confirmed (see e.g., McGrath & Altman, 1966). Thus, the development of taxonomic systems can also contribute to theory development.

Although the chapters that follow focus mainly on taxonomic is-sues in human performance, it is also evident that any attempt to develop a taxonomy of human performance is but a piece of the problem of behavioral science, with parallel efforts needed by psy-chologists concerned with other functional variables such as moti-vation, perception, and social processes. There are encouraging signs that this is happening; for example, see Bloom (1956), Casper & Snizek (1980), Cattell (1960), Chambers (1963), Goldberg (1978), Hall (1972), McGrath & Altman (1966), McKelvey (1975), Nieva, Fleish-man, and Rieck (1978), Norman (1963), Sells (1963) and Uttal (1981). Some of these classificatory efforts in other areas of psychology are described in more detail in Chapter 14.

Recent empirical work developed up to now suggests that the most useful primary categories in contemporary taxonomic efforts appear to involve a rather large and steadily increasing set of narrower cate-gories. This was shown to be true in the fields of biology and of human learning. The increasing fractionization of categories, though it perhaps complicates life, is consistent with empirical work on the interrelationships among human task performances.

In the next two chapters we discuss issues in the development and evaluation of classificatory systems. We then examine how these is-sues have been addressed in a number of the taxonomic efforts to date.

References

Adams, J. A. *Learning and memory: An introduction.* Homewood IL: Dorsey Press, 1976.

Bloom, B. S. *Taxonomy of educational objectives: Cognitive domain* (Handbook I). New York: McKay, 1956.

Boring, E. G. *Sensation and perception in the history of experimental psychology.* New York: Appleton-Century, 1942.

Carr, H. A. The quest for constants. *Psychological Review*, 1933, *40*, 514–522.

Casper, W. B., & Snizek, W. E. The nature and types of organizational taxonomies: An overview. *Academy of Management Review*, 1980, *5*, 65–75.

Cattell, R. B. Evaluation interaction and non-linear relations by factor analysis. *Psychological Reports*, 1960, *7*, 69–90.

Cattell, R. B. Taxonomic principles for locating and using types and derived taxonomy computer program. In B. Kleinmuntz (Ed.), *Formal representation of human judgment.* Pittsburgh: University of Pittsburgh Press, 1968.

Chambers, R. M. Operator performance in acceleration environments. In N. M. Burns, R. M. Chambers, & E. Hendler (Eds.), *Unusual environments and human behavior.* London, England: Glencoe, 1963.

Chapanis, A. Relevance of laboratory studies to practical situations. *Ergonomics*, 1967, *10*, 557–577.

Cole, A. J. *Numerical taxonomy.* New York: Academic Press, 1969.

Cotterman, T. E. *Task classification: An approach to partially ordering information on human learning* (WADC Tech. Note 58-374). Wright Patterson Airforce Base, OH: Wright Patterson AFB, January 1959.

Crowson, R. A. *Classification and biology.* New York: Atherton, 1970.

Durkheim, E., & Mauss, M. De quelques formes primitives de classification. *Annee Sociologique*, 1901–1902, *6*, 1–72.

Fitts, P. M. Perceptual–motor skill learning. In A. W. Melton (Ed.), *Categories of human learning.* New York: Academic Press, 1964.

Fleishman, E. A. Performance assessment based on an empirically-derived task taxonomy. *Human Factors*, 1967, *9*, 349–366.

Fleishman, E. A. On the relations between abilities, learning and human performance. *American Psychologist*, 1972, *27*, 1017–1032. (a)

Fleishman, E. A. Structure and measurement of psychomotor abilities. In R. N. Singer (Ed.), *The psychomotor domain: Movement behavior.* Philadelphia, PA: Lea & Febiger, 1972. (b)

Fleishman, E. A. Toward a taxonomy of human performance. *American Psychologist*, 1975, *30*, 1127–1149.

Fleishman, E. A. Relating individual differences to the dimensions of human tasks. *Ergonomics*, 1978, *21*, 1007–1019.

Gagné, R. M. Human functions in systems. In R. M. Gagné (Ed.), *Psychological principles in system development.* New York: Holt, 1962.

Gagné, R. M. Problem-solving. In A. W. Melton (Ed.), *Categories of human learning.* New York: Academic Press, 1964.

Gagné, R. M. *Conditions of learning* (2nd ed.). New York: Holt, 1970.

Gagné, R. M. Domains of learning, *Interchange*, 1972, *3*, 1–8.

Gagné, R. M. Taxonomic problems of educational systems. In W. T. Singleton & P. Spurgeon (Eds.), *Measurement of human resources.* New York: Halstead Press, 1975.

Gagné, R. M. *The conditions of learning* (3rd edition). New York: Holt, Rinehart, & Winston, 1977.

Gilmore, J. S. C. Taxonomy and philosophy. In J S. Huxley (Ed.), *The new systematics.* Oxford: Clarendon Press, 1940.

Goldberg, L. R. *Language and personality: Developing a taxonomy of personality descriptive terms.* Eugene, OR: Institute for the Measurement of Personality, 1978.

Grant, D. Classical and operant conditioning. In A. W. Melton (Ed.), *Categories of human learning.* New York: Academic Press, 1964.

Guralnik, D. B. (Ed.). *Webster's new world dictionary of the American language* (2nd ed.). United States: Collins & World Publishing, 1978.

Hall, R. H. *Organizations.* Englewood Cliffs, NJ: Prentice-Hall, 1972.

Harlow, H. F. The formation of learning sets. *Psychological Review,* 1949, *56,* 51–65.

Hilgard, E. R., & Bower, G. H. *Theories of learning* (4th ed.). Englewood Cliffs, NJ: Prentice-Hall, 1975.

Hilgard, E. R., & Marquis, D. G. *Conditioning and learning.* New York: Appleton–Century, 1940.

Hill, W. F. Learning: *A survey of psychological interpretations.* San Francisco: Chandler, 1963.

Hull, C. L. *Principles of behavior.* New York: Appleton–Century, 1943.

Hull, C. L. *A behavior system.* New Haven, CT: Yale University Press, 1952.

Kimble, G. A. Categories of learning and the problem of definition: Comments on professor Grant's paper. In A. W. Melton (Ed.), *Categories of human learning.* New York: Academic Press, 1964.

Kraepelin, E. Der psychologische versuch in der psychiatrie. *Psychol. Arbeiten,* 1895, *1,* 1–91. (Boring, E. G. *A history of experimental psychology* [2nd ed.]. New York: Appleton– Century–Crofts, 1950)

Mayr, E. *Principles of systematic biology.* New York: McGraw–Hill, 1969.

McGrath, J. E., & Altman, I. *Small group research.* New York: Holt, 1966.

McKelvey, B. Guidelines for the empirical classification of organizations. *Administrative Science Quarterly,* 1975, *20,* 509–525.

Meister, D. *Behavioral foundations of system development.* New York: Wiley, 1976.

Melton, A. W. Learning. In W. S. Monroe (Ed.), *Encyclopedia of educational research.* New York: Macmillan, 1941.

Melton, A. W. The taxonomy of human learning: An overview. In A. W. Melton (Ed.), *Categories of human learning.* New York: Academic Press, 1964.

Melton, A. W. (Ed.). *Categories of human learning.* New York: Academic Press, 1964.

Michner, C. D., & Sokal, R. R. A quantitative approach to a problem in classification. *Evolution,* 1957, *11,* 130–162.

Miller, R. B. Taxonomies for training. In W. T. Singleton & P. Spurgon (Eds.), *Measurement of human resources.* New York: Halstead, 1975.

Mowrer, O. H. On the dual nature of learning: A reinterpretation of "conditioning" and "problem-solving". *Harvard Educational Review,* 1947, *17,* 102–148.

Mowrer, O. H. *Learning theory and behavior.* New York: Wiley, 1960.

Neyman, J. *First course in probability and statistics.* New York: Holt, 1950.

Nieva, V. F., Fleishman, E. A., & Rieck, A. *Team dimensions: Their identity, their measurement, and their relationships* (ARRO Final Tech. Rep. DAHC19-78-C-0001). Washington, D.C.: Advanced Research Resources Organization, November 1978.

Norman, W. T. Toward an adequate taxonomy of personality attributes. *Journal of Abnormal and Social Psychology*, 1963, *66*, 574–583.

Pearlman, K., Schmidt, F. L., & Hunter, J. E. Validity generalization results for tests used to predict job proficiency and training success in clerical occupations. *Journal of Applied Psychology*, 1980, *65*, 373–406.

Postman, L. Short term memory and incidental learning. In A. W. Melton (Ed.), *Categories of human learning*. New York: Academic Press, 1964.

Raven, P. H., Berlin, B., & Breedlove, D. E. The origins of taxonomy. *Science*, 1971, *174*, 1210.

Sarton, G. *The study of the history of science: Ancient sciences through the golden age of Greece* (Vol. 1). Cambridge, MA: Harvard University Press, 1952.

Schmidt, F. L., Gast-Rosenberg, I., & Hunter, J. E. Validity generalization results for computer programers. *Journal of Applied Psychology*, 1980, *65*, 643–661.

Schmidt, F. L., & Hunter, J. E. Development of a general solution to the problem of validity generalization. *Journal of Applied Psychology*, 1977, *62*, 529–540.

Schmidt, F. L., Hunter, J. E., & Pearlman, K. Task differences as moderators of aptitude test validity in selection: A red herring. *Journal of Applied Psychology*, 1981, *66*, 166–185.

Schmidt, F. L., Hunter, J. E., Pearlman, K., & Shane, G. S. Further tests of the Schmidt–Hunter Bayesian validity generalization procedure. *Personnel Psychology*, 1979, *32*, 257–281.

Sells, S. B. *Stimulus determinants of behavior*. New York: Ronald Press, 1963.

Simpson, G. G. *Principles of animal taxonomy*. New York: Columbia University Press, 1961.

Skinner, B. F. *The behavior of organisms: An experimental analysis*. New York: Appleton-Century, 1938.

Skinner, B. F. *Science and human behavior*. New York: Macmillan, 1953.

Sokal, R. R. Classification: Purposes, principles, progress, prospects. *Science*, 1974, *185*, 1115– 1123.

Sokal, R. R., & Sneath, P. H. A. *Principles of numerical taxonomy*. San Francisco: Freeman, 1963.

Theologus, G. C. Development of a taxonomy of human performance: A review of biological taxonomy and classification. JSAS *Catalog of Selected Documents in Psychology*, 1973, *3*, 23–24 (Ms. No. 319).

Thorndike, E. L. The law of effect. *Psychological Review*, 1933, *40*, 434–439.

Tolman, E. C. There is more than one kind of learning. *Psychological Review*, 1949, *56*, 144–155.

Underwood, B. J. The representativeness of rote verbal learning. In A. W. Melton (Ed.), *Cagegories of human learning*. New York: Academic Press, 1964.

Underwood, B. J., Borush, R. F., & Malmi, R. A. Composition of episodic memory. *Journal of Experimental Psychology—General*, 1978, *107*, 393–419.

Uttal, W. R. A taxonomy of visual processes. Hillsdale, NJ: Erlbaum, 1981.

Wood, P. J. A taxonomy of instrumental conditioning. *American Psychologist*, 1974, *29*, 584–597.

Woodworth, R. S. *Dynamics of behavior*. New York: Holt, 1958.

Zubin, J. Biometric assessment of mental patients. In M. M. Katz, J. O. Cole, & W. E. Barton (Eds.), *The role and methodology of classification in psychiatry and psychopathology* (U.S. Public Health Service Publication No. 1584). Washington, D.C.: U.S. Government Printing Office, 1968. (a)

Zubin, J. *Classification of human behavior.* Paper presented at the meeting of the
    Canadian Psychological Association Institute on Measurement, Classification and
    Prediction of Human Behavior, The University of Calgary, Alberta, Canada, June
    1968. (b)

CHAPTER 3

Conceptual Bases for Classifying Human Task Performance

In the previous chapter we described some of the taxonomic issues faced in scientific development, showed how these have been dealt with in the biological sciences, and discussed classification issues related to the behavioral sciences. Particular emphasis was given to the relevance of these issues to theoretical and methodological problems in general experimental psychology and, in particular, to areas of human learning. The present chapter, and the one that follows, provide a more intensive treatment of the taxonomic issues related to the classification of human task performance.

It appears useful to examine past attempts in the area of human performance in order to provide procedural guidelines for subsequent taxonomic efforts. Specifically, Chapter 3 examines approaches taken and problems encountered in attempting to develop systems of classification for organizing and understanding information about human task performance. This chapter describes the issues identified and the relationships between the purpose and content of the classification. Chapter 4 emphasizes the methodological considerations in actually developing classificatory systems, and concludes with a description of criteria for evaluating such systems.

Despite the documented need for taxonomic development in the field of human performance, a widely accepted and useful classification of human task performance has not yet evolved. It was our feeling (see Fleishman, Kinkade, & Chambers, 1972; Wheaton, 1973) that progress might be facilitated if we faced and attempted to clarify three complex taxonomic issues. Essentially, these issues relate to choices that must be made before taxonomic development can proceed. Specifically, these issues include: (1) the objectives to be served by a particular classificatory system; (2) the descriptive basis of the system; and (3) the analytical techniques used to establish and validate the system.

A review carried out by Wheaton (1973) early in our Taxonomy Project explored these and related issues as an aid to future efforts at task taxonomic development. This review, which has been extended and updated, forms the primary basis for portions of this chapter. Primary evidence in this review was literature dealing with the classification of different aspects of human performance on tasks. In reviewing these efforts, the intent was to acquire and synthesize information on representative descriptive and classificatory schemes that have been proposed, including the purposes and the approaches employed. Most of the schemes reviewed did not represent formal attempts at classification. Indeed, the majority discussed classification in rather general terms, whereas some of the others emphasized a completely descriptive approach (e.g., task analysis). Our goal in this chapter is not to describe the particulars of each system, but rather to examine the diversity of these systems and to attempt some synthesis and "state of the art" evaluation of the issues that emerged from this examination.

Classification: Process and Product

In Chapter 2 we made the distinction between classification as the *process* of systematically arranging subject matter into categories, and classification as the *product*, or set of formal categories, that emerges. Behavioral scientists attempting to organize information about tasks and performance should obviously be interested in classification both as process and as product. However, we seldom see this dual interest expressed (Pearlman, 1980). Emphasis is usually placed upon a discussion of alternative categories (products) rather than upon the systematic examination of the general principles and issues of the classification process. It is toward this latter area that psychologists must turn their attention.

We saw in Chapter 2 that the penchant of scientists to deal with the products of classification, at the expense of understanding the process, has handicapped other sciences as well. This penchant tends to result, on the one hand, in fragmentary and isolated attempts at classification that make generalization difficult and, on the other hand, in schemas that seldom progress beyond the conceptual level.

This was the conclusion with regard to such efforts in psychology and, in particular, the human performance area (Wheaton, 1973).

We attempt here to deal with considerations of classification as a process. Basic to the consideration of classification as a process are three of the major taxonomic issues described in Chapter 2. The first of these involves the *purpose* or objective that gives rise to the desire to classify. Why does the behavioral scientist attempt classification? What should be accomplished by such a complicated and time-consuming activity?

Having stated the purpose in undertaking classification, the behavioral scientist must next choose the appropriate *subject matter* and conceive of ways in which it can be most clearly and systematically described. In the areas of human performance, what will the descriptors be based upon—observed behaviors, hypothesized intervening processes, required abilities, responses measured, display control characteristics, or what? This, we shall see, brings in the problem of task definition.

Third, a *method* of classification must be developed. Thus, *criteria* for class inclusion or exclusion must be formulated and the applicability of various analytical techniques must be determined.

Only when these issues have been faced and resolved, can classification proceed on a logical and consistent basis. Moreover, it must be noted that the taxonomic issues of purpose, conceptual basis, and procedures are inextricably interwoven. Each step in the development of a classificatory system has implications for subsequent (and often preceding) steps. Thus taxonomic development is necessarily an iterative process. We shall discuss these issues in turn, in this and the following chapter.

Purpose of Classification

Individuals who attempt classification rarely view it as an end in and of itself. Rather, they view such systems as tools that might provide the increased ability to interpret, predict, or control some facet of performance (Fleishman, 1975; Meister, 1976). This is accomplished by understanding the relationships between that which is classified (e.g., tasks, mediating processes, performance) and selected variables in a particular area (e.g., distribution of practice, training regimens, environmental stressors) (Cotterman, 1959b).

Given the general purpose of establishing such relationships, the behavioral scientist faces an initial choice of objectives. The taxonomist may elect to develop a unique system of classification useful for a very specific area (e.g., the classification of tasks with respect to which training procedures are most effective in producing high levels of task performance). In this case, specific utility is perhaps maximized, but at the expense of generalizability of the system to other problem areas. For example, a specific taxonomy designed to be of use in understanding the effects on performance of different training procedures may contribute little to our understanding of the effects of environmental stressors on performance.

A second type of objective is for a classificatory system designed from inception to be general. In this case, the taxonomist develops a classification of behavior, tasks, or processes, then later attempts to organize a wider range of data in terms of this scheme. For example, one might first classify tasks and only then relate stressors, learning principles, or training regimens to each class of tasks in the system. Although one is not precluded from seeking specific applications for general taxonomies, the specific applications do not dictate the composition of the system. The hope is that such a classification will serve a variety of users by aiding in the interpretation, prediction, and/or control of a broader range of phenomena.

Implicit in this distinction of objectives is the notion that classifications may be viewed either as means toward a specific end, in which case they are clearly utilitarian, or they may be viewed as ends in themselves with eventual application being an essential, but independent, problem (Wheaton, 1973). In this sense, the general system may be more linked to theory development.

In the case of the utilitarian objective, the approach appears to be one of grouping tasks as a function of the effects of a selected set of variables on measures of task performance. Consequently, groupings of tasks can be achieved regardless of their intrinsic similarities and dissimilarities. On the other hand, in developing general classificatory systems, the approach is altogether different. Direct interest initially lies not in the similarity of *effects* upon task performance, but rather in the similarity of *characteristics* (intrinsic properties) of the tasks themselves.

A further implication of this distinction is that when a specific application dictates classification, a unique classificatory system will be required each time. Establishing the functions to effectively translate one system into another, in an attempt to synthesize, interrelate, and integrate data, would be extremely difficult. Conversely, developing a classificatory system based upon behavioral or task properties, without initial concern for area of application, leaves open the possibility of applying or testing the system's utility across several sets of variables (for instance, environmental effects or training methods). We should stress that, while the distinction between specific utilitarian and general theoretical classifications is useful, we are dealing with a spectrum of possibilities. The difference is one of emphasis. Any classification is likely to have both applied and theoretical implications.

UTILITARIAN CLASSIFICATIONS WITH SPECIFIC APPLICATIONS

Of those taxonomies that are on the specific end of the spectrum, those concerned with the usefulness of learning principles and training methods to tasks are most numerous (Annett & Duncan, 1967; Cotterman, 1959a, 1959b; Eckstrand, 1964; Stolurow, 1964). As a consequence, these investigators have categorized tasks into sets that are relatively homogeneous and invariant with respect to learning and training principles. Their objective is to supply training personnel with rationales for the selection of training programs for specific tasks.

Bloom (1967) attempted to develop a similar system for the educational community. By developing a classification of educational objectives, he intended to facilitate communication among those in the educational system about appropriate methods of instruction. Stevenson (1972) has called for a taxonomy of tasks to assist in generalizing results about procedures and environmental conditions for use in developmental psychology.

Other examples of classificatory schemes dealing with specific and important human engineering problems include Alexander and Cooperband (1965), Colson, Freeman, Mathews, and Stettler (1974), Fowler, Williams, Fowler, and Young (1968), Kidd (1962), and Meister and Mills (1971, pp. 425–439), who were working toward categories of tasks relatively invariant for principles of equipment design.

Some investigators have proposed taxonomies more in the middle of the specificity–generality dimension, in the sense that their classifications would provide for more than one specific application. Fitts (1962) viewed the objective of task classification to be the identification and application of important correlates of learning rate, performance level, and individual differences. Miller (1967, 1975) discussed classificatory systems that would permit the specification of selection and training requirements. Dunnette (1976), Dunnette and Borman (1979), Pearlman (1980), and McCormick (1976) have discussed the classification of jobs with similar applications in mind, including prediction of job success.

THEORETICAL CLASSIFICATIONS WITH BROAD APPLICATIONS

As pointed out earlier, classificatory systems may also be developed as autonomous structures that are only some time later to be related to other variables or "applied." Often the classificatory exercise is an integral and inextricable step in the development of theory. The resultant classificatory system provides a consistent conceptual framework, the elements of which eventually are to be utilized in the interpretation or prediction of behavioral phenomena. Although one is not precluded from seeking specific applications for such classifications, these applications should not dictate the composition and structure of the system.

Learning theorists provide many examples of attempts at developing generalized taxonomies (see Hilgard & Bowers, 1974; Marx & Hillix, 1979). The long-standing nature of this issue has led to the generation of a number of classifications and to periodic revisions (see Melton, 1964). However, no classificatory system has been proposed that effectively compares, contrasts, and interrelates the various categories (see Chapter 2). The result has been an absence of a general theory of learning, although the ramifications of the concept of *task* and its classification have received attention (e.g., Wickens, 1964).

The ability theorists have also worked on generalized taxonomies, attempting to isolate basic dimensions of behavior upon which a general theory of human performance might be based. They differ from the learning theorists in that they analyze relationships among responses, rather than stimulus–response relationships. However, in properly designed studies, the stimulus materials in the tests (or tasks) utilized receive careful attention, and programmatic work allows variations in the task materials studied. Examples are the research programs of Cattell (1971), Carroll (1976, 1980), Fleishman (1964, 1972b, 1978), Guilford (1967), and Guilford and Hoepfner (1971).

In summary, the distinction among alternative task classification systems in terms of two general types of objectives is important for future taxonomic efforts. When a specific application is intended, it often dictates the classificatory structure from the start. This approach seems to be one of grouping tasks as a function of the effects of a selected set of variables on measures of task performance. Consequently, grouping of tasks can be achieved regardless of their intrinsic similarities and dissimilarities. On the other hand, in developing classification systems designed to satisfy a much broader range of applications, the approach is altogether different. Direct interest initially lies not in the similarity of effects upon task performance, but rather in the similarity of characteristics of the tasks themselves. This distinction is rarely made in present research practice.

Bases of Classification

We now proceed from the objectives of classification to the bases of behavioral taxonomies; we proceed from the question of *why* we classify to *what* we classify. Because the subject matter to be classified in the systems studied has generally been the task, we focus on two issues. First, is there consistency in the definition and meaning of the concept *task?* Second, is there general agreement as to the bases upon which task description, differentiation, and classification can be accomplished?

DEFINITION OF TASK

Needless to say, a variety of definitions of task have been employed in the literature. These definitions differ among themselves on two major dimensions. First, task definitions vary greatly with respect to their *breadth of coverage.* At one end of this dimension are definitions that view the task as an integral part of, and indistinguishable from, the larger work situation. In this context, the task is the totality of the situation imposed upon the performer. For example, this definition would consider ambient stimuli as an integral part of the task. The other end of this dimension is represented by definitions that treat a task as a specific performance. In this case, for example, one task could be to "depress the button whenever the light comes on." Very different concepts may underlie definitions falling at either end of this dimension.

The other dimension is the extent to which tasks are defined as being either *external* to or an *intrinsic* part of the performer. Thus, some definitions take into account the propensity of the performer to redefine an imposed task in terms of personal needs, values, or experiences. In the grossest sense, these definitions treat a task as whatever the performer perceives the task to be. To that extent, the task is idiosyncratically and subjectively defined. On the other end of the dimension are those definitions that bypass the redefinition problem by defining the task in terms of what has been imposed upon the performer, whether this is a specific performance requirement or the total situation.

Applying these dimensions to any review of task classification studies is difficult (Wheaton, 1973). Although the concept of task is fundamental to most of the systems that have been reviewed (Farina, 1973; Wheaton, 1973), there are few rigorous attempts in this literature to define precisely what is meant by the concept.

In general, most investigators treat tasks as processes consisting of interrelated activities. For example, R. B. Miller (1967) states, "A task is any set of activities, occurring at the same time, sharing some common purpose that is recognized by the task performer [p. 11]." Teichner and Olson (1971) share this view, but their definition is more narrow. They define a task in terms of transfer of information between components of a person–machine system with emphasis on the operations performed on the information within a component. Roby and Lanzetta (1956) conceive of tasks as represented by a space of multiple dimensions in which each dimension describes some condition relevant to performance.

There is, however, another type of task definition that is employed by relatively few investigators. This type of definition imbues the concept of task with an objective existence clearly apart from the activities or processes which the operator subsequently brings into play. In this sense, the task is a set of conditions that elicits specific activities or processes. Hackman (1968) represents this point of view in his definition of a task:

> A task is assigned to a person (or group) by an external agent or is self-generated, and consists of a stimulus complex and a set of instructions which specify what is to be done vis-à-vis the stimuli. The instructions indicate what operations are to be performed by the performer(s) with respect to the stimuli and/or what goal is to be achieved [p. 12].

The extent to which these or any other definitions are "appropriate" can only be seen in the implications that they have for the problem of task classification. We should not attempt to debate about *the* definition of a task as if only one definition were possible. Rather, we must adopt or develop a definition that will serve as an adequate vehicle for classification. An adequate vehicle will permit the derivation of terms that reliably describe tasks and distinguish among them. These derived terms provide the conceptual basis for classification.

We must keep in mind that *task* is a conceptual construct similar to many others we find in the behavioral sciences (Meister, 1976). Some constructs are more useful than others in assisting us in predictions and generalizations about human behavior. This applies, as well, to constructs used to differentiate human tasks. We are dealing with deductions and inferences about task dimensions. The problem is to identify those conceptualizations of tasks, and their characteristics, that are most powerful in deriving meaningful predictions and generalizations about human performance. A related problem is the evaluation of the usefulness of this information in the solution of practical problems, such as the derivation of learning and design principles.

Every system of classification has as its foundation a set of terms to be used in the description and eventual classification of its subject matter. It was noted above that the investigators who were reviewed differed substantially on the basis for describing and classifying tasks (Meister, 1976; Wheaton, 1973). Yet, such differences are not unexpected when one considers the diversity of their objectives and the range of task definitions (explicit or implicit) they utilized. Nevertheless, these alternative bases must be examined carefully for task classification to determine whether they merely reflect preferences or whether they can be differentiated on more substantive grounds. Our purpose here is to give the reader an overview of the various conceptual bases employed, with examples of the different classificatory schemes. A more comprehensive and detailed description of these and other schemes will be presented in the chapters which follow.

To lend structure to the appraisal, we shall deal with four major conceptual bases underlying task description and classification as discussed by Hackman (1968), Altman (1966), and McGrath and Altman (1966). The first three of these conceptualizations focus on the description of the behaviors, processes, and abilities involved in task performance, whereas the fourth conceptualization emphasizes the elements, conditions, or components of the task.

BEHAVIOR DESCRIPTION APPROACH

In the *Behavior Description Approach* to task classification, categories of tasks are formulated based upon observations and descriptions of what operators actually do while performing a task. Emphasis is placed primarily upon a description of the operator's overt behaviors rather than upon what the operator is required or expected to do in order to reach criterion levels of performance. The data collected by time and motion analysts and by task analysts are representative of the descriptive information upon which this approach is based.

Although overt behaviors such as dial setting, meter reading, and soldering are most often employed, certain subjective (and primarily cognitive) terms are also permissible (e.g., analyzing, computing, and decision making). Variations are possible not only because of the sheer number of such terms, but also because many levels of description are possible (e.g., adjusts volume control, adjusts control, adjusts; depresses, depresses keys, types).

Relatively few descriptive systems have been developed that are based exclusively on operator behaviors or activities. Berliner, Angell, and Shearer (1964) developed a hierarchical descriptive system, with only the lowest or most specific level being oriented toward actual behaviors (e.g., inspects, computes, informs). In a more extensive development of this type of descriptive system, Reed (1967) has constructed a list of verbs that represent frequently encountered behaviors or activities occurring during task performance. Reed's list of activities is particularly impressive because of his attempt to minimize redundancy among terms and yet be fairly exhaustive in his coverage.

McCormick and associates (McCormick, 1976, 1979; McCormick, Jeanneret, & Mecham, 1972) have employed this descriptive approach in their studies of *worker-oriented job variables*. They have dealt with the specification of human behaviors (e.g., handling objects, personal contact with customers), as opposed to the more technological aspects of jobs, for the purpose of establishing common denominators across jobs. This effort has led to the development of the Position Analysis Questionnaire (PAQ), which represents a relatively objective job analysis technique. Each of 187 job elements in the PAQ is to be rated in terms of its relevance to the job. More recently, McCormick et al. (1972) attempted to specify the human attributes that are relevant to the kinds of activities or behaviors occurring in various jobs. This interest in human attributes represents a transition from the behavioral description approach to the ability requirements approach discussed later in this chapter.

Fine, beginning with his association with the U. S. Department of Labor, has also been interested in describing jobs on the basis of worker functions or behaviors (Fine, 1974). Terms of interest to him have included handling (things), analyzing (data), and negotiating (with people). Working with these and similar concepts, Fine is attempting a broad mapping of work behaviors along lines analogous to McCormick's job description efforts.

The extent to which the Behavior Description Approach employed by these and other investigators could serve as a basis for task classification is limited because in any relatively complex task a myriad of activities may be observed. Are descriptions of each component activity necessary to identify completely the task and distinguish it reliably from others? If each and every activity is not to be included, how are the most "critical" or "representative" activities to be chosen—on the basis of frequency of occurrence, duration, and criticality? As noted above, the system has been most often employed in the description of what people do on jobs.

Toward what ends would this type of system be most powerful? Hackman (1968) doubts whether it would be useful in understanding how tasks affect behavior. He states:

> It appears that some researchers concerned with job and task descriptions have, in effect, substituted a dependent variable class for what should be an independent variable class. That is, if we are interested in the effects of tasks and task characteristics on behavior, it is essential that we develop means of describing and classifying our independent variables (tasks) other than in terms of the dependent variables (behaviors) to which we ultimately wish to predict [p. 7].

With other purposes in mind, such as building an information retrieval system that catalogues the effects of selected environmental variables on specific types of behavior, this approach might be of use. This point reaffirms the previously made statement that acceptance or rejection of this (or any other approach) is only possible in light of one's purpose in classifying (Wheaton, 1973).

BEHAVIOR REQUIREMENTS APPROACH

In the *Behavior Requirements Approach*, emphasis is placed on the cataloguing of behaviors that *should* be emitted or which are assumed to be *required* in order to achieve criterion levels of performance. The performer is assumed to be in possession of a large repertoire of processes that, as required, will serve to intervene between stimulus events and output responses.

Many of the classificatory systems that were reviewed are based on this approach. There has been a great deal of interest in classifying the required intervening processes (e.g., functions and behaviors), cataloguing tasks in terms of the types of processes required and then relating the types of tasks that emerge to particular training methodologies. Although Gagné (1962, 1975) and Miller (1967, 1973) are perhaps most representative of this approach, others have made use of it. For example, Eckstrand (1964), Folley (1964), Annett and Duncan (1967), and E. E. Miller (1963, 1969) have all discussed or proposed the classification of tasks in terms of required behaviors. Considered collectively, these and related schemes hypothesize initial lists of the major types of behavioral processes required in task performance, consider techniques for their detection or identification, and specify additional factors (sequencing of behaviors, time constraints, etc.) that should be considered for complete description of tasks in behavioral terms.

Miller (1967, 1973) provides a list of terms typical of the types of processes or functions used to describe and differentiate among tasks. These include: a scanning function, identification of relevant cues, interpretation of cues, short-term memory, long-term memory, decision making and problem solving, and an effector response. Although many of these terms are undoubtedly familiar to the reader, there are difficulties involved in analyzing tasks on the basis of these or similar terms. Miller (1967) suggests that the definitions—even in their more extended and refined form—are ambiguous in observing activities. They lack handles for quantification. In spite of these difficulties, however, Miller feels that this approach has utility, particularly for procedure design and development of appropriate training sequences. Whether or not this system of description actually proves to be useful is as much a function of the knowledge and skill of its users as it is of the system itself. Although investigators who have developed such systems may employ them effectively, they must be made public before they can be properly assessed. Attempts to do this were subsequently made under the Taxonomy Project. Succeeding chapters describe these efforts.

ABILITY REQUIREMENTS APPROACH

In the *Ability Requirements Approach* tasks are to be described, contrasted, and compared in terms of the abilities that a given task requires of the individual performer. These abilities are relatively enduring attributes of the individual performing the task. The assumption is made that specific tasks will require certain abilities if performance is to be maximized. Tasks requiring similar abilities would be placed within the same category or would be said to be similar.

Fleishman (1964, 1972b), Guilford (1967), Guilford and Hoepfner (1971), French, Ekstrom, and Price (1963), and Ekstrom, French, and Harman (1979) have provided lists of abilities and their definitions within the perceptual–motor, physical performance, and cognitive domains. The ability requirements approach requires the analysis of tasks to determine the contributions of these abilities to task performance. Fleishman (1972a) suggests that the various abilities can be thought of as representing empirically derived patterns of response consistencies to task requirements varied in systematic ways.

The abilities approach is similar to the behavior requirements approach in that they both seek to identify the critical aspects of the individual intervening between stimulus and response. The abilities approach differs from the behavior requirements approach primarily in terms of concept derivation and level of description. Ability concepts are empirically derived through factor analytic studies or some other empirical clustering process and are treated as more basic units than the intervening processes of the behavior requirements approach.

A problem with the abilities and behavior requirements approaches stems from the subjective manner in which abilities and functions are semantically defined. Abilities (i.e., the factors on the basis of which the abilities are inferred) are empirically derived from patterns of response consistencies on different tasks. The empirical definition for each factor is mathematically derived and consists of the factor-loadings of each of the many tasks contributing to the factor. This type of empirical–mathematical definition has limitations when the factor-analyst wants to communicate the nature of the ability factors. As a consequence, the attempt is invariably made to translate the empirical–mathematical definition of each factor into a semantic definition by a labeling process.

The investigator carefully examines each task associated with a particular factor and develops a set of hypotheses as to what it is that tasks loading on a given factor have in common. Even though there may be many things in common, the researcher will inevitably try to summarize them by employing a single label (e.g., Perceptual Speed, Flexibility of Closure, Control Precision). The label will then be defined semantically in terms of the attributes that best represent the communality among tasks on a specific factor. For example, Fleishman (1964) provides a semantic definition of the factor labeled *Control Precision*.

> This factor is common to tasks which require fine, highly controlled, but not over-controlled muscular adjustments, primarily where large muscle groups are involved. . . . This ability extends to arm–hand as well as to leg movements. It is highly important in the operation of equipment where careful positioning of controls by the hands or feet are required. It is most critical where such adjustments must be rapid but precise [p. 16].

There is nothing capricious about this or any other ability definition. It was painstakingly developed from a rational analysis of tasks.

The ability description integrates a great deal of information about the common properties of ostensibly diverse tasks that require that ability. Too often, however, this information tends to be rather private, residing within the investigator who originally supplied the ability labels. As with the behavior requirements approach, the descriptive power of the ability requirements system may be increased if the investigator made the underlying communalities more public through detailed operational definitions of these ability or behavior requirement categories. The advantage of the abilities approach is the empirical base. The categories are obtained on the basis of correlations among actual human task performances.

In later chapters we present details of extensions of the abilities approach, developed in the Taxonomy Project, that attempt to make ability definitions more public, provide methods for establishing the reliability of abilities as classification categories, and examine their utility according to a variety of evaluation criteria.

TASK CHARACTERISTICS APPROACH

The fourth approach differs from the preceding approaches in terms of the type of task description that is attempted. The three approaches previously discussed are predicated upon task definitions that are process-, function-, behavior-, or performance-oriented. Consequently, appropriate descriptive terms are those that focus on the task performer's overt activities or internal processing. Different tasks will evoke different activities, will require different types and sequences of processing, and will place demands on various abilities. In other words, task description focuses on what transpires between input and eventual output.

The *Task Characteristics Approach* is based upon a rather different conceptualization of the task. The approach is predicated upon a definition that treats the task as a set of conditions that elicits performance (Farina & Wheaton, 1973). These conditions are imposed upon the operator and have an objective existence quite apart from the activities they may trigger, the processes they may call into play, or the abilities they may require of the operator. Having adopted this point of view, appropriate descriptive terms are those which focus on the task per se. The assumption is made that tasks can be described and differentiated in terms of intrinsic, objective properties which they may possess. These properties or characteristics may pertain to the goal toward which the operator works, relevant task stimuli, instructions, procedures, or even to characteristics of the response(s) or the task content. The obvious problem is the selection of those task components which are to be described, as well as the particular terms or parameters by means of which description is to be accomplished.

Studies by Cotterman (1959b), Fitts (1962), Farina and Wheaton (1973), and Stolurow (1964) are representative of attempts to pursue the task characteristics approach. These explicitly considered prototype task classifications are based, at least in part, upon the description of task properties per se. Stolurow (1964), for example, developed a limited prototype classification of paired associate and serial learning tasks. Based upon his system of classification he was able to explore the effects of certain principles of learning (e.g., massed and distributed practice) with respect to different categories of tasks. Preliminary data suggested that the effects of massed and spaced practice were relatively homogeneous within certain of his task categories. Types of descriptors upon which he based task categories are number and sequence of stimuli and responses, stimulus and response limits, meaningfulness, and qualitative relationships between stimulus and response.

Although several investigators (e.g., Arnoult, 1963; Hackman, 1968; Sells, 1963) have considered this approach as potentially useful, it has also been argued that the approach is unfeasible because of the difficulty in selecting a manageable set of descriptors. From the enormous number of descriptors available, how does one decide upon which terms to use? Lacking criteria for choices about types or levels of description, the approach could be unfeasible because of the staggering amount of work involved.[1] An extension of this argument suggests that the approach would eventually dissolve into S–R reductionism, permitting study of the trees (S–R relationships), but providing little information about the forest (task performance) (Wheaton, 1973).

Meister (1976) has provided a number of suggestions regarding the choice of task characteristics for defining properties that differentiate one task from another. Tasks may vary along a number of continua. Some of these, described by Meister, are: temporal relations (includ-

---

[1]In Chapter 2 we indicated a similar problem faced by biological taxonomists. For example, Michner and Sokal (1957) employed 11,834 characteristics to differentiate among 97 species of bees!

ing duration and sequence), divisibility, organization, automation (degree of manual or equipment implementation), dependencies, complexity (number of subtasks or elements, S–R connections), difficulty, and criticality. Some of the characteristics such as complexity and organization have multiple dimensions. Task difficulty is a superordinate characteristic defined by the interrelations among all other task characteristics. An important contribution by Meister is his attempt to summarize some evidence on the relation of variations in these generic task characteristics to learning and performance.

Farina and Wheaton (1973), under the Taxonomy Project, conceptualized tasks as having several components: explicit goals, procedures, input stimuli, responses, and stimulus–response relationships. In order to differentiate among tasks, the components of a task were treated as categories within which to devise task characteristics or descriptors (e.g., stimulus duration, number of output units, number of procedural steps). Scaling methods have been developed to provide definitions and quantitative estimates of these characteristics for a variety of tasks (see Fleishman, 1975). Mirabella and Wheaton (1973) have already shown how variations in such task dimensions can predict performance during skill acquisition and transfer across tasks. This work, and extensions of it, will be described in a later chapter.

ADDITIONAL CONCEPTUAL BASES FOR CLASSIFICATION

The above presentation of the conceptual bases of classification was organized around four conceptions of task. We should emphasize that the task classification systems reviewed do not necessarily fall neatly into these four categories (see Chapters 5, 6, and 7). And there are other systems that have relevance to human task performance which have not been considered, for example, those based on physiological processes or indices, although there is some evidence of their relevance to task classification (see Teichner & Olson, 1971). For example, Teichner and Olson (1969) have been able to show how correlated physiological measures (ambient partial pressure of oxygen and blood oxygen saturation) are, in turn, correlated with decrements in various kinds of task performances.

Beside human task performance itself, however, there are other aspects of the field of human performance that could benefit from taxonomic development. For instance, there are a large number of methods for the collection and analysis of data. These require classificatory systems in their own right and would seem to be much in need of such taxonomic development. A significant effort at classification in this area is the operational analysis approach of Verplanck (1968), in which he sought to identify and compare the operations that are performed in various laboratory research studies as a basis for deriving generalizations among studies.

In addition, the units, measures, and measurement techniques can provide the basis for classification systems of their own. Swain (1980), for example, has pointed out the need for methods of classifying errors in performance and Chambers (1963) has developed categories for performance degradation measures. It would appear that the problem here may not be so much a lack of measures, but as Grether (1968) has pointed out, the lack of a basis for comparison among them.

SUMMARY OF BASES OF CLASSIFICATION

In summary, we have seen that tasks can be defined in several ways, particularly in regard to: the scope of definition; the extent to which tasks may be treated as objective entities, clearly apart from the operators who perform them; and the extent to which tasks are viewed as processes or structures. We have also seen that there are, at present, few guidelines for selecting a particular definition or a particular approach to classification.

It remains to be seen how the several bases of task classification relate to the various purposes of classification. Once the objective bases have been identified, these issues become researchable questions. For example, which conceptual basis is more likely to furnish a general taxonomic system of tasks to assist our generalizations across a variety of human performance areas? Is the system more likely to improve predictions in the specific areas of learning and training? If we are interested in how changes in task properties affect performance, is the task characteristic approach more useful? If we are interested in generalizing from laboratory tasks to field tasks regarding organismic variables (e.g., drugs), or environmental stressors (e.g., noise), are we better off with task classification schemes based on task properties or on the human abilities or functions required by those tasks? If we wish to build an information retrieval system in an area of human performance, which conceptual basis of categorization will lend itself more readily to a useful synthesis of the data base? In developing job families, for selection, transfer, and promotion, which system of classifying tasks will lead to better choices of test predictors or to better chances of skill transfer within the job families developed?

Our division into four primary conceptual bases of task classification does not rule out other bases (e.g., physiological descriptive systems) and should not minimize the likelihood that taxonomic systems in the future will, to some extent, incorporate several conceptual schemes (see Dunnette, 1976; Fleishman, 1978; and Peterson & Bownas, 1982). Beginnings have already been made in classifying the elements in one conceptual system in terms of elements in other systems. Thus, task characteristics may be classified in terms of human functions or abilities presumed to be required by various types of tasks (e.g., Fleishman, 1975; Gagné, 1975; R. B. Miller, 1973; Berliner, Angell, & Shearer, 1964). Other work has shown that systematic relationships can be established between experimental manipulations of task characteristics and the ability category of those tasks (Fleishman, 1957; Wheaton, Eisner, Mirabella, & Fleishman, 1976; Fingerman, Eisner, Rose, Wheaton, & Cohen, 1975; Rose, Fingerman, Wheaton, Eisner, & Kramer, 1974). And moderate success has been achieved in classifying task characteristics in terms of training principles (e.g., Gagné, 1975; E. E. Miller, 1969; R. B. Miller, 1975; Stolurow, 1964).

The establishment of such linkages across the various conceptual bases for classification provides implications for future taxonomic development. However, our present problems are more immediate. We still need to face the issues relevant to the procedures for developing task classifications and the criteria for evaluating such systems. We turn to these problems in the next chapter.

References

Alexander, L., & Cooperband, A. S. *A method for system analysis using statistical decision theory.* Santa Monica, CA: SDC, August 1965.

Altman, I. Aspects of the criterion problem in small group research: The analysis of group tasks (Vol. 2). *Acta Psychologica*, 1966, *25*, 199–221.

Annett, J., & Duncan, K. D. Task analysis and training design. *Occupational Psychology*, 1967, *41*, 211–221.

Arnoult, M. D. The specification of a "social" stimulus. In S. B. Sells (Ed.), *Stimulus determinants of behavior.* New York: Ronald Press, 1963.

Berliner, D. C., Angell, D., & Shearer, J. *Behaviors, measures, and instruments for performance evaluation in simulated environments.* Paper delivered for a symposium and workshop on the Quantification of Human Performance, Albuquerque, New Mexico, August 1964.

Bloom, B. S. Taxonomy of educational objectives. In *The classification of educational goals: Cognitive domain (Handbook 1)*. New York: McKay, April 1967.

Carroll, J. B. Psychometric tests as cognitive tasks: A new "structure of intellect." In L. Resnick (Ed.), *The nature of intelligence*. Hillsdale, NJ: Lawrence Erlbaum, 1976.

Carroll, J. B. *Individual difference relations in psychometric and experimental cognitive tasks* (Tech. Rep. 163). Chapel Hill, NC: The L. L. Thurstone Psychometric Laboratory, University of North Carolina, April 1980.

Cattell, R. B. *Abilities: Their structure, growth, and action*. Boston: Houghton Mifflin, 1971.

Chambers, R. M. Operator performance in acceleration environments. In N. M. Burns, R. M. Chambers, & E. Hendler (Eds.), *Unusual environments and human behavior*. London: Glencoe, 1963.

Colson, K. R., Freeman, F. S., Mathews, L. P., & Stettler, J. A. *Development of an information taxonomy of visual displays for Army tactical data systems* (Research Memo 74-4). Arlington, VA: U.S. Army Research Institute for the Behavioral and Social Sciences, 1974.

Cotterman, T. E. *Task classification: An approach to partially ordering information on human learning* (WADC TN 58-374), Wright-Patterson AFB, Ohio, January 1959. (a)

Cotterman, T. E. *Problems in describing and categorizing tasks for determining training needs*. Paper presented at Ohio Psychological Association, Dayton, Ohio, October 1959. (b)

Dunnette, M. D. (Ed.). *Handbook of industrial and organizational psychology*. Chicago, IL: Rand McNally, 1976.

Dunnette, M. D., & Borman, W. C. Personnel selection and classification systems. *Annual Review of Psychology*, 1979, *30*, 477–525.

Eckstrand, G. A. *Current status of the technology of training* (AMRL-TR64-86). Wright Patterson AFB, Ohio, September 1964.

Ekstrom, R. B., French, J. W., & Harman, H. H. Cognitive factors: their identification and replication. *Multivariate Behavioral Research Monographs*, 1979, (No. 79-2), pp. 1–84.

Farina, A. J., Jr. Development of a taxonomy of human performance: A review of descriptive schemes for human task behavior. *JSAS Catalog of Selected Documents in Psychology*, 1973, *3*, 23 (Ms. No. 318).

Farina, A. J., Jr., & Wheaton, G. R. Development of a taxonomy of human performance: The task characteristics approach to performance prediction. *JSAS Catalog of Selected Documents in Psychology*, 1973, *3*, 26–27 (Ms. No. 323).

Fine, S. A. Functional job analysis: An approach to a technology for manpower planning. *Personnel Journal*, 1974, *53*(11), 813–818.

Fingerman, P. W., Eisner, E., Rose, A. M., Wheaton, G. R., & Cohen, F. *Methods for predicting job-ability requirements: Ability requirements as a function of changes in the characteristics of a concept identification task* (Vol. 3) (AIR Tech. Rep. 75-1). Washington, D.C.: American Institutes for Research, 1975.

Fitts, P. M. Factors in complex skill training. In R. Glaser (Ed.), *Training research and education*. Pittsburgh: University of Pittsburgh Press, 1962.

Fleishman, E. A. Factor structure in relation to task difficulty in psychomotor performance. *Educational and Psychological Measurement*, 1957, *17*, 522–532.

Fleishman, E. A. *The structure and measurement of physical fitness*. Englewood Cliffs, NJ: Prentice-Hall, 1964.

Fleishman, E. A. On the relation between abilities, learning, and human performance. *American Psychologist*, 1972, *27*, 1017–1032. (a)

Fleishman, E. A. Structure and measurement of psychomotor abilities. In R. N. Singer (Ed.), *Psychomotor domain: Movement behavior.* Philadelphia: Lea & Febiger, 1972. (b)

Fleishman, E. A. Toward a taxonomy of human performance. *American Psychologist*, 1975, *30*(12), 1127–1149.

Fleishman, E. A. Relating individual differences to the dimensions of human tasks. *Ergonomics*, 1978, *21*(12), 1007–1019.

Fleishman, E. A., Kinkade, R. G., & Chambers, A. N. Development of a taxonomy of human performance: A review of the first year's progress. *JSAS Catalog of Selected Documents in Psychology*, 1972, *2*, 39 (Ms. No. 111).

Folley, J. D., Jr. *Development of an improved method of task analysis and beginnings of a theory of training* (NAVTRADEVCEN 1218-1), Port Washington, NY: U.S. Navy Training Services Center, June 1964.

Fowler, R. L., Williams, W. E., Fowler, M. G., & Young, D. D. *An investigation of the relationship between operator performance and operator panel layout for continuous tasks* (Report AMRL-TR-68-170). Wright–Patterson AFB, OH: Aerospace Medical Research Laboratories, December 1968.

French, J. W., Ekstrom, R. B., & Price, L. A. *Kit of reference tests for cognitive factors.* Princeton, NJ: Educational Testing Service, 1963.

Gagné, R. M. Human functions in systems. In R. M. Gagné (Ed.), *Psychological principles in system development.* New York: Holt, Rinehart, & Winston, 1962.

Gagné, R. M. Taxonomic problems of educational systems. In W. T. Singleton & P. Spurgeon (Eds.), *Measurement of human resources.* New York: Halstead Press, 1975.

Grether, W. F. Engineering psychology in the United States. *American Psychologist*, 1968, *23*, 743–571.

Guilford, J. P. *The nature of human intelligence.* New York: McGraw-Hill, 1967.

Guilford, J. P., & Hoepfner, R. *The analysis of intelligence.* New York: McGraw-Hill, 1971.

Hackman, J. R. Tasks and task performance in research on stress. In J. E. McGrath (Ed.), *Social and psychological factors on stress.* New York: Holt, Rinehart & Winston, 1968.

Hilgard, E., & Bowers, G. *Theories of learning.* Englewood Cliffs, NJ: Prentice Hall, 1974.

Kidd, J. S. Human tasks and equipment design. In R. Glaser (Ed.), *Psychological principles in system development.* New York: Holt, Rinehart & Winston, 1962.

Marx, M. H., & Hillix, W. A. *Systems and theories in psychology* (3rd ed.). New York: McGraw-Hill, 1979.

McCormick, E. J. Job and task analysis. In M. D. Dunnette (Ed.), *Handbook of industrial and organizational psychology.* Chicago, IL: Rand McNally, 1976.

McCormick, E. J. *Job analysis: Methods and applications.* New York: AMACOM, 1979.

McCormick, E. J., Jeanneret, P. R., & Mecham, R. C. A study of job characteristics and job dimensions as based on the Position Analysis Questionnaire (PAQ). *Journal of Applied Psychology*, 1972, *56*, 347–368.

McGrath, J. E., & Altman, I. *Small group research: A synthesis and critique of the field.* New York: Holt, 1966.

Meister, D. *Behavioral foundations of system development.* New York: Wiley, 1976.

Meister, D., & Mills, R. G. Development of a human performance reliability data system. *Annals of reliability and maintainability.* New York: American Society of Mechanical Engineers, 1971.

Melton, A. W. The taxonomy of human learning: Overview. In A. W. Melton (Ed.), *Categories of human learning.* New York: Academic Press, 1964.

Michner, C. D. & Sokal, R. R. A quantitative approach to a problem in classification. *Evolution,* 1957, *11*, 130–162.

Miller, E. E. A classification of learning tasks in conventional language (Report AMRL-TR-63-74). Wright-Patterson AFB, OH: Aerospace Medical Research Laboratory, July 1963.

Miller, E. E. A taxonomy of response processes (Technical report 69-16). Fort Knox, KY: Human Resources Research Organization, September 1969.

Miller, R. B. Task taxonomy: Science or technology? In W. T. Singleton, R. S. Easterly, & D. C. Whitfield (Eds.), *The human operator in complex systems.* London: Taylor & Francis, 1967.

Miller, R. B. Development of a taxonomy of human performance: A user-oriented approach. *JSAS Catalog of Selected Documents in Psychology,* 1973, *3*, 26 (Ms. No. 322).

Miller, R. B. Taxonomies for training. In W. T. Singleton, & P. Spurgeon (Eds.), *Measurement of human resources.* New York: Halstead, 1975.

Mirabella, A., & Wheaton, G. R. *Effects of task index variations on transfer of training criteria.* NAVTRAEQUIPCEN 72-C-0126-1, Orlando, FL: U.S. Navy Training Equipment Center, September 1973.

Pearlman, K. Job families: A review and discussion of their implications for personnel selection. *Psychological Bulletin,* 1980, *87*, 1–28.

Peterson, N. G., & Bownas, D. A. Skill, task structure and performance acquisition. In M. D. Dunnette & E. A. Fleishman (Eds.), *Human performance and productivity, human capability assessment* (Vol. 2). Hillsdale, NJ: Lawrence Erlbaum, 1982.

Roby, T. B., & Lanzetta, J. T. Work group structure, communication, and group performance. *Sociometry,* 1956, *19*, 105–113.

Reed, L. E. *Advances in the use of computers for handling human factors task data* (AMRL-TR-67-16). Wright-Patterson AFB, OH: Aerospace Medical Research Laboratories, April 1967.

Rose, A. W., Fingerman, P. W., Wheaton, G. R., Eisner, E., & Kramer, G. *Methods for predicting job-ability requirements: II Ability requirements as a function of changes in the characteristics of an electronic fault-finding task* (AIR Tech. Rep. 74-6). Washington, D.C.: American Institutes for Research, 1974.

Sells, S. B. Dimensions of stimulus situations which account for behavior variance. In S. B. Sells (Ed.), *Stimulus determinants of behavior.* New York: Ronald Press, 1963.

Stevenson, H. W. Taxonomy of tasks. In F. J. Monks, W. W. Hartop, & J. DeWit (Eds.), *Determinants of behavioral development.* New York: Academic Press, 1972.

Stolurow, L. M. *A taxonomy of learning task characteristics* (AMRL-TDR-64-2). Wright-Patterson AFB, OH: Aerospace Medical Research Laboratories, 1964.

Swain, A. D. *Development of human error rate data bank* (SC-R-70-4286). Albuquerque, NM: Sandia Laboratories, October 1980.

Teichner, W. H., & Olson, D. E. *Predicting human performance in space environments* (NASA Contractor Report No. CR1370). Washington, DC: National Aeronautics & Space Administration, June 1969.

Teichner, W. H., & Olson, D. E. A preliminary theory of the effects of task and environmental factors in human performance. *Human Factors,* 1971, *13*, 295–344.

Verplanck, W. S. *Operational analysis of behavioral situations* (AF-AFOSR-1269-69-67). Knoxville, TN: University of Tennessee, 1968.

Wheaton, G. R. Development of a taxonomy of human performance: A review of classificatory systems relating to tasks and performance. *JSAS Catalog of Selected Documents in Psychology*, 1973, *3*, 22–23 (Ms. No. 317).

Wheaton, G. R., Eisner, E. J., Mirabella, A., & Fleishman, E. A. Ability requirements as a function of changes in the characteristics of an auditory signal identification task. *Journal of Applied Psychology*, 1976, *6*(6), 663–767.

Wickens, D. D. The centrality of verbal learning: Comments on Professor Underwood's paper. In A. Melton (Ed.), *Categories of human learning.* New York: Academic Press, 1964.

CHAPTER 4

odological Issues in Developing
and Evaluating
Classificatory Systems

Procedures for Classification

eated the taxonomic issues of purpose and conceptual basis,
w in a position to consider the problem of how to proceed
ification. How are human tasks, regardless of how they are
o be arranged systematically into groups or categories?
exceptions (see e.g., Cattell, Coulter, & Tsujioka, 1966; Coul-
ell, 1966; Hammer & Cunningham, 1980), behavioral scien-
not discussed the issues in developing alternative pro-
or classification in the light of taxonomic objectives and
atter.

hat an objective has been stated and that a conceptual basis
ption has been chosen, four issues arise in actually develop-
sificatory system. First, the domain of relevant attributes
specified in relation to the conceptual base and the pro-
r selecting descriptors lying in this domain should be de-
Second, it is mandatory that the tasks be classified as relia-
ssible; this, in turn, depends upon the ability to define task
s objectively and operationally. Third, classification may
n qualitative or quantitative grounds; in other words, class-
epresent different kinds of things (e.g., tracking tasks or
naking tasks) or they may represent differences in degree
ect to dimensions they have in common (e.g., monitoring
ssified by either complexity or frequency of stimuli). Fourth,

criteria to assess the adequacy and utility of the classificato
must be selected and applied. We deal with these issues i

Defining the Descriptor Domain

The first issue that must be addressed in formulating an
classification is specification of the nature of the descri
form the basis for the classification. In such attempts, the c
base being employed by the taxonomist must serve as the
source of guidance. Although it is difficult to provide a gr
guidance in this regard, there are at least two steps that ma
to help ensure an adequate specification of the domain.

Initially, the relevant concepts should be reviewed and
into well-defined hypotheses bearing on the nature of the
that should be considered relevant within the classificatol
Subsequently, the literature pertaining to these hypothe:
with qualitative observations of the phenomena, can be em
specify a preliminary attribute domain and its associatec
tors, which will be subject to further refinement as the t
effort progresses. However, at this point, it is importan
domain be defined rather broadly to ensure that important
and descriptors yielding unique information are not disre
this preliminary stage.

Once the domain has been specified, albeit in a rather lo
some decisions must be made as to exactly what attribute
scriptors are selected for evaluation. There are basically tl
egies that might be employed in this attempt.

First, the taxonomist might attempt to evaluate all th
descriptions. Generally, this approach is likely to be fea:
when a relatively limited domain of attributes and descri
concern or there is a great deal of redundancy in the in
contained in the potential descriptors.

When the domain is sizable, a second strategy might be
in which an attempt is made to obtain a random sampl
attribute descriptors incorporated in the domain. Although
egy is characterized by a certain statistical elegance, it is
value if the domain is poorly specified.

The third strategy entails an attempt to specify signi
tributes and descriptors in the sense that they are likely to
ate the relevant classes and/or are of some practical conce
the context of the classification attempt. This strategy
tionally been emphasized in the behavioral sciences (e.g.,

Schoenfeldt, 1979), and it is especially likely to be useful in exploratory or applied research efforts where relatively little is known about the characteristics of the various classes and/or the domain of descriptors is believed to be sizable.

Of course, the choice of any one of these strategies should be guided by the context of the research effort. However, the selected procedure should result in a set of descriptors that are potentially capable of identifying the underlying classes and so will serve as a foundation for the construction of a valid and stable classificatory system.

Operational Definitions, Objectivity, and Reliability

Regardless of the descriptors serving as the basis for classification, ideally they should be defined in operational terms permitting some form of quantitative assessment. That is, they should be reasonably objective. Kimble (1964) points out that the reliability with which distinctions among attributes can be made is largely a function of the extent to which they have been operationally defined. For example, Stolurow (1964) presented a series of task descriptions to a sample of judges. They were to analyze the tasks with respect to a list of quasi-operationally defined characteristics (e.g., number of stimuli, stimulus sequence, meaningfulness). Although interjudge agreement was not reported, this may have been less than adequate, as Stolurow later expressed the wish to redefine his descriptors more carefully. In our Taxonomy Project and in our later research, we have encountered similar difficulties in attempting to analyze tasks in terms of ability requirements. However, it was possible to increase interrater reliability coefficients by careful attention to definitions and their distinctions (Theologus & Fleishman, 1973; Theologus, Romashko, & Fleishman, 1973; Fleishman & Hogan, 1978).

These examples stress the need to develop objective and concise definitions that will permit clear and consistent distinctions among descriptors, initially, and among categories of tasks, ultimately. Other steps in this direction have been taken by Teichner and Olson (1969) and Teichner and Whitehead (1973). They attempted to make behavior requirement terms (e.g., searching, switching, coding, and tracking) more objective and unambiguous, defining each type of task semantically and then operationally referencing each type of task in terms of a criterion response measure associated with it (e.g., probability of detection, reaction time, percentage of correct responses, time on target).

The requirement for concise and objective definition of terms becomes increasingly critical if the system is to be used by a broad range of specialists. The descriptive terms may be completely unfamiliar to many of these individuals, or too familiar, as in the case of the popular terms *decision making* and *problem solving*. Everyone has a personal meaning for these terms. As a consequence, it is desirable to train users in the meaning of nomenclature. However, the effectiveness of this training can only be as good as the definitions being learned. Objectivity of definitions bears directly on the reliability and precision with which the selected subject matter can be classified.

Different types of reliability indices need to be applied in the development and evaluation of the individual descriptors and in their use as a system. Traditional psychometric concepts of standard error of measurement, interrater agreement, test–retest and split-half reliability, and profile similarity are appropriate here (see e.g., Anastasi, 1982; Guilford & Fruchter, 1978). In our review of existing systems, we found that these types of reliability were often not determined (see Chapters 5, 6, and 7).

Hence, the development of any viable classificatory system, including those involving the field of human performance, is predicated upon reliable operational definitions of the relevant descriptors. In taxonomic efforts involving other areas of the behavioral sciences, additional considerations should be addressed in constructing the descriptor domain. These considerations include the measurement format and the validity of the descriptors, as well as the extent to which such descriptor measurements are free from the contaminating influences of extraneous variables. In fact, Jackson and Messick (1958) have suggested that the value of a classificatory system can be destroyed by a failure to examine and control such contaminating influences, which are, more often than not, attributable to poor operationalization.

Qualitative and Quantitative Classification

This section focuses on the systems of measurement typically applied to descriptors and on the implications they have for the structural and functional characteristics of the resulting classificatory system. Also discussed are issues related to the specific procedures utilized in developing classificatory systems.

The taxonomic issues of purpose, conceptual bases, and procedures are inextricably interwoven (Wheaton, 1973). Each step in the development of a classificatory system has implications for subsequent (and often preceding) steps. This interdependency is particularly noticeable when one attempts to specify the functional and structural nature of the system. Thus, the purpose for which classification is attempted has implications for the *definitions* of tasks. In turn, these task definitions determine directly the appropriate conceptual bases for task description and differentiation. Furthermore, the degree to which classificatory descriptors can be defined operationally and objectively appears to have implications for the system of measurement to be employed during classification.

QUALITATIVE CLASSIFICATION

As a minimum requirement, the descriptors employed in the differentiation and classification of tasks must permit nominal scaling. That is, a judge must at least be able to determine whether each descriptor applies or does not apply to the particular task being examined. In such qualitative (or absolute) classification, the judge is required to make a series of decisions about the presence or absence of a set of descriptors that are treated as attributes of the tasks. Examples of qualitative classification are the assignment of library accession numbers and the controlled vocabularies and thesauri of document reference services.

Classification based upon these types of decisions about the presence or absence of an attribute can proceed in two ways, which biologists call monothetic or polythetic classification (Sokal & Sneath, 1963). In *monothetic* classification, the taxonomist defines each type of task or category in terms of a unique and usually small set of attributes such that possession of these features is both necessary and sufficient for membership in the group so defined. The groups that result are termed monothetic groups because each grouping has a unique set of defining attributes.

The taxonomist who employs this method of classification is essentially providing a priori weightings to a large set of attributes. Thus, a *monitoring task* may be defined as a task in which attributes A and B are present, and a *tracking task* as one in which attributes X, Y, and Z are judged present. In other words, a weight of one is assigned to

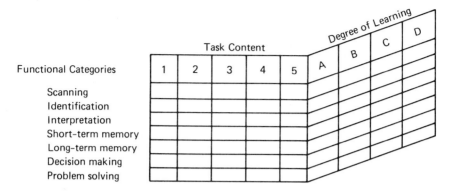

Figure 4.1 A taxonomic grid. Adapted with permission from Taylor & Francis Ltd. © R. B. Miller, Task taxonomy: Science or technology? In W. T. Singleton, R. S. Easterly, & D. C. Whitfield (Eds.), *The human operator in complex systems*. London: Taylor & Francis, 1967.

those attributes that define a particular type of task and a weight of zero to those attributes not included in the definition of that same type of task. Finding attributes X, Y, and Z present in a specific task (e.g., aiming a visually sighted antiaircraft weapon) indicates that the task can be categorized as a tracking task. This is essentially how Teichner and Whitehead (1973), for instance, might decide whether a particular specimen or unit is a searching, switching, coding, or tracking task. If the response measure involves "number of targets detected," it is, by definition, a searching task; if it involves "reaction time," then it is, by definition, a switching task; if it involves "time on tracking," it is a tracking task, and so forth.

In *polythetic* classifications, investigators examine the overall pattern of features that can be attributed to each specimen. Tasks that have the greatest number of shared features (e.g., attributes A through Z) are placed within the same category. No single attribute is either essential to group membership or insufficient to make a particular task a member of the group. Taxonomists who pursue this approach contend that any particular task will require some set of descriptors from the total set of descriptors, for example, a set of abilities from the total set of abilities, or some set of processes from a larger set. Classification proceeds as if a checklist were being employed.

An example of polythetic qualitative classification, based on a nominal scale of measurement, is provided in the work of R. B. Miller (1967). Figure 4.1 illustrates a prototype taxonomic grid, in Miller's system, consisting of three axes (the particular descriptors accom-

TABLE 4.1

Qualitative Task Description[a]

	Sampled Tasks							
Descriptors	1	2	3	4	5	6	7	8
A	+	+	+	+	+	0	+	0
B	0	0	+	+	+	0	+	0
C	+	+	+	0	+	0	0	+
D	0	0	0	+	+	0	0	+

[a]Adapted with permission from Wheaton, G. R. Development of a taxonomy of human performance: A review of classificatory systems relating to tasks and performance (American Institutes for Research Tech. Rep.) *JSAS Catalog of Selected Documents in Psychology,* 1973, *3,* 22–23. (Ms. No. 317).

panying each axis are intended to be illustrative only). Judges would be required to examine tasks with respect to each axis of description. Attributes on each axis would be judged present or absent, yielding a unique configuration. Tasks having identical or similar configurations would be said to belong to the same class, category, or taxon.

Regardless of which particular approach is chosen, classification of tasks on qualitative grounds is clearly possible, given a set of reasonably well defined descriptors whose presence or absence can be determined reliably for any particular task. Although only a few investigators have actually attempted systematic task classification, most of those reviewed (see Chapters 5, 6 and 7, as well as Wheaton, 1973; Farina, 1973) treat the process of classification as the categorization of tasks based on the pattern of attributes that they are judged to possess. Because many investigators seem, initially, to be interested in qualitative classification, it is important that its implications for the classificatory structure be understood.

Let us illustrate with a descriptive system based on four attributes: A, B, C, and D. In assessing the presence or absence of these descriptors in a sample of tasks, the configurations shown in Table 4.1 could be obtained.

With respect to Task 6 in Table 4.1, it is clear that it is similar to no other configuration because it does not include any of the attributes in the system. This configuration immediately suggests that additional attributes need to be found for inclusion in the system. To the extent that one has confidence that the system is reasonably complete, this configuration suggests that the task falls outside the domain of behaviors, functions, abilities, or characteristics under consideration.

In Table 4.1, there are two tasks that are identical; Tasks 1 and 2 have precisely the same configurations. They belong to the same category or class by virtue of the presence of attributes A and C, and the absence of attributes B and D. But what can be inferred from the remaining tasks and the configurations of attributes associated with them? We could conclude that the remaining tasks represent unique types or categories. With repeated sampling, other tasks might be found which exhibit one of these remaining configurations or other configurations. The extension of this argument is that there is a class for each possible configuration of attributes. For n attributes there are 2^n possible configurations. As n becomes large, the number of possible categories would become extremely large. Ultimately, such a system would generate classes permitting extremely fine distinctions among tasks. In the extreme case, the distinctions would become so precise as to provide classes consisting of single tasks!

Consequently, the taxonomist must develop this classificatory system to get around the *reductio ad absurdum* problem. The approach is one of placing *similar* tasks within the same category. However, when one deals with the types of data shown in Table 4.1, the determination of task similarities becomes extremely complex. The particular criterion of similarity that is chosen is often an arbitrary matter. There is no compelling logic for the adoption of one criterion over others. Consequently, for the data shown in Table 4.1, a number of alternative groupings are possible depending on how one chooses to define "similarity."

When classificatory systems are based on nominal data, similarity may be expressed in terms of the number of common attributes relative to the total number of attributes under consideration. However, this approach to the definition of similarity may not always be ideal. For instance, as has been pointed out, the resulting definition of similarity is highly contintgent on both the specific number and the nature of the attributes under consideration. Moreover, this approach implicitly disregards the possibility that attributes may be present in differing degrees, and these degrees of similarity may dramatically influence our conceptions of just what constitutes sufficient similarity between certain objects for inclusion in a single category. Additionally, when there is potential for sampling error in judgments regarding the presence or absence of an attribute, it is to some extent logically necessary to examine such differences in degree. The legitimacy of these concerns regarding the precision of measurement must be evaluated with respect to one's ultimate purpose in developing the classificatory system. If one's intention is to index the experimental literature, then categories that differ in the absolute presence or absence of attributes may suffice. However, if one's interest is in manipulating a task parameter and predicting the effect of such a manipulation upon performance, then task attributes that differ in degree are likely to be a more appropriate basis for classification.

QUANTITATIVE CLASSIFICATION

In quantitative (or relative) classification, our judgments concerning the presence or absence of elements are stated in degree. Thus, ratio, interval, or, more commonly, ordinal scales of measurement are employed in describing the attributes to make statements concerning differences among objects as to the amount or degree to which the attributes are present. The use of these higher-level scales requires increasing sophistication in the nature of the operationalized descriptors employed to access the degree to which these attributes are present. Consequently, a number of new statistical concerns arise. The primary quantitative issues in task classification are the need for reliable measures of task characteristics, indices of similarity, and methods of grouping or clustering on the bases of these indices.

MEASURES   Here we shall explore some of the initial considerations in developing a quantitative system of classification. A first step would be to try to select a set of descriptive dimensions common to or applicable to a wide variety of tasks. If this selection is successful, then all task specimens might be described in terms of each dimension. Figure 4.2 illustrates how the use of common dimensions would permit a profile of dimensional values to be developed for each task under investigation. More important, because all tasks would be evaluated with respect to all dimensions, tasks would be distinguished on the basis of *degree*.

In our review of task classifications in areas of human performance (see Chapters 5, 6, and 7), few specific classifications were found to be based explicitly upon the quantitative scaling of task descriptors. However, because most taxonomists begin with a qualitative approach, and because behavior taxonomy is in the rudimentary stage, it would be premature to conclude that interest in quantification is lacking. For example, with sufficient rigor in the definitions, a qualitative system could be made quantitative by having judges rate

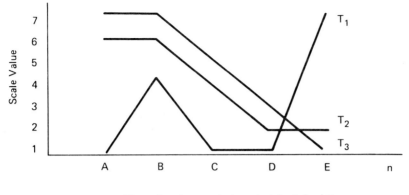

Dimensions (e.g., task characteristic, behavior
description, function, ability)

Figure 4.2 Illustrative task profile data. Reprinted with permission from Wheaton, G. R. Development of a taxonomy of human performance: A review of classificatory systems relating to tasks and performance (American Institutes for Research Tech. Rep.). *JSAS Catalog of Selected Documents in Psychology*, 1973, *3*, 22–23. (Ms. No. 317.)

or scale each descriptor in terms of its involvement in a particular task. Other measurements might proceed in terms of counts (e.g., number of controls) or in terms of other quantitative dimensions (e.g., level of force required). We found that quantitative classification was more advanced in the case of certain of the approaches examined (e.g., the Ability Requirements Approach) and that some of these methods could be extended to the other approaches (e.g., the Task Characteristics Approach). We shall see in later chapters that efforts on the Taxonomy Project, and more recent efforts, have produced considerable progress along these lines (Farina & Wheaton, 1973; Fleishman, 1975; Theologus *et al.*, 1973; Fleishman & Hogan, 1978).

In Chapter 2, we mentioned the increased development and application of numerical taxonomy procedures in biology (see Cole, 1969; Jardine & Gibson, 1971; Sokal & Sneath, 1963). Numerical taxonomy refers to those mathematical techniques intended to identify clusters of data points in multidimensional space. If the measure set contains relevant variables, objectively evaluated and spanning a substantial dimensionality, then members of clusters will share functional or structural characteristics. Silverman (1968) recommends that the numerical taxonomic procedures used in biology be employed in the generation of classes of tasks. Such procedures would base task comparison and classification on operational and quantitative grounds. There have been many developments and applications of quantitative methods for determining profile similarity (e.g., Cronbach & Gleser, 1953), and for clustering of variables in the behavioral sciences (e.g., Cureton, Cureton, & Durfee, 1970; Harman, 1967; Johnson, 1967; McQuitty, 1960; Ward & Hook, 1963; Ball & Hall, 1967).

For the problem of classifying tasks, we need both indices of similarity between measures taken from tasks and algorithms and methods for grouping these indices. These requirements cannot be neatly separated. There exist many different indices of similarity, ranging from the correlation coefficient to the generalized distance function most favored by biologists. The abundance of clustering techniques has been demonstrated by Ball (1965), who reviewed 27 techniques reported in the literature between 1960 and 1965. However, there have been few attempts to relate the logic and purposes of these various methods to the objectives of taxonomic development in the behavioral sciences. Examples of such attempts are found in Baker (1972), Coulter and Cattell (1966), Dubin and Champoux (1970), Owens and Mumford (1983), Owens and Schoenfeldt (1979), and Pratt and Canfield (1975).

Although the treatment of such issues is certainly relevant to quantitative methods needed for classifying human tasks, within the space of this chapter we give the reader only a glimpse of some of them. The reader is referred to Cattell, Coulter, and Tsujioka (1966) for the most comprehensive and sophisticated discussion of quantitative issues and methods relevant to taxonomic development in the behavioral sciences.

SIMILARITY INDICES   An important problem in classification is determining the degree of similarity between task dimensional profiles. Those profiles having the greatest similarity are placed within the same class. Quantitative classification techniques allow measurement of the similarity among the sample units to be classified. This is generally accomplished by multidimensional scaling, cluster analysis, latent structure or facet analysis, or discriminant function techniques. Each sample is located in hyperspace as a function of its values on the set of dimensions used to describe it. Those samples that are located in the same general space tend to cluster or to fall into classes or categories. Depending on the specific procedure used, the choice of a particular criterion for cluster size is sometimes arbitrary. However, once clusters are generated, the differences between them can be described in terms of their distances from one another along each dimension of description. An oversimplified representation of classes developed in this manner is shown in Figure 4.3.

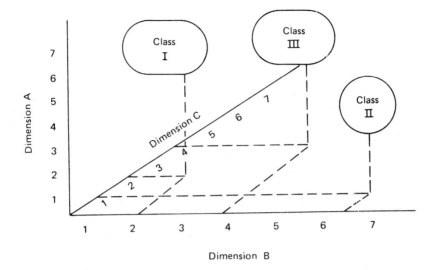

Figure 4.3 Numerical classification. Reprinted with permission from Wheaton, G. R. Development of a taxonomy of human performance: A review of classificatory systems relating to tasks and performance (American Institutes for Research Tech. Rep.). *JSAS Catalog of Selected Documents in Psychology*, 1973, 3, 22–23. (Ms. No. 317.)

There is a need to select the proper combinations of similarity indices and grouping algorithms for particular purposes. Nearly all clustering algorithms operate upon a matrix of intersubject similarity measures. However, there are a number of alternatives to the measurement of similarity. Earlier, it was pointed out that nominal data reflecting the relative frequency of shared attributes may be used as a basis for defining similarity. The biological taxonomist has been concerned primarily with the presence or absence of a characteristic in a specimen; occasionally characteristics having several states are observed. As a result, the numerical taxonomist in biology tends to use similarity measures depending upon frequency counts, such as agreement or matching indices.

Sokal and Sneath (1963) have reported a variety of matching indices depending on such data. Earlier, biologists utilized a simple measure of similarity (S) between pairs of organisms, using the expression:

$$S = \frac{n_s}{n_s + n_d}$$

is the number of features possessed by both organisms and
number of features possessed by one organism and not the
h organism is scored as positive (+) or negative (−) for each
n comparing two organisms, the computer is directed to
) as a similarity and (+ −) or (− +) as a difference, ignoring
ches. Beers and Lockhart (1962) pointed out the limitations
cedure in scoring certain properties that cannot be consid-
simply present or absent and in restricting the scoring of sim-
positive responses only.

noted earlier, relationships defined by such frequency-
tis.ics may not be sufficient for many purposes. This is par-
rue in the behavioral sciences where presence or absence is
ofter a relative than an absolute matter. The more common
indices in the behavioral sciences attempt to employ ordi-
to measure the relative distance between subjects. Here the
measured form an n-dimensional space on which each sub-
e located relative to all the other subjects on each of the
measured.

rity measure commonly used to summarize these relation-
he square of the Euclidean distance between two subjects in
where X_{ij} is a measure, i a characteristic, and j is the
index:

$$D^2 = \sum_{i=1}^{n} (X_{ij} - X_{ij})^2$$

er the distance between subjects on the various characteris-
reater their similarity. When the characteristics are mea-
a number of different scales, the problem of a common
ses. The usual solution to this problem is to standardize
ble before calculating the distance measures.

his D^2 measure is employed, it is sensitive to the overall
attribute measurements and so considers the elevation
and shape of the measurements in defining similarity. These
of profile similarity are presented in Figure 4.4.

nes, when defining similarity, taxonomists and researchers
ted only in the shape of a profile. In this case, the problem
matching is essentially one of clustering subjects (e.g.,
se sine vectors are alike; thus, a measure of similarity is
such distance measures are frequently used in the behav-
es, although the product moment correlation coefficient is

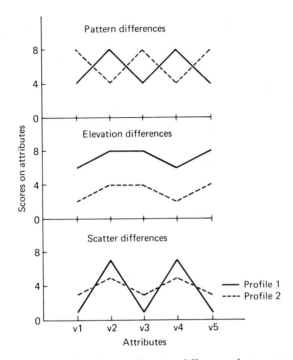

Figure 4.4 Pattern, elevation, and scatter differences between two

used more extensively as a similarity measure. Matrices tion coefficients can be analyzed by most clustering algor

Finally, it should be noted that, for nominal measures vant attributes, there are nonparametric alternatives to th and the correlation coefficient. More specifically, eithe square or one of the nonparametric contingency coefficient employed in the definition of similarity.

CLUSTERING Cluster analyses may or may not be neces development and evaluation of taxonomic systems. As we later chapters, some systems can be developed on the basis theoretical formulations and tested and modified in terms ber of internal and external criteria. Whether theoretica pirically derived, the classificatory system must conform cal criteria of all classificatory systems (e.g., mutually exc internally homogeneous categories, exhaustive and de characteristics).

Cluster analytic techniques are particularly useful when there is no theoretical scheme or model to guide an analyst through a large matrix of data representing indices of agreement in the properties or scores of the attributes examined. However, clustering techniques can be used to confirm, refine, or revise a priori theoretical classification schemes. These techniques search out the systematic (or latent) structure of a data matrix (Ball, 1965; Johnson, 1967). Further, it would be clearly impossible to expect to discover, by inspection, the structure of a large data matrix without using a search procedure specifically designed for that purpose.

By *structure* we mean the orderly groupings of data points in the data matrix. Each grouping (or cluster) contains data points that are more like each other than data points outside of the group (Ball, 1965; Bonner, 1964). A major contribution of cluster analysis is its ability to reveal such natural groupings. The groups are defined by the data themselves; they are not formed by the use of some external criterion of classification (Friedman & Rubin, 1967).

All clustering techniques employ two basic steps in order to define subsets or types of attributes in the matrix of attributes. The first step is the *putting together* of attributes that go together to form clusters. This is commonly done by using measures of association between all attributes taking two at a time in the matrix of attributes. Whatever the measure of association, the higher the value of that measure, the more alike are the attributes measured. (For distance measures, the smaller the distance, the more alike are the attributes.)

The second basic step in clustering techniques is the determination of the *boundaries* between clusters of attributes. When distance measures are used, the boundary is established by determining how far from a central point (some kind of average or representative point) any attribute can be and still be a member of a cluster. For similarity measures, a threshold level of measured association determines cluster membership. When the measured association of an attribute with one or all existing members of a cluster exceeds the threshold value, the attribute is included in the cluster. Otherwise, it is not. In both instances, the boundary is somewhat arbitrary because the maximum distance and the threshold level of association may be arbitrarily set, but generally there is some statistical or rational criterion.

In general, clustering techniques use measures of association to form clusters. The clustering techniques also specify the manner in which *likeness* or *closeness* of data points is to be determined, thereby establishing boundaries between types that permit unequivocal assignment of each data point to one and only one type. With these two basic steps in mind, we can see clearly that the objective of clustering techniques, as defined by Ball (1965), is the sorting of the set of data patterns into subsets such that each subset contains data points that are as much alike as possible. More specifically, the objective of classification is to identify categories of such a nature that every task (object, person) in the category is in some way more like some other task (object, person) in that category than it is like some task not in that category.

The literature relevant to grouping algorithms is extensive and the distinctions between techniques are not always clear-cut. The comprehensive survey of grouping and related techniques by Ball and Hall (1968) derived four classes of procedures: dimensionalizing the similarity matrix, nonhierarchical methods, hierarchical methods, and connectivity methods. Techniques that dimensionalize the similarity matrix are based upon principal components or factor analysis (see Harman, 1967). They perform what Greene and Carmone (1970) term metric reduced space analysis. These dimensionalizing techniques yield only the final clusters of objects and no hierarchical structure is involved. Stephenson's (1936) Q factor analysis and the clustering techniques of Tryon (Tryon, 1939; Tryon & Bailey, 1970) are of this type. The nonhierarchical methods are clustering techniques that depend upon establishing cluster centers; then the clusters grow in size by merging other objects into the clusters. Again, the end product is a set of clusters of objects. Psychometric techniques for profile analysis are of this type (see Cronbach & Gleser, 1953).

The hierarchical methods produce a tree structure that depicts the grouping performed at several iterations of the analysis (McQuitty, 1960). Connectivity methods are based upon developing a linkage between an object and a group. For example, if an object pair is encountered in the ranked list, and one member has a prior group membership, the connection results in the other member joining the group. The Johnson (1967) MIN algorithm belongs to this class of techniques as does Dissimilarity Linkage Analysis developed by Dubin and Champoux (1970).

Additional classes of statistical clustering techniques are Fisher's (1936) discriminant analysis and Rao's (1971) cluster analysis. These techniques yield clusters of objects on the basis of a similarity measure, but depend upon an a priori definition of the number of clusters rather than upon deriving the number of clusters from the data. Hence, they are not highly useful in empirically defining categories. However, they often serve as a useful adjunct, especially in evaluating the statistical adequacy of a clustering solution in assigning new entities to a previously defined set of clusters.

Many of the basic algorithms, concepts, and applications of grouping were pioneered by McQuitty. The basic grouping algorithm developed by McQuitty (1960) is called *Hierarchical Linkage Analysis*. This technique is identical to Johnson's (1967) MAX procedure and to Sorensen's (1948) early applications of numerical taxonomy in biology. Under this algorithm, the similarity indexes are rank ordered and a grouping procedure is employed. The results are presented in a tree structure. A variation of this algorithm, called *Hierarchical Syndrome Analysis* (McQuitty, 1960), differs in that a replacement procedure is applied to the similarity matrix at each iteration. When two subjects are grouped, the corresponding rows and columns of the similarity matrix are merged and replaced by a single row and column of similarity values. Thus, as grouping takes place, the size of the similarity matrix is reduced.

The grouping algorithms developed by McQuitty were based upon what he called the classification assumption. This assumption stated that for a given grouping of subjects, the individual members of the group have in common all of the characteristics that the pair in the group with the smallest similarity index have in common. Initially, this classification assumption depended upon the use of a similarity index that was an agreement index; hence, it stated the number of characteristics in common. Later it was assumed to hold for similarity coefficients, such as correlation coefficients, in which a count of the number of characteristics held in common was not possible.

A different approach to hierarchical grouping is used by Ward (1963). The similarity measure employed is the square of the score differences, d^2, summed over the set of scores. The grouping algorithm is based upon an optimization function rather than upon the rank order of the values of the similarity index. The optimization function determines the average similarity to be gained by merging two subjects, groups, or a subject and a group, and is calculated for all possible mergings at each iteration. The grouping yielding the maximum value of this function is then performed. The procedure is repeated until all subjects have been merged into a single group and the hierarchy completed. Ward's use of an optimizing function is important because it leads toward grouping algorithms that attempt to develop the best hierarchy in the presence of uncertainty in the data.

In the behavioral sciences, factor analysis methods have been the most common procedure for identifying clusters in large data matrixes of correlation coefficients. These developments have been applied primarily in areas of test development and in studies of human abilities and personality. Discussions of these methods are beyond our present scope and can be found elsewhere (Harman, 1967). However, the fundamental issues are relevant to procedures of task classifications. These applications have been largely in developing classificatory systems utilizing the abilities approach and will be discussed in later chapters.

APPLICATIONS A number of numerical taxonomic methods may be used interactively, or as cross checks of content, in developing quantitatively based classifications. A good example has recently been presented by John, Karmel, Corning, Easton, Brown, Ahan, John, Harmony, Prichep, Toro, Gerson, Bartlett, Thatcher, Kaye, Valdes, & Schwartz (1977). These investigators developed a methodology called *neurometrics* to provide quantitative information about brain activity. The aim was to gather data sensitive to a variety of brain functions and to quantify and classify profiles of these brain functions into clusters sharing common features. These goals were achieved using combinations of multiple discriminant function analysis, step-wise factor analysis, and other multivariate techniques. The new categories developed helped to integrate a great deal of information regarding symptomologies, dysfunctions, disease, and learning disabilities, and have potential to improve choices of intervention strategies. A recent example of the use of discriminant function analysis in taxonomic analysis has been provided by Bekoff and Hill (1975).

For our present purposes, there are numerical taxonomic techniques available that have not been applied extensively to taxonomic issues in the behavioral sciences. These should be more fully explored, especially in light of the difficulties that psychologists have in assessing the similarity among qualitatively derived categories. This is true in areas of human performance research as well as in other areas of psychology. Without the use of such procedures, it may be difficult to develop a classificatory system that can be quantitatively established and that can specify fully the relationships across and between levels.

We suspect that any comprehensive classificatory system for human performance will always be based on some combination of qualitative and quantitative approaches. Thus, in analyzing any task situation, the first question to be asked is, "Is some variable present or absent?"; then, if present, "How much?" and "On what measurement basis can it be expressed?" Also, if present, "Does the variable relate to some other variable?" If it does, "In what way?" and "What type of quantitative relationships can be expressed?" Later in this volume, we see how the methodology developed in connection with the Abilities Requirements Approach to task classification followed a sequence such as this.

Criteria for Evaluating Classificatory Systems

Assume for the moment that the behavioral taxonomist has dealt successfully with many of the preceding issues. The purpose of the classificatory system has been explicitly stated, the subject matter to be classified has been chosen, the descriptors have been carefully selected and defined, and one of several alternative clustering procedures has been utilized. How may the adequacy of the resulting classificatory system be judged? What criteria have been suggested for this evaluation?

Our reviews of the literature indicate that methods for evaluating classificatory systems have been particularly neglected. Because of this neglect and because evaluation seems so necessary for taxonomic progress, we have devoted considerable effort to (1) identifying methods and criteria for taxonomic evaluation, and (2) applying some of these methods and criteria to the evaluation of various descriptive and classificatory schemes that have been developed. This section describes the methods and criteria for evaluation that were identified. The application of such criteria is described in subsequent chapters in conjunction with each description of a particular scheme.

There are essentially three primary kinds of criteria for evaluation. The first we call *internal validity*, that is, whether the system is logical and parsimonious within itself. The second we call *external validity*, that is, whether the system is capable of accomplishing its intended purpose or predicting a behavioral effect. The third involves *use rate*, that is, whether the system is actually used by scientists and technologists in the fields of interest. Internal and external validity are necessary but not sufficient conditions for creating a high use rate of the system. How well the system is "human engineered" will have significant impact on its utility.

INTERNAL VALIDITY

As far as internal validity is concerned, there are several criteria. The first, *reliability* of the classifications, has already been described. Descriptors must be defined and treated within a system of measurement so that they can be evaluated reliably. Regardless of the descriptive bases or the techniques employed in classification, it is essential that descriptor values be assigned reliably. Additionally, reliability of the system, as a system, needs to be evaluated.

In no sense is this a redundant operation. When assessing the reliability of the classificatory system as a whole, the concern is with the degree to which the entities are assigned to the same category despite random fluctuations in the sampling of descriptors and/or numerical scores. The reliability of these differential assignments is highly dependent on adequate coverage of the relevant attribute–descriptor domain, as well as on the degree of true category differentiation and the degree of differentiation resulting from the measurements in use. If adequate conceptual and empirical differentiation is obtained, even individual measures of only moderate reliability may yield a reliable classification. In this sense, poor system reliability, when reliable individual measures are in use, suggests a need for conceptual reevaluation. On the other hand, poor system reliability, given a set of unreliable measures, can reflect either poor measurement or poor conception. Thus, careful attention should be given to both these issues when evaluating classification procedures.

Once the formal process of classification has been initiated, a second criterion for internal validity, inherited from biological taxonomists, is called into play. This criterion involves the desirability of having *mutually exclusive* classes on the same horizontal level, so that it is possible to place any entity into only one grouping. This criterion is most readily satisfied in monothetic qualitative systems, and is hardest to achieve in quantitative systems. Behavioral taxonomists are not in complete agreement as to the necessity of mutual exclusivity (Annett & Duncan, 1967). Some investigators stress this criterion, attempting to achieve it through careful formal definition of categories. Others seem to de-emphasize it, finding it to be unrealistically constraining (Dubin & Champoux, 1970), at least during initial stages of classificatory development. One should probably strive for eventual exclusivity of classes, but one should also be willing to accept less rigor during initial efforts.

A third internal criterion concerns the extent to which classification is *exhaustive.* Powerful classifications are those in which every sample or unit of subject matter can be placed somewhere. Annett and Duncan (1967) identify two reactions to this criterion by behavioral taxonomists. Some start by considering a tremendous range of tasks with the objective of accounting for each in their systems. Others are interested initially in classifying a smaller set, providing a "catchall" category for tasks that cannot immediately be located within their formal framework. Again, while exhaustive classification is an ultimate objective, it is perhaps unrealistic during initial efforts. It is this continuing search for both mutually exclusive classes and exhaustive classification that seems to lead to the constant revision and modification found in healthy systems of classification.

A final internal criterion that should be examined when classificatory systems are being evaluated reflects a somewhat subjective yet highly important consideration. Here we refer to the fact that the attributes that distinguish a category member from the general population (as well as the relationship among and within the categories) should fall into an interpretable and meaningful pattern, given a knowledge of relevant literature, the data base, and the purpose of classification. The categories contained in the classification may be viewed as highly complex constructs in the sense specified by Cronbach (1971) and thus are amenable to an internal-construct validation effort. Less formally, the empirical characteristics of the classification should "make sense" to the informed reviewer.

EXTERNAL VALIDITY

The second type of criteria, external validity, pertains to how well the classificatory system achieves the objectives for which it is designed. Relevant criteria may vary as a function of the purpose, conceptual base, and use of the taxonomic scheme. For example, for systems designed as information retrieval aids, some assessment should be made of the efficiency and accuracy with which studies can be retrieved that are relevant to the particular users' interests and problems (see Chapter 8). If designed as an aid in scientific prediction, the evaluation must come in the form of its usefulness as an aid for interpreting and integrating research results (e.g., Levine, Romashko, & Fleishman, 1973). Subsequent evaluations of the system involve laboratory testing of generalizations across tasks defined in terms of the classificatory system developed (Theologus *et al.*, 1973) and in the prediction of complex task performance from laboratory data (Farina & Wheaton, 1973). An issue that should be addressed in such attempts is the generality or robustness of the classificatory system. A number of strategies might be used to assess the characteristics of the system. Thus, the extent to which the relationships in the system are employed and supported in construct validation efforts, and are maintained in samples or on measures that were not used in formation of the classification, can be evaluated. Additionally, the extent to which the members of new samples can be accurately assigned to a single category can be evaluated in a manner analogous to the cross validation of discriminant functions. Finally, similar classifications developed over the years might be examined to determine the degree of overlap and so generate information bearing on the convergent validity of the classification system.

Other forms of evaluation could derive from assessment of the usefulness of the system for planning research programs to fill in missing data and for specifying how research should be reported to permit greater generalization. One factor impeding this use of a classificatory system is that researchers tend to avoid publishing "no difference found" studies (as if they were failures) and no publication medium is generally available for them. In principle, however, a Type II error creates just as serious a bias as a Type I error. For the purposes of evaluating a classificatory system, it is important to know whether a given condition produces no difference in a class of tasks. The extent to which such data are unavailable in the literature limits how well we can evaluate the application of a classificatory system to this literature.

Ultimately, any behavioral classification scheme must make the "match" between specific categories and behavioral effects. The degree to which the match can be made will determine the predictive power of the system. At one level, a statement might concern whether or not a particular training or environmental variable would affect performance. At another and more sophisticated level, it might be possible to predict the direction and magnitude of effect. We have attempted to show how quantitative systems, in particular, would meet this criterion.

UTILITARIAN CRITERIA

R. B. Miller (1967) and E. E. Miller (1969) have stressed the need to evaluate emerging classifications in terms of their utility and efficiency. A taxonomic system should promote communication among its users, whether laboratory researchers, applied psychologists, or those who must apply the system. It should assist heuristically in solving the applied problems described in Chapter 1 (e.g., decisions in personnel selection, system design, training). Time and training required to learn the system, and costs of implementing the system, are additional criteria emphasized by R. B. Miller (1973). He argues that perhaps the ultimate criterion is the degree of acceptance that the systems come to enjoy, that is, their use rate; if the classificatory system is to be of value, it must be used by a large number of people. Effective handling of the issues discussed previously would certainly contribute to the achievement of such a goal. However, one would hope that scientific truth is somewhat independent of people's ability to see and apply it!

References

Anastasi, A. *Psychological testing.* New York: MacMillan, 1982.

Annett, J., & Duncan, K. D. Task analysis and training design. *Occupational Psychology,* 1967, *41,* 211–221.

Baker, F. B. Numerical taxonomy for educational researchers. *Review of Educational Research,* 1972, *42,* 345–358.

Ball, G. H. Data analysis in the social sciences: What about the details? *Proceedings of the fall Joint Computer Conference,* 1965, 533–559.

Ball, G. H., & Hall, D. J. *Background information on clustering techniques.* Working Paper, Stanford Research Institute, Menlo Park, California, July 1967.

Beers, R. J., & Lockhart, W. R. Experimental methods in computer taxonomy. *Journal of General Microbiology,* 1962, *28,* 633–640.

Bekoff, M., & Hill, H. L. Behavioral taxonomy in canids by discriminant function analysis. *Science,* 1975, *190,* 1223–1224.

Bonner, R. E. On some clustering techniques. *IBM Journal of Research and Development,* 1964, *8*(1), 22–32.

Cattell, R. B., Coulter, M. A., & Tsujioka, B. The taxonometric recognition of types and functional emergents. In R. B. Cattell (Ed.), *Handbook of multivariate experimental psychology.* Chicago: Rand McNally, 1966.

Cole, A. J. *Numerical taxonomy.* New York: Academic Press, 1969.

Coulter, M. A., & Cattell, R. B. Principles of behavioral taxonomy and the mathematical bases of the taxonome computer program. *British Journal of Mathematical and Statistical Psychology,* 1966, *19,* 237–269.

Cronbach, L. J. Test validation. In R. L. Thorndike (Ed.), *Educational measurement.* Washington, DC: American Council on Education, 1971.

Cronbach, L. J., & Gleser, G. C. Assessing similarity between profiles. *Psychological Bulletin,* 1953, *50,* 456–473.

Cureton, E. E., Cureton, L. W., & Durfee, R. C. A method of cluster analysis. *Multivariate Behavior Research,* 1970, *5,* 101–116.

Dubin, R., & Champoux, J. E. *Typology of empirical attributes dissimilarity linkage analysis (DLA)* (Scientific Technical Report No. 3), Office of Naval Research Contract N00014-69-A-U200-9001. Irvine, CA: University of California, Graduate School of Administration, 1970.

Farina, A. J., Jr. Development of a taxonomy of human performance: A review of descriptive schemes for human task behavior. *JSAS Catalog of Selected Documents in Psychology,* 1973, *3,* 23 (Ms. No. 318).

Farina, A. J., Jr., & Wheaton, G. R. Development of a taxonomy of human performance: The task characteristics approach to performance prediction. *JSAS Catalog of Selected Documents in Psychology,* 1973, *3,* 26–27. (Ms. No. 323)

Fisher, R. A. *Statistical methods for research workers.* (6th ed.) Edinburgh: Oliver & Boyd, 1936.

Fleishman, E. A. Toward a taxonomy of human performance. *American Psychologist,* 1975, *30*(12), 1127–1149.

Fleishman, E. A., & Hogan, J. C. *Taxonomic methods for assessing the physical requirements of jobs: The physical abilities analysis approach.* (ARRO Technical Report 3012/R78-6). Washington, DC: Advanced Research Resources Organization, June 1978.

Friedman, H. P., & Rubin, J. On some invariant criteria for grouping data. *Journal of the American Statistical Association,* 1967, *62,* 1159–1178.

Greene, P. E., & Carmone, P. J. *Multidimensional scaling and related techniques in marketing analysis.* Boston: Allyn and Bacon, 1970.

Guilford, J. P., & Fruchter, B. *Fundamental statistics in psychology and education* (6th ed.). New York: McGraw Hill, 1978.

Hamer, R. M., & Cunningham, J. W. Cluster analyzing profile data confounded with interrater differences: A comparison of profile association measures. *Applied Psychological Measurement,* 1979, *5,* 63–73.

Harman, H. H. *Modern factor analysis* (2nd ed.). Chicago: University of Chicago Press, 1967.

Jackson, D. N., & Messick, S. Content and style in personality assessment. *Psychological Bulletin,* 1958, *55,* 243–252.

Jardine, N., & Gibson, R. *Mathematical taxonomy.* New York: John Wiley, 1971.

John, E. R., Karmel, B. Z., Corning, W. C., Easton, P., Brown, D., Ahan, H., John, M., Harmony, T., Prichep, L., Toro, A., Gerson, I., Bartlett, F., Thatcher, R., Kaye, H., Valdes, P., & Schwartz, E. Neurometrics. *Science,* 1977, *196*(4297), 1393–1410.

Johnson, S. C. Hierarchical clustering schemes. *Psychometrika,* 1967, *32,* 241–254.

Kimble, G. A. Categories of learning and the problem of definition: Comments on Professor Grant's paper. In A. W. Melton (Ed.), *Categories of human learning.* New York: Academic Press, 1964.

Levine, J. M., Romashko, T., & Fleishman, E. A. Evaluation of an abilities classification system for integrating and generalizing human performance research findings: An application to vigilance tasks. *Journal of Applied Psychology,* 1973, *58,* 149–157.

McQuitty, L. L. Hierarchical linkage analysis for the isolation of types. *Educational and Psychological Measurement*, 1960, *20*, 55–67.

Miller, E. E. *A taxonomy of response processes* (TR-69-19). Ft. Knox, KY: Human Resources Research Organization. September 1969.

Miller, R. B. Task taxonomy: Science or technology? In W. T. Singleton, R. S. Easterly, & D. C. Whitfield (Eds.), *The human operator in complex systems*. London: Taylor & Francis, 1967.

Miller, R. B. Development of a taxonomy of human performance: A user-oriented approach. *JSAS Catalog of Selected Documents in Psychology*, 1973, 26 (Ms. No. 322).

Owens, W. A., & Mumford, M. D. *Biodata subgroups over a twenty year period*. Athens, GA: University of Georgia Press, 1983.

Owens, W. A., & Schoenfeldt, L. F. Toward a classification of persons. *Journal of Applied Psychology*, 1979, *66*(5), 569–607.

Pratt, S., & Canfield, M. The evaluation contract: "Participative systems actualization research." In M. Guttentag, & E. L. Struening (Eds.), *Handbook of evaluation research* (Vol. II). Beverly Hills, CA: Sage Publications, 1975.

Rao, M. R. Cluster analysis and mathematical programming. *Journal of the American Statistical Association*, 1971, *66*, 622–626.

Silverman, J. *New techniques in task analysis* (SRM-68-12). San Diego, CA: U.S. Naval Personnel Research Activity, 1968.

Singleton, W. T., R. S. Easterly, & D. C. Whitfield (Eds.) *The human operator in complex systems*. London: Taylor & Francis, 1967.

Sokal, R. R., & Sneath, P. H. A. *Principles of numerical taxonomy*. San Francisco, CA: Freeman Press, 1963.

Sorensen, T. A method of establishing groups of equal amplitude in plant sociology based on similarity of species content. *Biolical Skrifter*, 1948, *5*, 1–34.

Stephenson, W. The inverted factor technique. *British Journal of Psychology*, 1936, *26*, 344–361.

Stolurow, L. M. *A taxonomy of learning task characteristics* (AMRL-TDR-64-2), Wright-Patterson AFB, OH: Aerospace Medical Research Laboratories, 1964.

Teichner, W. H., & Olson, D. E. *Predicting human performance in space environments* (NASA Contractor Report No. CR1370). Washington, DC: National Aeronautics & Space Administration, June 1969.

Teichner, W. H., & Whitehead, J. Development of a taxonomy of human performance: Evaluation of a task classification system for generalizing findings from a data base. *JSAS Catalog of Selected Documents in Psychology*, 1973, *2*, 26–27 (Ms. No. 324).

Theologus, G. C., & Fleishman, E. A. Development of a taxonomy of human performance: Validation study of ability scales for classifying human tasks. *JSAS Catalog of Selected Documents in Psychology*, 1973, *3*, 29 (Ms. No. 326).

Theologus, G. C., Romashko, T., & Fleishman, E. A. Development of a taxonomy of human performance: A feasibility study of ability dimensions for classifying human tasks. *JSAS Catalog of Selected Documents in Psychology*, 1973, *3*, 25–26 (Ms. No. 321).

Tryon, R. C. *Cluster analysis*. Ann Arbor: Edwards, 1939.

Tryon, R. C., & Bailey, D. E. *Cluster analysis*. New York: McGraw Hill, 1970.

Ward, J. H., Jr. Hierarchical grouping to optimize an objective function. *Journal of the American Statistical Association*, 1963, *58*, 236–244.

Ward, J. H., Jr., & Hook, M. E. Application of a hierarchical grouping procedure to a problem of grouping profiles. *Educational and Psychological Measurement*, 1963, 23, 69–82.

Wheaton, G. R. Development of a taxonomy of human performance: A review of classificatory systems relating to tasks and performance. *JSAS Catalog of Selected Documents in Psychology*, 1973, 3, 22–23 (Ms. No. 317).

CHAPTER 5

Classificatory Systems for Describing Human Tasks: Behavior Description

Many investigators have attempted to describe human task behavior. The next three chapters examine some specific systematic descriptive and classificatory systems that have been devised. These chapters draw on and extend an earlier review carried out by Farina (1973) in connection with the Taxonomy Project. This examination was conducted in the hope of finding classificatory systems on which to build. However, most schemes found were primarily descriptive in nature. It will be recalled from Chapter 2 that a classificatory system, a set of categories or taxa, is the end result of the process of classification. These taxa are formed by ordering or arranging entities into groups on the basis of their relationships based on observable or inferred properties. Thus, although classificatory systems encompass description, they go beyond it by involving an explicit methodology for grouping units into taxa after a comparison of similarities and dissimilarities among these units.

Although our emphasis here is on tasks, descriptive and classificatory systems of jobs have also been included as a secondary source of information because of their general relevance. There is a large variation in the degree of development across the schemes reviewed. Some investigators have suggested descriptive terms, generally undefined, that they consider to be useful. Others have contributed more by providing well-defined descriptors and specifying the relationships among them. Although some have made empirical efforts to develop their schemes, few have progressed to the point at which their schemes are capable of evaluation in both quantitative and qualitative terms. In general, only those schemes that are fairly well developed are included in the next three chapters. Some systems are covered in greater detail in later chapters of the book. These more detailed presentations are reserved for taxonomic developments that later evolved from the Taxonomy Project or from more recent developmental efforts.

Comparative evaluation of these systems poses a problem because they were not at equivalent stages of development at the time of review and, therefore, evaluative criteria could not be applied uniformly. The premises that guided the evaluation of the systems included the following:

1. Descriptors, whether at the taxon level or some other level of description, should be defined as precisely and objectively as possible.
2. Descriptors should be applied reliably; that is, intra- and interindividual agreement should be assessed in determining the adequacy of the system.
3. It should be feasible to actually apply the system to human tasks.
4. There should be some evidence of the validity of the system for its objectives.
5. Quantification of the descriptors is very desirable.

Classification should involve more than pinning a label on something. In Chapter 2, we distinguished the labeling action or identification of an object (allocating or assigning an additional, unidentified object to the correct class) from classification (the ordering or arranging of objects or entities into groups or sets on the basis of their relationships based on observable or inferred properties). The labeling action is but the last step in a sequence, and the label itself could be a neutral descriptor (e.g., "B-24") as well as a more conventional designator (e.g., "problem solving"). Also, classification is a process involving multiple dimensions. Classification results in placing a task in a hyperspace where its position reflects values on many dimensions.

Task analysis activities result in a wealth of information and data, combinations of which may be used as dimensions to categorize human task performance. Reed (1967) has identified 45 different types of information generated from task analysis. These types, which Reed has suggested are linked to human behavior, performance, equipment, or the workplace, are presented in Table 5.1.

The systems described in the following three chapters are grouped according to the four approaches to defining tasks presented in Chapter 3. In this chapter, we describe *behavior description* systems, in

TABLE 5.1

Types of Information Generated from Task Analysis[a]

1. Phase	25. Date of information
2. Phase segment	26. Information revision index (1, 2, 3,
3. Function (verb–object)	. . .)
4. Job	27. Personnel classification
5. Tasks	28. Task sharing classification
6. Task elements	29. Machine output
7. Indentures	30. Human output
8. System	31. Psychological processes (behavioral
9. Subsystems	processes)
10. Components	32. Task criticality
11. Subcomponents	33. Task area environment
12. Sub-subcomponents	34. Prerequisite training requirements
13. Parts	35. Training requirements
14. Job location	36. Training media
15. Frequency of job performance	37. Training equipment characteristics
16. Tools, equipment, fixtures, supplies	38. Hardware status
required	39. Equipment number
17. Number of personnel required to	40. Performance characteristics of
perform task (minimum)	equipment
18. Hazards that may be encountered	41. Cost
19. Communication	42. Accuracy of task performance
20. Difficulty index	43. Reliability of task performance
21. Skill requirements	44. Mission–function of hardware
22. Knowledge requirements	45. Task prerequisites
23. Time to perform task	
24. Source of information	

[a]Reproduced with permission from Reed, L. E. *Advances in the use of computers for handling human factors task data* (AMRL-TR-67-16). Wright Patterson Air Force Base, Ohio: Aerospace Medical Research Laboratories, Wright Patterson Air Force Base, April 1967.

Chapter 6 *behavior requirement* systems and, in Chapter 7, we present those descriptive systems using *ability requirements* or *task characteristics* as a basis for classification.

In Chapter 3, we defined *behavior description* schemes as those that deal with human task behavior per se, that is, the actual behaviors emitted or activities performed. In this conceptual approach to task classification, categories or types of tasks are formulated based upon observations and descriptions of what operators actually do while performing a task. Emphasis is placed primarily upon a description of the operator's overt behaviors in response to the task rather than on an analysis of what the operator is required or expected to do in order to produce criterion levels of performance (see Wheaton, 1973). All these classificatory schemes are attempts to arrive at systems that dimensionalize specific behaviors (such as setting dials and reading meters) into broader categories. Many of these schemes come from efforts to relate task behaviors to conditions of training, although others are derived from research involved with (1) selecting optimal methods and measures of job performance, (2) specifying human–machine interactions, or (3) determining occupationally related education.

Berliner: Hierarchical Model—Behaviors, Activities, and Processes

Berliner, Angell, and Shearer (1964) sought to develop a behavioral classification scheme in which categories would be meaningful for selecting optimal methods of measuring performance in military jobs. They felt that most previous classificatory systems had been devised with the purpose of relating task behavior to conditions of training and that a scheme more specific to performance measurement was needed.

The descriptors chosen for their scheme are arranged in a hierarchical fashion based upon behavioral processes, activities, and specific behaviors. Table 5.2 presents their scheme. The system has four major behavioral processes encompassing six broad types of activities under which are subsumed some 47 specific behaviors. The specific behaviors are represented by action verbs that are felt to be recognized widely, although fairly distinct from one another. The specific behaviors were selected for being (1) reliably identifiable, (2) simple acts with quantifiable properties, and (3) involved in a variety of jobs.

The varying amounts of specificity in the system were instituted deliberately. In general, the authors found high interrater reliability when either a few broad categories or many specific ones were used. The utility of each of these extremes used alone was questionable, however, because the scheme with only a few categories did not provide for a high level of differentiation and the multicategory scheme treated everything as unique. Their compromise was to construct a multilevel classification scheme that presumably possessed the benefits found at several levels of specificity.

The scheme was constructed by asking judges to group the specific behaviors into tentative larger categories, called "process" categories, that were devised by the project staff. An iterative, refining

TABLE 5.2

Berliner Classificatory Scheme[a]

Processes	Activities	Specific behaviors
Perceptual processes	Searching for and receiving information	Detects Inspects Observes Reads Receives Scans Surveys
	Identifying objects, actions, events	Discriminates Identifies Locates
Mediational processes	Information processing	Categorizes Calculates Codes Computes Interpolates Itemizes Tabulates Translates
	Problem solving and decision making	Analyzes Calculates Chooses Compares Computes Estimates Plans
Communication processes		Advises Answers Communicates Directs Indicates Informs Instructs Requests Transmits
Motor processes	Complex–continuous	Adjusts Aligns Regulates Synchronizes Tracks
	Simple–discrete	Activates Closes Connects

(*continued*)

TABLE 5.2 *Continued*

Processes	Activities	Specific behaviors
		Disconnects
		Joins
		Moves
		Presses
		Sets

phase occurred, and the resulting scheme includes those behaviors whose placement into process categories was agreed upon by at least six of eight judges, each sorting independently. Berliner *et al.* (1964) did not assess the reliability with which the scheme could be used in categorizing real-world tasks.

The specific behaviors serve as an entry point into the scheme; having selected one behavior, the activities and processes are predetermined. No definitions are presented for any of the terms in the scheme. The possibility that users may have different "private" definitions, even at the specific behavior level, is presumably accounted for and/or assessed by the estimates obtained of interjudge reliability. It is in a scheme of this type that the work of Reed (1967) and Oller (1968) has its greatest value. They have developed a glossary of 130 action verbs, each defined as precisely as possible, along with a cross-referenced system of synonyms; a similar glossary, minus the synonyms, is provided for nouns.

Quantifiable measures are obtainable for each of the specific behaviors in the scheme. The general types of measures are: (1) times (start, completion, and duration), (2) errors (omission, commission, magnitude, and direction), (3) frequency data, (4) workload, and (5) motion dynamics.

Berliner *et al.* (1964) complete their system by categorizing the types of instruments available for the above measures. The final system finds expression in a three-dimensional matrix (Figure 5.1) described by Rabideau (1964), consisting of behaviors, measures, and instruments. The cells of the matrix contain specific statements relevant to performance measurement and evaluation.

Christensen and Mills (1967) applied the Berliner *et al.* (1964) scheme in an effort to determine what operators do in complex sys-

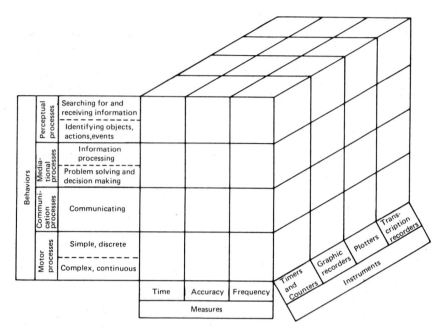

Figure 5.1 Matrix of behaviors, measures, and instruments relevant to performance evaluations. Reproduced with permission from *Human Factors*, 6, 1964, Rabideau, G. F. Field measurement of human performance in man–machine systems, p. 270. Copyright (1964) by the Human Factors Society, Inc.

tems. Specifically, they wanted to describe the activities of systems operators in psychological terms and to provide estimates of the proportion of time spent on each activity. They found satisfactory agreement between two independent raters who classified the activities of nine operators having different jobs. Interrater agreement estimates, generated using rank order techniques, yielded a median Rho of .78, with a range of .29–1.00. Christensen and Mills had the following suggestions for improving rater reliability:

1. Define operator activities in clear, unequivocal terms and in sufficient detail.
2. Use a standard set of activity descriptors when generating job descriptions.
3. Use raters who are familiar with the jobs they are rating.

In summary, in this "lexical" approach of Berliner *et al.* (1964), there are terms that are presumably related, via a hierarchical structure, to other terms; although the terms are not precisely defined, the scheme has utility. The simplicity of Berliner's scheme readily invites application. Frequent application, in turn, could lead to the standard usage of terms that is currently lacking. However, standardization in and of itself can provide only a limited amount of progress. It is not sufficient that everyone is using the same terms; the terms must have common meaning, and the structure in which they are embedded should be a valid and useful representation of the real world.

Willis: Input–Output Hierarchical Model

Willis (1961) had as his objective the derivation of training device implications from the interaction of a limited set of learning principles and a classificatory scheme for behavior. Willis developed a three-level, hierarchical classificatory scheme in which specificity and detail of description increase as one proceeds down through the levels. Figure 5.2 illustrates the behavioral scheme, which follows a general input–output model. His descriptors are a mixture of observable behaviors and unobservable functions.

His method of rational analysis to determine training implications initially employed a matrix consisting of the 19 Level III behavior categories and 13 common principles of learning. To avoid the need to discuss training implications for each of the 247 cells of this 19 × 13 matrix, he took two steps to reduce the number of relevant cells to be studied. In the first step, Willis dropped back to Level II headings; this permitted him to treat his 19 behavior descriptors as belonging to six families. For each learning principle, he then identified the member(s) of each family for which a particular principle would have the greatest degree of predictive or explanatory power. This operation identified 29 cells as relevant to the analysis. A similar operation was performed that focused on the principles. The principles were grouped into three classes, those relating to (1) stimulus manipulation, (2) response manipulation, and (3) experimental conditions. Cells were then identified for which these classes were most predictive. In short, Willis reduced the gross number of cells to be discussed by examining their potential relevance, first in terms of six behavioral families, and then in terms of three classes of learning principles. Willis focused attention on only those cells that were selected by both previous operations.

These steps produced 25 cells, and training implications were developed for each. A sample discussion is presented here for a cell formed by the behavior "nonverbal detection" in the Level II family of Discrimination–Nonverbal Cues and the learning principle "reinforcement schedule" (see Willis, 1961).

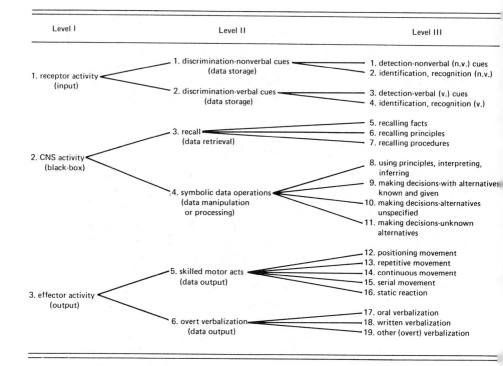

Figure 5.2 Willis input–output hierarchical model. Reproduced with permission from Willis, M. P. *Deriving training device implications from learning theory principles* (NAVTRADEVCEN 784-1). Port Washington, NY: USNTDC, 1961.

> *Implication:* In training for detection of nonverbal cues, provision should be made for intermittent (as opposed to uniform) reinforcement.
> *Basis:* Operational detection of nonverbal cues probably involves a substantial amount of nonreinforcement. Training under conditions of intermittent reinforcement would provide increased resistance to such potential extinction conditions.

Although Willis provides no definitions for his behavioral decriptors, which are relatively abstract, the learning principles are spelled out in detail. Currently, no provision exists for establishing the reliability with which analysts can assign behaviors from a task analysis into Willis' scheme, nor has any formal assessment been made of the validity of the "implications" for actual training-device decisions.

Lumsdaine: Five Learning Categories

In his treatment of training objectives, Lumsdaine (1960) used a classification that speaks indirectly to the question of describing human task behavior. Lumsdaine (1960) provides the following categories as "things to be learned," but they are also globally descriptive of task behavior.

1. *Identifying.* Pointing to or locating objects and locations, naming them, or identifying what belongs together, either physically or in words and symbols.

2. *Knowing principles and relationships.* Understanding a statement of relationship, as demonstrated by the ability to state, illustrate, and recognize its implications. Often this is a statement that tells how a cause produces an effect or how a result can be predicted from several component factors. It may involve knowing the rules of what to do when a contingency occurs.

3. *Following procedures.* Knowing how to carry out a rather fixed sequence, such as a preflight check, starting a car, or making a well defined type of calculation.

4. *Making decisions or choosing courses of action.* Applying conceptual rules or principles as a basis for making decisions involved in diagnosing or interpreting complex situations. Sometimes this involves perceptual discriminations that are learned or acted on directly without reasoning.

5. *Performing skilled perceptual–motor acts.* Performing acts that are quite simple (using basic hand tools) or acts that are quite difficult (manipulating the controls of an airplane). Often, the simpler skills provide necessary steps in more complex tasks that require following lengthy procedures.

Currently, there is no evidence available regarding the reliability or validity of this set of descriptors.

Chambers: Error Performance Categories

A very specific type of behavior description approach is found in the work of Chambers (1963). After reviewing the technical literature on perceptual, motor, and cognitive performance, he proposed a set of 19 categories representing characteristic degradations that may occur for any given behavior as a result of encountering acceleration stress (e.g., stress encountered driving an automobile, or flying an airplane or spacecraft). Some categories are increases in error amplitude, response lags, and perceived disintegration of the perceptual field or display. Chambers (1963) suggested that these error performance categories, when recorded during repeated trials, could be useful in evaluating the effectiveness of acceleration environment training procedures, even though they are highly variable, very difficult to measure, and extremely sensitive to subtle changes in the environment.

Theologus, Wheaton, and Fleishman (1974) rearranged Chambers' classificatory scheme into five areas, each of which incorporates several degradation subcategories, in order to organize the literature regarding the effects of noise on performance. These five broad classes are:

1. Changes in the distribution of performance over time (including lapses, escape, queuing).
2. Changes in accuracy of performance (increases in error amplitude, failure to detect, stereotyping).
3. Changes in the distribution of performance among tasks and within tasks (falling off, omissions).
4. Decreases in rate of performance (changes in phasing, response lags).
5. Increases in rate of performance (sudden changes in rate or frequency, inadvertent control inputs).

After categorizing the noise literature on the basis of these descriptors, Theologus *et al.* (1974) concluded that the bulk of the research had been concerned with decreases in performance rate and increases in error. A major finding of the review was that noise stressor research had been limited to seven of the 19 subcategories of performance decrement; only one-third of the potential forms of performance degradation had been examined vis-à-vis noise stress.

Although Chambers' classificatory scheme has been demonstrated as being useful in organizing the noise stress literature and in identifying needed areas for future research efforts, there is no evidence available as to the reliability or validity of the scheme per se. Consequently, further evaluation of Chambers' system is needed.

The "Meister Taxonomy"

A rather detailed classificatory system was developed for a fairly specific application, namely, the "man–machine" system of a hypothetical multicrew, Extended Earth Orbital Scientific Laboratory (Finley, Obermayer, Bertone, Mesiter, & Muckler, 1970). In addition to providing structure for this specific application (the method by which human behavior is classified within "man–machine" systems), this was an attempt to derive a general task taxonomic method. This method, called the *"Meister Taxonomy,"* is a form of task

TABLE 5.3

Four Classificatory Systems and Representative Categories: "Meister Taxonomy"[a]

Human Behavior Classificatory Systems (I–III)
  I. Functions: subsystem management
    Involves monitoring and control of specific vehicle subsystems as distinguished from overall vehicle navigation. May involve display monitoring, communication, data recording and analysis, or decision making. Probably will *not* involve continuous perceptual motor activity.
  II. Tasks: tracking
    Determination of position of own and/or target vehicle. (Tracking involves geographic position only and not subsystem status monitoring.)
      1. Visual tracking only
      2. Visual tracking plus position plotting (recording)
  III. Behavioral elements: motor responses
      1. Depress single control
      2. Turn single rotary control
      3. Adjust control to specified value
      4. Activate bank of controls (in series or all at one time)
      5. Type message on keyboard
      6. Insert object
      7. Remove object
      8. Lift object
      9. Move object
     10. Place object
     11. Open or close door, hatch, or access plate
     12. Connect or disconnect
     13. Write
Task dimensional classificatory system (IV)
  IV. Initiating stimulus
      1. Type (visual; auditory; kinesthetic)
      2. Mechanism (directly viewed event; display; written material)
      3. Characteristics (alpha numerics; raw stimuli; coded stimuli; changing or moving stimulus; static stimulus; multiple characteristics such as visual plus auditory)
      4. Information presented (quantitative, qualitative, content)
      5. Duration (persistent; short-lived)
      6. Number (single; multiple)

---

[a]Adapted from Finley, D. L., Obermayer, R. W., Bertone, C. M., Meister, D., and Muckler, F. A. *Human performance prediction in man–machine systems: A technical review* (Vol. 1, NASA CR-1614). Canoga Park, CA: The Bunker–Ramo Corporation, August 1970.

analysis, but one that is intended to improve upon traditional methods by introducing standardization into behavioral description.

This approach actually includes four classificatory systems, three representing different levels of description of human behavior and the fourth representing dimensions of task characteristics. Examples of one category for each of the four classificatory systems are shown in Table 5.3 (adapted from Finley *et al.*, 1970). The first level of behavioral description is that of function. The second is that of the tasks themselves. The third level is that of behavioral elements, of which the four major types are motor responses, perceptual–motor responses, mediational responses, and communication responses. The fourth classificatory system, the task dimensional one, consists of the major categories of initiating stimulus, response requirements, feedback, and task context.

The "Meister Taxonomy" is one of the most detailed of the classificatory systems that has been developed. It goes beyond straight description of human task performance to comparisons of tasks on multiple dimensions before assigning them to categories based on similarities or dissimilarities. Only limited evaluative information is available on this system. Project staff members were given lists of microlevel task descriptors for two manned space flight activities (Finley *et al.*, 1970). They were also given three classificatory systems developed by Meister (1976), Alluisi (1967), and Miller (1962). The latter two are of the behavioral requirements type and, therefore, are described in the next chapter. The staff members attempted to classify each task descriptor using each of the three schemes. Specifically, the second level of the "Meister Taxonomy," the tasks themselves, was used because it represented approximately the same level of detail as the level of the other two systems. The analysts had a high degree of interrater reliability using the "Meister Taxonomy," and they found the scheme quite easy to apply. The Alluisi classificatory system also generated high interanalyst agreement for all of its categories, with one exception, but the analysts felt that the categories were too general and did not cover sufficiently the domain of human tasks. The analysts had low interrater reliability using the Miller classificatory system and felt that the categories were too general and too vaguely defined. They concluded that the usefulness of the Miller system would be a function of the intuition and the depth of experience of the person applying the scheme.

Bennett: Semantic Classificatory Approach

Bennett (1971) developed a classificatory system using what he calls a semantic approach, involving consensus judgments about tasks as the basis for classifying. First, he pretested descriptions of 20 tasks on 100 college students in terms of task familiarity to them and relevance to three hypothesized dimensions: ideas, people, and things. Of these, 10 tasks were selected for use. Each task description consisted

TABLE 5.4

Factor Loadings from Principal Components Factor Analysis of Intercorrelations Among Bennett's Verbs[a,b]

Cognitive		Social		Procedural		Physical	
Decide	.85	Talk	.91	Operate	.72	Carry	.73
Judge	.83	Interact with		Follow pro-		Walk	.73
Analyze	.74	people	.88	cedures	.72	Handle	.55
Plan	.73	Answer	.84	Use equipment	.69	Write	− .47
Compute	.68	Ask	.78	Handle	.54		
Think	.67	Listen	.71	Do	.52		
Interact		Persuade	.68	Interact with			
with data	.55	Use equipment	− .40	things	.51		
Synthesize	.51			Read	.41		
Read	.45						
Adjust	.45						

[a]Reproduced with permission from *Human Factors, 13*, Bennett, C. A. Toward empirical, practicable, comprehensive task taxonomy, © 1971, Pergamon Press, Ltd.
[b]Only factor loadings over .4 are displayed.

of one or two sentences, for example, "Using a hand mower you are to mow a small lawn."

Next Bennett searched many task analysis reports and articles for worker-oriented verbs. Out of a list of 200 verbs, 25 were chosen to represent a comprehensive list, for example, "interact with people," "handle," "write." Thirty-six college students judged the applicability of each of the 25 verbs to each of the 10 tasks using a 4-point scale ranging from "not at all applicable" to "extremely applicable." Product-moment correlations were computed for each pair of verbs comparing the extent of agreement in their applicability ratings across the 10 tasks, and a principal-components factor analysis was performed. The results are shown in Table 5.4 (from Bennett, 1971). All verbs had at least one loading of .4 or more, and three verbs (*handle, read, use equipment*) had two such loadings. Table 5.4 shows four factors that emerged: Cognitive, Social, Procedural, and Physical.

Bennett (1973) considered these four factors to be broad task dimensions that he defined as follows: (1) physical—high-energy-expenditure tasks involving a few, simple tools; (2) procedural—repetitious, low-energy-expenditure tasks, sometimes involving complex equipment; (3) social—tasks involving interpersonal communication; and (4) cognitive—tasks for which internal activity (which might be called *thinking*) is crucial and for which the nature of the response (e.g., oral or written) may not be critical.

In a follow-up research investigation, Bennett (1973) had five groups of students judge 50 occupations on (1) the applicability of verbs chosen to represent the previously found task types, and (2) several other variables, including the number of years it would take for 50% of the workers to be displaced by advanced technology. Median judgments for each scale were determined and intercorrelated. After factor analysis, Bennett (1973) concluded that the four factors, which had been independent dimensions at the task level, collapsed into two bipolar dimensions: Cognitive versus Physical dimension; Social versus Procedural dimension. Thus, Bennett suggested that when tasks were put together into occupations, there is a tendency for occupations to involve either cognitive or physical tasks and either social or procedural tasks. Further, in the cognitive–social area, occupations are likely to be more resistant to automation.

In another research investigation, Bennett (1973) had 46 judges (members of the Human Factors Society) evaluate 25 functions (e.g., drive a car, simple reaction time, play a game, bear children) as to the applicability of the verbs representing the four task dimensions, the quality of machine performance if automated, and so forth, for a total of 12 judgments per function. A factor analysis of the judgments resulted in two factors—Automation and Humanness. The cognitive and social task factors loaded high and negatively on Automation, whereas the procedural factor had a high positive loading. This finding was consistent with Bennett's earlier study regarding the relationship of the task factors to automation resistance. Thus, there is at least some validity to the forecast that technological change will have less effect on jobs with functions characterized as cognitive or social.

Bennett's results may well be dependent upon the particular tasks, functions, occupations, and worker-oriented verbs used. Therefore, it would be useful to replicate this approach with different tasks, functions (and functions at the same level of generality), occupations, and verbs to see if the same factorial structures emerge. Additionally, it would seem worthwhile to use alternative populations of judges.

Christal: Comprehensive Occupational Data Analysis Program (CODAP)

There are a number of job analysis methods that involve the description and grouping of job tasks. Typically, a job incumbent checks the activities he or she performs on a task inventory. These tasks may be rated in terms of frequency of performance, importance to the overall job, and so forth. These task descriptive approaches to job analysis have been reviewed by McCormick (1979).

A primary development in this area is represented by the work of
Christal and his associates at the Air Force Human Resources Laboratory (e.g., Christal, 1972; Morsh & Christal, 1966; Morsh, 1964;
Morsh & Archer, 1967). The approach was designed for collecting and
organizing task level information for hundreds of occupations involving the assignment of thousands of individuals. The approach involves a task inventory method with specially designed computer
programs to cluster the information for a variety of personnel
purposes.

Such task inventories are often initially constructed from printed
materials, such as training manuals, available job descriptions, and
so forth. The first task list is reviewed by groups of senior supervisors
who revise task language and add new tasks. The revised task list is
subjected to a field review of samples of supervisors who may add,
modify, or delete tasks. In the Air Force program (Christal, 1974),
24–100 supervisors may review the task list before the final inventory
is developed. The task lists may average around 500 tasks; however,
as the respondent only marks the tasks actually performed, the inventory can be completed in a reasonable period of time.

Typically, the Air Force attempts to obtain a sample of 2000 or
more job incumbents. The incumbents check those tasks that are
performed as a normal part of the job, and add significant tasks if
they are not included on the list. Each incumbent also rates the tasks
performed on a 7-point relative-time-spent scale. These relative-time-
spent ratings are converted into estimated percent time values.

To evaluate the wealth of task data obtained through these inventories, the Occupational Research Division of the Air Force Human
Resources Laboratory developed the Comprehensive Occupational
Data Analysis Program (CODAP) system. Work on the CODAP analysis system has proceeded over the past 20 years resulting in well over
40 general purpose computer programs. One program prepares a
consolidated job description indicating the percentage of group
members performing each task, the average percentage of work time
spent on the task by those who perform it, and the percentage of
group time spent on each task. Christal (1974) has stated that such a
consolidated description of the work performed by individuals during their first year or two on the job is particularly useful for designing the curricula for entry level vocational training.

One of the most powerful CODAP programs identifies and describes all the types of jobs that exist in an occupational area. The
program starts with over 2000 individual job descriptions and compares each job with every other job. Similar jobs are then grouped

into clusters and job descriptions are prepared for each cluster. Thus, CODAP classifies jobs by their similarities in the percentage of time spent on various task activities. Christal (1974) noted that such analyses are particularly helpful in identifying needed changes in currently defined occupational categories. Another program uses factor ratings in conjunction with task data to compute the difficulty level or the grade level requirement of each job.

The United States Air Force has surveyed over 200,000 enlisted persons in 150 occupations using this behavior description approach. Christal (1974) noted that one of the primary payoffs from these occupational data was in the specifications of behaviors to be trained. Also, the occupational data revealed that certain forms of training were not necessary for effective job performance, thus resulting in considerable dollar savings.

CODAP has been adopted by the Marine Corps, the Navy, and the Coast Guard, as well as by a variety of universities and governmental organizations. One local government, Prince Georges County, Maryland (Gambardella & Alvord, 1978), has prepared a manual to facilitate the adoption of this approach by other organizations.

The occupational data supplied by CODAP is useful for training and job classification systems, as well as for defining ladders of career progression and identifying needed job redesign projects. McCormick (1976) reports that the system has respectable reliability. The median reliability coefficients for 35 samples representing 10 career fields and a total of 9822 cases were: percentage performing the tasks, .98; and time spent performing the tasks, .96. Although Christal (1969) reports some encouraging validity results, empirical evidence of external validity is needed.

The CODAP system was not intended as a theory-based classificatory system, but was developed as a pragmatic approach, applying computer technology to large-scale occupational data. Although useful in a variety of personnel systems applications, CODAP is not strictly a classificatory system, in the sense we have used the term here, because generic taxa and general task dimensions are not identified. The indiviudal task statements are not yet organized into broader functional behavior categories that might provide a basis for predicting human performance and for generalizing human performance data in a variety of areas.

McCormick: Position Analysis Questionnaire

McCormick and his associates (1964, 1979; McCormick, Jeanneret, & Mecham, 1972) have done extensive work in establishing dimensions of job performance and categorizing jobs accordingly. The rationale for this research rests on the assumptions that "there is structure and order within the domain of human work; that dimensions of that structure can be identified; and that individual jobs can be characterized in terms of such dimensions. . . . For each such dimension there are underlying requirements of human attributes that would be required for successful performance on the job dimensions" (McCormick, 1964, p. 1). McCormick took the approach of characterizing jobs in terms of the human behaviors involved rather than describing them by reference to technological activities (e.g., drilling, cutting, welding). Jobs are defined by job elements with elements describing some general work activity, work condition, or job characteristic. Thus, although we have chosen to include McCormick's system in our discussion of behavior description approaches, the nature of the job elements suggests that the system could be included as a task characteristics approach as well. Further, because McCormick's recent research efforts involve the derivation of job dimensions from human attribute data, a portion of his system will be presented in our discussion of ability requirements approaches to classifying tasks and jobs.

Based on his earlier work, McCormick developed a job analysis instrument, the Position Analysis Questionnaire (PAQ), which consists of 187 worker-oriented job elements (McCormick, 1979). The job elements are organized into six categories or divisions. The first three categories generally represent a Stimulus–Organism–Response (S–O–R) model of human behavior. Table 5.5 shows these six categories plus examples of the human elements within each. The PAQ represents a classification scheme for human job behavior. Each job element is rated on a scale considered appropriate to the content of the element. Examples of the scales are Extent of Use, Importance to the Job, and Amount of Time. One study of PAQ reliability was done by having two analysts independently use it on 62 different jobs (Jeanneret & McCormick, 1969). The average reliability was .79, which suggests a reasonably high degree of interrater consistency.

As McCormick (1976) has noted, "Each such element, of course, can be thought of as a job descriptor by itself. But further, such job elements can be subjected to statistical analyses (such as factor and principal components analyses) to identify broader descriptors" (p. 673). Three such studies have been conducted (Jeanneret & McCormick, 1969; Marquardt & McCormick, 1973, 1974) using different forms of the PAQ to derive job dimensions, that is, broader categories of human behavior that cut across various jobs (McCormick, 1979). One study (Marquardt & McCormick, 1974) was based upon PAQ job data for 3700 jobs. An overall or general analysis was carried out with

TABLE 5.5

Six Divisions of the Position Analysis Questionnaire with Job Element Examples[a]

---

1. *Information input.* (Where and how does the worker get the information he uses in performing his job?)
   Examples: Use of written materials
              Near-visual differentiation
2. *Mental processes.* (What reasoning, decision making, planning, and information processing activities are involved in performing the job?)
   Examples: Level of reasoning in problem solving
              Coding–decoding
3. *Work output.* (What physical activities does the worker perform and what tools or devices does he use?)
   Examples: Use of keyboard devices
              Assembling–unassembling
4. *Relationships with other persons.* (What relationships with other people are required in performing the job?)
   Examples: Instructing
              Contacts with public or customers
5. *Job context.* (In what physical or social contexts is the work performed?)
   Examples: High temperature
              Interpersonal conflict situations
6. *Other job characteristics.* (What activities, conditions, or characteristics other than those described above are relevant to the job?)
   Examples: Specified work pace
              Amount of job structure

---

[a]Reprinted, by permission, from (1) *Job analysis: Methods and applications*, by Ernest J. McCormick, © 1979 by AMACOM, a division of the American Management Association, p. 144, all rights reserved; and (2) McCormick, E. A., Jeanneret, P. R., & Mecham, R. C. Position Analysis Questionnaire, © 1969 by Purdue Research Foundation, West Lafayette, Indiana 47906.

the ratings for the 3700 jobs on virtually all of the PAQ job elements (182 out of 187). Other analyses were carried out separately for the job elements within each of the six divisions of the PAQ. The results of these principal component analyses, that is, the resulting factors or categories, were similar to those in the first column of Table 5.6. This table presents the results of more recent principal component factor analyses conducted by Mecham (1977). The data presented in the second column of this table are discussed in Chapter 7, which deals with ability requirements approaches to classification.

Fine: Functional Job Analysis

Fine (1963, 1974) has also been interested in describing jobs on the basis of worker functions or behaviors. Originally his work was done

TABLE 5.6

Summary of PAQ Job Dimension Titles[a]

Job dimensions based on job data[b]	Job dimensions based upon attribute profile data[c]	
Division 1: Information input		
1. Perceptual interpretation	A1–1	Visual input from devices or materials
2. Input from representational sources	A1–2	Evaluation of visual input
3. Visual input from devices or materials	A1–3	Perceptual input from processes or events
4. Evaluating–judging sensory input	A1–4	Verbal or auditory input and interpretation
5. Environmental awareness	A1–5	Nonvisual input
6. Use of various senses		
Division 2: Mental processes		
7. Decision making	A2–6	Use of job-related knowledge
8. Information processing	A2–7	Information processing
Division 3: Work output		
9. Using machines, tools, or equipment	A3–8	Manual control and coordination activities
10. General body vs. sedentary activities	A3–9	Control and equipment operation
11. Control and related physical coordination	A3–10	General body/handling activities
12. Skilled or technical activities	A3–11	Use of foot controls
13. Controlled manual or related activities		
14. Use of miscellaneous equipment or devices		
15. Handling, manipulating, and related activities		
16. Physical coordination		
Division 4: Relationships with other persons		
17. Interchange of judgmental and related information	A4–12	Interpersonal communications
18. General personal contact	A4–13	Signal or code communications
19. Supervisory, coordination and related activities	A4–14	Serving or entertaining
20. Job-related communications		
21. Public-related personal contacts		
Division 5: Job context		
22. Potentially stressful or unpleasant environment	A5–15	Unpleasant physical environment
23. Personally demanding situations	A5–16	Personally demanding situations
24. Potentially hazardous job situations	A5–17	Hazardous physical environment

(*continued*)

TABLE 5.6 *Continued*

Job dimensions based on job data[b]	Job dimensions based upon attribute profile data[c]
Division 6: Other job characteristics	
25. Nontypical vs. typical day work schedule	A6–18 Work schedule I
	A6–19 Job responsibility
26. Businesslike situations	A6–20 Routine and repetitive work
27. Optional vs. specified apparel	activities
28. Variable vs. salary compensation	A6–21 Attentive or discriminating work demands
29. Regular vs. irregular work schedule	A6–22 Work attire
30. Job demanding responsibilities	A6–23 Work schedule II
31. Structured vs. unstructured job activities	
32. Vigilant or discriminating work activities	
Overall dimensions	
33. Decision, communication, and general responsibilities	(No overall analyses made)
34. Machine and equipment operation	
35. Clerical and related activities	
36. Technical and related activities	
37. Service and related activities	
38. Regular day schedule vs. other work schedules	
39. Routine and repetitive work activities	
40. Environmental awareness	
41. General physical activities	
42. Supervising or coordinating other personnel	
43. Public, customer, and related contact activities	
44. Unpleasant, hazardous, or demanding environment	
45. Unnamed	

[a]The dimensions based on job data and on attribute profile data are arranged by PAQ division in parallel columns for comparative purposes. Within any given division there may be dimensions based on the two sources that may be identical, or nearly so. However, the ordering and numbering of dimensions within each division is not intended to reflect corresponding dimensions.

[b]Reprinted with permission from Mecham, R. C. *Technical manual for the Position Analysis Questionnaire.* February 1977. PAQ Services, Inc. 1625 N. 100 E., Logan, Utah 84321.

[c]Reprinted with permission from Marquardt, L. D., & McCormick, E. J. *The Job dimensions underlying the job elements of the Position Analysis Questionnaire (PAQ), Form B.* Lafayette, Ind.: Occupational Research Center, Dept. of Psychological Services, Purdue University, Report No. 4, June 1974.

to develop a systematic classification of occupations for the United States Employment Service *Dictionary of Occupational Titles* (3rd edition, 1965), the basic instrument for classifying workers in the United States (Fine, 1951, 1955a, 1955b). This work was originally undertaken to improve job placement and counseling for workers registering for employment at local employment services offices (Fine, 1974). Thus, Fine's purpose was to develop a uniform and consistent way of describing what workers are expected to do. His approach was to standardize the *language* of job descriptions. Initially, he drew a distinction between the language of worker behavior (what the worker does) and outcomes (results of the worker's action or what gets done). Worker behaviors (action verbs and objects) and outcomes (products and/or purposes) used together in a sentence are the basic descriptive components in a task statement (for example, "Listens to running engine in order to determine malfunction"). Fine (1974) recommended that action verbs be modified by the means (tools, methods, equipment) required by the immediate objective of the action and by some indication of prescription and discretion in the worker instructions.

In researching the 4000 job descriptions that were the basis for his work, Fine established that what workers do, they do in relation to Data, People, and Things. In each of these three categories there are only a relatively small number of distinguishable functions ranging from simple to complex. For example, in relation to Data, the worker functions include compare, copy, compute–compile, analyze, innovate–coordinate, and synthesize (eight functions, in all, on six levels). Data include information, ideas, facts, statistics, specification of output, knowledge of conditions, techniques, and mental operations. The worker functions are hierarchical and ordinal; therefore, if a worker compiles data, the job includes the requirements of lower functions such as comparing and copying, although it excludes the requirements of higher worker functions such as analyzing. In relation to Things (i.e., physical interaction with and response to tangibles, touched, felt, observed, and related to in space), there are 10 functions (e.g., handling–feeding, offbearing–tending) on three levels. In relation to People, there are 12 functions on seven levels for a total of 30 defined functions (see Fine & Wiley, 1971; Fine, 1973, 1977). The defined functions in each of the three categories are organized into ordinal scales. Figure 5.3 provides a summary chart of Fine's worker function scales (Fine, 1977).

In addition to providing a *level* dimension reflecting the relative complexity or simplicity of a task, the analyst also makes use of an *orientation* dimension expressing the relative involvement of the

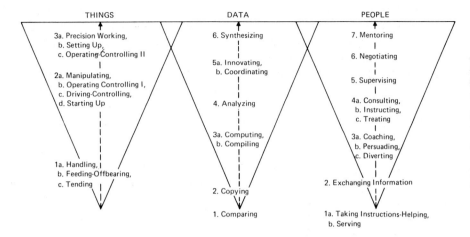

Figure 5.3 FJA scales for controlling the language of task statement: Summary chart of worker function scales.

Note: (1) Each hierarchy is independent of the others. It would be incorrect to read the functions across the three hierarchies as related because they appear to be on the same level. The definitive relationship among functions is within each hierarchy, not across hierarchies. Some broad exceptions are made in the next note. (2) The Data hierarchy is central because a worker can be assigned even higher Data functions although Things and People functions remain at the lowest level of their respective scales. This is not so for Things and People functions. When a Things function is at the third level (Precision Working), the Data function is likely to be at least Compiling or Computing. When a People function is at the fourth level (Consulting), the Data function is likely to be at least Analyzing and possibly Innovating or Coordinating. The case is similar for Supervising and Negotiating levels in the People hierarchy. Mentoring in some instances can call for Synthesizing. (3) Each function in its hierarchy is defined to include the lower-numbered functions. This is more or less the way it was found to occur in reality. It was most clear-cut for Things and Data, and only a rough approximation for People.

Reprinted with permission from Fine, S. A. *Job analysis for heavy equipment operators*. Washington, D.C.: International Union of Operating Engineers, 1977.

worker in terms of Data, People, and Things. Orientation is reflected by the analyst's assigning a percentage in units of five to each of the three functions, totaling 100%.

These worker function scales became the heart of the Functional Job Analysis (FJA) conceptual system, which also includes four other ordinal scales containing five to eight levels: Worker Instructions, Reasoning Development, Mathematical Development, and Language. All the scales are applied in task analysis by selecting the appropriate levels to reflect the descriptive material in the task statement. The levels selected are the basis for achieving precision in description and consensus. They are also the basis for systematically comparing and measuring the requirements of any task in any job.

FJA provides the basis for the method of job analysis used by the United States Employment Service. The basic manual describing its job analysis procedures is the *Handbook for Analyzing Jobs* (U.S. Department of Labor, 1972). Each job in the fourth edition of the *Dictionary of Occupational Titles* (U.S. Department of Labor, 1977) is accompanied by worker function ratings of the tasks performed in the occupation in relation to Data, People, and Things. As McCormick (1979) has noted, "It should be pointed out that the practice of USES in the use of functional job analysis consists of assigning levels to jobs . . . on the basis of the analysis of the total job. On the other hand, Fine and Wiley propose the application of the formulation to individual tasks, and, by integration across tasks, to the entire job" (p. 113).

Although quantitative information on reliability and external validity is needed, FJA has met the criterion of utility. A recent study for the U.S. Department of Housing and Urban Development used FJA to cluster job tasks into broader performance functions as a basis for performance standards used by supervisors for performance appraisal. Jobs examined included managers, environmental officers, field economists, community planners, and cost analysts. In other studies, the system was used to lay the groundwork for apprentice training programs, and the development and design of performance tests for heavy equipment operators and drillers for oil and gas (Fine & Eisner, 1980, 1981). FJA has been shown to be useful in sorting, reformulating, and grouping large numbers of task statements developed from CODAP or similar procedures into a more limited number of broader FJA-type task statements. This is accomplished by shifting the focus to the behavior required of the worker (Fine, Holt, & Hutchinson, 1974).

Stone and Yoder: Job Information Matrix System

Another approach to providing standardized job information is the Job Information Matrix System (JIMS) (Stone & Yoder, 1970). JIMS entails collecting job information in the following five categories:

1. What the worker *does*
2. What the worker *uses*
3. What *knowledge* the worker must have
4. What the *responsibilities* of the worker are
5. What the *working conditions* of the job are

The exact type of information to be collected in each of these categories is tailor made for specific occupational areas. Therefore, for a given occupational area, the analyst is presented with a standardized list of tasks and is asked to rate how often the worker performs each one.

The analyst is also required to provide an open-ended description of the tasks of the job that occupy a major portion of the worker's time. In so doing, the analyst is to use, when possible, the action verbs representing worker functions hierarchically organized in Functional Job Analysis by Data, People, and Things. To determine what the worker uses, the analyst has a listing of equipment, tools, work aids, and so forth. The analyst reviews the task description and the description of what the worker uses to infer required knowledge. Working conditions are described by forms used for the United States Employment Service involving physical demands and environmental conditions.

McCormick (1979) evaluates JIMS as a promising technique, but one that, at this stage, necessarily must be viewed as a model because it has been fully developed for only a few occupational specialties. Extending coverage to the full range of occupations will be a major undertaking.

Cunningham: Occupation Analysis Inventory

Cunningham and his associates (Heath, Cunningham, & Augustin, 1975; Pass & Cunningham, 1975) have had a long-term effort underway called the Ergometric Research and Development Project. Their purpose is to develop a quantitative occupational taxonomy that can be used to determine occupationally related education and guidance. In other words, they want to describe and classify jobs for educational purposes. Therefore, they have investigated the clustering of occupations with similar educational requirements (Riccobono & Cunningham, 1974a, 1974b; Riccobono, Cunningham, & Bosse, 1975; Pass & Cunningham, 1975a).

A job analysis approach is used with data collected by the Occupation Analysis Inventory (OAI). This instrument contains 622 individual work elements that fall into five generalized categories. These categories, which are derived from an information processing model, are: information received, mental activities, observable behaviors, work outcomes, and work context (Neeb, Cunningham, & Pass, 1971). These five categories were subdivided into selected conceptual frameworks pertaining to human behavior and work technology; work elements were developed for each of the subcategories. The OAI attempts to achieve as much specificity in occupational description as possible (i.e., content loading) while retaining its applicability to the entire occupational spectrum. The OAI is one of the few quantitatively based systems for describing, comparing, and classifying jobs and occupations.

Most of the individual work elements are rated on three scales: significance to the job, extent of occurrence, and applicability. As with McCormick's PAQ, the OAI contains not only behavioral work elements, but also job characteristic elements (e.g., context information). Consequently, Cunningham's system, although largely a behavior description approach, also overlaps with task characteristic approaches. Additionally, Cunningham's research with the OAI, involving the identification of job dimensions from human attribute data, has led us to describe a portion of his system in the chapter dealing with ability requirements approaches to job classification.

As one part of the Ergometric Research and Development Project, a study was conducted to derive empirically the human work dimensions inherent in the 602 work elements (Boese & Cunningham, 1976). Using the OAI, ratings were obtained on 1414 jobs in five major occupational categories. Eight factor analyses were done on the data in each of the eight separate sections of the inventory (e.g., information received, mental activities). The result was 132 first-order work dimensions. An overall factor analysis of these dimensions produced 28 higher-order dimensions. Not only did most of the first-order and higher-order dimensions seem easily interpretable and easily labeled, but also empirical measures of factorial stability indicated that the dimensions were reasonably stable. These factors and examples of high-scoring jobs are presented in Table 5.7. Quantitative profiles on these dimensions can be derived for any job or occupation rated on the OAI. As noted earlier, Cunningham's OAI also enables the identification of quantitative profiles on attribute dimensions (see Chapter 7; Cunningham, Boese, Neeb, & Pass, 1983).

Cunningham and his associates have conducted several studies to test the validity of the OAI work dimension and attribute dimension profiles. The studies have shown significant relationships between OAI work dimension and attribute requirement scores for occupations and various behavioral potentials of job holders in those occupations measured by tests and inventories (e.g., abilities, interests, needs, satisfactions). Cunningham concludes that OAI profiles are meaningful, reliable, and have construct validity.

In another study, Cunningham and his associates intercorrelated the previously mentioned 1414 jobs based upon their OAI work dimension scores. A hierarchical cluster analysis of the job intercor-

TABLE 5.7

Rotated Higher-Order Factors Derived from the Job-Rating Data of the Occupation
Analysis Inventory: Coefficients of Congruence and Examples of High-Scoring Jobs[a]

Higher-order factor code and title[b]	Examples of high-scoring jobs
Ij–1: Human development, assistance, and conflict resolution (.79)	School principal, case worker, social director
Ij–2: Sales, service, and public relations (.91)	Salesperson (sporting goods), bartender, director of recreation (hotel)
Ij–3: Routine semantic and symbolic activities: clerical activities (.95)	Personnel secretary, correspondence clerk, medical secretary
Ij–4: Biological or health-related activities (.94)	Obstetrical consultant, dentist, veterinarian
Ij–5: Mechanical repair, maintenance, and operation (.94)	Aircraft and engine mechanic, production mechanic (tin cans), service station mechanic
Ij–6: Activities related to visual aesthetics (.91)	Layout artist, art coordinator, cloth designer
Ij–7: Utilization and processing of numerical data (.92)	Savings operations officer, portfolio investment analyst, accountant
Ij–8: Botanical activities (.90)	Orchard supervisor, cranberry grower, game farm manager
Ij–9: Activities related to physical science and technology (.83)	Quality control pharmacist, pilot control operator (chemistry), industrial waste inspector
Ij–10: Electrical or electronic repair, maintenance, and operation (.91)	Radio mechanic, aircraft electrician, communications electrician
Ij–11: Building or repairing structures (.76)	Maintenance carpenter, bricklayer, shipfitter
Ij–12: Ue of technical–scientific devices (.73)	Air traffic control specialist, bio-instrumentation technician, physicist
Ij–13: Working with animals (.90)	Head animal keeper (amusement and recreation), pet salesperson, dairy farm hand
Ij–14: Improving or monitoring the physical performance, capability, or adjustment of others (.65)	Occupational therapist, physical therapist, physical education teacher
Ij–15: Food preparation or processing (.76)	Short order cook, chef, school lunch supervisor
Ij–16: Technical planning and drawing (.94)	Tool designer, naval architect, thermodynamics engineer
Ij–17: Assembly and fabrication activities (.85)	Module assembler (electronics), small products assembler, electric motor assembler
Ij–18: Environmental maintenance and planning (.66)	Hydrologist, air and water control director, waste treatment consultant
Ij–19: Performing arts activities (.82)	Music director, musician (instrumental), executive producer

TABLE 5.7 *Continued*

Higher-order factor code and title[b]	Examples of high-scoring jobs
Ij–20: Uninterpretable (.72)	—
Ij–21: Uninterpretable (.49)	—
Ij–22: Vehicle and mechanized equipment operation (.77)	Heavy equipment operator, fork-lift truck operator, chauffeur
Ij–23: Organizing and supervising the work of others (.72)	Warehouse manager, airline lounge manager, corporation president
Ij–24: Uninterpretable (.76)	—
Ij–25: Instructing (.49)	College faculty member, secondary school teacher, computer operations instructor
Ij–26: Material handling or arrangement (.44)	Storeroom clerk, stock clerk, receiving clerk
Ij–27: Uninterpretable (.53)	—
Ij–28: Verbal communication (.38)	Survey worker, psychiatrist, columnist

[a]Reproduced with permission from Boese, R. R. and Cunningham, J. W. Systematically derived dimensions of human work. *JSAS Catalog of Selected Documents in Psychology*, 1976, *6*, 57 (Ms. No. 1270).

[b]The coefficient of congruence appears in parentheses at the end of each higher-order factor title.

relations produced 25 broad, major job clusters, subsuming 88 narrower clusters. Statistical analyses of the major clusters revealed moderate to substantial within-cluster homogeneity, intercluster discriminability, and cluster stability. Further, the cluster structure related meaningfully to the worker traits cited in the *Dictionary of Occupational Titles*. Consequently, the OAI appears to form a useful occupational classificatory system. In addition to these applications to occupational clustering, efforts have been proposed to apply the OAI to the development of occupational interest scales. In fact, some scales have been developed.

Although the OAI and the PAQ are quite similar, there are two differences (McCormick, 1979). One is that the OAI includes many work elements that have specific technologically identified associations, such as medical activities and electrical repair activities. The other is that the OAI has work elements that deal with work goals, such as mechanical devices installed or assembled.

Classificatory Systems for Supervisory and Managerial Performance

A number of investigators have been concerned with the description of supervisory and executive work activities as a means of identifying patterns to guide the categorization of managerial jobs. A review of these is beyond the scope of this book. For a recent review the reader is referred to the revision of Stogdill's *Handbook of Leadership* by Bass (1981). For our present purposes, we have selected some of the most programmatic work that has focused on categorization of behaviors performed by individuals in management positions.

LEADER BEHAVIOR DESCRIPTION

The Ohio State Leadership Studies and later studies extending this research represented the first programmatic attempt to describe and categorize tasks carried out by individuals in supervisory and management positions (see, e.g., Shartle, 1949, 1956; Hemphill, 1950; Fleishman, Harris, & Burtt, 1955; Fleishman, 1953a, 1953b, 1953c; Shartle & Stogdill, 1948; Stogdill & Shartle, 1955; Stogdill, Wherry & Jaynes, 1955; Shartle, Stogdill, & Campbell, 1949; Stogdill & Coons, 1957; Halpin & Winer, 1956). The behavior of executives and supervisors in a wide variety of businesses and military organizations was studied by interview and questionnaire to determine the scope of supervisory performance and to identify the kinds of activities that the supervisors and managers performed. These activities were then grouped into broader dimensions, usually through factor analysis methods applied to the interrelations of task behaviors. In an early study, 14 activities were identified from an analysis of such data. These activities were named and defined in terms of specific behaviors. For example, *public relations* is defined as those acts that are designed to (1) inform outside persons regarding the program and functions of the organization, (2) obtain information regarding public sentiment, or (3) create a favorable attitude toward the organization. Some of the other categories identified included *planning* and *supervision of technical operations*.

In a later study, various managerial jobs were analyzed as a function of the percentage of time spent on the 14 activities. Thus, Shartle *et al.* (1949) used this list of activities to study the work patterns of heads of naval organizations and of the executives of business firms. In other studies, Stogdill *et al.* (1955) investigated 470 naval officers in 45 positions in 47 organizations and found the job tasks to group into eight "generic" clusters of positions: public relations representatives, professional consultants, personnel administrators, technical supervisors, directors of decision makers, schedule procedure makers, maintenance administrators, and coordinators. Although Shartle (1956) acknowledged the utility of such groups for selection and training purposes, he noted that "other studies are needed to discover further how executive positions may be classified" (p. 95).

Under the direction of Hemphill (1950), members of the Ohio State Leadership Studies generated 1800 statements descriptive of a wide range of supervisory behaviors. These specific activities were categorized by staff into 10 generic behavioral dimensions: Recognition, Initiation, Organization, Representation, Communication Up, Communication Down, Domination, Fraternization, Production Emphasis, and Integration. An original form of the *Leader Behavior Description Questionnaire* consisted of 150 items in which respondents described supervisors in terms of frequency of each behavior (always, often, never). The questionnaire was scored in terms of the 10 categories.

In subsequent studies (Fleishman, 1951, 1953; Halpin & Winer, 1957), it was found that these dimensions were highly intercorrelated and two primary dimensions were identified by factor analysis to account for these leader behaviors. The first factor was labeled *Consideration*, defined as

> behavior indicating mutual trust, respect and a certain warmth and rapport between supervisor and his/her group. This does not mean that this dimension reflects a superficial "pat-on-the-back, first name calling" kind of human relations behavior. This dimension seems to emphasize a deeper concern for group members' needs and includes such behavior as allowing subordinates more participation in decision-making and encouraging more two-way communication. (Fleishman & Harris, 1962, p. 43)

The second factor initially was labeled *Initiating Structure*. Later the label was shortened to *Structure*, and the factor was defined to include

> behavior in which the supervisor organizes and defines group activities and his relation to the group. Thus, he/she defines the role he/she expects each member to assume, assigns tasks, plans ahead, establishes ways of getting things done, and pushes for production. This dimension seems to emphasize overt attempts to achieve organizational goals. (Fleishman & Harris, 1962, p. 44)

These studies resulted in shorter forms of the questionnaire measuring these dimensions, utilizing items (behaviors) identified as most diagnostic of Consideration and Structure (see Stogdill & Coons, 1957; Halpin & Winer, 1957; Fleishman, 1953a, 1953b, 1969, 1972).

A large number of studies have been carried out on the relationships of Consideration and Structure with various organizational consequences, such as productivity of work groups (Fleishman, Harris, & Burtt, 1955), intraunit and interunit organizational stress (Oaklander & Fleishman, 1964), and turnover and grievance rates (Fleishman & Harris, 1962). The dimensions have helped integrate data about leadership in a wide variety of settings. These studies are summarized in Fleishman (1973). The extensive work of Fiedler (1973) and the Institute for Social Research at the University of Michigan (Kahn & Katz, 1960) identified similar dimensions. However, the studies summarized by Fleishman (1973) stress measures derived from behavior descriptions.

Landy and Trumbo (1980) have indicated that "the general findings of the Ohio State Studies have been replicated a number of different times, with different instruments, different theoretical approaches and different subject populations" (p. 439). Although a number of the follow-up studies have proposed additional factors, generally Consideration and Structure account for approximately 80% of the variance in leader behavior, leading Landy and Trumbo to conclude that "there is little doubt that consideration and initiating structure represent reliable phenomena in the measurement of leader behavior" (p. 439). Kerr, Schriesheim, Murphy & Stogdill (1974) propose that these dimensions remain the best means of leader classification to date. In view of these conclusions, it appears that any classificatory system for managerial jobs will need to include dimensions relating to Consideration and Structure.

CLASSIFICATORY SYSTEMS FOR MANAGERIAL JOBS

A number of other factor analytic studies have been directed toward identifying common work dimensions with the hope of categorizing managerial jobs according to similarities in their factorial structure. Hemphill (1959) pioneered the development of such an empirically based classificatory system of managerial jobs. In Hemphill's study, each of 93 executives representing several corporations (e.g., American Telephone & Telegraph, Westinghouse Electric Corporation, Standard Oil of Ohio) responded to a questionnaire indicating to what extent 575 position elements were a part of his job (only male executives were included in the study sample). The subjects represented several position levels (upper, middle, and beginning management) and functional areas (research and development, sales, manufacturing, general administration, and industrial relations). A factor analysis of the correlations of the questionnaire responses led to the identification of 10 dimensions. These 10 dimensions could be measured by 191 position elements. Position elements included position activities, responsibilities, demands, and re-

TABLE 5.8

Dimensions for Managerial Work Identified by Hemphill[a]

---

 1. Providing a staff service in a nonoperative area
 2. Supervision of work
 3. Internal business control
 4. Technical aspect of products
 5. Human, community, and social affairs
 6. Preservation of assets
 7. Long-range planning
 8. Personal demands
 9. Exercise of broad power and authority
10. Business reputation

---

[a]Adapted from Hemphill, J. K. *Leader behavior description.* Columbus, OH: Personnel Research Board, Ohio State University, 1950.

strictions and characteristics. Hemphill (1959) suggested that all executive positions were constituted partially by these position elements. He cautioned that the 10 dimensions did not completely cover any position. He suggested that "there will remain parts of the job that are outside the range of the dimensions and that may be relatively unique to the company or the business situation at a given point in time" (p. 65). The 10 dimensions, however, are considered to be relatively independent of function, managerial level, responsibilities, and local situation.

Hemphill (1959) indicated that each job had a pattern of position elements that could be examined for similarities and differences with profiles of other jobs. The dimensions are listed in Table 5.8. Some of these identified dimensions, such as Human, Community and Social Affairs, and Personal Demands, seem to relate to the Consideration dimension of leadership (see Fleishman & Harris, 1962), whereas others relate to the Structure dimension (e.g., Supervision of Work, Long Range Planning, Exercise of Broad Power and Authority).

In 1976, there was an attempt to build upon Hemphill's pioneering work involving the development of a classificatory system for managerial jobs. Tornow and Pinto (1976) recognized the "need for systematic research on the dimensions and groupings of tasks and jobs to develop a meaningful structure of human work" (p. 410). They attempted to replicate Hemphill's research while correcting some methodological limitations (e.g., the small number of positions sampled, the application of an inappropriate method for interpretation of the factors, and the absence of a cross-validation sample).

Tornow and Pinto (1976) asked 433 incumbents representing 28 functions, 3 levels, and 6 companies to complete a questionnaire developed to describe the job content of executive and managerial positions. An appropriate factor analysis of responses revealed 13 independent job factors. Positions in a holdout sample were then compared and grouped into 10 homogeneous clusters in terms of similarities and differences in their 13 factor profiles. A cross validation of these results showed that 73% of the cluster assignments for the 56 holdout positions matched the behavioral descriptions of those positions.

The factors from the two studies showed considerable overlap, although the factor labels were not identical. For example, Hemphill's Long Range Planning and Personal Demands are similar to Tornow and Pinto's Strategy Planning and Complexity and Stress. Four of the factors in the Tornow and Pinto study were extremely similar to Hemphill's Staff Service, Supervision, Internal Business Control, and Products–Services Responsibility. The factors that were unrelated to any in Hemphill's study were Coordination of Other Organizational Units and Personnel, and Advanced Counseling. Tornow and Pinto (1976) suggested that differences in factor structure could easily be attributable to differences in research methodology. Both taxonomic investigations have demonstrated that managerial jobs do have common work dimensions that may be used as the basis for a classificatory system.

In this chapter, we have summarized descriptive and classificatory schemes that categorize tasks and/or jobs on the basis of actual behaviors emitted or activities performed. In Chapter 6, we present approaches to classifying human task performance on the basis of behavior requirements and the associated intervening functions or processes.

References

Alluisi, E. A. Methodology in the use of synthetic task to assess complex performance. *Human Factors*, 1967, *9*, 375–384.

Bass, B. M. *Stogdill's handbook of leadership* (revised and expanded edition). New York: Free Press, 1981.

Bennett, C. A. Toward empirical, practical, comprehensive task taxonomy. *Human Factors*, 1971, *13*, 229–235.

Bennett, C. A. The human factors of work. *Human Factors*, 1973, *15*(3), 281–287.

Berliner, D. C., Angell, D., & Shearer, J. W. *Behaviors, measures, and instruments for performance evaluation in simulated environments*. Paper presented at a symposium and workshop on the quantification of human performance, Albuquerque, New Mexico, August 1964.

Boese, R. R., & Cunningham, J. W. Systematically derived dimensions of human work. *JSAS Catalog of Selected Documents in Psychology*, 1976, *6*, 57 (Ms. No. 1270).

Chambers, R. M. Operator performance in acceleration environments. In N. M. Burns,

R. M. Chambers, & E. Hendler (Eds.), *Unusual environments and human behavior.* London: Glencoe, 1963.

Christal, R. E. Comments by the chairman. In *Proceedings of 19. Division of Military Psychology Symposium: Collecting, analyzing, and reporting information describing jobs and occupations.* (77th Annual Convention of the American Psychological Association.) Lackland Air Force Base, TX: Personnel Research Division, Air Force Human Resources Laboratory, September 1961, 77–85.

Christal, R. E. *New directions in the Air Force occupational research program.* Lackland AFB, TX: USAF, AFHRL, Personnel Research Division, 1972.

Christal, R. E. *The United States Air Force occupational research project* (AFHRL-TR-73-75). Lackland AFB, TX: USAF, AFHRL, Occupational Research Division, 1974.

Christensen, J. M., & Mills, R. G. What does the operator do in complex systems? *Human Factors,* 1967, *9*, 329–340.

Cunningham, J. W., Boese, R. R., Neeb, R. W., & Pass, J. J. Systematically derived work dimensions: Factor analyses of the Occupation Analysis Inventory. *Journal of Applied Psychology,* 1983, *68*, 232–252.

Farina, A. J., Jr. Development of a taxonomy of human performance: A review of descriptive schemes for human task behavior. *JSAS Catalog of Selected Documents in Psychology,* 1973, *3*, 23 (Ms. No. 318).

Fiedler, F. E. Personality and situational determinants of leader behavior. In E. A. Fleishman and J. G. Hunt (Eds.), *Current developments in the study of leadership.* Carbondale, IL: Southern Illinois University Press, 1973.

Fine, S. A. *A pilot study to develop a functional classification structure of occupations.* Paper presented at the meeting of the American Psychological Association, Chicago, September 1951.

Fine, S. A. Functional Job Analysis. *Personnel Administration and Industrial Relations,* Spring 1955. (a)

Fine, S. A. A structure of worker functions. *Personnel Guidance Journal, 34*(2), 1955, 66–73. (b)

Fine, S. A. *A functional approach to a broad scale map of work behaviors* (HSR-RM-63/2). McLean, VA: Human Sciences Research, Inc., September 1963.

Fine, S. A. *Functional Job Analysis: An approach to a technology for manpower planning.* Paper presented at the meeting of the International Institute for Labour Studies, Geneva, Switzerland, February 1973.

Fine, S. A. Functional job analysis: An approach to a technology for manpower planning. *Personnel Journal,* 1974, *53*, 813–818.

Fine, S. A. *Job analysis for heavy equipment operators.* Washington, DC: International Union of Operating Engineers, 1977.

Fine, S. A. & Eisner, E. J. *Performance appraisal in the Department of Housing and Urban Development: A functional analysis approach.* Washington, DC: Advanced Research Resources Organization, July 1980.

Fine, S. A., & Eisner, E. J. *Development of a task bank, performance standards, and performance-based tests for drillers for gas and oil.* Washington, DC: Advanced Research Resources Organization, June 1981.

Fine, S. A., Holt, A. M., & Hutchinson, M. F. *Functional Job Analysis: How to standardize task statements.* Kalamazoo, MI: W.E. Upjohn Institute for Employment Research, October 1974.

Fine, S. A., & Wiley, W. W. *An introduction to Functional Job Analysis: A scaling of selected tasks from the social welfare field.* Washington, DC: W.E. Upjohn Institute for Employment Research, 1971.

Finley, D. L., Obermayer, R. W., Bertone, C. M., Meister, D., & Muckler, F. A. *Human performance prediction in man–machine systems: A technical review* (Vol. 1, NASA CR-1614). Canoga Park, CA: The Bunker–Ramo Corporation, August 1970.

Fleishman, E. A. *Leadership climate and supervisory behavior.* Columbus, OH: Ohio State University Personnel Research Board, 1951.

Fleishman, E. A. The description of supervisory behavior. *Journal of Applied Psychology*, 1953, *36*, 1–6. (a)

Fleishman, E. A. The measurement of leadership attitudes in industry. *Journal of Applied Psychology*, 1953, *37*, 153–158. (b)

Fleishman, E. A. Leadership climate, human relations training, and supervisory behavior. *Personnel Psychology*, 1953, *6*, 205–222. (c)

Fleishman, E. A. Difference between military and industrial organizations. In R. M. Stogdill & C. L. Shartle (Eds.), *Patterns of administrative performance.* Ohio State University Bureau of Business Research Monograph, 1955, *R-81*.

Fleishman, E. A. *Manual for the Leadership Opinion Questionnaire.* Chicago, IL: Science Research Institute, 1969.

Fleishman, E. A. *Manual for the Supervisory Behavior Description Questionnaire.* Washington, DC: Management Research Institute, 1972.

Fleishman, E. A. Twenty years of consideration and structure. In E. A. Fleishman & J. G. Hunt (Eds.), *Current developments in the study of leadership.* Carbondale, IL: Southern Illinois University Press, 1973.

Fleishman, E. A., & Harris, E. F. Patterns of leadership behavior related to employee grievances and turnover. *Personnel Psychology*, 1962, *15*, 43–56.

Fleishman, E. A., Harris, E. F., & Burtt, H. E. *Leadership and supervision in industry.* Columbus: Ohio State University, Bureau of Educational Research, 1955.

Gambardella, J. J. N., & Alvord, W. G. *TI-CODAP: A computerized method of job analysis for personnel management.* Prince Georges County, MD: Project Report, 1978.

Halpin, A. W. & Winer, B. J. A factorial study of the leader behavior descriptions. In R. M. Stogdill & A. E. Coons (Eds.), *Leader behavior: Its description and measurement.* Columbus: Ohio State University, Bureau of Business Research, 1957.

Heath, W. D., III, Cunningham, J. W., & Augustin, J. W. Ability correlates of systematically derived occupational variables: A repeated study. *JSAS Catalog of Selected Documents in Psychology*, 1975, *5*, 354 (Ms. No. 1153).

Hemphill, J. K. *Leader behavior description.* Columbus, OH: Personnel Research Board, Ohio State University, 1950.

Hemphill, J. K. Job description for executives. *Harvard Business Review*, 1959, *37*(5), 55–67.

Jeanneret, P. R., & McCormick, E. J. *The job dimensions of "worker oriented" job variables and of their attribute profiles as based on data from the Position Analysis Questionnaire* (Rep. No. 2). West Lafayette, IN: Occupational Research Center, Dept. of Psychological Sciences, Purdue University, June 1969.

Kahn, A. L., & Katz, D. Leadership practices in relation to productivity and morale. In D. Cartwright & A. Zander (Eds.), *Group dynamics: Research and theory* (2nd ed.). Evanston, IL: Row, Peterson, 1960.

Kerr, S., Schriesheim, C. A., Murphy, C. J., & Stogdill, R. M. Toward a contingency theory of leadership based upon the consideration and initiating structure literature. *Organizational Behavior and Human Performance*, 1974, *12*, 62–82.

Landy, F. J., & Trumbo, D. A. *Psychology of work behavior.* Homewood, IL: Dorsey Press, 1980 (Revised edition).

Lumsdaine, A. A. Design of training aids and devices. In J. Folley (Ed.), *Human factors methods for system design* (AIR-290-60-FR-225). Pittsburgh, PA: American Institutes for Research, 1960.

McCormick, E. J. *The development, analysis, and experimental application of worker-oriented job variables* (Final Report: ONR Nonr-1100 [19]). Lafayette, IN: Purdue University, 1964.

McCormick, E. J. Job and task analysis. In M. D. Dunnette (Ed.), *Handbook of industrial and organizational psychology.* Chicago: Rand McNally, 1976.

McCormick, E. J. *Job analysis: Methods and applications.* New York: American Management Association, AMACOM, 1979.

McCormick, E. J., Jeanneret, P. R., & Mecham, R. C. *Position Analysis Questionnaire.* West Lafayette, IN: Purdue Research Foundation, 1969.

McCormick, E. J., Jeanneret, P. R., & Mecham, R. C. A study of job characteristics and job dimensions as based on the Position Analysis Questionnaire (PAQ). *Journal of Applied Psychology,* 1972, *56*(4), 347–368.

Marquardt, L. D., & McCormick, E. J. *Component analyses of attribute data based on the Position Analysis Questionnaire* (Rep. No. 2). Lafayette, IN: Occupational Research Center, Dept. of Psychological Sciences, Purdue University, 1973.

Marquardt, L. D., & McCormick, E. J. *The job dimensions underlying the job elements of the Position Analysis Questionnaire* (PAQ), form B (Rep. No. 4). Lafayette, IN: Occupational Research Center, Department of Psychological Sciences, Purdue University, June 1974.

Mecham, R. C. *Technical manual for the Position Analysis Questionnaire.* Logan, UT: PAQ Services, Inc., February 1977.

Meister, D. *Behavioral foundations of system development.* New York: Wiley, 1976.

Miller, R. B. Task description and analysis. In R. M. Gagné (Ed.), *Psychological principles in system development.* New York: Holt, Rinehart & Winston, 1962.

Morsh, J. E. Job analysis in the United States Air Force. *Personnel Psychology,* 1964, *17,* 1–17.

Morsh, J. E., & Archer, W. B. *Procedural guide for conducting occupational surveys in the United States Air Force* (USAF PRL-TR-67-11, AD-664-036). Lackland Air Force Base, TX: USAF Personnel Research Laboratory, 1967.

Morsh, J. E., & Christal, R. E. *Impact of the computer on job analysis in the United States Air Force* (USAF TR-66-19). Lackland Air Force Base, TX: USAF Personnel Research Laboratory, 1966.

Neeb, R. W., Cunningham, J. W., & Pass, J. J. *Human attribute requirements of work elements: Further development of the Occupation Analysis Inventory* (Center Research Monograph No. 7). Raleigh, NC: Center for Occupational Research, University of North Carolina, 1971.

Oaklander, H., & Fleishman, E. A. Patterns of leadership related to organizational stress in hospital settings. *Administrative Science Quarterly,* 1964, *8,* 520–532.

Oller, R. G. *Human factors data thesaurus: An application to tasks data* (AMRL-TR-67-211). Wright Patterson Air Force Base, OH: Aerospace Medical Research Laboratories, March 1968.

Olson, H. C., Fine, S. A., Myers, D. C., & Jennings, M. C. The use of Functional Job Analysis for establishing performance standards for heavy equipment operators. *Personnel Psychology,* 1981, *34,* 351–364.

Olson, H. C., Fine, S. A., Myers, D. C., & Jennings, M. C. *Training standards project: Phase III—The development of performance-based tests for backhoe, front-end loader, grader, and scraper operators.* Washington, DC: Advanced Research Resources Organization, December 1978.

Pass, J. J., & Cunningham, J. W. *Occupational clusters based on systematically derived work dimensions: Final Report* (Ergometric Research and Development Report No. 16). Raleigh, NC: North Carolina State University, Center for Occupational Education, 1975. (a)

Pass, J. J., & Cunningham, J. W. A systematic procedure for estimating the human attribute requirements of occupations. *JSAS Catalog of Selected Documents in Psychology*, 1975, *5*, 353 (Ms. No. 1151). (b)

Rabideau, G. F. Field measurement of human performance in man–machine systems. *Human Factors*, 1964, *6*, 663–672.

Reed, L. E. *Advances in the use of computers for handling human factors task data* (AMRL-TR-67-16). Wright Patterson Air Force Base, OH: Aerospace Medical Research Laboratories, April 1967.

Riccobono, J. A., & Cunningham, J. W. Work dimensions derived through systematic job analysis: A study of the Occupation Analysis Inventory. *JSAS Catalog of Selected Documents in Psychology*, 1974, *4*, 145–146 (Ms. No. 806). (a)

Riccobono, J. A., & Cunningham, J. W. Work dimensions derived through systematic job analysis: A replicated study of the Occupation Analysis Inventory. *JSAS Catalog of Selected Documents in Psychology*, 1974, *4*, 146 (Ms. No. 807). (b)

Riccobono, J. A., Cunningham, J. W., & Boese, R. R. Clusters of occupations based on systematically derived work dimensions: An exploratory study. *JSAS Catalog of Selected Documents in Psychology*, 1975, *5*, 352. (Ms. No. 1150)

Shartle, C. L. Leadership and executive performance. *Personnel*, 1949, *25*(5), 375–376.

Shartle, C. L. *Executive performance and leadership*. Englewood Cliffs, NJ: Prentice-Hall, 1956.

Shartle, C. L., Stogdill, R. M., & Campbell, D. T. *Studies in naval leadership*. Columbus, OH: The Ohio State University Research Foundation, 1949.

Stogdill, R. M. & Coons, A. E. *Leader behavior: Its description and measurement*. Columbus: Ohio State University, Bureau of Business Research, 1957.

Stogdill, R. M., & Shartle, C. L. Methods of determining patterns of leadership behavior in relation to organization structure and objectives. *Journal of Applied Psychology*, 1948, *32*, 286–291.

Stogdill, R. M., & Shartle, C. L. *Methods in the study of administrative leadership*. The Ohio State University Bureau of Business Monograph, 1955, R-80.

Stogdill, R. M., Wherry, R. J., & Jaynes, W. E. A factorial study of administrative performance. In R. M. Stogdill & C. L. Shartle (Eds.), *Patterns of administrative performance*. The Ohio State University Bureau of Business Research Monograph, 1955, R-81.

Stone, C. H., & Yoder, D. *Job analysis, 1970*. Long Beach, CA: California State College, 1970.

Theologus, G. C., Wheaton, G. R., & Fleishman, E. A. Effects of intermittent, moderate intensity noise-stress on human performance. *Journal of Applied Psychology*, 1974, *59*, 539–547.

Tornow, W. W., & Pinto, P. R. The development of a managerial job taxonomy: A system for describing, classifying and evaluating executive positions. *Journal of Applied Psychology*, 1976, *61*(4), 410–418.

U.S. Department of Labor Manpower Administration. *Handbook for analyzing jobs* (Stock No. 2900-0131). Washington, DC: U.S. Government Printing Office, 1972.

U.S. Department of Labor Employment and Training Administration. *Dictionary of occupational titles*. Washington, DC: U.S. Government Printing Office, 1977.

Wheaton, G. R. Development of a taxonomy of human performance: A review of classificatory systems relating to tasks and performance. *JSAS Catalog of Selected Documents in Psychology*, 1973, *3*, 22–23 (Ms. No. 317).

Willis, M. P. *Deriving training device implications from learning theory principles* (NAVTRADEVCEN 784-1). Port Washington, NY: USNTDC, 1961.

CHAPTER 6

Classificatory Systems for Describing Human Tasks: Behavior Requirements

In Chapter 3, we defined behavior requirements schemes as emphasizing behaviors that should be emitted or that are assumed to be required in order to achieve criterion levels of performance. The human operator is assumed to be in possession of a large repertoire of processes or functions that intervene between stimulus events and output responses and enable those stimulus–response configurations to come into play (see Wheaton, 1973). Systems that classify such behaviors may include terms like identification, scanning, procedure following, short-term memory, and problem solving. Detailed rules and procedures for recognizing these functions, in terms of stimulus and response requirements, are often present in these schemes. More recent work from cognitive psychology, employing experimental research methods to categorize process variables, falls under this approach as well. In this chapter, we present a variety of descriptive schemes using behavior requirements as a basis for the classification of human task performance.

R. B. Miller: Task Strategies Approach

R. B. Miller (1962) has proposed a behavior requirements scheme. It is an attempt to go beyond task description (a process that produces a detailed picture of what physically occurs) to a task analysis that attempts to abstract behavioral implications from this physical description, resulting in a specification of required behaviors. Task analysis involves two basic components: a descriptive scheme of behavior, and a set of rules to determine if a behavior category is relevant to the task in question.

Miller's early descriptors are presented in Chapter 11, which summarizes his *Task Strategies Approach*. The descriptors refer to activities or functions that the operator engages in to meet the demands placed on the operator by the task. The four minimum system descriptors are *input reception, memory, processing,* and *output effectors.* These functions are defined in general terms that do not suggest either rules or operations for assessing their applicability to a given task or for quantifying the degree to which a given function is involved. For example, *processing* is defined as involving interpretation (i.e., the referencing of stored information to give meaning to data that seem incomplete or inadequate for selecting an effort or action), as well as problem solving or decision making.

The rationale underlying his scheme is that of an information-processing model, and the activities Miller initially proposes are essentially covert, internal processes. Miller acknowledges their intuitive, rational nature and views them as a heuristic tool invented for a specific purpose. For him, task analysis is a clinical exercise, a creative enterprise, because the recording process itself involves value judgments and reflects only portions of the total situation. His descriptive scheme, therefore, is an invention, not a discovery in nature and, like any tool, its effectiveness depends as much on the knowledge and skill of the user as on any of its intrinsic properties (Miller, 1966).

Because the level of specificity of the definitions of Miller's descriptors was originally quite low, it is perhaps unreasonable to expect a high degree of specificity in the abstract, covert realm of internal processes. Miller (1966) himself has characterized his earlier definitions as "overlapping," "ambiguous," and "lacking handles for quantification." However, he also stressed that their test lies in utility rather than in validity in the conventional sense. In fact, Miller's early system has demonstrated some usefulness in predicting the kinds of errors likely to occur in new task situations and the conditions leading to increases in such errors.

Angell, Shearer, and Berliner (1964), who had judges assign some 40 tasks into categories using several classificatory schemes, including Miller's, reported low interjudge agreement. However, Miller's system was greatly extended in his later work to include more precisely defined task functions and their associated work strategies. These developments, which we call the *Task Strategies Approach*, are discussed in Chapter 11. These extensions of Miller's system occurred as a part of the Taxonomy Project and in subsequent work.

Folley: Human Activities Defining Training Needs

Folley (1964a, 1964b) developed a method of task analysis specifically designed to aid in the development of training devices and programs. This focus on training purposes only (as opposed to collecting data for all personnel systems) reduces both the amount and the kinds of information to be collected. This modified method of task analysis is associated with a theory of training developed by Folley (1964b).

Means are generally lacking for converting systematically task description data into behavioral data. Folley responded to this gap by merging the task description process and the task analysis process, thus defining *task analysis* as a process that produces a task description. He specified that task analysis is something one does, whereas a *task description* is a product, a thing, a body of information, or a set of statements about a task that characterizes that task in terms of selected attributes. Given this approach, one does not generate task description data and then try, in some unspecified manner, to impose a behavioral scheme upon the data such as with the system developed by Miller (1962). Rather, the task is analyzed and described in terms of the scheme from the beginning. This method focuses on identifying the presence or absence of specified human activities (behaviors); physical descriptions and information not immediately relevant to training decisions are omitted.

Folley's view of a task is that it can be described in terms of five classes of attributes. These are:

1. The extent to which each of five types of "ongoing activities" is required in the task
2. The temporal, sequential, and causal relationships among these activities
3. Characteristics of the detailed behaviors that constitute the activities
4. Contingencies that might affect task performance
5. Disruptive conditions under which the task might have to be performed

The class of most interest here is the first because it contains the behavioral descriptors. There are five such descriptors or activities that characterize the task with respect to training needs, plus a non-task-related activity category. They are:

1. Procedure Following
2. Continuous Perceptual Motor Activity
3. Monitoring
4. Communicating
5. Decision Making and Problem Solving

Each activity is defined and its critical aspects are listed. For example, *Procedure Following* (PF): performing a sequence of discrete steps, each of which has an identifiable beginning point and an ending point.

The critical aspects of following a procedure are (Folley, 1964b):

1. Knowing what to do next (performing a specified sequence of activities). The sequence of activities may be fixed or branched. In a *Fixed Sequence*, the steps are always done in the same order regardless of the outcome of the steps (unless contingencies occur). Electronic equipment turn-on procedures are good examples of Fixed Sequences. In a *Branched Sequence*, which step is done next depends, at least in some cases, on the outcome of a (preceding) step or steps. Check and adjustment procedures for electronic equipment are usually Branched Sequences.

2. Ability to perform the individual steps required. Six kinds of steps are identified:

a. Setting a control to a single specified position
b. Reading a display
c. Observing a display reaction and operating a control to set the display to a certain point
d. Fastening or unfastening a connector or fastener
e. Putting an object into position or removing it from position
f. Obtaining an item of information from a reference document

In addition to deciding whether an activity is involved in a task, the analyst is required to estimate two quantities for each activity: (1) the proportion of total task time the activity involves, and (2) the degree of the operator's attention required by the activity. A fair degree of precision is achieved for these descriptors by defining the activity, listing its critical aspects or the subactivities that comprise it, and giving examples of the activity. No evidence is provided on the reliability of applying these descriptors to a task.

In summary, Folley created a method for analyzing tasks in terms of a specified set of behavioral descriptors, which are a mixture of functions and observable acts. These descriptors, plus nonbehavioral aspects of the task, are related to the development of training devices and training programs by means of a theory of training.

E. E. Miller: Four-Category Classificatory System for Perceptual–Motor Tasks

E. E. Miller (1969) developed a four-category task classification system for perceptual–motor type tasks. His purpose in doing so was to develop an efficient way to determine what training methods are most appropriate for various types of tasks. The four categories in his scheme are:

1. *Reactive–adjustive tasks* require responding to a series of cues. There is an underlying continuum for the stimulus and response, and the response directly alters the stimulus dimension. Tracking tasks fall into this category. A common example is steering a car.
2. *Reactive–choice tasks* involve choosing from a set of appropriate responses. An example is typing.
3. *Developmental–procedural tasks* involve performing a series of steps in fixed order. An example is flight procedures in an airplane.
4. *Developmental–skilled performance tasks* require attaining progressively more skill in controlling an ever-changing process. An example is batting a ball.

Miller (1969) also developed a classificatory system for training strategies. By creating a matrix using the two classification systems, one for tasks and the other for training strategies, Miller could fulfill his purpose of assessing which training methods are most appropriate for a given type of task. Table 6.1 shows this matrix. The number in each cell refers to a paragraph describing the interaction between type of task and training method. For example, the following is a description of Cell 3:

> In learning *developmental-procedural* tasks, the main feature is to remember what to do, not to perform with high skill. The stimulus problems are those of remembering gross distinctions, rather than of sharpening fine distinctions. Thus, terminology drill might be appropriate, or the demonstration of tolerance limits, or recall of differences. Yet these would probably be a matter of associating words with various cue states. The gradual narrowing of a discrimination would be more likely to be involved in other kinds of learning—those that involve quantitative rather than qualitative performance requirements [Miller, 1969, p. 28].

TABLE 6.1

Interactions of Task Categories with Training Strategies[a,b]

	Task category			
	Reactive		Developmental	
Training strategy	Adjustive	Choice	Procedural	Skilled performance
A. Operational Conditions of Practice				
1. Representation of task environment				
a. Unmodified				
b. Modified				
(1) Stimulus predifferentiation	(1)	(2)	(3)	(4)
(2) Response practice under progressively more difficult conditions	(5)	(6)	(7)	(8)
2. Analysis into subtasks	....	(9)	....	
3. Performance requirements information	(13)	(12)	(10)	(11)
4. Supplementary knowledge of results	....	(14)	....	
5. Incentive manipulations				
B. Progress Diagnosis				
1. Utilizing knowledge of results				
a. Clarify goal state	....	(15)	....	
b. Call attention to subgoals	....	(16)	....	
c. Supplementary (early) knowledge	....	(17)	....	
2. Process conception	....	(18)	....	
3. Response set for effective feedback				
a. Movement consistency	....	(19)	....	
b. Avoid responses which mask feedback				
4. Overt response patterns	....	(20)	....	
5. Sensitivity to cue indicating moment for response	....	(21)	....	
6. Response anticipation	....	(22)	....	

[a]Each number in the table refers to the text paragraph in Miller (1969) in which that particular interaction is discussed; e.g., Stimulus Predifferentiation, as applied to *reactive-adjustive* tasks, is discussed in paragraph 1. When a number covers all four task categories, that training strategy is discussed for all tasks in the paragraph indicated; e.g., Analysis into Subtasks is discussed in paragraph 9, for all four task categories.

[b]Reprinted with permission from Miller, E. E. *A taxonomy of response processes* (HumRRO Tech. Rep. 69–16). Alexandria, VA: Human Resources Research Organization.

Although Miller presented no evaluative data for his classificatory system, he acknowledged the strong need to generate such data for his system as well as for all such systems.

Alluisi: Seven Critical Functions Assessed by
Multiple-Task Performance Battery

In attempting to assess complex performance, Alluisi (1967) reasoned that there are critical human functions that are required for overall system performance. He embodied these functions in standardized task situations that can be combined into a test battery (Multiple-Task Performance Battery or MTPB; see Adams, 1958; Adams, Levine, & Chiles, 1959; Chiles, Alluisi, & Adams, 1968). The functions and their representative tasks are shown in Table 6.2. Chiles (1982) has noted that Alluisi's system has been characterized as "a synthetic work approach." Selected tasks can be presented in any combination desired, and indiviudal tasks can be varied in relation to both time constraints and task-difficulty parameters.

TABLE 6.2

Alluisi's Critical Functions and Representative Tests[a]

Performance function	Specific tasks (tests)
Watch keeping	Warning-lights monitoring
	Blinking-lights monitoring
	Probability monitoring
Memory (short and long term)	Arithmetic computations
Sensory–perceptual	Visual target-identification
Procedural	Code-lock solving
Communication	Not currently measured directly; possibly being tapped by arithmetic computations display
Intellectual	None as yet; a modified version of code-lock solving may serve as test task
Perceptual–motor	None as yet[b]

[a]Reprinted with permission from *Human Factors*, 9, Alluisi, E. A. Methodology in the use of synthetic tasks to assess complex performance, © 1967, Pergamon Press, Ltd.

[b]Morgan and Alluisi (1972) have stated that "research has been underway to develop tasks for direct measurements of performances of . . . perceptual–motor functions" (p. 838).

The tasks, which are fully described in Morgan and Alluisi (1972), were selected in accordance with the following criteria:

1. Content validity
2. Face validity
3. Sensitivity to genuine performance changes
4. Engineering feasibility
5. Reliability
6. Flexibility–ease in modifying the stimuli presented and responses recorded
7. Workload variability
8. Trainability (easily learned after a short familiarization period)

Alluisi's functions include both internal processes and external activities, the latter encompassing a mixture of observable and covert behaviors. The functions presumably are represented by the tasks (tests), and, consequently, operationally defined by describing what the operator does when performing them. Reliability data within Alluisi's scheme are available for performance measures on the tasks themselves. Adequate reliabilities were achieved using test–retest methods (see Alluisi, 1967).

Four forms of validity were cited by Alluisi as relevant to his scheme. He concluded that the scheme has content validity because the tasks employed in the battery logically represent the seven functions. Although no specific evidence is provided regarding face validity, one might assume that the tasks have been accepted by the subjects as valid.

To achieve construct validity, the functions should be essentially independent or orthogonal. Therefore, performance on the tasks representing different functions should show low intercorrelations. On the basis of an analysis, it was concluded that the tasks are independent and do measure different things. Alluisi feels that assumption of independence among the functions may be desirable in a psychometric sense but is not essential from a systems point of view because the functions that are components of the system interact to produce the performance output.

Predictive criterion-related validity remains unassessed, due to Alluisi's conviction that no empirical way exists for validating the results obtained from the task battery. He maintains that, until the basic problem of what criterion measures should be used to assess operator performance on complex meaningful tasks is solved, there is no way of evaluating the scheme's predictive validity.

Alluisi's approach is not a conceptual scheme for describing human behavior in task situations. He postulates that certain functions are essential in complex system performance and seeks to identify measures of these functions. It was not his intention to develop a method for determining which functions are actually required in specific real-world tasks or for quantifying and differentiating among those functions. Consequently, Alluisi's descriptors are not particularly useful for examining a new task to determine which functions are required. They have been useful in examining the effects of such variables as illness and organismic stresses (see, for instance, Alluisi, Thurmond, & Coates, 1971; Coates, Thurmond, Morgan, & Alluisi, 1972; Coates & Kirby, 1982), forced rest and sleep–wakefulness cycling, endurance and work–rest scheduling, and other environmental, task, and situational stresses on sustained performance (see Morgan, Brown, & Alluisi, 1970; Alluisi & Morgan, 1982).

Gagné: Categories of Learning Processes

For many years, Gagné (1972, 1977; Gagné & Briggs, 1979) has proposed that researchers concentrate on the identification and refinement of the domains of learning and their associated performance objectives and outcomes. Gagné views learning not only as *content* or subject matter, but also as a *process* of acquiring modifications in existing knowledge, skills, habits, or action tendencies. Gagné has suggested that, by classifying learning processes, the varieties of learning that occur in the classroom will become more manageable. He also has criticized some of the previously identified categories, such as cognitive learning, rote learning, discovery learning, and concrete vs. symbolic learning as "limited in usefulness because they are not well differentiated either by means of the operations required to establish them, or by the consequences to which they lead" (Gagné, 1972, p. 2).

Based on his own research, Gagné has proposed five categories of learning processes: Intellectual Skills, Cognitive Strategy, Verbal Information, Attitude, and Motor Skills. These are presented in Table 6.3. Intellectual Skill is subdivided into five additional categories: problem solving or higher order rule, rule, defined concept, concrete concept, and discrimination. (Some of the subcategories appear to

TABLE 6.3

Gagné's Categories of Learning Outcomes[a]

Category	Performance	Example
Intellectual Skills		
Problem Solving (Higher-Order Rule)	Generate a solution to a novel problem	Predicting rainfall, given conditions of location and terrain
Rule	Apply the rule to a specific example	Demonstrating that water changes state at 100°C
Defined Concept	Classify an object or situation in accordance with a definition	Classifying a "city," using a definition
Concrete Concept	Identify a class of object characteristics, objects, or events	Identifying an equilateral triangle
Discrimination	Distinguish object features as same or different	Distinguishing printed "bs" from "ds"
Cognitive Strategy	Originate novel problems and solutions	Originating a novel plan for disposing of fallen leaves
Verbal Information	State facts, generalizations, or descriptions	Stating how blood is circulated in the body
Attitude	Choose a course of action toward some person, object, or event	Choosing swimming as a preferred exercise
Motor Skills	Execute a skilled motor performance	Planning the edge of a board

[a]Adapted with permission from Table 3.1, Gagné, R. M., *Essentials of learning for instruction.* New York: Holt, Rinehart & Winston, 1974.

resemble the human functions of sensing, identification, and interpretation described earlier by Gagné, 1962.)

Gagné (1972) has provided definitions for each of his domains:

Intellectual Skills involve discriminations, concepts and rules, and their elaborations. Neither practice nor context improve their learning. Rather, the learning of Intellectual Skills is enhanced by the prior acquisition of prerequisite skills.

Cognitive Strategies are internally organized skills that govern the individual's behavior in learning, remembering, and thinking (see Bruner, 1970). They are directed toward self-management of learning and thinking and obviously differ from Intellectual Skills, which are oriented toward the learner's environment. Cognitive Strategies are continually refined with practice as the learner encounters situations that require learning, remembering, and solving or defining problems.

Verbal Information involves learning facts, principles, and generalizations that are needed for continued learning within a particular subject area. Additionally, this category involves larger, organized bodies of information (or knowledge) that must be acquired not only for further learning in a particular area, but also for learning across areas and for thinking in general. The crucial requirement for the attainment of Verbal Information appears to be the presentation of material within an organized, meaningful context.

Attitudes constitute another type of learning process identified by Gagné. These are not learned by practice nor are they affected by a meaningful context. However, they may be modified by human role models.

Motor Skills are the capabilities that mediate organized motor performances like tying shoelaces and printing letters. These skills can be improved with practice over long periods (see Fitts & Posner, 1967).

Gagné suggested that generalizations of research findings can be made within these learning process domains, regardless of the nature of the subject matter. However, generalization across the domains "is at best a highly risky business and likely to be quite invalid" (Gagné, 1972, p. 4). Gagné warned that, although the domains had been formulated on the basis of research, future research investigations undoubtedly will result in their refinement. He suggested that conclusions about the extent of generalizability would need to be drawn only after the examination of research results from many content areas. Research will establish the generalizability (or lack thereof) of learning conditions and learning outcomes across the domains.

Gagné has indicated that the learning process will differ between age groups. Instructional techniques for one group may not be effective for another group, due to varying degrees of development of the various domains.

Gagné believed that one of the major practical applications of his classificatory system pertained to instructional design. He indicated that "the domains are classes of instructional objectives, each of which requires a different set of critical conditions to ensure efficient learning, and each of which implies the need for a different sort of situation for its assessment as a learning outcome" (Gagné, 1972, p. 7). Only with such relationships identified for a given domain will educators be able to identify appropriate instructional techniques and to measure effectively learning performance.

Primoff: Job Element Method

Primoff (1959, 1970, 1971, 1972, 1973) developed the job element method for analyzing federal government jobs while serving as a psychologist in the Personnel Research and Development Center of the United States Civil Service Commission (now the Office of Personnel Management). The approach involves a structured job analysis method that results in the description of a job in terms of elements and subelements. Primoff (1975) has defined a *job element* as a worker characteristic that influences success in a job. Elements may be "a knowledge, such as knowledge of accounting principles; a skill, such as skill with woodworking tools; an ability, such as ability to manage a program; a willingness, such as willingness to do simple tasks repetitively; an interest, such as interest in learning new techniques; or a personal characteristic, such as reliability or dependability" (Primoff, 1975, p. 2).

Primoff (1955) applied his method initially to the analysis of trade and industrial jobs to determine appropriate selection criteria. He has identified 56 elements for federal trade and labor jobs that are listed in the U.S. Civil Service Commission Handbook X–118C (U.S. Civil Service Commission, 1969). Some of these elements include "Ability to Do the Work of the Position Without More Than Normal Supervision," "Knowledge of Welding," "Use of Measuring Instruments (Mechanical)," and "Ability to Interpret Instructions, Specifications, Including Blueprint Reading." Primoff (1975) has also identified 137 generic elements for office positions. Some examples are "Ability to Gain Cooperation," "Ability to Learn New Procedures," "Desire to Learn Technical Field," "Grammar," and "Initiative and Aggressiveness." The list of 137 elements also includes complex supervisory elements such as "Training and Preparing Employees to Work." This element refers to the ability to teach, train, and explain to employees thoroughly and clearly the correct methods, work and sequences, changes in methods of work, and so forth. Abilities defined include "makes sure employees understand by questioning them," and "develops skills of workers." These more complex elements for supervisory jobs were developed by Daniel B. Corts, an associate of Primoff's at the U.S. Civil Service Commission.

Job elements and subelements are generated by subject matter experts who may be incumbents, supervisors or other individuals who have had an opportunity to observe superior, average, and inferior workers in action. After identifying job elements through the application of previously developed standardized lists such as those described for trade and office jobs or through brainstorming sessions (or a combination of these procedures), each element is rated.

If the ratings are to be used to select a test battery to assess the critical job elements, the ratings are made on a 3-point scale:

0   The element is not present in the job. Value = 0
√   The element is present in the job but not of extreme importance. Value = 1
+   The element is present and of extreme importance to the job. Value = 2

The ratings of the several raters are then added together. These values are used to derive an estimate of the validity (the J–Coefficient) of one or more standardized tests. The J–Coefficient is obtained through a mathematical formula that involves

> correlating weights assigned through job analysis to specific job elements (expressed in psychological terms) against 'beta' weights of tests designed to measure each element. The latter weight is determined by expert judgment influenced by a growing body of empirical data where test scores are treated as the dependent variable and job elements as the independent variable in a multiple regression equation. In this sense, it is a measure of the correspondence of the content of the job, as judged by competent analysts, and the job-relevant content of the tests [Guion, 1976, pp. 808–809].

The beta weights for various standardized tests are contained in an easily read matrix having job elements as rows and tests as columns. Of course, in some cases, a cell of the matrix will be blank where the job element and the standardized test are not correlated.

Primoff's approach has been identified by Guion (1976) as a form of synthetic validity that Balma (1959) has described as "the inferring of validity in a specific situation from a logical analysis of jobs into their elements, a determination of test validity for these elements, and a combination of elemental validities into a whole" (p. 395). Guion (1976) has suggested that once jobs have been analyzed into their components, and test correlates of the elements identified and combined to form a test battery for a given job, the evaluation of the scheme depends upon the "degree of correspondence between predicted and actual performance on a composite criterion" (p. 808). McCormick (1976) reported that in such evaluative studies in which the J–Coefficient has been used to select the test battery and where the batteries have been involved in criterion-related validity studies, the comparisons indicated that the J–Coefficient approach is a "reasonably satisfactory method for developing test batteries" (p. 690).

Primoff (1975) also has applied his job element method to developing new testing instruments for a given job. When developing job relevant tests, job elements generated by subject matter experts are rated on the following scales:

Barely acceptable workers (B)
+ all have   Value = 2
√ some have   Value = 1
0 almost none have   Value = 0

To pick out superior workers (S)
+ very important   Value = 2
√ valuable   Value = 1
0 does not differentiate   Value = 0

Trouble likely if not considered (T)
+ much trouble   Value = 2
√ some trouble   Value = 1
0 safe to ignore   Value = 0

Practical, demanding this element, we can fill (P)
+ all openings   Value = 2
√ some openings   Value = 1
0 almost no openings   Value = 0

The S, T, and P ratings are used in deriving an *item index*. McCormick (1979) has described the subsequent process as follows:

> These indexes and the ratings on the fourth factor (B) for the individual raters are then summarized for all raters and converted to percentages related to all items. In turn, items with percentages above 50 on both the item index and on factor B (with some exceptions) are used as the basis for construction of test items. In general terms, a test developed from this basis would then have items which are relatively representative of the more important elements of the job in question [pp. 258–259].

Primoff's Job Element Method has been useful not only in the selection and design of written examinations, but also in the construction of applicant rating schedules and self assessment forms. The approach has been widely used throughout federal, state, and local governments. It is likely that many of the elements in Primoff's system are highly intercorrelated and would reduce to clusters of broader functional categories of behavior requirements. Such research might allow a better assessment of the utility of the system for generalizing and predicting human task performance across jobs.

Hunt: Cognitive Correlates Approach

Earl Hunt and his associates (Hunt, Frost, & Lunneborg, 1973; Hunt, Lunneborg, & Lewis, 1975) have been interested in comparing similarities and differences in performance of high and low ability individuals on a variety of tasks. The tasks examined include many paradigms of current interest in cognitive psychology such as choice reaction time and the Posner letter-matching task. Pellegrino and Glaser (1979) have labeled Hunt's work the *cognitive correlates* approach.

Subjects are divided into high and low ability groups based upon measures of verbal and quantitative reasoning. Hunt (1978) has found that individuals high in verbal ability can make faster letter comparisons on the Posner task than individuals low in verbal ability. Carroll (1979) has noted that "we cannot tell from Hunt's findings what aspects of the verbal abilities are correlated with . . . the parameters of the experimental task. . . . One alternative explanation . . . is that there is an essential link between the mental speed aspect of the experimental task and the speededness aspect of the verbal aptitude test" (p. 30). Carroll (1979) further suggested that careful design using the correlational, factor-analytic method could yield "useful information about the construct validity of the verbal and quantitative aptitude tests that have been used as correlates of the experimental task data" (p. 30).

Sternberg (1979a) has questioned the usefulness of the cognitive correlates approach to understanding and categorizing task performance. He stated, "I find it very difficult to believe, on merely intuitive grounds, that the simple tasks used in the cognitive psychologist's laboratory bear much relation to the complex tasks found on aptitude tests or to the still more complex tasks required in everyday and in academic life" (p. 69). Nonetheless, because of the positive results of Hunt (1978) regarding interrelationships between group aptitudes and abilities and task performance, it would seem that a comprehensive classificatory system, based upon a behavioral requirements approach, would need to explain and incorporate these findings.

Carroll: Coding Scheme for Cognitive Tasks
Appearing in Psychometric Tests

Carroll (1979) has recognized the need to identify the mental processes that people use in performing ability and aptitude tests. He has suggested that "many items presented in conventional aptitude tests are highly similar, if not identical, to tasks studied in experimental cognitive psychology, and that the analysis of such tasks ought to help in understanding what is measured by aptitude and ability tests in which such tasks are to be found as items" (p. 31).

Carroll (1976) developed a uniform system for coding the characteristics of the tasks represented by items in a sample of tests taken from the Educational Testing Service Kit of Reference Tests for Cognitive Factors (French, Ekstrom, & Price, 1963). This coding system reflects an information-processing model of cognition. Task characteristics that are coded include the types of stimuli presented (e.g., number of stimulus classes, completeness, interpretability), the kinds of overt responses that are required to demonstrate performance (e.g., number and type, response mode, criterion of response acceptability), relevant aspects of sequencing of subtasks within the task (number of occasions, temporal structure), types of operations and strategies that will probably be employed in central processing (e.g., type or description, specifications in task instructions, determination of acceptable performance), and probable ranges of relevant temporal parameters (e.g., duration, individual differences in duration, criterion for termination).

After coding 48 tests, Carroll (1976) analyzed the codes to isolate distinctive patterns of codes for the 24 previously identified factors (French, et al. 1963). Carroll (1979) referred to this approach as a logical analysis of construct validity. He concluded that "nearly all pairs of tests from the same factor had one or more codes in common . . . and that patterns of these codes were generally distinct from factor to factor" (Carroll, 1976, p. 41).

This logical coding of tasks in terms of their processes, contents, and strategies represents a behavior requirements approach to task classification. Carroll (1976) acknowledged that he has not yet determined the intercoder reliability of the system. Based upon his initial, encouraging results at matching task codes with common factors, it seems likely that further research will be undertaken. Carroll (1979) has characterized his preliminary analysis as "somewhat speculative" and called for "the necessary empirical evidence for the information processing components" of task performance (p. 31).

Sternberg: Componential Metatheory and Analysis

Sternberg (1979b) has developed an information-processing theory of mental abilities. The theory organizes mental abilities into four levels: composite tasks, subtasks, information processing components, and information-processing metacomponents (see Figure 6.1). The

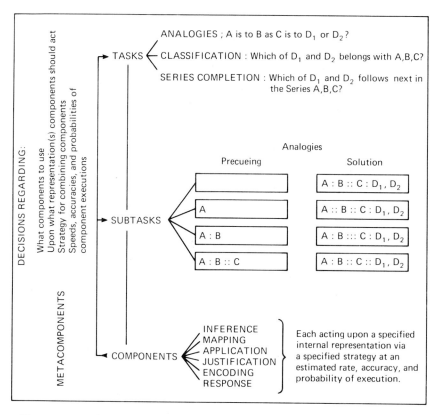

Figure 6.1 Outline of Sternberg's theory of mental abilities. Copyright (1979) by the American Psychological Association. Reprinted with permission from Sternberg, R. J. The nature of mental abilities. *American Psychologist*, 1979, *34*(3), 214–230. (b).

theory is of particular interest to us because of its emphasis upon categorizing tasks by their required components or processes and metacomponents.

Sternberg (1979b) differentiated the information-processing approach from the differential approach to the study of mental abilities. (We shall examine the latter approach more closely under our discussion of taxonomic systems involving ability requirements.) Specifically, he stated,

> Investigators pursuing the differential approach have sought [an] understanding of the nature of mental abilities by studying relationships between patterns of individual differences in scores on psychometric ability tests. The basic idea motivating this approach is that a relatively small number of

latent abilities are responsible for observed variation among individuals on these tests. Understanding of abilities is to be had by discovering in the test data the sources of individual differences variation. Discovery of these sources has typically been by means of correlational techniques, especially factor analysis. Investigators pursuing the information-processing approach have sought understanding of the nature of mental abilities by studying patterns of performance on cognitive tasks with systematically varied attributes. These variations in task attributes, rather than variations in subject attributes, have provided the basis for inferring the nature of mental abilities [p. 214].

Sternberg (1979b) added that the approaches that seem most viable for understanding mental abilities integrate differential and information-processing techniques in some way.

In Sternberg's theory, the first level pertains to the composite task as the subject views it. Tasks are selected for research based on four criteria proposed by Sternberg and Tulving (1977): quantifiability, reliability, construct validity, and empirical validity. Using these criteria, Sternberg and his associates selected the following *tasks* to investigate task performance of adults and children and associated mental abilities: analogies, classifications, series completions, metaphorical completions and ratings, linear syllogisms, categorical syllogisms, and conditioned syllogisms. Performance on these tasks is quantifiable in terms of response time to solution and error rate in solution. The tasks have been demonstrated to yield reliable performance, with reliability estimates across individuals and across tasks generally exceeding .90. The tasks are construct valid as they are selected by Sternberg's componential theory of reasoning, and they have been shown to be empirically valid indicators of the mental abilities they were designed to measure.

Sternberg (1979b) finds that a listing of individual scores on these tasks is "theoretically barren." Consequently, he decomposes tasks into *subtasks* involving a subset of information processing components that are involved in the full task. For example, analogies (A:B::C:D) are decomposed by a method known as precueing (Sternberg, 1977). An analogy is divided into four subtasks, using zero, one (A), two (A:B), or three (A:B::C) precues. Subtask scores are then correlated with scores on standard reasoning tasks such as those included in intelligence tests. Sternberg (1979b) suggested that analysis of such subtasks reveals more about mental abilities than the study of composite tasks alone.

Subtasks are then broken down further into components. A *component* is defined as an elementary information process that operates on internal representations of objects or symbols. Sternberg (1977) noted that a component or process may translate a sensory input into a conceptual representation, transform one conceptual representation into another one, or translate a conceptual representation into a motor output. Sternberg (1979b) uses the term *componential metatheory* to refer to the "schematization of the nature of mental abilities," whereas *componential analysis* refers to "the methodology used to fill in the substantive details of the various levels of the schematization" (p. 221).

Components are divided into three categories: (1) *general components* that are required for performance on all tasks within a given universe; (2) *class or group components* that are required for performance of classes of tasks within the task universe; and (3) *specific components* that are required for performance of single specific tasks within the task universe. Components perform at least five different functions. Sternberg (1979a) has suggested that, although there are 15 types of components (three classes × five functions), only 10 have theoretical interest.

Analysis at the component level enables the detailed specification of task performance including identification of (1) the component processes, (2) the internal representation of information on which the component processes act, (3) the strategies by which different component processes are combined, and so forth.

Sternberg (1979b) has suggested that tasks used to measure mental abilities can be arranged hierarchically. The placement of tasks in the hierarchy is determined by the class components used to perform each task. The successive levels of the hierarchy differ in task complexity, with higher levels representing greater complexity. Tasks at a given level are of equal complexity, but may differ in class components used for task completion. Such a hierarchy based on a componential theory of mental abilities guides the selection of tasks for research purposes to confirm or refute the theory. Sternberg (1979b) labeled the underlying theory the "unified componential theory of human reasoning." He suggested that reasoning, a major aspect of intelligence, comprises a relatively small number of information-processing components.

The final level of mental abilities in Sternberg's theoretical framework is that of *metacomponents*. These controls determine what occurs at the componential level. They are described by Sternberg (1979a) as "higher-order control processes that are used for planning how a problem should be solved, for making decisions regarding alternative courses of action during problem solving and for monitoring solution processes. These metacomponents are sometimes referred to collectively as an 'executive' or a 'homunculus'" (p. 71).

Sternberg believes that the analysis of mental abilities at the four levels of composite tasks, subtasks, components, and metacomponents will provide valuable information regarding the structure and content of mental abilities. His research is of particular relevance to our discussion of classificatory systems because of his efforts to develop a taxonomy of task performance from the knowledge of underlying components or processes and metacomponents determining that performance. Although the task hierarchy that Sternberg has developed is of theoretical interest, empirical research is needed to support the model. Sternberg (1979b) himself has noted, "An intelligent taxonomy of these tasks can be formed only after we know the components and metacomponents that enter into them. Similarly, an intelligent taxonomy of components requires understanding of the metacomponents controlling them, and we have almost no understanding of activities at the metacomponential level" (p. 228).

Posner: Taxonomy of Information-Processing Tasks

Posner (1964) has proposed a taxonomy of information-processing tasks categorizing all tasks on the basis of one dimension, namely, the relationship between the amount of input information and the amount of output information. Using this dimension, Posner (1964) identified three categories of tasks (see Figure 6.2):

1. *Information Conservation.* The amount of input information is the same as the amount of output information. A conservation task, such as the standard choice reaction time situation, requires the subject to preserve all stimulus information for perfect performance.
2. *Information Reduction.* The amount of input information is greater than the amount of output information. In a reduction task, the subject is required to map more than one stimulus point into a single response. The loss of information in this situation is not error, but is required by the task.
3. *Information Creation.* The amount of input information is less than the amount of output information. In the creation task, the subject is required to map a single stimulus point into more than one response.

Posner (1964) acknowledged the similarity of his scheme to that of Hunt (1962), who divided tasks into those requiring complete infor-

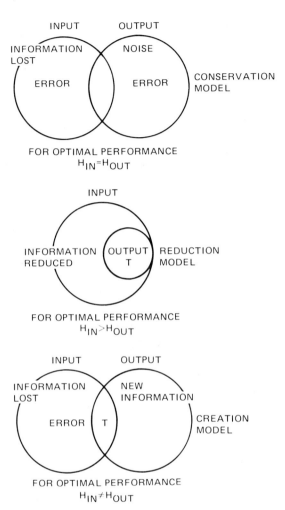

Figure 6.2 Posner's proposed taxonomy of information-processing tasks. Copyright (1964) by the American Psychological Association. Reprinted with permission from Posner, M. I. Information reduction in the analysis of sequential tasks. *Psychological Review*, 1964, *71*(6), 491–504.

mation transmission (rote learning), information reduction (concept learning), and information production (probabilistic learning). Posner (1964) also recognized that his classificatory scheme and that of Hunt captured Bartlett's (1959) verbal distinction between "closed-system thinking," in which the solution is implicit in the problem (such as in the reduction model, adding number stimuli to obtain a sum), and "open-system thinking," in which the subject uses the available evidence to leap beyond the input and provide a creative solution (such as in the creation model). Similarly, Bruner (1957) recognized the presence of the creation model when he suggested that "the most characteristic thing about mental life is that one constantly goes beyond the information given" (p. 41).

Posner (1964) noted that a classificatory "system is of little value unless it can be shown that the tasks falling within a category obey the same general rules" (p. 493). Posner added that information-conservation tasks had been widely studied and that the investigations had been useful in demonstrating relationships for that task category. He has urged more investigation of tasks falling within the information reduction and creation categories.

Posner's own research (1962) with information-reduction tasks, and that of others summarized in his 1964 article, suggested the following principles. If the task requires complete representation of the stimulus in the response (or *condensation*), the amount of information reduced is related directly to difficulty both during learning and in the utilization of previously learned rules. However, if the task allows the subject to ignore some information in the stimulus (or *gating*), the direct relation between reduction and difficulty is found during learning, but may not occur after the rule is learned. Further experimental work is required to clarify the relationships between information transmission, task difficulty, and other variables, for the various task categories identified by Posner.

Levine and Teichner: Information–Theoretic Approach

The behavior requirements approach to task classification developed by Levine and Teichner (1973) is based on a theoretical model that provides for a systems language common to tasks. Information processing is seen as the common denominator, in which a task is defined in terms of types of information transferred between sources and receivers. The types of terms used include classes of constraints on stimulus and response events, amount of redundancy, and types of relations between input and output.

Because this methodology was developed under the Taxonomy Project, the approach is described more fully in Chapter 10 of this book. Work on this approach has led to the description of methods for evaluating its utility.

Teichner and Whitehead: Criterion Measures Approach

As part of the Taxonomy Project, Teichner and Whitehead (1973) developed a behavior requirements approach that they labeled the *Criterion Measures Approach*. Although this approach is discussed more fully in Chapter 9 of this book, a brief description is provided in this section.

The Criterion Measures Approach to task classification categorizes tasks in terms of dependent operator response measures. For example, one class of task performance, called *switching*, is defined by measures indicating the latency or reaction time of the operator's response. Another, called *coding*, is defined by the percentage of correct responses made, and a *searching* category is defined by probability of detection. There are subcategories for these types of broad categories.

The Criterion Measures Approach has received some empirical evaluation in so far as the classificatory scheme has been applied to tasks utilized previously in several areas of research on learning (e.g., effect of schedules of practice) and on the effects of environmental factors (e.g., noise). Encouraging results have been obtained. As an illustration, it was possible to organize the literature on distributed practice in terms of these categories. Different functions were obtained, depending on the task categories. For example, for simple coding tasks, performance change was a linear function of intertrial interval. For successive coding tasks, there was an increase in percentage improvement with increased practice distribution, followed by a decrease. Chapter 9 provides a detailed description of the studies involving this classificatory scheme, and also describes work needed to assess further the method's viability.

In this chapter, we have described a number of schemes that classify human task performance on the basis of inferred functions or processes necessary for effectve performance. In the next chapter we review other schemes that also rely on intervening processes to classify human task behavior. These processes, labeled *abilities*, are derived through empirical correlational–experimental research, using such techniques as factor analysis, and, as such, are distinct from the processes described in this chapter. Chapter 7 also describes classificatory schemes in which the descriptors are the objective properties of the task, per se, with human task performance categorized on the basis of task characteristics.

References

Adams, O. S. *Aircrew fatigue problems during extended endurance flight: Phase I* (WADC Tech Rep. 57-510). Dayton, OH: USAF Wright Air Development Center, 1958.

Adams, O. S., Levine, R. B., & Chiles, W. D. *Research to investigate factors affecting multiple-task psychomotor performance* (WADC Tech. Rep. 59-120). Dayton, OH: USAF Wright Air Development Center, 1959.

Alluisi, E. A. Methodology in the use of synthetic task to assess complex performance. *Human Factors*, 1967, *9*, 375–384.

Alluisi, E. A., & Morgan, B. B., Jr. Temporal factors in human performance and productivity. In E. A. Alluisi and E. A. Fleishman (Eds.), *Human performance and productivity. Vol. 3. Stress and performance effectiveness*. Hillsdale, NJ: Lawrence Erlbaum, 1982.

Alluisi, E. A., Thurmond, J. B., & Coates, G. D. Behavioral effects of infectious diseases: Respiratory Pasteurella Tularensis in man. *Perceptual and Motor Skills*, 1971, *32*, 647–668.

Angell, D., Shearer, J. W., & Berliner, D. C. *Study of training performance evaluation techniques* (AIR-D-81-3/64-TR). Palo Alto, CA: American Institutes for Research, 1964.

Balma, M. J. The development of processes for indirect or synthetic validity. A symposium: I. The concept of synthetic validity. *Personnel Psychology*, 1959, *12*, 395–396.

Bartlett, F. C. *Thinking: An experimental and social study*. New York: Basic Books, 1959.

Bruner, J. S. Going beyond the information given. In *Contemporary approaches to cognition*. Cambridge, MA: Harvard University Press, 1957.

Bruner, J. S. The skill of relevance and the relevance of skills. *Saturday Review*, April 18, 1970, pp. 66–68; 78–79.

Carroll, J. B. Psychometric tests as cognitive tasks: A new "structure of intellect." In L. Resnick (Ed.), *The nature of intelligence*. Hillsdale, NJ: Lawrence Erlbaum, 1976.

Carroll, J. B. Measurement of ability constructs. In A. P. Maslow (Ed.), *Construct validity in psychological measurement: Proceedings of a colloquium on theory and application in education and employment*. Washington, DC: Office of Personnel Management, and Princeton, NJ: Educational Testing Service, October 1979.

Chiles, W. D. Workload, task, and situational factors as modifiers of complex human performance. In E. A. Alluisi and E. A. Fleishman (Eds.) *Human performance and productivity. Vol. 3. Stress and performance effectiveness*. Hillsdale, NJ: Lawrence Erlbaum, 1982.

Chiles, W. D., Alluisi, E. A., & Adams, O. S. Work schedules and performance during confinement. *Human Factors*, 1968, *10*, 143–196.

Coates, G. D., & Kirby, R. H. Organismic factors and individual differences in human performance and productivity. In E. A. Alluisi and E. A. Fleishman (Eds.) *Human performance and productivity. Vol. 3. Stress and performance effectiveness*. Hillsdale, NJ: Lawrence Erlbaum, 1982.

Coates, G. D., Thurmond, J. B., Morgan, B. B., Jr., & Alluisi, E. A. Behavioral effects of infectious diseases: Phlebotomus fever in man. *Journal of Applied Psychology*, 1972, *56*, 189–201.

Fitts, P. M., & Posner, M. I. *Human performance*. Belmont, CA: Brooks/Cole, 1967.

Folley, J. D., Jr. *Development of an improved method of task analysis and beginnings of a theory of training* (NAVTRADEVCEN 1218-10). Port Washington, NY: USNTDC, June 1964. (a)

Folley, J. D., Jr. *Guidelines for task analysis* (NAVTRADEVCEN 1218-2). Port Washington, NY: USNTDC, June 1964. (b)

French, J. W., Ekstrom, R. B., & Price, L. A. *Manual for kit of reference tests for cognitive factors.* Princeton, NJ: Educational Testing Service, June 1963.

Gagné, R. M. Human functions in systems. In R. M. Gagné (Ed.), *Psychological principles in system development.* New York: Holt, Rinehart & Winston, 1962.

Gagné, R. M. Domains of learning. *Interchanges,* 1972, *3*(1), 1–8.

Gagné, R. M. *Essentials of learning for instruction.* New York: Holt, Rinehart & Winston, 1974.

Gagné, R. M. *The conditions of learning* (3rd ed.). New York: Holt, Rinehart & Winston, 1977.

Gagné, R. M., & Briggs, L. J. *Principles of instructional design.* New York: Holt, Rinehart & Winston, 1979.

Guion, R. M. Recruiting, selection and job placement. In M. D. Dunnette (ed.), *Handbook of industrial and organizational psychology.* Chicago: Rand McNally, 1976.

Hunt, E. B. *Concept learning: An information-processing approach.* New York: Wiley, 1962.

Hunt, E. B. Mechanics of verbal ability. *Psychological Review,* 1978, *85,* 109–130.

Hunt, E. B., Frost, N., & Lunneborg, C. E. Individual differences in cognition: A new approach to intelligence. In G. Bower (Ed.), *The psychology of learning and motivation* (Vol. 7). New York: Academic Press, 1973.

Hunt, E. B., Lunneborg, C. E., & Lewis, J. What does it mean to be high verbal? *Cognitive Psychology,* 1975, *7,* 194–227.

Levine, J. M., & Teichner, W. H. Development of a taxonomy of human performance: An information-theoretical approach. *JSAS Catalog of Selected Documents in Psychology,* 1973, *2,* 28 (Ms. No. 325).

McCormick, E. J. Job and task analysis. In M. D. Dunnette (Ed.), *Handbook of industrial and organizational psychology.* Chicago: Rand McNally, 1976.

McCormick, E. J. *Job analysis: Methods and applications.* New York: American Management Association, AMACOM, 1979.

Miller, E. E. *A taxonomy of response processes* (HumRRO Tech. Rep. 69-16). Fort Knox, KY: Human Resources Research Organization, September 1969.

Miller, R. B. Task description and analysis. In R. M. Gagné (Ed.), *Psychological principles in system development.* New York: Holt, Rinehart & Winston, 1962.

Miller, R. B. *Task taxonomy: Science or technology?* Poughkeepsie, NY: IBM, 1966.

Morgan, B. B., Jr., & Alluisi, E. A. Synthetic work: Methodology for assessment of human performance. *Perceptual and Motor Skills,* 1972, *35,* 835–845.

Morgan, B. B., Jr., Brown, B. R., & Alluisi, E. A. *Effects of 48 hours of continuous work and sleep loss on sustained performance* (Report No. ITR-70-16). Louisville, KY: University of Louisville Performance Research Laboratory, 1970.

Pellegrino, J. W., & Glaser, R. Cognitive correlates and components in the analysis of individual differences. *Intelligence,* 1979, *3,* 187–219.

Posner, M. I. *An informational approach to thinking* (Technical Report, Office of Research Administration Project 02814). Ann Arbor, MI: Office of Research Administration, April 1962.

Posner, M. I. Information reduction in the analysis of sequential tasks. *Psychological Review,* 1964, *71*(6), 491–504.

Primoff, E. S. *Test selection by job analysis: The J–Coefficient, what it is, how it works* (2nd ed.) (Test Technical Series No. 20). Washington, DC: U.S. Civil Service Commission, 1955.

Primoff, E. S. The development of processes for indirect or synthetic validity: IV. Empirical validations of the J-Coefficient: A symposium. *Personnel Psychology,* 1959, *12,* 413–418.

Primoff, E. S. *Research on efficient methods in job-element examining: Report No. 1— research on the additive checklist.* Washington, DC: U.S. Civil Service Commission, 1970.

Primoff, E. S. *Summary of job-element principles: Preparing a job-element standard.* Washington, DC: U.S. Civil Service Commission, 1971.

Primoff, E. S. *Preliminary draft: The J-Coefficient procedure.* Washington, DC: U.S. Civil Service Commission, 1972.

Primoff, E. S. *Introduction to J-Coefficient analysis.* Washington, DC: U.S. Civil Service Commission, 1973.

Primoff, E. S. *How to prepare and conduct job element examinations* (Tech. Study 75-1). Washington, DC: Government Printing Office, 1975.

Sternberg, R. J. *Intelligence, information processing, and analogical reasoning: The componential analysis of human abilities.* Hillsdale, NJ: Erlbaum, 1977.

Sternberg, R. J. The construct validity of aptitude tests: An information-processing assessment. In A. P. Maslow (Ed.), *Construct validity in psychological measurement: Proceedings of a colloquium on theory and application in education and employment.* Washington, DC: U.S. Office of Personnel Management, Princeton, NJ: Educational Testing Service, October 1979. (a)

Sternberg, R. J. The nature of mental abilities. *American Psychologist,* 1979, *34*(3), 214–230. (b)

Sternberg, R. J., & Tulving, E. The measurement of subjective organization in free recall. *Psychological Bulletin,* 1977, *84,* 539–556.

Teichner, W. H., & Whitehead, J. Development of a taxonomy of human performance: Evaluation of a basic classification system for generalizing findings from a data base. *JSAS Catalog of Selected Documents in Psychology,* 1973, *2,* 26–27 (Ms. No. 324).

U.S. Civil Service Commission, Bureau of Policies and Standards, Standards Division. *Job qualification system for trades and labor occupations* (Handbook X118-C). Washington, DC: USCSC, 1969.

Wheaton, G. R. Development of a taxonomy of human performance: A review of classificatory systems relating to tasks and performance. *JSAS Catalog of Selected Documents in Psychology,* 1973, *3,* 22–23 (Ms. No. 317).

CHAPTER 7

Classificatory Systems for Describing Human Tasks: Abilities and Task Characteristics

In this chapter, we examine a variety of descriptive schemes using operator variables (ability requirements) and situational variables (task characteristics) as bases for the categorization of human task performance. We then conclude with an overview of the systems presented in Chapters 5, 6, and 7, and discuss their implications for taxonomic research and development.

Ability Requirements

The third conceptual basis for describing and classifying human task performance, which we presented in Chapter 3, is the *ability requirements approach*. In this approach, tasks are described, contrasted, and compared in terms of the abilities that they require of the operator. Abilities are relatively enduring attributes of the individual performing the task. Specific tasks are said to require certain ability profiles if performance is to be maximized with respect to established criteria. Tasks requiring similar ability configurations (both in terms of type and amount) are placed within the same category (Fleishman, 1966). Abilities differ from behavior requirements (or functions) primarily in terms of concept derivation and level of description. A primary source of information for the definition of an ability is experimental factor-analytic research of individual differences in task performance.

The field of research on human abilities has, overall, had much attention devoted to it over the years. Almost all of this research is related in one way or another to taxonomic issues because it is devoted to identifying categories of abilities and then determining the relationships of these abilities to each other and to task performance. In other words, a major part of the effort in this field is devoted to developing useful systems for simplifying and understanding human cognitive and psychomotor abilities. In a recent review of this field, Horn (1976) divided the descriptive and classificatory systems in the field into two broad groups: (1) those derived from analyses of the interrelationships among various types of performance, and (2) those derived from behaviors characteristic of different ages of development (e.g., Piagetian systems). The most significant recent development in the second group is the new attention being paid to development during adulthood, rather than only in childhood (Bond & Rosen, 1980). Although little integration has occurred across these two broad groups of systems, there is no need to regard them as in competition, and, actually, they could be used to complement one another. In this section, attention is directed toward those systems falling into the former group that have been sufficiently developed to be regarded as having taxonomic qualities.

GUILFORD: STRUCTURE OF INTELLECT

A number of investigators have been concerned with defining the nature of intelligence as well as with describing the interrelationship between intelligence and task performance. Spearman (1927) suggested a two-factor theory of intelligence, consisting of a general factor that permeates all tests of intellectual aptitude, and specific factors that are found only in single aptitude tests or tasks. In contrast, Thurstone (1938) viewed intelligence as composed of a small set of primary mental abilities, including Verbal Comprehension, Number, Spatial Visualization, Word Fluency, Perceptual Speed, Reasoning, and Memory. Cattell (1941, 1963) and Horn (1968) described two broad factors as indicators of intelligence. *Crystallized Intelligence* indicates the extent of acculturation as it determines human abilities; it is best measured by tests of vocabulary, reading comprehension, and general information. *Fluid Intelligence* indicates a pattern of neural– physiological and incidental learning influences; it is best measured by tests of abstract reasoning, such as visual analogies, classifications, and series problems. Fluid Intelligence declines with brain damage and aging in adulthood.

Another factorial theory of intelligence is based upon a monumental program spanning more than 25 years of research. This program was conducted by Guilford in the area of cognitive abilities

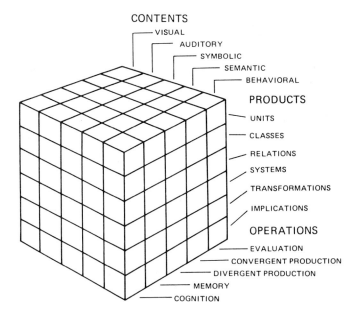

CONTENTS
— VISUAL
— AUDITORY
— SYMBOLIC
— SEMANTIC
— BEHAVIORAL

PRODUCTS
— UNITS
— CLASSES
— RELATIONS
— SYSTEMS
— TRANSFORMATIONS
— IMPLICATIONS

OPERATIONS
— EVALUATION
— CONVERGENT PRODUCTION
— DIVERGENT PRODUCTION
— MEMORY
— COGNITION

Figure 7.1 Guilford's Structure-of-Intellect model. Reprinted with permission from *Way beyond the IQ*, by J. P. Guilford. Copyright © 1977, Creative Education Foundation, Inc., Buffalo, New York.

(1956, 1959). Although his interest centered on the theoretical nature of intelligence, the model he developed of the Structure of Intellect is relevant to the description of tasks in terms of an information-processing model.

Guilford (1977) developed a morphological model that organizes intellectual abilities along three dimensions. Figure 7.1 presents the model and shows the basic dimensions of Operations, Products, and Contents. *Operations* refer to major kinds of intellectual activities or processes, that is, things that the organism does with raw materials of information; information is defined as that which the organism discriminates, that is, each item of information is different from every other item so that the organism can distinguish one item from another. *Products* are forms that information takes in the organism's processing of it. *Contents* refer to broad classes or types of information discriminable by the organism. In an information-processing context, the Contents dimension represents inputs, the Operations dimension reflects the processing of or acting upon the inputs, and the Products dimension represents the outputs. Table 7.1 summarizes the definitions of the categories of Operations, Products, and Contents.

TABLE 7.1

Category Definitions for Guilford's Parameters (Operations, Products, and Contents) in
the Structure-of-Intellect Model[a]

Operations

Cognition (C). Immediate discovery, awareness, rediscovery, or recognition of
information in its various forms; comprehension, or understanding.

Memory (M). Fixation of newly gained information in storage. The operation of
memory is to be distinguished from the memory store.

Divergent Production (D). Generation of logical alternatives from given information, where the emphasis is upon variety, quantity, and relevance of output from
the same source. Likely to involve transfer recall (instigated by new cues).

Convergent Production (N). Generation of logical conclusions from given information, where the emphasis is upon achieving unique or conventionally best outcomes.
Likely that the given information fully determines the outcome.

Evaluation (E). Comparison of items of information in terms of variables and
making judgments concerning criterion satisfaction (correctness, identity,
consistency).

Contents

Auditory (A). Information instigated directly from stimulation of the inner ear in
the form of sensations, or indirectly in the form of images.

Visual (V). Information instigated directly from stimulation of the eye in the form
of sensations, or indirectly in the form of images.

Symbolic (S). Pertaining to information in the form of denotative signs having no
significance in and of themselves, such as letters, numbers, musical notations,
codes, and words (as ordered letter combinations).

Semantic (M). Pertaining to information in the form of conceptions or mental
constructs to which words are often applied. Most notable in verbal thinking and
verbal communication, but not necessarily dependent upon words. Meaningful
pictures also convey semantic information.

Behavioral (B). Pertaining to information, essentially nonfigural and nonverbal,
involved in human interactions, in which the attitudes, needs, desires, moods,
intentions, and thoughts of others and of ourselves are involved.

Products

Units (U). Relatively segregated or circumscribed items or "chunks" of information having the character of a "thing". May be close to Gestalt psychology's "figure
on a ground."

Classes (C). Conceptions underlying sets of items of information grouped by virtue
of their common properties.

Relations (R). Connections between items of information based upon variables or
points of contact that apply to them. Relational connections are more definable
than implicational connections.

Systems (S). Organized or structured aggregates of items of information; com-
plexes of interrelated or interacting parts.

Transformations (T). Changes of various kinds (redefinitions, shifts, transitions, or
modifications) in existing information.

Implications (I). Circumstantial connections between items of information, as by
virtue of contiguity or any condition that promotes "belongingness."

[a]Adapted with permission from Guilford, J. P. & Hoepfner, R., *The analysis of intelligence.* New
York: McGraw–Hill, 1971.

Each cell in the model represents a hypothetical factor (or ability) related to intelligence. The 5 Operations × 6 Products × 5 Contents solid contains 150 such factors of which more than two-thirds have appeared in factor-analytic studies as of 1971 (see Guilford & Hoepfner, 1971; Guilford, 1977). There exists one or more tests designed to measure each of the demonstrated factors. The factorial descriptions are interesting in their own right, and provide concise definitions of each ability.

The application of Guilford's work to the description of human task behavior entails the following steps. To find which factors (descriptors) are required in a particular task, one must employ a battery of reference tests for the established factors. In one study, for example, tasks designated as problem solving in nature did not reveal a problem solving factor, but rather loaded on already established factors, such as Verbal Comprehension, Conceptual Foresight, Originality, and Semantic Elaboration (Merrifield, Guilford, Christensen, & Frick, 1962). The point is that the term *problem solving* does not represent a unitary behavior distinct from all other behaviors; rather, it can be analyzed in terms of less complex, component behaviors.

In summary, Guilford's approach is that of classical factor analysis. His morphological model can profitably be viewed as a detailed information processing scheme, with the "cells" providing succinct descriptions of covert behaviors. Each behavior is a composite of an operation or activity performed upon some content or type of information to yield a product. The fact that tests exist for measuring many of these behaviors provides the scheme with a more objective base than many of the other schemes discussed thus far. The tests used to measure specific factors (over 200 tests are involved in Guilford's factors) also are used to assess the reliability of the classificatory system. The system remains the most complete taxonomic system for describing intellectual functioning. Guilford's landmark work has extended our knowledge about the diversity of cognitive functions and their dimensions and methods of measurement, and has provided numerous hypotheses for future taxonomic research (see Guilford, 1977). Meeker (1981) established an SOI Institute to implement and evaluate Guilford's model in child education. She and her colleagues have translated items from IQ tests (Binet, Wechsler) into SOI ability factors, and are constructing curricula based SOI books to develop these abilities.

PAWLIK'S RESEARCH

Pawlik and his associates at the University of Hamburg have worked with Guilford's model in attempting to establish "an equally representative though theoretically more parsimonious empirical framework for cross-relating individual differences in cognition" (Pawlik, 1981, p. 6). Pawlik selected or developed tests to represent systematically the three dimensions (Operations, Contents, Products) of Guilford's morphological model. During this process, care was taken to cross-reference additional factors of intelligence identified in the past in reviews by Pawlik (1973), French (1951) and Guilford and Hoepfner (1971). These measures, arranged in batteries of between 19 and 74 tests, were administered in four studies involving a total of 1160 subjects. The factor analysis and transformation analysis of factors obtained for different subject samples and variable domains led the researchers to conclude that the Structure of Intellect model and similar theories postulating an extensive number of cognitive factors could be simplified. Pawlik's research (1981) indicated the existence of a limited number of basic factors of cognition that were replicable. He provided definitions for six of the eight factors identified in his research:

1. *Numerical Facility:* Individual differences in dealing with numbers (simple arithmetic, arithmetical reasoning)
2. *Visual Perception:* Individual differences in tests involving visual stimulus material. Tests loading on this factor include simple tests of perceptual speed, comparison-length estimation, and perceptual scanning, as well as complex tests of spatial visualization and perceptual closure.
3. *Convergent Reasoning:* Individual differences in inductive and deductive reasoning, whether the stimulus is figural, verbal or a symbol
4. *Convergent Verbal Aptitude:* Individual differences in tasks requiring active or passive use of one's own native language, as well as individual differences in passive (receptive) linguistic aptitudes
5. *Divergent Verbal Aptitude:* Individual differences in tests of verbal and semantic fluency (ease and speed in expressing oneself and in producing words meeting a certain formal or semantic requirement)
6. *Divergent Reasoning:* Individual differences in the production of new ideas and new modes of thinking, as opposed to the application of overlearned rules of thought. Tests requiring flexibility, semantic redefinition, sensitivity to problems, and ideational fluency load on this broad factor of creative performance.

The remaining two factors are Associative Memory and Immediate Memory Span.

These eight independent factors representing individual differences in cognition have been identified reliably across studies. Pawlik (1981) reported that the average congruence coefficient was .92, with a standard deviation of .04. Pawlik and his associates are now in the process of designing a "multifactor test battery" to assess individual differences in these eight identified components of cognition.

FRENCH, EKSTROM, AND PRICE: KIT OF REFERENCE TESTS FOR COGNITIVE FACTORS

In 1963, the Educational Testing Service (French, Ekstrom, & Price, 1963) developed a kit of reference tests for 24 commonly known aptitude and ability factors (e.g., Flexibility of Closure, Word Fluency, Memory Span). The kit was intended to provide research workers with a standard set of tests for defining the factors. The rationale behind the kit was that the use of these tests would facilitate comparison and interpretation across various factorial studies of human performance. In the absence of any such standard tests, it is difficult to decide whether certain factors are operating to produce performance when the factors are being measured in different ways. The 1963 French, Ekstrom, and Price kit has served as a basis for the initial development of several cognitive ability requirement classificatory systems, including those by Fleishman (1975; Theologus & Fleishman, 1973) and Harman (1975).

In 1973, Ekstrom reviewed the research involving the 24 factors. Ekstrom (1973) concluded that Length Estimation, Mechanical Knowledge, Semantic Redefinition, Sensitivity to Problems, Spatial Scanning, Figural Adaptive Flexibility, and Spontaneous Semantic Flexibility were either too narrow or too poorly defined by their reference tests. Further, Flexibility of Closure and Speed of Closure could not be differentiated adequately. Additionally, Associative Fluency, Expressional Fluency, Ideational Fluency, and Word Fluency were too closely related, as well as related to Originality. Finally, General Reasoning was related strongly to the other reasoning factors, whereas the Spatial Orientation and Visualization factors were difficult to distinguish from one another. Based on Ekstrom's results, Dunnette (1976) suggested that only 10 factors be retained:

1. Flexibility and Speed of Closure
2. Fluency
3. Inductive Reasoning
4. Associative (Rote) Memory
5. Span Memory

6. Number Facility
7. Perceptual Speed
8. Syllogistic (Deductive) Reasoning
9. Spatial Orientation and Visualization
10. Verbal Comprehension

Ekstrom (1973) added some possible new factors based upon her literature review: Automatic Processes, Behavioral Relations and Systems, Chunking Memory, Concept Formation, Integration, Visual Memory, and Verbal Closure.

HARMAN: COGNITIVE AND TEMPERAMENT FACTORS

More recently, Harman (1975) and his associates at the Educational Testing Service (ETS), under contract with the Office of Naval Research, have expanded upon the work of French et al. (1963). The 4-year project resulted in the further definition and refinement of the cognitive domain of human abilities, identifying 23 factors with accompanying reference tests. A second accomplishment was the beginning of a comparable structure of human abilities in the personality domain. Twenty-eight temperament factors were identified, with 26 having reference scales developed either by ETS or by other researchers. Table 7.2 lists the 23 cognitive factors and the 28 temperament factors.

The 1963 French, Ekstrom, and Price Kit of Reference Tests for Cognitive Factors served as a starting point for Harman's research. Other cognitive and noncognitive factors were identified at a conference of specialists in the areas of factor analysis and human assessment in 1971. Additional factors were discovered after a comprehensive literature review. For a factor to be considered "established," it had to be identified in at least three analyses performed in at least two different laboratories.

Items were either adopted or prepared as markers for the various factors and packaged for pretesting. The field tests supplied information on test reliability, some normative data, and verification of the effectiveness of the marker tests in identifying the postulated factors.

These pilot tests and the accompanying factor analyses resulted in a kit of factor-referenced cognitive tests and a guide to factor-referenced temperament scales. Harman (1975) described the development of the cognitive kit as follows:

> The Kit of Reference Tests for Cognitive Factors involved, in large measure, the revision and updating of material that had been under development for

TABLE 7.2

Cognitive and Temperament Factors Identified as a Phase of a Research Project of the Educational Testing Service[a]

Cognitive Factors	Temperament Factors
CF, Closure, Flexibility of	Ac General Activity
DS Closure, Speed of	Ag Agreeableness
CV Closure, Verbal	Al Alertness
FA Fluency, Associational	Au Autistic Tendency
FE Fluency, Expressional	Ca Calmness vs. Anxiety
FF Fluency, Figural	Co Concentration
FI Fluency, Ideational	De Dependability
FW Fluency, Word	Do Dominance
I Induction	Em Emotional Maturity
IP Integrative Processes	Es Emotional Stability
M Memory, Associative	Gs Gregariousness
MS Memory Span	In Individualism
MV Memory, Visual	Me Meticulousness
N Number	Mo Morality
P Perceptual Speed	Na Need for Achievement
RG Reasoning, General	Ob Objectivity vs. Paranoid Tendency
RL Reasoning, Logical	Om Open-mindedness vs. Dogmatism
S Spatial Orientation	Pe Persistence
SS Spatial Scanning	Po Poise vs. Self-Consciousness
V Verbal Comprehension	Rt Restraint vs. Rhathymia
VZ Visualization	Sc Self-Confidence
XF Flexibility, Figural	Se Sensitive Attitude
XU Flexibility of Use	So Sociability
	Ss Self-Sufficiency
	Su Surgency
	Th Thoughtfulness
	To Tolerance of Human Nature vs. Cynicism
	Wb Well-being vs. Depression

[a]Reprinted with permission from Harman, H. H. *Final report of research on assessing human abilities* (PR–75–20). Princeton, NJ: Educational Testing Service, 1975.

more than 20 years, with the last published version in 1963. Of course, there had to be introduced some new 'established' factors, and tests to measure them had to be developed. Hence, the new publication is very similar in form to the preceding one but has been improved to provide more ready accessibility as well as the inclusion of the latent factors found in the literature and substantiated in field tests [p. 11].

Harman acknowledged that the development of reference materials for the noncognitive domain was not nearly as complete as the development of the reference materials for the cognitive factors. However, he noted that cognitive factors had been the focus of ETS research for more than 20 years, whereas temperament factors were a new research endeavor.

Ekstrom, French, and Harman (1979) have provided a recent description of further efforts by the researchers at the Educational Testing Service to refine the cognitive factors. Their research demonstrated that the new factors of Verbal Closure, Visual Memory, and Figural Fluency were clearly distinctive. Integrative Processes was somewhat distinct, but difficult to separate from some of the reasoning factors. A proposed Concept Attainment factor was not replicated adequately.

McCormick (1979) has noted that there is no single list of human abilities "representing a reasonably complete inventory of attributes or qualities. However, the combination of Fleishman's listing (see below) and that of ETS probably represents the best available approximation to such an inventory." (p. 203). Chapter 12 describes the attempt to synthesize the better-established ability factors into an ability requirements classificatory system.

FLEISHMAN: ABILITY REQUIREMENTS APPROACH

A longstanding program of research involving the identification of perceptual–motor ability requirements in human task performance has been conducted by Fleishman and his colleagues (Fleishman, 1964, 1972, 1975a, 1978; Theologus & Fleishman, 1973; Theologus, Romashko, & Fleishman, 1973). Tasks are categorized according to the human capacities required to perform them effectively. The most recent developments involving this scheme are described in Chapter 12; only the beginnings of the *Ability Requirements Approach* are presented here.

The general objective of this work has been "to define the fewest independent ability categories which might be most useful and meaningful in describing performance in the widest variety of tasks" (Fleishman, 1967, p. 352). Fleishman distinguishes abilities from skills. An *ability* refers to a more general capacity of the individual related to performance in a variety of human tasks. Fleishman stated, "The fact that individuals who do well on task A also do well in tasks B and C but not in tasks D, E, and F indicates, inferentially, a common process involved in performing the first three tasks distinct from the processes involved in the latter three. To account for the observed consistencies, an ability is postulated" (p. 352). Thus, an ability is a general trait of the individual that has been inferred from certain response consistencies. Both learning and genetic components under-lie ability development. In contrast, a *skill* is defined as the level of proficiency on a specific task or group of tasks. The development of a given skill or proficiency on a given task is predicated in part on the possession of relevant basic abilities.

Fleishman's methodology for identifying human abilities involves a whole series of interlocking experimental-factor analytic studies. Fleishman (1978) described this methodology as follows:

> Essentially, this is laboratory research in which tasks are specifically de-signed or selected to test certain hypotheses about the organization of abili-ties in a certain range of tasks. The experimental battery of tasks is admin-istered to several hundred subjects, and the correlation patterns examined. Subsequent studies tend to introduce task variations aimed at sharpening or limiting our ability factor definitions [p. 1009].

Thus, in defining ability factors, Fleishman and his colleagues are really linking together information about task characteristics with ability requirements. Their work has resulted in a number of princi-ples relating these two concepts. For example, it is possible to say that an ability called *Multilimb Coordination* is common to tasks in-volving two hands or hands and feet, and so forth in operating equip-ment. However, that ability does not extend to tasks in which the body was in motion, as in certain athletic activities. One may say that a person possesses the ability or, alternatively, that the task requires, involves, or elicits the use of the ability.

Fleishman's earlier work (1964, 1966) involved the identification of human abilities in the physical and psychomotor domains. Landy and Trumbo (1980) have noted that "Fleishman and his associ-ates . . . have been extremely successful in refining our understand-ing of psychomotor and sensorimotor tests . . . through a program of careful and exhaustive research" (p. 86). A similar program of re-search was conducted in the physical proficiency area. Eleven psy-chomotor factors and nine physical factors were identified initially. Table 7.3 presents the abilities identified, their definitions, and ex-amples of tests or tasks requiring each ability.

Each of these factors resulted from factor analysis of the intercor-relations of a large number of tests or tasks given to large numbers of subjects. A given factor represents the loadings of different tests. These loadings are examined to label the ability common to the vari-ous task performances. Reference tests are constructed and refined for each factor or hypothetical ability.

Future research efforts with ability requirements area have pro-ceeded in a variety of areas (see, e.g., Fleishman 1972, 1975a). These

TABLE 7.3

Psychomotor and Physical Proficiency Factors Resulting from Fleishman's Factor Analytic Studies[a]

Psychomotor factors

Control Precision

The ability to make fine, highly controlled muscular movements required to adjust the position of a control mechanism. Examples of control mechanisms are joy sticks, levels, pedals, and rudders. A series of adjustments may be required, but they need not be performed simultaneously. This ability is most critical where adjustments must be rapid, but precise. Adjustments are made to visual stimuli and involve the use of a single limb, either arm–hand or leg.

Examples: Rotary Pursuit Test; operate a joy stick to steer an aircraft.

Multilimb Coordination

The ability to coordinate the movement of a number of limbs simultaneously. Best measured by devices involving multiple controls. (Hands, feet, or hands and feet).

Examples: Complex Coordination Test; operate a bulldozer.

Response Orientation

This factor is general to visual discrimination tasks. These tasks involve rapid recognition of the direction (north, south, east, west) indicated by a particular visual stimulus (e.g., an arrow) followed by the appropriate motor response chosen from several alternatives. The response may be simple or complex (push a button and pull a switch vs. push a button). This ability appears to be most critical when the conditions are highly speeded.

Example: Flip different switches in response to different colored lights appearing on a display panel.

Reaction Time

This ability represents the speed with which the individual can provide a single motor response to a single stimulus when it appears. It is independent of the mode of presentation (auditory or visual) and also of the type of motor response required. Response cannot involve alternate choices.

Example: Depress a button as soon as possible after hearing a buzzer.

Speed of Arm Movement

The speed with which an individual can make a gross, discrete arm movement where accuracy is minimized. There is ample evidence that this ability is independent of reaction time.

Example: Move a series of control levers to new positions in rapid succession.

Rate Control

Involves the timing of continuous anticipatory motor adjustments relative to changes in speed and/or direction of a continuously moving target or object. Actual motor response to change (rather than verbal estimate) is necessary. Extends to tasks involving compensatory as well as following pursuit and to those involving responses to changes in rate.

(*continued*)

TABLE 7.3 *Continued*

Psychomotor factors

Example: Track a moving target by keeping a circle around a dot which changes in
speed and direction of movement.

Manual Dexterity

The ability to make skillful, well directed arm–hand movements in manipulating
fairly large objects under speeded conditions.

Examples: Minnesota Rate of Manipulation Test; use hand tools to assemble an
aircraft engine.

Finger Dexterity

The ability to make skillful, controlled manipulations of objects small enough to
be handled with the fingers.

Examples: Purdue Pegboard Test; assemble peg, washer, and collar units and insert
them in small holes.

Arm–Hand Steadiness

The ability to make precise arm–hand positioning movements in which strength
and speed are minimized. It extends to tasks that require steadiness during
movement as well as those that require a minimum of tremor while maintaining a
static arm position.

Examples: Arm Tremor Test; perform retinal surgery.

Wrist–Finger Speed

The ability to make rapid pendular (back and forth) and/or rotary wrist movements in which accuracy is not critical.

Example: Tapping Test.

Aiming

The ability to make highly accurate, restricted hand movements requiring precise
eye–hand coordination.

Example: Make a dot in a series of very small circles on a printed test.

Physical proficiency factors

Extent Flexibility

The ability to extend or stretch the body. Tests that load on this factor require
stretching of the trunk and back muscles as far as possible, without speed, either
laterally, forward, or backward.

Example: Twist as far around as possible, touching the scale on the wall.

Dynamic Flexibility

Common to tasks that require rapid and repeated trunk and/or limb movements.
Emphasizes both speed and flexibility.

Example: Without moving your feet, bend and touch a spot on the floor, stand up,
twist, and touch a spot on the wall behind as rapidly as possible.

(continued)

TABLE 7.3 *Continued*

Physical proficiency factors

Explosive Strength

Common to tasks that require expenditure of a maximum of energy in one or a series of explosive acts. This factor emphasizes the mobilization of energy for a burst of effort, rather than continuous strain, stress, or repeated exertion of muscles.

Examples: Broad jump; sprint 50 yards.

Static Strength

Common to tasks that require the exertion of maximum strength against a fairly immovable external object, even for a brief period. It is general to different muscle groups (hand, arm, back, shoulder, leg) and to different kinds of tasks.

Examples: Squeeze a grip dynamometer as hard as possible; lift heavy objects.

Dynamic Strength

The ability to exert muscular force repeatedly or continuously over time. It represents muscular endurance and emphasizes the resistance of the muscles to fatigue. Tests loading on this factor tend to emphasize the power of the muscles to propel, support, or move the body repeatedly or to support it for prolonged periods.

Examples: Pull-ups; scale a wall.

Trunk Strength

This is a second, more limited, dynamic strength factor specific to the trunk muscles, particularly the abdominal muscles.

Examples: Leg-lifts; sit-ups.

Gross Body Coordination

The ability to perform movements simultaneously that involve the entire body.

Example: Holding the ends of a short rope in each hand, jump over the rope without tripping, falling or releasing the rope.

Gross Body Equilibrium

The ability to maintain or regain body balance, especially in situations in which equilibrium is threatened or temporarily lost.

Example: Walk a narrow rail without falling off.

Stamina (Cardiovascular Endurance)

The ability to exert sustained physical effort involving the cardiovascular system.

Examples: Run a distance of one mile as fast as you can; extinguish a building fire.

---

[a]Adapted with permission from Fleishman, E. A. Structure and measurement of psychomotor abilities. In R. N. Singer (Ed.), *Psychomotor domain: Movement behavior*, Philadelphia: Lea & Febiger, 1972; and from Fleishman, E. A. The structure and measurement of physical fitness. Englewood Cliffs, NJ: Prentice Hall, 1964.

efforts, which are described in detail in Chapter 12, include (1) the identification of human abilities in the sensory, perceptual, and cognitive domains; (2) the prediction of various training measures and other aspects of task performance through the use of ability concepts; (3) the exploration of the effects of stress, diet, anoxia, noise, and drugs on performance on a variety of reference tasks for abilities in the perceptual, motor, sensory, and cognitive areas; (4) the refinement of methods for estimating ability requirements, including the construction of ability requirements scales and binary decision flow diagrams; (5) the evaluation of the utility of ability requirements in classifying tasks, including the capacity of this classificatory system to organize data in the human performance literature; and (6) the determination of job-relevant tests.

McCormick: Position Analysis Questionnaire (PAQ)—Job Dimensions from PAQ Attribute Profile Data

McCormick also employs a number of human attributes, some of which were derived originally from factor-analytic work. In two research studies, one involving Form A of the Position Analysis Questionnaire (Mecham & McCormick, 1969) and the other involving Form B (Marquardt & McCormick, 1972), industrial psychologists rated the relevance of 76 human attributes to the job elements of the PAQ using a 6-point scale. (Most of the 37 abilities of Theologus et al., 1973, were included.) Interrater reliabilities ranged from the upper .80s to the lower .90s for teams of 8 to 18 raters per attribute. Median ratings on the 76 attributes constituted the attribute profile for a given job element.

The attribute profiles for the job elements were correlated, and principal component analyses were carried out separately for the job elements in each of the six divisions of the PAQ. The results of these principal component analyses, the factors or categories reflecting common profiles of attribute requirements for each division, are shown in Column 2 of Table 5.6. There is some similarity between the factor structure based on job data or job elements and the factor structure based on attribute profile data for the job elements.

Cunningham: Occupation Analysis Inventory (OAI)—Job Dimensions from OAI

Cunningham, Tuttle, Floyd, and Bates (1971) and Pass and Cunningham (1975) rated the 622 work elements in the Occupational

TABLE 7.4

Higher-Order Job Dimensions (Factors) of Attribute Requirement Profiles of the Work
Elements of the Occupation Analysis Inventory (OAI)

Dimension	Title of work dimension
H–1	Machine operation, maintenance, and repair
H–2	Development and supervision of others
H–3	Mathematical/symbolic activities
H–4	Health/biological activities
H–5	Representation and production of figural arrangements and relationships
H–6	Activities related to the aesthetic appearance of others
H–7	Agricultural/botanical activities
H–8	Clerical activities
H–9	Verbal communication: writing and speaking
H–10	Performing and visual art decorative activities
H–11	Material processing and modification
H–12	Business/sales activities
H–13	Work activities requiring balance and body coordination
H–14	Health-related interaction and responsibility
H–15	Construction and assembly activities
H–16	Planning and innovation
H–17	Direct interpersonal communication
H–18	Electrical/electronic maintenance, repair and operation
H–19	Measuring, testing, and inspecting activities
H–20	General tool usage
H–21	General physical labor

[a]Adapted with permission from Neeb, R. W., Cunningham, J. W., & Pass, J. J. *Human attribute
requirements of work elements: Further development of the Occupation Analysis Inventory* (Center
Research Monograph No. 7). Raleigh, NC: Center for Occupational Research, University of North
Carolina, 1971; with revised factor titles from Neeb, R. W., Cunningham, J. W., & Pass, J. J. Human
attribute requirements of work elements: Further development of the Occupation Analysis Inventory. *JSAS Catalog of Selected Documents in Psychology*, 1974, *4*, 145 (Ms. No. 805).

Analysis Inventory on 103 human attributes constituting an Attribute
Requirement Inventory. The attributes were categorized as general
vocational capabilities, cognitive abilities, psychomotor abilities,
sensory capacities, interests, and needs. Attribute profiles for each
work element were derived from mean ratings of 9 or 10 raters.

Principal component analyses of the intercorrelations of the attribute profiles for the work elements were carried out for each section of the OAI. These analyses resulted in 77 factors or job dimensions. A higher-order factor analysis resulted in 21 higher-order
dimensions. These are presented in Table 7.4. The derived linkages
between the OAI work elements and the 103 measurable human at-

tributes expand the capability of the OAI. Any job or occupation rated on the OAI can be described quantitatively in terms of its scores on factors representing different types of work activities and conditions or in terms of its estimated requirements for various human attributes.

Task Characteristics

A fourth approach to the classification of tasks differs from the preceding approaches in terms of the type of task description that is attempted. This approach is predicated on a definition of the task as a set of conditions that elicits performance. These conditions are imposed on the individual and have an objective existence quite apart from the activities they may trigger (behavior description), the processes or functions they may call into play to achieve criterion performance (behavior requirements), or the abilities they may require (ability requirements). Having adopted this point of view, appropriate descriptive terms are those that focus on the objective properties of the task per se, such as characteristics of the goal toward which the operator works, relevant task stimuli, instructions, procedures, or the task content. The problem is not only the selection of those components to be described, but also the selection of the parameters by means of which description is to be accomplished. This approach has, in the past, received the least attention of the four types of classificatory systems, although, as we have seen, a number of the schemes labeled as behavioral description approaches also rely on task characteristic descriptors (e.g., McCormick, Cunningham).

Studies by Cotterman (1959), Fitts (1962), Stolurow (1964), Hackman and Oldham (1975), and Farina and Wheaton (1973) are perhaps the most representative of attempts to pursue the task characteristics approach. They explicitly considered prototype task classifications based, at least in part, upon the description of task properties. In addition to an interest in the process or functions evoked by a task, they were also concerned with morphological description.

COTTERMAN: TASK CLASSIFICATORY SCHEME TO GENERALIZE PRINCIPLES OF HUMAN LEARNING

Cotterman (1959) has called for the development of a classificatory scheme to categorize tasks that humans have to learn. He felt that such a scheme would be useful in generalizing principles of human

TABLE 7.5

Cotterman's Illustrative Categories of Learning Situations or Tasks[a]

Tracking or Continuous Adjustment:	Concurrently with continual quantitative variation in one or a set of specified input qualities, continual quantitative variation through infinite degrees in one or a set of specified output qualities occurs, such as to minimize continually the input variation.
Skilled Act (Single Criterion Response):	For each succeeding occurrence of essentially the same discrete input, a discrete output drawn from an infinite set occurs, such as to result in a secondary input event that deviates minimally from a specified limit expressed in terms of an input quality.

[a]Adapted with permission from Cotterman, T. E. *Task classification: An approach to partially ordering information on human learning* (WADC TN 58-374). Wright Patterson Air Force Base, OH: Wright Patterson Air Development Center, 1959.

learning from one task situation to another, thus solving many practical training problems.

Cotterman recognized three sets of variables as operating in a learning environment: basic variables (such as degree of prior experience or learning, reinforcement, and knowledge of results), task variables (such as size of stimulus population and size of response population), and subject variables (characteristics of subjects). He equated these three sets of variables to the traditional ones of principles of learning (basic), individual differences (subject), and tasks (tasks). Cotterman proposed that a rational approach be used to categorize tasks to reflect the interaction between task and basic variables. Specifically, Cotterman recommended that a large, representative sample of human learning tasks be sorted after a review of their similarities and differences as to "(1) which commonalities among tasks permit the prediction that the effects of a given set of basic variables would be unchanged and (2) which differences do not significantly affect the operation of those variables" (p. 4). Thus, for tasks within a given category, the effects of a given principle of human learning could be generalized to be the same, whereas for tasks in different categories, the effects of a given principle of learning could not be generalized. The underlying assumption of this classificatory scheme is that there are some aspects of the task that do not affect the operation of some principles of human learning; that is, for all tasks subsumed under a category, certain principles of learning remain reasonably invariant.

Cotterman (1959) suggested that a general description of task stimuli and responses and the transformations that occur would enable the appropriate categorization of a task. He presented an illustrative classificatory scheme of learning situations or tasks. Table 7.5 provides several examples of the categories in Cotterman's scheme. As Cotterman himself noted, his scheme is not refined and is not intended to serve as a hypothetical categorization of tasks to be evaluated empirically. Rather, it is simply an example of how abstract definitions of task categories may be generated. Although Cotterman proposed various methodologies for generating such a classificatory system as well as criteria for evaluating such a system, his scheme does not constitute such a system. In its current stage of development, Cotterman's scheme is of theoretical interest. However, further development is required before the scheme has practical usefulness.

FITTS: TWO CLASSIFICATORY SYSTEMS FOR SKILLED TASKS

Although Fitts (1962) recognized skill as a continuous interplay of input, output, and feedback processes, he felt that a taxonomy of skilled tasks could begin with a consideration of the "conditioning existing prior to the initiation of some behavior sequence of interest" (p. 178). Fitts noted that an adequate task taxonomy for skilled tasks would identify important correlates of such variables as learning rate and performance level, resulting in substantial theoretical and practical contributions.

Fitts described two classificatory systems based on task characteristics. The first contains only three categories based upon two gross descriptors: (1) the degree of gross body involvement and (2) the extent of external pacing activity. The first category of skilled tasks contains those in which the body is at rest at the beginning of a response sequence and the individual initiates a behavior pattern in relation to a stable set of environmental objects. In the second category, either the individual body is in motion while the environment is stable or the body is stable and the environment is in motion when the behavior sequence begins. In the third category, both the individual's body and the environmental conditions change immediately prior to the initiation of the behavior sequence.

In the second classificatory system described by Fitts (1962), tasks are characterized by their (1) stimulus and response sequences (including their degree of coherence, continuity, frequency, and complexity); (2) stimulus coding (the particular size, color, pitch, or other characteristic of the stimulus); (3) response coding (the force, amplitude, or other characteristics of the response); (4) code transformations; (5) nature and amount of input; (6) kind and quantity of external feedback; (7) kind of internal (proprioceptive) feedback; (8) dynamics of physical systems (including machine lags); and (9) overall task complexity (e.g., number of separate sources of input or feedback information, number of external systems with separate dynamics, number of separate actions that must be taken sequentially and concurrently).

This latter classificatory system is based upon Fitts' analytic approach to skilled performance, which considers the individual engaged in skilled performance as part of one or more closed loop systems involving (1) only the individual, (2) the individual and an interacting environment, and (3) the individual and an interacting machine.

STOLUROW: TASK CHARACTERISTICS AND LEARNING PRINCIPLES

Stolurow (1964) succeeded in developing a limited prototype classification of paired associate and serial learning tasks. Based on his system of classification, he was able to explore the effects of certain principles of learning with respect to different categories of tasks. Preliminary data suggested that the effects of massed and spaced practice were relatively homogeneous within certain of the task categories. This is especially interesting when one considers the types of descriptors upon which Stolurow based task categories. These included number and sequence of stimuli and responses, stimulus and response limits, meaningfulness, and qualitative relationships between stimulus and response.

HACKMAN AND OLDHAM: JOB CHARACTERISTICS MODEL OF WORK MOTIVATION AND THE JOB DIAGNOSTIC SURVEY

Hackman and Oldham (1975, 1976) have built a job characteristics model of work motivation, shown in Figure 7.2. Basically, the model suggests that personal and organizational outcomes (i.e., high internal work motivation, high satisfaction with the work, high quality work performance, and low absenteeism and turnover) are the result of three critical psychological states that must be present simultaneously for the positive outcomes to be realized. The critical psy-

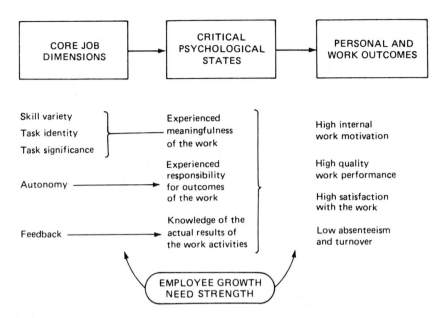

Figure 7.2   The job characteristics model of work motivation. Reproduced with permission from Hackman, J. R. & Oldham, G. R. Motivation through the design of work: Test of a theory. *Organizational Behavior and Human Performance*, 1976, *16*, 250–279.

chological states are created by five core dimensions or job characteristics. Jobs may be categorized according to the extent to which they reflect similarities or differences on these five characteristics, which are defined by Hackman and Oldham (1975) as follows:

1. *Skill Variety.* The degree to which a job requires a variety of different activities in carrying out the work, which involve the use of a number of different skills and talents of the employee

2. *Task Identity.* The degree to which the job requires completion of a "whole" and identifiable piece of work, that is, doing a job from beginning to end with a visible outcome

3. *Task Significance.* The degree to which the job has a substantial impact on the lives or work of other people, whether in the immediate organization or in the external environment

4. *Autonomy.* The degree to which the job provides substantial freedom, independence, and discretion to the employee in scheduling the work and in determining the procedures to be used in carrying it out

5. *Feedback From The Job Itself.* The degree to which carrying out the work activities required by the job results in the employee obtaining direct and clear information about the effectiveness of his or her performance

The classificatory system developed by Hackman and Oldham (1975) is derived logically from expectancy theory (see Hackman & Oldham, 1974b, 1976; Hackman & Lawler, 1971). The expectancy theory of work motivation states that the likelihood that an individual will engage in a particular behavior is enhanced to the extent that the individual believes that the behavior will lead to reward that the individual personally values (see Porter & Lawler, 1968; Vroom, 1964). These rewards may be intrinsic or extrinsic. Hackman and Lawler (1971) suggested that certain characteristics of the job, such as skill variety, task identity, autonomy, and feedback, will enhance the intrinsic motivation of workers who desire higher need satisfaction. Thus, certain characteristics lead to critical psychological states, which in turn lead to positive outcomes in both attitudes and behavior (e.g., satisfaction, performance, and attendance).

Hackman and Lawler (1971) used a measuring instrument called the Yale Job Inventory in their earlier research. This was later refined and replaced by Hackman and Oldham (1974a, 1975) by the Job Diagnostic Survey (JDS). This survey obtains measures of each of the five job core characteristics, and combines them into a total Motivating Potential Score (MPS) by the following formula:

$$\frac{\text{Skill Variety} + \text{Task Identity} + \text{Task Significance}}{3} \times \text{Autonomy} \times \text{Feedback} = \text{MPS}$$

Thus, the Job Diagnostic Survey may compare jobs by subscores on the five core dimensions or by their total Motivating Potential Scores. Figure 7.3, drawn from Hackman and Suttle (1977), provides an illustration of these comparisons. The Job Diagnostic Survey also contains measures of "feedback from agents" and "dealing with others."

The Survey requires respondents to give their perceptions regarding the amount of each job characteristic that is present in their jobs. In another section, respondents indicate the accuracy of a number of statements regarding the characteristics of their jobs. The JDS also measures the three critical psychological states and affective reactions to the job.

Aldag, Barr and Brief (1981) provide a comprehensive review of the literature involving the psychometric evidence for the JDS. The following summary of the evidence is based upon their review.

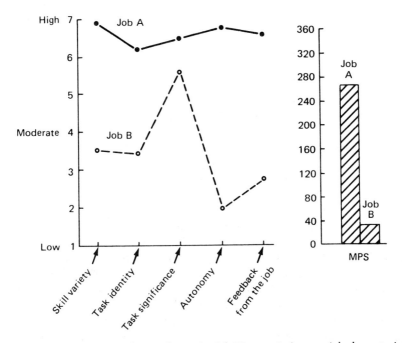

Figure 7.3 Comparison of two jobs on the Job Diagnostic Survey: job characteristic subscores and motivating potential scores. Reproduced with permission from Hackman, J. R. & Suttle, J. L. *Improving life at work: Behavioral science approaches to organizational change.* Goodyear Publishing Company, 1977.

Ten studies have investigated the internal consistency of the JDS. The mean reliability is .68. Convergent validity has been investigated in seven studies, with interesting results. Although incumbent and supervisory perceptions of the job do not always highly agree, the JDS has been shown to correlate well with other measures of task characteristics, such as the Job Characteristic Inventory of Sims, Szilagyi and Keller (1976), and measures drawn from the sociological literature. Discriminant validity has been investigated in 10 studies. The average intercorrelation between the job characteristic dimensions across these studies was .36.

Sixteen studies have investigated the empirical validity (what Aldag *et al.,* 1981, label *substantive validity*) of the JDS. Based on their review, Aldag *et al.* (1981) concluded, "Substantive validity is not clear. Whereas relationships of job attributes to employee's affective reactions were positive and often significant, those to employee's performance were consistently significant in only two cases" (p. 422).

One possible explanation for the confusing results regarding empirical validity has been proposed by Oldham, Hackman, and Pearce (1976). Their research results demonstrated that two variables—the need state of the employee and the level of employee satisfaction with the work context (pay, job security, and relationships with peers and supervisors)—moderate the relationship between job characteristics and personal and work outcomes.

Factor-analytic investigations of the Job Diagnostic Survey have resulted in mixed findings. Hackman and Lawler (1971) found four dimensions, Hackman and Oldham (1975) used five, and Sims et al. (1976) found six. Dunham (1976) factor-analyzed the responses of 3610 exempt employees who responded to the JDS. Using oblique rotations, he found that only one factor, Job Variety, (representing job complexity), accounted for 83% of the explained variance. However, a clean four-factor solution also was obtained, although it added little to the explained variance. The factors were labeled Feedback, Task Significance, Task Identity, and Task Variety–Autonomy.

Dunham, Aldag, and Brief (1977) factor-analyzed the responses of 5945 individuals. In only 2 of 20 samples did the researchers identify five job dimensions. Results in the other samples varied dramatically, with some containing the same factors as the five specified by Hackman and Oldham (1975), some containing combinations of those factors, and others containing totally new factors or job characteristics.

There have been a number of other challenges to the theory (see Landy & Trumbo [1980]), including those pertaining to the formula for the calculation of the MPS (Dunham, 1976) and to the moderating effects of growth need strength (Brief & Aldag, 1975). Cascio (1978) noted that "these results suggest that both the dimensionality and the theory of job characteristics, as presently formulated, may require revision" (p. 358). Hopefully, the necessary research and revisions will be undertaken to modify the theory and the Job Diagnostic Survey so that the survey can fulfill the two purposes for which it was originally designed: (1) to aid in the diagnosis of jobs before undertaking a job design or enrichment effort, and (2) to assess the effects of redesigned jobs on the job incumbents.

FARINA AND WHEATON: TASK CHARACTERISTICS APPROACH

Farina and Wheaton (1973) developed a task characteristics classificatory system, called the Task Characteristics Approach, as part of the Taxonomy Project. This system, described in detail in Chapter 13 of this book, has proceeded to the measurement stage with some empirical evaluation.

Briefly, a model was developed to characterize tasks in terms of the general components of goal, stimuli, responses, and the relationships among these variables. Within these components, major components of a task were identified and treated as categories within which to devise task characteristic descriptors.

Each characteristic was cast into a rating scale format that presented a definition of the characteristic and provided a 7-point scale with defined anchor points along with examples for each point. Nineteen scales were developed and evaluated in a series of three reliability studies. In general, it was found that a subset of scales having adequate reliability emerged consistently in the three studies.

The paradigm used to determine whether the task characteristics were correlates of performance for which predictive relationships might be established was that of "postdiction." The results of two postdiction studies were encouraging in so far as significant multiple correlations were obtained between task-characteristic ratings and performance measures on a variety of different tasks. Although a final interpretation of these findings must await cross-validation, it does appear possible to describe tasks in terms of a task-characteristic language that is (1) relatively free of subjective and indirect descriptors found in many other systems, and (2) shown to represent important correlates of performance. Some subtle differences among tasks were identified and those differences were related systematically to variations in performance. These encouraging results and later studies that show the usefulness of this Task Characteristics Approach in training device development are described more extensively in Chapter 13.

Implications for Future Taxonomic Development

In this and the two preceding chapters, we have summarized a variety of descriptive systems ranging from those with highly detailed and specific descriptors with well-defined interrelationships to those with general descriptors and categories found typically in the experimental literature (e.g., motor skills, cognitive skills). We have reviewed the classification of human performance on the basis of overt behaviors, on the basis of internal processes (or covert behaviors), and on the basis of a combination of these two (e.g., McCormick,

Cunningham). Behavior description systems and behavior requirements schemes were the most prevalent. Substantially fewer schemes using ability requirements as a basis for classification were identified. This is probably due to the elaborate research procedures required to establish ability constructs. Fewer schemes relying on task characteristic descriptors were located, possibly because of the greater interest of psychologists in human responses and processes than in situational variables.

A number of the systems (e.g., Information–Theoretic, Criterion Measures, Task Strategies) have a common definition of a "task" as an information transfer, deriving this definition from information-processing theory. Other systems may have greater similarities than are readily apparent from the labels assigned to their descriptors. In fact, one of the major impediments in advancing task taxonomic state of the art is the use of a plethora of verbal terms that may or may not be directly equated. Meister (1976) has made the following observation with respect to the state of the art of task taxonomies:

> Any task taxonomy is based on a concept of the behaviors inherent in the task and how they function; thus, it is limited by our conceptual rigidities. Since Western behavioral concepts are couched almost exclusively in verbal terms, the task taxonomies developed have been equally verbal. Consequently, differences among taxonomies often turn out to be largely semantic—for example, the contrast between "scan" and "survey." Although there may well be subtle differences involved in the actual behaviors represented by these two terms, the differences are extremely difficult to define either observationally or descriptively [p. 101].

Taxonomists must strive for more semantic consistency, or for more refined operational definitions of verbal descriptors, to facilitate taxonomic developments.

Based upon our review, a number of conclusions were reached that influenced later classificatory efforts in the Taxonomy Project. First, it became apparent that neither highly specific nor highly general categories would be most useful in generalizing principles across tasks. Second, although the schemes reviewed differed dramatically in their degree of development and evaluation, generally we found little empirical evaluation of the extent to which the descriptive systems could improve prediction and generalization about factors affecting human performance, a major raison d'être for classifying human task performance in the first place. Third, our review strengthened our belief in the need for the establishment of adequate measurement techniques for the classificatory schemes that we develop. Although many of the schemes surveyed were primarily qualitative, there was evidence of a trend toward quantitative description. A sample of the variety of measures found in the various approaches includes proportion of total task time involved, degree of attention required of operator, errors (omission, commission, magnitude, direction), importance over time, amount of specific ability required by task and possessed by operator, difficulty level (complexity), general presence–absence of descriptor unit (ability, function, activity), time (start, completion, and duration), and frequency. Finally, after a review of the arguments for and against various approaches, we became convinced that more than one provisional approach was needed. We decided to include more than one provisional approach in our conceptual development of a taxonomic system of human task performance.

The decision to develop a number of *alternative* taxonomic systems, based on different rationales about common factors in task performance, may in retrospect appear obvious, but at the time it was an insight that provided a major advance toward the solution of some taxonomic problems. These approaches eventually developed into the *Criterion Measures Approach*, the *Information–Theoretic Approach*, the *Task Strategies Approach*, the *Ability Requirements Approach*, and the *Task Characteristics Approach*. Some of these approaches are essentially empirically inductive, whereas others involve testing of a priori theoretical formulations. Each of these approaches is described in detail in succeeding chapters of this book.

In the development of these alternative taxonomic systems, there were several primary considerations kept in mind that were intended to enhance the quality of the resulting taxonomic work done prior to this program. One such consideration was that extensive effort was made to translate some of these approaches into usable *measurable* systems. Some approaches did not reach this stage of development, but, for at least one approach, some fairly sophisticated methods were developed. Additionally, major attention was also given to the development of *criteria* and *evaluative systems* for testing the reliability, validity, and utility of these approaches. A third consideration included defining the requirements for *data bases* that could be used in evaluating the capabilities of the various taxonomic systems to integrate the experimental literature. It was believed that the development and validation of any taxonomy of human performance is highly dependent on the data in the existing literature. Consequently, attention was given to an information system providing access to the research relevant to the classification of human performance. Problems of indexing and classifying, formating, search vocabulary, and cross-referencing, and the needed technology were dealt with, and prototype attempts to build a data base of previous research findings in several areas of human performance were conducted. These efforts will be described in detail in the next chapter.

References

Aldag, R. J., Barr, S. H., & Brief, A. P. Measurement of perceived task characteristics. *Psychological Bulletin*, 1981, *90*(3), 415–431.

Bond, L. A., & Rosen, J. C. (Eds.). *Competence and coping during adulthood*. Hanover, NH: New England University Press, 1980.

Brief, A. P., & Aldag, R. S. Employee reactions to job characteristics: A constructive replication. *Journal of Applied Psychology*, 1975, *60*, 182–186.

Cascio, W. F. *Applied psychology in personnel management*. Reston, VA: Reston, 1978.

Cattell, R. B. Some theoretical issues in adult intelligence testing. *Psychological Bulletin*, 1941, *38*, 592. (Abstract)

Cattell, R. B. Theory of fluid and crystallized intelligence: A critical experiment. *Journal of Educational Psychology*, 1963, *54*, 1–22.

Cotterman, T. E. *Task classification: An approach to partially ordering information on human learning* (WADC TN 58-374). Wright Patterson Air Force Base, OH: Wright Patterson Air Development Center, 1959.

Cunningham, J. W., Tuttle, T. C., Floyd, J. R., & Bates, J. A. *The development of the Occupation Analysis Inventory: An "ergometric" approach to an educational problem* (Center Research Monograph No. 6). Raleigh, NC: Center for Occupational Education, North Carolina State University, 1971.

Dunham, R. B. The measurement and dimensionality of job characteristics. *Journal of Applied Psychology*, 1976, *61*, 404–409.

Dunham, R. B., Aldag, R. J., & Brief, A. P. Dimensionality of task design as measured by the Job Diagnostic Survey. *Academy of Management Journal*, 1977, *20*, 209–223.

Dunnette, M. D. Aptitudes, abilities and skills. In M. D. Dunnette (Ed.), *Handbook of industrial and organizational psychology*. Chicago: Rand McNally, 1976.

Ekstrom, R. B. *Cognitive factors: Some recent literature* (Technical Report No. 2, ONR Contract NO0014-71-C-O117, NR 150-329). Princeton, NJ: Educational Testing Service, 1973.

Ekstrom, R. B., French, J. W., & Harmon, H. H. Cognitive factors: Their identification and replication. *Multivariate Behavioral Research Monographs*, 1979 (No. 79-2), pp. 1–84.

Farina, A. J., Jr. Development of a taxonomy of human performance: A review of descriptive schemes for human task behavior. *JSAS Catalog of Selected Documents in Psychology*, 1973, *3*, 23 (Ms. No. 318).

Farina, A. J., Jr., & Wheaton, G. R. Development of a taxonomy of human performance: The task characteristics approach to performance prediction. *JSAS Catalog of Selected Documents in Psychology*, 1973, *3*, 26–27 (Ms. No. 323).

Fitts, P. M. Factors in complex skill training. In R. Glaser (Ed.), *Training research and education*. Pittsburgh: University of Pittsburgh Press, 1962.

Fleishman, E. A. *The structure and measurement of physical fitness*. Englewood Cliffs, NJ: Prentice-Hall, 1964.

Fleishman, E. A. Human abilities and the acquisition of skill. In E. A. Bilodeau (Ed.), *Acquisition of skill*. New York: Academic Press, 1966.

Fleishman, E. A. Performance assessment based on an empirically derived task taxonomy. *Human Factors*, 1967, *9*, 349–366.

Fleishman, E. A. Structure and measurement of psychomotor abilities. In R. N. Singer (Ed.), *The psychomotor domain: Movement behavior*. Philadelphia: Lea & Febiger, 1972.

Fleishman, E. A. Toward a taxonomy of human performance. *American Psychologist*, 1975, *30*(12), 1127–1149. (a)

Fleishman, E. A. *Development of ability requirement scales for the analysis of Bell system jobs*. Bethesda, MD: Management Research Institute, October 1975. (b)

Fleishman, E. A. Relating individual differences to the dimensions of human tasks. *Ergonomics*, 1978, *21*(12), 1007–1019.

French, J. W. The description of aptitude and achievement tests in terms of rotated factors. *Psychometric Monographs*, 1951 (No. 5).

French, J. W., Ekstrom, R. B., & Price, L. A. *Manual for kit of reference tests for cognitive factors*. Princeton, NJ: Educational Testing Service, June 1963.

Guilford, J. P. The structure of intellect. *Psychological Bulletin*, 1956, *53*, 267–293.

Guilford, J. P. Three faces of intellect. *American Psychologist*, 1959, *14*, 469–479.

Guilford, J. P. *The nature of human intelligence*. New York: McGraw-Hill, 1967.

Guilford, J. P. *Way beyond the IQ*. Buffalo, NY: Creative Education Foundation, 1977.

Guilford, J. P., & Hoepfner, R. *The analysis of intelligence*. New York: McGraw–Hill, 1971.

Hackman, J. R., & Lawler, E. E. Employee reactions to job characteristics. *Journal of Applied Psychology Monograph*, 1971, *55*, 257–286.

Hackman, J. R., & Oldham, G. R. *The Job Diagnostic Survey: An instrument for the diagnosis of jobs and the evaluation of job redesign projects* (Tech. Rep. No. 4). New Haven, CT: Yale University, Department of Administrative Services, 1974. (a)

Hackman, J. R., & Oldham, G. R. *Motivation through the design of work: Test of a theory* (Tech. Rep. No. 6). New Haven, CT: Yale University, Department of Administrative Services, 1974. (b)

Hackman, J. R., & Oldham, G. R. Development of the Job Diagnostic Survey. *Journal of Applied Psychology*, 1975, *60*(2), 159–170.

Hackman, J. R., & Oldham, G. R. Motivation through the design of work: Test of a theory. *Organizational Behavior and Human Performance*, 1976, *16*, 250–279.

Hackman, J. R., & Suttle, J. L. *Improving life at work: Behavioral science approach to organizational change*. Santa Monica, CA: Goodyear Publishing Company, 1977.

Harman, H. H. *Final report of research on assessing human abilities* (PR-75-20). Princeton, NJ: Educational Testing Service, 1975.

Horn, J. L. Organization of abilities and the development of intelligence. *Psychological Review*, 1968, *75*, 242–259.

Horn, J. L. Human abilities: A review of research and theory in the early 1970s. In M. R. Rosenzweig & L. W. Porter (Eds.), *Annual review of psychology* (Vol. 27). Palo Alto, CA: Annual Review, 1976.

Landy, F. J., & Trumbo, D. A. *Psychology of work behavior*. Homewood, IL: Dorsey, 1980 (Revised edition).

McCormick, E. J. *Job analysis: Methods and applications*. New York: American Management Association, AMACOM, 1979.

Marquardt, L. D., & McCormick, E. J. *Attribute ratings and profiles of the job elements of the Position Analysis Questionnaire (PAQ)*. (Report No. 1). West Lafayette, IN: Department of Psychological Sciences, Purdue University, 1972.

Mecham, R. C., & McCormick, E. J. *The rated attribute requirements of job elements in the Position Analysis Questionnaire* (Rep. No. 1). Lafayette, IN: Occupational Research Center, Department of Psychology Sciences, Purdue University, 1969.

Meeker, M. The SOI Institute based on Guilford's "Structure-of-Intellect" model. *Education*, 1981, *101*, 302–309.

Meister, D. *Behavioral foundations of system development*. New York: Wiley, 1976.

Merrifield, P. R., Guilford, J. P., Christensen, P. R., & Frick, J. W. The role of intellectual factors in problem solving. *Psychological Monographs*, 1962, *76*, (10, Whole No. 529).

Neeb, R. W., Cunningham, J. W., & Pass, J. J. *Human attribute requirements of work elements: Further development of the Occupation Analysis Inventory* (Center Research Monograph No. 7). Raleigh, NC: Center for Occupational Research, University of North Carolina, 1971.

Neeb, R. W., Cunningham, J. W., & Pass, J. J. Human attribute requirements of work elements: Further development of the Occupation Analysis Inventory. *JSAS Catalog of Selected Documents in Psychology*, 1974, *4*, 145 (Ms. No. 805).

Oldham, G. R., Hackman, J. R., & Pearce, J. L. Conditions under which employees respond positively to enriched work. *Journal of Applied Psychology*, 1976, *61*(4), 395–403.

Pass, J. J., & Cunningham, J. W. A systematic procedure for estimating the human attribute requirements of occupations. *JSAS Catalog of Selected Documents in Psychology*, 1975, *5*, 353 (Ms. No. 1151).

Pawlik, K. Faktorenanalytische Personlichkeitsforschung. (Factor analytic personality research). In *Kindlers Enzyklopadie der Psychologie des 20. Jahrhunderts*, Zurich, 1973, 617–712.

Pawlik, K. *Differential psychology of learning and cognition*. Paper presented at the meeting of the Chinese Psychological Association, Peking, December 1981.

Porter, L. W., & Lawler, E. E., III. *Managerial attitudes and performance*. Homewood, IL: Irwin, 1968.

Sims, H. P., Szilagyi, A. D., & Keller, R. T. The measurement of job characteristics. *Academy of Management Journal*, 1976, *19*, 195–212.

Spearman, C. *The abilities of man*. New York: Macmillan, 1927.

Stolurow, L. *A taxonomy of learning task characteristics* (AMRL-TD-12-64-2). Wright Patterson Air Force Base, OH: Aerospace Medical Research Laboratories, January 1964.

Theologus, G. C., & Fleishman, E. A. Development of a taxonomy of human performance: Validation study of ability scales for classifying human tasks. *JSAS Catalog of Selected Documents in Psychology*, 1973, *3*, 29 (Ms. No. 326).

Theologus, G. C., Romashko, T., & Fleishman, E. A. Development of a taxonomy of human performance: A feasibility study of ability dimensions for classifying human tasks. *JSAS Catalog of Selected Documents in Psychology*, 1973, *3*, 25–26 (Ms. No. 321).

Thurstone, L. L. *Primary mental abilities*. Chicago: University of Chicago Press, 1938.

Vroom, V. H. *Work and motivation*. New York: Wiley, 1964.

CHAPTER 8

Data Bases and Taxonomic Development

An enormous amount of human performance research data has been generated over the years, and large quantities of new research data are added each year. We have already pointed out the need for classificatory systems to introduce order into this information so that investigators may draw conclusions from these data. A sophisticated data base would contain meaningful categories of independent and dependent variables and could deal with functional relationships between them, allowing the user to integrate diverse information, extract behavioral principles, or even develop mathematical models.

This chapter examines the role data bases can play in developing and evaluating classificatory systems, as a tool in the pursuit of taxonomic development. As Korotkin, Krebs, and Darby (1972) have said:

> The development and validation of any taxonomy of human performance is highly dependent upon the data in the existing literature, i.e., the results of experimental studies. However, if research is to be useful, it must itself be organized. Therefore, the first step, and a necessary prerequisite to the classification of human performance, is the classification of the many studies dealing with human performance [p. 47].

One use for a human performance data base is the evaluation of alternate provisional taxonomies. Each taxonomy is intended to identify meaningful classes of human performance; the data base can indicate whether relationships have, in fact, been found to exist among the classes of human performance as defined by the classificatory system. For example, in the case of an abilities scheme, the information system can retrieve studies that have used the tasks requiring the same abilities. These studies can then be examined to determine the consistency of findings in this class of tasks.

In sum, a data base can perform several useful functions in science. It can tell the researcher what relevant studies have already been performed and what results were found. It can provide information from related studies that allows integration of findings and drawing of overall conclusions. The contents of the data base can suggest useful categories for classificatory systems. Lastly, the data base can be used to evaluate various taxonomic systems.

In order to understand how data bases can be used to accomplish these functions, it is necessary to understand a variety of concepts and developments in the field of information science. Therefore, this chapter first reviews relevant aspects of information science and then turns to specific issues in data base development. Finally, it describes a preliminary attempt, in our Taxonomy Project, to build a data base to be used in taxonomic development.

Relevant Aspects of Information Science

In a typical automated scientific information data base, standard citations along with author-provided abstracts constitute the only retrievable information. The kinds and amounts of additional information that should be included are a function both of the particular needs for which the data base is implemented and of the particular kinds of intended uses. If the only intended use is for the requestor to obtain a list of relevant references, then perhaps no more information is necessary than standard citations. If, on the other hand, the requestor desires information with regard to data and results of scientific reports, then it is necessary to provide far more information. Inputting research data provides the capability of retrieving standardized sets of data for any particular study or for several studies in order to investigate functional relationships between dependent and independent variables. Furthermore, such data permit the identification of gaps in existing knowledge; the integration of this kind of data might lead to new hypotheses for scientific testing and generate additional ideas regarding the directions in which research should proceed.

Types and Forms of Information

In considering the roles that the data bases of a scientific field play in its taxonomic development, there are two aspects of the data bases that, to some extent, must be considered separately. One is the form of the actual data or information, and the other is the way in which the information is classified and organized. The information itself exists in a number of forms that can be placed on a continuum according to the extent to which the information has been condensed. This continuum ranges from the one extreme of the raw data themselves, through the intermediate position of some form of summary statistics, to the other extreme of highly condensed results reported in professional publications. The physical medium in which the information is stored also varies according to this dimension. Raw data are usually stored on coding sheets, computer cards, tape, or disks, and highly condensed information is usually stored in books or journals.

The manner in which a body of information may be organized is the aspect that is most directly relevant to taxonomy; indeed, the classification of research literature (or any literature) by subject matter is a taxonomic endeavor. However, the procedures for subject classification, as part of information science, have not been derived directly from taxonomic principles but have been of a more ad hoc nature. Moreover, procedures for subject classification within library science have been dictated more by the state of the art in information storage and retrieval technology than by the formal principles of taxonomy. This is understandable considering that even the most elegant classificatory system based upon taxonomic logic will be useless to a librarian if the technology does not exist to implement the system. Fortunately, however, the technology of information storage and retrieval recently has been advancing by leaps and bounds, particularly with the advent of sophisticated computer technology, so that there are few technological constraints left on implementing any type of classificatory system.

It should be noted that formal subject classifications of research information have been developed almost exclusively for one end of the information dimension, the highly condensed form published in the research literature. Relatively less classificatory effort has gone into organizing the other end of the dimension, the raw data themselves. This state of affairs is changing, however, with profound implications for future taxonomic developments. Licklider (1965), in discussing how libraries must change in the future if they are to be effective, has made a strong and convincing argument for treating all information alike, regardless of its medium of communication. His point is that a library exists to provide information, that is, to provide answers to questions, or to tell the user if there is no answer available (to expose gaps in research knowledge). Libraries, as presently organized, cannot do this effectively because they classify and store information by the physical unit in which it is contained, such as book or journal. In other words, they are largely *bibliographic* retrieval systems, with little interest in the development of *information* retrieval systems. The best that a library user can do presently is to retrieve all books and articles that may contain relevant information on a given subject and then to search within those units for the information. To achieve this long-range goal, Licklider emphasizes that libraries must modify their entire method of physical storage of information as well as their existing methods for classifying that information to accommodate the various media. Thus, he points to the interdependence of storage and retrieval technology with classificatory system development.

SECONDARY ANALYSIS

Another indication that taxonomic developments in the future will have to encompass information in varying forms and stored in various media is the secondary analysis movement. Secondary analysis entails reanalyzing raw data gathered for some other purpose and applying it to answer different research questions from those addressed in the original study.

An example is a study that used secondary analysis to determine that greater differentials in the presidential vote were associated with newspapers than with other media (Robinson, 1975). This relationship was measured by linking election survey data from the Center for Political Studies archives to records of newspaper presidential endorsements, for five successive presidential elections. This is an example not only of secondary analysis of data over time, but also of the comparison of survey data with outside records.

Other examples of secondary analysis that represent the state of the art, and have attained significant visibility, include secondary analyses of the Coleman study (Mosteller & Moynihan, 1972), of the Ohio–Westinghouse Headstart evaluation (Campbell & Erlebacher, 1970), and of the Pygmalion in the Classroom study (Elashoff & Snow, 1971).

Hyman (1972) classified the benefits of secondary analysis into three groups: practical, social, and theoretical. The *practical* benefits include economizing on money, time, and personnel, because raw data collection is such an expensive, time-consuming part of research. *Social* benefits include the lessening of research intrusions upon a general public that is already sensitive to such intrusions, making it financially possible for researchers to work independently, and providing a comparatively inexpensive vehicle for training future researchers. Benefits for *theory* and substantive knowledge include: an enhanced understanding of the process of change by searching for trends in the data; examining problems comparatively by contrasting (for instance, data from two similar studies on different populations); improving general knowledge through replication and enlargement; and extending theory. Regarding this last aspect, Hyman (1972) writes:

> When an investigator focuses on a concept in designing a new inquiry he points himself in the right direction, but his vision is narrowed. He selects the few indicators that hit the center of his target idea. The secondary analyst starts at the other end. He must examine a diverse array of concrete indicators, assorted specific manifestations of behavior or attitude, apparently tangential bits and pieces that he hopes will fit into some larger domain. He is compelled to think broadly and abstractly in order to find overarching concepts or categories within which these varied specific entities can be contained. He is likely to be more exhaustive in his definition of a concept, to think about it not only in his accustomed ways, but in all sorts of odd ways. Vicariously, he is immersed in the thought processes of others, some being products of the same milieu and period, and some far removed from him in time and place [pp. 23–24].

The mechanical issues pertaining to secondary analysis can be subdivided into three sets: those associated with data production (primary analysis); data acquisition, storage, and retrieval (archiving); and data consumption (secondary analysis). Of all the activities entailed in producing data in the primary analysis process, the two most important ones for secondary analysis are the documentation and dissemination of data. Documentation entails making available the coding of the data so that any other researcher can read and reuse the data. Lack of proper documentation is the biggest barrier presently existing to secondary analysis. Anyone who has tried to reuse even his or her own personal data at some later date can testify to this fact. Procedures for data documentation are rarely taught or even mentioned in courses on research methodology. Consequently, in organized archives a very large proportion of the time often is spent working with the primary analyst to produce proper documentation. In the Survey Research Archives at the University of Michigan, for instance, the dialogue between the archivists and the primary analyst to produce documentation can last as long as two years.

In addition to the raw data, data bases frequently contain additional information, such as (1) demographic information on the sample, (2) criterion information on the sample (e.g., individual performance test scores or group criteria such as aggregate safety records),

(3) questionnaire items, or (4) experimental tasks. Any reliability, validity, and scale property characteristics available can be stored with the actual questionnaire items or experimental tasks. There has been some impetus in psychology in archiving psychological measures and scales (apart from archiving results obtained using them). This impetus has developed from the realization that approximately 70% of the psychological and sociological measures, once published, are never used again even by the authors (Chun, Cobb, French, & Seashore, 1973). Because to some extent this represents wasted effort, the ready availability of an archive of measures might serve to redirect this energy into the utilization, validation, and refinement of existing measures. Chun *et al.* (1973) concluded that this problem is so detrimental to the progress of social science research that they proposed the development of a National Repository of Social Science Measures. A step in this direction has been taken with the publication of a directory of psychological measures (Chun, Cobb, & French, 1975). Lastly, although it is conventional to store the raw data, it is becoming more common also to store the summary statistics that the primary analyst computed, such as means, standard deviations, and correlations. This saves some duplication of effort on the secondary analysts' part.

META-ANALYSIS

Glass (1976, 1977, 1981) strongly advocates practicing an advanced form of secondary analysis—*meta-analysis*—which refers to the statistical analysis of many individual analyses from different studies to integrate findings and draw overall conclusions. Glass states:

> We need more scholarly effort concentrated on the problem of finding the knowledge that lies untapped in completed research studies. We are too heavily invested in pedestrian reviewing where verbal synopses of studies are strung out in dizzying lists. The best minds are needed to integrate the staggering number of individual studies. This endeavor deserves higher priority now than adding a new experiment or survey to the pile [1976, p. 4].

Meta-analysis facilitates taxonomic development by enabling comparisons of the phenomena in question across data bases collected in many research inquiries. An example is a meta-analysis conducted on the research dealing with class size and academic achievement (Glass & Smith, 1979). There have been hundreds of studies done on the relationship between number of students in a classroom and their academic achievement; the results of this body of research are self-contradictory and confusing. Using meta-analytic statistical techniques, the authors were successful in integrating this literature and drawing conclusions. For instance, they determined that, other things being equal, more is learned in smaller classes. Moreover, this relationship is slightly stronger at the secondary grades than in elementary school. The relationship does not differ, however, across schools or pupil I.Q. Other examples of meta-analysis include (1) the comparative studies of primitive cultures conducted using the Yale Human Relations Area File, which is a large compendium of data collected by social anthropologists; and (2) the studies of organizations using the case studies compiled in the Yale Technology Project (Burns, 1967).

Before meta-analysis emerged as a field in its own right, there were essentially two approaches taken to integrating research findings. In the first approach, all relevant studies are located, the majority are eliminated on the basis of various methodological flaws, and general conclusions are drawn from the few that remain. This approach is unsatisfactory for two reasons. One is that even studies with methodological flaws, taken in the aggregate, may produce very strong results. Another is that the conclusions necessarily are based on the methodological and philosophical opinions and biases of the reviewer. The other approach is somewhat quantitative, but, as Glass points out, it is too weak for the complexity of the problem:

> Statistically significant vs. non-significant findings are classified by one, or perhaps two, attributes of the studies. There is little to recommend this attack on the problem. It is biased in favor of large-sample studies that may show only weak findings. It is not suited to the task of answering the important questions of how large an effect a particular treatment produces, or among several effective treatments which is most effective. The "vote taking" approach frequently produces only perplexing results [1976, p. 6].

Meta-analysis is directed toward a quantitative aggregation of research findings and a description of the relationships among study findings and characteristics. There are a variety of techniques available to conduct a meta-analysis. One set of approaches involves the use of the raw data from the studies (Light & Smith, 1971). However, in many instances, the raw data are no longer available or do not meet certain statistical assumptions. Consequently, a variety of meta-analytic techniques have been developed that allow the analyst to use summary statistics, by applying statistical methods to statistical findings (Glass, 1977). Some of these techniques, such as multiple regression, are sophisticated. However, others (for example, tables, graphs, measures of location and spread, and scatter diagrams) are relatively simple descriptive techniques that aid the analyst's ability to perceive patterns in the data.

The use of secondary analysis and meta-analysis has implications for the process of psychological research itself (Miller, 1976). Psychological research has been a highly individualistic activity, with a great deal of personal freedom for each researcher. The secondary or meta-analysis, however, is dependent upon what is available in the data base. Therefore, the primary analyst must now consider the long-range potential of each study conducted, as well as devote more time to documentation and quality control. Success in taxonomic development is dependent on the quality of data bases. The quality of data bases, in turn, is dependent on the quality of studies, including the documentation of those studies.

There are numerous indications that secondary analysis and meta-analysis will play a larger role in the behavioral sciences. For example, within political science, secondary analysis is a major activity; a number of large data archives have been developed to make raw data sets available for general consumption. Bryant and Wortman (1978) argue strongly for expanding the use of meta-analysis in psychology. Hunter, Schmidt, and Jackson (1982) already have expanded greatly the use of meta-analysis in the behavioral sciences.

If the use of data bases for secondary and meta-analysis becomes wide-spread, another likely result is cross-fertilization of knowledge, at least by those data bases servicing mixed groups of users. An existing example is the National Clearinghouse for Alcohol Information (Uprichard, 1974). That data base consists of all publications pertaining to alcoholism. Users comprise a highly disparate group including biochemists, paraprofessional alcoholism counselors, educators, law enforcement officers, medical personnel, psychologists, people with alcoholism in their families, geriatric specialists, and social workers. Thus, an information system can have the salutary effect of breaking down some of the barriers to information flow that frequently separate disciplines or separate laboratory researchers from both applied researchers and practitioners.

Deutsch (1970) presents a far-reaching discussion of the need for secondary analysis and meta-analysis in the social sciences and provides numerous examples of their use. He concludes that social science has to improve its capacity to "remember relevantly and effectively by a whole order of magnitude" that in the next half century this may be "a matter of life and death for all of us," and that "social science data archives will provide an indispensable contribution." (1970, p. 38).

The search for deriving principles of behavior by developing appropriate categories can be greatly facilitated by secondary and meta-analysis. In the area of human task performance, meta-analyses for deriving broader principles of task performance from data across a number of diverse studies have been successful in showing the potential for several classificatory systems (see, for example, Fleishman, 1975).

Issues in Data Base Development

Developing a data base requires obtaining the information itself, creating a classificatory system, and developing or applying the technology for indexing, storing, and retrieving the information. A data base is a type of human–machine system in which the human components include those who operate and maintain the system as well as those who use the system. Data base development can be performed best if principles of systems design are employed. Systems analysis begins with a functional analysis to describe the purpose and uses of the system components and their interrelationships.

It would be impossible here to touch on all the technological issues pertaining to data base development in general; with the exponential increase in information, the field of information science and technology has expanded rapidly. However, we review some of the issues in information science that are most pertinent to the development of a human performance data base. These can be subdivided into issues pertaining to classification and indexing, data base structure, software and hardware, and human engineering.

CLASSIFICATION AND INDEXING

The basic purpose of an index is to operationalize a classification system. From a practical standpoint, the aim is to maximize the likelihood that the indexer and searcher will use the same terms when referring to the same concept or to the contents of a document or study. The subject matter indexes used in books and libraries and the thesauri used by document retrieval services represent the beginnings of refined descriptor systems. However, it is possible to improve substantially the comprehensiveness, organization, and content of such systems. This may be accomplished by selecting and hierarchically arranging descriptors so that they correspond to information that a user requires to locate only those studies of interest.

Many indices, perhaps most, have not been developed on the basis of an explicit classificatory system that was available or developed beforehand. However, many of them do represent implicit classificatory schemes. Ramsey-Klee, Richman, and Wiederhold (1975) describe the historical evolution of the relationship of classification to indexing in library and bibliographic retrieval applications:

> The historical rationale behind classification theory is to organize all knowledge into groups of related items where the related items are brought together by carefully applied principles of division. When the theory of classification is applied to indexing, the indexing terms chosen to describe the items of information usually are selected before any indexing is begun. The relationship among the selected indexing terms is set in a rigid fashion and arranged in a logical order starting from the very general and going to the specific, with the specific always being included in the general. Some examples of classification schemes are Ranganathan's Colon Classification, Dewey's Decimal Classification, and the Universal Decimal Classification. However, with the expansion of knowledge and the concomitant diffuseness of meaning of an item of information, the clear and logical distinctions between classes and groups became more difficult. . . . With the recognition that an item of information has a diffusion of meaning and can be looked at from a different point of view depending on user needs and areas of interest, the rigidity of the traditional classification theory was not practical. The current use of word classification is any method creating relations, generic or other, between individual semantic units, regardless of the degree of hierarchy, or more simply, it is the putting together of like things. The classes (or groups) determined should be recognizable and nameable. Therefore, word classification now is applied to any indexing language in which the relationships between terms are indicated. The advantage of the hierarchical form that results from the classification process draws attention to omissions and incomplete hierarchies. It also imposes a discipline that helps to avoid loose terminology [pp. 59–60].

Search of a data base can occur in one of two basic ways, either with or without vocabulary control. Vocabulary control entails limiting in some way the terms that are used for indexing and/or searching. If no vocabulary control is used, the search is called *natural language retrieval*, which means that there is no limit to the terms that may be used. If a data base has a natural language search capability, the user may pick any word or combination of words, and the data base will provide all documents that contain those words or combinations. Natural language retrieval has been made possible only by advanced computer technology.

There are two basic approaches to vocabulary control, although many data bases incorporate some elements of each. One approach is called *precoordinated*, which means that the vocabulary is developed by subject matter experts to represent a logical and comprehensive structure that will cover the data base contents. The other approach is called *postcoordinated*, in which a machine develops the vocabulary based on the frequency and pattern of usage of terms in the data base. Vocabulary control can be imposed in several different combinations: both the index and search vocabulary can be controlled;

TABLE 8.1

Extract of Controlled Vocabulary for a Human Performance
Data Base (Alphabetical Listing)[a]

A

ABSENCE	AFTER EFFECTS
ABSOLUTE	AFTERNOON
ACCELERATION	AGE
ACCOMODATION	AGING
ACCUMULATION	AGREEMENT
ACCURACY	AIR
ACHIEVEMENT	AIRCRAFT
ACOUSTIC	(see also: SPACECRAFT)
(see: SOUND)	ALCOHOL
ACQUISITION	ALERTING
(see also: LEARNING)	ALERTNESS
ACTION POTENTIAL	(see also: ATTENTION)
ACTIVATION	ALIGNMENT
ACTIVITY	(see also: ADJUSTMENT)
ACUITY	ALPHA
ADAPTATION	ALTERNATION
ADDITION	ALTERNATIVE
ADJUSTMENT	ALTITUDE
(see also: ALIGNMENT)	AMBIENT
ADULT	AMBIVALENCE
ADVERSE	AMOUNT
ADVICE	AMPLITUDE
(see also: DIRECTION)	ANALOG
AFFECT	ANALYSIS
(see: EMOTION)	

[a]Reproduced with permission from Chambers, A. N., Krebs, M. J., & Shaffer, E. J. *Development of a taxonomy of human performance: A document and information indexing and retrieval approach to classification.* Project report. Washington, D.C.: American Institutes for Research, October 1969.

one or the other can be controlled whereas the other is natural; or they both can be natural.

When precoordinated vocabulary control is used, there are a variety of options. The simplest is the *alphabetic subject index*, which is a list of all index terms in alphabetical order. If such a list includes "See also" references, this mechanism implicitly introduces a modest amount of classification. Another option, the *hierarchical index*, is a list of all index terms given based on their relationships to one another. Therefore, this represents a classificatory system. Examples of an alphabetic subject index and a hierarchical index for the field of human performance are shown in Tables 8.1 and 8.2. Both types require a great deal of preparatory work and substantive knowledge on the part of the indexer.

With the advancement of computer technology, postcoordinated

TABLE 8.2

Examples of Indexing Descriptors and Codes for Human Performance Research studies[a,b]

Subject matter		Units and measures		Treatment	
Code	Descriptor	Descriptor	Code	Descriptor	Code
Classes of Independent Variables					
1.	Operations				
2.	Equipment				
3.	Personnel				
4.	Environment				
4.1	Physical				
4.1.1	Pressure				
4.1.2	Thermal				
4.1.3	Contaminants/toxicants				
4.1.4	Radiation				
4.1.5	Acceleration				
4.1.6	Reduced/zero gravity				
4.1.7	Vibration				
4.1.8	Noise				
4.1.8.1	Medium				
4.1.8.1.1	Atmosphere (=air, ambient)				
4.1.8.1.2	Hydrosphere (=underwater)				
4.1.8.1.3	Communication equipment				
4.1.8.2	Range	Cycles per second	A		
		Hertz	B		
4.1.8.2.1	Infrasonic				
4.1.8.2.2	Sonic (=audible)				

4.1.8.2.3	Ultrasonic		
4.1.8.3	Frequency	Cycles per second	A
4.1.8.3.1	Constant (=steady) (see also pitch)	Hertz Octave Band (see also Mel)	B C
4.1.8.3.2	Variable		A
4.1.8.4	Intensity (=amplitude) Acoustic pressure (See also: Loudness)	Decibels (See also Phon, Sone)	
4.1.8.4.1	Constant		
4.1.8.4.2	Variable		
4.1.8.5	Duration	Second, minutes	A
4.1.8.5.1	Single (=Discrete)	On/Off cycle	
4.1.8.5.2	Continuous		
4.1.8.5.3	Intermittent (=Discontinuous, Interrupted) (See also: Random, Aperiodic)		
4.1.8.5.4	Impulsive (=Bursts)		
4.1.8.6	Spectrum	Hertz	A
4.1.8.6.1	Pure	Octave Band	B
4.1.8.6.2	Narrow Band	Power Density	C
4.1.8.6.3	Broad Band (=White noise)		
4.1.9	Terrain		*Treatments, for example, might include:
4.1.10	Electricity		
4.1.11	Magnetism		independent
4.1.12	Confinement		randomized
4.1.13	Isolation		stratified
4.1.14	Day/Night Cycles		controlled
4.1.15	Drugs		
4.2	Social		Also, the parameters may be: unknown

(continued)

TABLE 8.2 *Continued*

Subject matter		Units and measures		Treatment	
Code	Descriptor	Descriptor	Code	Descriptor	Code
5.	Selection			uncontrolled	
6.	Training			ignored	
Classes of Dependent Variables					
7.	Physical Responses				
8.	Physiological Responses				
9.	Psychological Responses				
9.1	Performance (objective)				
9.2	Behavior (subjective)				
10.	Pathological Responses				
10.1	Physical				
10.2	Psychological				

[a]Reproduced with permission from Chambers, A. N., Krebs, M. J., & Shaffer, E. J. *Development of a taxonomy of human performance: A document and information indexing and retrieval approach to classification.* Project report. Washington, D.C.: American Institutes for Research, October 1969.
[b]Adapted with permission from Chambers, A. N. *Development of a taxonomy of human performance: A heuristic model for the development of classification systems,* 1973. American Institutes for Research Technical Report. Reproduced in *JSAS Catalog of Selected Documents in Psychology*, 1973, 3, 24–25 (Ms. No. 320).

systems have become popular. Here, a machine performs word indexing by extracting all substantive words in the title, abstract, and/or
text. Thus, there is minimal vocabulary control. A common example
is the Key Word in Context (KWIC) index. Such an index lists each
substantive or key word every place it appears in the text, sur-
rounded on each side by the other words in the text, for the length of
one line. This provides contextual information to the person doing
the search.

Another indexing option is the thesaurus, which introduces more
vocabulary control and some precoordinated indexing into a postcoordinated index. Thesauri contain the descriptors in alphabetic
order, and also display nonaccepted terms in the alphabetic sequence. "Use" references to the accepted terms tell a user if a term is
not part of the vocabulary and identify the equivalent accepted term.
They indicate generic relationships by BT (broader than) and NT
(narrower than) references. RT (refer to) notations suggest similar
terms or general relationships among terms. Sometimes the alphabetic list is supplemented by a fully hierarchical list and the two are
cross-referenced (Salton, 1975; Soergel, 1974; Lancaster, 1972;
Ramsey-Klee *et al.*, 1975).

A step beyond postcoordinate indexing is mathematical classification, which is the automated derivation of classes of terms (Prywes &
Smith, 1972). Using various mathematical clumping and clustering
techniques, a classificatory system is built a posteriori, based on the
content of the data base itself. In general, however, it has been found
that these methods produce results somewhat inferior to manually
constructed thesauri and classificatory systems (Lancaster, 1972).

DATA BASE STRUCTURE

Another basic element of a data base is its structure. The data base
structure should be designed in accordance with the contents of the
data base and the usage patterns, as well as hardware capability, if
the data base is to be computerized. Any data base is composed of
data elements that are grouped into records, then subsequently
grouped into files. One of the main challenges in data base design is
to construct efficient file structures.

There are six basic methods of file organization (Wiederhold, 1977).
The minimal, most unstructured method is the *pile file*, in which data
are collected in the order in which they arrive. The records may not
contain the same data elements and may be of variable length. In a
sequential file, the data elements are restricted to a predetermined set

of attributes; therefore, each record contains the same type of information, usually in the same order. The data records are also ordered into a specific sequence. The *indexed sequential file* adds an index so that access can be made either via the sequence or via the index. A *multi-indexed file* can only be accessed through its indexes; it does, however, provide several different indexes that allow access. A *direct file* structure is so named because it closely relates the attribute value that is used to search to the physical capabilities of direct access mechanisms. It is suitable for applications such as directories, where record sizes are small and fixed and the data are always accessed by a single key attribute. Lastly, *multi-ring files* are used when the requirement is to identify sets of records with a common attribute. Pointers are used to identify the subsets. Once the overall data base structure has been set, a data base schema is developed that describes the organization in terms of files, records, and the relationships between them. In computerized systems, the schema must be readable by the data base system.

There are a variety of other considerations that affect decisions about data base structure. Two key ones are reliability and privacy. *Reliability* includes quality of information retrieval, as well as ensuring that the contents will not be inadvertently eliminated. Deliberately introducing redundancy of information is one way of coping with these problems. Also, some method of error correction must be available. With respect to *privacy*, the traditional distinction is made between permission to read data and permission to write data. In most information systems, permission to read data is granted to all users, whereas permission to write data is granted in very limited fashion. There are seven different types of access privileges that can be granted: reading, executing (using a program or procedure), changing (the traditional writing function), deleting, extending (adding information to a file), moving data fields, and verifying the existence of data elements (Wiederhold, 1977). In certain data bases, even permission to read is restricted. Almost any type of data object can be "locked" through a variety of methods.

Other issues affecting data base structures are the growth and retirement of the data base contents (Salton, 1975). Sometimes data can be added simply within the existing schema. At some point, however, a reconfiguration is needed. There are many reclustering operations suitable for deciding how to rearrange the information. Retirement of information may be needed to make room for new information, because of obsolescence of the information, or because of a change in the scope of the contents of the data base. Again, there are several retirement policies and associated techniques available for making these decisions.

SOFTWARE AND HARDWARE

It should be kept in mind that data bases need not be computerized. In fact, for simple ones, it is usually preferable not to do so. However, most of the data bases lend themselves to computer application, especially with declining hardware costs and simplified programming techniques. The software and hardware operationalize the data base, including the indexing and search vocabularies, and thus determine the efficiency and capabilities of the data base. Moreover, software capabilities are partially dependent upon hardware capabilities. The requirements for the software will differ significantly depending upon the form of the information (e.g., natural text, summary statistics) and upon the nature of the indexing and search vocabularies. If these vocabularies, for example, are refined beyond the descriptive level to the quantitative level, the software must have additional capabilities.

The dramatic increase in storage capabilities of computer hardware has revolutionized the technology of information science. This increase is driven primarily by the rapid progress in design and application of integrated circuits. A data base designer must consider whether the organization of the information dictated by the indexing vocabulary is efficient in terms of the file storage capabilities of the equipment. Moreover, the vocabulary must be reasonable in terms of the operating system characteristics, the communication requirements, and the anticipated user load (e.g., is the hardware capable of time-sharing among many users simultaneously?). In sum, as with any system, the decisions regarding design of the various subsystems must be based on their interdependencies, and this will be an iterative process. Therefore, the decision whether to use a particular formal classificatory system for indexing and/or searching, or to use some alternative form of vocabulary, is in part dependent upon the capabilities of the available software and hardware. Moreover, decisions regarding the classificatory scheme are dependent upon the last of our four data base issues: the human engineering requirements of the data base operator and users.

HUMAN ENGINEERING ISSUES IN DATA BASE DEVELOPMENT

Two characteristics of the indexing and search vocabularies will be important in meeting the requirements of operators and users. First, the vocabulary will affect the efficiency with which the system is operated and used. For example, a well-constructed hierarchical classificatory system usually is easier to employ for both indexers and users than a straight alphabetic list. Second, the vocabulary will affect how much the system is used. In most cases, data base use is voluntary, so a revealing measure of data base effectiveness is the extent to which it is used. Therefore, data base development should be predicated on a thorough user needs analysis, touching on the following areas: the problems that users must solve as part of their jobs (e.g., basic research, policy formulation); the kind and amount of information they need; the forms the information is in; the media and units in which the information is stored; the manner in which users can best access the data base (the search vocabulary); the most convenient modes for users to receive the information (e.g., cathode ray tube [CRT] terminal screen, hard-copy computer printout); and how users would like to interact with the data base (e.g., interactive, batch-processing, through a human intermediary).

There is a major challenge in doing a user needs analysis of any yet-to-be-constructed data base, namely, that it is hard to obtain answers to the above questions directly from the potential users. It is difficult for potential users to know what characteristics they would like in a data base with which they have had no experience. For example, it would be hard to imagine whether one would feel more comfortable with the output on a CRT screen or in hard copy unless one has had the opportunity to try these alternative modes. Almost all analyses of information needs and uses in science and technology are descriptive rather than experimental; they are based on information collected from scientists using diaries, interviews, observations, or questionnaires. These methods, although contributing some information about user needs, are not entirely satisfactory. They may confuse what a scientist thinks he or she needs with what he or she actually uses or would use.

One attempt to cope with this problem is demonstrated as part of a feasibility study on developing a research information system for Navy personnel surveys (Ramsey-Klee et al., 1975). In this instance a mock-up was created that simulated what the designer believed the ultimate system would look like, with samples of actual search and retrieval problems. Demonstrations were held with small groups of potential users. This "straw man" approach gave the users a chance to see the archive's intended capabilities and requirements and thus allowed them to react to a concrete system.

Another way of grappling with this problem is illustrated by a series of experimental studies run to assess the extent to which biologists would use an information retrieval system and how that system should be constructed to facilitate its use (Van Cott & Kinkade, 1968). This research, carried out by Taxonomy Project staff, simulated information retrieval systems by using humans to fulfil each of the information retrieval functions of the system, even though ultimately many of those functions would be mechanized. Such an approach minimizes cost and enables one to try differing design configurations to determine their effects on user behavior, prior to computerization.

To complicate matters further, the preferences of users usually change once they have had some practice with the system. Moreover, the technological state-of-the-art is always changing. Thus, a well designed system will contain several levels of sophistication for user interaction with the data base. In the case of the vocabulary, this means that the search vocabulary for the uninitiated user must include explicit, elaborately defined terms and cross-references, whereas the search vocabulary for the veteran user can be a mere skeleton. A well-constructed data base must have a built-in capacity to be changed.

EXAMPLES OF INFORMATION SYSTEMS FOR
PSYCHOLOGISTS

There are a large number of computerized information storage and retrieval systems available to psychologists. Many of these were developed by and for particular organizations and individuals. However, a number are available for general use. Among the more common ones are the PSYCINFO and PSYCSCAN Services of the American Psychological Association, the National Technical Information Service (NTIS) of the Department of Commerce, the MEDLARS/MEDLINE System of the National Library of Medicine, and the Educational Resources Informational Center (ERIC) of the National Institute of Education. These systems allow the user to obtain citations and abstracts of reports using a comprehensive key word system. In essence, these data bases are input–output devices to store information. The key words are cross-referenced. Citations and abstracts are sufficient information in many instances; for other instances, however, they are not. Depending upon user needs, there is a large variety of other information that might be useful, such as details of approaches, tasks used, and findings. More detailed classificatory systems need to be developed to index these kinds of information.

We have touched briefly on a number of issues that, sooner or later, must be addressed by those who would develop a data base in the field of human performance. In this review, we have gone beyond issues directly pertaining to classificatory systems and indexing vocabularies, and have discussed data base structure, software, hardware, and human engineering issues. We have considered this broad spectrum of issues because a data base is an information system, and all these issues are interdependent. Therefore, the choice of a classificatory system to organize the information in the data base will influence and be influenced by the data themselves, the available software, the available hardware, and the users' needs, as well as the not inconsequential matter of relative costs. Thus, data base development truly represents a classic example of systems design.

Development of Human Performance Data Bases

EFFORTS UNDER THE TAXONOMY PROJECT

The Taxonomy Project included a prototypical data base effort as part of the plans for evaluating some of the provisional classificatory approaches developed (see Fleishman, Kinkade, & Chambers, 1972). The method involved classification of the tasks from the data base into the categories provided by the particular classificatory system. Evaluation then consisted of seeing whether (1) scientific generalizability of the findings was improved; (2) new relationships among the variables were uncovered; (3) predictions of human task performance were obtained; and/or (4) the efficiency with which information could be retrieved from the data base was enhanced. It should be noted that there is one fundamental problem using this, or any other human performance data base, for evaluation of a classificatory approach. The extent to which a classificatory scheme can be used to perform these functions is not only dependent on the quality of the scheme, but also on the quality of the data base itself; therefore, such evaluation is actually a joint test of both the classificatory scheme and the data base.

Information retrieval systems believed most appropriate for these purposes were to have certain characteristics. The data base (1) uses the whole article rather than abstracts; (2) allows for the plotting of functional relationships of interest to the user; (3) focuses on specific dependent variables; (4) is screened for quality and adequacy of description by an experienced professional; and (5) is an open-ended file with the capability to incorporate new findings without major revisions.

If the body of experimental literature is to be useful for the evaluation of provisional classificatory approaches, it must be organized so that individual documents can be retrieved selectively and compared on many different bases. Whether or not this retrieval and comparison of studies is feasible depends upon: (1) the relevance of the literature included in the data base; (2) the extent to which the data present in the research reports can be quantified adequately; (3) the consistency of the results across reports dealing with the same topic; and (4) the utility of the system used for classifying the data originally.

PROCEDURES In the Taxonomy Project, the effort was made to develop a document indexing and retrieval system that involved indexing a fairly large number of research studies. The system attempted to enhance document retrieval and comparison by taking into account the preceding factors, which were believed to contribute to such comparisons. The combination of the research studies themselves, along with the indexing and retrieval system, produced a Human Performance Data Base potentially useful in evaluating task classification systems as they were developed (an example is provided in Chapter 9).

The initial step in the development of the Human Performance Data Base (Korotkin & Chambers, 1969) was the collection of hard copies of research studies on human performance in the following subject matter areas:

1. Environmental areas
   a. Atmospheric thermal environment
   b. Auditory noise environment
2. Training areas
   a. Knowledge of results
   b. Massed vs. distributed practice
3. Psychophysiological areas
   a. Psychoactive drugs
   b. Alcohol

These areas were selected on the basis of several criteria:

1. The existence of a relatively large number of research studies in the area

2. The absence of any major attempt to systematize the results in the area
3. A fairly wide variety of tasks employed in studies in the area
4. Interest on the part of the scientific and technical community in the area

Approximately 600 studies were collected that met these selection criteria.

The second step was to develop a controlled vocabulary, or subject matter index (Chambers, Krebs, & Shaffer, 1969). The use of a controlled vocabulary limits the universe of acceptable descriptors and thus improves the consistency with which documents are indexed in the data base system. It also ensures compatibility between the indexer and the data base user, acting as a bridge by establishing a common vocabulary. Initially, this vocabulary was confined to an alphabetical listing of terms; Table 8.1 illustrates a portion of this alphabetical listing. The long-term goal was to develop a hierarchical list. A critical consideration was to construct a classificatory scheme that would be capable of growth and modification.

The criteria employed in the development of this vocabulary were as follows:

1. The terms should be limited to those that are generally used in the research literature.
2. Every effort should be made to use preferred terms, and indicate other terms that are equivalents.
3. Hierarchical levels for descriptors eventually should be developed to permit selective search.
4. The hierarchical vocabulary must provide for orderly growth so that additional categories may be added, or existing categories may be reversed, without disturbing the overall structure.
5. Descriptor terms should be standardized and consistent (for instance, insofar as possible, all terms should be expressed as nouns, in singular form).

Considerable attention was given to the controlled vocabulary because this was thought to be crucial to the successful development of the indexing and retrieval system. Perhaps the feature that most distinguished this vocabulary from many others is that it was based on the specific needs of the *user* rather than on the content of the documents alone.

Concurrent with the development of the vocabulary, an indexing format was designed. Its purpose was to provide the indexer with a systematic method for selecting and entering descriptors in a form that would identify the study being indexed. The format provided for entering information such as accession number; citation of author, title, source, and date, (conventional indexing); independent variables; dependent variables; subjects; apparatus; tasks; controlled parameters; and comments.

The original plans included extracting just the important information from each study. For example, the noise literature could be scored with a "plus" if noise had an incremental effect on performance, a "zero" if there was no significant effect, and a "minus" if there was a decrement in performance. However, it was found that the extraction of such simplified information can be misleading. Having the entire study available frequently provides meaningful contextual information that facilitates interpretations. Therefore, the decision was made to provide the user with the research documents themselves, rather than surrogates, sorted on the basis of the indexing descriptors.

The next step was to index studies. The information was put on punch cards to facilitate the retrieval of citations and abstracts. Figure 8.1 summarizes the input cycle of the data.

Once the data base was organized in this manner, it was possible to retrieve studies on the basis of types of tasks, apparatus, or any of the other indexing descriptors or combinations thereof. Such selective retrieval facilitates comparisons of similarities and differences between the studies. These comparisons help to explain the clusterings (or lack of clusterings) of tasks or abilities that have been predicted from alternative classificatory schemes.

This data base was used in evaluating two of the classificatory approaches in the Taxonomy Project. One was the evaluation of the Criterion Measures Approach for predicting the effects of noise on performance and massed versus distributed practice. Another was the evaluation of the Abilities Requirements Approach to predict the results of experimental findings involving the effects of (1) alcohol, and (2) signal types on task performance. These results are described in Chapters 9 and 12, respectively.

If the number of studies used to make these comparisons were increased, it would become necessary to develop computerized retrieval programs to facilitate these efforts. Figure 8.2 illustrates how a retrieval cycle can be computerized. Here, it should be noted, the user has the option of receiving printouts of citations or abstracts.

LESSONS LEARNED There were a number of lessons learned and conclusions drawn from this experience with developing a Human Performance Data Base (Korotkin, Krebs, & Darby, 1972). It was

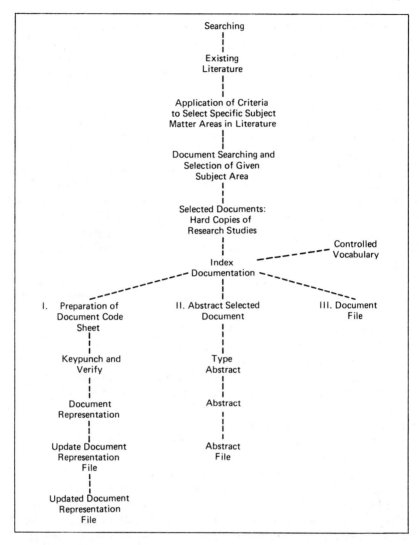

Figure 8.1   Input cycle. Revised with permission from Korotkin, A. L., & Chambers, A. N. *A human performance data base for evaluation of taxonomies.* Paper presented at the American Psychological Association Convention, Washington, D.C., 1969.

concluded that, in such data base development efforts, the following issues need to be addressed:

1. *Potential users and their problem areas.* Who are the potential users and what are their areas of application?
2. *Kind and amount of information.* What types of information do

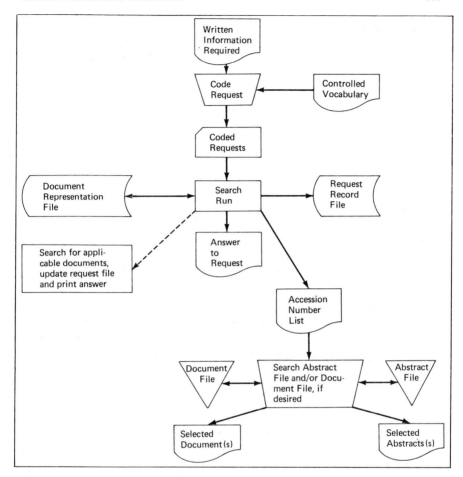

Figure 8.2 Output cycle. Reproduced with permission from Korotkin, A. L., & Chambers, A. N. *A human performance data base for evaluation of taxonomies.* Paper presented at the American Psychological Association Convention, Washington, D.C., 1969.

the users need to solve their problems? At what level of detail and in what format is this information most useful?
3. *Input–output considerations.* How will the users access the data base and in what ways will the data be delivered?
4. *Requirements for modification and refinement of the data base.* How does the data base need to be changed to match changing user requirements and changes in the available information?

Although the data base was developed as an evaluation tool, it may also be useful in its own right. For example, it might provide information that would enable a user to determine fully the relevance of a particular study to his or her own needs. Or, in the applied domain, the data base might serve as a primary source of decisions concerning selection, training, and equipment design. A refined, hierarchical descriptor system could make information for all purposes more explicit and systematic.

In order to produce an explicit and systematic indexing system, categories of variables that should be taken into account in the prediction of human performance must be identified. Theoretically, we should be able to identify in each study what variables are operating and which of them have a significant effect on performance. In practice, of course, the identification of all these variables in a research report is extremely difficult, but this does not negate the logic of the approach. The reasons that this approach may be possible are as follows:

1. In any given subject matter category, there may be only a few independent variables operating at a significant level to account for the results of any given study. Thus, not every element that could possibly function as a variable in a given situation needs to be indexed for a given study.
2. The ambiguities in interpreting research reports have not developed overnight; therefore, one should not expect to eliminate them overnight. However, if we are more fully aware of what is required in the way of information and standardization to make comparisons across studies meaningful, progress will be made toward correcting the situation.
3. The theoretical formulations underlying human behavior are improving, so that the logic of the classificatory system can be revised continually to better reflect our knowledge of the functional relationships between variables within and among categories.

Thus, the classificatory system for the data base should not only include the categories of independent, intervening and dependent variables that account for human performance, but it should also begin to consider what is known and needs to be known about their functional relationships. Qualitative classification of variables within these categories is only one place to begin. What is eventually needed, of course, is a model of the quantitative functional relationships among these variables. Because the state of the art is still primarily at the qualitative level, however, let us examine in greater detail how a qualitative hierarchical indexing system might aid in moving in the direction of a quantitative functional model of human performance.

If one wishes to refine classificatory systems beyond the descriptive level, many additional problems must be faced. The first of these is the derivation of variables within each of the classes that can be identified, manipulated, and measured in an unambiguous and consistent manner. Second, there are similar problems with respect to establishing relationships between variables in the independent, intervening, and dependent classes. Third, there is a vast compounding of the manipulation and measurement problems when we combine variables to account for more "real life" situations. Fourth, there are problems arising from gaps in the research literature. Either research is unavailable in certain areas, or it is reported in a fashion that is difficult to interpret or compare with other studies.

AN EXAMPLE   Assuming that a reasonably large number of studies is indexed, it should be possible to sort and to compare studies literally on a variable by variable basis, using suitable computerized retrieval programs. For example, it might be discovered that the reason why some reviewers conclude that noise has no long-term effects on performance, whereas others conclude that it has such effects, might be due to the types of tasks employed, or to the duration of the exposure, or to some other basis that might be very difficult for a reviewer to discern. If the development of even a sample indexing system of this type is successful, we might be encouraged to extend it from a technique for comparing research studies for the derivation of generalizations, to a technique for matching conditions in applied problem areas (such as human engineering) with research studies, thus assessing the relevance of research to the solution of problems.

An example of a hierarchical vocabulary that would be appropriate for a human performance data base was provided by Chambers (1973), under the Taxonomy Project. Table 8.2 illustrates this indexing system for independent variables, showing in detail how one particular variable, "Physical Environment," might be broken down into subclasses. For example, let us say that an indexer was indexing a study in which "noise" was the only independent variable. The indexer would use 4.1.8 and then proceed to level 4 (4.1.8.1) to indicate the "Medium" (atmosphere, hydrosphere, or communication equipment). Next the "Range" (4.1.8.2) would be indicated, and then the units in which the range is expressed (Column 2, Cycles per second). The indexer would continue in a similar manner through all the subclasses, identifying all appropriate subject matter codes and their associated units and measures. The indexer would also indicate through use of the treatment descriptors whether the subject matter had been treated as a variable, controlled in some fashion, or was ignored or unknown.

The advantage of this approach is that the user can look systematically for all possible bases of comparison across studies that might account for similarities and differences in results. Chambers (1973) constructed a set of provisional classifications of a wide variety of human performance descriptors in the form of a controlled vocabulary similar to the format in Table 8.2. These include descriptors for human responses, performance capabilities, operations, equipment and materials, personnel, physical environments, social environments, selection, training, human physical moderators or mediators, physiological moderators, and psychological moderators.

OTHER EFFORTS TO DEVELOP HUMAN PERFORMANCE DATA BASES

There have been several other efforts to develop human performance data bases (e.g., Reed & Wise, 1967; Swain, 1970; Swain & Guttman, 1980). Blanchard (1973), in particular, developed detailed requirements and specifications for a data bank in support of a program to improve methods for quantifying human performance reliability. There were several components to this effort. The first was a survey of user needs for such data to produce a list of user requirements. Findings included the need for (1) valid and generalizable data, (2) ease of retrievability of data, (3) emphasis on design trade-off analysis (the relative costs of various design options), and (4) a format that would be equally responsive to users with behavioral or engineering backgrounds. The second component was a determination of input data requirements. The following general model for input data requirements was identified: (1) data on both time and accuracy should be presented as continuous distributions; (2) data should be available at the task element level of specificity; (3) data should be available on both discrete and continuous behaviors; (4) data on equipment reliability should be available; and (5) information on external system operational requirements should be provided. If the data base includes maintenance as well as operational activities, then time-based performance data, both corrective and preventive, should be included on the maintenance activities.

In addition to the general model input requirements, there were unique model requirements, such as for micro-level behavioral data in some instances. Using both of the above sets of requirements, a conceptual model of the data base was developed. This process included the consideration of the need for long-range development of such a system to allow for evolution. For example, it was felt that several different data bases, integrated with one another, would eventually be needed.

Out of the above conceptual process, specifications for implementation of the data base were developed. The data base specifications included the following seven components:

1. Procedures for Using the Data Base
2. Behavioral Master Index (pertaining to human behavior)
3. Engineering Master Index (pertaining to equipment function)
4. Behavioral Slave Index
5. Engineering Slave Index
6. Data Insert
7. References

A preliminary three-order classification scheme was developed to form the basis of the Behavioral and Engineering Master Indexes. The Slave Indexes relate directly to the Master Indexes and are the primary mechanism for accessing the data. A sample of part of the Behavioral Master Index is presented in Table 8.3. The first level in this classificatory system consists of generic categories of human behavior (Perceptual Processes 1.0, Perceptual–Motor Processes 2.0). The second level categories represent a wide variety of human capabilities (Visual 1.1., Auditory 1.2, Tactile 1.3). The third level consists of relatively specific behaviors (Detect presence of one or more stimuli 1.1.1). Each Slave Index lists all the studies that fall within each third-order category.

A sample of part of the Engineering Master Index is displayed in Table 8.4. This index pertains to behaviors performed by machines, whereas the former index pertains to those performed by people. The first order of equipment categories in the Engineering Master Index consists of major types of equipment (Visual Displays 1.0, Auditory Displays 2.0). The second order consists of more specific types of equipment that exist within each major category (Indicator Lights 1.1, Scalar Displays 1.4). The third order consists generally of parts of each type of equipment (Single Status 1.1.1, Multiple Status 1.1.2).

The basic storage and retrieval unit is the Data Insert, which includes index and coding information, the data source, the important

TABLE 8.3

Behavioral Master Index (Sample)[a]

1.0 Perceptual Processes
    1.1 Visual
        1.1.1 Detect presence of one or more stimuli (radar target, indicator light)
        1.1.2 Detect movement of one or more stimuli
        1.1.3 Detect change in basic stimulus presentation (status, alpha–numeric)
        1.1.4 Detect variation in stimulus characteristics (color, shape, size)
        1.1.5 Recognize stimulus characteristics and identify or classify stimulus types
        1.1.6 Locate stimulus in a field containing other stimuli of varying similarity
        1.1.7 Discriminate two or more stimuli on basis of relative characteristics
        1.1.8 Read materials and obtain information or instructions
        1.1.9 Read displays and obtain alpha–numeric information
    1.2 Auditory
        1.2.1 Detect presence of one or more aural stimuli (sonar signal, aural alarm)
        1.2.2 Recognize stimulus characteristics and identify or classify stimulus types
        1.2.3 Detect a variation or change in stimulus characteristics (pitch, amplitude, harmonics)
        1.2.4 Discriminate two or more stimuli on basis of relative characteristics (pitch, amplitude, quality, harmonics)
    1.3 Tactile
        1.3.1 Identify control(s) by discriminating among various shape codes
2.0 Perceptual–Motor Processes
    2.1 Discrete
        2.1.1 Activate or set one or more controls according to displayed information
        2.1.2 Mark position of object(s) on a device or surface according to displayed information
        2.1.3 Manipulate control to position one or more stimuli at a discrete location according to displayed information
        2.1.4 Change stimulus characteristics by manipulating control (gain, brightness)
        2.1.5 Introduce new stimuli or remove old stimuli by manipulating control (information display updating)
    2.2 Continuous
        2.2.1 Adjust control(s) to maintain coincidence of two moving stimuli (pursuit tracking)
        2.2.2 Adjust control(s) to compensate for deviation in one moving stimulus (compensatory tracking)
        2.2.3 Input data or information by manipulating one or more controls (alpha–numeric keyboard)
        2.2.4 Align two or more stimulus presentations to achieve balanced or steady-state condition
        2.2.5 Regulate the level or rate of a process, event, or output according to displayed information

[a]Reproduced with permission from Blanchard, R. E. *Requirements, concept and specification for a Navy human performance data store* (Report No. 102-2). Santa Monica, CA: Behaviormetrics, April 1973, pp. 81–82.

TABLE 8.4

Engineering Master Index (Sample)[a]

1.0 Visual Displays
   1.1 Indicator Lights (transilluminated)
      1.1.1 Single status
      1.1.2 Multiple status
      1.1.3 Lighted pushbutton displays
   1.2 Sequential Access Digital Readouts
      1.2.1 Electromechanical drum counters
      1.2.2 Flag counters
   1.3 Random Access Digital Readouts
      1.3.1 Segmented matrices
      1.3.2 Cold cathode tubes
      1.3.3 Edge-lighted plates
      1.3.4 Projection readouts
      1.3.5 Back-lighted belt displays
      1.3.6 Light-emitting diode displays (LED)
   1.4 Scalar Displays (dials, gauges, meters)
      1.4.1 Moving pointer, fixed scale
      1.4.2 Fixed pointer, moving scale
   1.5 CRT Spatial Relation Displays
      1.5.1 Radar displays
      1.5.2 Sonar displays
   1.6 CRT Alphanumeric–Pictorial Displays
      1.6.1 Computer output displays
      1.6.2 Television output displays (CCTV)
      1.6.3 Infrared sensor displays
      1.6.4 Low-light-level TV displays
   1.7 CRT Electronic Parameter Displays
      1.7.1 Waveform displays
      1.7.2 Bargraph displays
      1.7.3 Analog computer output displays
   1.8 Status Displays
      1.8.1 Plot boards
      1.8.2 Map displays
      1.8.3 Projected displays (static or dynamic)
      1.8.4 Matrix boards
      1.8.5 Large screen displays
   1.9 Hard Copy Readout Displays
      1.9.1 Printers
      1.9.2 Recorders
      1.9.3 Plotters
2.0 Auditory Displays
   2.1 Electromechanical
      2.1.1 Bells
      2.1.2 Buzzers
      2.1.3 Horns
      2.1.4 Sirens
   2.2 Electronic
      2.2.1 Electronic tones and signals
      2.2.2 Recorded signals directions (tape)

---

[a]Reproduced with permission from Blanchard, R. E. *Requirements, concept and specification for a Navy human performance data store* (Report No. 102-2). Santa Monica, CA: Behaviormetrics, April 1973, pp. 89–90.

DIN	93	E/ST	GRB/AAW	Variable Class	TS	Data Source	S-3	DB	2-1
DIN Ref.	R-65	Related Refs.	R-22, 54, 79			Related DIN's	89, 167		
BSI Code	1.1.1	Detect presence of one or more stimuli		ESI Code	1.5.1	CRT Radar Displays			
Behavior				Device					
Monitor radar scope and detect aircraft signal at unknown position.				PPI-Scan Radar					

Data Source Description

AAW laboratory simulation of an enemy raid on a
destroyer to determine detection capability as a function of tracking load.
Sixteen subjects performed 2-hour tasks on each of 5 continuous days. One
new target occurred every two minutes and one old target disappeared every
two minutes, on the average (at destroyer's position). Subjects were required
to detect new targets while simultaneously tracking old targets. Target presentations were presented by computer.

Operational Factors

Mission: Aircraft surveillance for airborne intercept
Enemy Mission: Penetration with stand-off weapons (hypothetical)
Threat Level: None
Countermeasures: None

Equipment Factors

Study used actual CIC equipment as installed on board Type DD962 class
destroyers. PPI scope, 7 inches in diameter with P-7 phosphor. Gain and
bias setting performed by operator. Equipment layout exact replica of
DD CIC space

Task Factors

Individual scope monitoring; variable load stress from low to near saturation
in terms of target tracks; continuous 2-hour task duration; load considered
slightly stressful but does not approximate combat stress levels; task complexity considered low; high fidelity stimulus characteristics

Personnel Factors

Subjects were graduates of RD Class C school with 12 to 24 months fleet
experience. Subjects selected randomly from 21 destroyer RO's. Age range:
21–26. Time-in-service: 18–36 months. Motivation level: moderate to high.

Environmental Factors

Standard ambient light, noise, and temperature conditions in CIC spaces.
Ship motion, vibration and sea state effects not represented.

Figure 8.3 Example of Data Insert for dynamic simulation data. Reproduced with
permission from Blanchard, R. E. *Requirements, concept and specification for a Navy
human performance data store* (Report No. 102-2). Santa Monica, CA: Behaviormetrics,
April 1973, pp. 103–104.

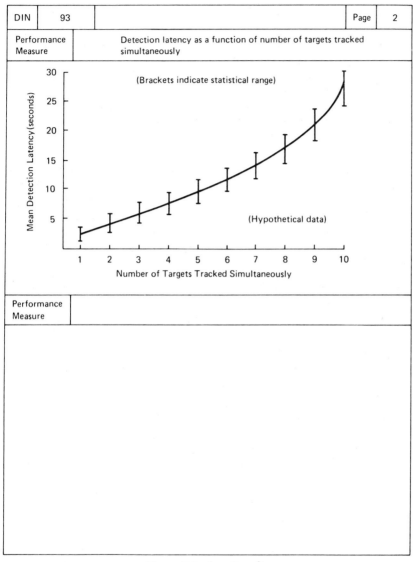

Figure 8.3 (*continued*)

performance shaping factors, and graphics presenting the findings. An example is shown in Figure 8.3.

Blanchard (1973) defined the "References" component as including all studies abstracted in the form of Data Inserts. After assigning numerical codes to the bibliographic entries, they are ordered sequentially.

Blanchard (1973) summarized the access process for this human performance data base as follows:

> Access to specific data (one or more Data Inserts) is accomplished by (1) selecting the desired first, second, or third order classification number from the appropriate Master Index; (2) advancing to the appropriate Slave Index and scanning the list of available Data Inserts for relevant studies and data. These data insert numbers would be used to interrogate the store and retrieve the desired information.

In 1963, the Aerospace Medical Research Laboratories and the National Aeronautic and Space Administration initiated an effort to explore and develop techniques for the efficient handling and processing of human factors task data. The overall purpose was to help ensure early human factors input into the design of aerospace systems. The goals of this effort were as follows (Reed & Wise, 1967, pp. 183–184):

1. *Improve communications:* provide a means for having information where and when it is needed
2. *Reduce redundancy:* alleviate the problem of duplication of data through a continuous exchange of information within a system development team and between systems
3. *Improve accessibility:* provide a common store from which the user may retrieve selectively
4. *Provide dynamic data:* provide a data base that is current and frequently updated
5. *Provide basic tools:* provide the user with a pool of analytic and simulation tools
6. *Provide standardization:* provide standardization of the language and procedures

After the formulation of goals, the next step performed was the development of a detailed functional flow diagram for the human factors task data handling system. This diagram was intended to facilitate the identification of areas requiring research (see Figure 8.4). Based on this functional flow analysis, the following five areas of needed research were identified:

1. Formulation of an indexing–classification scheme for human factors task data
2. Investigation of vocabulary and thesaurus techniques for control of storage and retrieval
3. Experimentation on computer storage, updating, and retrieval techniques to task data

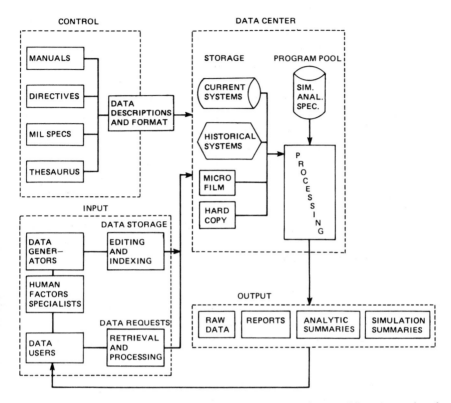

Figure 8.4 Human factors task data handling system: Functional flow. Reproduced with permission from Reed, L. E., & Wise, F. H. Report on automated human factors task data handling research. *Human Factors*, 1967, *9*, 181–186.

4. Evaluation of the applications of analysis and simulation techniques
5. Experimentation on current awareness notification

A thesaurus for the system was prepared (Oller, 1968). This thesaurus represents the introduction of a controlled vocabulary for accessing the data in the system. Also included were rules for regulating the use of the terms. In addition, users' and controllers' operating guides were prepared (Reardon, 1968).

IMPORTANCE OF DATA BASES

Based on our review, we conclude that data bases in science are important for a number of reasons. They represent the accumulation of knowledge; they document what has been studied; they make available findings of individual studies as well as findings for similar studies; they allow further hypotheses to be drawn; they allow conclusions to be reached; and they highlight gaps in the literature. The subject of data bases is tied closely to the subject of taxonomy. On the one hand, classification assists in the organization, indexing, storage, and retrieval of information in the data base. On the other hand, the data base can be used to evaluate alternate provisional classificatory approaches; the ability to do so is dependent on the extent and quality of the data in the data base. Gaps in the literature will mean gaps in the data base, in which case the data base cannot be used to evaluate certain parts of the classificatory scheme. Poor quality of the research literature, if it goes undetected, presents an even greater problem because it could cause an erroneous evaluation of a provisional classificatory approach. For example, a scheme might predict certain outcomes for certain classes of tasks, and the data base might not support this prediction only because it contains faulty research data.

There has been increasing interest in developing human performance data bases. Considerable conceptual effort has been directed at the problem. Thus far, however, most of the efforts have stopped short of a full scale implementation of a human performance data base.

We have reviewed efforts and needs in this area because they seem crucial to fully developed efforts in evaluating task classificatory systems. The next chapter describes some rudimentary attempts to utilize the limited data base developed within the Taxonomy Project. For various reasons, the data base efforts carried out under the Taxonomy Project had to be limited. However, our current evaluation is that this effort was useful in laying out some of the requirements of such data bases, and some methods for developing them in areas of human performance. These efforts also allowed us to specify how such data bases might be used to evaluate the utility of task taxonomies in enhancing our predictions of human performance.

References

Blanchard, R. E. *Requirements, concept and specification for a Navy human performance data store* (Report No. 102-2). Santa Monica, CA: Behaviormetrics, April 1973.

Bryant, F. B., & Wortman, P. M. Secondary analysis: The case for data archives. *American Psychologist*, 1978, *33*, 381–387.

Burns, T. The comparative study of organizations. In V. H. Vroom (Ed.), *Organizational design and research; methods of organizational research*. Pittsburgh, PA: University of Pittsburgh Press, 1967.

Campbell, D. T., & Erlebacher, A. E. How regression artifacts in quasi-experimental evaluations can mistakenly make compensatory education look harmful. In J. Hellmuth, (Ed.), *Compensatory education: A national debate* (Vol. 3). New York: Brunner/Mazel, 1970.

Chambers, A. N. Development of a taxonomy of human performance: A heuristic model for the development of classification systems. *JSAS Catalog of Selected Documents in Psychology*, 1973, *3*, 24–25 (Ms. No. 320).

Chambers, A. N., Krebs, M. J., & Shaffer, E. J. *Development of a taxonomy of human performance: A document and information indexing and retrieval approach to classification*. Project report. Washington, DC: American Institutes for Research, October 1969.

Chun, K., Cobb, S., & French, J. R. P., Jr. *Measures for psychological assessment: A guide to 3,000 original sources and their applications*. Ann Arbor, MI: Institute for Social Research, University of Michigan, 1975.

Chun, K., Cobb, S., French, J. R. P., Jr., & Seashore, S. Storage and retrieval of information on psychological measures. *American Psychologist*, 1973, *23*, 592–599.

Deutsch, K. W. The impact of complex data bases on the social sciences. In R. L. Bisco (Ed.), *Data bases, computers, and the social sciences*. New York: Wiley (Interscience), 1970.

Elashoff, J. D., & Snow, R. E. (Eds.). *Pygmalion reconsidered*. Worthington, OH: Jones, 1971.

Fleishman, E. A. Toward a taxonomy of human performance. *American Psychologist*, 1975, *30*(12), 1127–1149.

Fleishman, E. A., Kinkade, R. G., & Chambers, A. N. Development of a taxonomy of human performance: A review of the first year's progress. *JSAS Catalog of Selected Documents in Psychology*, 1972, *2*, 39 (Ms. No. 111).

Glass, G. V. Primary, secondary and meta-analysis of research. *Educational Researcher*, 1976, *5*(10), 3–8.

Glass, G. V. Integrating findings: The meta-analysis of research. In L. S. Shulman (Ed.), *Review of research in education* (Vol. 5). Itasca, IL: Peacock, 1977.

Glass, G. V., McGaw, B., & Smith, M. L. *Meta-analysis in social research*. Beverly Hills, CA: Sage, 1981.

Glass, G. V., & Smith, M. L. Meta-analysis of research on class size and achievement. *Educational Evaluation and Policy Analysis*, 1979, *1*, 2–16.

Hunter, J. E., Schmidt, F. L., & Jackson, G. B. *Meta-analysis: Cumulating research findings across studies*. Beverly Hills, CA: Sage, 1982.

Hyman, H. H. *Secondary analysis of sample surveys: Principles, procedures, and potentialities*. New York: Wiley, 1972.

Korotkin, A. L., & Chambers, A. N. *A human performance data base for evaluation of taxonomies*. Paper presented at the American Psychological Association Convention, Washington, D.C., 1969.

Korotkin, A. L., Krebs, M. J., & Darby, C. A. Development of a human performance data base. In E. A. Fleishman, R. G. Kinkade, & A. N. Chambers (Eds.), *Development of a taxonomy of human performance: A review of the first year's progress*. *JSAS Catalog of Selected Documents in Psychology*, 1972, *2*, 39 (Ms. No. 111).

Lancaster, F. W. *Vocabulary control for information retrieval*. Washington, DC: Information Resources Press, 1972.

Licklider, J. C. R. *Libraries of the future*. Cambridge, MA: MIT Press, 1965.

Light, R. J., & Smith, P. Accumulating evidence: Procedures for resolving contradictions among different research studies. *Harvard Educational Review*, 1971, *41*, 429–471.

Miller, W. E. The less obvious functions of archiving survey research data. *American Behavioral Scientist*, 1976, *19*, 409–418.

Mosteller, F. M., & Moynihan, D. P. (Eds.). *On equality of educational opportunity*. New York: Vintage Books, 1972.

Oller, R. G. *Human factors data thesaurus* (AMRL-TR-67-211). Wright-Patterson Air Force Base, OH: Aerospace Medical Research Laboratories, March 1968.

Prywes, N. S., & Smith, D. P. Organization of information. In C. A. Cuadra & A. W. Luke (Eds.), *Annual Review of Information Science and Technology* (Vol. 7). Washington, DC: American Society for Information Science, 1972, 103–158.

Ramsey-Klee, D. M., Richman, V., & Wiederhold, G. *Feasibility of and design parameters for a computer-based attitudinal research information system* (NPRDC TR 76-9). San Diego: Navy Personnel Research and Development Center, August 1975.

Reardon, S. E. *Computerized human factors task data handling techniques. User's and controller's operating guides* (AMRL-TR-67-226). Wright-Patterson Air Force Base, OH: Aerospace Medical Research Laboratories, March 1968.

Reed, L. E., & Wise, F. H. Report on automated human factors task data handling research. *Human Factors*, 1967, *9*, 181–186.

Robinson, J. P. Awakening a "sleeper" variable via secondary analysis. *Public Opinion Quarterly*, 1975, *39*, 411–412.

Salton, G. *Dynamic information and library processing*. Englewood Cliffs, NJ: Prentice-Hall, 1975.

Soergel, D. *Indexing languages and thesauri: Construction and maintenance*. Los Angeles: Melville, 1974.

Swain, A. D. Development of a human error-rate data bank (SC-R-70-4286), Albuquerque, NM: Sandia Laboratories, July 1970.

Swain, A. D. & Guttman, H. E. *Handbook of human reliability analysis with emphasis on nuclear power plant operations* (SAND 80-0200/NUREG CR-1278). Albuquerque, NM: Sandia Laboratories, October 1980.

Uprichard, E. M. The national clearinghouse for alcohol information. In P. Zunde (Ed.), *Information utilities proceedings of the 37th ASIS annual meeting* (Vol. 2). Washington, DC: American Society for Information Science, 1974.

Van Cott, H. P., & Kinkade, R. G. Human simulation applied to the functional design of information systems. *Human Factors*, 1968, *10*, 211–216.

Wiederhold, G. *Database design*. New York: McGraw-Hill, 1977.

CHAPTER 9

The Criterion Measures Approach

In earlier chapters, we have discussed how different conceptions of human tasks, and different purposes of classification, can lead to different kinds of task classificatory systems. The state of the art was such that there was no compelling reason to select one system over another for more intensive development. Consequently, in the Taxonomy Project the decision was made to develop several alternative systems, and, insofar as possible, to evaluate their utility for a variety of basic and applied purposes.

Chapters 9 through 13 describe, in turn, five different approaches that received special attention in the Taxonomy Project (Fleishman & Stephenson, 1972). These are called the Criterion Measures, Information-Theoretic, Task Strategies, Ability Requirements, and Task Characteristics approaches. Research on a number of them continues today, and these chapters emphasize their current status.

Ideally, the kind of data base development described in the preceding chapter should serve as a basis for evaluating the comparative utility of each system for organizing human performance information in ways that improve our predictions of human task performance. The first approach we describe, the *Criterion Measures Approach*, makes some use of the limited data base developed and discussed in Chapter 8. This chapter provides one prototype of how existing performance data can be utilized to evaluate a taxonomic system and illustrates some of the problems encountered in human performance data base development and application.

The Classificatory System

The Criterion Measures Approach, a term adopted in the Taxonomy Project (Teichner & Whitehead, 1973; Fleishman, Teichner, &

Stephenson, 1972), falls at the interface of two of the conceptual approaches to task classification described in Chapter 3. Thus, the approach emphasizes *behavior requirements*, in focusing upon a set of human functions required for task performance; consequently the scheme was categorized as such in Chapter 6. However, the approach also emphasizes *behavior description*, in operationalizing these functions in terms of specific dependent response measures.

The initial formulation, termed an *information approach*, was presented by Teichner and Olson (1969). The contention of the approach is that if a system is diagramed as a set of interacting person–machine components, "we can think of information or data as being transmitted between components and as being operated upon or processed within components" (Teichner & Olson, 1969, p. 4). From that conceptualization, a *task* is defined as the transfer of information between components and a *process* as the operation performed on the information within a component. The information transfer between the person and machine components of the system identifies four major classes of tasks: machine–person, person–machine, machine–machine, and person–person.

The task-descriptive terms derived are applicable to these four major classes of tasks and can be applied regardless of the level of analysis and the class of task. These terms represent different kinds of information transfer. Specifically, Teichner and Olson (1969, 1971), held that each of the four classes of tasks is characterized by one of four functionally different types of information transfer: *searching*, the sequential scanning of one or more signal sources; *coding*, the naming of a detected signal; *switching*, the occurrence of a discrete action that causes a state change in the next system component; and *tracking*, the alignment of a response with a changing input. The coding category is divided into the three subcategories of *simple*, *group*, and *successive* coding. Table 9.1 presents the detailed descriptions developed for the six categories.

A unique aspect of this taxonomic approach is that the task activities described above were defined by dependent measures. As shown in Table 9.1, the descriptive measures used were *probability of detection* for searching, *reaction time* for switching, *percent correct* for coding, and *time on target* for tracking. Teichner and Olson (1971) provided a modification to the basic scheme by adding a fifth task activity called *sensing*. This activity referred to the *sensory probability of detection*. The procedure of defining task activities in terms of dependent measures permits actual data in the literature to be incorporated into the classificatory system with relative ease. This tax-

TABLE 9.1

The Criterion Measures Classificatory System[a]

I. *Searching:*	The exposure of a sensor to positionally different signal sources or to one source at different times. Searching is receptor orienting or signal seeking. It may be *simple orienting*, as when the ears are positioned to enhance reception of a novel stimulus, or *successive orienting*, also called scanning. Examples are monitoring, reconnaissance, and target seeking.
Descriptive Measure:	Probability of detection
II. *Switching:*	A discrete action that changes the state of the next component in a system. Examples are turning anything on or off, go or no-go, or, in general, making a discrete, selective action involving categorical choices. In a system sense, switching should be described as the time between the initiation of the signal and the completion of the switching response. However, this time will depend critically on the characteristics of the switch used. For example, movement time will be longer, the longer the required switch movement or the greater the required torque. Because these factors cannot be anticipated, they must be estimated from specific analysis of the system of interest. Aside from these factors, switching responses vary in time from the initiation of the signal to the initiation of the response, that is, in reaction time.
Descriptive Measure:	Reaction time or latency
III. *Coding:*	The naming or identifying of a detected signal. A. *Simple coding* involves the attachment of a name to characteristics of a stimulus, such as color, pitch, direction of movement, or position. B. *Group coding* refers to the grouping of stimulus characteristics into a single classification, such as silverware for knives, spoons and forks. C. *Successive coding* implies a syntax or set of rules used to relate or transform names or codes, such as translating language and computing.
Descriptive Measure:	The percent of correctly coded responses or some equivalent, such as the percent of error
IV. *Tracking:*	Alignment of a response with a changing input. Tracking may be pursuit or compensatory, as conventionally used. Examples of tracking are steering, aiming, walking, and tuning. The measure used will be the percentage decrement in time on target. The use of a relative measure is dictated by the fact that actual time on target will depend on target dimensions and, therefore, must be determined uniquely.
Descriptive Measure:	Time on target or integrated error

[a]Adapted with permission from Teichner, W. H. & Whitehead, J. Development of a taxonomy of human performance: Evaluation of a task classification system for generalizing findings from a data base. (American Institutes for Research Tech. Rep.) *JSAS Catalog of Selected Documents in Psychology*, 1973, 2, 26–27 (Ms. No. 324).

onomic approach has been labeled the Criterion Measures Approach because of the use of dependent measures to operationally define the task activities.

Evaluation of the System

Chapter 8 described the development of a human performance data base for evaluating the effectiveness of provisional taxonomic systems in integrating the experimental literature. The basic notion, which we stressed in earlier chapters, is that a taxonomic system should be translatable into an indexing system. This indexing system should allow entry into the available literature in such a way that the tasks used in a large variety of studies can be classified (Chambers, 1973; Korotkin & Chambers, 1973). The data pertaining to these task categories then can be examined for consistencies between and within classes. Do alternative systems improve the kinds of generalizations that can be made about the performance effects of certain variables of interest? If such systems could be developed, especially if they are made computer compatible, there would be important implications for retrieving principles of human performance applicable to current and future tasks.

In this chapter, we present findings from an attempt to apply the Criterion Measures classificatory system to a portion of the existing literature on learning and environmental effects contained in the human performance data base developed in the Taxonomy Project (Teichner & Whitehead, 1973). The objective was to see if, by organizing the literature into the system's categories, it would be possible to ascertain functional relationships between certain independent variables and task performance. It is important to keep in mind that the success of such an attempt was dependent not only upon the usefulness of the classificatory system, but also upon the relevance and quality of the research literature in the data base. The two learning variables investigated were the effects of "different schedules of practice" and "knowledge of results" (KOR); the environmental factor investigated was "the effect of different noise intensities on performance."

The Criterion Measures Approach used by Teichner and Olson seemed particularly well suited to this kind of evaluation because it (1) provided a small set of operationally defined task classes; (2) required a minimum of qualifications needed to classify the tasks used in the literature; and (3) was designed for expression in terms of relationships between variables known to have received considerable study. It was assumed that further subclassifications would develop empirically from attempts to collate the results of studies into a single class. Those studies within a class that could be expressed by the same relationships would be defined as the same in kind, whereas those that required different relationships would be defined as a different subclass. The Criterion Measures Approach would be useful, when applied to previously unclassified sets of data from different studies, if it can be shown that data falling into the same category depend upon the same independent variables.

Teichner and Whitehead (1973) describe some conditions required to examine these data. To use the different studies in the literature for this purpose, it is necessary to assume that nonsystematic differences between studies at common levels of an independent variable are due to random error. With this assumption, one may average across studies in an attempt to find a systematic relationship between averaged dependent measures and the levels of the independent variable at which the averages fall. Relationships should be revealed as a result of these procedures if the following conditions hold:

1. The independent variable has a systematic effect.
2. The independent variable can be or is dimensionalized on a quantitative scale having at least rank order properties.
3. The descriptions of the independent and dependent variables are precise enough for interstudy comparisons.
4. The test or experimental procedures are an adequate basis for drawing conclusions from the results.

Even if none of the above conditions holds except the third one, the application of a useful classificatory system to a set of performance results still provides important information. If a sufficient number of studies is available for use, and if those studies extend over a reasonable range of the independent variable, classification indicates whether the variable has a systematic effect and, possibly, the nature of that effect. If no functional relationship is determined, it provides an organization of the data with which one can determine where the weight of evidence falls. At the very least, if the range of the studies is very limited, there are indications of where more research is needed.

THE LITERATURE BASE

The data to which we applied the classificatory system were drawn from three sets of experimental reports included in the human performance data base developed in the Taxonomy Project. Specifically, the reports included data from studies of (1) the effects of massed and distributed practice carried out between 1914 and 1968 inclusive (n = 87); (2) the effects of knowledge of results carried out between 1938 and 1968 inclusive (n = 148); and (3) the effects of acoustic noise carried out between 1929 and 1968 inclusive (n = 70).

Each study was evaluated for both sufficient precision of description of tasks and procedures and experimental adequacy. Sensory studies and studies involving complex tasks that were combinations of categories were not used. Finally, because the experimental conditions varied widely among studies with respect to other factors, no study was accepted unless it had a control group; it was then possible to make decisions about the effect of the experimental conditions that were used.

This "quality filter" phase of the study cannot be overemphasized. One alternative approach was to index all studies, as is done in many current bibliographic and human engineering data files. However, it became readily apparent that quality control of studies was essential to afford any meaningful test of this taxonomic system.

APPLICATION OF THE CLASSIFICATORY SYSTEM TO
STUDIES OF THE EFFECTS OF PRACTICE SCHEDULES

The studies of practice schedules are those in the learning literature that compare different distributed practice schedules with continuous (massed) practice over an equivalent practice period. Of the 87 studies on massed versus distributed practice examined by Teichner and Whitehead (1973), 35 were eliminated based upon the criteria described earlier. The studies varied widely in the amount of practice given and in the number of data points provided for the different stages of learning for each practice condition (massed or distributed). The measure used was the arithmetic mean, which was calculated for the last four trials of each condition, regardless of the number of trials employed. All further discussion, except where noted otherwise, is based upon such values.

As a first step, Teichner and Whitehead coded the results according to whether distributed practice produced an increment (+) in performance, no effect (0), or a decrement (−), when compared to the massed control condition of the experiment. Because many studies had more than one distributed condition, a total of 111 experimental comparisons was available. Figure 9.1 presents some of the results.

The figure shows that most of the tasks were classified as the simple coding type. Most of these were studies of verbal learning. No

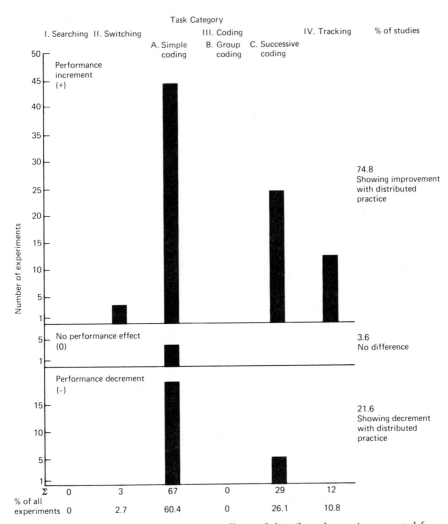

Figure 9.1 Distribution of qualitative effects of distributed practice reported for 111 experimental comparisons. Adapted with permission from Teichner, W. H., and Whitehead, J. Development of a taxonomy of human performance: Evaluation of a task classification system for generalizing findings from a data base (American Institutes for Research Tech. Rep.). *JSAS Catalog of Selected Documents in Psychology*, 1973, 2, 26–27 (Ms. No. 324).

studies fell into either searching or group coding and only 2.7% were categorized as switching. For the three remaining task categories, the weight of the evidence favors distributed practice as the learning condition that produces improved performance.

Figure 9.1 does not reveal whether or not the instances of no effect and of decrement are the result of poor choices of comparison between massed and distributed conditions. Thus, if the function of distributed practice reaches a limit, and if the control and experimental groups were both selected near the limit, no difference might occur. Similarly, it is possible that beyond some limit of intertrial interval, destribution of practive might be decremental compared to

Because the time between trials is a dimensionalized variable, it was desirable to analyze the data in a way that tests the classificatory system's ability to show trends and, hopefully, functional relations. To achieve this, several steps had to be taken. First, studies not providing quantitative data were eliminated from further analysis. For the remaining studies, a common metric had to be developed to allow plotting functional relationships across studies. The common measure used was the percent change of each experimental comparison from its control condition.

It was found that studies varied markedly with regard to selection of a control condition. What was treated as a distributed practice condition in one study may have been used as a massed practice condition in another. To handle this problem, the studies were grouped into class intervals of the massed control condition (0–3 seconds, 4–7 seconds, 8–10 seconds). The few studies that used massed control conditions longer than ten seconds between trials were excluded.

EFFECTS WITH SIMPLE CODING TASKS   The results for simple coding tasks were examined in detail. The data to be grouped and averaged represented an enormous variety of confounding of the effects of different variables on performance. Nevertheless, inspection of these data showed that the weight of the evidence favored the distribution of practice schedule. Furthermore, when compared with the shortest interval of massed practice (0–3 seconds) the amount of improvement, on the average and without regard to any other consideration, increases as distribution increases.

To investigate this further, Teichner and Whitehead averaged the values across experiments at fixed conditions of distributed practice and plotted them as a function of the interval between the distributed trials. These results are shown in Figure 9.2a. The results show that,

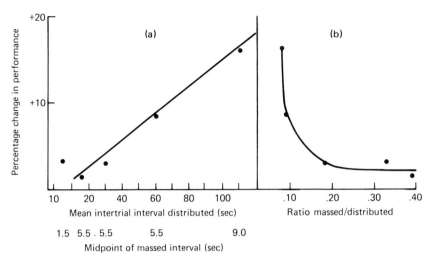

Figure 9.2 Percentage change in performance as a function of (a) mean intertrial interval and (b) ratio of intertrial intervals for 61 experimental comparisons among simple coding tasks. Reproduced with permission from Teichner, W. H., and White-head, J. Development of a taxonomy of human performance: Evaluation of a task classification system for generalizing findings from a data base (American Institutes for Research Tech. Rep.). *JSAS Catalog of Selected Documents in Psychology*, 1973, 2, 26–27 (Ms. No. 324).

on the average, the percentage improvement with practice is proportional to the length of the interval between practice trials in the distributed condition. However, the figure also shows that as the distributed interval increased in these studies, the control intervals of the massed practice trials also increased. Since this measure is increasing, it follows that the percent change can be expressed as a function of the ratio of the two (massed or distributed) conditions. Furthermore, since the change is linear, the ratio function must be nonlinear. To examine this, the values were plotted as a function of the ratio of the massed condition to the distributed condition. This is shown in Figure 9.2b. It is clear from the result that the greater the difference between the massed and distributed conditions, the greater the improvement in performance. The function is reasonably smooth and confirms the linearity suggested by Figure 9.2a. The finding that the categorization of diverse tasks falling into the simple coding category could provide such a synthesis of the data from many separate experiments is certainly encouraging.

EFFECTS WITH SUCCESSIVE CODING TASKS Teichner and White-head (1973) next examined studies classified in terms of another task category, successive coding. The studies available tended to use intertrial intervals of either 0 or 2 seconds as the massed control group condition. Trial plots of the mean percent change suggested that the relationships were not the same across studies with the different control conditions, as was the case for simple coding. Therefore, means were plotted separately for studies having a 0-second control and a 2-second control, as shown in Figure 9.3.

The relationships in Figure 9.3 for the successive coding tasks are more complex than the plot for simple coding tasks. The lines, drawn by eye, represent an attempt to express the trends that are suggested. That is, both sets of data represent an increase in percentage improvement in performance with increasing distribution, followed by a decrease in percentage improvement. The fits are reasonably good, but clearly more work is needed to determine what functions really apply. Meanwhile, the trends of Figure 9.3 may serve as hypotheses. These hypotheses are reasonable if one considers the nature of the

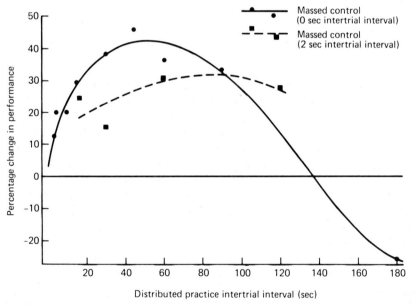

Figure 9.3 Percentage change in performance as a function of mean intertrial interval for 23 experimental comparisons among successive coding tasks. Reproduced with permission from Teichner, W. H., and Whitehead, J. Development of a taxonomy of human performance: Evaluation of a task classification system for generalizing findings from a data base (American Institutes for Research Tech. Rep.). *JSAS Catalog of Selected Documents in Psychology*, 1973, *2*, 26–27 (Ms. No. 324).

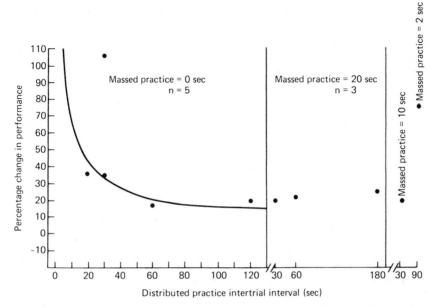

Figure 9.4 Percentage change in performance as a function of intertrial interval for tracking tasks. Reproduced with permission from Teichner, W. H., and Whitehead, J. Development of a taxonomy of human performance: Evaluation of a task classification system for generalizing findings from a data base (American Institutes for Research Tech. Rep.). *JSAS Catalog of Selected Documents in Psychology*, 1973, *2*, 26–27 (Ms. No. 324).

successive coding task. This is a task in which successive responses depend upon previous responses, so that there is a contingent probability between successive stimuli, as opposed to simple coding in which each stimulus is an independent event. Under the conditions of successive coding, short-term memory is expected to be a very important cognitive process, as postulated by Teichner and Olson (1969). The longer the intertrial interval, the greater the risk of decrement due to forgetting. On this basis, the decreasing effect of distribution would be overcome by the increasing effect of forgetting. The result would be a curve which first increased and then decreased as, in fact, is suggested in Figure 9.3.

TRACKING TASK RESULTS   The effects of the distributed practice schedules with tasks classified as tracking are shown in Figure 9.4. The data are those from ten studies that were considered to have produced acceptable quantitative results, or that used massed control groups with not more than 20 seconds between trials. The figure shows the effects of comparisons made against control conditions having zero time between trials (i.e., continuous massed practice), two seconds between trials, ten seconds between trials, and twenty seconds between trials. These four conditions are arranged from left to right according to the number of studies available for each. Teichner and Whitehead (1973) fitted the smooth line by eye to the 0-second control comparisons, ignoring the higher of the two 30-second distributed conditions on the assumption that, because it is out of the range of all other studies, it is unrepresentative.

Figure 9.4 shows that distributed practice produces better performance than massed practice under all conditions in which comparisons were made. The results also suggest that the gain expected with the more distributed condition decreases as the intertrial interval associated with it increases. The smooth line provides a general statement of that relationship. The curve suggests that the effect of increasing distributed condition intervals decreases to a limit. However, it is possible that with intervals longer than those studied, the curve might continue its drop to some point at which, relative to a smaller interval, the distributed condition would be deleterious.

Thus, the gain in performance attributable to the more distributed condition appears to be less the longer the distributed interval. To investigate this further, as well as to seek a single dimension along which to place the various studies, the data of five studies were plotted as a function of the ratio of the massed interval to the distributed interval. The results of this operation are shown in Figure 9.5, in which all five studies are ordered systematically regardless of the length of the intervals used. The function, drawn by eye, drops rapidly and flattens out between .10 and .20. Teichner and Whitehead concluded that the greater the difference between the massed and distributed intervals, the greater the gain associated with the distributed condition, until the ratio of the two approaches .20. They also conclude that after that value there is a small gain (15%) regardless of the difference, although this gain seems negligible from inspection of the tracking task curve.

These results must, of course, be qualified by the procedures that were used to develop the comparison measure. In particular, variations due to the different amounts of practice used are confounded in the measure. The means, based upon the last four practice trials, are necessarily sensitive to the steepness of the learning curve at these trials. Thus, studies that provide extensive practice are likely to show smaller differences between the massed and distributed conditions than studies with fewer trials, because the latter are more likely to be

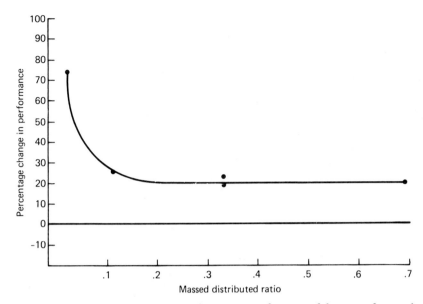

Figure 9.5   Percentage change in performance as a function of the ratio of massed to distributed intertrial intervals for tracking tasks. Reproduced with permission from Teichner, W. H., and Whitehead, J. Development of a taxonomy of human performance: Evaluation of a task classification system for generalizing findings from a data base (American Institutes for Research Tech. Rep.). *JSAS Catalog of Selected Documents in Psychology*, 1973, *2*, 26–27 (Ms. No. 324).

at a steep part of the learning curve. The use of the percentage difference equalizes this factor only in part. On the other hand, the systematic nature of the results suggests that these other considerations are not enough to obscure the effects of the intertrial interval, when the data are organized in this manner.

APPLICATION OF THE CLASSIFICATORY SYSTEM TO KNOWLEDGE OF RESULTS STUDIES

The second learning research area investigated by means of the Criterion Measures classificatory system was that of the effects of knowledge of results (KOR) on performance. Although it is generally accepted that learning reaches a higher level when the learner is provided with knowledge of results, there are difficulties with many of these studies that limit their usefulness in the data base. Teichner and Whitehead (1973) described some of these problems as they attempted to classify these previous studies by means of the Criterion Measures Approach. First of all, there are a variety of ways in which

KOR has been provided. The subject might be informed only when something is right in some sense, only when something is wrong in some way, or when actions are both right and wrong. Other possibilities include information on the direction and the amount of error. Because performance might depend differentially upon these various KOR conditions, Teichner and Whitehead examined their effects separately.

Another kind of problem arose because the literature allows only qualitative comparisons of KOR. KOR is not often dimensionalized in terms of amount. In counting the comparisons, Teichner and Whitehead ignored the manner of providing KOR (for example, whether it was provided verbally, or with signal lights or buzzers). As before, studies failing to provide a control group or those that appeared to be based upon inseparable experimental confoundings were rejected. Those studies that did provide more or less acceptable conditions yielded 60 experimental comparisons. Figure 9.6 summarizes the results in terms of whether KOR produced a relative gain, no effect, or a decrement for each of the eight possible KOR parameter combinations (A through H) for the various classes of tasks. The figure shows the frequency with which each of the eight possible kinds of KOR (A–H) was provided in the various studies found in the literature. For example, the most frequent kind of KOR (E) involves providing "correct and error" information (48.3% of studies). The next most frequent kind of KOR (B) involves providing "correct and direction" information (23.3% of studies).

Figure 9.6 shows that the most frequently made comparisons involved simple coding tasks (31.7%). No "group coding" studies were found at all. The figure also shows that the nature of KOR provided varied with the task. In most studies using tracking tasks only "correct" information was provided, whereas for studies using simple or successive coding tasks, both "correct" and "error" information were used as KOR conditions. Studies using searching tasks used "correct" and "error" information; these studies used "correct and error" slightly more frequently as the KOR manipulations than any other kind, with "error" a close second.

Figure 9.6 shows that KOR aided learning in nine comparisons of "search" task performance and had no effect in four comparisons. On the other hand, none of these nine comparisons used the same KOR conditions as the four that had no effect. It appears, therefore, that a conclusion favoring KOR for "searching" must be limited to the "error" only or to the "correct and error" kinds of KOR information.

KOR was beneficial in nine out of fifteen comparisons with

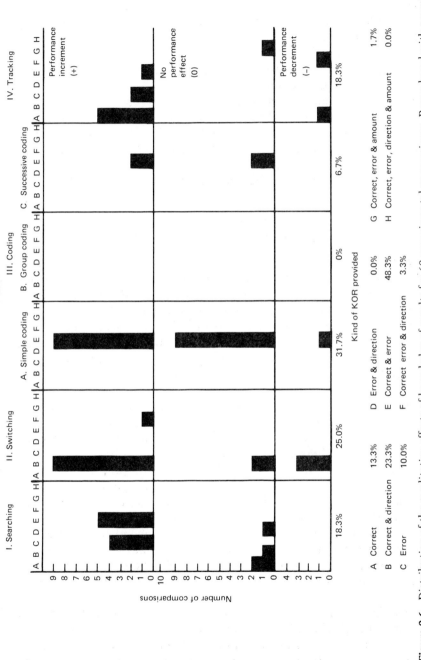

Figure 9.6 Distribution of the qualitative effects of knowledge of results for 60 experimental comparisons. Reproduced with permission from Teichner, W. H., and Whitehead, J. Development of a taxonomy of human performance: Evaluation of a task classification system for generalizing findings from a data base (American Institutes for Research Tech. Rep.). *JSAS Catalog of Selected Documents in Psychology*, 1973, 2, 26–27 (Ms. No. 324).

"switching" tasks in which KOR was expressed as "correct and direction" and one case of "correct, error, and direction." For tracking tasks, some form of KOR did aid "tracking," in eight out of the eleven comparisons. For the one form of KOR used in experiments with either "simple" or "successive" coding tasks, there was no clear superiority for the KOR condition.

Figure 9.6 demonstrates that the weight of the evidence favors KOR as a facilitator of performance, but the effect depends upon the category of task and the form of KOR employed. Because the data reported do not lend themselves to a meaningful quantitative analysis, Teichner and Whitehead restricted their conclusions to the presence or absence of KOR rather than to the amount of KOR.

APPLICATION OF THE CLASSIFICATORY SYSTEM TO STUDIES ON THE EFFECTS OF NOISE

Their review of the scientific literature on the effects of noise on human performance led Teichner and Whitehead to the conclusion that this literature, in terms of scientific rigor, left much to be desired for use in a data base suitable for taxonomic study. Aside from studies that were rejected because of poor or ambiguous procedures, a large number of studies was rejected for a failure to specify the noise levels used! These included studies with limited descriptions of control conditions (e.g., "quiet") as well as those that presented noise at a specific level from a speaker to a subject, but at an unspecified, undetermined, or variable distance and position. The "quiet" control condition in many studies represented the experimental noise condition in other studies. A major problem was the diversity of noise conditions used; these included continuous, intermittent, pure tone, broad band sound, and so forth. Sometimes the precise conditions were unspecified and the noise often passed through unspecified impedances before reaching the subject. Some studies did not specify whether the level was measured at the source or at the subject.

The first step taken by Teichner and Whitehead to organize the noise intensity literature was to plot the frequency of improvements, decrements, and no effects reported, for each Criterion Measures task category. The results for each of the task classes are shown in Figure 9.7.

It can be seen from this figure that none of the studies fell into the "group coding" class. For the remaining task classes, the most frequent result was a failure to show an effect of noise. Furthermore, improvements were almost as frequent as decrements. Figure 9.7

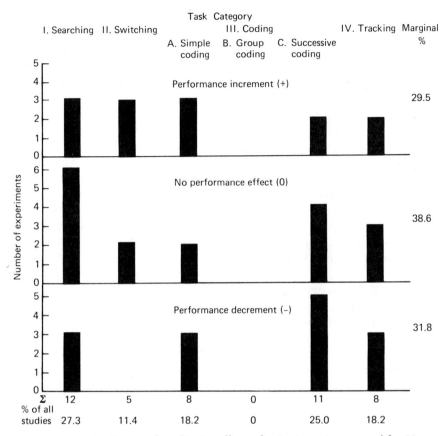

Figure 9.7 Distribution of qualitative effects of noise intensity reported for 44 experimental comparisons. Reproduced with permission from Teichner, W. H., and Whitehead, J. Development of a taxonomy of human performance: Evaluation of a task classification system for generalizing findings from a data base (American Institutes for Research Tech. Rep.). *JSAS Catalog of Selected Documents in Psychology*, 1973, 2, 26–27 (Ms. No. 324).

suggests that the intensity of noise has no significant effect upon performance, regardless of the type of task, when the tasks are classified according to the Criterion Measures classificatory system. The minimal effect of noise on performance was emphasized earlier by Kryter (1970), although Broadbent (1957, 1978) and others reported significant performance decrements due to increased noise intensity. More recent reviews (e.g., Gawron, 1982) stress the possible dependence of noise effects upon subject and task characteristics.

Teichner and Whitehead were not content with these summary

conclusions. To investigate the possibility that continued exposure to noise might produce a decrement, the studies in Figure 9.7 were coded according to cumulative effects of noise (no effect, no effect followed by a decrement, improvement followed by decrement, and so on). These refinements did not result in changing the conclusions drawn from Figure 9.7.

A further attempt was made to investigate the possibility that quantitative results might reveal more systematic trends than were evident from the qualitative comparisons. For each study, a percent change measure was determined. The studies were then further sub-divided according to the level of the quiet control conditions. It was possible to do this for 18 studies. The three coding studies reported decrements. For the five switching studies allowing such compari-sons, one showed no effect, three showed an improvement, and one a decrement. Plots of five tracking studies showed no effect when the experimental condition was 100 dB compared to a control between 60–75 dB, with three other tracking studies showing small, but sig-nificant, decrements.

Although there is some hint here that increasing noise intensity is more likely to produce decrement for tracking and coding tasks than for switching tasks, these effects are still not reliable. The results are presented as an illustration of one of the first attempts to apply a task classification to the experimental literature on noise. The attempt to apply this classificatory system to the noise literature was not very successful, either because the data base was inadequate or because the Criterion Measures Approach had limited utility for this purpose. We shall see in a later chapter that performance on tasks developed to represent different categories in an Ability Requirements classi-ficatory system did show differential effects when performed under intermittent noise conditions (Theologus, Wheaton, & Fleishman, 1974).

Some Conclusions

The Criterion Measures Approach was shown applicable to the clas-sification of tasks in the literature surveyed by Teichner and White-head. This is a general conclusion based upon ease of application, and was true regardless of the area examined. A primary finding was that the system made it possible to organize the literature on distributed practice in terms of (1) functional relationships and (2) the effects of different functions for different task categories. In fact, some hitherto unreported relationships were suggested. It is important to note that these principles are general to operationally defined task categories in which each category contains a variety of different tasks.

The application of the classificatory system to studies of massed vs. distributed practive led to several interesting functional relationships. For *simple coding tasks*, performance change was a linear function of intertrial interval in the range of 10 to 110 seconds, with massed practice periods of 1.5 to 9 seconds. When these results were plotted as a function of the ratio of the massed condition to the distributed condition, it was indicated that the greater the difference between the two conditions, the greater the improvement in performance. For successive coding tasks, on the other hand, it was determined that there was an increase in percentage improvement in performance with increasing distribution, followed by a decrease in percentage improvement.

Results with *tracking tasks* suggested that distributed practice produces better performance than massed practice and that the gain to be expected with the more distributed condition decreases as the intertrial interval associated with it increases. This result was true, however, only for comparisons made against control conditions having zero time between trials (that is, continuous practice). When performance was plotted as a function of the ratio of massed to distributed practice, it was apparent that the greater the difference between the massed and distributed intervals, the greater the gain that was associated with the distributed condition.

The application of the classificatory system to studies on the effects of knowledge of results and the effects of noise did not provide as clear a set of relationships as was the case for massed versus distributed practice. Although the weight of the evidence indicated that knowledge of results did result in improved performance, whether or not it really aided performance depended upon the task and the form of knoweldge of results employed. The data did not lend themselves to a meaningful quantitative analysis, so these conclusions must be restricted to the presence or absence of knowledge of results rather than to the amount of KOR.

In terms of the task categories, it was apparent that switching tasks provided the most consistent results. For these tasks, knowledge of results aided performance. For the other types of tasks (searching, simple coding, successive coding, and tracking) the data did not indicate any systematic increment or decrement in performance as a result of providing knowledge of results.

With respect to the noise literature, it was apparent that the most frequent result was a failure to show consistent effects of noise on tasks in any category. The effects of noise either were not demon-strated or did not exist; other task classificatory systems may be more useful in identifying the effects of noise, if any.

The above relationships are merely illustrative of the types capable of development with such systems. It is important also to note that, had the tasks been grouped without regard to the separate taxonomic categories, these functional relationships would have been obscured and few generalizations about performance would have been possible.

Other classificatory systems can now be applied to the distributed practice literature for evaluation. Other systems may or may not survive the test of application, or they may be even more successful, or they may serve to reveal still other kinds of relationships. An important result of these studies, of course, is the identification of a useable literature and the reduction of studies to those that are reasonably acceptable on scientific grounds.

The Criterion Measures Approach for task classification has not yet received a comprehensive evaluation. For example, we do not know the reliability with which individuals can assign tasks to the categories developed. The developers of the system assumed that their definitions of the task categories, in terms of "unequivocal" dependent response measures, minimized the need for such evaluation. The investigators (Teichner & Whitehead, 1973) commented that ease of application of the method decreases for those tasks that Teichner and Olson (1971) defined as combinations of the simpler tasks. Finally, the system is not complete in that it does not encompass all types of perceptual, motor, and cognitive tasks.

Subsequent to the work carried out on the Taxonomy Project, Teichner and his associates extended the data base development into other areas of human performance. They attempted to organize a great deal of this information as a basis for developing empirical models and quantitative principles for predicting human performance (Teichner & Olson, 1971; Teichner & Krebs, 1970, 1972a, 1972b, 1974a, 1974b; Teichner, 1972, 1974; Teichner & Mocharnuk, 1974). Essentially, these studies attempt to plot the data from diverse studies in the literature (e.g., reaction time, vigilance, effects of environmental stressors) and to identify regularities in the data across studies. Wherever possible, these data are converted to common scales, plotted, and functions fitted to the summarized data. Gaps in the data are identified and theoretical principles developed for testing, with a view to further iterations that will improve performance prediction. The classifications of the tasks in these diverse studies have been guided largely by the Criterion Measures classificatory system.

Although definite conclusions about the ultimate utility of these derived functions cannot yet be drawn, it is clear that these investigations have refined many relationships. For example, the general nature of search time functions for visual target acquisition (Teichner & Krebs, 1974b; Teichner & Mocharnuk, 1974), and the nature of the functions for specific conditions affecting reaction time to light signals were clarified. A number of these findings are relevant to the prediction of performance on new tasks and to the design of tasks for future use (Teichner, 1974). More importantly, these studies show the potential for organizing human performance data bases in a systematic and quantitative manner to enhance human performance prediction.

References

Broadbent, D. E. Effects of noise on behavior. In C. M. Harris (Ed.), *Handbook of noise control.* New York: McGraw–Hill, 1957.

Broadbent, D. E. The current state of noise research: Reply to Poulton. *Psychological Bulletin* 1978, *95,* 1052–1067.

Chambers, A. N. Development of a taxonomy of human performance: A heuristic model for the development of calssification systems. *JSAS Catalog of Selected Documents in Psychology,* 1973, *3,* 24–25 (MS No. 320).

Fleishman, E. A., & Stephenson, R. W. Development of a taxonomy of human performance: A review of the third year's progress. *JSAS Catalog of Selected Documents in Psychology,* 1972, *3,* 40–41 (MS. No. 113).

Fleishman, E. A., Teichner, W. H., & Stephenson, R. W. *Development of a taxonomy of human performance: A review of the second year's progress. JSAS Catalog of Selected Documents in Psychology,* 1972, *2,* 39–40 (MS No. 112).

Gawron, V. J. Performance effects of noise intensity, psychological set, and task type and complexity. *Human Factors,* 1982, *24*(2), 225–243.

Korotkin, A. L., & Chambers, A. N. *A human performance data base for evaluation of taxonomies.* Paper presented at the annual meeting of the American Psychological Association, September 1969.

Kryter, K. D. *The effects of noise on man.* New York: Academic Press, 1970.

Teichner, W. H. *Predicting human performance III: The detection of a simple visual signal as a function of time of watch,* (Technical Report 72-1). Albuquerque, NM: Department of Psychology, New Mexico State University, June 1972.

Teichner, W. H. *Quantitative models for predicting human visual/perceptual/motor performance* (Final Report). Albuquerque, NM: Department of Psychology, New Mexico State University, October 1974.

Teichner, W. H., & Krebs, M. J. *Predicting human performance: I. Estimating the probability of visual detection,* (Technical Report No. 1). Washington, D.C.: American Institute for Research, November 1970.

9. The Criterion Measures Approach

Teichner, W. H., & Krebs, M. J. Laws of the simple visual reaction time. *Psychological Review*, 1972, *79*, 344–358. (a)

Teichner, W. H., & Krebs, M. J. *Predicting human performance IV: Choice reaction time*, (Technical Report 72-2). Albuquerque, NM: Department of Psychology, New Mexico State University, December 1972. (b)

Teichner, W. H., & Krebs, M. J. Laws of visual choice reaction time. *Psychological Review*, 1974, *81*, 75–98. (a)

Teichner, W. H., & Krebs, M. J. Visual search for simple targets. *Psychological Bulletin*, 1974, *81*, 15–28. (b)

Teichner, W. H., & Mocharnuk, J. B. *Predicting human performance VII: Visual search for complex targets*, (TR-74-2). Albuquerque, NM: New Mexico State University, Dept. of Psychology, April 1974.

Teichner, W. H., & Olson, D. *Predicting human performance in space environments* (NASA Contr. Report CR–1370). Washington, D.C.: National Aeronautics and Space Administration, June 1969.

Teichner, W. H., & Olson, D. E. A preliminary theory of the effects of task and environment factors in human performance. *Human Factors*, 1971, *13*(4), 295–344.

Teichner, W. H., & Whitehead, J. Development of a taxonomy of human performance: Evaluation of a task classification system for generalizing findings from a data base. *JSAS Catalog of Selected Documents in Psychology*, 1973, *2*, 26–27 (Ms. No. 324).

Theologus, G. C., Wheaton, G. R., & Fleishman, E. A. Effects of intermittent, moderate intensity noise-stress on human performance. *Journal of Applied Psychology*, 1974, *59*, 539–547.

CHAPTER 10

The Information-Theoretic Approach

The information-theoretic classificatory approach is based on a general model derived from information-processing theory. The model establishes a set of definitions and describes relationships for a variety of parameters used to classify tasks. Many classificatory approaches begin with empirical relationships from which the abstract concepts and categories that form the basis of the classificatory system are inferred and defined. In contrast, the information-theoretic approach derives concepts and categories deductively from the theoretical information-processing model before attempting to apply the approach to empirical observations.

The *Information-Theoretic Approach*, also labeled the systems language approach, was developed by Levine and Teichner during the Taxonomy Project and is described in a series of papers and reports that form the basis of the present chapter (Levine & Teichner, 1970, 1972, 1973; Teichner, 1969). This chapter (1) summarizes the Information-Theoretic Approach, after defining key terminology in the system and describing the bases or dimensions for task classification; (2) relates the system to information-processing theory; (3) presents methods for evaluating the viability of the system for classifying tasks; and (4) describes practical applications of the Information-Theoretic Approach, including its relationships to other provisional classificatory systems.

Definitions of Key Terminology in the Information-Theoretic Approach

Levine and Teichner (1973), following the earlier logic of Shannon and Weaver (1949), define a *task* as a transfer of information between an information source and a receiver in any system that can be construed as an information channel. Whereas a task is defined as a transfer of information between components, the operation on the information or data within a component is a *process*. Processes, which appear at a more general level of systems analysis, may be subdivided into tasks.

Figure 10.1 provides two different levels of description of a system analysis to clarify the distinction between processes and tasks. Part A presents the System Information Transfer Function. System input flows from the display to the human to the control to the machine, where it appears as system output. The human and machine components are labeled processes, which are then broken down in Part B. Process A, occurring within the human component, becomes the Human Information Transfer Function; Process B, occurring within the machine component, becomes the Machine Information Transfer Function. These processes are subdivided into tasks, as there are now transfers of information between components that did not exist in Part A. Thus, Teichner (1969) concluded that "underlying processes" must be capable of description in exactly the same terms as tasks at more detailed levels.

Under the Information-Theoretic Approach, human and machine tasks must be defined in precisely the same manner, as a transfer of information. Teichner (1969) suggested that we need only one definition for the concept of task to cover both human and machine components. He noted, "If the model fits for situations involving people, then it is useful for that purpose and people can be said to be involved in tasks as defined. The model may fit situations which do not involve people, however, and these too would be called task situations" (1969, p. C-3). Thus, the information-theoretic classificatory approach is intended to provide a model for classifying all tasks, human and machine.

Levine and Teichner (1973) suggested that it is convenient to deal with the transfer of information between each two successive components of a system separately. Thus, they designated four major tasks: machine–human; human–human; human–machine; machine–machine. Teichner (1969) noted that the information flow is always in the direction of machine–human–machine–machine. This information flow is represented in Part B of Figure 10.1. Psychologists are concerned with the study of human behavior. Therefore, they are not as interested in the investigation of machine–machine tasks, except to the extent that such information transfers affect later transfers of information dealing with human components.

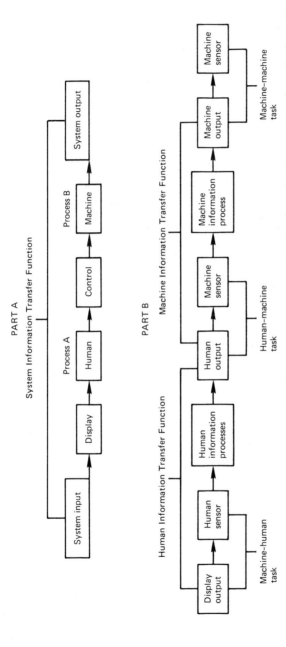

Figure 10.1 Human–machine system at two levels of description: Process and task. Adapted with permission from Teichner, W. H., and Olson, D. *Predicting human performance in space environments* (NASA Contractor Report No. CR 1370). Washington, D.C.: National Aeronautics and Space Administration, June 1969.

The model underlying the Information-Theoretic Approach is not concerned with the description of tasks as defined by the involvement of processes. Rather, it is concerned with classifying tasks *qua* tasks, whether those tasks involve transfers of information between components of the central nervous system, between machine components, or between a combination of human and machine components.

DIMENSIONS FOR CLASSIFICATION IN THE INFORMATION-THEORETIC APPROACH

In this information-processing approach to task classification, the tasks are categorized according to four dimensions: (1) the nature of the constraints that are imposed by the tasks or the restrictions placed on the random sampling of stimulus and response events at the source and at the receiver; (2) the location of the constraint, whether on the input (source) or on the output (receiver); (3) the amount and form of informational redundancy in the stimulus and/or response ensemble; and (4) the relationship between the amount of information in the input and the amount of information in the output.

Levine and Teichner (1972) noted that all tasks falling within a constraint class will be more similar to one another than tasks in different classes. Further, all tasks falling within a constraint class will exhibit similar functional relationships between redundancy and information transfer, whereas these functional relationships will differ across constraint classes.

NATURE OF CONSTRAINTS   Under the Information-Theoretic Approach, all tasks are characterized as imposing constraints or restrictions on the random sampling of stimulus and response events (see also Garner, 1962). These constraints are the structure that defines the task as a unique situation. Constraints structure the task by limiting the amount of information transfer. A *constraint* is defined as a sampling rule distinguishing the stimulus (response) set from the set that would result from random sampling from the population of stimulus (response) events.

The classificatory scheme differentiates between internal and external constraints. *Internal constraints* represent restrictions on how events are sampled. Examples include sampling rules such as stratified sampling, purposive sampling, and sampling without replacement. *External constraints* represent restrictions on sampled events. Teichner (1969) provided the following examples of external constraints:

1. *Combination constraint:* sample only *n* at a time
2. *Rate constraint:* sample no faster than at a given rate
3. *Range constraint:* sample only within a specified range of values
4. *Similarity–dissimilarity constraint:* sample only combinations having no common elements
5. *Probability constraint:* sample only events having probabilities greater than a specified probability
6. *Sequence constraint:* sample only sequences with some specified sequential restriction (e.g., no unique event can occur twice in succession).

Other kinds of external constraints have been identified for potential study but not described fully. They are: frequency constraint, conditional constraint, distributional constraint, relational constraint, spatial constraint, size of unit of input constraint, time constraint, and delay constraint.

A theoretical requirement of the information-theoretic classificatory approach is the specification of all possible sampling constraints. Teichner believed that constraints would differ for machine and human receivers, with human task performance influenced by such external constraints as the spectral sensitivity of the eye and ear, size of the visual field, empirical attention span, memory span, and coordination ability. All these variables act to limit the reception of transmitted events.

Figure 10.2 presents *nature of classes of constraint* as the first dimension for categorizing tasks within the Information-Theoretic Approach. Classes of tasks are, thus, established initially on the basis of classes of constraints. The number of task classes is dependent on the number of possible classes of constraints operating on sampling from the source and from the receiver.

LOCATION OF CONSTRAINT: INPUT OR OUTPUT The operation of a constraint at the input (source) or output (receiver) is the second major dimension for the classification of tasks under the Information-Theoretic Approach. Five kinds of constraints have been identified. Two of these operate on input: (1) constraints on input due to restrictions on random sampling of stimuli from source (e.g., rules specifying how the stimulus population is sampled or which stimuli are sampled), and (2) constraints on input prescribed by task requirements (e.g., presentation rate, stimulus range). Three kinds of constraints operate either directly or indirectly on the output: (3) constraints imposed on the receiver or operator by the task requirements (e.g., respond to every third input), (4) constraints imposed by the

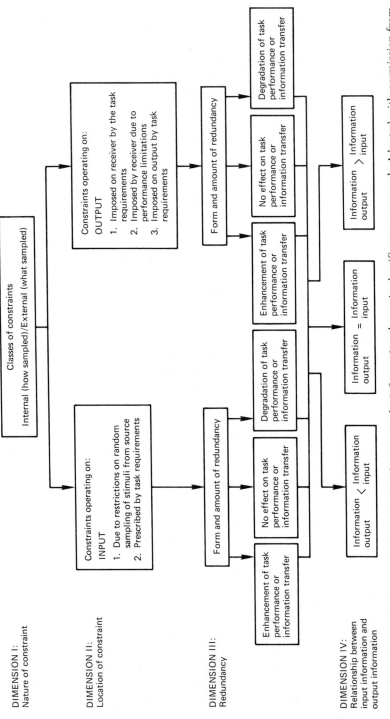

Figure 10.2 Four dimensions for task classification in the information-theoretic classificatory approach. Adapted with permission from Levine, J. M., and Teichner, W. H. *Development of a taxonomy of human performance: An information-theoretic approach* (American Institutes for Research Tech. Rep.). *JSAS Catalog of Selected Documents in Psychology,* 1973, 3, 28, (Ms. No. 325).

receiver due to performance limitations (e.g., encoding and decoding limitations), and (5) constraints imposed on the output by task requirements (e.g., response ensemble characteristics). Figure 10.3 summarizes the operation of these five constraint categories on components of a communication model. The figure provides the kinds of constraints, generic samples of those constraints, and specific examples for the task labeled *pattern recognition*.

The constraining process occurring in Figure 10.3 has been described as follows (Levine & Teichner, 1972):

> Input constraints relate to restrictions on the random generation of stimuli and the size of the stimulus ensemble (1, 2). In order to constrain the input, the stimuli of the task must be either a smaller sample of some total stimulus population as perceived by the receiver or an entire stimulus population but one whose individual stimuli occur with unequal probabilities. Output constraints with the exception of the specification of the response ensemble (by task requirements, 5) are imposed by the receiver of the stimulus set. These constraints are imposed in an attempt to structure performance in accordance with the requirements of the task (3). Such constraints are sampling restrictions implemented by the receiver either purposely to satisfy task requirements (3) or necessarily as a result of the receiver's limitations in the receipt or processing of stimuli from the source (4) [p. D–3].

Figure 10.2 presents *location of constraint* as the second dimension for categorizing tasks within the Information-Theoretic Approach.

REDUNDANCY   The third dimension for categorizing tasks in the Information-Theoretic Approach is *redundancy*. Constraints, whether imposed on input or output, introduce redundancies into sampled events (see Garner, 1962), that is, into the information contained in the stimulus and/or response sets. Redundancy can vary in form and amount (Levine & Teichner, 1973, p. 9):

> The particular form of redundancy is determined by the *specific* sampling rule through which the constraint operates. The precise amount of redundancy is a function of the number of alternatives in the stimulus or response sets relative to the number in the population, and their probabilities of occurrence. Redundancy, then, is introduced into input information when the stimuli generated occur with unequal probabilities, or are a smaller set of stimuli than *could* have been generated from the population. Redundancy is generated in output information in a like manner.

The Information-Theoretic Approach hypothesizes that, given the nature and location of the constraint, tasks can be classified in terms of increasing amounts of redundancy that affect information transmission between the source and the receiver. Further, different constraint classes will generate forms of redundancies that differentially will influence information transmission or task performance. These forms of redundancy may result in the enhancement of information

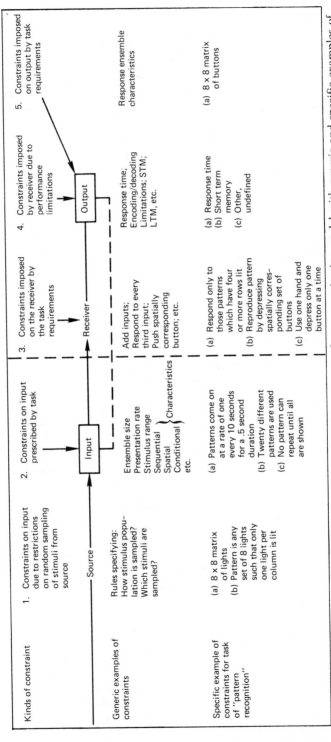

Figure 10.3 Operation of five constraint categories on components of a communication model with generic and specific examples of constraints. Adapted with permission from Levine, J. M., and Teichner, W. H. *Development of a taxonomy of human performance: An information-theoretic approach* (American Institutes for Research Tech. Rep.). *JSAS Catalog of Selected Documents in Psychology,* 1973, 3, 28, (Ms. No. 325).

transmission, in no effect on information transmission, or in the degradation of information transmission. The interrelationships among constraints, redundancies, and task performance have been explained by Teichner (1969) as follows: "As external constraining increases, redundancy increases and [task] complexity increases [resulting in performance degradation]. As internal constraining increases, redundancy increases but [task] complexity decreases [resulting in performance enhancement]." (p. C–4)

Figure 10.2 presents *redundancy* as the third dimension for categorizing tasks within the information-theoretic classificatory approach, as well as the possible effects of various amounts and forms of redundancy on task performance or information transmission.

RELATIONSHIPS BETWEEN INPUT INFORMATION AND OUTPUT INFORMATION   Figure 10.2 also presents the relationship between quantities of input and output information as the fourth and final dimension for classifying tasks. After task completion, the amount of input information is compared to the amount of output information. Employing three broad categories of information-processing tasks originally identified by Posner (1964), tasks are categorized as those requiring (1) information conservation (information output = information input), (2) information reduction (information output < information input), or (3) information creation (information output > information input). Thus, output information may be less than, equal to, or greater than input information. Further, the relationship between redundancy and the amount of information transmitted may differ as a function of the relationship between input and output information.

When information in the output is less than information in the input, the amount of information transmitted is less than the maximum amount possible. This implies constraints present in the receiver that are not present at the source. For example, a range constraint (sample only within a specified range of values) might be operating, but unaccounted for by known range type constraints, such as the eye's physiological limitations. To explain the constraint, an underlying mechanism is postulated, such as attention, which would impose the observed range constraint. This mechanism would be viewed as present in the receiver.

When information in the output is greater than information in the input, the communication system has more sources than can be accounted for by the observer. For example, if there is only one external source, then other sources must be internal to the receiver. Levine

TASK (Information transfer)	Information reduction	Information conservation	Information creation
	Information output $<$ Information input	Information output $=$ Information input	Information output $>$ Information input
	Input constraints	Input constraints	Input constraints
	Restrictions from source Task requirements	Restrictions from source Task requirements	Restrictions from source Task requirements
Output constraints	None A B C D...etc.	None A B C D...etc.	None A B C D...etc.
Task requirements on receiver	None	None	None
	A	A	A
Performance limitations	B *	B	B
	C	C	C
Task requirements on output	D . . .	D . . .	D . . .
	etc.	etc.	etc.

*For any cell, the effects of increasing amounts of redundancy on information transmission are evaluated and the resulting effects on task performance (enhancement, degradation, or no effect).

Figure 10.4 Interaction of four dimensions of classification of the Information-Theoretic Approach. Adapted with permission from Levine, J. M., and Teichner, W. H. *Development of a taxonomy of human performance: An information-theoretic approach* (American Institutes for Research Tech. Rep.). *JSAS Catalog of Selected Documents in Psychology*, 1973, *3*, 28, (Ms. No. 325).

and Teichner (1973) provided an example of this relationship between input and output information. They suggested that successive inputs from a single external source might be operated on internally to produce a third event, with all three events being reported by the receiver. For example, in a human performance situation, the external source might present the numerical events "2" and "3", with the receiver reporting "2 and 3 are 5." The third event, "5," could be accounted for by postulating an underlying process called "computation" or "addition."

When output information equals input information, there is no need to assume the operation of any receiver constraints, whether due to performance limitations or internal processes.

Figure 10.4 illustrates the interaction of the four dimensions in the Information-Theoretic Approach. Tasks are structured by classes of input and output constraints. Once the constraints have been identified, it is possible to determine the form and amount of redundancy and the effects of redundancy on information transfer. Redundancy affects task complexity, which results in performance enhancement, degradation, or no effect on performance or information transfer. The relationship between redundancy and information transfer is affected by the nature of the relationship between information input and information output, or whether the completed task results in information conservation, information reduction, or information creation.

SUMMARY OF THE INFORMATION-THEORETIC CLASSIFICATORY APPROACH

The information-theoretic classificatory approach is based on a general model derived from information-processing theory. The model provides a systems language common to all tasks, whether human or machine. In all cases, a task is defined as an information transfer between a source (input) and a receiver (output). This definition parallels the traditional S–R relationship. Although this relationship may be dependent on underlying processes, the Information-Theoretic Approach suggests that these processes are simply a series of intervening tasks that can be broken down at a more specific level of systems analysis.

The model establishes a set of definitions and describes relationships for a variety of parameters used to classify tasks. Specifically, any given task may be assigned to a category based on (1) the nature of the constraints imposed (restrictions on *which* events and *how* events are sampled in the stimulus configuration and response ensemble), (2) the location of the constraints (operating on the source or input, or on the receiver or output), (3) the amount and form of redundancy introduced by the constraints, and (4) the relationship between the amounts of input and output information. Tasks falling within a specific category are more like one another than tasks in different categories. Furthermore, once a task is assigned to a category, the functional relationships among the parameters on which performance depends can be identified. Thus, the model provides a logic: information transfer or task performance within a given category, defined by the nature and location of the constraints, is dependent on the amount of redundancy and the relationship between input–output information.

Whereas many classificatory approaches are inductive in nature, the Information-Theoretic Approach is essentially deductive, deriving concepts and categories from an information-processing model before examining empirical observations.

Relationship of the Information-Theoretic Approach to Information-Processing Theory

The information-theoretic classificatory approach incorporates an information-processing model, and thus derives many of its concepts from information-processing theory. Information theory formalizes and quantifies many of the concepts, providing formulae for their measurement. These formulae have been adopted by the developers of the Information-Theoretic Approach and used in their efforts to evaluate the viability of the model underlying this classificatory scheme.

The Information-Theoretic Approach defines a task as an information transfer between two system components after a communicative act. Levine and Teichner (1973) suggested that transmitted information is that portion of the uncertainty in the stimulus that is reduced as reflected in the response. In fact, under the Information-Theoretic Approach, information transmission is partially dependent on the relationship between the amount of information in the input and the amount of information in the output.

Information theory quantifies the concept of uncertainty, suggesting that the uncertainty about the outcome of any act is related to the number of possible outcomes that exist and the probability associated with the possible occurrence of each of these outcomes:

$$H = - \sum_1^n p_i \log_2 p_i$$

where H is the average actual uncertainty, n the number of alternatives, and p the probability of the occurrence of the ith event or stimulus. Under the Information-Theoretic Approach, this formula is used to derive stimulus and response uncertainty (or conversely, the amount of stimulus or response information). These variables and their relationships to information transmission have been described as follows (Levine & Teichner, 1973, p. 8):

> The [amount of] information [at the stimulus or source], H(X) is a function of the number of alternative events contained [within] the source and their probabilities. The [amount of] information [at the response or receiver], H(Y), is defined in terms of the number of events the receiver can exhibit and their probabilities. The amount of information transmitted, H(XY), is a function of the joint probabilities of selecting source events and observing receiver events.

The Information-Theoretic Approach suggests that, after tasks have been classified by the nature and location of constraints, those constraints will result in various amounts and forms of redundancy that will affect task performance. In evaluating the model, redundancy is treated as an independent variable and its effects on information transmission (symbolized as H_T) are examined for a given constraint. In information theory, the concept of redundancy also is quantified. Redundancy is defined mathematically as a difference between actual uncertainty and maximum uncertainty, where maximum uncertainty, H_{MAX}, exists whenever outcomes of the event are equiprobable. Thus, Redundancy = $H_{MAX} - H(X)$ in absolute bits. Redundancy may also be expressed as a percentage after subtracting the ratio of actual or present uncertainty to maximum uncertainty from 1.0.

$$\text{Redundancy} = 1 - \frac{H(X)}{H_{MAX}} \times 100 = \text{percentage}$$

Consequently, if actual uncertainty equals maximum uncertainty, redundancy equals zero. Redundancy is created whenever any selection process (a process that involves sampling from a stimulus–response population) retains maximum uncertainty while reducing actual uncertainty. Redundancy may be manipulated by holding actual stimulus uncertainty constant and varying maximum stimulus uncertainty. Thus, the influence of redundancy on task performance or information transfer is not confounded by the possible effects of actual stimulus uncertainty. This procedure is suggested in the approach recommended by Levine and Teichner (1973) for evaluating the information-theoretic model. Such manipulations provide information on the relationship between redundancy and information transmission for various input constraints. However, for output constraints, redundancy cannot be manipulated because it is apparent only after performance. Consequently, it is necessary to calculate H_T, information transmission, under several conditions of maximum response uncertainty, and then to determine the amount of redundancy in the response or output information, as well as the amount of transmitted information.

In the next section, we shall see how these concepts and their mathematical definitions supplied by information-processing theory are useful in evaluating the efficacy of the Information-Theoretic Approach to task classification.

Evaluation of the Information-Theoretic Model

For any proposed classificatory scheme, it is necessary to evaluate the underlying model to determine its utility for classifying tasks accurately, which, in turn, allows researchers to identify correctly the relationships and parameters influencing task performance. Levine and Teichner (1973) suggested that there is no point to classifying tasks, except to be able to denote the relationships involved when a new task is classified.

A fairly elaborate plan for the evaluation of the feasibility and validity of the model underlying the Information-Theoretic Approach to task classification has been proposed. The approach involves a two-fold, iterative process, with both theoretical and empirical activities. This process is described as follows (Levine & Teichner, 1972):

> On the one hand, a strictly theoretical activity will be carried forth by computer simulation of sampling constraints and the determination of the relationship between amount of redundancy and transmitted information (H_T) under a variety of constraint conditions. On the other hand, a series of empirical investigations will be accomplished using tasks which allow the experimenter to manipulate input constraints and require the subject to provide output constraints. The influence of redundancy upon information transmission will be determined empirically and compared to the results of the computer simulation. If agreement is found, we will have evidence for the viability of the system [p. D–5].

Five major steps for implementing this evaluation program have been outlined: (1) conceptualization of classes of constraints, (2) development of a laboratory task, (3) design of a series of experiments, (4) development of computer programs, and (5) matching of computer and experimental results. Progress made towards the completion of each of these steps is described more fully in the sections that follow.

CONCEPTUALIZATION OF CLASSES OF CONSTRAINTS

We have already noted that a theoretical requirement of the Information-Theoretic Approach is the specification of all possible sampling constraints. The number of task categories is dependent on the number of constraint categories. Although the conceptualization of all constraints is of theoretical interest, as a practical matter only a certain number of classes of constraints can be investigated. Consequently, the researchers must, after examining many possible constraint categories, select judiciously only several of these for subsequent experimentation.

Although the information-theoretic model covers both human and machine tasks, the researchers chose to focus on those classes of constraint that exist in human performance situations. The interest is in the questions of which classes of constraints operate in human performance situations, and the relationships between those constraints and information transfer or task performance as redundancy (and, consequently, the complexity of the task) is varied. The basic postulate is that the effect of any constraint on human task performance is a function of the redundancy introduced by the constraint.

Most human performance situations are those in which the human receiver provides output constraints (e.g., size of the visual field, empirical attention span). Consequently, the researchers' interest is in specifying which classes of constraint the receiver can represent.

There is a need to limit theoretical and empirical evaluations of the model to tasks involving the simultaneous operation of (1) a single input constraint and a single output constraint, (2) a single input constraint and no output constraint, or (3) a single output constraint and no input constraint. In addition to limiting the number of constraints examined in the early investigations of the viability of the information-theoretic model, the constraints selected should be easily quantifiable. This implies that the task employed in the investigation should be one in which input and output information are easily quantified.

By limiting initial investigations to only a few easily quantified constraints, it is possible to investigate the viability of the model under relatively simple circumstances. If the model is viable, constraint conditions can be increased in complexity. On the other hand, "if . . . the model proves to be invalid, it can be modified or discarded on the basis of a minimal research effort" (Levine & Teichner, 1973, p. 18).

DEVELOPMENT OF A LABORATORY TASK

To evaluate the model adequately, it is necessary to develop a versatile laboratory task providing for easy manipulation of input and output specifications. Although the model can accommodate any kind of task, a decision was made by the researchers to base the preliminary evaluation of the model on the results of a laboratory task that involved discrete responses. The discrete tasks were to be generated by selecting stimuli and establishing the appropriate responses to them. There is a need for the model to be subjected to such simple experimental evaluation before it can be applied to more complex operational tasks.

The apparatus, the Sequential Information-Processing Programmer, which was built to serve as the laboratory task to test the basic assumption of the information-theoretic model, is depicted in Figure 10.5. An 8 × 8 matrix of lights serves as the stimulus configuration. Through the use of a grid, the size of this matrix may be reduced to any $n \times m$ configuration. Visual signals are presented automatically in a time-controlled fashion, either simultaneously or sequentially. The response console is a corresponding 8 × 8 matrix of buttons. Responses and response latencies may be recorded automatically onto punched tape as they occur. Redundancy can be manipulated on both the input and output sides. The researchers also can manipulate stimulus light and response button compatibility (S–R compatibility). This device provides the researcher with the flexibility of imposing and manipulating a wide variety of constraints on the input or the output.

Using this device, Levine and Teichner (1970) conceptualized an example of the interplay between the sample rules and the resulting amount of actual input uncertainty, which determines the amount of stimulus redundancy. Maximum stimulus uncertainty for the 8 × 8 matrix exists when no sampling rules are specified and, therefore, each of the 64 cells contains one bit of information for a total of 64

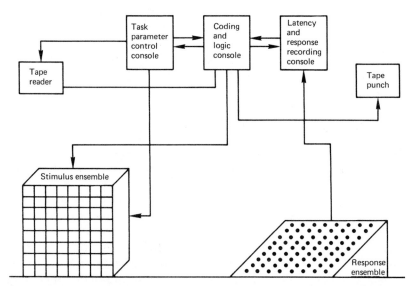

Figure 10.5 Sequential information-processing programmer. Reproduced with permission from Levine, J. M., and Teichner, W. H. *Development of a taxonomy of human performance: An information-theoretic approach (American Institutes for Research Tech. Rep.). JSAS Catalog of Selected Documents in Psychology,* 1973, *3,* 28, (Ms. No. 325).

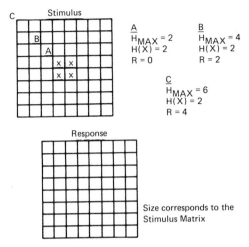

$$\underline{A}$$
$$H_{MAX} = 2$$
$$H(X) = 2$$
$$R = 0$$

$$\underline{B}$$
$$H_{MAX} = 4$$
$$H(X) = 2$$
$$R = 2$$

$$\underline{C}$$
$$H_{MAX} = 6$$
$$H(X) = 2$$
$$R = 4$$

Size corresponds to the
Stimulus Matrix

Figure 10.6 Examples of redundancy manipulation through manipulation of maximum stimulus uncertainty. Adapted with permission form Levine, J. M., and Teichner, W. H. *Development of a taxonomy of human performance: An information-theoretic approach* (American Institutes for Research Tech. Rep.). *JSAS Catalog of Selected Documents in Psychology,* 1973, *3,* 28, (Ms. No. 325).

bits. Different sampling rules then generate different amounts of actual input uncertainty, H(X), as follows:

A. Only 1 of the 64 cells can be activated
$$H(X) = \log_2 64 = 6 \text{ bits}$$
B. Exactly 1 cell per column is to be activated
$$H(X) = 8 \log_2 8 = 24 \text{ bits}$$
C. Exactly 1 cell per column adjoining another cell is to be activated
$$H(X) = \log_2 8 + 7 \log_2 3 = 14 \text{ bits}$$

Levine and Teichner also have provided an example of manipulating maximum stimulus uncertainty, H_{MAX}, while holding actual stimulus uncertainty constant. This example is shown in Figure 10.6. For this example, the probabilities of occurrence of the stimuli are equal. Redundancy, it will be recalled, also can be manipulated by assigning the cells unequal probabilities of occurrence.

DESIGN OF A SERIES OF EXPERIMENTS

After the equipment was developed, three experiments were conceptualized involving the control of selected constraints. These experiments were designed to be conducted iteratively along with corresponding computer simulations. They involve the tasks of signal detection, pattern identification, and pattern classification. As conceptualized, the primary independent variable is stimulus redundancy. Subjects would be required to perform the discrete information-processing task while input constraints and redundancy are varied. Task performance or information transmission would then be evaluated, including the possible operation of output constraints as determined by the response ensemble and/or constraints imposed by the subjects themselves. The results of the amount of information transmission in the experiments would be compared to the outcomes of the associated computer simulations. To date, none of these experiments has actually been carried out as a test of the information-theoretic model. These experiments are designed to answer three research questions: (1) What kinds of human constraints are operating and what are their effects on human performance? (2) What kinds of experimenter-imposed constraints influence human performance and in what manner? (3) Do the laboratory results agree with the theoretical results?

In summary, the primary research investigations involve (1) the identification of the nature and location of the classes of constraints operating in human performance situations and (2) the determination of the kind of relationships existing between them and information transfer as redundancy is varied.

DEVELOPMENT OF COMPUTER PROGRAMS

Future research involving the Information-Theoretic Approach should include the development of computer programs to simulate the effects of constraint classes on the random sampling of events and the effects of redundancy manipulations. The effects of these manipulations on task performance or information transmission should then be compared to the results from the experimental laboratory tasks.

The use of computer simulations to evaluate theoretical propositions has gained increasing popularity among researchers. Hilgard and Bower (1974) describe this technique. Specifically, psychological theories are formulated in the format of programs for high-speed computers. "The aim of the enterprise is to get such a programmed computer to go through a series of 'actions' which in some essential ways resemble or simulate the cognitive and/or behavioral actions of a real subject performing some task" (Hilgard & Bower, 1974, p. 428). Researchers believe that if the machine accurately simulates relevant aspects of an organism's behavior, then the simulation constitutes a genuine explanation of that behavior. This is the logic underlying the use of computer simulations.

A major advantage of the use of computer simulations to test psychological theories is the speed and accuracy with which computers operate. Additionally, as Hilgard and Bower (1974) suggested, when it is programmed to operate according to a theory, the computer becomes another realization of that theory. Computer simulations are particularly well suited for testing information-processing models such as that underlying the information-theoretic classificatory approach.

The developers of the Information-Theoretic Approach intended to employ computer simulation to investigate the influence of constraint classes on information transmission (H_T), using the following steps (Levine & Teichner, 1973, p. 19):

1. Postulate a task having a 1:1 input–output relationship.
2. Impose a constraint (sampling rule) on the stimulus population or response population or both, with the initial population consisting of equiprobable alternatives.
3. Sample combinations of stimulus and response alternatives according to the constraint rules.
4. Generate an output of frequencies of occurrence of computer-drawn samples.
5. Compute H_T.
6. Repeat to get an average H_T and $\nabla\,^2H_T$.
7. Compute $H(X)$, $H(Y)$, $1 - H(X)/H_{MAX}$.
8. Using the same constraint, repeat steps 2 through 7 manipulating amount of input redundancy (through changes in maximum uncertainty).
9. Plot H_T as a function of redundancy for the constraint class.
10. Repeat steps 2 through 9 for 1: n and n:1 relationships.
11. Repeat steps 1 through 10 for additional constraints.

Matching of Computer and Experimental Results

The results generated from the computer simulations reflecting the information model's theoretical propositions should agree with the results of the series of laboratory experiments. If they do not, the researchers may postulate the operation of classes of human-imposed constraints, that is, hypothesize that the presence of these constraints accounts for the differences in the two sets of results. These hypothetical constraints may be introduced into a new computer simulation to determine if the theoretical outcome can then be matched with the laboratory performance data. By this iterative process, human-imposed constraints, and their effects on performance, will be identified. Further, the functional relationships between input redundancy and information transmission will be identified for these and other classes of constraint. It will be recalled that the basic postulate of the Information-Theoretic Approach is that the effect of any constraint on task performance or information transfer is a function of the redundancy introduced by that constraint.

Teichner (1969) noted that, in those instances in which the theoretical result and the laboratory result agree, "the model fits at that point, ie., there are tasks of that sort in human affairs and they are describable by the logic of the model" (p. C–7). He added that by the use of such a limited theoretical and empirical approach to the determination of the viability of the model, the researchers avoid the necessity of developing the model in its entirety. Rather, researchers can concentrate on only those aspects of the model that they expect to have relevance to human performance.

Practical Applications of the Information-Theoretic Approach

With its emphasis on system analyses, such as those presented in Figure 10.1, it is reasonable for the information-theoretic classificatory approach to be viewed as particularly helpful for understanding the relationships between components in human–machine systems. In this regard, J. E. Uhlaner, former Director of the United States Army Behavior and Systems Research Laboratory, has stated, "The particular language system discussed is most useful in its application to equipment design problems which must consider performance in man–machine interactions" (Levine & Teichner, 1973, ii).

In contrast to this narrow view, the developers of the Information-Theoretic Approach have suggested a broad range of practical applications. They suggested that the information-theoretic system language potentially can be developed to the point at which it will be useful for any one of a variety of applied decisions, such as selection, equipment design, or training, rather than being useful for one or two types of applied decisions, as seems to be the case with other provisional classificatory approaches (Fleishman & Stephenson, 1970).

The major practical advantage of this system is that the present model for task classification has the potential of predicting performance for humans on tasks not yet researched and for hardware not yet built. This may be done by analyzing potential constraints for the new or modified task. These constraints are used to relate the task to others of similar constraint composition for which performance data are available. These data can be used to predict performance on the new task. Furthermore, performance on the new task may be estimated by computer simulation techniques when the constraints that restrict performance are properly identified and described.

An additional potential application of the Information-Theoretic Approach involves the integration and generalization of human performance research findings.

Relationships to Other Provisional Classificatory Systems

The information-theoretic classificatory approach can be compared to three other provisional classificatory schemes developed under the Taxonomy Project, namely, the Criterion Measures Approach, the Ability Requirements Approach, and the Task Characteristics Approach, as well as to a fourth approach undertaken later by Teichner (1974).

The Criterion Measures Approach, developed by Teichner and Olson (1969), and the Information-Theoretic Approach are based on the same fundamental definition of a task as an information transfer. The schemes, however, differ in their methodological approach to task classification. Teichner noted that the Criterion Measures Approach starts with the empirical side and builds up to abstract concepts. It goes from the specific to the general. In contrast, the Information-Theoretic Approach is based on a general theoretical model from which propositions are derived for testing. Consequently, scheme development proceeds from the abstract to the empirical. Fleishman, Teichner & Stephenson (1970) have described the model as a set of definitions, relationships, and classes that has meaning in the same sense that a mathematical or logical system has meaning. In this sense, the system is complete before any attempt is made to apply it to observations. For this reason, the Information-Theoretic Approach is not subject to the same inventive revisions as are possible using the Criterion Measures Approach. The Information-Theoretic Approach is clearly a priori whereas the Criterion Measures Approach may be characterized as a posteriori. The Criterion Measures Approach, which classifies tasks in terms of basic performance categories (e.g., tracking, switching, searching, coding), is described more fully in Chapter 9.

Research was begun on the theoretical relationships between the systems language of the Information-Theoretic Approach and the language systems of the Ability Requirements Approach and the Task Characteristics Approach. Briefly, the Ability Requirements Approach attempts to classify a task in terms of the human abilities required for performance. It is assumed that a profile of basic abilities can be identified to account for task performance. It is suggested that performance on tasks with similar ability profiles will be similar. Additionally, if the ability profile of a new task is known, predictions can be made regarding task performance by reviewing performance data for tasks having comparable ability profiles (see Theologus, Romashko, & Fleishman, 1973). This approach is described in Chapter 12.

The Task Characteristics Approach attempts to classify tasks on the basis of their similarities in terms of task characteristics (see Farina & Wheaton, 1973). It is assumed that a profile of task characteristics can be identified to account for task performance. It is suggested that performance on tasks with similar task characteristic profiles will be similar. Additionally, if the task characteristic profile of a new task is known, predictions can be made regarding task performance by reviewing performance data for tasks having comparable task characteristic profiles. This approach is discussed in Chapter 13.

From the beginning, the researchers involved in the Taxonomy Project believed that the Information-Theoretic Approach was more general and, consequently, that it would eventually encompass these other two provisional classificatory approaches. It was recognized that, for this process to occur, it would be necessary to translate and combine the three language systems (Fleishman, Teichner, & Stephenson, 1973). This process involves the specification of the kinds of, and the degree to which, task characteristic and operator ability variables impose limitations or constraints on performance. The Information-Theoretic Approach dovetails with the other provisional classificatory systems by providing a mathematical framework within which abilities and other performance limiting factors can operate predictively. Further, once the translation process is completed, future research plans involve an evaluation of the integrated classificatory system. Such an integrated system provides a bridge between general scientific studies and applied needs, because concepts and findings of the Ability Requirements and Task Characteristics approaches may be translated into a common systems language of relevance to design engineers and system equipment planners. Further, this language permits human performance and machine performance to be specified in terms of identical parameters by systems personnel.

A fourth provisional classificatory approach developed by Teichner (1974) is partially an outgrowth of the Information-Theoretic Approach. This scheme also borrows heavily from Teichner and Olson (1969). A task is defined as an information transfer. Tasks are classified according to the subtasks or functions involved in them and according to the operations performed on information within the subtasks.

The taxonomy is derived from a revision of Donders's (1868) law, which states:

$$\text{Choice Reaction Time (CRT)} = a + T_{S-S} + T_{S-R} + c$$

where a is a constant portion of reaction time associated with stimulus encoding, T_{S-S} the time required for stimulus codes when more than one is involved, T_{S-R} the time required to translate from the final stimulus code to the response code, and c the response execution or the time required for activities associated with the selection of a motor program to execute the response. Because a and c always will be involved, tasks can differ functionally in only three ways: (1) they include both the S–S and S–R translations, (2) they include only the S–R translation, or (3) they include neither translation.

Teichner characterized the operations performed on information within the subtasks as compression, conservation, classification, and creation. Three of these operations parallel those identified by Posner (1964) and are described in an earlier section of this chapter. (We equated classification with condensation.) Teichner added a new process, *compression*, defined as qualitatively different from condensation, although both result in a reduction of information. This classificatory system needs further refinement before an adequate evaluation can be made of its approach to task classification.

The information-theoretic or systems language approach, based on an information theory model, with a set of definitions and relationships among parameters affecting performance and classes, has several advantages. The scheme encompasses both human and machine tasks, defining tasks as information transfers. The approach is potentially useful for solving a vast array of practical problems, including equipment design and selection procedure and training program development. Additionally, the possibility of this approach encompassing other provisional classificatory approaches, such as the Ability Requirements Approach and the Task Characteristics Approach, may be the scheme's greatest usefulness. This integration may occur through a common systems language for task performance.

For these advantages to be realized fully, the theoretical model must be demonstrated to have some empirical support. While fairly elaborate plans have been made for a two-fold, iterative evaluation process involving theoretical (computer simulation) and empirical (series of experiments) activities, the evaluative work for this approach has not begun. At least the equipment (the Sequential Information Processing Programmer) was developed which would allow a minimal research effort bearing on the model's validity or invalidity. Future research efforts are needed to test the model's viability under both simple and complex circumstances. Perhaps it will be possible to predict task performance from a knowledge of the operational constraints for various levels of informational redundancy.

References

Donders, F. C. Die schnelligkeit psychischer processe. *Arch. Anat. Physiol.*, 1868, 657–681.

Farina, A. J., & Wheaton, G. R. Development of a taxonomy of human performance: The task characteristics approach to performance prediction. *JSAS Catalog of Selected Documents in Psychology*, 1973, 3, 26–27. (Ms. No. 323).

Fleishman, E. A., & Stephenson, R. W. Development of a taxonomy of human performance: A review of the third year's progress. *JSAS Catalog of Selected Documents in Psychology*, 1970, 3, 1–68. (Ms. No. 113).

Fleishman, E. A., Teichner, W., and Stephenson, R. W. Development of a taxonomony of human performance: A review of the second year's progress. *JSAS Catalog of Selected Documents in Psychology*, 1972, 2, 39–40. (Ms. No. 112).

Garner, W. R. *Uncertainty and structure in psychological research.* New York: Wiley, 1962.

Hilgard, E., & Bower, G. *Theories of learning.* Englewood Cliffs, N.J.: Prentice–Hall, 1974.

Levine, J. M., & Teichner, W. H. *A systems language for task classification.* Unpublished manuscript, March 1970.

Levine, J. M., & Teichner, W. H. Plans for the development of a systems language. In E. A. Fleishman, W. H. Teichner, & R. W. Stephenson, Development of a taxonomy of human performance: A review of the second year's progress. *JSAS Catalog of Selected Documents in Psychology*, 1972, 2, 39–40. (Ms. No. 112).

Levine, J. M., & Teichner, W. H. Development of a taxonomy of human performance:

An information-theoretic approach. *JSAS Catalog of Selected Documents in Psychology*, 1973, *3*, 28, (Ms. No. 325).

Posner, M. I. Information reduction in the analysis of sequential tasks. *Psychological Review*, 1964, *7*, 491–504.

Shannon, C. E., & Weaver, W. *The mathematical theory of communication*. Urbana, Il.: University of Illinois Press, 1949.

Teichner, W. H. *An information-theoretic approach to task classification*. Paper presented at the meeting of the American Psychological Association, Washington, D.C. September 1969.

Teichner, W. H. *Quantitative models for predicting human visual/perceptual motor performance* (Technical Report NMSU-ONR-TR-74-3). Las Cruces: New Mexico State University, Department of Psychology, October 1974.

Teichner, W. H., & Olson, D. *Predicting human performance in space environments* (NASA Contract Report No. CR 1370). Washington, D.C.: National Aeronautics and Space Administration, June 1969.

Theologus, G. T., Romashko, T., & Fleishman, E. A. Development of a taxonomy of human performance: A feasibility study of ability requirements for classifying human tasks. *JSAS Catalog of Selected Documents in Psychology*, 1973, *3*, 25–26. (Ms. No. 321).

CHAPTER 11

The Task Strategies Approach

Although the Criterion Measures Approach and the Information-Theoretic Approach to the classification of human performance were largely derivations from the field of experimental psychology, the Task Strategies Approach developed by R. B. Miller (1973) was an outgrowth of his work involving task analysis.

Researchers and practitioners alike have an interest in task analysis activities that provide information for better personnel systems. Thus, task information generated from these descriptive and analytic procedures is useful for the development of selection and performance appraisal procedures and training curricula, as well as for the design of equipment, simulators, and human–machine systems.

Task Analysis versus Task Description

Farina (1973) distinguished between the concepts of task description and task analysis. He views *task description* as a subprocess of task analysis, focusing on the production of a detailed picture of what physically occurs (e.g., push buttons) in the interaction of humans and machines within a system environment. In contrast, *task analysis* is a process that attempts to abstract behavioral implications from this description. Thus, task description concentrates on behavior description information (e.g., overt response activities) and non-behavioral information, such as characteristics of equipment, tools, or supplies, whereas task analysis attempts to identify the related behavioral requirements of the operator.

Miller (1962) advocated a similar distinction between these two processes. He suggested that task description is based on a Stimulus–Response–Feedback (S–R–F) paradigm, specifying over time the cues the human should perceive in the task environment and the related responses that should be made. This task-description process results in the identification of the following components for each task element: (1) an indicator on which the activity-relevant indication appears; (2) the indicator or cue that elicits a response (stimulus); (3) the control object to be activated; (4) the activation or manipulation to be made (response); and (5) the indication of response adequacy (feedback). Miller criticized this S–R–F model, suggesting that, for a full understanding of performance, it is necessary to analyze the role of intervening or organismic variables, functions, and processes (S–O–R–F). Like Farina, Miller views task analysis as the identification of the behavioral requirements needed for task completion. These behavioral requirements (functions, processes) form the basis of the behavioral structure of a task.

Working within the Taxonomy Project, Miller (1973) proposed that four dimensions be given consideration when categorizing human task performance. These dimensions are: task functions, task content, task environment, and level of learning. His own work in building such a classificatory scheme has focused primarily on the identification and refinement of task functions and their associated task strategies that result in more effective performance. Consequently, this system has been labeled the *Task Strategies Approach*. It relies largely on behavioral requirements as the mechanism for task classification (Miller, 1973, 1974).

In this chapter, we present Miller's (1962) earlier conceptualization for the analysis of intervening processes when describing human task performance. His work with task analysis led to a preliminary formulation of the behavioral structure of a task. We shall review this structure and its functional categories in its generic form and in its applications to real-world task situations. We shall see that this early conceptualization aided Miller in formulating his transactional definition of a task, which is the cornerstone of the Task Strategies Approach. Using a particular methodology, Miller developed a list of 24 task functions that he called a transactional *systems task vocabulary*. This list was later refined and work strategies were identified for each function through a process of analysis and synthesis of task information. We describe representative work strategies for various task functions and demonstrate how work strategies may be applied within particular job contexts. After a discussion of some of the practical applications of the Task Strategies Approach, we evaluate this descriptive system of task classification in light of the criteria established in Chapter 4. Much of the material summarized in this chapter is drawn from two technical reports prepared by Miller (1973, 1974).

Behavioral Structure of a Task

Table 11.1 presents the generalized task structure developed from Miller's earlier analysis of task performance. This structure, which has been expanded extensively in later work, represents the functions that an operator uses to meet the demands of the task. It is important to note that these functions, or covert internal processes, were "invented," not discovered or derived from empirical data.

The underlying conceptual model for Miller's generalized task structure views the human performer as an information-processing system. Consequently, as with any adaptive or programmable system, there are four minimum system functions: input reception, memory, processing, and output effectors. Table 11.1 demonstrates that, for two of these functions, a variety of subfunctions are specified. Miller (1973, pp. 2–3) describes the sequencing of these functions as follows:

> [The human information processor] must *scan* [the] environmental field . . . to detect task relevant cues and perhaps filter these cues through irrelevancies and disturbances. Cues must be responded to as message entities or patterns or organizations which are relatively stable and can have names attached to them—these are *identifications*. . . . When the data presented to the human seem incomplete or inadequate for selecting an effector action, reference information stored in the human may be necessary to interpret the pattern of cues—give it "meaningfulness" in terms of task context.
>
> Since the [human] must respond to data in the immediate (or not so immediate) past, as well as to data active on the sense organs, a buffering capability is necessary for storing transient task information. The coding of the contents of the buffer is not necessarily the same as the form in which the data are apprehended—indeed this would be inefficient from many standpoints. In any event, the function of *short term memory* is a necessary postulation.
>
> The information content of "procedures" or programs is stored in *long term memory*. These contents are used in processing input data, complex mediating processes, and organization and selection of output processes. Long term memory is, of course, the equivalent of the content of what has been learned and its associative linkage structure with all orders ot task data.
>
> If an input or stimulus pattern does not immediately lead to the selection of an "appropriate" response, further mediating activities must occur. These processing activities [are] called [problem solving].
>
> Motor and other *effector processes* are output activities.

TABLE 11.1

Behavioral Structure of a Task[a]

Goal Image	
Input	Reception of Task Information
	Scan and Detect
	Identification
	Noise Filtering
Memory	Retention of Task Information
	Short-term Retention
	Long-term Retention
	Memory for Codes
Processing	Interpretation and Decision Making
Output	Motor Response Mechanisms

[a]Adapted with permission from Miller, R. B. (1) Task description and analysis. In R. M. Gagné (Ed.), *Psychological principles in system development.* New York: Holt, Rinehart and Winston, 1962. *(2) Development of a taxonomy of human performance: Design of a systems task vocabulary* (American Institutes for Research Tech. Rep.). *JSAS Catalog of Selected Documents in Psychology,* 1973, *3,* 29–30 (Ms. No. 327).

Taken as a whole, these functions suggest that the human, as an information processor, transmits information in the form of messages through a series of behaviors or transactions. For this reason, as we shall see later in this chapter, the functions in his generalized task structure have been labeled a transactional *systems task vocabulary.*

APPLICATION OF MILLER'S FUNCTIONS: AN EXAMPLE

To clarify the application of the functions in his generalized task structure to task accomplishment, Miller (1973) used an illustration of a soldier in the field charged with removing rust spots from any metal part of a rifle with rust remover and a swab. The *goal image* is the criterion level of performance to be achieved; in this case, a clean rifle may be defined either as one with no rust spots or with some other set of perceptual references as to the appearance and feel of the rifle. The criterion level is not likely to be absolute. The condition of acceptability may differ across performers, in this case, soldiers, and as a function of the environmental conditions. For example, although a clean rifle may be a matter of life and death in combat, demands of the combat situation on the soldier may make cleaning a lower priority. Under usual circumstances, the goal set affects the performance of the task, including the class of messages accepted, the program selected for processing, the selection of material from memory content, and the selection of a class of output activities. As an example, when we are thirsty, we look for signs leading to water; we attempt to recall or deduce how the available cues were used to find water in the past and we select those actions that we expect will lead us to water. Motivational variables also interact with the goal image to affect human task performance.

To return to our example of the soldier, once the goal image has been established, a *scan and detect* mechanism is instituted to differentiate work cues in a neutral field. This entails inspecting the metal parts of the rifle for places that do not meet the task criterion level of "clean." The scanning function may be preceded by a procedural set-up, such as ensuring the right amount of light to aid visibility. The actual scanning may be a habit sequence for examining segments of the field, such as the barrel or the breech. If the soldier detects a deviation from the smooth, bright surface of the barrel, it may or may not be identified as rust. Once a deviation has been perceived, the soldier must determine whether the deviation is rust, dirt, a shadow, or something else. The soldier also may use additional scanning modes. For example, the soldier may rub the suspected area with a finger; if it is rough, the chances increase that it is rust.

The naming operation may result in a mnemonic aid for a complex sensory impression and, thus, use less short-term storage capacity. Applying the label *rust* tells the soldier to check the name against other labels on the can of rust remover and in the table of contents of the rifle manual. Although the naming or *identification* of the suspected area as rust is an important function, an even more important role of this process is serving as a cue for the next response. Thus, the identification of the rust spot may initiate the procedural task of reaching for the rust remover and swab.

Having identified the area as rust, the soldier might next scan and detect the work area to locate the swab before picking it up. This concern with such detail reflects a micromotion task-analysis. While this scan and detect action might well be discarded as irrelevant to anything "important," this would be an act of judgment on the part of the task analyst. In any task analysis, the analyst is involved in innumerable instances of similar judgments. Thus, task description and task analysis never can be complete in terms of data collection. The analyst must choose an appropriate balance between microactions and macroactions. Consequently, in any task analysis, there may be several loops of scan–detect–identify before a next step in the task structure is entered, depending on the level of task description desired by the analyst.

Once the soldier identifies the area as rust, an act of *interpretation* may be involved before the cleaning responses are activated. A single rust spot may suggest to the soldier that the rifle has been exposed to moisture and that there are probably more rust spots. The inference "exposure to moisture, hence more rust spots" implies the addition of information currently in the soldier's head to the information contained in the observation of a rust spot, resulting in the drawing of a conclusion. Thus, *conclusions* are the products of interpretation.

Interpretations may be viewed as hypotheses regarding how a number of different cues are interrelated because of some pattern projected on them (like an overlay) by the operator. An interpretation involves a generalization or conceptual classification and abstraction. Typically, the operator is searching for generalizations about identifiable task activities. As a result of interpretation, the soldier may rescan the field previously examined, using greater care (e.g., by examining smaller areas at a time). The soldier also may take apart the activating mechanism and reexamine the bore of the rifle for rust.

It is entirely possible that a procedure previously learned by the soldier may eliminate the need for interpretation. For example, the soldier may be taught, "whenever you find a single rust spot on any part of your rifle, disassemble it completely and clean it completely, using rust remover." Such a procedure leads directly to action without the application of further interpretive functions.

Once the soldier decides to clean the rifle, the soldier's long-term memory provides the information for selecting and using the rust remover and swab to remove the rust. The contents of long-term memory are recalled through a process of accessing the relevant content and converting that content into a task action directly, as in automatic motor performance, or indirectly, by means of verbal content, imagery, or both. Stored information is summoned on the basis of identified and interpreted cues, with that information linking the cue to the task response. Miller suggests this function be called *long-term memory for procedures*, as it applies to scanning habits, detection, identification, and interpretation.

In contrast, *short-term memory* is defined as the application of stored information both peculiar and relevant to the task cycle. Short-term memory may assist in interpretation. For example, the soldier may recall walking briefly beside a shallow river during the day and, thus, account for the rust. In cleaning the rifle, short-term memory carries the location of the rust spot on the rifle while the soldier is getting the swab and soaking it in rust remover. Additionally, more or less continuously, the soldier recalls which parts of the rifle have been cleaned and which remain to be cleaned.

In some instances, the recall of procedures does not, in and of itself,

eliminate choices. In still others, the operator has not learned a procedure that can be recalled or generalized to the demands of the
particular task situation.[1] Thus, the rust removing soldier may
choose to clean the first identified spot of rust, to do a complete job of
using rust remover on all the metal parts, or to delay cleaning until a
few more rust spots have been identified. If the rust remover does not
remove the entire rust spot, the soldier has another decision to make.
The decision as to when to stop cleaning is based on the soldier's
perception of the result of the cleaning efforts vis-à-vis the standard
adopted earlier as part of the goal image. Some amount of *decision
making* enters into every task, even one that is highly routinized. The
importance of the decision-making behavior is dependent on the context and purpose of the task. Decision making logically follows an
interpretation; in fact, it may even be part of the interpretation as
selection of one of several hypotheses. Decision making has particular operational significance when contingencies arise (unexpected
task environments, operator overloads, error by human or machine)
for which the operator lacks a procedure for choice and action in
long-term memory. For even the most artifically simple task, there
may be a great variety of contingencies that can beset every cycle of
the task and the task's behavioral context. It is the capacity to deal
with the great proportions of these contingencies that differentiates
good from poor performers. Often, the operator contributes stored
information to facilitate the decision-making process. Decisions typically reflect real-life trade-offs among values that are qualitatively
and quantitatively complex.

Once all information has been received and processed, often in
combination with stored information, the operator is ready to produce a *motor response*. Few modern tasks require high orders of dexterity. For instance, in our example of cleaning a rifle, the motor
elements of the task tend to be procedural. Grossly inadequate motor
performances often lack adequate task strategy in terms of recalled
procedure, such as setting down the rifle before moistening the swab
with the solvent, and finding a level spot to place the open bottle of
solvent before opening it. Although much motor behavior requires
less skill, the public's image of motor behavior is usually that of the
performance of a virtuoso pianist, a billiard champion, a skiing

---

[1]The problems caused by the absence of such procedures suggest that training
should focus on imposing the ability requirement to "invent good procedures." That is,
the operator may have to be able to compensate for what the operator did not learn in
training.

champion, or an expert race car driver. Motor considerations are indeed significant in delicately timed operations. In complex skills, however, the utility of separating perceptual from motor components is often dubious.

This analysis of a soldier's activities with a rifle illustrates the intermeshing of the functional components of the generalized task structure with real-life behaviors. The functions follow logically in the sequence of goal orientation, identification, interpretation, short-term memory, long-term memory, decision making (or problem solving), and motor activity. Practically no procedural step was taken without some manifestation of each and every function.

In his more recent work, Miller (1982b) suggested that there are more or less standard variables that recur in each task cycle as part of the generalized task structure. With continued practice, an operator internalizes these task variables as a kind of implicit model for apprehending and holding in mind task-relevant information during task performance. These learned tendencies to respond selectively to recurring variables and conditions in a given information-processing transaction are labeled *task formats*. This concept is similar to that of set or expectancy previously discussed in the psychological literature.

Miller believed that the commonality-oriented task structure approach was the best way to proceed in the search for a classificatory system to categorize human task performance. This task structure obviated the need for artificial boundaries between one task and another. His conceptualization proposes a statement of the job mission with a starting point and a structure; within some range of variation, these tend to be constant from one mission cycle to another. Thus, practically every human task has some degree of all the constituent functions presented in the task structure. Certain tasks weight more highly on some functions than on others. However, Miller (1973) added that "even a piano mover should *scan and detect* a marble on the stairs, *interpret* its potential significance, and devise a foot-moving *strategy* that will avoid its untoward possibilities" (p. 3).

Although convinced of the generality of his task structure and the commonalities across human task performance, Miller warned against an oversimplified view of human tasks. For instance, when a computer analyst attempts to automate a human information-processing task and to compare the outcome with the work of even a below average human, the variety and complexity of the simplest human acts are revealed. Undoubtedly, this variety and complexity of human task performance are partially responsible for Miller's later elaboration of his classificatory scheme from the four generalized functions in Table 11.1 to the 25 he defined in a later report (Miller, 1974).

Evaluation of Miller's Preliminary Formulation of the Behavioral Structure of a Task

Farina (1973) suggested that a task analysis system such as the behavioral structure identified by Miller (1962) requires two basic components to become operational. The first is a descriptive schema of behavior such as that outlined in Table 11.1. The second is a set of rules specifying the reference operations for determining whether a particular behavioral or functional category is relevant to a given task in question. Farina added that, at the very least, these rules conceivably could be contained within the definitions of the behaviors comprising the schema. In other words, if the behaviors are defined objectively and precisely, the task analyst's attention can be directed explicitly to specific characteristics that, in effect, define the presence or absence of a particular behavior in a work situation. As presented in Table 11.1, Miller's behavioral functions lack precision. The definitions do not provide the level of specificity that would dictate the rules for assuming the applicability of a particular process to a given task. Furthermore, there are no rules for quantifying the degree to which a particular function is required for effective task performance. Miller (1967) himself has characterized his definitions as "overlapping," "ambiguous," and "lacking handles for quantification."

However, the real evaluation of this scheme should be made not on the basis of the amount of detail devoted to definitions of the functional categories, but rather on the basis of the scheme's utility in an operational task setting. Farina does acknowledge that Miller and his associates have had modest success in applying his scheme to work situations, such as identifying conditions likely to lead to increases in errors, and adapting complex human activities so that new applications for computers can be conceptualized. Nonetheless, Angell, Shearer & Berliner (1964) found little agreement among judges using the system to assign some 40 tasks into the categories of various classificatory systems. The low reliability obtained from the application of Miller's behavioral structure may be due not just to the lack of precision in the functional definitions, but also to the intuitive, rational nature of the system. This task analysis system involves a clinical exercise (a creative enterprise because of the interactions and contingencies occurring in task situations), so that the recording process itself involves value judgements and reflects only portions of the total situation (see Farina, 1973).

In light of the lack of adequate functional definitions and rules for applying those functions to real task situations, as well as the resulting need for analyst judgment in applying Miller's (1962) scheme, it may be concluded that the preliminary formulation has serious limitations. However, as we shall see, later efforts were directed toward improving some of the deficiencies associated with this preliminary formulation, thus strengthening its contribution to the description and classification of human task performance.

A Transactional Definition of Task

Prior to adopting a definition for the construct "task," Miller (1973) reviewed a number of the major kinds of reference images associated with that term. These include (1) defining a task in a real-world context of human purpose, interruption, ambiguity, motivation, noise, concomitance, and contingencies; (2) equating a task with a relatively pure laboratory activity; (3) viewing a task as a set of abilities which are statistically derived from empirical data (as in the Ability Requirements Approach); (4) defining a task as a set of transactions or task functions that result in a sequence of work stages directed toward a work activity (as in the Behavioral Requirements Approach); and (5) equating a task with the transmission of bits of information from one system component to another (as in the Information-Theoretic Approach).

For the development of his classificatory system, the latter two reference images (transaction or function and information transmission) were incorporated into a unified transactional definition of task. Thus, tasks were viewed as involving transactions, especially information-processing transactions, and defined as follows: "A task consists of a series of goal-directed transactions controlled by one or more 'programs' that guide the operations by a human operator of a prescribed set of tools through a set of completely or partially predicted environmental states" (1973, p. 11). This definition implies that the task is characterized not only by a succession of transactional relationships between the operator and the environment, but also by a succession of behavioral states within the operator. The definition combines structural factors (programs) and process activities (transactions), leading to an inference that every task cycle is unique. A classificatory scheme, identifying the commonalities of tasks, would have to be superimposed on this definition.

Miller (1973) examines the components of this transactional definition of a task in greater detail. His use of the term *series* implies setting the task boundaries. A useful starting point for identifying the beginning of a task series is the initiating operation of establishing a set including a given pattern of intentions, expectations, and preparatory responses. The series is completed with a sense of accomplishment of the performance cycle, that is, with a subjective state of an opportunity seized or missed.

In contrast to this subjective feeling of task completion, the goal image provides an objective standard against which to evaluate task accomplishment. *Goal direction,* derived from the goal image, establishes criteria for determining relevant cues and appropriate responses in the situation.

A *transaction* is a process on a task message that creates a change of state and, consequently, defines the condition of a subsequent response or of a goal state. A *program* is a relationship between a state or condition (stimulus), a tool, and an action to be taken with that tool (response). If the relationship involves subsets of response alternatives to planned environmental contingencies, the program is more elaborate and may involve decision making or problem solving. Programs may be preplanned or improvised. If situations involving improvised programs are repeated, those programs may become procedural. In terms of learning theory, a response once relatively low in the hierarchy becomes higher in the hierarchy. Programs may inhibit as well as activate responses.

Prescribed tools include instruments that (1) enable something to be made; (2) permit the sensing and interpreting of an environmental state (e.g., the ear or eye); (3) enable an action to be taken to change an environmental state to facilitate reaching a goal state; or (4) access more information about the state of affairs relative to the task.

Environmental states are the conditions that separate a goal state from a present state. They are also the environmental conditions under which the task transactions must be performed. They may help or hinder the mechanisms for performing the task, including the activities of the human operator.

This transactional definition of task could possibly be faulted for its attempt at all-inclusiveness. However, any reference image for "task" intended to generalize to the world of work must provide for the integration of psychological variables and environmental variables in the operational setting of which the task is only one such variable. The definition Miller supplies certainly meets this requirement.

Dimensions for Categorizing Task Information

Miller's transactional definition of task has implications for the design of any descriptive system attempting to categorize tasks to enable generalizations regarding human task perormance from setting to setting. The definition suggests four major dimensions for categorizing task information: (1) task content, (2) task environment (prescribed tools and environmental states), (3) level of learning (e.g., the state of development of the programs), and (4) discriminable task functions (transactions). Miller (1973) suggested that unless "performance is characterized in dimensions such as these, judgments about [the] applicability of data sets to each other will produce necessarily vague or potentially misleading generalizations" (p. 14). On the basis of these four dimensions, performance could be indexed into a reference library of tasks with great utility for researchers and practitioners alike. We shall describe briefly three of the task dimensions before presenting the extensive work involving both the development of the fourth dimension (task functions) and the associated task strategies.

Task content is defined as the kind of information the operator must use. It pertains to the subject matter of the task. Whereas an ideal taxonomy of human performance would be content free, a more conservative classificatory approach would include a statement regarding task content. Miller questioned whether a taxonomic dimension of task content could be established, suggesting that factor-analytic methods might be applied to enable the researcher to differentiate task structure (behavioral functions) from task content and to relate or discriminate among the various kinds of task content. Until such statistical methods are refined, the relevance of the content of one task to the content of another task will be based to a greater extent on connotation than on denotation. Although some diverse tasks (e.g., decoding a program from Fortran into ordinary English and decoding a telegrapher's Morse code into English) may involve the same structured operations, their unique subject matter results in quite different behavioral problems relevant to selection, training, and job aids.

Under the dimension of *task environment*, two separate concepts are included. One is the physiological and psychological environment of the operator in terms of stress, impairment, or handicap. The second is other goal-directed activities that are more or less congruent with the subject task.

Occasionally, the environment may have deleterious physiological effects on the operator, which potentially can threaten the effectiveness of task performance. These effects are ameliorated partially by the fact that the operator rarely is performing at the maximum performance limits, either in terms of physical work or in terms of information-processing. Consequently, the operator has substantial reserve capacities available for greater arousal, reserves that can result in quantitative and qualitative improvements in performance. Thus, the operator compensates by applying greater effort when feeling physiologically below par. For example, workers are still able to perform even when suffering from a headache, a slight fever, or a hangover. However, if a task demands a maximum effort from the operator when the operator is in optimal shape physiologically, any physiological change altering the operator's condition will result in inadequate task performance. Some kinds of activity may deteriorate from the effects of the task environment more quickly than others. For example, drowsiness may affect vigilance and field of scan more severely than it affects performance of a well-learned, serialized procedure. The extent to which a physiological stressor or deteriorator affects task performance depends on the extent to which the operator performs (or needs to perform) the given task at a high degree of arousal.

The effects of psychological stressors on operator performance can be assumed similar to those of physiological stressors. The operator, under conditions of psychological stress, may exhibit more effort to counterbalance those effects and to manitain performance levels. If, under normal circumstances, the task requires maximum concentration and effort, the effects of psychological stressors cannot be counteracted and performance decrements (either quantitative or qualitative) undoubtedly will occur.

A task performed congruently with another task ("time-shared" tasks) may have different implications for selection, training evaluation, procedural design, and work space design, than a task performed independently. Miller (1973) provides a real-world example of simultaneous performance of a variety of goal-directed activities, the second type of task environment:

> While the mechanic is diagnosing a fault by organizing symptoms and making inferences, he is also setting up test instruments, comparing test readings with nominal values, searching for references in a manual, watching the clock signalling an overrun of allowable maintenance time, and so on. He becomes fatigued by awkward positions, exasperated by test probes that fall off, anxious about inadvertently touching a high voltage line, or about turning on power and, due to an error on his part, blowing out the entire equipment [p. 13].

Tasks must be viewed in a holistic context containing not only congruent activities, but antecedent and subsequent activities as well. All concurrent activities undertaken by the operator sum into one "task." Generalizations regarding principles associated with task functions must be qualified based on knowledge of the task environment, that is, a description of the other goal-directed activities associated with the task function.

The third dimension identified by Miller for the classification of human task performance is *level of learning*. Fleishman (1957, 1966, 1967), Fleishman and Ellison (1969), Fleishman and Hempel (1954, 1955), and Fleishman and Rich (1963) have offered evidence that tasks are performed with qualitative and quantitative differences by individual operators at different levels of practice. Individual differences after a skill has been learned are not the same as those demonstrated during the early stages of learning. Miller (1973) provides the following hypothetical example of this phenomenon:

> A student who is rapid at rote verbalization of procedures may quickly master the early stages of a procedural ability, but as greater speed is required and the verbal mediators have to drop out of the behavior, the individual with better "eye-muscle" learning ability will surpass the good verbal learner [p. 18].

High degrees of practice lead to the automatization of habits and, consequently, the deletion of much verbal–conceptual mediating behavior. Thus, the habit, in the form of a skill, represents a different response from that previously demonstrated when the response was performed as verbal-mediated behavior. Consequently, there are at least two levels of learning, mediated and nonmediated. Not only are there different ability implications at different levels of learning, but also unique human engineering and training implications.

Miller suggested that level of learning has an oblique, but significant, relationship to the task functions used to describe human performance. Specifically, the higher the degree of practice with a given population of stimulus situations, the lower the complexity of the kind of task function (or number of processing transactions) that mediates the response to the stimulus situation. Task situations, which at one stage of practice consist of almost formal decision making behavior, shift to interpretation and finally to identification. As an example, we can contrast the process of diagnosis of a common illness by an intern with that of one who has diagnosed thousands of patients. The former must detect, identify, and interpret clusters of symptoms before reaching a decision regarding the ailment, whereas the latter is able to identify by name the common ailment as soon as the patient is observed, without invoking more elaborate task functions. The larger the universe of variations and the larger the number of variables in that universe, the greater the amount of practice required to move from a higher level of functioning to a lower level of information-processing for effective performance. Additionally, subtle differences or unique interaction effects among variables also inhibit the application of the more elementary task functions. Thus, level of learning has important implications for generalizing performance data from one situation to another. In his earlier work, Miller criticized the learning research literature for its overconcentration on the behavior of the novice performer in cognitively deprived tasks and its neglect of the examination of skilled performers in cognitively complex situations.

In summary, Miller has suggested categorizing task information by (1) describing the task content or subject matter; (2) identifying the task environment, including physiological and psychological stressors on the operator and external conditions imposed by time-shared tasks; (3) recognizing the level of learning stipulated for the task, taking into account the fact that different amounts of practice result in changes in the nature of the application of the task functions required for effective performance; and (4) naming the task function (through procedures described in the following sections of this chapter). These four dimensions parallel the components of Miller's transactional definition of task.

Task Functions: Development of a Systems Task Vocabulary

Miller proposed *task functions* as a fourth dimension to categorize human task performance. After clarifying the relationship between task functions and transactions, we present some guidelines and procedures for analysts wishing to invent or adopt task function terminology. We summarize Miller's classificatory approach, which involves 25 task functions, and relate this scheme to his earlier formulation of the behavioral structure of a task. Finally, we provide some guidance regarding the appropriate use of the *systems task vocabulary*, which is reproduced in its entirety as Appendix A.

The names and definitions of the task functions characterize transactions. A transaction is defined as a process on a task message that creates a change of state and, consequently, defines the condition of a subsequent response or of a goal state. A transaction begins when a stimulus field is searched and a potentially relevant task stimulus is detected. A series of transactions or functions may follow in identifying the components of the message, interpreting it, and selecting courses of action. Ultimately, some action results in an effector operation on the environment.

A message may be natural (e.g., a roadway), symbolic (e.g., instruction in an English text), or a combination. A *message* is defined as embodying a unit of structure of information; *structure* refers to syntactic rules and relations. Thus, a declarative statement is one kind of message. Its syntactic elements are the subject, predicate, and object. Messages have semantic (reference or meaning), syntactic (structure) and pragmatic (utility) dimensions. Messages are transmitted in a medium that imposes constraints on what is being communicated, such as on the particular pattern of information or speed of transmission. The set of rules for selecting or interpreting the symbols that transmit the content of the message may be viewed as a code. If the receiver (human or machine) shares the same rules for decoding a message as the source that encoded the message, it is assumed that the message will reach its maximum level of potential effectiveness. Because messages exist in time, they must be in a state of being transmitted, stored, processed, or in some combination of these states. This fact represents a highly significant consideration in the development of a set of consistent, operational definitions of task function.

Guidelines and Procedures for Invention or Adoption of Functional Categories

Miller believed that a useful systems task vocabulary would need to provide an exhaustive list of information-processing functions representing all classes of system transactions. The scientific method is effective in revealing common physical structures and properties of objects, but the adaptive functions acquired by purposeful human entities are essentially an arbitrary imposition made by the analyst. Thus, discriminable task functions typically represent an invention of the analyst. Previous descriptive listings of functions or processes had included a sufficient number of terms in the glossary to be of use to a particular class of specialists. Terms generally were invented as needed, resulting in a great proliferation of technical terms and a large variety of vocabularies.

To assist in the development of the classificatory system of task functions, a variety of practical guidelines and procedures were established to be exercised in the invention and/or adoption of functional categories. These procedures, which represent techniques for mapping or naming system behavior, were required to stabilize the growth and proliferation of taxonomic glossaries. Although someday a taxonomic glossary might be derived from classical behavioral research methods, in the interim practical guidance for glossary development is needed. This guidance represents a rationale for creating a descriptive and analytic terminology for general system behavior. Miller (1973) suggested that the analyst wishing to develop, add, or change terminology, should do the following:

1. Assume the human is an information processor, capable of coding one class of information into another class of information, where the second class is symbolic of the first. Symbols, when communicated between system components, are messages. Thus, humans are message processors.

2. Limit the size of an analytic, descriptive vocabulary to 25 to 30 terms. A vocabulary of this size is believed to be of sufficient utility. Fewer terms would be preferred, but there is a trade-off with the need for precision when describing human task behavior. The terminology should be sufficiently complete to enable the full description of the chain of functions between system input and output, that is, to show what has to be done to the inputs of the system to convert the information into outputs. The same vocabulary should be applicable to describing internal system functions. Analysts will have a difficult

time differentiating 25–30 task functions, so a limit on the number of task functions is required for human convenience in learning and application.

3. Assume that a workable vocabulary for human tasks will also be a workable vocabulary for machine tasks in human–machine systems. Thus, the terminology will be independent of the mechanism that performs the function. It is highly desirable for analysts to use the same terminology in both contexts. This notion of a common definition of tasks and task processes for both humans and machines also characterizes the Information-Theoretic Approach to task classification (see Chapter 10, and Miller, 1982a).

4. Stipulate that identifiable transaction operations are required in the definitions of the terms in the vocabulary. The terminology should reference transactional definitions that point both to the transformation operation and to the information necessary to make the transformation denoted by the term. The analyst should be able to justify the term selected on the basis of the identified transactions.

5. Stipulate that the terms need not be mutually exclusive. The activities denoted by one term may be component activities of another term. This results from the fact that the functions are derived from a conceptual model providing for the continuous flow of information. This model implies linking transactions that result in some redundancy of terms. However, Miller suggested that the redundancy is a small price for comprehensiveness.

6. Assume the necessity of judgment in applying these terms to the real world. Thus, it is expected that the terms will be characterized by some degree of ambiguity when applied to real-life situations.

7. Design the terminology to be applicable to gross, as well as to fine, levels of system operation. Both micro and macro operations should be capable of analysis by the systems task vocabulary.

8. Provide a vocabulary that permits the specification of system objectives in qualitative and quantitative terms. The vocabulary may suggest a basis for the development of quantification or measurement techniques for the various task functions.

With these considerations in mind, Miller developed his 24 task functions in the systems task vocabulary. Specifically, he held in his mind an image of a generalized information-processing system. The system was described as having receptor input channels, a processing facility, a modifiable memory for both data and procedures, and output facilities. The system included the capability to transmit symbolic messages. Transactions or messages result in responses or physical work mechanisms. The generalized information-processing system exists in an environment. The concept of system goal is side-stepped by treating the goal as resulting from a supersystem design entity. This supersystem not only imbues an implicit purpose that directs the design of the system facilities, but it also affects the control programming of those facilities.

The invention of Miller's functional categories was facilitated by an imaginary sequencing of activities performed on a message from the time it is available for entering as an input (where it competes with irrelevancies) to the time an appropriate or inappropriate response is emitted. The development of his processing concepts was aided by sampling from different kinds of message format and content, which imply different treatments by the system in selecting appropriate outputs. Messages may be incomplete (missing information), contain irrelevant data or false information, or require code translation or decoding in the form of conceptual and logical operations. Some messages have to be combined with others. Further, the source of the message may be either the environment or the memory of the system. All these variations in message format and development have different implications for the design of task functions.

Using the conceptual model of a generalized information-processing system, a function was defined by stating the significant feature of: (1) the input mode, message or source; (2) the processing rules or operations for translating the input into the output; and (3) the output condition or result of the operation. Thus, as with operational definitions in general, the name of the function becomes merely a mnemonic handle for the analyst once the transactions have been defined.

THE SYSTEMS TASK VOCABULARY

Using the above rationale and procedures, Miller (1973) created a descriptive and analytical terminology to represent the functions operating in a generalized information-processing system. The 24 task functions he identified and defined are presented in the left-hand column of Table 11.2. In the right-hand column are listed Miller's earlier functional categories, opposite their more recent counterparts. Goal Image and Motor Response Mechanisms do not have direct referents. However, in his later formulation of the systems task vocabulary, Miller (1974) added a new task function, Goal Image, or a picture of a task well done. Miller believed that his list of functions was relatively exhaustive of the classes of information-processing en-

TABLE 11.2

Miller's Systems Task Vocabulary[a]

Task functions[b]	Preliminary task functions
	Goal Image
1. *Message.* A collection of symbols sent as a meaningful statement.	
2. *Input Select.* Selecting what to pay attention to next.	
3. *Filter.* Straining out what does not matter.	Noise Filtering
4. *Queue to channel.* Lining up to get through the gate.	
5. *Detect.* Is something there?	
6. *Search.* Looking for something.	Search and Detect
7. *Identify.* What is it and what is its name?	Identification
8. *Code.* Translating the same thing from one form to another.	Memory for Code
9. *Interpret.* What does it mean?	Interpretation and Decision Making
10. *Categorize.* Defining and naming a group of things.	
11. *Transmit.* Moving something from one place to another.	
12. *Store.* Keeping something intact for future use.	Long-Term Retention
13. *Short-Term Memory (buffer).* Holding something temporarily.	Short-Term Retention
14. *Count.* Keeping track of how many.	
15. *Compute.* Figuring out a logical or mathematical answer to defined problem.	
16. *Decide–Select.* Choosing a response to fit the situation.	Interpretation and Decision Making
17. *Plan.* Matching resources in time to expectations.	
18. *Test.* Is it what it should be?	
19. *Control.* Changing an action according to plan.	
20. *Edit.* Arranging or correcting things according to rules.	
21. *Display.* Showing something that makes sense.	
22. *Adapt/Learn.* Making and remembering new responses to a learned situation.	
23. *Purge.* Getting rid of the dead stuff.	
24. *Reset.* Getting ready for some different action.	
	Motor Response Mechanisms

[a]Adapted with permission from Miller, R. B. (1) *Development of a taxonomy of human performance: Design of a systems task vocabulary* (American Institutes for Research Tech. Rep.). *JSAS Catalog of Selected Documents in Psychology*, 1973, *3*, 29–30 (Ms. No. 327). (2) *A method for determining task strategies* (Tech. Rep. AFHRL-TR-74-26). Washington, D.C.: American Institutes for Research, May 1974.

[b]The colloquial phrase for each term is intended as a mnemonic aid, not as a definition.

gaged in by humans in task environments. The one notable omission was the concept of *power*. Physical operations on signals require energy and entail energy loss or change; the psychological analogue of physical power is motivation.

Definitions of the 25 task functions, including the extended definition of Goal Image, are presented in an appendix to this book. Table 11.3 provides an illustration of one of these definitions, for the function *Detect*. The information provided for the 25 functions varies in terms of the level of descriptive detail and the nature of the format. For each of the functions, a mnemonic aid and a generalized definition are presented. For some functions, concrete examples of real-world behaviors involving the functions are provided, whereas others contain descriptive diagrams or paradigms, comments, notes, or summaries. For several, Miller discusses purpose, for others he provides a description of associated properties, variables, factors, requirements, subfunctions, difficulties, and so forth. For some, he discusses necessary trade-offs. Additionally, strategic principles for a large number of functions are derived. In his later work, these principles form the basis for the development of task strategies.

USE OF THE SYSTEMS TASK VOCABULARY

Miller suggested the manner in which his functional language should be used. A scenario is prepared of the sequence of activities in the operational use of the system. This sequence of actions is represented by a flow diagram in systems language. The flow diagram represents the sequence of transactions, from a given input condition or pattern of conditions, through the system components, to the output. Initially, the cue initiating a task "set" is identified. Miller (1973) explains:

> The next step in the scenario may be a request for a format for entering a query of a given class. This sets in motion another train of functions or activities, i.e., another sequence of processing flow functions is initiated. This sequence is diagrammed like the first, but a different pattern of information functions will be drawn. As additional steps in the operational scenario arise, they are similarly analyzed for their information-processing content and operations [p. 32].

The scenario is time-ordered, permitting the identification of concurrences. This allows the identification of patterns of activities that must be performed together. Additionally, it enables the identification of activities that must be brought together to permit a decision to be made. The combining of the processes that must occur within

TABLE 11.3

Definition of Miller's Task Function *Detect*[a]

Detect

Definition   Is something there?

Procedures and mechanisms for sensing the presence or absence of a cue or condition requiring that some form of action be taken by the system. Detection requires the discrimination of an action-stimulating cue from some background of stimulation. What is detected may consist of normal work cues, or of exceptions (such as errors). The source of these cues may be inputs to the system or feedback from the monitoring of outputs. The sensing function does not analyze or classify the cue.

Note: Detecting, as defined here, is confined to a sensing operation that excludes interpreting activities. In human terms, detecting results in sensing a stimulus to which attention will be paid. In many practical situations, however, detecting and identifying are a single process. (see *Identify*)

Scanning and Detecting

Unless the sensor is part of a fixed channel, it must scan segments of its environment so that the sensor is exposed to signals. The sensor is preset to respond to certain kinds of change or discontinuity in the field being scanned.

Principles

1. The response lag of the detecting device must be less than the cycle time of the stimulus to be detected.
2. The greater the contrast between the stimulus to be detected and its background, the greater the reliability of detection.
3. For given kinds of signal patterns to be detected, some scan patterns and frequencies are better than others.
4. In human behavior, what will be detected is related to "set" or pre-established tendencies to respond. More simply, we tend to notice what we expect to see, or what we are looking for, or what we are attending to. A number of principles in addition to item 2 influence human detection, as well as other sensing and perceptual behavior.[b]

Comment

In digital processing activities Detect and Identify cannot be separated. But in analog activities a sensor may detect a pattern of frequencies representing a speaking voice, but not be able to identify it or its content.

---

[a]Adapted with permission from Miller, R. B. *Development of a taxonomy of human performance: Design of a systems task vocabulary* (American Institutes for Research Tech. Rep.). *JSAS Catalog of Selected Documents in Psychology*, 1973, *3*, 29–30 (Ms. No. 327).

[b]See the chapter on perception in any general psychology text.

each step in the scenario sequence with all the steps in the scenario results in a time-ordered mapping of the information-processing required for either the hypothetical system or for an actual system in an operational environment. This functional mapping has to be revised with each step in the physical design of the system. Each physical facility imposes its own pattern of requirements on the system: its own channel capacity, delay functions, reliabilities, and limitations.

Work Strategies: Behavior and Task Strategies

While working on the Taxonomy Project, Miller (1973) identified strategic principles for many of his 25 task functions. These principles were later expanded into *work strategies* that were viewed as implicit in the job activities of highly proficient performers. In subsequent work, Miller (1974) contrasted work strategies, or higher order competencies, with simple procedural rules identified by his earlier task analysis procedure. Work strategies are optimizing procedural rules or principles to cope with uncertainties and scarce resources (including time). These competencies ensure that the procedures include, but are not restricted to, "tricks of the trade," which professional performers have developed. Such competencies enable the performer to be more effective at less personal cost. Thus, the operating strategies enable the performer to become a more efficient processor. Work strategies could be subdivided into two groups:

1. *Behavior Strategies:* techniques that maximize the operator as a processing resource. These techniques specifically offset certain types of error, increase the amount of task information the operator can process in a given amount of time, or increase operator reliability of performance. As an example, Miller described a driver who increases range and frequency of scanning behavior when anxious at reaching the goal. The driver's actions are directed at deliberately compensating for the tendency to use tunnel perception under stress.
2. *Task Strategies:* techniques for coping more effectively and efficiently with the uncertainties of a work environment.

All work strategies are constructed through trade-offs. A given layout of a problem in a work setting must depict a class of actions or a given action in a variety of circumstances. The strategic principle appears to be a compromise between a benefit and a cost, between one benefit and another, or one cost and another. Additionally, the strategy may be perceived as a compromise between short-term objectives and longer term objectives, or between task objectives and mission objectives.

In later work, Miller (1974) extended his earlier task analysis procedures to identify and describe work strategies for each of his 25 information-processing task functions. These strategies would lead to levels of competence above that of the bare procedural mastery of a task, insofar as they would differentiate between skilled and unskilled performance on a variety of tasks.

In Table 11.3, we presented a definition of the task function *Detect*. One of the principles listed for that function states, "In human behavior, what will be detected is related to 'set' or pre-established tendencies to respond. More simply, we tend to notice what we expect to see or what we are looking for, or what we are attending to." Miller (1974) transformed this principle into a work strategy for a formal training program designed to teach the Detect task function. Specifically, he suggested that operators learn "models of threat," which include dynamic factors in a task that need to be sampled at some frequency and range in order to assume some probability of survival or effectiveness. Thus, the principle recognizes the role of *set* in the application of the task function Detect. The work strategy involves instructing the operator to establish a set for detecting certain factors that might inhibit the operator's effective performance. Table 11.4 provides several additional work strategies for a number of the task functions. (For a more complete description of the work strategies he has developed, see Miller, 1974.)

Miller (1974) also provided examples of the application of task strategies for particular jobs: strategies for a parts procurement buyer; strategies for disassembling, inspecting, and reassembling a device for workers in a repair shop; strategies for loading and unloading a delivery truck for drivers; strategies for setting up a filing system for a supervising secretary; and strategies for visual inspection of a complex part for employees in an inspection room in a large electronics manufacturing facility. Table 11.5 presents the strategy for setting up a filing system. (The other extensive behavioral examples of applying task strategies within a real-world context are presented in an appendix to Miller's 1974 report. Brief examples of strategy applications are also presented for activities involving clerical work, heavy lifting, the controlled swing of an ax or hammer, matching patterns in wallpapering, cutting a large grassy area with a tractor power-mower, and pole vaulting.)

Although work strategies can be learned on the job if the operator is provided with the time and the opportunity, their development could be facilitated through training. After a discussion of the analyt-

TABLE 11.4

Representative Work Strategies for Some of Miller's Task Functions[a]

INPUT SELECT

In psychological terms, Input Select means what is next noticed or paid attention to. It is related to the process of scan and detect. The fewer the alternatives in message format, the more readily can irrelevant (to a given context) messages be rejected. Factors that influence message selection include perceived congruence with goal image; with prevailing set; with a hypothesis; with a demand for immediate response; and for immediacy of goal and closure. After a sense of closure, messages relevant to the preceding tasks will tend to be disregarded.

Habitual input selection structures, while necessary in degree for efficiency, have liabilities. *Strategies imbedded by training or used deliberately by the operator in operations consist of:*

1. Having a mental map of the task cycle and mission well enough in mind that one can "tag" message for context outside those of the moment.

2. On occasion, deliberately interrupting preoccupations of the moment to examine overall status, and, thereby, possibly modifying criteria of message relevance.

3. Learning that rapidly changing variables require more frequent sampling priority.

4. Remembering to relate status messages to strategic (longer-term) goals, as well as to tactical (short-term) goals.

5. Standardizing the maximum intervals when any message source will be sampled.

6. Scanning messages in advance of having to respond to them.

7. Sampling frequently when a resource of uncertain capability is used.

8. Collecting and grouping messages that build up the "complete" context for a response of large commitment.

9. Giving special priority to garbled messages.

It is of course possible to program training exercises in such a way that the operator is forced to acquire these strategies to compensate for the liabilities he acquires in processing "normal" messages and normal message sequences. But the operator must acquire sufficient facility with the normal operations that he has enough attention left over for coping with these interruptions to the ordinary flow of events.

EDIT

Editing is applying rules for arranging and symbolizing information in messages according to prescribed formats. An example is a customer giving an order in narrative prose which the clerk translates into the content on an office order form.

(continued)

TABLE 11.4 *Continued*

After a high degree of practice in editing messages into output formats, the format tends to become a tyrant to what the operator will accept as input from an environment. Exceptions become rejected or force-fitted into the format. Furthermore, the editor tends to disregard components in the messages he edits that are not the subject of his formatting rules; he may disregard content even when common sense might show it is important for him not to do so.

Task strategies should aim to provide the editor, insofar as feasible, a structure of output that is compatible with input structure and its variations. Thus, the waiter in a restaurant offers a menu in which classes of items are listed in the same order in which he sets down the order to the chef. Again where feasible, the editor should be enabled to cope with exceptional conditions not anticipated by his format; this may consist at least of a cell for entering a "comment." It is usually difficult for an operator to apply a number of rules at the same time, so he should be taught to sequence (where feasible) the classes of information to which editing rules are applied. Thus, editing a text for the meaning of its content makes it difficult to edit for typographical errors, and vice versa. Separate passes with different "set" (rule prepotency) should be made. If editing time is at a premium, the sequence should be prioritized from the most important aspect for editing to the least important, according to the recipient's criteria of importance.

TEST

Testing consists of the rules and procedures for deciding on the integrity or acceptability of a signal, message, or mechanism. As an operation, it includes sensing and measuring attributes of the signal, comparison with a reference value for the signal, decision as to whether the signal is in or out of tolerance, and an indication of that decision. The foregoing transactional variables indicate potential sources of test inadequacy, especially when a test is regarded as a sample of performance.

The operator will tend to omit tests under stress, unless they are learned as integral to the "critical path" in performance. He will tend to limit the range of his test samples and tend to use only "normal" input and output values, rather than tests for range and variety of input and output. If the test indicator is not a go, no-go device, but permits the use of judgment with qualitative criteria, the judgment will be influenced by "belief" and wishful thinking. The operator will tend to selectively test devices with which he has had difficulties and scan the others. The motivation of maintenance specialists to keep a professional integrity in their testing activity depends in part on their ethics (motivation) to "do it right" for its own sake. An awareness of this factor in training may enable reinforcing it.

In operations, *a number of strategies are applicable.* One is the collection, indexing, and retrieval of experience data that may serve as predictive data. A system may be checked out with a minimum number of tests by using data about its logical and physical pathways, connections, and dependencies. This principle extends to diagnostic testing where there are two major logical (as contrasted with empirical) strategies. One is the binary search or "half-split" principle. The other is symptom pattern analysis based on deductions from the sharing of good and bad outlets.

(continued)

TABLE 11.4 *Continued*

Training should attempt to mitigate the error tendencies that seem ubiquitous in empirical findings. The troubleshooter settles too soon on a hypothesis of what is wrong; he fails to look at symptoms directly available; he neglects positive as well as negative signs; he makes tests erratically; he is strongly influenced by his experience pattern, especially of dramatic instances; he repeats tests unnecessarily; he makes specific subsystem tests before general tests that justify them; he tends to be inefficient in setting up input conditions that will enable a variety of tests and deductions. Many of these tendencies would be diminished if the trouble shooter had a strategic model of procedure that guided his optimum sequencing of each next test. Each test would at a given stage of inquiry give him the most information about the system's status.

*a*Adapted with permission from Miller, R. B. *A method for determining task strategies* (Tech. Rep. AFHRL-TR-74-26). Washington, D.C.: American Institutes for Research, May 1974.

ical procedure for determining and/or devising work strategies from task functions, we shall summarize Miller's suggestions for the instruction of task strategies. It should be noted that Miller has identified the training implications of many of the work strategies that he developed for his 25 task functions. He believed that the training programs should attempt to optimize work strategies in order to facilitate strategy application in the system environment.

PROCEDURE FOR DETECTING OR INVENTING WORK STRATEGIES

Miller (1974) developed a procedure for determining and/or inventing work strategies that distinguish skilled from unskilled performance of a given task. The process involves analyzing the job, identifying the goal or mission and major steps, and displaying them in transactional or information-processing terms. To the extent that the task and work requirements can be expressed in transactional terms, the analyst can then apply the 25 task functions and reference the previously developed work strategies associated with the relevant functions. It is impractical for the analyst to engage in the analysis of microactivities. Rather, the major actions and their related task functions should be identified. The strategies associated with these major activities and functions should form the basis for training curricula. A particular work strategy should be evaluated as to how adequately the strategy fulfills the criteria for the accomplishment of the goal or mission.

Whereas the process for identifying work strategies associated with information-processing task functions is greatly facilitated by Miller's classificatory system, in other cases functions are identified for which no work strategy reference material exists. In these cases, work strategies must be developed by a two-phase process of analysis and synthesis of job information. (Miller undoubtedly followed a similar procedure for the identification of the work strategies for his 25 information-processing functions.)

The *analysis phase* begins with an examination of the operating conditions to determine whether a work strategy can be useful. Strategies are appropriate particularly when work conditions require multiple reasonable response alternatives and also involve (1) uncertainty about preliminary operational conditions; (2) uncertainty about the capability of a task resource; (3) more than one goal variable; or (4) efficiency and dependability as desired standards for evaluating performance. In determining whether strategies are useful, analysts are encouraged to ask such questions as: Are errors in misjudging a state of affairs critical? Is the resource precious? Once the analyst determines that it is worthwhile to develop a strategy based on this earlier analysis of the operating conditions, then the job information is reviewed at the work segment or duty module level. The analyst abstracts the functions or operations or strategic significance; identifies the independent and dependent variables in the task; simplifies assumptions regarding the roles of secondary variables by assuming they operate as constants; and makes some extremely simple action models, such as diagrams relating dependent and independent variables in a transactional model.

After completion of these activities, the analyst shifts from the analysis phase into the *synthesis phase,* which leads to the invention of a work strategy. The strategic principle may appear from the inspection of conditions of uncertainty and risk, or from the disproportionate difference between a given magnitude of outcome when it is a reward or when it is a penalty. The analyst should: (1) induce or select the strategic principle; (2) test the logic of the principle (the principle should be fairly simple in concept and not result in the necessity of naming many qualifying variables when applied to more complex situations); (3) extend the strategic principle to real-life work behaviors and situations; (4) realistically assess the principle; (5) devise an instructional module to facilitate principle acquisition during training; and (6) test the adequacy of the strategy. The last step involves examining the relevance of the strategy to the task,

TABLE 11.5

Real World Application of Task Strategies: Strategy in Setting Up a Filing System for a
Supervising Secretary[a]

Work Environment. Whereas research organizations generally have stability and
permanence over extended periods of time, development groups in large organizations may often be ad hoc and relatively transient—existing for a period of between
nine months and three years. If it is a high activity project, and the project interacts
with a larger number of other projects sharing related goals, there is inevitably a
large flow of documentation. Documents include administrative memoranda and
directives as well as technical reports and technical advisory publications. The
distinction between administration and technical subject matter may often be
blurred, but a rule of thumb is that administrative operations deal with money,
deadlines, personnel and the organization's procedural rules for doing business.
Administrative memos are generally person-to-person or organization-to-organiza-
tion documents.

A supervising secretary was hired for Project M. One of her duties was to
"organize the files" which were admittedly in bad shape. She was to design a
workable filing system for all project documentation, both administrative and
technical.

Work Criteria. The following criteria applied to the secretary's filing system, *not* to
the operations whereby she develops a filing system.

Average time and effort (such as number of inquiries) required to classify and
file a document.

Average time and effort required to locate a document on demand by subject
matter descriptors, document source, approximate date of receipt, or some
combination of approximate descriptions of all of these. A modified form of the
same criterion might be: the number of documents retrieved after a fixed
amount of search time. The criterion applies only to the technical and administrative personnel, and their inquiries, in Project M.

What is NOT a Criterion Variable. It is not required that the classification system
correspond to any formal library or organizational classification system, nor that
the system be applied outside Project M. (This somewhat unrealistic qualification is
provided to clarify the strategy for reaching a solution. If this qualification were not
valid, the same principle would apply, but a secondary principle would be needed
for adapting the solution to other file classification structures.)

Organization Policy. Documents are to be made freely available to requestors, but
a sign-out procedure is used to identify who has borrowed specific documents from
the file. All memos and reports, even those that are addressed to an individual in
the department, eventually become part of the organizational file.

Operations and Work Flow.
1. All organizational documents received come across the project secretary's
   desk.
2. Documents are logged in. Administrative items are separated from technical
   items.

(*continued*)

TABLE 11.5 *Continued*

3. Each document is assigned a serial accession number as received.
4. Provisional subject matter descriptors are assigned to each document.
5. A physical location code is assigned for position in the file.
6. The document is routed to project personnel. The project staff may add or change the descriptors.
7. The document is returned to the filing secretary, who checks the document against the receiving code and then enters bibliographic data and physical file location of the document on reference cards and on subject matter cards for the catalogue. The document is placed in the physical file.
8. Requests are made for administrative documents.
9. Requests are made for technical documents.
10. Search is made for the requested documents and physically retrieved.

This work flow outlines the revised procedure, not the original one in which all documents were merely filed by the subject title given the document by the originator, and were then placed in folders arranged alphabetically.

Problem Using the Former Procedure. There was continuous doubt about how to classify incoming material. Some documents carried two subject matter titles, or the titles were of the compound type. Finally, a simplified "rule of precedence" was adopted: Take the first subject matter word in the title or document that seems to fit. This rule also caused some difficulties, but the exasperated secretary found arbitrary responses that reduced anxieties.

Problem Using the Former Procedure. Search by subject matter descriptor generally involved much time and frustration, and was less than 40 percent effective, even when the requestor was quite certain the subject matter was contained in some document in the collection. Attempts to search the files according to subject matter became rare.

Strategy Responses. The formulation of strategy requires a perception of operational objectives. The following rule applies. The only justification for storing information is to permit retrieval. (Although the rule may be self-evident, the practices it implies apparently are not.)

Strategy 1: Develop classification criteria and procedures to be applied to documents from the terms and subject matter descriptors used in retrieval demands. Contrast this strategy with its operational reference and empirical applications to the generally vain attempts to classify by document "content." The latter is practically a meaningless aspiration since there are virtually an infinite number of possible ways to create and apply taxonomies.

The secretary who was charged with setting up a revised filing structure interviewed the staff members of Project M and, with patience, elicited lists of topic titles they were likely to request. These terms together became the starting lists for classifying incoming documents. The list was modified as search requests were actually made, depending on whether the result was successful or otherwise.

There is, of course, a trade-off between the effort made in filing and the effort made to find a document when needed. More effort spent in classifying the

(continued)

TABLE 11.5 *Continued*

document before it is put away can reduce the effort required to locate it—if the filing operations are consistent with the retrieval operations.

There is another trade-off in storage and retrieval. Organizing collections of subject matter where objects are grouped in physical proximity because they share an attribute is good for browsing purposes. This organizing principle may, however, complicate retrieval if some other attribute is the basis for inquiry, or if a document is precisely identified. In the latter case, a straight accession order sequencing may be more convenient. This raises a secondary issue in strategy for storage and retrieval.

Strategy 2: Separate logical descriptions of objects and their relations from actual physical location of the objects. Cards and indexes are more readily manipulated, organized, and reproduced than are physical objects. It is only necessary that the physical "address" of an object be included in the index card(s) which describes the object.

This strategy, aimed at minimizing object handling and physical activities, has its trade-off since, for example, the preference for a given member of a set of objects may depend on observing and comparing it physically with other members of the same set.

Strategy 1 is generally applicable to information and communications viewed in a practical, task-oriented context. In effect, the selection of format, terms, symbols, and other attributes that make up a message or set of messages should be derived from the intended use of the message set, and from the expected needs of the user or message recipient. The same principle applies to the construction of job manuals and work instructions, reference indexes, messages to computer operators, memoranda, and even technical reports.

[a]Reprinted with permission from Miller, R. B. *A method for determining task strategies* (Tech. Rep. AFHRL-TR-74-26). Washington, D.C.: American Institutes for Research, May 1974.

including the relative importance of the strategic variables vis-à-vis the other task variables.

This relatively elaborate process of analysis and synthesis for the creation of work strategies can be abbreviated substantially. Sometimes mere observation of task performance will lead to insights regarding appropriate strategic principles. However, should the insight of the experienced analyst fail or should the analyst lack a sufficient degree of training and experience, then the rational procedure outlined above will facilitate the development of work strategies.

Most work strategies were related to the task functions and to the transactional model of an information-processing system, but a number of strategies simply do not fit the model. Miller categorizes these work strategies into two groups. In the first group, there are strategies that increase the effectiveness or benefit of the way the system copes with its environment; for example, effectiveness can be increased by making the history of the system's behavior available to the system components so that environmental conditions can be anticipated more accurately. In the second group are strategies that increase the efficiency (reduce cost) with which the system operates; for example, efficiency can be increased by policies that conserve system resources. A number of other work strategies were identified that do not fit the transactional model, but Miller has made no attempt to define them. They are developing or perceiving multiple options, drawing conclusions from data samples, use of musculature in work, using mechanical advantage, and pattern matching.

Once the work strategies have been identified, one must design training programs to teach them to operators, thus going beyond the instruction of simple procedural rules. Miller provided some suggestions for instructional programs attempting to teach work strategies.

INSTRUCTION OF WORK STRATEGIES

Few researchers have attempted to convert strategic principles into instructional plans for formal training programs. In some cases, the conversion from principle to training content may be fairly straightforward. However, Miller (1974) warns that "the art whereby an abstract concept, such as a principle, becomes reliably integrated into an operational competence is not to be taken for granted" (p. 31). Trainers should not attempt to teach all work strategies associated with all task functions. Rather, trainers should prioritize the strategies, selecting only those that are critical to some set of work requirements. Next, trainers must determine the appropriate instructional techniques for incorporating the work strategy into a reliable operator competence.

Miller (1974) provided some guidance for members of the training staff regarding the necessary stages for the instruction of work strategies and their appropriate sequence:

1. The trainees must be provided with a general picture or description of the task including its activities, environmental variables, and several examples of representative problem situations.
2. The trainee should be provided with a description of the information-processing structure of the task, including a list of task functions.

3. The variables to be optimized in performing the task should be clarified for the trainee.

4. The trainee should be presented with the work strategy stated as an optimizing principle and accompanied by simplified demonstrations and graphic displays.

5. The trainee should be given guidance regarding practical qualifications made in reaching decisions and the level of precision to be achieved in applying the strategy for practical purposes.

6. The trainee should be given an opportunity to practice the work strategy on highly simplified examples. By presenting many examples and allowing the trainee to practice the strategy, the strategy acquires mnemonic richness. It is assumed that the training of strategies would be more efficient, effective, and enduring if the trainee participated cognitively in performing the strategic principle. Thus, a training atmosphere that encourages trainee initiative in thought and action, in contrast to pedantic dogma and mechanical practice of rules, facilitates the acquisition of work strategies.

7. After practice with simplified examples, the trainee should be presented with diagrammatic representations of a variety of real-life examples.

8. The trainee should be exposed to a controlled progression culminating in realistic problems, although symbolically presented.

Next a controlled progression into the physical context of problems requiring the application of strategy is presented. Because strategies are effective only on a probabilistic basis, occasionally the strategy will fail in a complex situation. For this reason, it is necessary for the instructor to establish a climate of mutual trust so that the trainee will have confidence in himself or herself as well as in the instructor.

Although Miller advocated the above instructional process for teaching work strategies, he also noted that there would be varying instructional conditions for particular strategies. For instance, some strategies can be learned and applied simply from the presentation of a mechanical rule. Others will be learned only from the application of the strategic principle in the actual context of the task itself. The learning of decision-making strategies in complex situations would be made more efficient by extracting the decision-making aspect of the work and applying that strategy widely. Further, strategies for coping with behavior liabilities and limitations need extensive, repetitive practice in order to become automatic for the trainee.

There will be large individual differences among trainees in the learning and application of work strategies. Further, because the application of strategies involves trade-offs and requires judgments, no two trainees are likely to follow a given strategy in identical ways. Training programs must be designed to accommodate and encourage such individual differences.

With extended practice, the trainee adopts certain general behavior tendencies that are characteristic of skilled performance[2] and that reflect changes in the operator's strategy of processing information. These changes result in greater efficiency, effectiveness, reliability, and flexibility in performance.

Practical Applications of the Task Strategies Approach

Miller's earliest work was directed toward describing and analyzing military tasks and duties. Task description methodologies, which focused solely on overt stimuli, responses, and feedback, were regarded as inadequate for fully understanding human task performance. Consequently, he developed 24 task functions, which represented intervening processes of the operator, to clarify how system inputs become outputs. His transactional definition of task and the information-processing model underlying that definition and his systems task vocabulary make Miller's approach particularly effective in the context of system analysis. His task functions may deal with human behavior, with machine behavior, or with combinations of both. Consequently, those task functions have definite implications for the design of human–machine systems.

Miller's later expansion of his task analysis procedures led to the identification of work strategies (both behavior and task strategies) that distinguish skilled performance. Simply by analyzing the impor-

---

[2]For example, a progressive decrease in the amount of awareness or cognition needed to perform the task; an increase in the capacity to resolve uncertainties; an increase in the ability to group input data into meaningful units and to schedule output smoothly; a reduced dependence on specific real-time information in the task; and a progressive decrease in effort required to perform the task with an increase in stereotyped behavior.

tant task functions involved in a job, Miller is able to identify associated strategic principles that will lead to more effective and more efficient task performance. In addition to developing generalized work strategies for his extended list of 25 task functions, Miller presents specific examples of developing task strategies for skilled performance for five different jobs. He also provides brief accounts of essential differences in strategy between skilled and unskilled performers for six other jobs. This translation of abstract strategic principles into real-life situations may provide employers and workers alike with much needed guidance on how to improve performance. In essence, this represents an operational definition within a particular job context of the higher-order competencies that characterize the skilled performer. It also provides insights as to how skilled performers process information via particular work strategies in a more effective manner.

As we saw in the preceding section of this chapter, the contributions of Miller's classificatory system go beyond the mere identification of the competencies or work strategies of skilled performers. He also provides recommendations for individuals wishing to instruct others in the development and application of work strategies. Thus, one of Miller's goals was to facilitate the development of training programs that promote the attainment of highly skilled performance. He outlined a sequence of instructional stages to be followed in the training program to enable the trainees to go beyond the mere application of procedural rules to the application of work strategies to complex task situations. Miller also provided general guidance for trainers wishing to facilitate the instruction of strategic principles, including: the encouragement of trainee interaction and practice in a realistic context of the job; the establishment of confidence in the training conditions; the progression from easy to more complex examples; and the adaptation to individual differences in the application of work strategies. Miller's descriptive system is useful for system design and for the identification of work strategies for various job contexts, yet the greatest practical contribution of the scheme is the guidance provided to those wishing to teach work strategies. Previously, too little attention was paid to delineating behavioral differences between skilled and unskilled performers. The knowledge of these differences and the ability to teach trainees the competencies associated with skilled performance must contribute to the attainment of one of the nation's leading goals—high organizational productivity.

Evaluation of the Task Strategies Approach

In an earlier section of this chapter, we critiqued Miller's (1962) preliminary formulation of the behavioral structure of a task. We now evaluate Miller's (1973, 1974) more elaborate Task Strategies Approach against the criteria presented in Chapter 4.

No data are presented regarding the reliability of the Task Strategies Approach in categorizing human task performance. We do not know whether two independent analysts using this system would derive the same task functions and work strategies for a given set of task activities, or if the same analyst, on two different occasions, would reproduce the same functions or strategies when viewing the same work behaviors. We can be fairly certain that, due to the increased precision of the definitions accompanying the 25 task functions, the reliability of this system would be greater than the reliability of the preliminary formulation.

In Chapter 4, we indicated that it is desirable for a descriptive system to have mutually exclusive categories. However, Miller himself acknowledges that his task functions are overlapping. In his efforts to capture the continuous flow from input to response actions and all of the intervening processes, Miller created some categories that do not appear to be mutually exclusive. He was willing to accept a certain amount of redundancy in the descriptors to ensure that he provided a full description of the transactions involved in human task performance (see Miller, 1967).

We also suggested in Chapter 4 that classification should be exhaustive placing all subject matter into some class. We have seen that Miller's system appears to be exhaustive in identifying information-processing task functions and their associated work strategies. However, there are also a number of work strategies that do not fit the information-processing model underlying his task analysis. We may assume that these work strategies have other, possibly non-information-processing functions not covered by this classificatory system. Although the system does not meet the criterion of being exhaustive, it does seem to meet its objectives of identifying all information-processing task functions.

The later elaborations of the Task Strategies Approach begin to provide the needed match between specific categories and behavioral effects, another criterion for the evaluation of classificatory systems. Miller's real-life examples of the translation of strategic principles associated with task functions into work strategies (both behavioral and task) provide some evidence of external validity of the system. Further research is needed to demonstrate that the predicted work strategies do result in skilled performance in the real-world context.

The final criterion presented for the evaluation of a classificatory approach is utility, or the usefulness of the system in solving an applied problem. Certainly, the Task Strategies Approach has potential for meeting this requirement, both in its designation of work strategies for particular task functions and in its practical recommendations for the instructional design of training curricula to teach those strategies.

Miller (1967) himself has suggested that the ultimate criterion for evaluating a system is its degree of acceptance. The Task Strategies Approach has not been cited widely in the literature. Miller (1973) noted that his functions represent "examples of what is needed, rather than a final product" (p. 28). Perhaps when additional empirical evidence has been accumulated on task strategies and behavior strategies, the resulting refined analytical definitions of the task functions may gain greater acceptance in operational work settings.

References

Angell, D., Shearer, J. W., & Berliner, D. C. *Study of training performance evaluation techniques* (AIR-D-81-3/64-TR). Palo Alto, CA: American Institutes for Research, 1964.

Farina, A. J., Jr. Development of a taxonomy of human performance: A review of descriptive schemes for human task behavior. *JSAS Catalog of Selected Documents in Psychology*, 1973, *3*, 23 (Ms. No. 318).

Fleishman, E. A. A comparative study of aptitude patterns in skilled and unskilled psychomotor performances. *Journal of Applied Psychology*, 1957, *41*, 263–272.

Fleishman, E. A. Human abilities and the acquisition of skill. In E. A. Bilodean (Ed.), *The acquisition of skill.* New York: Academic Press, 1966.

Fleishman, E. A. Individual differences in motor learning. In R. M. Gagné (Ed.), *Learning and individual differences.* Columbus, OH: Merrill, 1967.

Fleishman, E. A., & Ellison, G. D. Prediction of transfer and other learning phenomena from ability and personality measures. *Journal of Educational Psychology*, 1969, *60*, 300–314.

Fleishman, E. A. & Hempel, W. E., Jr. Changes in factor structure of a psychomotor test as a function of practice. *Journal of Experimental Psychology*, 1954, *18*, 239–252.

Fleishman, E. A. & Hempel, W. E., Jr. The relation between abilities and improvement with practice in a visual reaction discrimination task. *Journal of Experimental Psychology*, 1955, *49*, 301–312.

Fleishman, E. A. & Rich, S. Role of kinesthetic and spatial visual abilities in perceptual–motor learning. *Journal of Experimental Psychology*, 1963, *66*, 6–11.

Miller, R. B. Task description and analysis. In R. M. Gagné (Ed.), *Psychological principles in system development.* New York: Holt, Rinehart, & Winston, 1962.

Miller, R. B. Task taxonomy: Science or technology? In W. T. Singleton, R. Easterby, & D. Whitfield (Eds.), *The human operator in complex systems*. London: Taylor & Francis, 1967.

Miller, R. B. Development of a taxonomy of human performance: Design of a systems task vocabulary. *JSAS Catalog of Selected Documents in Psychology*, 1973, *3*, 29–30 (Ms. No. 327).

Miller, R. B. *A method for determining task strategies* (Tech. Rep. AFHRL–TR–74–26). Washington, D.C.: American Institutes for Research, May 1974.

Miller, R. B. *A task analysis terminology for man-machine information systems*. Unpublished manuscript, 1982a. Available from Robert B. Miller, Colonial House, South Road, Poughkeepsie, New York 12601.

Miller, R. B. *Task formats in human behavior*. Unpublished manuscript, 1982b. Available from Robert B. Miller, Colonial House, South Road, Poughkeepsie, New York 12601.

CHAPTER 12

The Ability Requirements Approach

The genesis of the *Ability Requirements Approach* was presented in Chapter 7. In this approach, tasks are described in terms of the human abilities required to perform them effectively. The major programmatic research on the identification of human abilities also was discussed in the earlier chapter. The present chapter examines extensions of this work in relation to the broader issues of taxonomic development discussed elsewhere in this volume. The work includes that conducted in the Taxonomy Project, as well as the related programmatic work on human ability measurement that preceded and followed this project.

The Ability Requirements Approach probably has received more extensive development and evaluation than any other approach (Fleishman, 1982). This chapter describes the provisional abilities taxonomy and the measurement system that was developed for classifying tasks, and evaluates the Ability Requirements Approach according to a number of criteria and for a variety of basic and applied purposes.

Conceptual Background

One approach to taxonomic development in this area lies in the use of known parameters of human performance as a basis for describing and classifying tasks. A major source of information is the literature on human abilities identification. This extensive research is based on the intercorrelations obtained among task performances in a variety of performance areas (e.g., cognitive, perceptual, psychomotor). Here individual differences are exploited to gain insights about common processes required to perform different groups of tasks. Abilities are defined by empirically determined relations among these observed separate performances. Typically, correlational studies have been carried out in the psychometric tradition and, until recently, little attempt has been made to integrate the ability concepts developed there into the more general body of psychological theory (Fleishman, 1967a, 1972a).

To review briefly, *ability* refers to a more general capacity of the individual such as Verbal Ability or Spatial Visualization, related to performance in a variety of human tasks. These abilities are relatively enduring attributes of the individual performing the task (Fleishman, 1966; Gagné & Fleishman, 1959). The assumption is that specific tasks require certain abilities if performance is to be maximized. Tasks requiring common abilities would be placed within the same category. Factor-analytic studies or other clustering methods, based on the correlations among task (or test) performances, form the initial bases for identifying these ability dimensions.

Our reviews of other task classification attempts indicated that broad descriptors (such as "decision making" or "problem solving") or narrow categories (such as "rotates control knob") do not allow for dependable prediction of human performance. The reason may be that such descriptors bear little relationship to experimentally established results regarding human performance. These descriptors ignore our present knowledge of the nature and number of human performance categories. Present knowledge indicates that broad categories such as "problem solving" or "perceptual–motor" are not unitary processes, and that highly specific categories such as "rotates knob" are not general types of human performance. Thus, there is reason to doubt that systems based on categories such as these will be successful in allowing dependable predictions of human performance from one task to another.

For example, the broad category of *perceptual–motor* is likely to be relatively useless in generalizing from one perceptual–motor task to the next. Knowledge from research on correlations among human performances indicates a greater degree of specificity and a considerable diversity of function in this category (see Fleishman, 1964, 1972b). Manual Dexterity, Multilimb Coordination and Control Precision are a few examples of the many perceptual–motor abilities which have been experimentally shown to underlie the broad category of *perceptual–motor*. Not only have such abilities been identified, but they also have been found to be related to performance in a variety of human tasks. For example, Spatial Visualization has been shown to account for performance in such diverse tasks as aerial navigation, blueprint reading, and dentistry. Put in other terms, each of these tasks is, in part, describable in terms of that component of its performance that can be attributed to the ability Spatial Visualization. Thus, in choosing a level and basis for task description in terms of human performance, it would appear wise to capitalize on the experimental knowledge we already possess concerning basic human abilities.

Derivation of Human Abilities

In order to understand more fully the use of human abilities in task classification, it may be useful to describe some of the logic and technique for their derivation (see Fleishman, 1967b). Generally, in establishing a set of abilities, a subarea of human performance is studied in which tasks are designed specifically to tap certain hypothesized ability categories. These tasks are administered to a sample of subjects and the correlations among them are obtained and subjected to factor-analytic study. Based on this information, additional hypotheses are generated and further studies are conducted to sharpen the definitions of the categories. Many of these later studies introduce variations in the tasks to investigate the relationships between the task parameters (e.g., number or nature of stimuli) and the ability requirements (Fleishman, 1975, 1978). This may be done through an examination of correlations between performance on reference measures and performance on tasks in which parameters have been varied (e.g., Fleishman, 1957; Guilford & Hoepfner, 1966). Factor analysis methods of clustering are used to define the fewest independent ability categories that might be most useful and meaningful in describing performance in a wide variety of tasks.

It is perhaps not too extreme to state that most of the empirically based categorization of human skills comes from such correlational and factor-analytic studies. We can think of such categories as representing empirically derived patterns of response consistencies to task requirements varied in systematic ways. In a sense, this approach describes tasks in terms of the common abilities required to perform them. The fact that individuals who do well on Task A also do well on Tasks B and C but not on Tasks D, E, and F indicates, inferentially, a common process involved in performing the first three tasks distinct from the processes involved in the latter three. To account for the observed consistencies, an ability is postulated. Once postulated in this fashion, the definition of the ability must then be refined and its limits carefully specified by further research.

A prototype program in the area of perceptual–motor abilities was described by Fleishman (1964, 1972a, 1972b). A series of interlocking experimental factor-analytic studies attempted to isolate and identify the factors common in a wide range of perceptual–motor performances. Essentially, this was laboratory research in which tasks were specifically designed or selected to test certain hypotheses about the organization of abilities in a certain range of tasks. The experimental batteries of tasks were administered to several hundred subjects, and the correlation patterns examined through factor analysis methods. Subsequent studies introduced task variations aimed at sharpening or limiting the ability factor definitions. The purpose was to define the fewest independent ability categories describing performance in the widest variety of tasks.

Without reviewing the list of ability categories developed, we can say that a limited number (9 or 10 in the psychomotor area and 9 in the physical proficiency area) seemed to account for most of the variance in several hundred tasks investigated over many years. These abilities and their operational definitions are described in Chapter 7.

It may be useful to provide an example of how one examines the generality of an ability category and how one defines its limits. The specification of an ability category is an arduous task requiring programmatic work, using combinations of experimental and correlational methods. The definition of an ability called *Rate Control* provides an illustration. In early factor analysis studies of psychomotor tasks (e.g., Fleishman, 1954), it was found that this ability factor was found common to compensatory tracking (e.g., keep a horizontal line in the center of the dial by compensatory movements of a control) as well as to following pursuit tasks (e.g., keep a gun sight in line with a moving target). Figure 12.1a shows one such task. To test the generality of this factor, further tasks were developed to emphasize responses to stimuli moving at different rates, where these tasks were not conventional tracking tasks. For example, Figure 12.1b shows a task in which the subject had to *time* his or her movements in relation to different stimulus rates, but did not have to follow a target or compensate for the target's movement. The factor was found to extend to such tasks (Fleishman, 1958).

Later studies attempted to discover if emphasis in this ability is on judging the rate of the stimulus, as distinguished from moving a control at the appropriate rate. Figure 12.1c shows a task developed in which the only response is the timing of pressing a button in

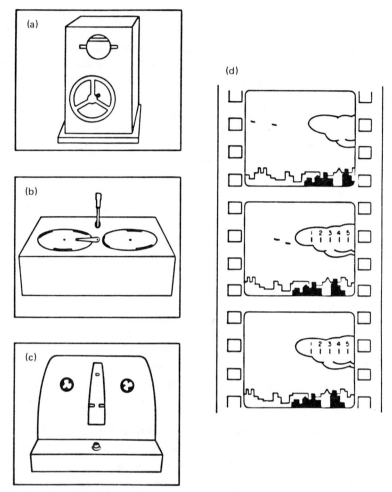

Figure 12.1 Examples of tasks used to evaluate the generality of Rate Control ability. (a) Single dimensional pursuit; (b) motor judgment; (c) visual coincidence; (d) stages in a sample item of the Estimation of Relative Velocities Test. Reprinted with permission from Fleishman, E. A. On the relation between abilities, learning, and human performance. *American Psychologist*, 1972, 27, 1017–1032. (a)

response to judgments about the location of stimuli moving at different rates. Performance on this task was found not to correlate with other Rate Control tasks. Finally, several motion picture tasks, such as the one in Figure 12.1d, were adapted in which the subject is required to extrapolate the course of an airplane moving across a screen. For example, in the test shown, the subject must judge the point at which the two planes meet (Points 1,2,3,4, or 5). The only response required is marking with a pencil on an IBM answer sheet. These moving picture tests, involving only judgments about stimulus rate, did not correlate with the group of tasks previously found to measure Rate Control. Thus, the definition of this Rate Control ability was expanded to include measures beyond tracking and pursuit tasks, but restricted to tasks requiring the timing of an actual adjustive movement to a changing stimulus (Fleishman, 1972a).

A similar history can be sketched for a variety of abilities identified. In reviewing our studies and those of others, it became apparent that, in defining these ability factors, we were linking up a great deal of information about task characteristics and ability requirements. It was possible to describe a number of principles relating task characteristics and abilities measured. For example, we now know that Multilimb Coordination is common to tasks involving simultaneous control of the actions of two hands, two feet, or hands and feet, but some feedback indicator of performance is required. Furthermore, this factor does not extend to tasks involving the body in motion, such as athletic tasks. We also know that fast reaction times are general to auditory and visual stimuli, but as soon as more than one stimulus or response is involved in such tasks, the ability required shifts to an ability called *Response Orientation*. Furthermore, it is useful to know that there are three primary strength factors, not confined to muscle groups but dependent on specific task requirements (see Fleishman, 1964). Thus, lifting, pulling, and pushing objects involve Static Strength, whereas jumping and sprinting involve Explosive Strength and tasks in which the muscles fatigue over time (push-ups, digging ditches) involve Dynamic Strength. Tasks with different characteristics bring into play other distinct physical abilities such as Stamina, Flexibility, Gross Body Coordination, and Equilibrium. All these studies also identified the task measurements most *diagnostic* of these ability categories (Fleishman, 1972b).

Although the work is not complete in all areas of human performance, it seems clear that substantial experimental effort has been devoted to identification of the basic human abilities. The result has been the establishment of sets of abilities encompassing much of the cognitive, perceptual, psychomotor, and physical areas of performance. This careful experimental process produced a set of abilities that varies in scope and specificity and provides insights into the nature and structure of human performance. Because these major areas of human performance already have been delineated in terms of ability dimensions, a significant step has been taken toward the adequate coverage of the range of human abilities required for performance on any type of task.

Thus, abilities provide a natural basis for describing and classifying tasks in terms of human performance requirements. However, we need to examine the extent to which the use of ability categories to describe tasks facilitates the generalization of research results on the effects of various independent variables on human performance. We also need to evaluate the extent to which these categories can be used reliably by behavioral scientists, human factors technologists, and other specialists in describing human tasks for a variety of purposes.

Development of Ability Dimensions and Measurement Systems

An important phase of the Taxonomy Project involved converting into measurement systems the abilities identified in our extensive reviews of the factor-analytic ability literature (Fleishman, 1975b; Theologus & Fleishman, 1973; Theologus, Romashko, & Fleishman, 1973). Objectives were (1) the derivation of a provisional classificatory system of unambiguously defined abilities, utilizing those abilities best substantiated in previous research, and (2) the development of a rating scale methodology by means of which the ability requirements of tasks could be described as a basis for classifying these tasks. This section reviews these developmental efforts as well as more recent evaluations of the approach.

A number of investigations were undertaken to determine the feasibility and usefulness of ability constructs in the analysis of tasks and jobs. The prototype model that resulted is a product of successive studies. It is important to mention that the end product has undergone a number of transformations, expansions, and revisions based on empirical guidance from these studies.

A pilot study in this series examined the utility of a prototypic methodology for classifying tasks on the basis of ability requirements (Theologus, Romashko, & Fleishman, 1973). Utility in this case was defined as agreement between raters on their ability ratings of a number of tasks. The research included generating ability lists, generating tasks to be rated in terms of abilities required, and obtaining ability ratings of the tasks from judges.

Generating Ability Lists

In the first step, a comprehensive literature review determined the cognitive, perceptual, psychomotor, and physical abilities previously identified in factor-analytic research.

One of the striking findings in the early review was the difficulty in moving from the factor analysts' definition of an ability to a more operational definition that could be used reliably by observers to estimate the ability requirements of a new task (Theologus, Romashko, & Fleishman, 1973). A large effort in our program involved the successive refinement of such definitions to improve the utility of these concepts in describing tasks. A host of different reliability studies has been conducted, beginning with the Taxonomy Project (Theologus & Fleishman, 1973; Theologus, Romashko, & Fleishman, 1973) and more recently by Fleishman (1975a, 1982), Fleishman and Hogan (1978), Myers, Gebhardt, Price, and Fleishman (1981), and Cooper, Schemmer, Gebhardt, Marshall-Mies, and Fleishman (1982). In these studies, individuals rated tasks in terms of cognitive, perceptual, and motor abilities. These descriptions ranged from laboratory tasks and training devices to jobs and job tasks in a variety of organizational settings. The goal has been to use the same ability concepts to describe both laboratory and real-world tasks within the same conceptual framework.

For the cognitive and perceptual domains, the primary sources were Guilford's work (1967) on the nature of intellect and the work of French (1951) and French, Ekstrom, and Price (1963) on cognitive and perceptual reference tests. From these sources 19 abilities were selected, based on the criterion that each ability was identified in a minimum of 10 individual studies. A definition for each of these 19 abilities was developed by integrating French's definition of a given ability with that of Guilford.

In the psychomotor area, abilities were selected from those factors analytically established by Fleishman (1954, 1958, 1962, 1964, 1972b). Also included in the preliminary ability list were the physical proficiency abilities derived from work by Fleishman (1964). Representative tests or tasks with the highest factor loadings on each ability factor were included as examples with each definition.

These abilities were merged into a single list and reviewed by psychologists for their comments. A series of interviews and discussions revealed a number of areas that merited further consideration. These included: (1) the need for a more comprehensive ability list; (2) the need to clarify vague and ambiguous definitions; and (3) the need to provide additional examples. In response to these comments, attempts were made to delineate more carefully the extent and limits of each ability in the list, and additional task examples were included with the ability definitions to better illustrate the abilities.

In still another effort to sharpen the abilities list, a variety of experimental studies were reviewed to determine whether any obvious areas of performance were not represented in the ability list. From this review it became apparent that the list was still incomplete, because some task elements could not be analyzed in terms of the existing ability list. Recognition of this fact led to the inclusion of a group of abilities that had not been studied to any great extent but nevertheless appeared to have wide applicability to human performance (e.g., Time Sharing and Attention). The result of these efforts was a list of 48 abilities with definitions and examples for each.

In addition to this list of specific abilities, a list of 12 general abilities was constructed. The purpose of this second list was to determine whether a wide variety of tasks could be analyzed effectively using fewer but broader ability categories. The list was developed by collapsing many of the similar specific abilities into more general descriptors. For example, several kinds of memory were collapsed into the single category called Memory; Finger and Manual Dexterity, and Arm–Hand Steadiness were collapsed into Dexterity; several psychomotor factors were collapsed into Precision of Movement; and so forth.

Pretests of Ability Rating Procedures

In order to refine further the two ability lists, a sample of judges next rated a set of task descriptions, utilizing rating scales. For each ability, the rater was required to rate the degree to which that ability was required by that task. The task descriptions were obtained from a review of experimental journals and technical reports.

The task selection process was based on several criteria: (1) completeness of task descriptions, (2) range of behaviors samples, and (3) a balance between real-world and laboratory tasks. The three real-world tasks employed a task analysis format in which the task procedures were presented sequentially. The three laboratory tasks were described in paragraphs that included information on subjects, apparatus, and procedures. The real-world tasks comprised the jobs of computer programmer, fire control leader, and sheet metal worker; the laboratory tasks were "problem similarity," "letter recognition," and "polar pursuit." Each category of task description included cognitive and psychomotor tasks.

To rate the task descriptions on the ability scales, a sample of 18 psychologists was randomly assigned to receive the general ability list (12 descriptors) or the specific ability list (48 descriptors). Each judge rated each of the six tasks on each of the abilities in the list assigned to them. The ratings were made by scoring an ability as present or absent in a given task and then, for those abilities rated as present, determining whether the ability was critical to individual differences in performance. Of primary importance at this stage were the opinions of the judges concerning the adequacy and comprehensiveness of the scales; these opinions were obtained in written form and in interviews.

In general, the results of this small-scale examination of the abilities approach, coupled with the judges' comments, indicated that the approach to task classification was feasible. A comparison of data obtained from the application of the two ability lists showed that the specific list of 48 abilities allowed for a more detailed and thorough analysis of the task descriptions without any loss in interjudge agreement. However, necessary modifications included greater specificity in the ability definitions to reduce apparent overlap among them, and the addition of memory abilities to the specific list. For the latter, the work of Christal (1958), Kelley (1964), and Guilford (1967) was utilized. Additionally, the instructions originally given to the 18 judges were revised, and a detailed explanation of the abilities approach was developed. Major sections included in this explanation were: (1) a background and rationale for the approach, (2) a description of the materials to be used, and (3) a schema for applying the abilities to tasks, as well as criteria for their application. These more detailed instructions were incorporated into the revision of a manual (Fleishman, 1975a) now called the *Manual for Ability Requirement Scales* (MARS).

EARLY RELIABILITY STUDIES

After completion of all revisions, a study was designed to reassess the ability rating scales, to evaluate statistical methods for analyzing the data, and to determine whether the judges could agree on the rating of the abilities required for performance on a given task (Theologus, Romashko, & Fleishman, 1973). Task descriptions for the six tasks selected for this study are shown in Table 12.1. The subjects were 25 psychologists with diverse specialties and 32 well-known experts in psychological measurement, chosen from the membership of the Division of Evaluation and Measurement (Division 5) of the American Psychological Association. The judges were required to rate each of the tasks on each of the abilities as "not involved," "baseline," or "critical" (rating 0, 1, and 2, respectively). *Base-line* was defined as the amount of the ability that an average person would exhibit; *critical* was defined as requiring more of the ability than exhibited by the average person.

For each of the 50 ability rating scales, several intraclass correla-

TABLE 12.1

Task Descriptions Used in the First Reliability Study[a]

Task title	Type	Performance category
Sheet metal worker	Real world	Psychomotor
Air traffic controller	Real world	Cognitive
Helicopter pilot	Real world	Cognitive–Psychomotor
Polar pursuit	Laboratory	Psychomotor
Letter recognition	Laboratory	Cognitive
Astronaut	Laboratory	Cognitive–Psychomotor

[a]Adapted with permission from Theologus, G. C., Romashko, T., and Fleishman, E. A. Development of a taxonomy of human performance: A feasibility study of ability dimensions for classifying human tasks (American Institutes for Research Tech. Rep.). *JSAS Catalog of Selected Documents in Psychology*, 1973, *3*, 25–26 (Ms. no. 321).

tion coefficients were calculated as measures of interjudge agreement or individual scale reliabilities. The reliability coefficients for groups of 25, 16, and 5 judges, and for a single judge, were calculated for each ability. In general, the intraclass correlations revealed that substantial reliability could be expected for the majority of the ability rating scales if they were employed by a panel of judges. In several, the scales exhibited low reliabilities when employed by a group of five judges or by an individual judge.

To obtain insight into the exact nature of the reliabilities, the distributions of the judges' ratings of each task on each ability were examined. The percentage of judges rating the task as a "zero," "one," or "two" was computed. "Agreement" was defined arbitrarily as 80% or more of the judges assigning the exact same ability rating to a given task. Agreement was most often obtained when the judges rated the ability with a zero. The predominance of zero ratings might have occurred because the sample of tasks employed in the pilot study did not cover a wide enough range of performance to require the use of all the ability scales.

The data also were analyzed for the degree of similarity between pairs of ability profiles on each of the tasks (Coulter & Cattell, 1966). For each sample of judges, a similarity correlation coefficient (r_p) was calculated on each task for every pair of profiles. Similarity coefficients also were calculated between the mean ability profiles, or the mean rating given by each group of judges to each task on each ability scale. As with the intraclass correlations, the r_p values indicated that a full panel of judges was required to achieve a stable rating. Low values of r_p between pairs of individual profiles indicated substantial differences in interjudge agreement. Interviews with the judges suggested two possible sources of this high intrajudge and interjudge error variance. The first involved ambiguity over the meaning of "average person". This criterion produced difficulty because the "average" could be considered either experienced or naive on a given task. A second difficulty was that some judges found it possible to account for the same task performance by means of two different abilities. Thus, there was a need to revise the ability scales to delineate more carefully the limits of each ability,and to provide judges with the specific nature of the distinctions between abilities.

Similarity coefficients also were calculated between the mean ability profiles obtained from the diverse group of psychologists and the experts in measurement. The mean profiles were developed by calculating the mean rating given by each group of judges to each task on each ability scale. All the obtained r_p values revealed significantly high agreement between the two groups of judges.

DEVELOPMENT OF SCALING PROCEDURES FOR ABILITY RATINGS

Although the results of this pilot study were encouraging, it was clear that the methodology for rating abilities required extensive developmental research. Subsequent modifications made in the ability scales included the careful specification of distinctions among abilities to reduce ambiguities in the definitions, and the revision of the scaling technique. The original list of abilities was reorganized into a set of 37 abilities by elimination and condensation. Definitions of most of the remaining abilities were reworked to include more operational terms. The rating scale was changed from three points to seven points, and a behaviorally anchored rating technique (Smith & Kendall, 1963) was employed that anchored both the high and low ends of the scale with definitions and task examples.

The development of these task anchors proceeded in three steps. First, staff members familiar with these abilities were asked to develop definition anchors for the high and low ends of each of the 37 ability scales. This was an iterative process and was terminated for a given ability scale when general agreement was reached. Panels of individuals were then assembled to generate examples of everyday occupational or laboratory tasks that would reflect high, moderate, and low levels of each ability. The intention was to develop task examples that were generally familiar and required no specialized information.

Using more than 1000 examples thus generated, a determination was made of the scale value of each example in order to place it at the appropriate point along its ability scale. To make this determination, judges were asked to rate each of the examples on the particular ability scale it was intended to reflect. These judges were permitted to reject any example that they believed was not representative of the scale. The mean rating for each example and its standard deviation were computed. The mean ratings of all the examples for a particular scale were then grouped as high, moderate, or low. Within each of these groups, examples with the smallest standard deviations were chosen to anchor the scale because these represented task examples showing the most agreement among the judges. It was possible to select a task anchor example with high, average, and low mean values on each ability scale with virtually no overlap in their rating distributions.

Figures 12.2 and 12.3 illustrate the format utilized. Figure 12.2 shows the manual page providing the definition, rating scale, and distinctions made for the ability *Verbal Comprehension*. A similar format was provided for each of the 37 abilities. Figure 12.3 presents illustrations for the ability *Static Strength*. Table 12.2 presents the 37 abilities and the definitions utilized in this study.

A second pilot study involved two groups of graduate students. Group 1 (n = 19) was asked to rate a set of tasks on the ability scales now anchored with definitions and task examples. Group two (*n* = 22) was given the identical rating task, but their ability scales were anchored only with definitions. The judges were instructed to follow a two-stage rating procedure. First, they had to decide whether an ability was required for the performance of the task. If their decision was "no," they would proceed to the next ability scale. In making these ratings, the judges were told to estimate the lowest amount of an ability a person could possess and still produce errorless performance.

Six task descriptions were chosen: air traffic controller, sheet metal worker, astronaut, helicopter pilot, automobile driver, and basketball player. To assess whether there was a relationship between interprofile similarity and familiarity with the tasks involved, the judges were asked to rate familiarity of each task description on the following seven-point scales: (1) degree of understanding, (2) completeness of task description, (3) clarity of task description, (4) degree of familiarity, (5) degree of experience, and (6) degree of proficiency.

The results showed significant increases in scale reliability over the reliability from the first pilot study, especially in the intraclass cor-

VERBAL COMPREHENSION

This is the ability to understand English words and sentences.

How Verbal Comprehension Is Different From Other Abilities

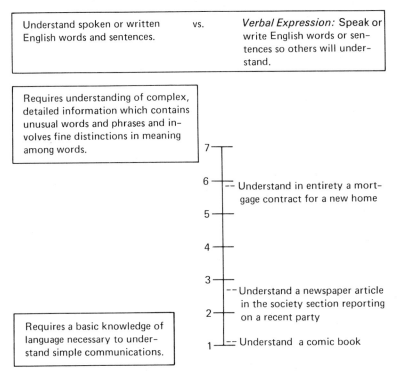

Understand spoken or written English words and sentences.   vs.   *Verbal Expression:* Speak or write English words or sentences so others will understand.

Requires understanding of complex, detailed information which contains unusual words and phrases and involves fine distinctions in meaning among words.

7
6 —— Understand in entirety a mortgage contract for a new home
5
4
3
-- Understand a newspaper article in the society section reporting
2   on a recent party
1 —— Understand a comic book

Requires a basic knowledge of language necessary to understand simple communications.

Figure 12.2 Definition and ability rating scale for Verbal Comprehension. Adapted with permission from Theologus, G. C., Romashko, T., and Fleishman, E. A. Development of a taxonomy of human performance: A feasibility study of ability dimensions for classifying human tasks (American Institutes for Research Tech. Rep.). *JSAS Catalog of Selected documents in Psychology*, 1973, 3, 25–26 (Ms. No. 321).

relation coefficients for small groups of judges. Intraclass correlations revealed that the improvement in scale reliability was attributed mainly to improved ability definitions, better defined scales, and more detailed rating instructions. An examination of the percentage distributions of the judges' ratings revealed that, in general, large samples of judges (19 or 22) still were required to achieve substantial scale reliability. However, for about half the scales, smaller groups of judges ($n = 5$) produced reliability coefficients greater than zero.

STATIC STRENGTH

This is the ability to use muscle force to lift, push, or carry objects.
This ability can involve the hand, arm, back, shoulder, or leg.

How Static Strength Is Different From Other Abilities

Use muscle force against *objects*.	vs.	*Dynamic Strength and Trunk Strength:* Use muscle power repeatedly to hold up or move the body's own weight.
Use *continuous* muscle force, without stopping, up to the amount needed to lift, push, pull, or carry an object.	vs.	*Explosive Strength:* Gather energy to move one's own body to propel some object with *short bursts* of muscle force.
Does *not* involve the use of muscle force over a *long* time.	vs.	*Stamina:* *Does* involve physical exertion over a long time.

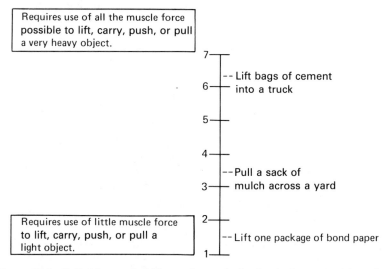

Figure 12.3 Definition and ability rating scale for Static Strength. Adapted with permission from Theologus, G. C., Romashko, T., & Fleishman, E. A. Development of a taxonomy of human performance: A feasibility study of ability dimensions for classifying human tasks (American Institutes for Research Tech. Rep.). *JSAS Catalog of Selected Documents in Psychology*, 1973, *3*, 25–26 (Ms. No. 321).

For each of the two samples of judges and on each of the tasks, a value of interprofile similarity (r_p) was calculated for every pair of task ability profiles. The results indicated substantially greater agreement between profiles over the earlier pilot study. The impact of the increase in scale reliability was seen in this substantial increase in interjudge agreement on the ability profiles for each task. No strong relationships were found between interprofile similarity and ratings of familiarity with the task.

Three conclusions drawn from this research reflected directly on the utility of the scaling methodology developed to describe tasks in terms of types and amounts of human abilities. First, it became apparent that a seven-point scale, using definitions of high and low requirements as scale anchors, provides a statistically reliable tool for assessing amount of ability requirement. This method proved significantly more reliable than previous qualitative discrete rating categories. Although differences observed with the addition of task example anchors were small, this methodological development required further research before the scaling format was finalized. Second, the fact that familiarity with the task description to be rated and the interrater profile similarity were independent suggests that personal experience with the task is not an essential prerequisite for using the scales. Finally, it appeared that this scaling methodology can be used by raters who do not have specific expertise in psychological assessment methods.

CONSTRUCT AND PREDICTIVE VALIDITY

A number of studies have been conducted that are relevant to the validity of the Ability Requirements Approach for classifying human tasks. Theologus and Fleishman (1973) conducted an evaluation of validity in two different ways. First, they examined the *construct validity* of the scales by determining the relationships between ability scales and the empirically derived ability factors they were designed to represent. A panel of 9 judges was asked to rate descriptions of each of 38 tasks, used in an earlier study (Fleishman, 1954), on each of the 37 scales. These data indicated that, of the eight ability categories examined, seven abilities demonstrated significant agreement between the independent ratings and the empirical loadings.

Predictive validity of the ability scales was estimated by whether the judges' ability ratings were correlates of actual task performance (Theologus & Fleishman, 1973). A multiple regression analysis was performed for each task in which the mean ability ratings were the predictor variables and task performance was the criterion. The mean performance levels of 400 subjects on each of the 38 tasks were used from the Fleishman (1954) study. The performance data on 27 of the 38 tasks could be converted to a common measure of "number of units produced per unit time." The units varied across tasks and included such things as number of openings negotiated, number of

TABLE 12.2

Human Ability Definitions[a]

---

1. VERBAL COMPREHENSION   This is the ability to understand language. It is concerned with the understanding of individual words as well as words as they appear in context, i.e., in sentences, grammatical patterns and idiomatic phrases. In terms of communication, this ability is limited to the receiver of information; it does *not* apply to the sender or communicator.

2. VERBAL EXPRESSION   This is the ability to utilize language (either oral or written) to communicate information or ideas to another person or persons. It requires the production and utilization of individual words or of words in context (i.e., in phrases, sentences, etc.) to express ideas or factual information. Neither the actual production of the ideas nor questions relating to *the quality of an idea* are included under this ability. The ability is concerned *solely* with the *quality of the communication* of such ideas. Quality of communication can be thought of as depending upon factors such as (1) size of one's vocabulary, (2) knowledge of distinctions among words, and (3) knowledge of grammar and syntax.

3. IDEATIONAL FLUENCY   This is the ability to produce a number of ideas concerning a given topic. It is only concerned with the *number* of ideas produced and does *not* extend to the quality of those ideas.

4. ORIGINALITY   This is the ability to produce unusual or clever responses related to a given topic or situation. It is the ability to improvise solutions to problems or to develop procedures in situations where standard operating procedures do not apply. This ability is concerned with the *degree of creativity of responses* and does not deal with the number of responses made.

5. MEMORIZATION   This is the ability to memorize and retain new information which occurs as a regular or routine part of the task. These new bits of information must be memorized to properly accomplish or carry out the task. This ability does not extend either to the memorization of the task procedures or to the recall of any information previously learned outside of the given task situation.

6. PROBLEM SENSITIVITY   This is the ability to *recognize* or *identify* the *existence* of problems. It includes the specification of the problem as a whole as well as recognition of the elements of the problem. This ability encompasses all types of problems whether they be figural, symbolic, or semantic. However, the ability does *not* include any of the reasoning necessary for the solution of a problem.

7. MATHEMATICAL REASONING   This is the ability to reason abstractly using quantitative concepts and symbols. It encompasses reasoning through mathematical problems in order to determine appropriate operations which can be performed to solve them. It also includes the *understanding or structuring* of mathematical problems. The actual manipulation of numbers is *not* included in this ability.

8. NUMBER FACILITY   This is the ability to manipulate numbers in numerical operations; for example, add, subtract, multiply, divide, integrate, differentiate, etc. The ability involves both the speed and accuracy of computation.

9. DEDUCTIVE REASONING   This is the ability to apply general concepts or rules to specific cases or to proceed from stated premises to their logical conclusions. This ability can also be termed syllogistic reasoning or analytic reasoning in that progression is from the *whole to the parts*.

10. INDUCTIVE REASONING   This is the ability to find the most appropriate

---

(*continued*)

TABLE 12.2 *Continued*

general concepts or rules which fit sets of data or which explain how a given series of individual items are related to each other. It involves the ability to synthesize disparate facts; to proceed logically from *individual cases to general principles.* It also involves the ability to form hypotheses about relationships among items or data.

11. INFORMATION ORDERING   This is the ability to apply rules or objectives to given information in order to arrange that information into the best or most *appropriate sequence.* The types of information considered under this ability include numbers, letters, words, pictures, procedures, sentences, and mathematical or logical operations. Rules or objectives for ordering *must first be provided* to the operator or subject in the task.

12. CATEGORY FLEXIBILITY This is the ability to produce alternative groupings or categorizations for a set of items, based upon rules or specifications produced by the individual who is carrying out the categorization. Each alternative group must contain at least two items from the initial list, but any specific set of alternative groups need not contain all of the items from the initial list.

13. SPATIAL ORIENTATION   This is the ability to *maintain one's orientation* with respect to objects in space or to *comprehend the position* of objects in space with respect to the observer's position. The question posed is often "If the environment looks like this, what is my position?"

14. VISUALIZATION   This is the ability to manipulate or transform the visual images of spatial patterns or objects into other spatial arrangements. It requires the formation of mental images of the patterns or objects as they would appear *after certain specified changes* such as unfolding, rotation, or movement of some type. The transformation or set of transformations the observer is asked to make may involve either entire spatial patterns or objects or parts of those patterns or objects. The observer predicts what an object, set of objects, or pattern would look like after the specified changes were actually carried out.

15. SPEED OF CLOSURE   This ability involves the speed with which a set of apparently disparate sensory elements can be combined and organized into a single, meaningful pattern or configuration. The operator must combine *all* the elements presented from a single source of information into a meaningful configuration. The operator is *not told* what he or she is trying to identify; the elements appear to be disparate. This ability applies to all senses with the restriction that elements to be combined must be presented within the *same sensory modality.*

16. FLEXIBILITY OF CLOSURE   This is the ability to identify or detect a *previously specified* stimulus configuration which is embedded in a more complex sensory field. It is the ability to isolate the specified relevant stimulus from a field where distracting stimulation *is intentionally included* as part of the task to be performed. *Only one* information source is utilized. This ability applies to all senses with the restriction that both the relevant and distracting stimulation must occur *within the same sense modality.*

17. SELECTIVE ATTENTION   This is the ability to perform a task in the presence of distracting stimulation or under monotonous conditions without significant loss in efficiency. When distracting stimulation is present in the task situation, it is not an integral part of the task being performed, but rather is extraneous to the

(continued)

TABLE 12.2 *Continued*

task and imposed upon it. The task and the irrelevant stimulation can occur either within the same sense or across senses. Under conditions of distracting stimulation, the ability involves concentration on the task being performed and filtering out of the distracting stimulation. When the task is performed under monotonous conditions only concentration on the task being performed is involved.

18. TIME SHARING   This is the ability to utilize information obtained by shifting between two or more channels of information. The information obtained from these sources is either integrated and used as a whole, or retained and used separately.

19. PERCEPTUAL SPEED   This ability involves the speed with which sensory patterns or configurations can be *compared* in order to determine identity or degree of similarity. Comparisons may be made either between successively or simultaneously presented patterns or configurations, or between *remembered* or standard configurations and *presented* configurations. The sensory patterns to be compared must occur *within the same sense* and not between senses.

20. STATIC STRENGTH   This ability involves the *degree* of muscular force exerted against a fairly immovable or heavy *external object* in order to lift, push, or pull that object. Force is exerted *continuously* up to the amount needed to move the object. This ability is general to different muscle groups (e.g., hand, arm, back, shoulder, leg). This ability does not extend to prolonged exertion of physical force over time and is not concerned with the number of times the act is repeated.

21. EXPLOSIVE STRENGTH   This is the ability to expend energy in one or a series of explosive muscular acts. The ability requires a mobilization of energy for a *burst* of muscular effort, rather than continuous strain, stress, or repeated exertion of muscles. The ability may be involved in propelling the body as in the activities of jumping or sprinting, or in throwing objects for distance.

22. DYNAMIC STRENGTH   This ability involves the power of arm and trunk muscles to repeatedly, or continuously support or move the *body's own weight.* Emphasis is on resistance of the muscles to performance decrement when put under repeated or continuous stress.

23. STAMINA   This ability involves the capacity to maintain physical activity over *prolonged* periods of time. It is concerned with resistance of the *cardiovascular system* (heart and blood vessels) to breakdown.

24. EXTENT FLEXIBILITY   This is the ability to extend, flex, or stretch muscle groups. It concerns the *degree of flexibility* of muscle groups, but does *not* include repeated or speed flexing.

25. DYNAMIC FLEXIBILITY   This is the ability to make repeated trunk and/or limb flexing movements where both *speed* and *flexibility* of movement are required. It includes the ability of these muscles to recover from the strain and distortion of repeated flexing.

26. GROSS BODY EQUILIBRIUM   This is the ability to maintain the body in an upright position or to regain body balance especially in situations where equilibrium is threatened or temporarily lost. This ability involves only *body balance;* it does *not* extend to the balancing of objects.

27. RESPONSE ORIENTATION   This is the ability to select and initiate the appropriate response relative to a given stimulus in the situation where *two or more*

(*continued*)

TABLE 12.2 *Continued*

stimuli are possible and where the appropriate response is selected from *two or more* alternatives. The ability is concerned with the *speed* with which the appropriate response can be *initiated* and does not extend to the speed with which the response is carried out. This ability is independent of mode of stimulus presentation (auditory or visual) and also of type of response required.

28. REACTION TIME   This ability involves the *speed* with which a *single motor response* can be initiated after the onset of a *single stimulus*. It does *not* include the speed with which the response or movement is carried out. This ability is independent of the mode of stimulus presentation (auditory or visual) and also of the type of motor response required.

29. SPEED OF LIMB MOVEMENT   This ability involves the *speed* with which discrete movements of the arms or legs can be made. The ability deals with the speed with which the movement can be carried out after it has been initiated; it is not concerned with the speed of initiation of the movement. In addition, the precision, accuracy, and coordination of the movement is not considered under this ability.

30. WRIST–FINGER SPEED   This ability is concerned with the *speed* with which discrete movements of the fingers, hands, and wrists can be made. The ability is not concerned with the speed of initiation of the movement. It is only concerned with the speed with which the movement is carried out. This ability does not consider the question of the accuracy of the movement, nor does it depend upon precise eye-hand coordination.

31. GROSS BODY COORDINATION   This is the ability to *coordinate* movements of the *trunk and limbs*. This ability is most commonly found in situations where the entire body is in motion or being propelled.

32. MULTILIMB COORDINATION   This is the ability to coordinate the movements of two or more limbs (e.g., two legs, two hands, one leg and one hand). The ability does *not* apply to tasks in which trunk movements must be integrated with limb movements. It is most common to tasks where the body is at rest (e.g., seated or standing), while two or more limbs are in motion.

33. FINGER DEXTERITY   This is the ability to make skillful, coordinated movements of the fingers where manipulations of objects may or may not be involved. This ability does *not* extend to manipulation of machine or equipment control mechanisms. Speed of movement is *not* involved in this ability.

34. MANUAL DEXTERITY   This is the ability to make skillful, coordinated movements of a hand, or of a hand together with its arm. This ability is concerned with coordination of movement within the limb. It may involve manipulation of objects (e.g., blocks, pencils), but does not extend to machine or equipment controls (e.g., levers, dials).

35. ARM-HAND STEADINESS   This is the ability to make precise, steady arm-hand positioning movements where both strength and speed are minimized. It includes steadiness during movement as well as minimization of tremor and drift while maintaining a static arm position. This ability does *not* extend to the adjustment of equipment controls (e.g., levers, dials).

36. RATE CONTROL   This is the ability to make timed, anticipatory motor adjustments relative to *changes* in the speed and/or direction of a continuously

(*continued*)

TABLE 12.2 *Continued*

moving object. The purpose of the motor adjustments is to intercept or follow a
continuously moving stimulus whose speed and/or direction vary in an *unpredictable*
fashion. This ability does not extend to situations in which both the speed and
direction of the object are perfectly predictable.

37. CONTROL PRECISION   This is the ability to make controlled muscular
movements necessary to adjust or position a machine or equipment control mechanism. The adjustments can be anticipatory motor movements in response to
changes in the speed and/or direction of a moving object whose speed *and* direction
are perfectly predictable.

*a*Adapted with permission from Theologus, G. C., Romashko, T., and Fleishman, E. A. Development of a taxonomy of human performance: A feasibility study of ability dimensions for classifying
human tasks (American Institutes for Research Tech. Rep.). *JSAS Catalog of Selected Documents in
Psychology*, 1973, 3, 25–26 (Ms. No. 321).

matchings accomplished, number of items completed, and number of
pins placed. In these tasks, the subject had to complete as many units
as possible within a fixed period of time. Because the time period
varied across tasks, a time base of one second was chosen, and the
mean performance scores were converted to the average number of
units produced per second.

In selecting ability scales for use as predictors, three criteria were
employed: (1) the scales had to have high reliability, in terms of
intraclass correlations; (2) they had to have enough variability in
mean ratings across the 27 tasks to provide for some discrimination
among tasks; and (3) they had to possess some logical relationship to
performance on the tasks. Six scales were selected for analysis as a
result of this procedure.

A Wherry–Doolittle stepwise multiple regression was performed.
The resulting regression equation is shown below in raw score form.
(Gross Body Coordination, Manual Dexterity, and Arm–Hand Steadi-
ness are the abilities with the primary weights in this equation.)

$$Y = 5.03 - 2.37X_1 - 0.95X_2 - 0.74X_3$$

The multiple correlation cooefficient, corrected for small sample
bias, was 0.64, highly significant. Although cross validation was still
needed, this analysis indicated that the abilities scales were indeed
correlates of task performance, meeting one of the primary criteria
for taxonomic development discussed in Chapter 4.

Another category of investigations reflecting on the validity of the
ability scales for classifying tasks involves test validation in an employment situation. In validating tests for selected craft positions,
Zedeck (1976) used portions of the Abilities Analysis Scales to deter-

mine the validity of physical ability tests as predictors of performance on job tasks. These tests typically represent the marker tests
for the specific ability determined through factor analysis (Fleishman, 1964). The scales were administered to determine the abilities
necessary for the job. Reference tests corresponding to each of these
abilities were specified and criteria to be predicted were determined
across jobs. Applicants were then tested on the measures, placed into
training school (independent of test performance), trained, and later
evaluated on the criterion job tasks. A multiple stepwise regression
equation was computed, yielding a significantly high multiple correlation of .41. This indicated that, in a field study, Physical Abilities
Analysis provided estimates of job requirements useful in selecting
valid predictors of job success.

Similar findings were obtained in a predictive validity study conducted by Jones and Prien (1978), who identified ability requirements using the ability rating scales with a sample of analysts. They
identified tests that loaded on the required abilities and administered the test battery to a sample of applicants in entry-level jobs.
Significant correlations were obtained between the composite physical test scores and ratings of physical proficiency ($r = .40, p < .01$)
and ratings for overall performance ($r = .38, p < .01$) after 60 days on
the job. These data suggest a valid relationship between abilities
identified by this methodology, the tests selected on this basis, and
subsequent job performance.

Other studies by Hogan, Ogden, and Fleishman (1978), Myers, et al.
(1981), and Cooper et al. (1982) have confirmed that tests selected on
the basis of ability analyses of job tasks have significant predictive
validity in a wide variety of settings. Taken together, these findings
are supportive of the construct and predictive validity of the Ability
Requirements Approach.

Recent Developments

NEW SCALES

The development and refinement of the ability scales has been a
continuing effort. New scales have been developed and additional
methods for improving the methodology have been examined and
incorporated. Two studies sought to expand and improve the abilities
analysis with regard to current and anticipated jobs in a large utility
company (Fleishman, 1975a; Fleishman, Cobb, & Spendolini, 1976).

Starting with the 37 scales developed earlier, job analysts and abilities specialists reviewed descriptions of the range of jobs under consideration in the company and recommended specific areas of analysis expansion. For example, Verbal Comprehension was split into two components: Written Comprehension and Oral Comprehension. Verbal Expression was split into Written Expression and Oral Expression. Trunk Strength, from previous research (Fleishman, 1964), was added to the coverage of physical abilities. Several abilities in the interpersonal area were added, such as Persuasion and Social Sensitivity. Each of these new scales was developed according to the prototype procedures used to create the original ability scales.

Additional ability scales have been developed in the sensory–perceptual domain, in particular for vision and audition (Hogan, *et al.* 1978; Schemmer, 1982). Table 12.3 lists the abilities and scales available for inclusion in recent forms of the Manual for the Ability Requirements Scales (MARS). Appendix B contains the updated definitions for these categories.

Tasks Categorized

Additionally, scale values for thousands of tasks have been obtained and included in a task bank classified according to the ability taxonomy. Appendix C contains examples of these. Tasks scaled now represent a wide range of occupational tasks. This data base of tasks classified by ability category, called the Task Abilities Bank (TAB), is maintained by the Advanced Research Resources Organization in Washington, D.C.

Agreement among Respondents

Reliability issues in terms of agreement among groups of raters have been discussed. A related issue is agreement between different respondent groups using the ability rating scales. Studies have been accumulating that demonstrate high agreement between incumbents, supervisors, and job analysts who use these scales to describe the same jobs. In analyses of three civil service jobs in New York city, Romashko, Brumback, Fleishman, and Hahn (1974) found a high correlation (.69) between ratings made by incumbents and assistant foremen for the sanitation job. The correlation between the rank orders of ratings made by incumbents and supervisors for the parking enforcement agent job was also .69. Correlations between the rank orders of ratings between incumbents and officers for the firefighter job was .64. Romanshko, Hahn, and Brumback (1976), in assessing

TABLE 12.3

Abilities in Recent Forms of the Manual for Ability Requirements Scales (MARS)[a,b]

1. Oral Comprehension	27. Finger Dexterity
2. Written Comprehension	28. Wrist–Finger Speed
3. Oral Expression	29. Speed of Limb Movement
4. Written Expression	30. Selective Attention
5. Fluency of Ideas	31. Time Sharing
6. Originality	32. Static Strength
7. Memorization	33. Explosive Strength
8. Problem Sensitivity	34. Dynamic Strength
9. Mathematical Reasoning	35. Trunk Strength
10. Number Facility	36. Extent Flexibility
11. Deductive Reasoning	37. Dynamic Flexibility
12. Inductive Reasoning	38. Gross Body Coordination
13. Information Ordering	39. Gross Body Equilibrium
14. Category Flexibility	40. Stamina
15. Speed of Closure	41. Near Vision
16. Flexibility of Closure	42. Far Vision
17. Spatial Orientation	43. Visual Color Discrimination
18. Visualization	44. Night Vision
19. Perceptual Speed	45. Peripheral Vision
20. Control Precision	46. Depth Perception
21. Multilimb Coordination	47. Glare Sensitivity
22. Response Orientation	48. General Hearing
23. Rate Control	49. Auditory Attention
24. Reaction Time	50. Sound Localization
25. Arm–Hand Steadiness	51. Speech Hearing
26. Manual Dexterity	52. Speech Clarity

[a]Adapted with permission from (1) Fleishman, E. A. *Development of ability requirements scales for the analysis of Bell System jobs*. Bethesda, MD: Management Research Institute, 1975(a), and (2) Schemmer, F. M. *Development of rating scales for selected visual, auditory, and speech abilities*. Washington, D.C.: Advanced Research Resources Organization, 1982.
[b]See Appendix B for most recent definitions of abilities.

the police officer job in Philadelphia, obtained similar correlations between ratings for incumbents and officers (.75), between incumbents and experts (.66), and between officers and experts (.81). Similarly, correlations between ability ratings made by foremen and incumbents for the jobs installer–repairman, splicer, and lineman were .79, .87, and .68, respectively (Zedeck, 1975). In another study, ratings by experts of the physical abilities in a number of entry-level jobs, yielded high interrater reliability (.82) across all jobs studied and scales used (Jones & Prien, 1978).

Recent studies found similar levels of agreement between incumbents, supervisors, and job analysts in the use of these ability scales for describing the requirements of 15 benchmark jobs in the county of San Bernardino, California (Hogan *et al.*, 1978); 20 jobs in a large public utility (Inn, Schulman, Ogden, & Sample, 1982); 7 different military occupational specialties (e.g., military police, hospital corpsman) (Myers, Gebhardt, Price, & Fleishman, 1981); lineman and maintenance positions in the electric power industry (Cooper *et al.*, 1982); shipboard jobs (e.g., gunner's mates and bosun's mates in the Navy) (Gebhardt, Jennings, & Fleishman, 1981); and court security officers in New York state (Myers, Jennings, & Fleishman, 1981).

Abilities Analysis reliability has also been assessed by replication. Zedeck (1975) reported high agreement between raters in San Diego and in Sacramento for abilities required in installer–repairman (.68), splicer (.50), and lineman (.50) jobs. Hogan *et al.* (1978) analyzed an entry-level gorcery warehousing job, order selector, across three different warehouses in different cities, using Abilities Analysis ratings. There were no significant mean rating differences across abilities and warehouses except for the Extent Flexibility scale. It was determined subsequently that differences in the heights of the shelves accounted for the differences in these ratings of required Flexibility. Thus, these methods were shown to be sensitive to the differences in job requirements.

Interrater agreement with current versions of these scales, used to describe jobs and tasks in a wide variety of industrial, governmental, and military settings, tend to be in the .80s and .90s (see Hogan *et al.*, 1978; Myers *et al.* 1979; Myers *et al.* 1981; Gebhardt *et al.*, 1981; Cooper *et al.*, 1982).

DECISION AIDS IN ESTIMATING ABILITY
REQUIREMENTS

In addition to the rating scale approach to ability identification and classification, a parallel system was developed. This system utilizes binary decision flow diagrams to simplify decisions by observers when estimating the ability requirements of a task (Fleishman & Stephenson, 1972). The purpose is to reduce the level of information processing and decision making on the part of the rater. Figure 12.4 gives a truncated example of these attempts for an area of perceptual–motor abilities. This approach requires the observer to make a series of branching, binary decisions that result in assessing the presence or absence of an ability. More elaborate decision charts were developed by Fleishman and Stephenson for other areas of motor and physical performance as well as for various cognitive and perceptual domains.

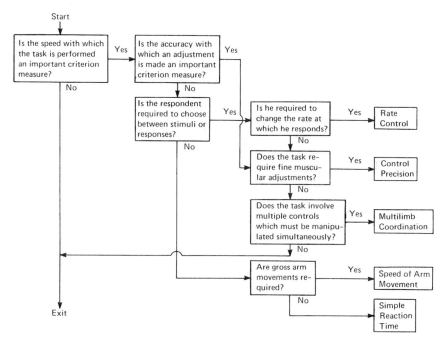

Figure 12.4 Portion of binary decision flow diagram for ability identification and classification. Adapted with permission from Fleishman, E. A. and Stephenson, R. W. Development of a taxonomy of human performance: A review of the third year's progress (American Institutes for Research Tech. Rep.). *JSAS Catalog of Selected Documents in Psychology*, 1972, *48*, 1–68 (Ms. No. 113).

Mallamad, Levine, and Fleishman (1980) recently extended this work to include ability definitions, distinctions, and task examples. They also assessed the psychometric properties of this approach. Figure 12.5 presents one example from their diagrams. This particular assessment device was found to be reliable with groups of judges and effective in reducing some of the "false positives" in identifying abilities in tasks that sometimes occur using the scaling technique. The study showed that these diagrams are best used as a supplementary method, because the scaling of "amount" of an ability requirement must still be done. The method is particularly suitable for adaptation to computer-interactive administration and scoring. Such computer adaptation, utilizing the ability classificatory system described, already is being attempted using an Apple II computer.

The preceding sections provide the conceptual framework, methodological background, and psychometric characteristics of a measurement system for utilizing the ability classificatory approach in

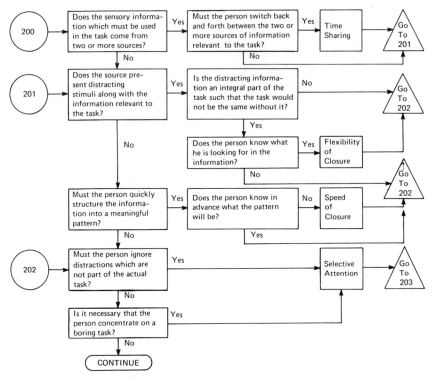

Figure 12.5 Portion of a decision flow diagram dealing with some perceptual abilities. Adapted with permission from Mallamad, S. M., Levine, J. M., and Fleishman, E. A. Identifying ability requirements by decision flow diagrams. *Human Factors*, 1980, *22*(1), 57–68.

describing and classifying tasks. The results generally are supportive of the operational utility of the method for describing tasks reliably in terms of the types and amounts of abilities required for performance. Later in this chapter, we review some specific uses for these methods in the solution of a number of research and applied problems.

Evaluating the Utility of Ability Requirements in Integrating Research Data

VIGILANCE STUDIES

One way to evaluate a taxonomic system is in terms of its capacity to organize a portion of the data found in the human performance literature (Levine, Romashko, & Fleishman, 1973). In one study our objective was to examine the feasibility of structuring an area of literature according to the abilities required for task performance. The area of human performance selected for examination was sustained attention in monitoring tasks, the so-called vigilance literature. *Vigilance* generally is considered to involve a change in the detection of infrequent signals over prolonged periods of time. Our idea was to examine the tasks used in these previous studies, to rate them in terms of the abilities scheme using our scales, and to classify the studies in terms of the abilities required by the tasks used. The next step was to examine the data within and between these categories of tasks to see if improved generalizations could be made about factors affecting vigilance performance.

The vigilance area was selected for study for several reasons. First, although a variety of different tasks has been used in previous vigilance research, the range of tasks is not as great as in many other areas. Consequently, the number of different abilities involved is not likely to be large and this, in turn, would reduce the complexity of the evaluation. Second, a reasonably large number of studies has been reported on the effects of several selected independent variables on vigilance performance. Obviously, it is important that enough studies be available to provide a sufficient number of data points within task categories. Third, a common dependent measure is employed in nearly all vigilance studies, namely, detection accuracy.

The study was designed to examine (1) the extent to which performance in vigilance tasks could be differentiated on the basis of abilities, and (2) whether improved generalizations about the effects of independent variables in vigilance performance were possible as a result of such task classifications.

Four abilities were required for the different task performances in this area, with two, Perceptual Speed and Flexibility of Closure, predominating. Figure 12.6 provides illustrative results when the data for such tasks are partitioned according to levels of an independent variable, whether the signals were auditory, visual, or both. We have plotted percent of target detections at 30-minute intervals throughout the first 180 minutes of the vigilance task. It can be seen that regardless of whether the ability category was Perceptual Speed or Flexibility of Closure, overall performance under auditory conditions was superior to visual conditions. Furthermore, the visual plus auditory condition was markedly superior to either auditory or visual presentation in number of targets detected.

The important results show that the functions obtained vary with

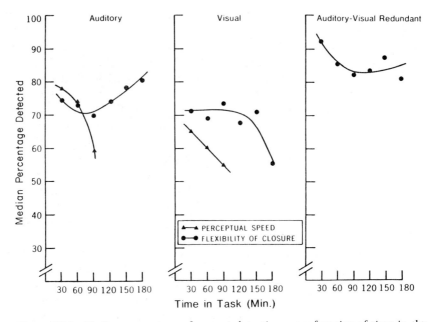

Figure 12.6 Median percentage of correct detections as a function of time in the task and ability category for different sensory modes. Adapted with permission from Levine, J. M., Romashko, T., and Fleishman, E. A. Evaluation of an abilities classification system for integrating and generalizing findings about human performance: The vigilance area. *Journal of Applied Psychology*, 1973, *58*, 147–149.

the type of task as defined by our ability ratings. For the auditory condition Perceptual Speed tasks show a severe performance decrement with time in the task. On the other hand, there was a very small performance decrement for Flexibility of Closure tasks within the first 90 minutes, and an increment in performance accuracy beyond that time. The function describing performance with time in the task for Perceptual Speed studies was similar in the visual condition and the auditory condition. However, for tasks requiring Flexibility of Closure, the function in the visual condition was almost the reverse of that for the auditory condition.

Similar analyses were made for other variables, such as signal rate. Although the data provided are preliminary, and in several instances functions are based on only a few data points, it was nevertheless possible to infer that the effects of the independent variables on performance in a vigilance task are in part a function of the class of task imposed upon the subjects. It has been demonstrated that when studies are categorized by abilities required by the task, relationships between performance and time in the task differ markedly as a function of the selected independent variables. It should be emphasized that, despite the differences among specific tasks in terms of equipment, displays, response requirements, and so forth, the classificatory system enabled an integration of results and the development of functional relationships that were otherwise obscured.

Further support of the utility of the abilities classification system for organizing data and predicting performance on diverse visual-monitoring tasks has been provided by Parasuraman (1976).

ALCOHOL STUDIES

Another study, along these same general lines, was conducted on the effects of alcohol on human performance (Levine, Kramer, & Levine, 1975). As before, the effort was designed to categorize the existing literature on alcohol effects into task groups in order to determine whether alcohol effects differ as a function of type of tasks. Tasks described in the literature on alcohol effects were grouped together on the basis of the abilities required to perform the task using the ability rating scale procedures developed. A preliminary set of abilities was chosen representing the cognitive, sensory–perceptual, and psychomotor domains. After the tasks in these studies were grouped according to abilities measured, performance on these tasks as a function of amount of alcohol dosage and time since dosage were examined for each function of class of tasks.

Figure 12.7 depicts performance as a function of dosage, for the ability categories of Selective Attention, Perceptual Speed, and Control Precision. The performance decrement relative to control groups for increasing dosage levels is plotted. The plots are in terms of grams of alcohol per kilogram of body weight. The number of data points is small, because of the limited number of studies found in the literature, and therefore conclusions and interpretations were made with caution. However, each point is an average of several studies and there is a striking similarity in the rate of performance deterioration with increasing alcohol dosages for the Perceptual Speed and Control Precision tasks. The situation is somewhat different, however, for tasks involving Selective Attention. The data suggest that performance on tasks involving this cognitive ability is impaired more seriously with increases in dosage. Other results suggest that the greatest impact of alcohol on performance occurs when an hour or more elapses between administration of alcohol and task performance. Further, when these conditions prevail, the Selective Attention and Perceptual Speed tasks are most hampered by alcohol and the Control Precision tasks least hampered. Taken together, these results

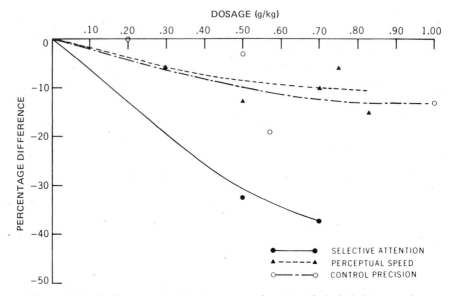

Figure 12.7 Median percent decrement as a function of alcohol dosage and predominant ability. Adapted with permission from Levine, J. M., Krammer, G. G., and Levine, E. N. Effects of alcohol on human performance: An integration of research findings based on an abilities classification. *Journal of Applied Psychology*, 1975, *60*, 285–293.

indicate that the rate and degree of deterioration are a function of both dosage levels and task categories. Although the results are not as clear as those found for the vigilance research, knowledge of the task categories appears to improve the prediction that can be made about human performance. Again, despite differences among the specific tasks in the literature in displays, response requirements, performance indexes, techinque of alcohol administration, and so on, the categorization of tasks used in these different studies according to ability requirements, appears to allow an integration of results and the development of functional relationships that otherwise may be obscured.

Predicting Learning and Performance Levels

Earlier studies attempted to use ability concepts to predict various learning measures and other aspects of task performance (e.g., Fleishman, 1957, 1964; Fleishman & Ellison, 1969; Fleishman & Hempel, 1954, 1955; Fleishman & Rich, 1963). In general, these studies with a variety of practice tasks showed that the role of various abilities at different stages of learning could be traced. Some abilities predicted early learning and others predicted later learning. Thus, some of the taxonomic criteria proposed by Fitts (1962) were met by the ability concepts, because they were shown to be related to learning rates, performance levels, and individual differences. We had special interest in identifying abilities predicting eventual high proficiency levels in such skills. These studies have used, but have not been confined to, combinations of experimental and factor analysis designs.

In a typical study, 200–300 subjects received a battery of reference tests known to sample certain abilities (as defined in the taxonomic work described). These same subjects then received practice on a more complex criterion task to be learned. Through the use of factor-analytic techniques, applied to the correlations obtained between ability tests and scores during learning trials, the abilities from the reference ability tests were identified. The factor loadings of successive trial scores on the criterion task on these factors defined by the reference tasks then were examined. A variety of multivariate and regression techniques was used to confirm the general findings.

In general, these studies, with a great variety of practice tasks, show that: (1) the particular combinations of abilities contributing to performance on a task may change as practice on this task continues; (2) these changes are progressive and systematic and eventually become stabilized; (3) in perceptual–motor tasks, for example, the contribution of nonmotor abilities (e.g., verbal or spatial) may play a role early in learning, but their contribution relative to motor abilities decreases systematically with practice; (4) there is also an increase in a factor specific to the task itself, not common to the more general abilities.

Figure 12.8 illustrates one set of results (Fleishman & Hempel, 1955) using a task in which the subject had to learn to respond as quickly as possible to patterns of signal lights, in which the correct switch depended on the particular combination of colored lights presented. It was found that while spatial and verbal abilities contribute to performance during early trials (shown by high factor loadings), their contribution decreases until late in learning. At this stage, the contribution of two motor abilities, Rate of Movement and Reaction Time, not measured by the task early in learning, increases in importance. At advanced proficiency levels, the latter are the main abilities related to performance. The results also showed the increasing importance of a within-task factor confined to trials on the practiced task and not shared with the reference tests.

When we compare learning on this task for groups differing in their levels of different abilities (Figure 12.9), we find that certain ability

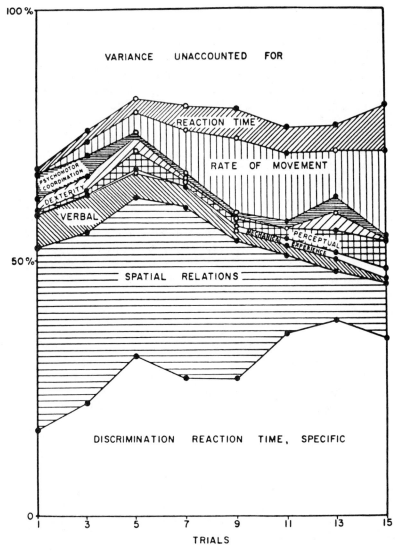

Figure 12.8 Percentage of variance represented by loadings on each factor at different stages of practice on the discrimination reaction time task. Reprinted with permission from Fleishman, E. A. and Hempel, W. E., Jr. The relation between abilities and improvement with practice in a visual discrimination reaction task. *Journal of Experimental Psychology*, 1955, 49, 301–312.

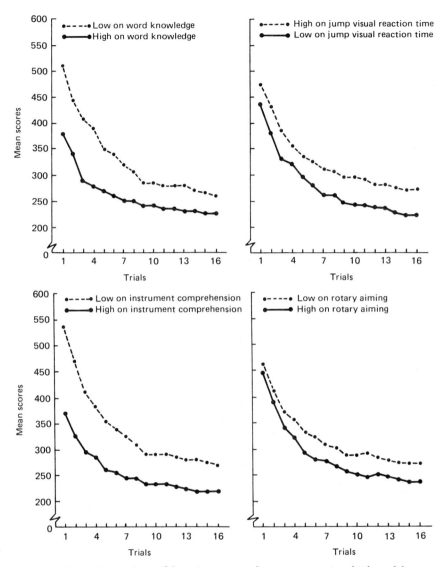

Figure 12.9 Comparison of learning curves for groups scoring high and low on different ability test measures. Reprinted with permission from Fleishman, E. A. and Hempel, W. E., Jr. The relation between abilities and improvement with practice in a visual discrimination reaction task. *Journal of Experimental Psychology*, 1955, *49*, 301–312.

tests discriminate between individuals high and low in proficiency on the learning task mainly early in learning, whereas other abilities discriminate better at advanced levels of learning.

These results were obtained with a great variety of tasks and methods and were found to extend to perceptual tasks, verbal tasks, and concept-formation and problem-solving tasks. Other studies replicated these findings using more complex tasks, such as job simulators (Parker & Fleishman, 1960) and actual training and job situations (Fleishman & Fruchter, 1960). Reviews of test validities predicting job performance over time also supported these findings (Ghiselli & Haire, 1960).

Clearly, the possibility of different ability requirements for initial stages of learning and for final stages of proficiency can have important implications for the prediction of ultimate task performance. Such shifts also have implications regarding the nature of skill training and the emphasis that should be placed on various stages of practice. If the abilities required by a task change during the course of the learning period, a clear distinction between final proficiency and proficiency during training must be maintained in developing predictive instruments. Also, it may be possible to increase the efficiency of skill training by concentrating throughout the training period on those abilities required for final proficiency, rather than on those abilities required only in the early stages of skill acquisition.

Actually, Parker and Fleishman (1961) have already tried to manipulate training content, in an experimental study involving a highly complex flying simulation task, so that the training would correspond to the abilities that were operational at different stages of learning. The learning curves show that the group given such special training learned at a faster rate and reached a higher level of proficiency than did matched groups given more traditional instruction for this task.

This work that relates abilities to more general performance phenomena led us to conclude that this kind of taxonomic system might be worth future development. For reviews of this research, see Fleishman (1966, 1967a).

Development of Laboratory Tasks Standardized by Ability Measured

EFFECTS OF DRUGS

As another illustration, we developed laboratory tasks representative of the various categories in the ability requirements classificato-

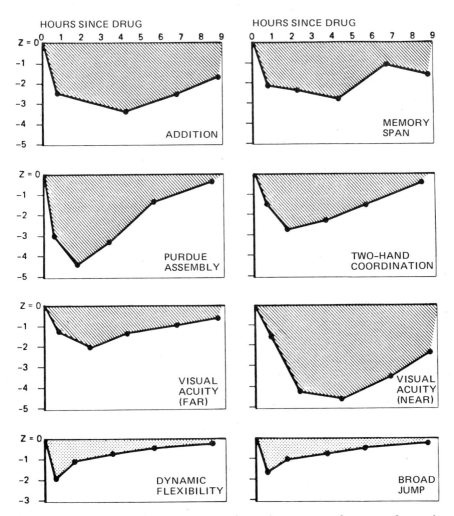

Figure 12.10 Effects of a given dosage of scopolamine on performance of several different tasks involving different abilities. Adapted with permission from Elkin, E. H., Fleishman, E. A., Van Cott, H. P., Horowitz, H., and Freedle, R. O. *Effects of drugs on human performance: Research concepts, test development, and preliminary studies* (Report AIR-E-25-10/65-AR-I). Washington, D.C.: American Institutes for Research, 1965.

ry system. Such "standardized tasks," representing the ability dimensions, were used in laboratory studies of various factors affecting human performance. Thus, we studied the effects of a variety of drugs and dosages on measures of a variety of reference ability tasks. Figure 12.10 provides a few illustrations of such results with a given dosage of the drug scopolamine (Elkin, Fleishman, Van Cott, Horo-witz, & Freedle, 1965). Different effects were obtained according to the task performed in a variety of cognitive, perceptual, and motor areas, that is, some abilities within each area were more affected than others by the same dosage of the drug. The absolute perfor-mance decrement, time to reach maximum effect, and time to re-cover, depended on the ability measured. For example, the physical abilities of Dynamic Flexibility and Explosive Strength (Broad Jump Task) showed only slight effects, whereas the motor abilities of Multi-Limb Coordination (Two-Hand Coordination Task) and Finger Dex-terity (Purdue Assembly Task) showed marked effects. Such findings show why the general category "motor skill" is too broad. Similar findings in the program were found for a variety of other drugs, such as magnesium-pemoline and ritalin, that may enhance or degrade performance (Baker, Geist, & Fleishman, 1967).

EFFECTS OF NOISE

Similar studies were conducted on the effects of different noise stressors (Theologus, Wheaton, & Fleishman, 1974). The device

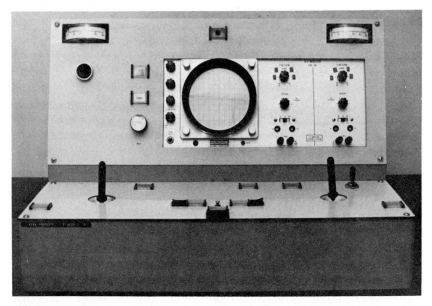

Figure 12.11 The perceptual–motor console. Reprinted with permission from The-ologus, G. C., Wheaton, G. R., and Fleishman, E. A. Effects of intermittent, moderate intensity noise-stress on human performance. *Journal of Applied Psychology*, 1974, *59*, 539–547.

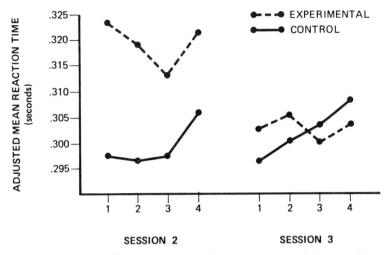

Figure 12.12 Effect of random (session 2) versus patterned (session 3) noise on Reaction Time task. Adapted with permission from Theologus, G. C., Wheaton, G. R., and Fleishman, E. A. Effects of intermittent, moderate intensity noise-stress on human performance. *Journal of Applied Psychology*, 1974, *59*, 539–547.

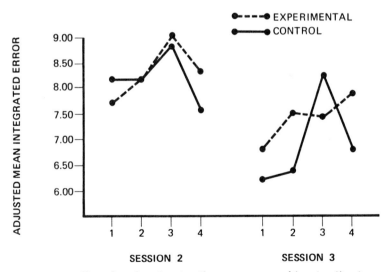

Figure 12.13 Effect of random (session 2) versus patterned (session 3) noise on Rate Control task. Adapted with permission from Theologus, G. C., Wheaton, G. R., and Fleishman, E. A. Effects of intermittent, moderate intensity noise-stress on human performance. *Journal of Applied Psychology*, 1974, *59*, 539–547.

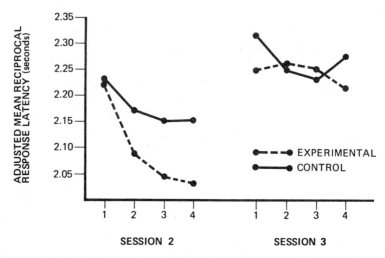

Figure 12.14 Effect of random (session 2) versus patterned (session 3) noise on Time-Sharing task. Adapted with permission from Theologus, G. C., Wheaton, G. R., and Fleishman, E. A. Effects of intermittent, moderate intensity noise-stress on human performance. *Journal of Applied Psychology,* 1974, *59,* 539–547.

shown in Figure 12.11 was designed to measure the different psychomotor abilities identified. It was found that random, intermittent, moderate-intensity noise (85 dB) is more likely to affect performance on tasks emphasizing some of these abilities than others. Figure 12.12 shows the significant effect of random intermittent noise on the mean reaction time and the absence of any effect on this measure for the patterned noise of the same intensity. However, Figure 12.13 shows that on the rate control task (tracking), no effect of either type of noise is demonstrated. Figure 12.14 illustrates that for a time-sharing task there is no noise effect at first, but the effects appear to be cumulative during continued exposure. The results illustrate differential effects according to task category. Thus, improved generalizations of research data are possible if careful specifications of our task categories are utilized, with ability concepts holding the key.

Utility of the Abilities Classificatory System

Job Analysis and Test Development

In terms of the criterion of utility, the ability system for describing human tasks is applicable to a variety of applied problems. As a method of job analysis and test development, it has been employed in a range of studies determining the requirements of firefighters, grocery warehouse clerks, telephone line workers, probation officers, refinery workers, Army and Navy occupational specialities, accountants, inspectors, and maintenance personnel. Tests selected to map onto the abilities identified have been shown to have criterion-related validity (Hogan, Ogden, & Fleishman, 1979; Myers, Gebhardt, Price, & Fleishman, 1981; Cooper, Schemmer, Gebhardt, Marshall-Mies, & Fleishman 1982). The Abilities Analysis method of job analysis is particularly relevant to issues of content and construct validation, because it provides the basis for demonstrating the job relevance of the ability tests selected and their linkages to critical job tasks.

SETTING PERFORMANCE STANDARDS

These methods have been used as a basis for setting standards for assessing job performance. Specific tasks comprising a job are first evaluated with respect to their requirements for various ability factors. Tasks rated highest on the different scales across a wide variety of occupational specialities are then selected for work sample or criterion-referenced tests. Individuals who can perform these tasks can be assumed to be able to perform all other job tasks rated lower on the same ability scales. The scales provide a means for identifying the relevant tasks covering the abilities required by the job in a cost-effective, objective manner (e.g., Myers, Gebhardt, & Fleishman, 1979).

SETTING MEDICAL STANDARDS

A more recent development is the use of these methods in setting medical standards for physically demanding jobs. The medical examination, administered by physicians, is coming under increasing scrutiny for job relevance. Medical screening often is done without clear information about the job tasks and requirements. Current work underway attempts to link the ability requirements of job tasks with the diagnostic procedures utilized by examining physicans (Hogan, Ogden, & Fleishman, 1978; Gebhardt, Weldon, & Fleishman, 1981; Gebhardt & Weldon, 1982; Myers et al., 1981). The Ability Requirements Approach allows integration of such requirements across a great many jobs. Working with specialists in occupational medicine, physicians' manuals have been developed in which disqualifying symptoms are provided at each level of each physical ability requirement. As an example, in the orthopedic section of the manual, a job falling at level 5 on Dynamic Strength might disqualify individuals with "loose bodies in the knee." These levels were established at the task level across a great variety of tasks, but the taxonomy allowed their integration into the general ability categories. Using the manual developed by this process, the physician notes the rating of each job on each ability and can relate the symptoms and impairments observed in job applicants to the job-related guidance provided in the manual (Myers *et al.*, 1981). Figure 12.15 provides an illustrated page from the manual.

The method has particular implications in the areas of disability assessment, assignment of handicapped, and reassignment of disabled or rehabilitated individuals to jobs they can perform.

CLASSIFYING JOBS AND TASKS

The system described also appears to be useful as a method for classifying, grouping, and indexing jobs in terms of common ability requirements. Thus, diverse jobs involving many different types of tasks have been grouped according to the common abilities needed to perform them effectively (e.g, Hogan *et al.*, 1978). Table 12.4 presents a portion of this information. A data base of thousands of job tasks with empirically derived different abilities also has been developed. As new jobs containing similar tasks are analyzed, their ability requirements can now be estimated from this data base. Computer programs have been developed at the Advanced Research Resources Organization (ARRO) for matching tasks from new jobs with task information stored in the computer. The result is a profile of the ability requirements of the new job.

Summary Statement

In conclusion, tasks can be described in terms of the human abilities required to perform them. We discussed the rationale and methodology identifying these abilities and described a taxonomic system of abilities developed on the basis of current research. The efforts to develop measurement systems for estimating these requirements of tasks has produced a reliable system, with evidence of construct and predictive validity. The system is useful in predicting learning and performance levels, integrating research data in a variety of areas, and in developing standardized laboratory tasks. Generalizations

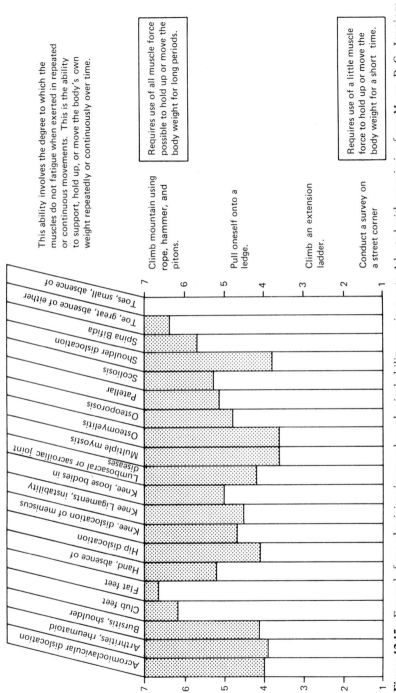

Figure 12.15 Example from physicians' manual on physical ability requirements. Adapted with permission from Myers, D. C., Jennings, M. C., and Fleishman, E. A. *Development of job-related medical standards and physical tests for court security officer jobs* (ARRO Final Report 3062/R81-3). Washington, D.C.: Advanced Research Resources Organization, September 1981.

TABLE 12.4

Partial List of Jobs Grouped According to Common Abilities Needed[a]

	Static Strength	Explosive Strength	Dynamic Strength	Trunk Strength	Stamina	Extent Flexibility	Dynamic Flexibility	Speed of Limb Movement	Gross Body Coordination	Gross Body Equilibrium	
7	Firefighter	Firefighter Officer						Officer			7
6	Attendant Operator Officer Clerk/Painter Laborer/Mechanic		Firefighter	Firefighter	Firefighter		Firefighter	Firefighter Attendant	Firefighter Officer	Firefighter	6
5	Custodian Nurse	Operator Attendant Mechanic Laborer Clerk/Painter	Officer Painter Operator Inspector Laborer	Operator Laborer Clerk/Officer Attendant Mechanic/Painter Custodian	Officer Operator Laborer Attendant Clerk/Painter	Mechanic Firefighter Attendant Painter Operator Laborer	Operator/Officer Attendant Laborer Painter	Operator Inspector Clerk Laborer/Nurse Painter	Operator Attendant Painter Laborer	Inspector Officer Painter Operator Laborer Attendant	5

A table displaying benchmark job titles positioned along vertical rating scales (marked 4, 3, 2, 1 on both sides), organized into columns:

Inspector	Custodian Inspector Nurse	Mechanic Attendant Clerk/Custodian	Nurse	Custodian Mechanic	Officer/Clerk	Clerk Mechanic Custodian	Mechanic	Inspector Clerk Custodian	Mechanic Custodian
		Nurse	Inspector	Nurse	Custodian Inspector Nurse	Nurse	Custodian	Mechanic Nurse	Clerk Nurse
				Inspector		Inspector	Social Worker		
Accountant Clerical		Attorney Clerical Social Worker Accountant	Clerical Social Worker Attorney Accountant	Attorney	Clerical		Clerical		
	Clerical Accountant Social Worker Attorney	Accountant		Clerical Social Worker Accountant	Social Worker Accountant Attorney	Clerical Attorney Accountant Social Worker	Attorney Accountant	Clerical Social Worker Attorney Accountant	Clerical Accountant Attorney Social Worker
Social Worker Attorney									

aAdapted with permission from Hogan, J. C., Ogden, G. D., and Fleishman, E. A. *Assessing physical requirements for establishing medical standards in selected benchmark jobs* (ARRO Final Report 3012/R78-8). Washington, D.C.: Advanced Research Resources Organization, June 1978.

about the effects of a number of independent variables on performance appear to be improved through use of the categories provided by the Ability Requirements Approach. The approach also has been useful in the solution of a number of applied problems, such as job analysis and personnel selection, clustering of jobs with common attributes, setting performance standards, and the development of medical standards linked to job requirements.

References

Baker, W. J., Geist, A. M., & Fleishman, E. A. *Effects of cylert (magnesium-pemoline) on physiological, physical proficiency, and psychomotor performance measures.* Washington, D.C.: American Institutes for Research, August 1967.

Christal, R. E. Factor-analytic study of visual memory. *Psychological Monographs,* 1958, *72*(13), Whole No. 466.

Cooper, M., Schemmer, F. M., Gebhardt, D. L., Marshall-Mies, J., & Fleishman, E. A. *Development and validation of physical ability tests for jobs in the electric power industry* (ARRO Final Report 3056). Washington, D.C.: Advanced Research Resources Organization, April 1982.

Coulter, M. A., & Cattell, R. B. Principles of behavior taxonomy and the mathematical basis of the taxonomic computer program. *British Journal of Mathematical and Statistical Psychology,* 1966, *19*, 237–269.

Elkin, E. H., Fleishman, E. A., Van Cott, H. P., Horowitz, H., & Freedle, R. O. *Effects of drugs on human performance: Research concepts, test development, and preliminary studies* (Report AIR-E-25-10/65-AR-1). Washington, D.C.: American Institutes for Research, 1965.

Fitts, P. M. Factors in complex skill training. In R. Glaser (Ed.), *Training research and education.* Pittsburgh, PA: University of Pittsburgh Press, 1962.

Fleishman, E. A. Dimensional analysis of psychomotor abilities. *Journal of Experimental Psychology,* 1954, *48*, 437–454.

Fleishman, E. A. Factor structure in relation to task difficulty in psychomotor performance. *Educational and Psychological Measurement,* 1957, *17*, 522–532.

Fleishman, E. A. Dimensional analysis of movement reactions. *Journal of Experimental Psychology,* 1958, *55*, 438–453.

Fleishman, E. A. The description and prediction of perceptual-motor skill learning. In R. Glaser (Ed.), *Training research and education.* Pittsburgh, PA: University of Pittsburgh Press, 1962.

Fleishman, E. A. *The structure and measurement of physical fitness.* Englewood Cliffs, NJ: Prentice-Hall, 1964.

Fleishman, E. A. Human abilities and the acquisition of skill. In E. A. Bilodeau (Ed.), *The acquisition of skill.* New York: Academic Press, 1966.

Fleishman, E. A. Individual differences in motor learning. In R. M. Gagné (Ed.), *Learning and individual differences.* Columbus, OH: Merrill, 1967. (a)

Fleishman, E. A. Performance assessment based on an empirically derived task taxonomy. *Human Factors,* 1967, *9*, 349–366. (b)

Fleishman, E. A. On the relation between abilities, learning, and human performance. *American Psychologist,* 1972, *27*, 1017–1032. (a)

Fleishman, E. A. Structure and measurement of psychomotor abilities. In R. N. Singer (Ed.), *Psychomotor domain: Movement behavior* (Chapter 4). Philadelphia, PA: Lea & Febiger, 1972. (b)

Fleishman, E. A. *Development of ability requirements scales for the analysis of Bell System jobs.* Bethesda, MD: Management Research Institute, 1975. (a)

Fleishman, E. A. Toward a taxonomy of human performance. *American Psychologist,* 1975, *30,* 1127–1149. (b)

Fleishman, E. A. Relating individual differences to the dimensions of human tasks. *Ergonomics,* 1978, *21*(12), 1007–1019.

Fleishman, E. A. Systems for describing human tasks. *American Psychologist,* 1982, *37*(7), 1–14.

Fleishman, E. A., Cobb, A. T., & Spendolini, M. J. *Development of ability requirement scales for the analysis of yellow page sales jobs in the Bell System* (Final Report). Bethesda, MD: Management Research Institute, 1976.

Fleishman, E. A., & Ellison, G. D. Prediction of transfer and other learning phenomena from ability and personality measures. *Journal of Educational Psychology,* 1969, *60,* 300–314.

Fleishman, E. A., & Fruchter, B. Factor structure and predictability of successive stages of learning Morse code. *Journal of Applied Psychology,* 1960, *44,* 96–101.

Fleishman, E. A., & Hempel, W. E., Jr. Changes in factor structure of a complex psychomotor test as a function of practice. *Psychometrika,* 1954, *18,* 239–252.

Fleishman, E. A., & Hempel, W. E., Jr. The relation between abilities and improvement with practice in a visual discrimination reaction task. *Journal of Experimental Psychology,* 1955, *49,* 301–312.

Fleishman, E. A., & Hogan, J. C. *Taxonomic method for assessing the physical requirements of jobs: The Physical Abilities Analysis approach* (ARRO Technical Report 3012/R78-6). Washington, D.C.: Advanced Research Resources Organization, June 1978.

Fleishman, E. A., & Rich, S. Role of kinesthetic and spatial-visual abilities in perceptual-motor learning. *Journal of Experimental Psychology,* 1963, *66,* 6–11.

Fleishman, E. A., & Stephenson, R. W. *Development of a taxonomy of human performance: A review of the third year's progress.* JSAS Catalog of Selected Documents in Psychology, 1970, *48,* 1–68 (Ms. No. 113).

French, J. W. The description of aptitude and achievement tests in terms of rotated factors. *Psychometric Mongraphs,* 1951 (No. 5).

French, J. W., Ekstrom, R. B., & Price, L. A. *Kit of reference tests for cognitive factors.* Princeton, NJ: Educational Testing Service, 1963.

Gagné, R. M., & Fleishman, E. A. *Psychology of human performance: An introduction to psychology.* New York: Holt, 1959.

Gebhardt, D. L., Jennings, M. C., & Fleishman, E. A. *Factors affecting the reliability of physical ability and effort ratings of Navy tasks* (ARRO Technical Report 3034/R81-1). Washington, D.C.: Advanced Research Resources Organization, February 1981.

Gebhardt, D. L., & Weldon, L. J. *Development and validation of physical performance tests for correctional officers* (ARRO Final Report 3080). Washington, D.C.: Advanced Research Resources Organization, September 1982.

Gebhardt, D. L., Weldon, L. J., & Fleishman, E. A. *Development of a physician's manual for assessing physical qualifications required in public safety jobs* (ARRO Final Report 3067). Washington, D.C.: Advanced Research Resources Organization, February 1981.

Ghiselli, E. E., & Haire, M. The validation of selection tests in the light of the dynamic character of criteria. *Personnel Psychology*, 1960, *13*(3), 225–231.

Guilford, J. P. *The nature of human intelligence*. New York: McGraw–Hill, 1967.

Guilford, J. P., & Hoepfner, R. *Structure of intellect factors and their tests* (Rep. No. 36). Los Angeles, CA: Psychological Laboratory, University of Southern California, 1966.

Hogan, J. C., Ogden, G. D., & Fleishman, E. A. *Assessing physical requirements for establishing medical standards in selected benchmark jobs* (ARRO Final Report 3012/R78-8). Washington, D.C.: Advanced Research Resources Organization, June 1978.

Hogan, J. C., Ogden, G. D., & Fleishman, E. A. *The development and validation of tests for the order selector job at Certified Grocers of California, Ltd.: Technical report*, Vol. 1 (ARRO Technical Report 3029). Washington, D.C.: Advanced Research Resources Organization, August 1979.

Inn, A., Schulman, D. R., Ogden, G. D., & Sample, R. A. *Physical ability requirements of Bell System jobs* (ARRO Final Report 3057/R82-1). Washington, D.C.: Advanced Research Resources Organization, February 1982.

Jones, M. A., & Prien, E. P. A valid procedure for testing the physical abilities of job applicants. *Personnel Administrator*, 1978, *23*, 33–38.

Kelley, H. P. Memory abilities: A factor analysis. *Psychometric Monographs*, 1964 (No. 11).

Levine, J. M., Kramer, G. G., & Levine, E. N. Effects of alcohol on human performance: An integration of research findings based on an abilities classification. *Journal of Applied Psychology*, 1975, *60*, 285–293.

Levine, J. M., Romashko, T., & Fleishman, E. A. Evaluation of an abilities classification system for integrating and generalizing findings about human performance: The vigilance area. *Journal of Applied Psychology*, 1973, *58*, 147–149.

Mallamad, S. M., Levine, J. M., & Fleishman, E. A. Identifying ability requirements by decision flow diagrams. *Human Factors*, 1980, *22*(1), 57–68.

Myers, D. C., Gebhardt, D. L., & Fleishman, E. A. *Development of physical performance standards for Army jobs* (ARRO Final Report 3045/R79-10). Washington, D.C.: Advanced Research Resources Organization, November 1979.

Myers, D. C., Gebhardt, D. L., Price, S. J., & Fleishman, E. A. *Development of physical performance standards for Army jobs: Validation of the Physical Abilities Analysis methodology* (ARRO Final Report 3045/R81-2). Washington, D.C.: Advanced Research Resources Organization, April 1981.

Myers, D. C., Jennings, M. C., & Fleishman, E. A. *Development of job-related medical standards and physical tests for court security officer jobs* (ARRO Final Report 3062/R81-3). Washington, D.C.: Advanced Research Resources Organization, September 1981.

Parasuraman, R. Consistency of individual differences in human vigilance performance: An abilities classification analysis. *Journal of Applied Psychology*, 1976, *61*, 486–492.

Parker, J. R., Jr., & Fleishman, E. A. Ability factors and component performance measures as predictors of complex tracking behavior. *Psychological Monographs*, 1960, *74* (No. 503).

Parker, J. R., Jr., & Fleishman, E. A. Use of analytical information concerning task requirements to increase the effectiveness of skill training. *Journal of Applied Psychology*, 1961, *45*, 295–302.

Romashko, T., Brumback, G. B., Fleishman, E. A., & Hahn, C. P. *The development of a procedure to validate physical tests: Physical requirements of the parking enforcement agent's job* (Technical Report 2). Washington, D.C.: American Institutes for Research, March 1974.

Romashko, T., Hahn, C. P., & Brumback, G. B. *The prototype development of job-related physical testing for Philadelphia policeman selection.* Washington, D.C.: American Institutes for Research, 1976.

Schemmer, F. M. *Development of rating scales for selected visual, auditory, and speech abilities* (ARRO Final Report 3064). Washington, D.C.: Advanced Research Resources Organization, June 1982.

Smith, P. C., & Kendall, L. M. Retranslation of expectations: An approach to the construction of unambiguous anchors for rating scales. *Journal of Applied Psychology*, 1963, *47*(2), 149–155.

Theologus, G. C., & Fleishman, E. A. Development of a taxonomy of human performance: Validation study of ability scales for classifying human tasks. *JSAS Catalog of Selected Documents in Psychology*, 1973, *3*, 29 (Ms. No. 326).

Theologus, G. C., Romashko, T., & Fleishman, E. A. Development of a taxonomy of human performance: A feasibility study of ability dimensions for classifying human tasks. *JSAS Catalog of Selected Documents in Psychology*, 1973, *3*, 25–26 (Ms. No. 321).

Theologus, G. C., Wheaton, G. R., & Fleishman, E. A. Effects of intermittent, moderate intensity noise-stress on human performance. *Journal of Applied Psychology*, 1974, *59*, 539–547.

Zedeck, S. *Validation of physical abilities tests for PT&T craft positions: Program report with special emphasis on detailed job analysis* (Technical Report 5). New York: American Telephone and Telegraph, January 1975.

Zedeck, S. *Validation of physical abilities tests for PT&T craft positions: Preliminary final report* (Technical Report 7). New York: American Telephone and Telegraph, June 1976.

CHAPTER 13

The Task Characteristics Approach

We have seen that the key to establishing a classificatory system lies in developing a well-defined task-descriptive language. Previous chapters described efforts at developing task classification systems in terms of the *specific activities* an individual engages in while performing a task. Those who have taken this approach are more concerned with describing performance, responses, and dependent measures. Other chapters have dealt with classificatory systems that emphasize *resources of the individual* required for performance on the task. These may be functions, processes, or abilities on which the tasks make demands. Emphasis is on critical aspects of the individual intervening between features of the task and consequent performance. All these approaches deal with variables related to human intervention in task performance. Although we cannot fully assess these systems at this time, generalizations eventually may be made to the behaviors of individuals performing many different types of tasks.

It is possible, however, to conceptualize tasks per se, independent of the human operator's activities, abilities, or functions. For example, tasks can be characterized in terms of kinds of controls (e.g., rotary knobs, joy sticks), kinds of displays (e.g., indicator lights, digital readouts), or in terms of many other types of hardware with which individuals may interact during the operation of a system. These are only a few of the many characteristics that might be employed to describe tasks prior to their classification. In Chapters 3 and 7, we reviewed some previous attempts at classifying tasks using task characteristics. The present chapter describes some extensions of the *Task Characteristics Approach* carried out under the Taxonomy Project, as well as subsequent research efforts that bear on the utility of this scheme.

354

Essentially, this approach to developing a task-descriptive language treats the task as a critical subset of antecedent conditions of which performance is a function. Here the investigator attempts description in terms of the characteristics of the task confronting the operator (e.g., Cotterman, 1959; Folley, 1964; Jacobs, 1959; Stolurow, 1964). It was felt that this Task Characteristics Approach to classification could serve at least two important functions: (1) it might provide a more systematic method for handling large numbers of terms involved in task analysis data; and (2) it might provide a systematic structure for the matching of human functions with the task characteristics that place demands on those functions.

The decision to describe tasks in terms of task characteristics stemmed from the conviction that tasks in their own right represent a potent class of independent variables. Knowledge of how performance varies as a result of manipulating the characteristics of tasks provides a basis for estimating performance on other tasks whose characteristics can be described more precisely. Furthermore, as Hackman (1968) pointed out, this approach has the added advantage of describing the independent variables (tasks) in terms other than the dependent variables (behavior) we ultimately wish to predict.

This approach to developing a task-descriptive language seems appropriate for the type of taxonomy called for by Fitts (1962). In order to predict the performance that will result when a subject is exposed to a given situation, one must be able to describe fully those independent variables that are in effect. It is within the stimulus complex known as the *task* that many correlates of learning rate or proficiency level should be found.

This chapter draws on the major conceptual and methodological work carried out by Farina and Wheaton (1973) under the Taxonomy Project, and also includes later work. The chapter describes the classificatory system, the measurement system developed, the empirical evaluations made thus far, and some applications of the approach in accounting for human performance in actual tasks.

Development of the Task Characteristics System

During various stages of the Taxonomy Project, consideration was given to the manner in which descriptive data provided by the system were to be used in organizing tasks and consequent performance data. This issue was important because we believed that specification of the intended use of the descriptive data would culminate in a set of requirements for the language itself. Two major uses were identified: classification and prediction.

With respect to classification, we believed that task characteristics data would provide a basis for classifying tasks in terms of their observed similarities and dissimilarities. In this connection, we assumed the desirability of quantitative rather than qualitative bases for classification techniques. Thus, if descriptive profiles could be generated for tasks, it would be possible to express the similarity among them mathematically in terms of a matrix of similarity coefficients. These data could then be analyzed by cluster-analytic techniques to define clusters or classes of highly similar tasks. This emphasizes the need for a descriptive system that treats tasks in terms of quantitative profiles.

The second use for descriptive data involved the prediction of learning rates or proficiency levels on tasks. Emphasis here is not on classifying tasks, but on identifying those characteristics of tasks that are correlates of performance. These correlates represent evaluative criteria for the Task Characteristics Approach. The descriptive data could be utilized within a multiple regression context to relate variations in the characteristics of tasks to variations in performance.

Based on these considerations, Farina and Wheaton attempted to (1) develop a series of generically applicable quantitative rating scales for the description of various task characteristics, (2) determine the reliability with which these scales could be used to describe tasks, and (3) evaluate the feasibility of using the descriptive data as predictors of mean levels of performance on different tasks. We shall describe these efforts in turn.

Task Definition

Given the interest in predicting performance, a *task* was defined as a complex situation capable of eliciting goal-directed performance from an operator (Farina & Wheaton, 1973). Given this orientation, a task was conceived as having several intrinsic components, with each component possessing certain salient characteristics. These components were: an explicit goal, procedures, input stimuli, responses, and stimulus–response relationships.

An *explicit goal* was a specification of the state or condition to be achieved by the operator. The term "explicit" meant that the goal was presented to at least the operator and one independent observer, and that some objective procedure existed whereby the observer could verify whether or not the goal had been achieved. A task also had to include a statement of the means by which the goal was to be attained. The means consisted of *procedures*, which were statements specifying the types of *stimulus–response relationships* to be formed, and their sequencing. The task also had to contain a set of relevant *input stimuli* attended to by the operator. Finally, the statement of the task had to describe a set of *responses* contributing to goal attainment.

TASK CHARACTERISTICS

Given the requirement that a task possess these components, it followed that if a potential task did not possess all these components, then by definition it was not a task under the present system. Further, if an operator failed to perform in accordance with the specified procedures, the question of goal attainment for that task could not be raised. The operator, by definition, would not have performed the task in question; in fact, the operator would have performed a different task. This latter point led to a direct consideration of what made tasks different. That is, given that all tasks had the above components, what distinctions could be made among these common components? For example, what were characteristics of a task goal that, when measured in some fashion, would serve to differentiate among various task goals?

In order to differentiate among tasks, the five components of a task were treated as categories within which to devise task characteristics or descriptors. Development of these characteristics was, essentially, an inventive effort guided by the five components and certain other requirements. These requirements were that the characteristics should be common or applicable to most, if not all, types of tasks; be capable of being scaled in at least an ordinal manner; possess an acceptable degree of reliability; and require a minimum of training time on the part of the user. The result of the initial effort was a set of 25 characteristics distributed among the five task components.

Figure 13.1 clarifies these relationships among the terms *task, task components,* and *task characteristics.*

MEASUREMENT PROCEDURES

Once these 5 categories of task components were conceptualized and their 19 task characteristics specified, a measurement system was developed for describing diverse tasks in terms of this task characteristics taxonomic system. To accomplish this, each separate characteristic was cast into a rating scale format that (1) presented a definition of the characteristic, (2) provided a 7-point scale for rating

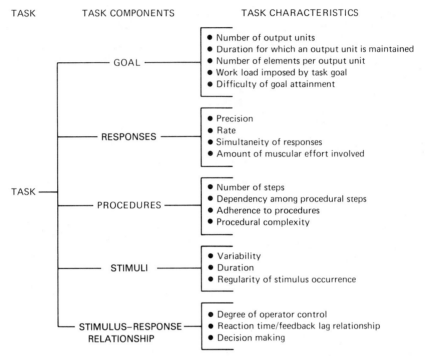

Figure 13.1 Relationship among the terms *task, components,* and *characteristics.* Adapted with permission from Farina, A. J., and Wheaton, G. R. Development of a taxonomy of human performance: The task characteristics approach to performance prediction (American Institutes for Research Tech. Rep.). *JSAS Catalog of Selected Documents in Psychology*, 1973, *3,* 26–27 (Ms. No. 323).

the degree to which a task involved this characteristic, and (3) provided specific task examples anchoring the high, low, and midpoints of each scale (Smith & Kendall, 1963). The task examples were drawn intentionally from a variety of contexts, including laboratory, recreational, and job tasks. The examples were scaled by groups of raters and selected for their mean values at different points on the task characteristic scale, as well as for their small standard deviations (reflecting high agreement among the raters).

Altogether, 25 such scales were developed originally. The scales underwent a number of revisions, deletions, and additions in a series of studies to determine their psychometric characteristics and their ability to predict task performance.

Appendix D presents the definitions of each task characteristic and reproduces in full the rating scales developed for their measurement.

TABLE 13.1

Task Characteristics Measured[a]

Scaling	Name
	1. Number of output units
	2. Duration for which an output unit is maintained
	3. Number of elements per output unit
	4. Work load imposed by task goal
	5. Difficulty of goal attainment
	6. Precision of responses
	7. Response rate
	8. Simultaneity of responses
	9. Degree of muscular effort involved
	10. Number of procedural steps
	11. Dependency of procedural steps
	12. Adherence to procedures
	13. Procedural complexity
	14. Variability of stimulus location
	15. Stimulus or stimulus-complex duration
	16. Regularity of stimulus occurrence
	17. Operator control of the stimulus
	18. Operator control of the response
	19. Reaction time and feedback lag relationship
	20. Feedback
	21. Decision making

[a]Reproduced with permission from Farina, A. J., and Wheaton G. R. Development of a taxonomy of human performance: The task characteristics approach to performance prediction (American Institutes for Research Tech. Rep.). *JSAS Catalog of Selected Documents in Psychology*, 1973, *3*, 26–27 (Ms. No. 323).

Since several original scales and definitions were revised, and others deleted, we have included the most recent versions. Table 13.1 presents the 21 task characteristics represented in the most recent list, and Figure 13.2 presents an example of one of the rating scales.

Reliability of the Measurement System

Farina and Wheaton (1973) carried out a series of studies on the reliability of the task characteristic rating scales. These studies examined questions such as interrater agreement, the differential reliability of different scales, numbers of raters needed to obtain acceptable reliabilities, and agreement among profiles obtained. An objective was to improve the reliabilities of the scales through clarifi-

1. Scale for NUMBER OF OUTPUT UNITS

The entire purpose of the task is to create output units. An output unit
is the end product resulting from the task. Output units can take different
forms. For example, sometimes the output unit is a physical object assembled from several parts. It may also take the form of a relationship
between two or more things, e.g., drive three car-lengths behind the car in
front of you. An output unit might also be a destination, e.g., run from here
to the corner, with the corner being the destination.

First, identify what the output unit(s) is in the present task. Now, judge
the number of such output units that someone performing this task is supposed
to produce.

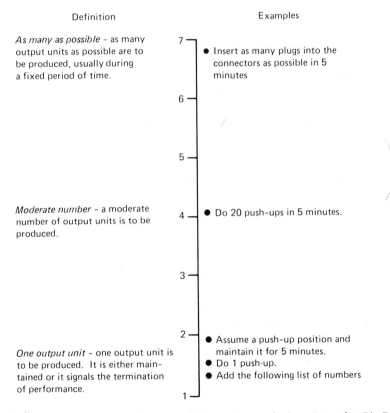

| Definition | Examples |

As many as possible – as many output units as possible are to be produced, usually during a fixed period of time.

7 — ● Insert as many plugs into the connectors as possible in 5 minutes

6 —

5 —

Moderate number – a moderate number of output units is to be produced.

4 — ● Do 20 push-ups in 5 minutes.

3 —

2 — ● Assume a push-up position and maintain it for 5 minutes.
● Do 1 push-up.
● Add the following list of numbers

One output unit – one output unit is to be produced. It is either maintained or it signals the termination of performance.

1 —

Figure 13.2 Example of task characteristic rating scale (see Appendix D). Reproduced with permission from Farina, A. J., and Wheaton, G. R. Development of a
taxonomy of human performance: The task characteristics approach to performance
prediction (American Institutes for Research Tech. Rep.). *JSAS Catalog of Selected
Documents in Psychology*, 1973, 3, 26–27 (Ms. No. 323).

TABLE 13.2

Reliability Estimates for 28 Judges Using Revised Scales to Rate 15 Tasks[a,b]

Rating scale[b]	Average (r_k)
1. Number of output units	.97
2. Duration of output units	.96
3. Number of elements	.91
4. Work load	.95
6. Precision of responses	.97
7. Rate	.91
8. Simultaneity of responses	.98
9. Effort	.58
10. Number of steps	.95
11. Dependency	.93
14. Variability	.96
15. Stimulus duration	.84
16. Regularity	.88
17. Stimulus control	.91
18. Response control	.82
20. Feedback	.78

[a]Adapted with permission from Farina, A. J., and Wheaton G. R. Development of a taxonomy of human performance: The task characteristics approach to performance prediction (American Institutes for Research Tech. Rep.). *JSAS Catalog of Selected Documents in Psychology*, 1973, *3*, 26–27 (Ms. No. 323).

[b]Numbering refers to Appendix D scale numbers.

cation of definitions, changes in task anchors on the rating scales, changes in instructions, rater training, and so forth.

The typical approach was to have groups of judges (research assistants, college students, or research psychologists) examine descriptions of tasks. Studies have included laboratory tasks, tests, training devices, and simulators. Subjects were presented written descriptions of the task instructions, procedures, and pictures.

In the first study, three judges rated 37 psychomotor tasks on 19 of the task characteristic scales. Interrater reliabilities of these scales for 3 subjects ranged from 0.00 to .90, but 12 scales had reliabilities above .50. Highest reliabilities were for the scales measuring duration of output uints (.90), number of output units (.84), work load (.70), variability of stimulus location (.74), precision of responses (.64), simultaneity of responses (.72), and number of procedural steps (.70). Inspection of the rating data showed that the three judges also were in strong agreement on the scale for adherence to procedures, but they were not able to differentiate among the tasks very effectively, as shown by the relatively small variance between tasks on this

TABLE 13.3

Measures of Task Characteristics Involving Enumeration[a]

---

1. Number of output units (UNIT)

The entire purpose of the task is to create output units. An output unit is the end product resulting from the task. Output units can take different forms. For example, sometimes the output unit is a physical object assembled from several parts. It may also take the form of a relationship between two or more things, such as drive three car-lengths behind the car in front of you. An output unit might also be a destination, such as run from here to the corner.

First, identify the output unit(s) for the present task. Now, count the number of such output units that someone performing this task is supposed to produce. Use the designation AMAP (As many as possible) if no actual limit exists.

2. Duration for which an output unit is maintained (DURA)

Once the operator has produced an output unit, he may be required to maintain or continue it for one of several time periods. For example, it can be maintained for as long as possible. Another alternative is that completing one output unit is a signal to leave it and go on to produce the next output unit. Or, after producing the output unit, performance ends.

Choose which of the following alternatives applies:

(1) Maintain unit as long as possible.
(2) Maintain unit as long as possible, but continue to produce additional units.
(3) Leave unit and go on to produce next unit.
(4) Production of unit signals end of task.

3. Number of elements per output unit (ELEM)

One way of describing an output unit is in terms of the number of elements involved in its production. By *elements* we mean the parts or components that comprise the output unit. In an addition problem, for example, the numbers to be added are the elements that comprise the output unit. In a more physical task, the elements could be parts to be assembled or apparatus to be manipulated.

Count the number of different displays and controls that are manipulated in producing a single output unit.

4. Simultaneity of responses (SIMU)

The responses that the operator makes in producing one output unit may involve one or more effectors (e.g., hand, foot, arm, voice). Depending on the task, these effectors may or may not be used simultaneously. For example, both hands (two effectors) are used simultaneously in playing a piano.

How many effectors are being used simultaneously during the present task?
zero_____   two_____   three_____   four_____

5. Number of responses (NO.R)

Earlier we were concerned about the number of elements (objects or components) involved in the production of one output unit. Now we want to consider the number of responses needed to produce one output unit. There is no necessary one-to-one relationship between objects and responses.

(continued)

TABLE 13.3 *Continued*

Count the number of responses or steps involved in producing one output unit for the present task. Enter this number on the answer sheet.

6. Rapidness of feedback (FEED)

For present purposes the term *feedback* refers to information that an operator may get about the correctness of a response. Consider the maximum number of responses the operator makes before receiving feedback on the status of output units. Enter that number on the answer sheet.

*a*Adapted with permission from Wheaton, G. R., Mirabella, A., and Farina, A. J., Jr. *Trainee and instructor task quantification: Development of quantitative indices and a predictive methodology* (NAVTRADEVCEN 69-C-0278-1). Orlando, Florida: U.S. Naval Training Device Center, January 1971.

scale. Overall, the results were encouraging for establishing reliability for a number of scales with a small number of judges.

Revisions were made in the original scales and a reduced set was utilized by 28 judges to rate 20 tasks on each scale. The findings are presented in Table 13.2. The results indicated high reliabilities of the task characteristic scales for a group of raters of this size. The results also indicated that ratings obtained from single judges were not reliable and that three judges appeared to be the minimum required for most scales.

A third study reported by Farina and Wheaton (1973) utilized ratings by two judges who evaluated a variety of tracking tasks described in technical reports, articles, and manuals. Revised task-characteristic scales were used. Based on experiences in the first two studies, measures of several characteristics were converted from rating scales to a procedure for enumeration or counting. These new measures are described in Table 13.3.

In addition to intraclass correlation coefficients (interrater reliability), similarity coefficients (Coulter & Cattell, 1966) were computed on the profiles generated by the two raters for each task. The primary finding was that 10 of the similarity coefficients were significant, implying agreement between judges' profiles. On 8 scales, the judges were in agreement at least 90% of the time. Only 3 scales failed to exhibit high interrater agreement, a significant similarity coefficient, or a high percentage (90%) of agreement.

SUMMARY OF RELIABILITY STUDIES

The results of assessing the reliability of the task characteristic scales are encouraging, but they are not conclusive. Interpretation of

TABLE 13.4

List of the Most Reliable Scales Within Each of the Three Studies[a,b]

3-Judge study	28-Judge study	2-Judge study
1. Number of output units	1. Number of output units	1. Number of output units
2. Duration for which an output unit is maintained	2. Duration for which an output unit is maintained	2. Duration for which an output unit is maintained
4. Work load imposed by task goal	4. Work load imposed by task goal	7. Response rate
8. Simultaneity of responses	6. Precision of responses	8. Simultaneity of responses
10. Number of procedural steps	8. Simultaneity of responses	10. Number of procedural steps
14. Variability of stimulus location	10. Number of procedural steps	11. Dependency of procedural steps
15. Stimulus or stimulus-complex duration	14. Variability of stimulus location	17. Operator control of the stimulus
		18. Operator control of the response

[a] Adapted with permission from Farina, A. J. and Wheaton, G. R. Development of a taxonomy of human performance: The task characteristics approach to performance prediction (American Institutes for Research Tech. Rep.). *JSAS Catalog of Selected Documents in Psychology*, 1973, 3, 26–27 (Ms. No. 323).
[b] Numbering refers to Appendix D scale numbers.

intraclass correlations is troublesome, when a small but consistent bias exists among raters in the use of a scale, and each rater assigns but one scale value to all tasks. In these instances, the question is whether the tasks studied were homogeneous with respect to those scales or whether the scales were insensitive to differences among tasks. Test–retest reliability, for example, would assess the consistency of an average rater in applying a particular scale. It does not address itself to the equally important question of how well the raters agree among themselves in their collective use of a scale. Similarly, the intraclass correlation coefficient shed some light on interrater agreement, but to do so appeared to require some unknown amount of heterogeneity among the rated tasks. Ideally, one would want each rater to be highly consistent in the use of a scale on a test–retest basis, and also to have raters in high agreement on the scale's use across tasks.

Regarding the particular scales evaluated in these studies, it appears that a subset of scales consistently emerged with adequate reliability. Table 13.4 shows the most reliable sets of scales.

In the three studies carried out by Farina and Wheaton (1973), there was a high degree of consistency between the reliable scales emerging from the 3-judge and 28-judge studies. Comparing this common subset to the reliable scales of the 2-judge study, four of the six again were reliable. Additional scales were reliable also, but these were employed only in the 2-judge study.

In general, consideration of these three reliability studies led the investigators to the following recommendations in the use of these scales: (1) the raters should have a background in psychology or human factors, or a good awareness of concepts such as stimulus and response; (2) at least three raters should be used in applying the scales in this form, with an average of their ratings used as the value assigned to the characteristic in question; (3) further development of the scales should include enumeration (counting) rather than rating for certain characteristics; and (4) an assessment of test–retest reliability is still needed.

Task Characteristic Correlates of Performance

A primary criterion for evaluating the Task Characteristics Approach was the extent to which the categories predicted learning or performance. For this purpose, Farina and Wheaton (1973) utilized a multiple regression model, in which task characteristic descriptors were treated as predictor variables. The model was based on the premise that descriptive terms could be selected that represented correlates of performance and, as such, could be used to predict average learning rates or proficiency levels on different tasks. The rationale underlying the regression approach was as follows. Suppose a single group of operators performed two different tasks yielding the same type of performance measures. If individuals' scores were averaged on each task and if the means for the two tasks differed, then, because identical subjects are involved, the difference between means could only be attributed to differences between the tasks themselves (assuming "environmental" and "subject" variables were identical in both situations). The difference between tasks would be specified in terms of task descriptors.

If the concept of differences between tasks and consequent differences between performance means were extended to a larger set of tasks, performed by the same operators under the same conditions, then a variable (P_m) would be created. A given value on this variable would represent the mean performance score associated with a particular task (m) within the set of tasks. It was hypothesized, therefore, that specific values for this variable could be predicted in terms of task characteristic scale values. The multiple regression equation required for that purpose would have the following form:

$$\bar{P}'_m = a_0 + a_1 X_{m1} + a_2 X_{m2} + \ldots + a_n X_{mn}$$

where $\bar{P}'_m$ is the predicted mean performance score on task m, a_n the regression weight for the nth task descriptor, and X_{mn} the value for task m on task descriptor n.

To accomplish these ends, however, it was necessary to impose a major restriction on the model. The tasks under investigation at any one time had to share a common response measure (e.g., reaction time, time on target, percent correct). This restriction had profound consequences, for it implied that different regression equations would be required to handle different types of performance measures. This would not have been the case had it been possible to describe different measures of perfromance in terms of a single common metric. The absence of this universal metric, however, made it necessary to categorize tasks in terms of the measures employed to describe performance on the tasks. The categories of performance described in Chapter 9 in the Criterion Measures Approach (see Teichner & Olson, 1971) were considered for this purpose. Separate regressions were anticipated for tasks yielding such diverse performance measures as probability of detection, reaction time, percentage correct, and percentage of time on target.

There are several consequences of the regression model for the descriptive system. The system had to contain multiple dimensions, each of which could be applied to any selected task. The dimensions had to be quantitative in nature and had to possess a reasonably high reliability. Apparently, these requirements were fulfilled, as described in the previous section. However, if the model were to aid in predicting parameters of performance, we needed to demonstrate whether the descriptive dimensions represented correlates of performance.

The paradigm used by Farina and Wheaton (1973) to determine whether the task characteristics were correlates of performance on which predictive relationships might be established was that of *postdiction*. Essentially, this involved selection of previous studies of tasks in which data on achieved performance levels were already available. Task characteristic ratings were made of the tasks used in these studies. These ratings then were entered into a multiple regression analysis to establish the extent to which they were related to the performance in question. The task descriptions in the literature were often too brief to use, but it was possible to obtain detailed descriptions either from a study's author, or by acquiring the references an author made to more detailed descriptions of the task or apparatus. Through these means, it was possible to provide the raters with explicit descriptions of the tasks to be rated. Two such studies were conducted by Farina and Wheaton (1973).

Both studies shared a number of common restrictions. First, in selecting studies for the two postdiction efforts, there was the need to have a common metric of performance within each study. Thus, for the first postdiction, the performance measure of all studies was expressed in terms of "the number of output units produced per unit time." The second postdiction used studies in which the common performance metric was "percentage of time on target."

The need for a common metric reduced the number of studies (and tasks) available for analysis. This posed some methodological problems for the investigators. For a regression analysis, the number of predictors should not approach the number of cases sampled. As the number of predictors (task characteristic scales) approaches the number of cases sampled (studies or tasks), the multiple regression coefficient becomes spuriously large and uninterpretable. Because this was the case initially in both postdictions, the decision was made to use only a selected set of the task characteristic indexes rather than the full set. For example, instead of using 19 indexes and 26 tasks in the first regression study, a smaller set of the 6 most reliable indexes was used.

FIRST POSTDICTION STUDY

The first postdiction study was based on data published by Fleishman (1954) in which 37 perceptual–motor tasks were administered to 300 subjects in a factor-analytic study. Applying the requirement for a common performance measure, the 37 tasks were screened carefully in order to determine the types of performance measures associated with them. Although several different measures were represented (for example, reaction time, percentage of time on target, and percentage correct), 26 of the tasks had one measure in common, which was designated as the "number of output units produced per unit time." The units varied and included such things as number of blocks moved, number of assemblies completed, number of taps made, and number of correct discriminations given. Common to these 26 tasks was the requirement that as many units as possible be produced during specified time periods. Because different amounts of time were allowed for completion of the various tasks, a common time frame was needed to provide a standard basis for comparison. The time unit chosen for this purpose was 1 second. Therefore, the performance score reported for each task was prorated to obtain the average number of units produced per second (thus, 98.5 units produced in 80 seconds equals 1.23 units per second). Table 13.5 lists the tasks rated and the average number of units produced per second for each task. It can be seen that the range is from 6.24 (Key Tapping) to .04 (Dynamic Balance).

The six most reliable scales were chosen for analysis. For each of these scales, the ratings provided by three judges were averaged to obtain a single value on each scale for each of the tasks. Table 13.6 presents the specific scales employed in the study, their intercorrelations, and their correlations with the criterion performance measure. Six rating-scale variables were entered into a Wherry–Doolittle stepwise regression analysis as predictors. The order in which the scales are listed in Table 13.6 represents their order of extraction based on the percent variance accounted for in the criterion measure (R^2). Although five scales emerged from the analysis, a point of diminishing returns in terms of percentage of variance accounted for was reached after extraction of the fourth scale. Consequently, a regression equation was written using only the first four scales listed in Table 13.6.

TABLE 13.5

Units Produced on the Tasks Rated[a]

Tasks	Average number of units produced per second
1. Two-plate tapping	3.98
2. Key tapping	6.24
3. Ten-target aiming	2.02
4. Rotary aiming	2.49
5. Hand-precision aiming	1.87
6. Visual reaction time	2.71
7. Auditory reaction time	2.86
8. Minnesota—placing	1.23
9. Minnesota—turning	1.49
10. Purdue pegboard—right hand	0.56
11. Purdue pegboard—both hands	0.87
12. Purdue pegboard—assembly	0.62
13. O'Connor finger dexterity	0.53
14. Santa Ana finger dexterity	1.80
15. Pin stick	1.26
16. Dynamic balance	0.04
17. Medium tapping	1.34
18. Large tapping	1.26
19. Aiming	1.81
20. Pursuit aiming I	2.32
21. Pursuit aiming II	1.76
22. Square marking	1.16
23. Tracing	1.89
24. Discrimination reaction time-printed	0.38
25. Marking accuracy	1.37
26. Verbal addition task	0.19

[a]Adapted with permission from Farina, A. J., and Wheaton, G. R. Development of a taxonomy of human performance: The task characteristics approach to performance prediction (American Institutes for Research Tech. Rep.). *JSAS Catalog of Selected Documents in Psychology*, 1973, 3, 26–27 (Ms. No. 323).

The regression equation was:

$$\bar{P}'_m = -1.064 + 1.245X_1 - 0.197X_2 - 1.072X_3 - 0.089X_4$$

where $\bar{P}'_m$ is the predicted mean number of output units produced per second, and X_1–X_4 the task characteristic scales 1 through 4 listed in Table 13.6.

The multiple-correlation coefficient for this analysis (based on four predictors) was $R = .85$ (significant at the $p < .01$ level). When the correction in R for small sample bias (Guilford, 1956) was applied, yielding a correlation of .82, the correlation was still significant

TABLE 13.6

Intercorrelation Matrix for the First Regression Analysis[a,b]

	2	3	4	5	6	7
1. Stimulus or stimulus-complex duration (15)	.01	−.06	−.12	−.10	.27	.78
2. Number of output units (1)		.07	.15	.12	−.70	−.19
3. Duration for which an output unit is maintained (2)			.45	−.07	−.38	−.26
4. Simultaneity of responses (8)				.55	−.23	−.28
5. Number of procedural steps (10)					.04	−.12
6. Variability of stimulus location (14)						.47
7. Criterion measure—number of output units produced per unit time						

[a]Adapted with permission from Farina, A. J., and Wheaton, G. R. Development of a taxonomy of human performance: The task characteristics approach to performance prediction (American Institutes for Research Tech. Rep.). *JSAS Catalog of Selected Documents in Psychology*, 1973, 3, 26–27 (Ms. No. 323).

[b]Numbers in parentheses refer to Appendix D scale numbers.

($p < .01$). The individual task characteristics showing highest correlations with actual performance on this diverse set of psychomotor tasks were the ratings of stimulus duration (.78), the variability of the stimulus location (.47), the simultaneity of responses (−.28), and the duration for which an output unit is maintained (−.26). However, one of these characteristics dropped out (i.e., the variability of the stimulus location) in the formation of the most predictive composite battery of scales, whereas another (i.e., number of output units) was added due to its contribution of unique variance in the prediction equation.

An index of forcasting efficiency was computed (Guilford, 1956). This indicates the degree to which predictions made by means of the regression equation were more accurate than those made merely from a knowledge of the mean of the criterion measures. The index for the correct R was 43%, indicating that use of the regression equation would be superior to using the mean alone.

SECOND POSTDICTION STUDY

The second postdiction study was based on data from the study of tracking tasks described earlier, in which 2 judges rated 20 tasks on 18 scales. The criterion measure common to the 20 tasks was the mean percentage of time on target achieved after 5 minutes of practice on the tasks. These tasks and their associated performance data were obtained from studies reported in the experimental literature.

TABLE 13.7

Intercorrelation Matrix for the Second Regression Analysis[a,b]

	2	3	4	5	6	7
1. Number of procedural steps (10)	.34	.90	.44	.75	.76	−.54
2. Precision of responses (6)		.25	.34	.61	.26	.30
3. Number of responses			.59	.60	.60	−.41
4. Number of output units (1)				.38	.22	.07
5. Simultaneity of responses (8)					.81	−.18
6. Number of elements per output unit (3)						−.46
7. Criterion measure—time on target achieved after 5 minutes of practice						

[a]Adapted with permission from Farina, A. J., and Wheaton, G. R. Development of a taxonomy of human performance: The task characteristics approach to performance prediction (American Institutes for Research Tech. Rep.). *JSAS Catalog of Selected Documents in Psychology*, 1973, 3, 26–27 (Ms. No. 323).
[b]Numbers in parentheses refer to Appendix D scale numbers.

The same procedure for selecting task-descriptive scales was followed. The reliable scales used are presented in Table 13.7, along with their intercorrelations. The order of the scales listed in the table paralleled the order in which the predictor variables emerged from the stepwise regression analysis. In terms of percentage of variance accounted for (R^2), diminishing returns were reached after the fourth predictor emerged.

The multiple R achieved was .79 ($p < .01$), which accounted for 63% of the variance. Correction for small sample bias yielded a $R = .73$ ($p < .05$). The index of forcasting efficiency for this corrected R was 32%. This percentage indicated that prediction using the regression equation would be superior to that made on the basis of knowledge of the mean of the criterion measures alone.

The regression equation was:

$$\bar{P}'_m = -1.484 - 19.056X_1 + 12.102X_2 + 4.213X_3 + 1.251X_4$$

where $\bar{P}'_m$ is the predicted mean percent time on target after 5 minutes of practice, and X_1–X_4 the task characteristic scales 1 through 4 listed in Table 13.7.

It can be seen that the major contributors to the prediction of the time-on-target performance measures, across a wide variety of tracking tasks, were the task characteristics of number of procedural steps, the precision of the response requirements, and the number of responses required. Table 13.8 compares the predictions achieved in the two postdiction studies.

TABLE 13.8

Comparison of Postdiction Studies 1 and 2[a]

	Uncorrected		Corrected		Forecasting efficiency	$P(_cR)$
	R	R_2	$_cR$	$_cR^2$		
Study 1	.85	.72	.82	.67	43%	.01
Study 2	.79	.63	.73	.53	32%	.05

[a]Adapted with permission from Farina, A. J., and Wheaton, G. R. Development of a taxonomy of human performance: The task characteristics approach to performance prediction (American Institutes for Research Tech. Rep.). *JSAS Catalog of Selected Documents in Psychology*, 1973, *3*, 26–27 (Ms. No. 323).

SUMMARY OF PERFORMANCE CORRELATES

It is apparent that these efforts were successful in both studies. The critical question of whether these results would hold up in the face of cross validation remains an open issue. Both studies show improved predictions over those achieved on the basis of knowledge of only the means of the respective samples.

Of interest also are the intercorrelations among the task characteristic measures. In most cases, these appear low enough to indicate they are conceptually independent as perceived by observers. However, some characteristics tend to go together in the limited range of tasks examined, such as number of output units and number of procedural steps, in the first postdiction study. There is also some overlap of simultaneity of responses with duration of output and number of procedural steps. Somewhat higher correlations emerge in the second regression analysis using only tracking tasks. Thus, tasks with a greater number of procedural steps tend to require a larger number of responses, and the number of simultaneous responses required is highly related to the number of elements per output units.

Data of this type should be helpful in understanding the structure of task characteristics and in redefining the smaller set of common characteristics useful in describing a large number of diverse tasks. This kind of analysis is needed for future work in evaluating the usefulness of a classificatory system based on task characteristics.

Farina and Wheaton (1973) have presented a model of performance (P) expressed as a function of the operator (O), the environment (E), and the task (T)—called POET. Given that the operator and the environmental components in their studies essentially were uncontrolled, or at least unknown, it is of special interest that the task components account for so much of the variance (67% and 53%).

Their model, for instance, suggests that uncontrolled variations in the operator and environmental components might mask the relationship between task characteristics and performance. This masking indeed may have been present. It was not as pronounced as expected, perhaps due to the fact that the operator and environmental components were controlled indirectly or almost held constant. For example, it could be assumed that any experimenter would attempt to ensure that environmental conditions such as room temperature, noise level, and level of illumination, were at least within some subjective zone of acceptance when setting up the experiment, unless these variables were part of the research design. Because the studies were chosen to avoid the presence of independent variables such as stress and drugs, it is reasonably safe to assume that the environmental component was fairly constant across studies. Furthermore, the use of mean performance scores on each task (obtained by averaging across individuals) tended to minimize the influence of individual difference variables.

Given the limitations inherent in the postdiction approach, these studies showed that selected task characteristics were correlates of performance. Use of the task definition described earlier, and the descriptive indexes derived from it, appears to provide a basis for systematically relating differences among tasks to variations in performance.

Correlates of Learning and Training Effectiveness

The previous section provides encouraging evidence that a quantified set of task dimensions serves as correlates of actual performance levels across a large number of diverse tasks. Thus, the Task Characteristics Approach appears to meet one of the criteria described in Chapter 4 for evaluating taxonomic systems in this area. A related criterion is the extent to which these systems predict learning and skill training.

It was possible to extend the series of studies described in the previous section to some specific issues in the design of training devices and in the prediction of their effectiveness for the U. S. Navy (Wheaton, Mirabella, & Farina, 1971; Wheaton & Mirabella, 1972). These studies allowed some evaluation of the predictions of skill acquisition and transfer of training that could be achieved from quantitative indexes of generic task characteristics. These studies also bear on the utility criterion for evaluation of the value of taxonomic systems in solving real-world problems.

Let us first examine some of the applied problems confronting individuals who are responsible for the design and development of effective training devices. During conceptualization of such devices, decisions must be made early concerning features of the operational task that should be incorporated into the trainer in order to make the device optimally effective for both the acquisition and transfer of skills. Complementary decisions are needed concerning those features of the operational task that can be eliminated to save costs. These are the issues of *fidelity of simulation* required for transfer of training to the operational equipment. Yet, objective means for deciding on a priori grounds what to include and what to eliminate never have been developed. In particular, quantitative methods are lacking with which to relate variations in trainer task characteristics to variations in the acquisition and transfer of skill. The pragmatic consequence of this situation is the incorporation into training devices and, especially, simulators, of as much realism as the state of the art and available dollars permit. Increasingly, the cost effectiveness of such a response to training needs has been questioned. The issues are described succinctly by Wheaton and Mirabella (1972).

A major stumbling block to the development of more objective and systematic approaches to device design is the lack of an acceptable method for analyzing and describing trainee tasks quantitatively. The Task Characteristics Approach described earlier in this chapter, based on the work of Farina and Wheaton (1973) in the Taxonomy Project, provides a start toward solving this problem. Farina and Wheaton demonstrated that it was possible to describe the critical features of a device reliably and along a number of quantitative dimensions. But, can measures of training effectiveness (rate of skill acquisition, level of transfer) be demonstrated to vary in some predictable manner as features of a training device are manipulated? Unless there is a relationship between these two sets of variables, prediction of effectiveness will not be feasible.

DEVELOPMENT AND EVALUATION OF QUANTIATIVE INDEXES

The first phase of the research program (Wheaton *et al.*, 1971) had three objectives. The first objective was to compile an initial set of quantitative indexes relating to selected characteristics of various human–machine tasks. The second was to determine whether the obtained indexes could be used to describe a sample of trainee tasks and to differentiate among them. The third was to develop a predictive methodology based on the task indexes and to assess its potential utility.

PROCEDURES USED As a first step to accomplish these ends, Wheaton *et al.* (1971) identified approximately 165 different trainers or simulators used by the Navy for instructional purposes. The equipment differed in terms of the basic content of training (e.g., vehicle control, fire control, navigation). The decision was made to focus on a more homogeneous subset of devices that would provide a better test of the overall methodology. If quantitative indexes could not be applied to a specific class of trainers, then there would be little hope of applying such indexes across many different types of devices. Navy sensor-based or surveillance systems were chosen for study, including such devices as sonar, radar, and electronic countermeasures trainers. The intention was to generate indexes that would provide for the quantitative description of other devices within the surveillance family.

The next step was to analyze the trainee tasks associated with these devices in order to determine the major subtasks performed by trainees. This analysis identified those features of the subtasks that might provide a basis for generation of task descriptive indexes of the four major trainee subtasks common to surveillance training devices. The first subtask identified was *procedural* in nature and involved receiver turn-on, set-up, and/or calibration in preparation for search activities. The second subtask, involving *monitoring* of the receiver, resulted in signal detection or target acquisition. In the third subtask, displayed signals were analyzed to permit target *identification* and classification. The fourth subtask involved *tracking* of the target in order to provide continuous or discrete information about target range and bearing. The reader will recognize that these are functional categories used in the behavior requirements approaches to task classification (see Chapter 6 and Chapter 11 on the Task Strategies Approach).

In selecting and developing quantitative indexes to be used in describing the four trainee subtasks, Wheaton *et al.* (1971) considered the critical task characteristics that, if manipulated, could be hypothesized to exert an appreciable effect on rate of acquisition or level of proficiency. Based on an examination of the four subtasks and on a review of the literature, two sets of indexes were generated. The first set consisted of generic indexes applicable to all of the trainee subtasks. The generic indexes included: (1) 13 of the task characteristic rating scales described earlier and presented in Appendix D, (2) the Display Evaluative Index (DEI), and (3) a set of panel layout and task-type indexes. The second set contained specific indexes developed to provide a more detailed description of each of the trainee subtasks.

An index within this second set was specific in the sense that it would apply to at least one, but not to all, of the trainee subtasks.

The Display Evaluative Index, developed by Seigel, Meihle, and Federman (1962), is a measure of the effectiveness with which information flows from displays via the operator to corresponding controls. It was derived originally from a set of assumptions about what constitutes efficient information transfer in display-control systems and is related to the information-theoretic concepts described in Chapter 10. The potential value of the index is demonstrated by its wide applicability. It has aided in the quantification of surveillance, fire control, and even communications systems (e.g., Siegel et al., 1962; Siegel & Federman, 1967). Moreover, the index has been partially validated against judgments by human engineering experts (Siegel et al., 1962; 1963).

The panel layout indexes developed by Fowler, Williams, Fowler, and Young (1968) are designed to provide description of two different aspects of human–machine tasks. One set is used to measure the extent to which general human engineering principles have been applied to the arrangement of controls and displays on a console. The second set relates to the degree to which different operations or task types, such as alternative actions or breaks in operational sequence, are embodied in a particular operator console. These indexes can vary independently of the DEI, which does not address itself to panel arrangements or types of panel operations.

To round out the initial set of generic indexes, seven additional measures were employed. Response actions were broken down into the following categories: (1) number of non-normal repertoire responses (Folley, 1964), (2) number of control activation responses, (3) number of feedback responses, (4) number of information-acquisition responses, and (5) number of instructor-initiated responses (Mackie & Harabedian, 1964). Two additional indexes were the number of redundant information sources processed simultaneously (Mirabella, 1969) and the time permitted for subtask completion. With the inclusion of the seven indexes just described, the generic set consisted of 29 separate measures. This set was felt acceptable for initial work in terms both of the number and variety of descriptors available.

In addition to the generic indexes, which cut across both training devices and trainee subtasks, Wheaton et al. (1971) developed an additional set of 25 descriptors specific to surveillance trainers. The items were selected because they appeared to have implications for device design decisions and because they appeared to be translatable directly into trainer design specifications. They included such items as signal-to-noise ratios, display-control ratios, and variations in target speeds. An additional set of 10 descriptors was related to the use of different training techniques. These included statements, for example, about the use of training tapes, adaptive techniques, and part-task training. Altogether, 29 generic indexes, 15 specific indexes, and 10 training technique descriptors were assembled by the investigators.

RESULTS OF VARIOUS INDEXES   All these indexes were applied to detailed task-analytic data collected on three U. S. Navy sonar devices. In general, application of the DEI was straightforward. Values could be obtained fairly quickly, reliability did not appear to be a problem, and the index differentiated subtasks and devices. The panel layout indexes also differentiated between and within subtasks, although several were difficult to apply and their reliability was questionable. Other generic indexes, including several of the rating scales, did not appear to provide for adequate differentiation among devices. Overall results were encouraging with respect to the generic indexes.

The results from applying the 15 specific and 10 training technique indexes generally were inconclusive. Many specific indexes could not be applied; even when they could they did not discriminate clearly among tasks or devices. Training indexes were simply binary statements about the presence or absence of part-task training capability, for instance.

This study demonstrated the feasibility of using a variety of quantitative indexes to describe salient characteristics of actual trainee subtasks. The importance of this demonstration is evident when one considers the nature of many of the quantitative indexes employed. First, several of the measures were related directly to features of a task familiar to design engineers. These were hardware and procedural features that might be reconfigured during the development of alternative designs. Modifications of these task characteristics would be reflected by changes in the values of many of the quantitative task indexes employed in the study. Second, and more importantly, these same task characteristics could be hypothesized to bear a relationship to measures of task performance, including rates of skill acquisition.

As a subsidiary analysis, the investigators examined the extent to which certain of the newer human engineering indexes would predict performance on the set of 22 tracking tasks. Earlier in this chapter (Table 13.7), we showed that the generic task characteristic scales predicted time on target performance across these diverse tasks, with an R of .73. Using five human engineering indexes, an R of .65 was achieved. The major contributions were primary predictors, duty cycle length, and work ratio, reflecting the distribution of practice dimension. When these indexes were combined with the generic task characteristic indexes, the multiple R was increased to .82.

Of special interest, Wheaton *et al.* (1971) found evidence that the generic task characteristics have their maximal predictive efficiency ($R = .78$) for the starting level of performance (first 5 minutes) relative to performance after 15 minutes on the tracking tasks ($R = .55$). However, the human engineering indexes (duty cycle and work ratio) made increasingly greater contributions to the amount of predicted variance as practice time grew longer. By including these predictors along with the original task characteristic predictors, it was possible to extend the predictive efficiency to interim levels of performance.

Therefore, this phase of the work indicated the possibility of developing quantitative profiles of tasks and of relating such profiles to measures of skill acquisition and performance in operational tasks. With such information, it might then be possible to predict the behavioral consequence of restructuring a task's profile of quantitative indexes. A basis would exist for predicting the effectiveness of alternative training device designs. All this was contingent, of course, on the demonstration of a relationship between the quantitative indexes and measures of performance.

PREDICTION OF SKILL ACQUISITION

In the next phase of this series, Wheaton and Mirabella (1972), examined the relationship between variations in quantitative indexes and corresponding changes, if any, in selected criterion measures. The objective was to examine the validity of the basic methodology of using quantitative task-index information to forecast the relative effectiveness of competing training-device designs.

The approach consisted of three interrelated activities. Quantification of devices in the field was continued, using a revised set of task characteristic indexes. The data obtained during this exercise were then used in conducting a two-pronged validation study consisting of a laboratory and a field effort. Before either validation effort could be initiated, quantitative task index data were obtained on an additional sample of 13 actual U. S. Navy training devices in use at different trainee stations around the United States. These data provided guidlines for the types and ranges of design characteristics to be manipulated in the laboratory. In addition, they were employed in the field validation effort as the predictor variables. The task-descrip-

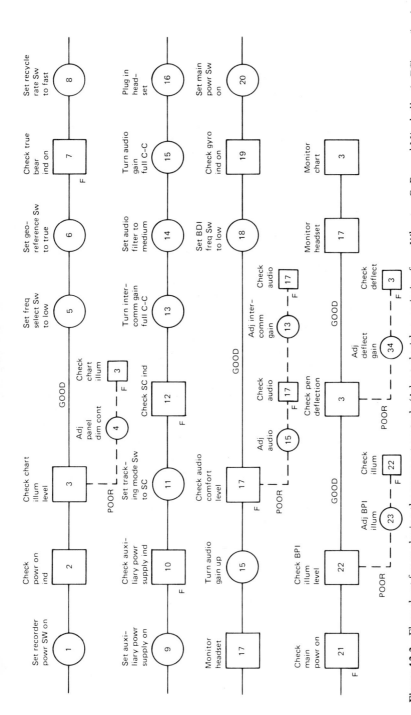

Figure 13.3 Flow chart for analyzing the sonar set-up task. (Adapted with permission from Wheaton G. R., and Mirabella, A. *Effects of task index variations on training effectiveness criteria* (NAVTRAEQUIPCEN 71-C-0059-1). Orlando, FL: Naval Training Equipment Center, October 1972.

tive data obtained for each subtask were then converted into flow charts for more convenient processing. Figure 13.3 presents an example of one type of flow chart for the sonar set-up subtasks.

After conversion of the task-descriptive data to flowchart form, the trainee tasks within each of the devices were analyzed in terms of a revised set of quantitative task characteristic indexes. The procedure used in quantifying the task characteristics required instructor personnel to perform and describe the primary and contingency actions comprising each of four trainee subtasks (set-up, search, localization, and classification).

For the laboratory validation, Wheaton and Mirabella developed a modularized, synthetic sonar trainer. This device could be configured readily into a large number of sonar trainers, varying in design characteristics but with a common set of functions. The trainer was designed to evaluate set-up behavior. An attempt was made to compile configurations that would vary as much as possible along the 17 design indexes selected for study. The synthetic trainer was constructed to represent a cross section of the 13 different U. S. Navy sonar devices previously task analyzed. The trainer consisted of 20 different modular panels representing sonar console functions. Alternatively designed panels could be interchanged, and thus used to manipulate the overall appearance of the trainer console.

Figure 13.4 shows the most complex configuration. For example, the panel at the top left represents the function of energizing the console. It consists of toggle switches, feedback lights, a rotary switch, and a meter. In other configurations, this particular panel might be replaced by one consisting of only one toggle switch and one feedback light. Similarly, most of the other panels were designed in "alternative forms." For each trainer, a specific set of procedures or sequence of responses was developed. These served to define "trainee" tasks analogous to the trainee set-up subtasks associated with actual sonar training devices.

Sixteen subjects were assigned randomly in groups of five to each of 12 experimental tasks. Following procedures outlined by Wheaton and Mirabella (1972), data were collected representing subjects' time and error performance during skill acquisition. On some tasks, pilot transfer of training data also was obtained.

The second prong of the dual validation attempt involved a study of the effectiveness of the 13 sonar training devices in the field. This field validation was pursued via structured interviews with experienced sonar instructors. The instructors were asked to rate the tasks trained on their devices against a set of synthesized comparison

Figure 13.4 Configuration of modular synthetic sonar trainer (complex configuration). Reprinted with permission from Wheaton, G. R., & Mirabella, A. *Effects of task index variations on training effectiveness criteria* (NAVTRAEQUIPCEN 71–C–0059–1). Orlando, FL: Naval Training Equipment Center, October 1972.

tasks. With respect to the subtasks found in each device, four specific judgments were made, including: (1) training time, (2) proficiency level, (3) degree of transfer of training, and (4) level of task difficulty.

In general, the results of the laboratory validation effort were very encouraging. Significant multiple correlations were obtained between the quantitative task indexes and speed and accuracy of performance during skill acquisition. Thus, an R of .78 was found between performance and a combination of the task characteristics E (number of different equipment elements), AA% (alternative actions present), and D% (number of display elements employed). A similar situation existed for predicting error scores (Rs as high as .89).

PREDICTION OF TRANSFER OF TRAINING

Having demonstrated that quantitative task-indexes could be related to skill acquisition, the investigators turned their attention to the issue of transfer of training (Wheaton & Mirabella, 1972). Could these same indexes predict transfer? How would the specific patterns of task characteristic predictors compare with those found to predict skill acquisition?

Using a synthetic trainer, such as that in Figure 13.4, trainees were put through 15 acquisition trials under the different task manipulations, given a half-hour break, and given 10 acquisition trials on transfer tasks. The initial acquisition data confirmed the high multiple correlations between selected task characteristics and performance at different stages of learning. The contributions of a particular task characteristic to performance also were replicated. Of primary importance was the finding that the high predictions extended to the transfer of training measures. These coefficients were even stronger than for acquisition (Rs from .75 to .91).

The validity of the task-index scores as predictors of performance during transfer has particular practical and theoretical significance. On the practical side, transfer is a primary criterion of training effectiveness. It is useful to identify task characteristics that predict learning, but ultimately a training device is to be evaluated in terms of its transfer to real-world tasks. On the theoretical side, learning theorists commonly invoke a task-similarity model to explain or predict transfer effects. However, similarity typically is unquantifiable except for very simple laboratory tasks. The results of the Wheaton and Mirabella studies provide an instance in which it was possible to quantify similarity among complex tasks and to predict performance and transfer on these tasks with very high validity. The data suggest that a linear regression model will provide good predictability of transfer of training criteria, using a set of task dimensions operationally defined and quantified.

RELATION OF TRAINING METHODS TO TASK
CHARACTERISTICS

Another potential value of quantifying task characteristics is their use as an aid to understanding how these characteristics interact with training methods. For example, the typical conclusion of studies of procedural training is that dynamic training on complex equipment is not cost effective; acquisition of skills and transfer to operational tasks are as good when mock-ups are used for training (Bernstein & Gonzalez, 1971; Prophet & Boyd, 1970).

Wheaton and Mirabella (1972) point out that quantitative task indexes such as those described above might help differentiate task complexity and serve as a basis for understanding how task complexity and training methods interact. These task dimensions can insure that training research on such questions will sample tasks over a broad range of complexity to assist in identifying interactions of training methods with types of tasks.

Wheaton and Mirabella (1972) found some support for interactions between task parameters and method of training. Thus, training method had a differential effect on more complex tasks, with "cold panel" presentation generating more errors than "hot panel" or pictorial presentations. Presence or absence of "task imbeddedness" generated different effects, depending on training method.

The potential significance of task quantification for studying such interactions is worth pursuing further. The unsatisfactory alternative commonly employed, for lack of a quantitative taxonomy, is to select training methods and tasks on an intuitive basis. The studies by Wheaton *et al.* are significant in providing a quantified and conceptual basis for future research in this area.

Current Status

Taxonomic systems based on the Task Characteristics Approach show considerable promise. This chapter has described the sequence of studies that built on earlier classification work discussed in Chapter 7. Starting with a definition that defined a task in terms independent of the human operator's behavior, abilities, or functions, a set of subcategories was derived and measures of each subcategory developed. These were refined and revised as a result of a number of studies concerned with their reliability and validity. It was possible to demonstrate the relation between the task characteristic measures and actual performance. Later research provided a methodology for the assessment of training effectiveness using quantified indexes of task characteristics. These efforts demonstrate the feasibility of such a methodology by relating variations in these indexes to skill acquisition and transfer of training. Although a definitive taxonomy of task characteristics is not yet available, a number of generic task dimensions and indexes have been derived and can serve as a basis for future work.

References

Bernstein, B. R., & Gonzalez, B. K. *Learning, retention, and transfer in military training* (NAVTRADEVCEN 69–C–0253–1). Orlando, FL: Naval Training Device Center, 1971.

Cotterman, T. E. *Task classification: An approach to partially ordering information on human learning* (WADC TN 58–374). Wright Patterson Air Force Base, OH: Wright Patterson Air Development Center, 1959.

Coulter, M. A., & Cattell, R. B. Principles of behavioral taxonomy and the mathematical basis of the taxonomic computer program. *British Journal of Mathematical and Statistical Psychology*, 1966, *19*, 237–269.

Farina, A. J., Jr., & Wheaton, G. R. Development of a taxonomy of human performance: The task characteristics approach to performance prediction. *JSAS Catalog of Selected Documents in Psychology*, 1973, *3*, 26–27 (Ms. No. 323).

Fitts, P. M. Factors in complex skill training. In R. Glaser (Ed.), *Training research and education*. Pittsburgh: University of Pittsburgh Press, 1962.

Fleishman, E. A. Dimensional analysis of psychomotor abilities. *Journal of Experimental Psychology*, 1954, *43*, 437–454.

Folley, J. D., Jr. *Development of an improved method of task analysis and beginnings of a theory of training* (NAVTRADEVCEN 1218–1). Port Washington, NY: U.S. Naval Training Device Center, June 1964.

Fowler, R. L., Williams, W. E., Fowler, M. G., & Young, D. D. *An investigation of the relationship between operator performance and operator panel layout for continuous tasks* (AMRL–TR–68–170). Wright Patterson Air Force Base, OH: Aerospace Medical Research Laboratory, December 1968.

Guilford, J. P. The structure of intellect. *Psychological Bulletin*, 1956, *53*, 267–293.

Hackman, J. R. Tasks and task performance in research on stress. In J. E. McGrath (Ed.), *Social and psychological factors in stress*. New York: Holt, Rinehart, & Winston, 1968.

Jacobs, P. I. *Meaning as a task dimension—A new technique of measurement and an application* (AF Project: 33 (616)-5965, Memorandum Report No. 7). Urbana, IL: University of Illinois Training Research Laboratory, February 1959.

Mackie, R. R., & Harabedian, A. *A study of simulation requirements for sonar operator trainers* (NAVTRADEVCEN 1320–1). Orlando, FL: U.S. Naval Training Device Center, March 1964.

Mirabella, A. Two-dimensional versus three-dimensional tracking under two modes of error feedback. *Human Factors*, 1969, *11*, 9–12.

Prophet, W. W., & Boyd, H. A. *Device-task fidelity and transfer of training: Aircraft cockpit procedures training* (Tech. Rep. No. 70–10). Fort Rucker, AL: Human Resources Research Organization, July 1970.

Siegel, A. I., & Federman, P. J. *Validation of the DEI technique for large-scale display evaluation* (RADC–TR–67 134). New York: Rome Air Development Center, Griffiss Air Force Base, May 1967.

Siegel, A. I., Miehle, W., & Federman, P. *Information transfer in display control systems IV: Summary review of the DEI technique* (Fourth Quarterly Report), Wayne, PA: Applied Psychological Services, 1962.

Siegel, A. I., Miehle, W., & Federman, P. *Information transfer in display control systems VII: Short computational methods for and validity of the DEI technique* (Seventh Quarterly Report). Wayne, PA: Applied Psychological Services, 1963.

Smith, P. C., & Kendall, L. M. Retranslation of expectations: An approach to the construction of unambiguous anchors for rating scales. *Journal of Applied Psychology*, 1963, *47*, 149–155.

Stolurow, L. *A taxonomy of learning task characteristics* (AMRL–TD–12–64–2). Wright-Patterson Air Force Base, OH: Aerospace Medical Research Laboratories, January 1964.

Teichner, W. H., & Olson, D. E. A preliminary theory of the effects of task and environmental factors in human performance. *Human Factors*, 1971, *13*, 295–344.

Wheaton, G. R., & Mirabella, A. *Effects of task index variations on training effectiveness criteria* (NAVTRAEQUIPCEN 71–C–0059–1). Orlando, FL: Naval Training Equipment Center, October 1972.

Wheaton, G. R., Mirabella, A., & Farina, A. J., Jr. *Trainee and instructor task quantification: Development of quantitative indices and a predictive methodology* (NAVTRADEVCEN 69–C–0278–1). Orlando, FL: U.S. Naval Training Device Center, January 1971.

CHAPTER 14

Taxonomic Developments in Related Areas

In the foregoing chapters we have described considerations involved in the development and applications of taxonomies of human performance. In Chapter 2 we examined taxonomic efforts in the biological sciences and described classification issues in the area of human learning. At one time or another, a number of other disciplines in the behavioral sciences have employed classification strategies in an attempt to gain some understanding of such diverse phenomena as the treatment of mental disorders and the characteristics of industrial organizations.

Because these investigations display many of the potential pitfalls and advantages inherent in any taxonomic effort, it would seem appropriate to review these classificatory schemes before returning to our overview of taxonomic systems in the area of human task performance. Some classificatory efforts have focused on highly specific research areas. For example, Utall (1981) has recently developed a taxonomy of visual processes and Woods (1974) has devised a taxonomy of instrumental conditioning. In this chapter, we present some of the more general taxonomic systems that have been undertaken.

Clinical Classification

One of the most extensive applications of classification strategies occurs within the realm of clinical psychology. Clinical classification has had a long history, stretching back to Kretchmer and Galen. It has traditionally focused on the assignment of individuals to certain categories of mental disease which are employed in clinical diagnosis. The relevant classification categories, such as *anxiety* and *schizophrenia*, have remained remarkably stable over the course of the last century, although certain modifications are apparent in the most recent version of the American Psychiatric Association's Diagnostic and Statistical Manual (DSM III) (see American Psychiatric Association, 1980; Million, 1983).

The current version of the DSM III attempts to classify disorders within five superordinate categories referred to as axes. Axes I and II are presented in Table 14.1 and reflect traditional psychiatric disorder and clinical syndromes, respectively. Axis III includes categories for assessing physical disorders relevant to patient care, while Axis IV contains categories of psychosocial stressors that might contribute to a disease and its treatment. Axis V provides categories for an individual's highest level of adaptive functioning.

The present version of the DSM III represents an advance over its predecessors in that it is behaviorally based. The DSM III is designed so that the individual's likelihood of membership in a category can be evaluated through ratings of observable behavior. In fact, specific

TABLE 14.1

Current DSM-III Disorder Categories: Axis I and Axis II[a]

Axis I	Axis II
Eating disorders	Paranoid
Affective disorders	Schizoid
Bipolar	Schizotypal
Major depression	Histrionic
Cyclothymic	Narcissistic
Dysthymic	Antisocial
Adjustment Disorder	Borderline
Senile and presenile dementias	Avoidant
Anxiety disorders	Dependent
Somatoform disorders	Compulsive–passive
Somatization	Passive–aggressive
Conversion	Atypical
Psychogenic pain	
Hypochondriasis	
Mental Retardation	
Psychosexual dysfunction	
Schizophrenia	
Substance-use disorders	
Paraphilias	

[a]Reproduced with permission from the American Psychiatric Association, *Diagnostic and statistical manual of mental disorders*, Third Edition, Washington, D.C.: American Psychiatric Association, 1980.

behavioral examples are provided to guide the rating process. Furthermore, the DSM III examines a far greater number of attributes and categories relevant to mental health than had been contained in past manuals, thus, providing a better and more comprehensive tool for clinical assessment. Until the publication of the most recent version of the DSM, the earlier categories tended to focus on biomedical or psychiatric concerns as opposed to psychological attributes (Cattell, 1983). Finally, through the inclusion of categories with positive connotations, such as those in Axis V, the DSM III avoids stigmatizing individuals through categorization. The diagnostic classifications resulting from the application of the DSM III provide the foundation for much of the professional practice in the clinical area.

While these classificatory developments are notable and laudatory, nonetheless, the publication of the DSM III has not been without controversy. This controversy centers on the qualitative or rational techniques employed in the derivation of the categories. In clinical classification, categories are selected to reflect current professional consensus concerning the syndromes observed in personality and mental disorders. Thus, the process of category construction is, in some respects, a political one, leading to debates between psychologists and psychiatrists as to whose syndromes will form the basis for the definition and treatment of mental disease. (Incoming patients, assigned to categories on the basis of ratings of behavioral observations, are provided particular treatments based upon category membership.)

The extensive research literature resulting from the application of this clinical classification system provides an excellent illustration of the advantages and pitfalls inherent in all classification efforts, especially those that are qualitative in nature. On the positive side, the availability of enduring, relatively stable, diagnostic categories has allowed clinicians to formulate a rich description of the various kinds of mental disease through ongoing research work. Moreover, it has permitted the clinical community to address the complex issue of individual disorders in a far more economical fashion than might otherwise be possible, simply by treating all individuals assigned to a given diagnostic category in a similar manner. There is little doubt that these two advantages, desirable outcomes for any classification effort, are of great importance in the clinical domain. They facilitate the application of the classificatory scheme, that is, the categorization of new members and the determination of appropriate actions after category assignment. Certainly, if application is the ultimate criterion of the success of a taxonomic scheme, then the DSM III can be characterized as a particularly successful classification effort.

On the other hand, we noted in Chapter 4 that a variety of other criteria should be used in the evaluation of a classificatory system. When we assess the clinical categories against these other considerations, they are generally found to be wanting (Cattell, 1983). Specifically, effective classification clearly requires an appropriate, justified, and well-defined set of attributes for category assignment. Unfortunately, there is a considerable amount of disagreement regarding the content and nature of the variables that should be employed in clinical classification (Kaplan, 1983; Williams & Spitzer, 1983). When this trend of vaguely defined attributes is coupled with (1) the complexity of behavioral manifestations of mental disorders, (2) the potential for true overlapping category assignments, and (3) the lack of well-specified attribute measures, the result is both poor category assignment (Meehl, 1954), and clinical categories lacking a sufficient degree of within-group homogeneity for predictive and treatment purposes (Cattell, 1983).

Thus, while containing relatively stable, diagnostic categories that are richly described in the literature and extensively applied, the end result of the clinical classification derived from qualitative techniques often is erroneous assignment of individuals. In essence, the lack of sufficient agreement as to what constitutes a legitimate category of mental disease limits the general acceptance of even the most well thought out qualitative classification scheme. As Cattell (1983) has pointed out, the most sensible approach to clinical taxonomic efforts at this point is likely to involve application of recent advances in clustering alogorithms in an attempt to provide a firm, consensual, empirical base for category formation, and a more accurate taxonomic description of individuals.

Personality Classification

The study of human personality is closely allied with clinical psychology, and over the course of the past century there has been a wide variety of systematic classification efforts focusing on the categorization of human traits, dispositions, and styles of behavior. These extensive classificatory schemes resulted from the proliferation of personality descriptors and the need for an organized approach to this unusually complex and diverse behavioral domain (Blashfield and Dragun, 1976; Jackson and Paunonen, 1980; Wiggins, 1979). These taxonomic efforts differ in a variety of ways, having two primary distinctions. First, they differ in the methods employed to develop the classificatory system, with some systems being derived from rational or qualitative procedures and others being developed empirically. A second difference among these classificatory schemes is the unit of classification. Some systems categorize behaviors; others focus on persons. We now present a brief review of some efforts representing these different classification strategies. We begin with behavioral classification.

EARLY IDENTIFICATION OF PERSONALITY DESCRIPTORS

One of the earliest attempts to classify behavioral manifestations of personality was the research investigation of Allport and Odbert (1936). These taxonomists reviewed nearly half a million terms in Webster's New International Dictionary (1924) in order to identify those that would distinguish the behavior of one human being from another. They eventually identified 17,953 descriptor terms. Norman (1967) later updated Allport and Odbert's original list, after reviewing Webster's Third New International Dictionary Unabridged (1961), expanding the original list to some 27,000 terms. Subsequently, this list was distilled to roughly 3600 terms that were held to represent stable traits, or as Wiggins (1976) defines them, "tendencies, proclivities, propensities, dispositions, and inclinations to act or not to act in certain ways on certain occasions" (p. 395).

GOLDBERG'S CLASSIFICATION OF DESCRIPTIVE TERMS

These initial behavioral descriptors have served as the basis for a series of taxonomic efforts. An excellent example is the research program of Goldberg (1975, 1978). By employing the terms identified in the earlier research by Norman (1967), Goldberg hoped to ensure the development of a systematic and comprehensive taxonomy of descriptive terms in personality theory that would facilitate scientific communication. Goldberg (1975) believes that this data base provides a nearly ideal foundation for taxonomic efforts since it provides a set of variables describing "individual differences that are of sufficient social significance, wide-spread occurrence, and distinctiveness to have been encoded and retained as descriptive predicates in the English language" (Goldberg, 1975, p. 4).

The specific objectives of Goldberg's project included (1) developing a taxonomic structure for those descriptors that refer to stable personality traits (e.g., *meek*); (2) controlling method-specific sources of variance (e.g., response biases, sets, or styles) in order to uncover those empirical structures in self and peer descriptions which are based solely on similarity of meaning; (3) learning as much as possible about the nature of the processes involved in descriptions of one's self and others (see Goldberg, 1978); (4) developing a taxonomic structure for moods or temporary states (e.g., *lonesome*) and for those referring to social roles and relationships, (e.g., *dangerous*); (5) determining the generality of the taxonomic structure of trait descriptive terms to other language communities in the United States and in other English speaking parts of the rest of the world; and (6) discovering the relationship between the taxonomic structures developed in this project and those under development elsewhere.

The initial steps consisted of culling through a master pool of more than 18,000 terms pertaining to attributes of people, and reducing it based upon several criteria. The remaining terms were sorted into three categories: (1) stable traits, (2) temporary states, and (3) social roles and relationships. The primary empirical analyses have been done on the first category. The 2800 stable-trait terms were divided into 14 lists of 200 each, and each list was given to a different sample of undergraduates. Students were asked to give a synonym or short definition of each word, to rate the extent to which the term is descriptive of themselves and of three self-selected peers, and to rate each term's social desirability. Subsequently, this 2800-item list was reduced to a more manageable list of 1710 descriptors. As in the Taxonomy Project described in this book, a variety of approaches were employed deliberately for rationally clustering and classifying these personality descriptors (Goldberg, 1975). For example, one set of analyses was directed at classifying personality descriptors simultaneously on two dimensions: descriptive and evaluative contrast. To illustrate:

Evaluative contrast	Descriptive contrast	
Good	Thrifty	Generous
Bad	Stingy	Extravagant

WIGGINS' INTERPERSONAL TAXONOMY

Wiggins (1979) has suggested that the most important categories of traits in need of taxonomic structure focus on interpersonal behavior. Building upon the work of Goldberg, as well as the earlier studies by Allport (1937; Allport & Odbert, 1936) and Norman (1967), he undertook the development of a taxonomy of trait descriptive terms in the interpersonal domain. Specifically, he classified all Goldberg's 1710 adjectives into seven a priori categories. This sorting process resulted in 800 terms that were identified as interpersonal. Wiggins then attempted to classify the terms into Leary's (1957) taxonomic system of interpersonal traits. Five hundred and sixty-seven adjectives were sorted into Leary's 16 categories with unanimous agreement across three raters. However, an analysis of this categorization led Wiggins to the conclusion that Leary's system had a number of theoretical gaps (i.e., the results of the taxonomic effort did not adequately correpond to the theoretical model of the interpersonal domain as defined by Foa and Foa [1974] and others).

After the disappointing results derived from the application of Leary's classificatory system, Wiggins (1979) developed his own categories—eight bipolar dimensions (dominant–submissive, arrogant–unassuming, calculating–ingenuous, cold–warm, quarrelsome–agreeable, aloof–gregarious, introverted–extroverted, and ambitious–lazy). All 1710 adjectives identified by Goldberg were assigned to one of the 16 bipolar interpersonal clusters based upon the results of a correlational analysis.

These 16 lists of adjectives were reviewed. Items clearly belonging to the interpersonal category were retained, otherwise the items were placed into one of eight other taxonomic categories (e.g., temperment, character). For each of the 16 interpersonal categories, the 25 best items, as determined from item–cluster correlations, were retained as the reference scale for that category. Three raters then selected the best 8 items in each of the 16 categories based on empirical and quasi-empirical procedures. (Each item had been correlated with its own 25-item cluster and with its 25-item opposite and orthogonal clusters and ordered within each category by the correlations obtained.) A set of 128 adjectives was selected for the eight bipolar scales (8 adjectives × 16 dimensions) that met the provisions of the structural theoretical model of the interpersonal domain, namely a two-dimensional real-space circumplex model (Guttman, 1954). This set of adjectives formed the basis of all of Wiggins' subsequent investigations. The scales were found to have satisfactory psychometric and structural characteristics and to be useful as reference points for the classification of variables in the personality area.

KIESLER'S INTERPERSONAL CIRCLE

A very recent extension of Wiggins' work in the domain of interpersonal behavior and theory has been provided by Kiesler (1983).

Kiesler constructed what he regards as a comprehensive taxonomy of the domain of two-dimensional interpersonal behavior, which he calls the 1982 Interpersonal Circle (see Figure 14.1). This circle integrates and expands the content of four major adult interpersonal inventory measures (La Force and Suczek's Interpersonal Checklist; Wiggins' Interpersonal Adjective Sides; Lorr and McNair's Interpersonal Behavior Inventory; and the Impact Message Inventory by Kiesler and his associates). The result is a "circle" taxonomy consisting of 16 segments, 128 subclasses, and 2 levels integrating 350 interpersonal behavior items developed by previous investigators. Kiesler believes this system provides a taxonomy of two-dimensional interpersonal behaviors to which existing and future measures or constructs may be compared, contrasted, and/or anchored.

Kiesler (1983) elaborates the range of theoretical, methodological, and empirical features necessary for developing this taxonomic circle system. These include the use of factor analytic findings yielding the 16 categories (segments); also categories at polar ends of circle diameters are classes of human behavior representing behavioral contrasts and are, hence, highly negatively correlated and show zero correlations with theoretically orthogonal segments. The circular arrangement reflects joint action of two basic interpersonal dimensions, control and affiliation, which define the vertical and horizontal axes of the circle respectively; each of the 16 categories reflects mathematically weighted combinations of these dimensions. Kiesler also specifies that empirical intercorrelations among the 16 categories should reveal a circumplex ordering (Guttman, 1954) wherein adjacent segments are positively correlated and opposite segments are negatively correlated. The degree of abnormality of a particular behavior is represented by its distance (radius) from the midpoint. Definitions and operationalizations of each level of a category should show minimal overlap with adjacent segments. Definitions should permit independent investigations to reliably cross-classify items from interpersonal measures.

Kiesler proceeds to provide the definitions, levels, subclasses, and numbers of items for each. He then uses the system to evaluate coverage and gaps in available interpersonal interaction measures. Emphasis in the system is on the construct of interpersonal "complementarity" in human interactions; the system provides a classificatory system for comparisons of opposing segments. Kiesler reviews previous conceptions of interpersonal complementarity and, using the taxonomy as a guide, derives a number of propositions of interpersonal theory as they apply in personality, psychopathology, and psychotherapy.

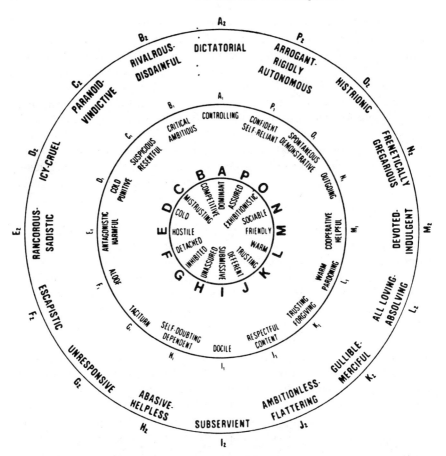

Figure 14.1 The 1982 Interpersonal Circle. Adapted with permission from Kiesler, D. J. The 1982 Interpersonal Circle: A taxonomy for complementarity in human transactions. *Psychological Review*, 1983, *90*, 185–214. Copyright 1983 by The American Psychological Association.

The foregoing systems represent consistent evolutionary progress over the years with investigators building on the work of their predecessors. Moreover, research in this area has begun to show a strong tendency to evaluate the appropriateness of initial rational classifications through well-thought-out empirical tests seeking to assess the validity of the relevant taxonomic structure. While these trends are laudable, some difficulties are apparent in these studies. First, no one system has gained any general acceptance in the field as a whole. Second, the amount of new knowledge provided by these research efforts is clearly open to question. For instance, the interpersonal work formulated by Kiesler (1983) is very similar to a circle formulated by Leary (1957) nearly 25 years ago. However, these limitations might be acceptable, given the restricted goals of these studies and the tendency of these taxonomic efforts to rely on a common core of preexisting descriptors.

A number of other taxonomic efforts in the personality domain have typically attempted to formulate categories of personality through observed empirical relationships among behavioral descriptors. These relationships are demonstrated through correlational and/or factor analytic methods. This classificatory approach has come to dominate the study of personality. While no attempt is made here to present a complete review of these efforts, the seminal investigations of Cattell, Guilford, and Eysenck are examined.

CATTELL'S CLASSIFICATORY DIMENSIONS

Cattell (1946) began his work with the list of trait descriptors prepared by Allport and Odbert (1936), and supplemented this list with certain additional descriptors culled from the psychiatric and clinical literature. The number of potential descriptors was reduced to 171 after review of the list (e.g., grouping synonyms). Ratings on these descriptors were then obtained for 100 adults and all rating dimensions yielding correlations in excess of .45 were grouped together into overriding clusters. Ratings on these behaviors were then obtained in a sample of some 200 adult males and subjected to a factor analysis. This analysis served to identify 12 factors or categories of behavior in the personality domain, and further research has served to bring this list up to 23 dimensions (Cattell, 1980). Some of the dimensions identified by Cattell include Expressiveness, Self-Sufficiency, Sanguineness, Group Dedication, and Dominance.

CLASSIFICATORY APPROACH OF GUILFORD AND ZIMMERMAN

Guilford and Zimmerman (1956) employed a somewhat different approach in their classification effort. Initially, item responses were obtained for a number of different personality measures. Subsequently, a set of judges was asked to group together those items which appeared to tap the same aspect of personality. This procedure resulted in some 69 clusters and a sample of 126 male and 87 females was then evaluated on each of the items incorporated in these clusters. Intercorrelations of the subjects' scores on these clusters, along with the subjects' status on a dichotomous sex variable then served as a basis for a factor analysis. These analyses resulted in 14 factors, which included Emotionality, Objectivity, Confidence, Sociability, and Restraint, among others. There is some overlap between the factors identified by Cattell and those identified by Guilford and Zimmerman.

EYSENCK'S CLASSIFICATORY SYSTEM

On the other hand, the categories identified by Eysenck do not display a great deal of similarity to the factors identified by either Cattell or Guilford and Zimmerman. Employing the factor analytic techniques of the "British School" Eysenck intercorrelated subjects' responses to the items in a series of personality tests and identified three primary factors that he has labeled Psychoticism, Neuroticism, and Introversion versus Extraversion. Further research employing a variety of other measures has served to suggest that abnormal individuals differ from normal individuals only in the degree to which they manifest these traits and that differences between clinical and normal populations on these dimensions are related to differences on a wide variety of other measures such as motor dexterity and body sway (Eysenck, 1951). One might ask why Eysenck has identified so few dimensions in comparison to Cattell and Guilford and Zimmerman. The differing results may be partially attributed to the divergent factor-analytic techniques employed by the British and American schools, as these methodologies seem to identify global and relatively specific dimensions, respectively.

INTEGRATIVE REVIEWS

Recently, a number of reviews have appeared attempting to synthesize the dimensions that have been identified by these quantitative efforts to classify behavior descriptive of human personality (French, 1973; Goldberg, 1971; Peterson & Bownas, 1982). French (1973) identified 28 factors that have appeared in at least three separate factor-analytic studies conducted by different investigators. However, as Peterson and Bownas (1982) have suggested, the composite list should be approached with some caution as the adequacy of this set of categories is contingent on the initial factor-analytic investigations. In that regard, it should be noted that some ambiguities exist when these studies are closely reviewed. Specifically, questions arise regarding (1) the comprehensiveness of the item bases; (2) the noncomparable nature of the factor rotations and the solution decisions; (3) the apparent inconsistencies in items contained in identical categories; and (4) low intercorrelations obtained among similar factors identified in different studies.

While recognizing the differences in the methodologies and factorial structures of the research investigations of Cattell, Guilford and Zimmerman, Eysenck, and in Royce and McDermott (1977) found sufficient commonalities to create an integrated, affective system from these taxonomic efforts. Their hierarchical structure of the human affective system is shown in Figure 14.2. The higher-order and the first-order factors presented in this hierarchy and their relationships to the earlier research investigations are extensively described in Royce and Powell (1983).

After concluding from their review that there was a need for a research investigation using a comprehensive item pool and a variety of factor rotation methods to identify basic personality constructs, Browne and Howarth (1977) conducted that study. Their research is summarized in Peterson and Bownas (1982). The 1726 items collected from 16 questionnaires were assigned to 20 Putative Factor Hypoth-

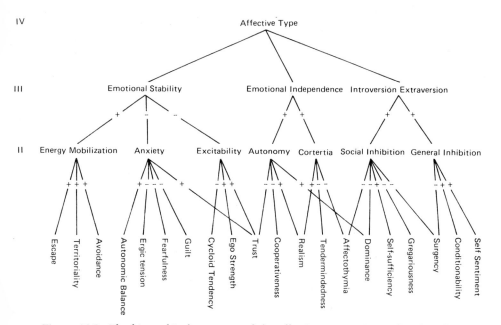

Figure 14.2 The hierarchical structure of the affective system. Reproduced with permission from Royce, J. R., & Powell A. *Theory of personality and individual differences: Factors, systems, and processes.* New York: Prentice–Hall, 1983.

TABLE 14.2

Personality Dimensions from Browne and Howarth Factor Analysis[a]

Social Shyness. Hesitancy to engage in social interactions with a lack of initiative in making new friends. Variance = 12.42.
Sociability. Enjoyment of and engagement in social activities; liking to be around and with people. Variance = 7.53.
Mood-swings Readjustment. Strong emotional moods without apparent cause, feeling listless and tired for no good reason, swings of happiness to depression, and often feeling just miserable. Variance = 6.5.
Adjustment–Emotionality. Nervous, easily rattled or upset, and worrying over possible problems. Variance = 6.18.
Impulsiveness. Impulsive actions, acting on the first thought that comes into one's head, being an "impulsive person," etc. Variance = 5.63.
Persistence. Persisting on a job until it is completed even when others have given up, not giving up easily, capability of working at a problem for more than an hour or two at a stretch. Variance = 5.45.
Hypochondriac–Medical. Complaints about state of physical health. Variance = 5.18.
Dominance I. Being easily downed in an argument, considered submissive, seldom fighting for one's rights, etc. Variance = 5.75.
Dominance II. Taking command, exerting leadership, swaying a group. Variance = 5.03.
General Activity. Interest in action and energy expenditure; preferring and enjoying many types of sports and sports that have "lots of action." Variance = 4.83.
Superego. A "social conscience" in terms of feeling that most people do an honest day's work for a day's pay, too many people take too much and give too little back to society, etc. Variance = 3.90.
Social Conversation. Talking with others a great deal, being considered a talkative person. Variance = 8.03.
Inferiority. Feelings of inferiority, not being successful, and failure to make favorable impressions on people. Variance = 7.05.
Cooperativeness–Considerateness. Inconveniencing one's self to oblige others, being a "Good Samaritan", becoming easily involved in straightening out other people's problems, etc. Variance = 4.10.

[a]This portion of the figure is abstracted from Browne and Howarth's (1977) description of the 15 factors that replicated across four rotations. The "variance" value given for each dimension refers to the mean eigenvalue obtained for that factor across the four separate solutions. Abstracted from Browne, J. A., & Howarth, E. A comprehensive factor analysis of personality questionnaire items: A test of 20 positive factor hypotheses. *Multivariate Behavioral Research*, 1977, *12*, 399–427.

eses (PFH) (representing a factor structure based on their literature review of personality classification). Twenty items were selected as the most representative of each PFH on the basis of item–factor relationships in the literature. The 400 items were placed in two questionnaires of 200 items each and administered to 1600 college students in 13 Canadian colleges. A resulting 401 × 401 correlation matrix (sex is the 401st variable) was factor analyzed. The authors concluded that 15 of the 20 PFHs were robust across differing rotation methods. These are presented in Table 14.2. Peterson and Bownas (1983) have suggested that the personality factors isolated by Browne and Howarth are the most promising set of descriptive categories within the personality domain.

RATIONAL CLASSIFICATORY TYPOLOGIES OF PERSONS

One of the earliest classificatory schemes involving the classification of persons in accordance with a preexisting rational categorization is the work of Jung (1923). Jung proposed a typology composed of four elements, including Introversion versus Extroversion, Sensation versus Intuition, Thinking versus Feeling, and Judgment versus Perception, reflecting an individual's characteristic means for adapting to the world. The Introversion versus Extroversion dimension is intended to reflect whether an individual directs his or her mental activities toward the external world or toward the internal world of ideas and experiences, whereas the Sensation versus Intuition index attempts to describe an individual's tendency to perceive the world as it is or the possibilities in it. Thinking versus Feeling refers to the individual's tendency to reach decisions on the basis of logic or by subjective values, and the Judgment versus Perception dimension reflects the tendency to judge others or approach others in an understanding manner. Jung held that individuals employed each of these dimensions, but preferred to use certain sequences of them in attempting to adapt to the world. For instance, an individual might be classified as extroverted, intuitive, thinking, and judgmental, rather than introverted, intuitive, thinking, and perceptive. Hence, these peculiar combinations were held to reflect mutually exclusive types of persons.

Relatively little research has been conducted employing Jung's typology. The Myers–Briggs type indicator has served to suggest that this taxonomy might have some descriptive value (Myers, 1962). However, research by Stricker and Ross (1964) has questioned whether there is a clear cut distinction among the various taxonomic categories included in this system.

Spranger has also attempted to categorize persons through his typology. This taxonomic system attempts to describe individuals in terms of their primary values which are held to be theoretical, economic, aesthetic, social, political, and religious. The Allport, Vernon, and Lindzey (1951) study of values attempted to implement this system. Research with this instrument has indicated that this taxonomy can provide a stable description of individuals which is relevant in the sense that it will predict other forms of criterion behavior (Kelly, 1955). Unfortunately, little evidence is available bearing on category differentiation.

Studies focusing on the classification of persons into rationally derived a priori categories remain relatively rare due to a number of difficiencies in the approach. Vague definition of categories, often resulting from armchair speculation, often leads to poor category differentiation with individuals falling between categories, rather than within a single category. While such imprecise categorization would tend to argue against this approach, these rational classifications have yielded some of our most stable and robust measures in the personality domain. When coupled with recent advances in the empirical classification of persons, this approach will be of substantial value.

EMPIRICAL CLASSIFICATIONS OF PERSONS

Attempts to classify persons on the basis of empirical data have also played an important role in the study of personality. The older work in this area typically relied on preexisting groups, such as sales personnel or neurotics, to define the categories of interest. Here, the behavior or experiences which differentiated known category members from the general population were used as a basis for predicting membership in any one of the relevant taxonomic categories.

This taxonomic approach for prediction of category membership was employed in the construction of the Strong–Campbell Interest Inventory (SCII) (Strong, 1946; Gough, 1976). In its current form, the SCII attempts to (1) predict membership in some 60 occupational categories (such as lawyer, and mathematician); (2) describe individuals in terms of 18 basic interests (e.g., teaching and religious interests); and (3) assign the individual to one or more of six occupational categories (reflecting realistic, enterprising, conventional, artistic, scientific, and intellectual occupations). The items used in this categorization process were derived by presenting long-term incumbents in a given occupational area with activities and occupational titles, which they rated as like, dislike, or indifferent. Those items which differentiated between group members and the general population served as a basis for developing a weighted key for prediction of category membership.

Research with the SCII has indicated that the instrument yields a stable categorization of individuals with substantial predictive power (Campbell, Borgen, Castor, Johanson & Peterson, 1968). Moreover, further studies by Schmidt (1975) suggest that, with minor modifications, the resulting classification of persons is quite accurate with high net utility. Interestingly, studies contrasting the SCII, and its empirical classification approach, with the Kuder Occupational Interest Survey (which is based on an empirical classification of behaviors) suggest that the empirical person-oriented strategy yields far better prediction (Lefkowitz, 1972). Certainly, the history of many similar empirical taxonomic efforts, such as the various life history keys and the Minnesota Multiphasic Personality Inventory (MMPI), tend to support the evidence bearing on the general effectiveness of this approach to classification.

Nevertheless, empirical efforts of this sort have been subject to a variety of criticisms. First, there are difficulties in obtaining a good understanding of the phenomena through these measures due to the complexity of the differentiating items. Second, the stability of these measures has often been questioned. Finally, it has been suggested that the categories employed in these efforts reflect preexisting, non-psychological constructs.

With the advent of classification algorithms, it has been possible to avoid this latter criticism to the empirical classification of persons. While relatively few studies in the personality area have attempted to employ this approach, one study of some significance was the California Longitudinal Study conducted by Block (1971). Essentially, the descriptive data accumulated for 84 men and 87 women at various points in their lives were reviewed by trained psychologists. Each subject was described in a series of Q sorts. This information then served as the basis for an inverse factor analysis clustering the Q sort data into general categories of personality development.

Table 14.3 presents a brief listing of the categories identified by

TABLE 14.3

Block's Classification of Personality Development[a]

Males	Females
Ego Resilients	Female Prototypes
Belated Adjusters	Cognitive Copers
Vulnerable Overcontrollers	Hyper-Feminine Repressives
Anomic Extraverts	Dominating Narcissists
Unsettled Under-Controllers	Vulnerable Under-Controllers
	Lonely Independents

[a]Reproduced with permission from Block, J. *Lives through time*. Berkeley, CA: Bancroft Books, 1971.

Block for the male and females included in his sample. Further analysis examining the characteristics of category members suggested that this was a robust classification in the sense that category members were differentiated on a wide variety of measures not included in initial category formation, and that these categories provided an interpretable pattern that allowed 60–80% of the individuals to be assigned to a single category. While Block's (1971) work suggests that this might be a promising approach for classifying persons, this classification strategy represents a relatively recent innovation and a review of the approach must therefore await further developments.

A Review of Personality Classification

As the foregoing paragraphs have pointed out, a variety of attempts have been made to classify personality. While no single approach to taxonomic development has proven to be universally successful with respect to the available criteria for the assessment of taxonomic schemes, the future does seem promising. Much of the requisite preliminary work has been accomplished and a systematic effort attempting to combine the relative advantages of each approach, while eliminating the disadvantages, might yield a more viable taxonomy than has heretofore been available.

Some support for this hypothesis may be found in the work of Gough (1956, 1976). In constructing the California Psychological Inventory (CPI), he employed both rational and quantitative techniques, using both behavior and persons as descriptors. Essentially, undergraduates were presented with behavioral descriptors, such as sociability, and asked to nominate friends who were either high or low on this quality. Subsequently, the items included in this scale (e.g., sociability) were selected partly on the basis of the extent to which they differentiated these high and low groups. Further research with the resulting CPI scales has shown it to be one of our best predictors in the noncognitive domain. This finding provides a strong argument for further integrative efforts along these lines, employing multiple classification strategies, in an attempt to more fully describe human personality.

Classificatory Systems Based on Biographical Data

A taxonomic effort closely related to the description of personality may be found in attempts to categorize people into homogenous classes based upon similarities in their life histories. A major project, carried out at the University of Georgia under the direction of Dr. William Owens, has attempted to assess the utility of taxonomic efforts of this sort in the description and assessment of human individuality. Briefly, this effort postulates that (1) individuality will be manifested in the individual's past behavior and experience; (2) it is a developmental phenomenon, and (3) similarity in a wide variety of past behavior and experience will provide an adequate definition of individuality in a global sense and define categories of individuals who differ from each other in a systematic fashion over the course of their lives.

To investigate this possibility, Owens (1976) formulated three biographical (biodata) instruments examining significant behavior and experiences occurring during childhood and adolescence, the college years, and young adulthood. These three instruments were subsequently administered to a sample of some 10,000 males and females at various points in their development. The subjects' responses to the items contained on each of these three instruments and the total item pool were then factor-analyzed. The subjects' scores on these factors served as the basis for a Ward and Hook (1963) clustering.

Results of an initial analysis focusing on the subjects' responses to the childhood and adolescence questionnaire are reported in Owens and Schoenfeldt (1979). This study indicated that roughly 75% of the total sample could be assigned to a single category through a cross-validated discriminant function which employed the subject clusters identified in the Ward and Hook analysis as criterion categories. It was also found that the members of a given category were differentiated from each other on a wide variety of measures not employed in the initial biodata clustering and that subgroup status was an excellent predictor of a wide variety of real world criteria, including academic performance, job performance, and drug abuse, among others.

Further research examining the results obtained in clustering item responses to all three of the instruments yielded a number of additional findings of some significance. First, it was found that this cross-time clustering yielded a higher classification rate than that obtained in the analysis of a single instrument. Second, the data indicated that each subgroup was associated with an interpretable pattern of differential characteristics and that this pattern was maintained on measures not employed in the initial analysis. Third, differences between the subgroups were associated with qualitative differences that appeared to be attributable to complex characteristic adaptive styles. Fourth, this classification showed a surprising amount of overlap with Block's (1971) classification, despite differences in nomenclatures and measurement procedures. These findings lead Mumford and Owens (1983) to argue that it is possible to formulate a valid taxonomy describing individuality as a developmental phenomena.

Table 14.4 presents a brief listing of the categories of individuals identified in the Mumford and Owens (1983) study. The nature of these data might be clarified by a specific example. The second female subgroup has been labeled Competent Nurturers. The differential characteristics of subgroup members indicated that they were reared in a warm, religious, upper class family in which the mother was socially active. They displayed substantial intellectual ability and a rather nutrient pattern of activities and interests. While somewhat introverted in high school, they were socially active and effective. In college, they became involved with religion and less involved with academics. They tended to acquire social service jobs after graduation. However, their successful marriages, religious activities, and community activities seemed to be the focus of their lives.

On a more global level, analysis of the subgroups' differential characteristics led to a number of salient conclusions. One central finding was that the stability of an individual's status on any given charac-

TABLE 14.4

Subgroups of Individuals Identified from Longitudinal Life History Data[a]

Males	Females
Channeled Concrete Achievers	Unscathed Adjusters
Upwardly Mobile Individuals	Competent Nurturers
Unrealistic Independents	Unconventional Successes
Virile Extraverts	Frustrated Incompetents
Analytical Adapters	Social Manipulators
Withdrawn Effeminates	Paternal Reactives
Insecure Socialites	Restricted Socializers
Constrained Careerists	Discontented Male Dependents
Ineffectual Authoritarians	Defensive Conformists
Religious Copers	"Orphaned" Adapters
Expansive Compensators	Unambitious Passives
Fortunate Approval Seekers	Social Copers
Adjustive Successes	Channeled Extraverts
Premature Conformists	Isolated Intellects
Bourgeois Outliers	Independent Achievers
	Insecure Bohemians
	Female Enuchs

[a]Reproduced with permission from Mumford, M. D., & Owens, W. A. Individuality in a developmental context: Some empirical and theoretical considerations. *Human Development*, 1983, *4*, in press.

teristic, as well as the predictive import of this characteristic, varied as a function of the individual's category membership. Moreover, it was found that the impact of any given behavior or experience on later development also varied with category membership. Additionally, because the members of different categories over the course of development might display nearly identical behaviors at a point in development, it was argued that individuality can only be fully defined on a cross-time basis.

The foregoing considerations also lead Mumford and Owens (1983) to argue that a taxonomic approach to the description of individuality is urgently needed. They view their research as an initial exploratory attempt to formulate such a taxonomy, although they have provided substantial evidence for the validity of their conceptualization.

Taxonomies of Environments and Situations

A great deal of attention has been focused on attempts to understand the interaction between the behavior of people and the environment. Frederiksen (1972) and Sells (1963a) both observed that the large majority of taxonomic work in the behavioral sciences has been directed at people (especially the large body of work that categorizes individual differences) rather than at situations. Tenopyr and Oeltjen (1982), in their recent *Annual Review of Psychology* chapter, noted the need for a taxonomy of situations and environmental dimensions. This need has also been recognized by Price and Blashfield (1975), Roberts, Hulin, and Rousseau (1978), Schneider (1978), Peters and O'Connor (1980), and Terborg, Richardson, and Pritchard (1980).

Frederiksen (1972) describes some of the efforts toward situational classification that have been undertaken, and reviews various methodologies that could be employed in such taxonomic efforts. He suggests that anyone embarking on development of a situational category scheme should first consult the outline developed by Sells (1963b). This outline, based on a scheme proposed by Sherif and Sherif (1956), describes the basic aspects of the total situation, including such categories as weather, social institutions, socioeconomic status, and information group structure.

An attempt has been made to classify human environments based on the underlying assumption that such a taxonomic approach will make it easier to assess the impact of environments on individual and group behavior, and vice versa (Insel & Moos, 1974; Moos, 1973). As part of this effort, six different ways of conceptualizing human environments have been suggested: (1) ecological dimensions, including physical factors such as geography, climate, and architecture; (2) dimensions of organizational structure, such as size and staffing ratios; (3) personal characteristics of inhabitants such as age and abilities; (4) behavior settings, or ecological units with both an environmental and a behavioral component; (5) functional or reinforcement properties of environments; and (6) psychosocial characteristics and organizational climate.

Moos and his associate conducted an extensive program to investigate further the dimensions of psychosocial characteristics of the environment. They developed perceived climate scales for eight different environments (e.g., psychiatric wards, classrooms). The common dimensions that emerged from empirical data from these scales across the eight environments were (1) relationship dimension—the extent to which the inhabitants help and support one another; (2) personal development dimensions—opportunities in the environment for personal growth and development of self-esteem; and (3) system maintenance and change dimensions—the extent to which the environment is clear in its expectations and maintains control, yet is responsive to change.

In a recent study, Peters, O'Connor, and Rudolf (1980) identified eight situational dimensions that represented a needed input or resource variable that could either inhibit or facilitate successful task performance. These dimensions include job-related information; tools and equipment; materials and supplies; budgetary support; required services and help from others; task preparation; time availability; and work environment. Four of these situational variables were experimentally manipulated to create facilitating and inhibitory treatment conditions. Significant effects on quality and quantity of performance were obtained for the relatively weak experimental manipulations, leading the authors to suggest "that in task situations which contain either a greater number of and/or more severe situational inhibitors, the effects on performance may be more pronounced" (p. 92). Clearly, in light of these encouraging results, more research is needed to determine the effects of various categories of situations on human task performance.

Taxonomies in Education

The development of educational objectives from which curricula can be designed occupies a major portion of the effort expended by educational administrators (see Hilgard & Bower, 1974, pp. 633–636). Curriculum planners often deal with large numbers of very specific educational objectives. The organization of these specific objectives through classificatory systems makes it much simpler and more effective to translate them into curricula (see, e.g., Gage, 1968; Gagné, 1972; 1975; Jenkins & Deno, 1968; Klausmeier & Goodwin, 1975). Gagné (1975) believes the application of a taxonomic approach to the field of educational objectives is much broader than curriculum development. He sees it as a systematic way to translate broad educational goals, based on the needs of society, into specific objectives for individual development. Without a taxonomic approach, broader educational goals based on societal needs frequently are not translated systematically or logically into specific objectives, resulting in educational systems that do not serve society.

A major taxonomic effort in this regard has been undertaken by Bloom, Krathwohl, and their associates (Bloom, 1956, 1967; Krathwohl, Bloom, & Masia, 1964). Their intent was to create a separate taxonomy of educational objectives for each of three domains: cognitive, affective, and psychomotor. The assumption is that a primary aim of schooling is the development of the ability to think. An objective of Bloom's cognitive taxonomy is to provide curriculum planners and teachers with an explicit, comprehensive set of categories to allow greater precision in translating this aim into practice. The taxonomy divides the cognitive domain (those behaviors involved in thought processes) into six main categories: knowledge, comprehension, application, analysis, synthesis, and evaluation. These categories are assumed to be hierarchical and cumulative. Each major category is defined and broken into subcategories containing more explicit and discrete behaviors. Table 14.5 shows the 21 separate behavioral categories that have been defined in the cognitive domain. These "educational objectives" (desired outcomes) represent categories of behaviors to be developed in all curriculum content areas.

The affective taxonomy of Bloom and his associates is divided into five major categories: receiving or attending, responding, valuing, organization, and characterization by a value complex. The categories are ordered along the dimension of internalization, that is, how much an attitude or emotion has been incorporated by an individual. Their psychomotor taxonomy is not yet developed fully.

Bloom's taxonomy, especially in the cognitive domain, has stimulated and influenced a great deal of research and practice, much of it bearing on the evaluation and validation of the taxonomic structures in the field (e.g., Jenkins & Deno; 1968; Kropp, Stoher, & Bashaw, 1966). Marksberry, McCarter, and Noyce (1969) analyzed the content

TABLE 14.5

Bloom's Taxonomy of Educational Objectives: Cognitive Domain[a]

1.00 Knowledge
    1.10 Knowledge of Specifics
        1.11 Knowledge of Terminology
        1.12 Knowledge of Specific Facts
1.20 Knowledge of Ways and Means of Dealing with Specifics
        1.21 Knowledge of Conventions
        1.22 Knowledge of Trends and Sequences
        1.23 Knowledge of Classifications and Categories
        1.24 Knowledge of Criteria
        1.25 Knowledge of Methodology
1.30 Knowledge of the Universals and Abstractions in a Field
        1.31 Knowledge of Principles and Generalizations
        1.32 Knowledge of Theories and Structures
2.00 Comprehension
    2.10 Translation
    2.20 Interpretation
    2.30 Extrapolation
3.00 Application
4.00 Analysis
    4.10 Analysis of Elements
    4.20 Analysis of Relationships
    4.30 Analysis of Organizational Principles
5.00 Synthesis
    5.10 Production of a Unique Communication
    5.20 Production of a Plan or Proposed Set of Operations
    5.30 Derivation of a Set of Abstract Relations
6.00 Evaluation
    6.10 Judgments in Terms of Internal Evidence
    6.20 Judgments in Terms of External Criteria

---

[a]Adapted with permission from Bloom, B. S. (Ed.) *Taxonomy of educational objectives: Cognitive domain.* New York: Longmans, Green, and Company, 1956.

of textbooks in language arts, mathematics, reading and social studies, according to the six major levels of the taxonomy. McFall (1964) and Pfeffer and Davis (1965) used the taxonomy as a method for classifying test items and achievement exams to identify the relative emphasis in course objectives and learning outcomes.

Klein (1972) developed tests to measure the separate behaviors defined by the cognitive taxonomy; the purpose was to evaluate if the behaviors defined by the taxonomy could be elicited in lower grade levels in a social studies course. Content validity and reliability and independence of the categories were evaluated and recommendations made for clarification and redefinition of the categories for the early grades studied.

A review of empirical validation of taxonomies of educational objectives in the cognitive domain can be found in Cox and Unks (1967). More recently, Stahl (1979) has been examining an alternative to Bloom's cognitive domain taxonomy for use in teacher training courses.

Taxonomies of Organizational Behavior

Much empirical research has been done in the field of organizational psychology, utilizing a large number of variables. Theoretical development is hindered by the lack of classificatory systems to organize these variables into a comprehensive framework, to facilitate communication across researchers, and to clarify appropriate applications of research findings for practitioners.

One taxonomic need in this field is a scheme to classify organizations. Two systems are those of Etzioni (1961) and Blau and Scott (1962). Both these schemes were derived rationally, and each is based on a single organizing dimension. The dimension for Etzioni is "compliance features of the organization," or the type of control structure within the organization. Etzioni's three categories are normative, utilitarian, and coercive. For Blau and Scott, the primary dimension is the "prime beneficiary served by the organization" (owners, members, clients, public-at-large).

Hall (1972) found that neither of these two classificatory systems was useful in differentiating organizations in terms of external relationships or change patterns. Because these are important aspects of organizational functioning, Hall concludes that these two schemes have very limited usefulness. Haas, Hall, and Johnson (1966) adopted an empirical approach to classification, using data from 75 organizations on 99 variables, the same data used to evaluate the Etzioni and Blau and Scott schemes. The determination of classes of attributes shared by the organizations resulted in a very different list than the rational taxonomies, including items such as financial condition and existence of racial restrictions on membership. Although this particular analysis was limited in scope, Hall (1972) argues for the continued pursuit of the empirical approach to classification of organizations.

Most organizational typologies are based on the objective characteristics of organizations. However, it also is possible to base them on the behavior of people within organizations. Herman, Hulin, and Dunham (1976) developed such a "response relevant typology." This approach emphasizes organizational characteristics relevant to employees' responses. Hunt (1970) summarized the various ways, both rational and empirical, in which organizations have been classified, including organizational inputs, outputs, and throughputs (i.e., technology), social function, form, and pattern of organizational activities. Almost all such attempts can be described best as descriptive schemes rather than well-developed classificatory systems. Carper and Snizek (1980) have provided a review of both rational and empirical taxonomies of organizations. They conclude that these approaches have been pursued independently and are in need of integration. Moreover, they note that the empirically constructed taxonomies have tended to be so problem specific that they lack broad applicability.

The field of organization development (OD) can be defined as the systematic application of behavioral science principles to organizations in order to enhance their effectiveness. The field is in a state of some confusion partly because of the diverse conceptualizations placed under the OD label. In an attempt to bring some order to the field, White and Mitchell (1976) developed a classificatory system based on the content of OD practice, using the methods of facet theory (Foa, 1961, 1965). A facet design is a logical system of classification

TABLE 14.6

A Facet Design for Organizational Development Research[a]

Facets	Elements
A. Recipient of change	1. The individual
	2. The subgroup
	3. The total organization
B. Level of expected change	1. Conceptual
	2. Behavioral
	3. Procedural
	4. Structural
C. Relationships involved in change	1. Intrapersonal
	2. Interpersonal
	3. Intragroup
	4. Intergroup
	5. Organizational

[a]Adapted with permission from White, S. E., & Mitchell, T. R. Organization development: A review of research content and research design. *Academy of Management Review*, 1976, *1*, 57–73.

that focuses attention on the common dimensions underlying the research findings. The OD research from 1964 to 1974 was reviewed using certain selection criteria. Out of this review, 67 studies were uncovered that included 147 different independent variables and 247 different dependent variables. Both authors independently classified the variables in terms of the facet design shown in Table 14.6. They were in agreement 90% of the time on the initial classification; the few differences were discussed and agreed upon. The result was a percentage distribution describing the number of dependent and independent variables falling into each category. Thus, it was possible to gain some picture of the kinds of variables studied in organizational development efforts. Using some of the methods for validating the facet structure, the authors found some empirical support for the use of the system to predict relationships found empirically among these variables.

Taxonomies of Work Motivation

Many models of work motivation may be viewed as attempts to identify and classify the content of motivation (see Ronen, Kraut, Lingoes, & Aranya, 1979). Some of these models deal with the classification of variables related to performance outcomes, while others focus on classifying individual needs. In a recent review, Campbell and Pritchard (1976) raised questions regarding the adequacy of the classifications used to group motivational variables.

CLASSIFICATION BASED ON OUTCOMES

Herzberg (Herzberg, Mausner, & Snyderman, 1959), classifies variables in work motivation into two primary groups. One grouping, intrinsic factors (motivators), reflects the *content* of work, and includes six components such as rewards for achievement, recognition, and advancement. The other grouping, extrinsic factors (hygienes), is related to job context, and includes seven components, including supervision, pay, co-workers, and job security.

Using factor-analytic techniques, Smith, Kendall, and Hulin (1969) have identified five key factors and Dawis, Lofquist, and Weiss (1968) reported 20 factors that reduced to intrinsic and extrinsic higher-order factors. Campbell and Pritchard (1976) believe Herzberg's two-factor model best summarizes the various results, but questions whether the domain of job outcomes has been adequately sampled.

CLASSIFICATIONS BASED ON NEEDS

Maslow's (1954) theory of need hierarchy, derived from clinical experience, groups needs into five classes: physiological, security, social, self-esteem, and self-actualization. However, factor analysis studies (e.g., Roberts, Walter, & Miles, 1971; Waters & Roach, 1973) have not supported Maslow's groupings. Alderfer (1972) has recast Maslow's groupings into three basic sets of needs called existence, relatedness, and growth, and has developed items that cluster into these three dimensions.

INTEGRATION OF WORK MOTIVATION CLASSIFICATIONS

Ronen, Kraut, Lingoes, & Aranya (1979) attempted to provide some integration of these previous efforts. They developed the schema in Figure 14.3 to show that the three theories are not contradictory, but

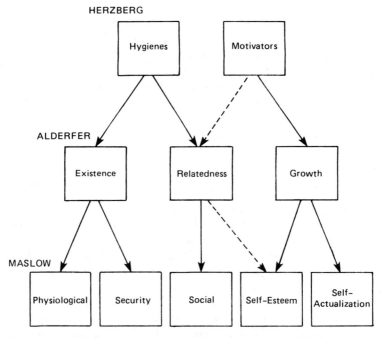

Figure 14.3 Comparison of three theoretical taxonomies of work motivation. Adapted with permission from Ronen, S., Kraut, A. I., Lingoes, J. C., & Aranya, N. A nonmetric scaling approach to taxonomies of employee work motivation. *Multivariate Behavioral Research*, 1979, *14*, 387–401.

represent alternative views of "how the pie should be cut" (p. 390). They then developed a questionnaire around 14 work goals selected to represent a wide variety of work-related expectations and administered it to 1800 repairmen and 800 sales personnel. The employees rated these 14 goals on their importance in an ideal job. Table 14.7 shows how each item was assigned, a priori, to the categories in the taxonomies of Maslow, Alderfer, and Herzberg.

The correlations were analyzed using Smallest Space Analysis, a nonmetric multidimensional scaling technique developed by Guttman (1968) and Lingoes (1973). In contrast to factor analysis, which treats correlations as a measure of common variance to be decomposed, this technique uses the correlation as an index of similarity. The simpler assumption of ordinal rather than interval measurement leads, in general, to dimensional parsimony. The focus is on the configuration of the variables, rather than on underlying dimensions, and emphasizes the interpretation of order relationships (see Karni & Levin, 1972).

The results by Ronen et al. (1979) were consistent with an intrinsic–extrinsic grouping, but also supported a modified Maslow model, in providing a more complex taxonomy of needs bearing on worker motivation. The methodology allowed the relationships among work goals to be diagnosed. Thus, it was found that some items in the extrinsic category, such as desirable area and personal time, were much more distant from other extrinsic facets, such as manager and coworkers, than the latter were from intrinsic facets such as recognition and use of skills.

Perhaps the main value of the Ronen et al. research is to show the value of nonmetric, multidimensional scaling techniques in taxonomic research, especially for testing relationships among variables where well-developed theories are available.

A Taxonomy of Team Functions

Nieva, Fleishman, and Rieck (1978) developed a provisional taxonomy of team functions. The taxonomy was developed after an extensive literature review of research on small groups and teams. The goal was to define the domain of team performance by focusing on performance dimensions that make effective, synchronized work possible. Their implicit assumptions were that certain common functions underlie many apparently diverse team performance settings,

TABLE 14.7

Questionnaire Wording of 14 Work Goals and Assignment to Various Motivational Taxonomies[a]

Work goal	Questionnaire wording	Category of various taxonomies		
		Maslow's	Alderfer's	Herzberg's
Physical	Have good physical working conditions (good ventilation and lighting, adequate work space, etc.)	Physiological and Security	Existence	Hygienes
Area	Live in an area desirable to you and your family			
Time	Have a job which leaves you sufficient time for your personal or family life			
Security	Have the security that you will be able to work for your company as long as you want to			
Benefits	Have good fringe benefits			
Earnings	Have an opportunity for high earnings			
Co-workers	Work with people who cooperate well with one another	Social	Relatedness	
Manager	Have a good working relationship with your manager			
Recognition	Get the recognition you deserve when you do a good job	Self-Esteem		Motivators
Advancement	Have the opportunity for advancement to higher level jobs		Growth	
Training	Have training opportunities (to improve your skills or to learn new skills)			
Autonomy	Have considerable freedom to adopt your own approach to the job	Self-Actualization		

TABLE 14.7 *Continued*

Work goal	Questionnaire wording	Category of various taxonomies		
		Maslow's	Alderfer's	Herzberg's
Skills	Fully use your skills and abilities on the job	Self-Actualization *(continued)*	Growth *(continued)*	Motivators *(continued)*
Challenge	Have challenging work to do—work from which you get a personal sense of accomplishment			

*[a]*Reproduced with permission from Ronen, S., Kraut, A. I., Lingoes, J. C., & Aranya, N. A nonmetric scaling approach to taxonomies of employee work motivation. *Multivariate Behavioral Research*, 1979, *14*, 387–401.

and that these would be exhibited in varying degrees depending on task requirements, as well as on team proficiencies. The team performance functions specify what a team does in the interactive effort to accomplish work. Four major categories of team performance functions were proposed:

Orientation functions involve the processes by which information necessary to task accomplishment is generated and distributed to relevant team members.

Organizational functions involve the processes necessary for the group members to perform their tasks in coordination. They include the processes by which the team members decide who is to do what and when, perhaps through team development of patterns or programs of coordinated behavior in response to the task environment.

Adaptation functions include the processes that occur as team members carry out accepted strategies, make mutual adjustments, and complement each other in accomplishing the team task. The capacity for mutually complementing performances provides one of the major advantages of teamwork over work by individuals. This category encompasses cooperation.

Motivational functions are processes involving defining team objectives related to the task and energizing the group towards these objectives. They determine the intensity with which members invest expectation and energy on behalf of the group. Team motivational functions encompass task-orientation.

For each function, a set of dimensions was developed. Table 14.8 presents the provisional taxonomy.

TABLE 14.8

Provisional Taxonomy of Team Performance[a]

 I. Orientation functions
   A. Information exchange about team goals
   B. Information exchange about team tasks
   C. Information exchange about member resources and constraints
   D. Information exchange of situational resources and constraints
 II. Organizational functions
   A. Matching member resources to task requirements
   B. Response coordination and sequencing of activities
   C. Activity pacing
   D. Priority assignment among tasks
   E. Load balancing of tasks by members
III. Adaptation functions
   A. Mutual critical evaluation and correction of error
   B. Mutual compensatory performance
   C. Mutual compensatory timing
 IV. Motivational functions
   A. Development of team norms
   B. Generating acceptance of team performance norms
   C. Establishing team-level performance-rewards linkages
   D. Reinforcement of task orientation
   E. Balancing team orientation with individual competition
   F. Resolution of performance-relevant conflicts

---

[a]Adapted with permission from Nieva, V. F., Fleishman, E. A., & Rieck, A. *Team dimensions: Their identity, their measurement, and their relationships.* (Final Technical Report, ARI Contract DAHC 19078-C-001). Washington, D.C.: Advanced Research Resources Organization, 1978.

One objective of this attempt was to convert the taxonomy developed to a measurement system for evaluating team proficiency. The general approach was patterned after the procedure described in Chapter 12 for estimating ability requirements. Scaling methods were developed to measure each dimension. Figure 14.4 presents an example of one such scale developed for a try-out with Army combat teams.

Preliminary studies were carried out to test the feasibility of the approach (Shiflett, Price, & Schemmer, 1981; Shiflett, Eisner, & Inn, 1981). The attempt was to determine if naive judges, given a short training experience, can detect these functions in actual team settings, and whether they can do so reliably enough for subsequent validation work. Videotapes were made of 13 team activities involved in Army motor crews and bridge platoon operations. These were viewed later in the laboratory by 19 subjects who rated the activities on selected scales. The study indicated that naive subjects can be trained to detect reliably the presence of such functions in at least

INFORMATION EXCHANGE ABOUT MEMBER RESOURCES AND CONSTRAINTS (IMR)

This is an information exchange function that serves to make team members aware of each others' resources and capabilities. It includes exchange of information about (a) team member/manpower status and (b) messages about physical/equipment resources. Information reflecting stable member skills as well as availability on a spontaneous basis is exchanged.

How IMR Is Different From Other Functions

Information regarding *internal* status of the unit	vs.	ISR-information about circumstances *external* to the unit; support, threat, environment
Ongoing exchange/*discovery* process with respect to member skills, resource availability	vs.	MMR-use of *known* information in role assignment/resource distribution to further task/mission completion

Task Conditions: Team Behavior Anchors:

Very complex task structure requiring high degree of information exchange about internal resources	Efficient exchange of available and critical information about team member and resource status

Breaking camp/10km march on cloudy night in dense terrain; no loss of equipment or personnel.

7 —
6 —

Total awareness of teammate whereabouts and status while under heavy shelling.

Conducting a large force assault

5 —

4 —

With enemy in immediate vicinity, team quickly and without detection clarifies and disseminates information about ammunition availability and distribution

3 —

2 —

Loading troops onto a truck

1 —

Team unintentionally fires at own member(s)

Very simple task requiring little exchange of information about resources	Minimal information exchange about internal status of unit

Using the 7-point scale, please rate:

The demands of the task you observe in terms of *need* for IMR:	The level of IMR you observe during team performance:
(Task: _____ _____)	(Behaviors: _____ _____)

Figure 14.4 Example of a Prototype Scale. Adapted with permission from Shiflett, S., Price, S., & Schemmer, F. M. *Toward a taxonomy of team functions: Concepts, operations, and issues* (ARRO Interim Report 3068). Washington, D.C.: Advanced research Resources Organization, April 1981.

two very different Army settings, although some categories and scales fell short of acceptable reliability levels. Some modifications in the categories were made. Although it is too early to evaluate these developments, it appears that a start has been made to develop a system for classifying group functions.

Summary Comments

It is not possible, in the limited space available, to provide a comprehensive evaluation of each of the taxonomic developments in the several areas of behavioral science described. However, we have, by our selection of these systems, emphasized the more concerted efforts discovered. It is hoped that this review has provided the reader with a better understanding of the status of classification efforts in these fields. The interested reader can pursue these developments in more depth, through the references we have brought together. The criteria and the conceptual and methodological issues described in earlier chapters can assist in a more comprehensive evaluation of these systems.

It can be said, from this review, that investigators in several areas of psychology, have recognized the need for taxonomic development. In many ways, this review is encouraging. Clearly, investigators are starting to give careful attention to the relevant conceptual and methodological issues and a number of studies have shown the careful systematic work required in taxonomic development. Progress has been made in developing classificatory systems, which may improve communication among scientists and practitioners, increase generalizations about human behavior, and improve the application of psychological principles.

References

Alderfer, C. P. *Existence, relatedness, and growth: Human needs in organizational settings.* New York: The Free Press, 1972.

Allport, G. W. *Personality: A psychological interpretation.* New York: Holt, 1937.

Allport, G. W., & Odbert, H. S. Trait names: A psycholexical study. *Psychological Monographs*, 1936, *47*, (1, Whole No. 211).

Allport, G. W., Vernon, P. E., & Lindzey, G. *Study of values.* Boston: Houghton Mifflin, 1951.

American Psychiatric Association. *Diagnostic and statistical manual* (3rd Edition). Washington, D.C.: American Psychiatric Association, 1980.

Blashfield, R. K., & Draguns, J. G. Toward a taxonomy of psychopathology: The purpose of psychiatric classification. *British Journal of Psychology*, 1976, *129*, 574–583.

Blau, P., & Scott, W. R. *Formal organizations: A comparative approach.* San Francisco: Chandler, 1962.

Block, J. *Lives through time.* Berkeley, CA: Bancroft Books, 1971.

Bloom, B. S. (Ed.) *A taxonomy of educational objectives. Handbook I: Cognitive domain.* New York: McKay, 1956.

Bloom, B. S. *Taxonomy of educational objectives. The classification of educational goals. Handbook I: Cognitive domain.* New York: McKay, 1967.

Browne, J. A., & Howarth, E. A comprehensive factor analysis of personality questionnaire items: A test of 20 positive factor hypotheses. *Multivariate Behavioral Research*, 1977, *12*, 399.

Campbell, D. P., Borgen, F. H., Caster, S. H., Johanson, C. B., & Peterson, R. A. Basic interest scales for the SVIB. *Journal of Applied Psychology Monographs*, 1968, *52*, 1–54.

Campbell, J. P., & Pritchard, R. D. Motivation theory in industrial and organizational psychology. In M. D. Dunnette (Ed.), *Handbook of industrial and organizational psychology.* Chicago: Rand McNally, 1976.

Carper, W. B., & Snizek, W. E. The nature and types of organizational taxonomies: An overview. *Academy of Management Review*, 1980, *5*, 65–75.

Cattell, R. B. *The description and measurement of personality.* New York: Harcourt Brace and World, 1946.

Cattell, R. B. Let's end the duel. *American Psychologist*, 1983, *38*, 769–777.

Cattell, R. B. *Personality and learning theory* (Vol. 2). New York: Springer, 1980.

Cox, R. C., & Unks, N. J. *A selected and annotated bibliography of studies concerning the taxonomy of educational objectives: Cognitive domain.* Pittsburgh: University of Pittsburgh, Learning Research and Development Center, 1967.

Dawis, R. V., Lofquist, L. H., & Weiss, D. J. A theory of work adjustment (A revision). *Minnesota Studies in Vocational Rehabilitation*, Vol. 23. Minneapolis: University of Minnesota, 1968.

Etzioni, A. *A comparative analysis of complex organizations.* Glencoe, IL: Free Press, 1961.

Eysenck, H. J. The organization of personality. *Journal of Personality*, 1951, *20*, 101–117.

Foa, U. G. Convergences in the analysis of the structure of interpersonal behavior. *Psychological Review*, 1961, *6*, 341–353.

Foa, U. G. New developments in facet design and analysis. *Psychological Review*, 1965, *72*, 202–274.

Foa, U. G. & Foa, E. B. *Societal structures of the mind.* Springfield, IL: Charles C. Thomas, 1974.

Frederiksen, N. Toward a taxonomy of situations. *American Psychologist*, 1972, *27*, 113–115.

French, J. W. *Toward the establishment of non-cognitive factors through literature search and interpretation.* Princeton, NJ: Educational Testing Service, 1973.

Gage, N. L. An analytic approach to research on instructional methods. In H. J. Klausmeier & C. W. Harris (Eds.), *Research and development toward the improvement of education.* Madison, WI: Dembar Educational Research Services, 1968.

Gagné, R. M., Behavioral objectives? Yes! *Educational Leadership*, 1972, *29*, 394–396.

Gagné, R. M. Taxonomic problems of educational systems. In W. T. Singleton & P.

Spurgeon (Eds.), *Measurement of human resources*. New York: Halstead Press, 1975.

Goldberg, L. R. A historical survey of personality scales and inventories. In P. McReynolds (Ed.), *Advances in psychological assessment*. New York: Science and Behavior Books, 1971.

Goldberg, L. R. *Toward a taxonomy of personality descriptive terms: A description of the O.R.I. Taxonomy Project* (ORI Technical Report Volume 15, No. 2). Eugene, OR: Oregon Research Institute, 1975.

Goldberg, L. R. Differential attribution of trait descriptive terms to oneself as compared to well liked, neutral and disliked others: A psychometric analysis. *Journal of Personality and Social Psychology*, 1978, *36*, 1012–1028.

Gough, H. C. *Manual for the California Psychological Inventory*. Palo Alto, CA: Consulting Psychologists Press, 1957.

Gough, H. Personality and personality assessment. In M. D. Dunnette (Ed.), *Handbook of industrial and organizational psychology*. Chicago: Rand McNally, 1976.

Guilford, J. P., & Zimmerman, W. S. Fourteen dimensions of temperment. *Psychological Monographs*, 1956, *70*, #10.

Guttman, L. A new approach to factor analysis: The radex. In P. R. Lazarsfeld (Ed.), *Mathematical thinking in the social sciences*. Glencoe, IL: Free Press, 1954.

Guttman, L. A general non-metric technique for finding the smallest coordinate space for a configuration of points. *Psychometrika*, 1968, *33*, 461–496.

Haas, E. J., Hall, R. H., & Johnson, N. J. Toward an empirically derived taxonomy of organizations. In R. G. Bowers (Ed.), *Studies on behavior in organizations*. Athens, GA: University of Georgia Press, 1966.

Hall, R. H. *Organizations*. Englewood Cliffs, NJ: Prentice Hall, 1972.

Herman, J. B., Hulin, C. L., & Dunham, R. B. *Developing a response relevant typology of organizations* (Technical Report 76-2). Champaign, IL: Department of Psychology, University of Illinois, April 1976.

Herzberg, F., Mausner, B., & Snyderman, B. *The motivation to work* (2nd Ed.). New York: Wiley, 1959.

Hilgard, E. & Bower, G. *Theories of learning* (4th Ed.). Englewood Cliffs, NJ: Prentice Hall, 1974.

Hunt, R. G. Technology and organization. *Academy of Management Journal*, 1970, *13*, 235–252.

Insel, P. M., & Moos, R. F. Psychological environments: Expanding the scope of human ecology. *American Psychologist*, 1974, *29*, 179–188.

Jackson, D. N., & Paunonen, S. V. Personality structure and assessment. *Annual Review of Psychology*, 1980, *31*, 503–551.

Jenkins, J. R., & Deno, S. L. On the critical components of instructional objectives. *Psychology in the Schools*, 1968, *5*, 296–302.

Jung, C. G. *Psychological types*. London: Rutledge and Kegan, 1923.

Kaplan, M. The issue of sex bias in DSM-III: Comments on articles by Spitzer, Williams and Kass. *American Psychologist*, 1983, *38*, 799–802.

Karni, E. S., & Levin, J. The use of smallest space analysis in studying scale structure. *Journal of Applied Psychology*, 1972, *56*, 341–346.

Kelly, L. E. Consistency of adult personality. *American Psychologist*, 1955, *10*, 659–681.

Kiesler, D. J. The 1982 interpersonal circle: A taxonomy for complementarity in human transactions. *Psychological Review*, 1983, 90(3), 185–214.

Klausmeier, H. J., & Goodwin, W. *Learning and human abilities: Educational psychology* (4th Ed.). New York: Harper & Row, 1975.

Klein, M. F. Use of taxonomy of educational objectives (cognitive domain) in constructing tests for primary school pupils. *Journal of Experimental Education*, 1972, *40*(3),
38–50.

Krathwohl, D. R., Bloom, B. S., & Masia, B. B. *Taxonomy of educational objectives.
Handbook II: Affective domain.* New York: McKay, 1964.

Kropp, R. P., Stoker, H. W., & Bashaw, W. L. The validation of the taxonomy of
educational objectives. *Journal of Experimental Education*, 1966, *34*, 69–76.

Leary, T. *Interpersonal diagnosis of personality.* New York: Ronald Press, 1957.

Lefkowitz, J. E. Comparison of the Strong Vocational Interest Blank and the Kuder
Occupational Interest Survey scoring procedures. *Journal of Counseling Psychology*, 1972, *17*, 357–363.

Lingoes, J. C. *The Guttman-Lingoes nonmetric program series.* Ann Arbor: Mathesis
Press, 1973.

Marksberry, M. L., McCarter, M., & Noyce, R. Relation between cognitive objectives
from selected texts and from recommendations of national committees. *Journal of
Educational Research*, 1969, *62*, 422–429.

Maslow, A. H. *Motivation and personality.* New York: Harper and Row, 1954.

McFall, R. W. The development and validation of an achievement test for measuring
higher level cognitive processes in general science. *Journal of Experimental Education*, 1964, *33*, 103–106.

Meehl, P. E. *Clinical vs. statistical prediction: A theoretical analysis and review of the
evidence.* Minneapolis: University of Minnesota Press, 1954.

Miller, R. B. Taxonomies for training. In W. T. Singleton & P. Spurgeon (Eds.), *Measurement of human resources.* New York: Halstead Press, 1975.

Millon, T. The DSM-III: An insiders perspective. *American Psychologist*, 1983, *38*,
804–814.

Moos, R. F. Conceptualizations of human environments. *American Psychologist*, 1973,
28, 652–665.

Mumford, M. D., & Owens, W. A. Individuality in a developmental context: Some
empirical and theoretical considerations. *Human Development*, 1983, *4*, in press.

Myers, I. B. *The Myers-Briggs type indicator manual.* Princeton, NJ: Educational Testing
Services, 1962.

Nieva, V. F., Fleishman, E. A., & Rieck, A. *Team dimensions: Their identity, their measurement, and their relationships* (Final Technical Report, ARI Contract DAHC
19-78-C-001). Washington, DC: Advanced Research Resources Organization, 1978.

Norman, W. T. *2,800 personality trait descriptors: Normative operating characteristics for
a university population.* Unpublished manuscript, University of Michigan, 1967.

Owens, W. A. Background data. In M. D. Dunnette (Ed.), *Handbook of industrial and
organizational psychology.* Chicago: Rand McNally, 1976.

Owens, W. A., & Schoenfeldt, L. F. Toward a classification of persons. *Journal of
Applied Psychology*, 1979, *64*, 569–607.

Peters, L. H., & O'Connor, E. J. Situational constraints and work outcomes: The influences of a frequently over-looked construct. *Academy of Management Review*, 1980,
5, 391–397.

Peters, L. H., O'Connor, E. J., & Rudolf, C. J. The behavioral and affective consequences
of performance relevant situational variables. *Organizational Behavior and Human
Performance*, 1980, *25*, 79–96.

Peterson, N. G., & Bownas, D. A. Skill, task structure, and performance acquisition. In
M. D. Dunnette & E. A. Fleishman (Eds.), *Human performance and productivity:
Vol. 1. Human capability assessment.* Hillsdale, NJ: Lawrence Erlbaum, 1982.

Pfeiffer, I., & Davis, O. L., Jr. Teacher-made examinations—What kind of thinking do they demand? *Bulletin of the National Association of Secondary School Principals,* 1965, *49,* 1–10.

Pinto, P. R. *Subgrouping in prediction: A comparison of moderator and actuarial approaches.* Unpublished doctoral dissertation, University of Georgia at Athens, 1970.

Price, R. H., & Blashfield, R. K. Explorations in the taxonomy of behavior in settings: Analysis of dimensions and classification of settings. *American Journal of Community Psychology,* 1975, *3,* 335–351.

Roberts, K. H., Hulin, C. L., & Rousseau, D. M. *Developing an interdisciplinary science of organizations.* San Francisco: Josey-Bass, 1978.

Roberts, K. H., Walter, G. A., & Miles, R. E. A factor analytic study of job satisfaction items designed to measure Maslow need categories. *Personnel Psychology,* 1971, *24,* 205–220.

Ronen, S. Cross national study of employees work goals. *International Review of Applied Psychology,* 1979, *28,* 1–12.

Ronen, S., Kraut, A. I., Lingoes, J. C., & Aranya, N. A nonmetric scaling approach to taxonomies of employee work motivation. *Multivariate Behavioral Research,* 1979, *14*(4), 387–401.

Royce, J. R., & McDermott, J. A multidimensional system dynamics model of affect. *Motivation and Emotion,* 1977, *1,* 193–224.

Royce, J. R., & Powell, A. *Theory of personality and individual differences.* Englewood Cliffs, NJ: Prentice Hall, 1982.

Ruda, E. S. *The effect of interpersonal similarity on management performance.* Unpublished doctoral dissertation, Lafayette, IN: Purdue University, 1970.

Schmidt, F. L. Probability and utility assumptions underlying the use of the Strong Vocational Interest Blank. *Journal of Applied Psychology,* 1975, *59,* 456–464.

Schneider, B. Organizational climate: An essay. *Personnel Psychology,* 1975, *28,* 447–479.

Schneider, B. Person-situation selection: A review of some ability-situation interaction research. *Personnel Psychology,* 1978, *31,* 281–297.

Sells, S. B. An interactionist looks at the environment. *American Psychologist,* 1963, *18,* 696–702. (a)

Sells, S. B. (Ed.) *Stimulus determinants of behavior.* New York: Ronald, 1963. (b)

Sherif, M., & Sherif, C. W. *An outline of social psychology* (Rev. ed.). New York: Harper, 1956.

Shiflett, S., Eisner, E., & Inn, A. *The identification and measurement of military team functions using videotaped segments of team activities* (ARRO Final Report 3068). Washington, D.C.: Advanced Research Resources Organization, September 1981.

Shiflett, S., Price, S., & Schemmer, F. M. *Toward a taxonomy of team functions: Concepts, operations, and issues* (ARRO Interim Report 3068). Washington, D.C.: Advanced Research Resources Organization, April 1981.

Smith, P. C., Kendall, L. M., & Hulin, C. L. *The measurement of satisfaction in work and retirement.* Chicago: Rand McNally, 1969.

Stahl, R. J. *The domain of cognition: A useful model for looking at thinking and instructional outcomes.* Unpublished Report, Tempe, AZ: Arizona State University, 1979.

Stricker, L. J., & Ross, J. An assessment of some structural properties of the Jungian personality typology. *Journal of Abnormal and Social Psychology,* 1968, *68,* 62–71.

Strong, E. K. *The vocational interests of men and women*. Stanford University Press, 1946.

Taylor, L. R. *A quasi-actuarial approach to assessment*. Unpublished doctoral dissertation, Lafayette, IN: Purdue University, 1968.

Tenopyr, M. L., & Oeltjen, P. D. Personnel selection and classification. In M. R. Rosenzweig, & L. W. Porter (Eds.), *Annual Review of Psychology*, 1982, *33*, 581–618.

Terborg, J. R., Richardson, P., & Pritchard, R. D. Person-situation effects in the prediction of performance: An investigation of ability, self-esteem, and reward contingencies. *Journal of Applied Psychology*, 1980, *65*, 574–583.

Uttal, W. R. *A taxonomy of visual processes*. Hillsdale, NJ: Lawrence Erlbaum, 1981.

Ward, J. H., Jr., & Hook, M. E. Application of a hierarchical grouping procedure to a problem of grouping profiles. *Educational and Psychological Measurement*, 1963, *23*, 69–82.

Waters, L. K., & Roach, D. A factor analysis of need fulfillment exams designed to measure Maslow need categories. *Personnel Psychology*, 1973, *26*, 185–195.

White, S. E., & Mitchell, T. R. Organization development: A review of research content and research design. *Academy of Management Review*, 1976, *1*, 57–73.

Wiggins, J. S. A psychological taxonomy of trait-descriptive terms: The interpersonal domain. *Journal of Personality and Social Psychology*, 1979, *37*, 395–412.

Williams, J. B., & Spitzer, R. L. The issue of sex bias in DSM-III: A critique of "A women's view of DSM III" by Marcie Kaplan. *American Psychologist*, 1983, *38*, 793–799.

Woods, P. J. A taxonomy of instrumental conditioning. *American Psychologist*, 1974, 584–597.

CHAPTER 15

Conclusion

In this concluding chapter, we provide a brief recapitulation of our principal findings. Also, we examine the potential usefulness of research linking two of the taxonomic systems examined, and present some implications for future efforts.

Overview

We began by highlighting the need for taxonomic development in the field of human performance. After reviewing problems in contemporary human performance research and application, we described the scientific–theoretical and applied–practical benefits to be derived from the development of a classificatory scheme for the tasks that people perform. These needs and objectives provided a set of criteria against which to evaluate the utility of particular systems of task classification. We were able to show in later chapters, that some systems were more generally useful than others in meeting these criteria.

In Chapter 2, we reviewed the role of taxonomic development in science, with particular emphasis on concepts and methods that have possible application to such developments in the behavioral sciences. We distinguished the *science* of classification from the *role* of classification in the development of scientific areas, and we discussed basic taxonomic concepts. The role of taxonomic concepts in biology was given particular attention for lessons relevant to classification in psychology and to taxonomic efforts in the area of human performance. We then examined some earlier taxonomic developments in psychological science, particularly in the field of human learning, and described their implications for taxonomic development in the field of human performance. It was concluded that work on taxonomies to synthesize research information had a long history in the natural sciences, but only a short one in the behavioral sciences. The changing nature of the categories used in the field of learning, particularly the increasing fractionization of categories, suggests that a parallel result may be found in classificatory schemes attempting to describe human task performance. Such a finding has not inhibited theoretical and applied developments in other sciences and should not be discouraging to the behavioral scientist, because increased precision of description and prediction is a consequence.

Chapter 3 provided a more intensive treatment of a number of complex taxonomic issues related to the classification of human task performance. We examined different classificatory approaches taken and problems encountered in attempting to develop systems of classification for organizing and understanding information about performance on human tasks. The examination of past attempts to classify human performance provided some procedural guidelines for subsequent taxonomic efforts. Specifically, we described the issues that emerged from early attempts at human task classification, including the relationships identified between the purpose and content of the classification. Four bases for conceptualizing human tasks were described, leading to different task classifications and models for task classification. These conceptual bases are *behavior description* approaches (e.g., handling objects), *behavior requirements* approaches (e.g., scanning, coding), *ability requirements* approaches (e.g., spatial ability) and *task characteristics* approaches (e.g., type of display).

We turned next, in Chapter 4, to the methodological considerations involved in developing and evaluating classificatory systems. We made distinctions between various kinds of qualitative and quantitative classifications. The desirability of quantitative classifications was stressed and we described appropriate procedures for dealing with issues of reliability, similarity indexes, clustering, and validity evaluation. We concluded with a description of procedures and criteria to be used for evaluating the internal and external validity of such systems.

In Chapters 5, 6, and 7, we examined some specific descriptive and classificatory systems devised by various investigators. These were, in turn, classified according to the four primary conceptual bases identified in Chapter 3. Although the review of systems was conducted originally in the hope of finding classificatory systems on which to build, the schemes identified were found to be primarily descriptive in nature. Classificatory systems encompass description, but go beyond it by involving an explicit methodology for grouping units into categories (i.e., taxa) after a comparison of similarities and dissimilarities. The review of classificatory schemes in these chapters was not limited to those dealing only with tasks, but encompassed those systems attempting to classify jobs as well. Although only those schemes that were fairly well developed were included in this review, we found considerable variation in the degree of development and empirical evaluation in the schemes presented. In some cases, the available schemes were limited by one or more factors such as imprecise descriptors, little measurement capability, or insufficient development for application to real-world tasks. Other approaches, however, offered considerable potential for further development.

In Chapter 8, we established the linkage of data bases to the subject of taxonomy. On the one hand, classification assists in the organization, indexing, storage, and retrieval of information in the data base. On the other hand, the data base can be used to evaluate alternative provisional classificatory systems. The chapter described some basic concepts for the development of human performance data bases relevant to the use and evaluation of task classification systems. The issues include those involved in designing a suitable data base, as well as the manner in which these can be employed in evaluating the utility of taxonomic systems under development. We described a preliminary attempt to build a data base of previous research findings as a basis for evaluating if generalizations could be improved when the data on factors affecting human performance were reorganized according to different classes of tasks.

The next five chapters presented some new attempts at developing classificatory systems for describing human tasks carried out in a research program directed by Fleishman and his colleagues. Because the state-of-the-art review suggested no compelling reason to select one system over another for more intensive development, a variety of alternative systems was developed and evaluated for several basic and applied purposes.

Chapter 9 provided one prototype of how existing performance data can be used to evaluate a taxonomic system. The system evaluated was called the *Criterion Measures Approach*. The chapter illustrated some of the problems encountered in human performance data base development and application. The Criterion Measures Approach, based on work by Teichner and Olson, was used to classify tasks administered in research on learning (e.g., effect of schedules of practice), and in research on the effects of environmental factors (e.g., noise). Utilizing developed data bases, the results from these studies were summarized within the categories of tasks provided by the classificatory system. Encouraging results were obtained; it was possible to organize the literature on schedules of practice in terms of the system's categories. Different functions were obtained, depending on these task categories. For example, for simple coding tasks, performance change was a linear function of intertrial interval. For successive coding tasks, there was an increase in percent improvement with increased practice distribution, followed by a decrease. We concluded that, had the tasks been grouped without regard to the separate taxonomic categories, the functional relationships would have been obscured and few generalizations about performance would have been possible. Subsequently, the data base development used with the Criterion Measures Approach was extended into other areas of human performance. In spite of these encouraging applications, the Criterion Measures Approach has not yet been subjected to a comprehensive evaluation (e.g., there is need for evidence of reliability of its categories).

Chapter 10 presented the *Information–Theoretic Approach*, originally developed by Levine and Teichner. The approach is atypical in that it is deductive rather than inductive, deriving concepts and categories from a theoretical information-processing model before attempting to apply the approach to empirical observations. We summarized the classificatory scheme, including the definitions of key terminology; described the bases or dimensions for task classification; related the approach to information-processing theory and its formulas; presented methods for evaluating the viability of this system for classifying human tasks; and described practical applications of the approach. We concluded that the approach is potentially useful for solving an array of practical problems, including equipment design, selection procedures, and training development. The possibility of this approach encompassing other provisional classificatory approaches may be the scheme's greatest usefulness. However, although fairly elaborate plans have been made for a two-fold, iterative evaluation process involving theoretical (computer simulation) and empirical (series of experiments) activities, the evaluative work has not begun. We suggested that the theoretical model should be tested to determine if it has any empirical support.

Chapter 11 described the *Task Strategies Approach*, based on the work of R. B. Miller. After a summary of Miller's early conceptualization of the structure of a task, we discussed his transactional definition of a task, which became the cornerstone of the Task Strategies

Approach. The 24 task functions contained in his original "systems task vocabulary" were expanded and refined to include "work strategies." Chapter 11 described these representative work strategies for various task functions and demonstrated their applications within particular job contexts. After evaluating the Task Strategies Approach against the criteria presented in Chapter 4, we concluded that, although reliability evidence has not been presented and the categories (task functions) are neither mutually exclusive nor exhaustive, the scheme provides the needed match between specific categories and behavioral effects. Specifically, real-life examples of the translation of strategic principles associated with task functions into work strategies provide some evidence of the external validity of the system. The Task Strategies Approach also has utility in that it provides practical recommendations for the instructional design of training curricula to teach work strategies. We suggested that the system might gain greater acceptance once additional empirical data have been collected to demonstrate that the predicted work strategies do result in skilled performance in a real-world context.

The *Ability Requirements Approach,* described in Chapter 12, has received more extensive development and evaluation than any other approach. Factor-analytic studies form the initial bases for these ability dimensions. Chapter 12 briefly described this derivation and showed how these concepts have been useful in a variety of human performance areas. We discussed the considerable efforts to develop operational definitions of the abilities and techniques for evaluating their application to task description. We described in detail the scaling and rating instruments developed for translating task behavior into ability requirements, and we reviewed studies on the reliability and validity of these instruments. Findings to date show that it is possible to develop a set of reliable, ability-based scales for classifying tasks; these scales are useful in describing both laboratory and operational tasks. This measurement system was shown to have construct and empirical validity. For example, task ratings were found to be correlated with actual factor loadings of the abilities rated; and multiple regression analyses indicated that ratings of abilities required are significantly related to performance on the rated tasks.

The Ability Requirements Approach also was evaluated in terms of its capacity to reorganize areas of the human performance literature in meaningful ways. Thus, improved generalizations about factors affecting performance in long-term monitoring tasks were obtained when the data were replotted according to the ability categories of the tasks. Similarly, the literature on the effects of alcohol on performance, when recast in terms of the ability requirements of the tasks examined, showed improved generalizations about dosage and time course effects. The Ability Requirements Approach has also demonstrated considerable utility in diverse applied settings. These methods have been used as a method of job analysis, as a basis for setting standards for assessing job performance, for grouping jobs and tasks into families, and for selecting tests with criterion-related validity. They also have been used to set medical standards linked to ability requirements for physically demanding jobs. In general, the evidence on the utility of this approach is encouraging.

Chapter 13 described some extensions of the *Task Characteristics Approach* carried out by Farina and Wheaton, as well as some later research, bearing on the utility of this approach, conducted with Mirabella. The system classifies tasks in terms of descriptors that are independent of the characteristics of the human operator. They developed a model to characterize tasks in terms of the general components of goal, stimuli, responses, and their relations. Within these components, major subcomponents of a task were identified and treated as categories within which to devise task characteristic descriptors, such as response rate and variability of stimulus location. Each characteristic was cast into a rating scale format with task examples at defined anchor points. A variety of scales was developed and evaluated in a series of reliability and performance studies. In general, subsets of scales had adequate reliability and significant multiple correlations were obtained between task characteristic ratings and performance measures on a variety of tasks. A final interpretation of these findings must await further cross-validation. However, it appears possible to describe tasks in terms of a task characteristic language that is relatively free of the subjective and indirect descriptors found in many other systems. Task characteristics were shown to represent important correlates of learning and performance in simulator and field settings. Later, it was possible to describe subtle differences among tasks and to relate such differences systematically to skill acquisition, measures of transfer, and variations in performance. These later studies suggest that this approach may be useful, especially in training device development, and may offer a basis for defining "fidelity of simulation" in terms of the common task characteristics identified.

Finally, Chapter 14 reviewed recent taxonomic efforts in other fields of psychology. Examples were drawn from such fields as personality, social, organizational, and educational psychology. Although these examples, for the most part, are in an early stage of development, they demonstrate parallel concerns by researchers in these fields.

Our discussion has indicated that no single system for classifying tasks will be useful for all basic and applied problems. On the basis of current research evidence, the abilities approach seems to have been evaluated against more criteria and to have a wider variety of applications. Approaches such as task characteristics and task strategies seem more directly applicable to training and equipment design. However, it is too early to reach conclusions on the relative utility of different systems, due to the uneven nature of the developmental and evaluative efforts made thus far. Much of what we have presented represents prototype attempts or first efforts that need to be followed up or improved. The efforts described provide some guidelines for future research.

Linking Abilities and Task Requirements

In our discussion of the abilities approach, we indicated how the identification of abilities, through combinations of experimental and correlational research, integrates a great deal of information regarding commonalities in task characteristics. For example, the characteristics of tasks with operator requirements of Verbal Ability, Spatial Visualization, Response Orientation, and Multilimb Coordination are now well understood. We can make fairly good estimates of the ability requirements of tasks from specifications of task characteristics.

The Task Characteristics Approach is an attempt to develop a language to describe tasks independent of the human operator, and to quantify the degree to which tasks possess these characteristics. A long-range objective of our program is to develop more systematic relations between abilities and task characteristics (Fleishman, 1967, 1978). One of the conclusions drawn from our review of alternative classificatory approaches is that a system linking task characteristics and ability requirements may be particularly fruitful in achieving a fuller understanding of human task performance.

Other psychologists, notably Dunnette (1976) and Peterson and Bownas (1982), have called for similar linkages. Peterson and Bownas proposed that jobs be analyzed in terms of a *job requirements matrix*. Specifically, such a matrix contains rows defined by the categories of tasks and columns containing the categories for human attributes. Each cell of the matrix represents the degree to which the ability is required for performing the particular task. Peterson and Bownas suggest that the linkage of task and ability taxonomies is "necessary in order to produce an operationally useful job-requirements matrix" (p. 86). The authors believe that such a matrix, prepared for a wide assortment of task and ability categories, can make substantial contributions to personnel management activities, including performance enhancement and productivity improvement.

We have encouraging results from studies indicating that it is possible to build up a body of principles about interactions of task characteristics with ability requirements through experimental–correlational studies in the laboratory (e.g., see Fleishman, 1975). In this research paradigm tasks that can be varied along specified task dimensions are developed. The tasks are administered to groups of subjects who also receive a series of reference ability tasks that are known to sample certain more general abilities (e.g., Spatial Orientation, Control Precision). Correlations between these reference tasks and scores on variations of the criterion task specify the ability requirements (and changes in these requirements) as a function of task variations. We summarize the results of such studies carried out in several areas of human performance.

PSYCHOMOTOR PERFORMANCE

In an earlier study of psychomotor performance (see Fleishman, 1957), the task characteristic varied was the degree of display–control compatibility. Subjects were required to press a button within a circular arrangement of buttons on the control panel in response to particular lights that appeared in a circular arrangement of lights on a display panel. The correct button depended on the relative position of the light. Subjects performed under 7 different conditions in which the display panel was rotated from the standard position of 0°, to displacements of 45°, 90°, 135°, 180°, 225°, and 270°. These same subjects also performed on a series of spatial, perceptual, and psychomotor reference tests.

The results showed systematic changes in the ability factors sampled by the criterion task as a function of degree of rotation of the display panel, from the fully compatible (0°) condition. Progressive rotation of the display panel shifted the ability requirements from Perceptual Speed to two other factors, Response Orientation and Spatial Orientation. Perceptual Speed was measured in the upright and slight displacement conditions. The other abilities were measured at larger display rotations. Here, individual differences along known ability dimensions were used to explore the relations between changes in task dimensions and the characteristics of people who can perform the tasks most effectively. Of course, these are problems faced every day by personnel, training, engineering, and systems psychologists.

PERFORMANCE ON PERCEPTUAL TASKS

A later study (Wheaton, Eisner, Mirabella, & Fleishman, 1976) has taken us a step closer in applying this paradigm to an operational task. The task, which is involved in the job of Navy sonar operator, consisted of auditory signal identification. Subjects were to determine the identity of a variety of complex sounds representing various types of ships. Each time a signal was presented, subjects had to determine whether it belonged to a cargo ship, warship, submarine, or lightcraft.

Two task characteristics were selected for manipulation, signal duration and signal-to-noise ratio. Nine different task conditions were generated according to a factorial arrangement of these two variables. Stimuli were presented for either 9, 6, or 3 seconds, and under one of three signal-to-noise ratios. Background noise was set at −5 dB, 0 dB, or +5 dB referenced to the intensity of the signal to be identified. Each of the 9 different task conditions generated in this manner was represented by a tape containing 100 signals, 25 for each ship category. A battery of 24 specifically selected tests was administered to all subjects prior to their involvement in the auditory signal identification criterion task. The battery contained tests representing a variety of well-established factors in the perceptual and cognitive ability domains of performance.

Upon completion of the battery, and following extensive training in identifying the ship sounds, subjects performed under the nine different criterion task conditions. It was found that the two characteristics really made a difference in performance: as signal duration and signal–noise ratio increase, signal detection decreases. But what of the relation of the ability factors to these changes in task characteristics?

Of the five separate ability factors that were identified in the test battery, an Auditory Perceptual ability was found to be most related to criterion task performance. Within each signal duration, the loadings on this factor increased as background noise grew louder. The same was generally true within each level of background noise where loadings on the Auditory Perceptual factor increased in magnitude as signal durations grew shorter. In other words, the contribution of this ability to individual differences in performance increased as the criterion task became more difficult. There appeared to be two critical levels for each task dimension. Thus, signal duration could be decreased from 9 to 6 seconds without much change in the Auditory Perceptual ability requirement, but a further decrease to 3 seconds increased this ability requirement substantially. Furthermore, at this short signal level, an increase in background noise to equal intensity produced a further requirement for this ability, beyond which an additional increase in sound level produced little effect on the ability requirement. Knowledge of these task conditions allows us to be much more precise in specifying the ability requirements for effective criterion performance.

PERFORMANCE ON REASONING TASKS

Another study in this program involved the extension of this paradigm to cognitive or higher order reasoning tasks (Rose, Fingerman, Wheaton, Eisner, & Kramer, 1974). Specifically, representative tasks faced by electronic troubleshooters and maintenance personnel were examined. The criterion task was an analog of a faultfinding or troubleshooting situation. Working with wiring diagrams, the subjects' task was to determine which one of a number of possible breakpoints actually was faulty. Each wiring diagram contained a number of logic gates, switches, and probe points. The subjects tested the points by "placing a light bulb" at various points in the circuit and pressing a switch or combination of switches.

The basic task was varied along two dimensions, formal difficulty and perceptual complexity of the wiring diagram. Variations in formal difficulty involved increasing the number of possible breakpoints and the number of logic gates. Variations in perceptual complexity involved changing the perceptual organization of the circuits. For example, a first level of difficulty was a left to right circuit with no crossed wires; a second level rearranged the locations of the switches on the same circuit, creating several crossed wires; and the third level changed the locations of both the switches and the logic gates. Subjects were given training in the mechanics of using the diagrams to test for breakpoints.

The task was analyzed according to the abilities hypothesized to contribute to task performance. A comprehensive battery of 21 ability tests was selected and administered to all subjects, who then performed on the 18 troubleshooting problems in a replicated 3 × 3 design. The order of presentation was counterbalanced.

Without going into details of the results and the analyses, the ability Flexibility of Closure was found related to performance and increased in importance as difficulty increased on both dimensions. A Syllogistic Reasoning ability remained stable across conditions, whereas Associative Memory and Induction abilities dropped out, but at different levels of perceptual complexity.

PERFORMANCE ON CONCEPT-IDENTIFICATION TASKS

The final study in our laboratory (Fingerman, Eisner, Rose, Wheaton, & Cohen, 1975) extended this work to changes in the characteristics of concept identification tasks. Such tasks are prototype problem-solving tasks (for example, aircraft or ship identification), in which a large number of targets must be classified based on attributes such as track on a radar display, visual silhouette, or sound. The study involved the formation and testing of hypotheses in order to identify a classification rule. As in previous work, all subjects performed on the criterion task under varying conditions and also received a battery of selected reference ability measures.

The analysis was extremely complex, involving multiple criterion measures. Performance was found to be affected markedly by increases in the two task dimensions, perceptual complexity and formal difficulty. However, most of the variance in criterion task performance could be accounted for by four abilities: Associative Memory, Flexibility of Closure, Syllogistic Reasoning, and Induction. Perceptual Speed and Speed of Closure had insignificant relations. The involvement of the different abilities varied as a function of the task manipulation. For example, prediction of performance from the subjects' Associative Memory scores increased as task difficulty increased, but remained constant for different levels of perceptual complexity. These studies demonstrated empirically that the patterns of abilities related to criterion performance may undergo changes as specific characteristics of a task are manipulated systematically. The results of the research with the cognitive tasks confirm Fleishman's earlier findings with psychomotor and with perceptual tasks and extended the principles to more realistic job-related tasks. If one were to predict from these abilities which individuals would do well on these tasks, the choices would depend on task characteristics.

IMPLICATIONS FOR VALIDITY GENERALIZATION

In Chapter 2, we indicated that some recent research efforts by Schmidt, and Hunter, and their colleagues, (Schmidt, Gast-Rosenberg, & Hunter, 1980; Schmidt, & Hunter, 1977; Schmidt, Hunter,

Pearlman, & Shane, 1979; Schmidt, Hunter, & Pearlman, 1981) suggest that relationships between cognitive abilities and criterion variables can be generalized (across situations and across jobs) to a greater extent than previously believed possible. Tenopyr and Oeltjen (1982) noted that "while the equations associated with the validity generalization model have changed somewhat since 1977, and alternative equations have been proposed by Callender and Osburn (1980), the conclusions from applying the model have not been affected by the use of different equations . . . Most of the between-study variance of validity coefficients was found to be artifactual and due primarily to differences in sample size" (p. 598).

The theory of situational specificity states that a test valid for a job in one organization or setting may be invalid for the same job in another organization or setting. Schmidt and Hunter (1981a, 1981b) interpreted their validity generalization research as showing this theory to be false. The underlying assumption of validity generalization is that situational characteristics, including task requirements, do not moderate test validities. How can the apparently conflicting results of the validity generalization research be reconciled with the research just described indicating moderating effects of particular task characteristics or the relations between ability measures and performance?

One possible solution was suggested by Tenopyr and Oeltjen (1982). They stated, "Validity generalization and situational specificity are not mutually exclusive hypotheses. While there is sufficient reason to conclude that validities generalize across a variety of jobs, there is insufficient evidence to reject the possibility of situational effects on the size of the validity coefficients" (p. 598). As we mentioned earlier in Chapter 2, Fleishman's (1975, 1978) explanation for his findings was that when the researcher has better control over the measurement of the criterion performance, it is possible to show that different task requirements can moderate test validities. Tenopyr and Oeltjen (1982) consider this explanation a plausible hypothesis worthy of further study. Specifically, they stated, "It appears that criteria such as supervisory ratings, which are subject to a large general factor, may lead to extensive generalizability, whereas those criteria which are more focused upon specific aspects of job behaviors and results may be associated with more situational specificity of validity" (p. 599).

As long as improved predictions of performance can be obtained through an understanding of task requirements (such as those improvements demonstrated in the research summarized earlier in this section), it seems reasonable to proceed with efforts to develop taxonomic systems to categorize tasks in terms of those moderating requirements.

Concluding Statement

Our book serves as a primer on the state of the art of taxonomic efforts pertaining to human task performance. A number of psychologists have called for the development of a taxonomy of human performance to facilitate generalizations of research, but until recently results have been limited. There have been few systematic attempts at taxonomic development and, to our knowledge, no comprehensive summary describing and evaluating alternative classificatory schemes. This book has attempted to provide that summary.

The book offered the opportunity to bring together, in a single volume, relevant contributions from diverse fields within psychology. These include efforts from experimental psychology, personnel psychology, psychometrics, training research, and systems design. Although taxonomic effort in the behavioral sciences appears to be in its infancy, our review described a number of encouraging developments. Some recent attempts at developing classificatory schemes to describe human task performance have explored more intensively complex taxonomic issues such as the establishment of system objectives, appropriate subject matter and methodology, and criteria for the evaluation of classificatory schemes. Further, some approaches appear to be proceeding on a more empirical basis in their development and evaluation with increased attention to quantification (i.e., measurement of descriptors), reliability, validity, and utility. These encouraging trends need to be continued.

We urge behavioral scientists, researchers, and practitioners to confront the taxonomic problems of their discipline. It is a safe assumption that the world of human tasks is not impossibly diverse. We are encouraged that systems for classifying such tasks do improve our predictions and generalizations regarding human task performance. If nature is more complex than we would like it to be, we need to take steps to organize and conceptualize it in ways that will make it more manageable.

References

Callender, J. C., & Osburn, H. G. Development and test of a new model for validity generalization. *Journal of Applied Psychology*, 1980, 65, 543–558.

Dunnette, M. D. Aptitudes, abilities and skills. In M. D. Dunnette (Ed.), *Handbook of industrial and organizational psychology*. Chicago: McNally, 1976.

Fingerman, P. W., Eisner, E., Rose, A. M., Wheaton, G. R., & Cohen, F. *Methods for predicting job-ability requirements: III. Ability requirements as a function of changes in the characteristics of a concept identification task*. (AIR Tech. Rep. 75-4). Washington, D.C.: American Institutes for Research, April 1975.

Fleishman, E. A. Factor structure in relation to task difficulty in psychomotor performance. *Educational and Psychological Measurement*, 1957, *17*, 522–532.

Fleishman, E. A. Development of a behavior taxonomy for describing human tasks: A correlational-experimental approach. *Journal of Applied Psychology*, 1967, *51*, 1–10.

Fleishman, E. A. Toward a taxonomy of human performance. *American Psychologist*, 1975, *30*, 1127–1149.

Fleishman, E. A. Relating individual differences to the dimensions of human tasks. *Ergonomics*, 1978, *21*, 1007–1019.

Peterson, N. G., & Bownas, D. A. Skill, task structure, and performance acquisition. In M. D. Dunnette, & E. A. Fleishman (Eds.), *Human performance and productivity: Human capability assessment* (Vol. 1). Hillsdale, N.J.: Lawrence Erlbaum, 1982.

Rose, A. M., Fingerman, P. W., Wheaton, G. R., Eisner, E., & Kramer, G. *Methods for predicting job-ability requirements II. Ability requirements as a function of changes in the characteristics of an electronic fault-finding task*. (AIR Tech. Rep. 74-6). Washington, D.C.: American Institutes for Research, August 1974.

Schmidt, F. L., Gast-Rosenberg, I., & Hunter, J. E. Validity generalization results for computer programers. *Journal of Applied Psychology*, 1980, *65*, 643–661.

Schmidt, F. L., & Hunter, J. E. Development of a general solution to the problem of validity generalization. *Journal of Applied Psychology*, 1977, *62*, 529–540.

Schmidt, F. L., & Hunter, J. E. Employment testing: Old theories and new research findings. *American Psychologist*, 1981, *36*,(10), 1128–1137. (a)

Schmidt, F. L., & Hunter, J. E. New research findings in personnel selection: Myths meet realities in the '80s. *Public Personnel Administration—Policies and Practices for Personnel Service*, 1981, *261*, 431–434. (b)

Schmidt, F. L., Hunter, J. E., & Pearlman, K. Task differences as moderators of aptitude test validity in selection: A red herring. *Journal of Applied Psychology*, 1981, *66*, 166–185.

Schmidt, F. L., Hunter, J. E., Pearlman, K., & Shane, G. S. Further tests of the Schmidt-Hunter Bayesian validity generalization procedure. *Personnel Psychology*, 1979, *32*, 257–281.

Tenopyr, M. L., & Oeltjen, P. D. Personnel Selection and Classification. In M. R. Rosenzweig, & L. W. Porter (Eds.) *Annual Review of Psychology*, 1982, *33*, 581–618.

Wheaton, G. R., Eisner, E. G., Mirabella, G., & Fleishman, E. A. Ability requirements as a function of changes in the characteristics of an auditory signal identification task. *Journal of Applied Psychology*, 1976, *61*, 663–676.

APPENDIX A

Miller's Terminology: Definitions for the 25 Task Functions Involved in a Generalized Information-Processing System[1]

MESSAGE A collection of symbols sent as a meaningful statement

A pattern of input symbols[2] that is "meaningful" and purposeful in that it activates (or can activate) some processing capability of the system in generating a useful response.

The formal features of a message consist of a set (as "vocabulary") of *elements* and of the *pattern* (syntax, grammar) in which the elements are arranged.

1. The elements or symbol set consist of a limited number of "defined" terms.
2. The patterning of the symbols are grammatical rules for organizing them into meanings.

Example: In human discourse the message unit is the sentence. A sentence consists of words (elements) patterned by rules of grammar. The meaning of a sentence is based on both the words chosen and their grammatical arrangement. An operational message consists, in its simplest form, of subject, predicate, and object, as in: "store number 9 in cell 12."

---

[1]Adapted with permission from: (1) Miller, R. B. Development of a taxonomy of human performance: Design of a systems task vocabulary. (Tech. Rep. AIR-72 6/2035-3/71-TRII). Silver Spring, MD.: American Institutes for Research, March 1971; and (2) Miller, R. B. A method for determining task strategies (Tech. Rep. AFHRL-TR-74-26). Washington, D.C.: American Institutes for Research, May 1974.

[2]A *symbol* is a pattern of signals that can initiate or direct a given processing action.

In system behavior, a message about a state (or stimulus condition) must ultimately be linked to a response action or response decision. In other words, "data" must eventually be linked to an instruction for operating with or on the data.

What is "data" and what is "instruction" content in a message is relative, not absolute. It is relative to the operations performed with or on the message by the system.

In operational terms, the "meaning" of a message is identified by the response it can or does generate.

A message is the smallest conceptual unit of action that produces a system response that is useful to a user of the system. This is in contrast to a *signal*, which is defined as an instigator of action localized to one or more system components.

Pressing a machine STOP button introduces a message. In effect, the message is: "Whatever the present activity or the state of affairs right now (subject) stop (predicate) it (object)." The linkage from the STOP button to the stop controls contains the *context* of the message introduced by pressing the STOP button.

INPUT SELECT   Selecting what
                                                              to pay attention to next

Rules for admitting a message or message channel into the internal system.

These rules may include system turn-on and turn-off schedules, or power-up on input lines.

Input select rules may operate at the information source to compose a message eligible for entry into the systems according to criteria of (1) format, (2) content.

Examples

1. Polling procedures for accepting from an input channel
2. Rejection of message lacking preestablished fields of information
3. Rejection of message containing illegal symbols
4. Composing of source message for entry to system
5. Selective response to patterns of auditory input signals
6. Rejection of a given signal-to-noise relationship

Variables in Designing Input Select Rules

1. Physical mode of sensing: auditory, optical, mechanical, electronic
2. The symbol set or vocabularies permissible for acceptance
3. The grammar or syntax variables that structure symbols into words,

fields, stimulus (data) or response (instruction) and other format characteristics

4. Channels to be made available from sensor to processor–memory
5. Size of chunk of information acceptable at one time, for example, symbol, word, sentence, information field length

Principles

1. The fewer alternatives in message form (symbol set, formats, and length of message), the cheaper and faster to decide to accept or reject. The penalty for limited, standard messages comes from increased limitations in range of message content and increased effort to compose messages within the constraints.
2. The smaller the alternatives allowed in message options, the greater the number of messages that may have to be stored and collated if a meaningful system action requires more information than a single message can carry.
3. The greater the rigidity of message structure, the fewer the users and the smaller the range of users.
4. In summary, there tends to be a tradeoff between the ease of accepting the processing messages by a system and the ease of generating and composing messages from the information source.

FILTER   Straining out what does not matter

Procedures for reducing or eliminating irrelevance and disturbance from signals and messages.

Principle

Signal or message elements that do not serve a system purpose are costly to transmit, process, store, and retrieve, and can interfere in carrying out system purposes.

Comment

Major sources of irrelevance (and inaccuracy) are usually at the human input to information-processing. For this reason, attention to a discipline for input formats (language terms, syntax, and user concept of purpose) is perhaps the most important type of filtering device for a processing system. Some degree of redundancy usually helps the human in composing and checking his own output (which is also a message to himself). This redundancy may be filtered out by the nonhuman portions of the system to which it is a nuisance.

QUEUE TO CHANNEL   Lining up to get through the gate

Rules to organize random arrivals at one or more entrance gates into a waiting line.

Purpose of Queuing Rules

1. To attempt to minimize extreme fluctuations in length of waiting lines
2. To minimize delay in assigning processing priority if the priority is not based on serial order of arrival
3. To minimize conflicts among those in the waiting line
4. To sample from waiting lines at a rate that optimizes between:
   a. arrival frequencies and average waiting times
   b. length of input messages
   c. system response capabilities (throughout time)
   d. number of channels required for given population of demand

Note: Queuing rules interact with INPUT SELECT rules for the formatting of messages into the system. They may interact with rules for the formatting of output in real time systems in which an input channel is also an output channel.

Principles

1. If no user ever has to wait at all, the system is probably more expensive than it needs to be, or is underutilized.
2. Human users can accommodate their expectations of delay and delay probability in getting attention.
3. Humans with different kinds of purpose will tolerate different kinds of delay in getting attention.
4. Where possible, message priority should be established without having to process all the messages, and ideally would occur immediately when the message (or sender) joined the queue.
5. Unused channels should be switchable to overcrowded queue lines, but without jeopardizing relative positions in the waiting line. Thus, diverting the tail of queue to a new ticket booth is unfair to those forward of the break.
6. Any evaluation of throughput speed of a system should include waiting line statistics.
7. Humans are probably less patient in waiting for attention than in any other context.
8. Unless constrained or trained to do so, humans will not spontaneously organize themselves or their inputs into a serial order according to arrival.
9. If more than one equally accessible entrance gate is available, newcomers should be directed so that all wait lines are of equal length.

10. Qualify item 9 above as follows: specialize queues for long and short inputs. A short input will endure a longer line if it is perceived to move quickly. Average waiting time for short (or fragmentary) messages should be less than for long (or complete) messages.

DETECT   Is something there?

Procedures and mechanisms for sensing the presence or absence of a cue or condition requiring that some form of action should be taken by the system.

Detection requires the discrimination of an action-stimulating cue from some background of stimulation.

What is detected may consist of normal work cues, or of *exceptions* (such as errors). The source of these cues may be inputs to the system, or feedback from the monitoring of outputs. The sensing function does not analyze or classify the cue.

Note: Detecting, as defined here, is confined to a *sensing* operation, which excludes interpreting activities. In human terms, detecting results in sensing a stimulus to which attention will be paid. In many practical situations, however, detecting and identifying are a single process. (See IDENTIFY.)

Scanning and Detecting

Unless the sensor is a part of a fixed channel, it must scan segments of its environment so that the sensor is exposed to signals. The sensor is preset to respond to certain kinds of change or discontinuity in the field being scanned.

Principles

1. The response lag of the detecting device must be less than the cycle time of the stimulus to be detected.
2. The greater the contrast between the stimulus to be detected and its background, the greater the reliability of detection.
3. For given kinds of signal patterns to be detected, some scan patterns and frequencies are better than others.
4. In human behavior, what will be detected is related to "set" or pre-established tendencies to respond. More simply, we tend to notice what we expect to see, what we are looking for, or what we are attending to. A number of principles in addition to Item 2 influence human detection, as well as other sensing and perceptual behavior.[3]

---

[3]See the chapter on perception in any general psychology text.

Comment

In digital processing activities detect and IDENTIFY cannot be separated. But in analog activities a sensor may detect a pattern of frequencies representing a speaking voice, but not be able to identify it or its content.

SEARCH   Looking for something

Rules for selecting a set of entities for inquiry, for sequencing an inquiry among members of the set to be searched, and rules for applying criteria of "same" or "different" between the objective (search image) for searching and the objects in the search set being examined.

Selecting a Set of Entities for Inquiry

The set of entities for inquiry make up the "universe" to be searched, like the file room or file drawer in which a document is sought. The search request must contain or embody a code that identifies and subdivides the physical or logical universe to be searched.

Sequencing an Inquiry

The rule or principle for selecting for examination each next member or element in the searchable set. For example, this may be done by serial order, binary techniques, probability, recency of insertion to the file set, index linkages, and others.

Matching Search Image and Object Examined

The search image is by definition the necessary and sufficient information for establishing either "yes, this is the object I want in this search set" or "no, I don't want this object in this search set." The process of making this decision will consist of a set of rules for sequencing a pattern of steps for trying to match successive attributes of the search image with the object examined. Matching may be a step-by-step comparing of each attribute of the search image with the object examined, or simultaneously on the principle of an optical mask. Undoubtedly both principles require the support of an indexing structure.

Comment

The identity that is searched may be coded by location, relative position, or category code. The identity also may be based on one or more physical characteristics if the information is analog.

IDENTIFY   What is it and what is its name?

Methods for characterizing a message by type or by source.
In ordinary usage, to identify is to recognize an object or entity and apply
some label to it.

Thus: Identify a sender, a Type I instruction, a location, a previously received message.

Identification requires a referencing action. This action produces the name
or similar symbolic response to attach to the sensed input.

(In human behavior, the content of this symbolic response may not always
be explicit: you "recognize" an individual and treat him as a "recognized"
individual even though you don't recall his name or other explicit reference in your experience with him.)

In information-processing, two sets of reference codes may be necessary.
One reference structure may apply to the universe outside the processing
system (for example, the name and address of the sender of the message). The
other reference structure is to the physical (and/or functional) location of the
message as an identity within the system. These two identity codes may
require a set of cross-referencing rules or codes.

Principles

1. The identifying operation generally requires information in addition to
   that necessary for the detecting operation.
2. Once an identification is made, cues inconsistent with that identification tend to be ignored.
3. In human behavior, expectancies and recent experiences strongly influence how a set of cues will be "identified" even though inconsistent cues
   are present.
4. The labels making up an "identity" may consist of one or more of the
   following kinds of symbols:
   a. Arbitrary serial number (library accession number of books, street
      numbers on buildings, serial numbers starting from zero and pro-
      gressing continuously).
   b. Individual or class name (George Washington, emergency code,
      shelf number of library book, title of book).
   c. Combination of class identity and individual identity (social se-
      curity number, which contains region digits and individual's digi-
      ts; changed part number consisting of original part numbers plus
      suffix).

Note: the most efficient and unambiguous labeling or identity coding,
from the standpoint of symbols required in an open-ended acquisition series,
is by ordinal number. The code name given to each new acquisition is one

increment larger in the symbol series than the previous acquisition, as 1, 2, 3, . . . n.

An object or message may have two cross-referenced identifications: an accession code (which is unambiguous) and a content or attribute code based on its attributes. The latter has high probability of ambiguity, but may simplify preliminary phases of search in a file.

CODE   Translating the same thing
                                                  from one form to another

Encoding and decoding: rules for translating messages in one symbolic form to another symbolic form, presumably without loss of information content.

Example: The decimal number 12 coded as the binary number 1100.

Recording of messages standardizes their symbolic format so that they can be processed by a standard device and a standard instruction set.

Properties

1. Symbols are more readily (cheaply) checked and corrected automatically in some codes than in others.
2. A small variety of symbols may be compensated by a large number of symbol positions. Thus, there are 10 different decimal symbols, but only two binary symbols. On the other hand, the decimal 12 is expressed in two symbol positions (the tens position and the units position), whereas the binary expression of the decimal number 12 requires four positions.
3. Coding may apply to a symbol (m), a word (MILE), an expression (the miles from New York to Chicago), or a statement (the message went from New York to Chicago). Position information may be coded (18° latitude, 42° longitude), but always requires a position reference to be explicitly or implicity identified.
4. Recoding is often necessary when changing from one type of transmission medium to another.
5. Recoding can eliminate redundancy from a set of symbols (or a language) and thereby increase system efficiency. These gains are somewhat reduced by the cost of logic for the recoding operations.

INTERPRET   What does it mean?

Rules for translating the symbolic context of a message into a reference or meaning, usually by addition of reference context from within the message itself, or reference context outside the message itself.

Examples

1. Automatic analysis and "recognition" of an English word as a pattern contained in the physical wave form of an utterance.
2. Human conclusion that the unannounced approach of foreign aircraft, detected and identified on radar screens, means invasion and war.
3. Human conclusion that a given pattern of symptoms signifies that a system failure must be caused by a programming error rather than a machine failure.
4. Language translation from Greek to English expressions.

Note: Interpreting requires response to a pattern of cues, and applies to events on conditions that go beyond the input data (or symbols) as such. The input data are only a part of the total information required to make the interpretation. This differentiates interpretation from decoding.

An interpretation is an inference about a condition, or state of affairs, or source of data.

Process Variables

1. Degree of statistical certainty of correctness required of the interpretation.
2. Amount of redundancy in the form of context available in the message.
3. Range of variability among elements in the pattern to be determined.
4. Proportion of irrelevant transients in the message that act as noise to interpretation.
5. Number of elements sufficient and necessary to make matches with a reference set (or "dictionary") of meanings or interpretations.
6. Number of alternative meanings or identifications in the reference set available for trying to make matches.
7. Opportunity for interpreter to query message source for additional information for testing hypotheses about an interpretation.

CATEGORIZE   Defining and naming a group of things

Rules for classifying data, information, or intelligence according to its source, format, purpose, or content in order to organize messages into meaningful groups, or in order to selectively retrieve them for decision making and control.

Examples

1. All messages about John Doe are categorized (labeled) "John Doe" and go into the "John Doe file."

2. Data describing the functions of a system are classified as *"input," "processing,"* or *"output."*
3. "Age of applicant" data are entered in the third "field" in each applicant's record.

Categorical Structures

A set of categories may be in the form of a list where each member category is independent of every other member ("age, height, weight"). A set of categories may be arranged in trees or hierarchies: "safe drivers under 25 years of age, safe drivers over 25 years of age."

Ambiguity in Classifying

Classification rules are unambiguous only when the classification is based on some arbitrary counting of discrete units (e.g. men with 5 children) or natural dichotomies (e.g., males or females) or physical location (e.g., cell 121). Rules for classifying by attribute (blond vs. brunet) are always ambiguous in application.

Design Principle for Category Structure

An efficient category structure is one which permits the largest number of purposes for using an information file to be performed with the fewest decision operations in (1) classifying incoming messages for the file and (2) in searching the file for messages relevant to purposes.

This principle suggests that a classification scheme for information coming into a system should be designed around the categories of purpose and the options of control available in the system or subsystem. In short, develop categories around the ways you will use the information, not on the ways in which messages may differ from each other. Control options tend to be fewer than the variety of input conditions requiring a control decision that selects a control option.

Example

A given control switch can be set in either position A or position B. No matter what varieties of information come into this mechanism, there are *only two* valid and useful categories for this information: Category A that sets it in Position A and Category B that sets it in Position B. (The argument that a category exists which is information that interferes with these choices is irrelevant.)

Comment

The central design issue in any information-retrieval system is category structure, and the interaction between filing categories and searching categories.

TRANSMIT   Moving something from one place to another

Rules and conditions for transmitting a message from one location to another.

Serial versus Parallel Transmission

In serial transmission, message elements are transmitted one after another, such as the dots and dashes of Morse code. In parallel transmission, the message as a whole, or chunks of it, is transmitted at the same time, such as the optical projection of an entire image through a lens. In wire facilities, parallel transmission is faster but costs more in hardware.

Bandwidth

This is the rate at which discriminably different elements at the receiver can be transmitted through a medium. Bandwidth is a measure of channel capacity to transmit signals. (It is also a term sometimes used to describe a processing throughput rate.) Greater bandwidth usually requires higher dollar cost.

Open versus Closed Transmission Lines

An open line (also called "dial-up") is one which is continuously open to a message source for transmission. A closed line requires the sender to request to be switched to an open path, or to wait until a path is periodically opened to him.

Coding and Buffering

Long distance transmission often requires changes in the physical form of the message, and in transmission rate. These changes require coding and decoding logic and physical changes in the signal carrying the message.

Tradeoffs

1. Speed of transmitting input messages in segments of all-at-once is a tradeoff against facility costs.
2. Reduction in mean waiting time to send a message is bought at higher cost whenever there are queues.
3. Local processing with fewer and shorter messages to transmit versus centralized processing with heavy communication traffic and facilities.
4. Error detection and correction operations impose redundancy in message content and delay in transmission throughput.
5. Identification of message (and message segments) by physical or logical location of source versus by code identification transmitted with the message or message parts.
6. Time slicing with fixed message length and predictable time of transmission versus total message transmission regardless of length but un-

predictable time of initiating transmission of any given message from an origin.

7. Polling each of multiple source channels in sequence in order to determine if a source message awaits transmission versus demand for attention signals to the message link and queuing lines.

STORE   Keeping something intact for future use

Rules for where and how to hold messages for retrieval, including rules for filing and retrieval search. The contents of storage are data, programs, or combinations of both.

Essential Operations

1. Labeling the stored content by code or physical position
2. Determining units of physical store required by the stored content
3. Locating the physical place of available storage space
4. Loading the content into the physical storage
5. Safeguarding from physical deterioration
6. Identification of the stored content
7. Selective unloading of the stored content

Tradeoffs

1. In nonassociative memories, as memory size increases, the information required for identification of a storage cell (or content) may become greater than the information content of the cell.
2. *Serial* access to stored information (e.g., magnetic tape) is cheaper in storage cost per message, but more costly in search time than *random* access (e.g., magnetic core).
3. The savings in processing gained from tables of precalculated answers is offset by time to search the table and by the filling up of physical storage space.
4. Simplicity and reliability in filing a message or message content (such as by serial access number) is counterbalanced by complexity and unreliability in searching for the message content.

Associative and Nonassociative Memory

In a nonassociative memory, the *label* or name attached to a message for filing or retrieval has no meaningful relevance to the content of the message. The label may be an arbitrary cell number or position (e.g., "message number 1101").

In associative memory, the content of the message is, in part or in whole, the symbolic basis for filing and/or retrieving the message, (e.g., "message containing 'winning horse'").

In nonassociative memory, selection logic in search applies only to message labels. In associative memory, selection logic in search applies to message content.

SHORT-TERM MEMORY   Holding something temporarily

Rules for holding in temporary storage a message or parts of a message for use at a later time during a task cycle, or for combining with other information during the cycle.

Examples

1. A human typist reading a sentence and holding it in mind while her fingers key the symbols.
2. A register in a computer.
3. The retention of symbols or messages in a buffering device for translating into a different transmittal rate or frequency.

Operations

These are equivalent in principle to those in STORE.

Comments

1. The greater the number of channels, variables, codes, and chunks of information input that must be integrated in order to reach a decision or select a response, the larger the short-term storage that is needed. Human short-term memory is limited, but can be functionally increased by practice and by regularizing or formatting the input, by mnemonic aids, and by map-like job aids.
2. The greater the variations among message sizes and message rates of transmitted and processing data, the more important the design of short-term storage facilities to the efficiency of the total system (e.g., time-shared, remote terminals).
3. Information elements in short-term storage must be addressable as parts to the decision to be reached or problem to be solved. These addresses use up system channel capacity (or bandwidth). Some address codes will be more efficient, than others in a given system. (For humans, standard spatial patterns—map-like or chart-like—are good as a matrix for displaying elements of information as they arrive.)
4. Short-term memory may store partial solutions in heuristic, semi-algorithmic problem solving, or in trying out strategies (e.g., troubleshooting and other diagnosis, or in game playing). If the human must make judgments and intervene in further steps, the codes and pattern in which partial solutions are displayed will be critical to human effectiveness in participation.
5. In human behavior, unaided short-term memory is flexible but unreliable.

Note: The concept of short-term storage is among the highest in importance to human problem-solving capability. The computer in conversational mode can be a great aid to the human in retaining and effectively displaying short-term task information in tasks such as information searching, diagnosing, decision making, and constructing.

COUNT   Keeping track of how many

Identifying an entity or unit of something and incrementing or decrementing a storage and readable device by a unit of magnitude.
The definition may be expanded as follows:

1. The counter must sense the presence of the entity to be counted. (This might include specialized detecting and identifying mechanisms.) The presence or absence of the entity or characteristic of the entity must be all-or-none.
2. Incrementing or decrementing some numerical value, which could be zero.
3. Storing the new count.
4. Displaying the count to a mechanism which reads it in order to fulfill some purpose of the system. The reading mechanism may be human or machine.
5. Resetting the counter when a new counting cycle is initiated. If the counter is not reset, a log must be kept of the count when a new cycle is entered.

COMPUTE   Figuring out a logical/mathematical
                                            answer to a defined problem

Rules for solving arithmetic and mathematical problems involving numerical data, or the logical reduction of logical statements (equations).

Comment

Any class of computation problems can be solved by a large variety of equally valid patterns of logical manipulation. The general tradeoff is space (number of channels holding and processing in parallel) versus time (number of operations performed in series). Computation requires both short-term memory (intermediate results) and long-term memory (sequence of logical instructions).

Operational Tradeoffs

1. Computing an answer by logical means versus obtaining the answer from a table in storage

2. Digital computation (counting) versus analog computation (adding or subtracting physically continuous properties, such as voltages)
3. Various specific mechanisms for given logical operations and few program instructions versus general purpose logical mechanisms and many program instructions
4. Parallel computing operations (with high speed but more facilities) versus serial computing operations (with lower speed and less facilities required)
5. Higher speed from local short-term storage of intermediate results (more facilities) versus lower speed by storing and retrieving intermediate results in long-term memory (fewer facilities)

PLAN   Matching resources in time to expectations

Rules for predicting what future sets of conditions will occur and what responses to make to them and in what order.

Planning is a subset of decision making.

Functions in Planning

1. Predicting the future, by using historical and present information to anticipate which of a set of alternative states will occur at some future moment or time interval
2. Exercising priority rules for determining which of several anticipated states to give priority of attention
3. Determining the set of response capabilities required for effective response to the expected condition or state
4. Scheduling the resource for making the response so that the resource is available when the expected condition occurs

Summary

The planner combines the functions of predictor, resource selector, and resource scheduler.

TEST   Is it what it should be?

Rules and procedures for deciding on the integrity of (1) a signal, (2) a message, (3) a mechanism.

A Signal Test is made as follows:

1. Sensing and measuring one or more attributes of the test signal
2. Comparing these measurements with a set of normative or reference values

3. Deciding whether the test signal fell within the prescribed tolerances for that signal
4. An indication of that decision

Note: A "mask" may be used to compare several variables in the signal set at one time.

A Message Test consists of:

1. Identifying the class of message
2. Deciding whether its contents do or do not match, according to:
   a. the reference set of symbol elements
   b. rules for combining symbol elements into words
   c. format rules for combining words into messages.

Note: Tests for the validity of the "meaning" or content of a message must be made in a context of "meaning" references. Ordinarily this requires a redundant expression of the message. A check and confirmation with the source is an example of such redundancy.

A Test of a Mechanism requires:

1. A controlled or known signal or signal pattern as input to a mechanism
2. Measurement of relevant characteristics of the corresponding output of the mechanism
3. A comparison of the input–output relationship with a set of reference values prescribed for that relationship
4. A decision as to whether or not the actual output falls within the prescribed tolerance limits

Note: A test may also be a decision based on a comparison of outputs from redundant mechanisms that use the same input.

CONTROL   Changing an action according to plan

Physical Control

Changing the direction, rate, or magnitude of a physical force that may be acting on objects, processes, or symbols. The stimulus may be embedded in a fixed serial order, or it may consist of feedback Test Signals.

Physical control is observed in the human nerve and muscle that manipulates a tool, in the electromagnetic yoke which directs the electron beam in a cathode ray tub.

Symbolic Control

The source of instructions as to what will be done next with what facility. Symbolic control appears when an instruction in a computer program reads and interprets an input message and, despite competing claims for a particular input channel, opens that channel to more messages from the source of that input message. Control resides in that instruction, in the location that holds that instruction, and in the physical mechanism that executes the command contained in that instruction.

Factors in the Process of Control

1. A signal of status based either an instruction count, or on test feedback
2. A decision or other selection mechanism for eliciting an instruction
3. The instruction that directs a change in some set of physical behaviors
4. The mechanism which converts the instruction into a physical action or initiates a train of physical actions
5. The jurisdiction (set) of physical actions which can be physically modified at some time by the instruction and its location

Note: The concept of control includes the function of coordination in time and space according to plan.

Feedback control implies both a monitoring–testing and an executive function.

EDIT   Arranging things according to rules

Rules for arranging information (or symbols) into a message according to prescribed formats.

Editing may have as its purpose the structuring of data or information for machine handling purposes or for human handling purposes.

Examples

1. Suppressing nonsignificant zeros
2. Breaking a chain of symbol elements into component strings
3. Arranging a listing of bookkeeping data into a display of rows and columns according to tabs and headings
4. Correcting a misspelled word or ungrammatical sentence

Note: Editing changes elements in the structure but not the operational content of a message, nor the symbol set by which the message is expressed.

DISPLAY   Showing something that makes sense

Arranging messages into a prescribed format and symbology for human perception and interpretation.

A convenient, but by no means exhaustive, distinction at a primitive level may be made between displays in symbolic forms such as:

1. Signals, such as a flashing light associated with a label or spatial position
2. Alphanumerics, such as words, phrases, and sentences in English
3. Graphics, such as pictures, maps, charts, and graphs

PURGE   Getting rid of the dead stuff

Rules for eliminating unwanted information from storage.

Example

All files except those marked with an asterisk, will be thrown out upon reaching their tenth year.

Requirement for Purging

As new messages arrive, storage space is used up and search time is increased. Methods for systematically clearing storage are therefore essential.

Purging Policy

Aside from the special case of legal requirements, files or messages are discarded when the probability of referring to them goes below some value, or when the importance of finding them shrinks to some value less than the cost of maintaining the message or file in a given medium.

Purging policy may specify how purged messages are to be abstracted and retained in condensed form, or statistically summarized and retained as a summary.

Purging policy may specify exceptions, and how exceptions to purging rules will be identified and treated.

Comment

Humans tend to be irrationally reluctant to discard their files except under conditions of space crisis or other pressure, and then they may be equally irrational in what they discard. Purging policy is a planned discipline against these tendencies.

RESET   Getting ready for some different action

Purging an old context of status and readiness in order to respond by substituting a new context of status and readiness.

Examples

A clock completes timing the runners in a foot race and is reset to zero in readiness for the next race. In another example, an English-speaking person is addressed in French and shifts his language context and speech patterns into French.

The reset operation is meaningless except as preparation for a new action context. It is therefore necessary for the system to identify the new context to which the reset is relevant. The mere return to zero of an indicator or control is irrelevant to a concluded action, but relevant to some next action.

Reset of Short-Term Memory

This is equivalent to turning the clock or indicator back to a zero setting in preparation for a new cycle or context of system action.

Reset of Instruction Readiness

A reset may include any changed readiness of a mechanism to respond. Thus, a new instruction set loaded into active memory and controls is a reset operation by this definition. The human who shifts from speaking English to speaking French has had a reset operation.

Note: The concept of reset makes the term "set" unnecessary. After the first occasion on which a mechanism is set, it can only be reset. Note that the expression set is used in the sense of "prepare."

DECIDE/SELECT   Choosing a response to fit the situation

Rules for selecting a response alternative to given states of affairs. Conceptually, the simplest decision mechanism is a two-way switch in which the input may be in one of two relevant states, each of which selects a response alternative.

In symbolic behavior, an operation implicit in a hardware mechanism must be a "compare" action. The decision results from the comparison of one or a set of input states, with reference criteria for each of a set of response alternatives. When a match is found between the input conditions and the criteria for a response alternative, that response is selected and the alternatives rejected.

Human decision making requires an extended analysis.

The variables of the "input state" consist of

+   goal variables and priorities
+   situation variables and their data content

The output variables are characterized by

+   the set of response alternatives and their respective implications

Another kind of information in probabilistic or ambiguous situations consists of

+   strategy rules for selecting a response alternative from any given
    input state

A strategy rule seeks the best fit between a "profile" of needs expressed in a
problem statement and the "profile" of capabilities of each of the response
alternatives.

Note: The term SELECT has the same operational meaning as DECIDE,
although its connotation emphasizes the executive action implied by the
choice reached in a decision.

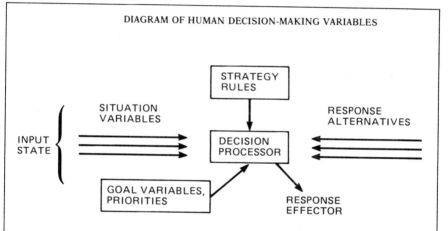

DIAGRAM OF HUMAN DECISION-MAKING VARIABLES

DIFFICULTIES IN HUMAN DECISION MAKING

Input State

1. Input variables are incomplete or include irrelevant variables.
2. Classification structure of input variables is inappropriate to this problem (potentially relevant information cannot be labeled properly).
3. Information is absent on one or more variables.
4. Information on various input variables arrives out of time phase.
5. Input noise disturbs the perception of relevant signals.
6. The meaning of the situation is not adequately interpreted (failure to
   organize data about the situation variables as a whole or pattern).

Goal Variables, Priorities

1. Goal variables are inadequately defined.
2. Incompatible priorities exist among goal variables.

Response Alternatives

1. The set of alternatives recognized is inadequate.
2. The definition and classification of alternatives is inadequate.
3. The premises for combining or compromising alternatives are inappropriate.
4. The data on consequences of respective response alternatives in this kind of situation are inadequate.

Strategy Rules

1. Processor is unable to identify and select appropriate strategy rule.
2. Strategy rules conflict.
3. No strategy rule is available for this combination of situation and recognized response alternatives.

Decision Processor

1. Short-term memory (buffer) is insufficient.
2. Logical capability to process all the data is inadequate.

Response Effector

1. No channel exists for transmitting or executing the chosen response.
2. There is no appropriate message code for converting output response into control behavior.

ADAPT/LEARN   Making and remembering new responses
                                          to a repeated situation

Structural modification of the behavior of a system as the result of experience, where the behavior change carries over from one cycle of operation to another.

A learned act requires that: Response B becomes substituted for Response A to Situation X, and that when Situation X recurs, Response B will tend to recur rather than the old Response A. The information handling process must account both for the acquisition and substitution of Response B for A when Situation X occurs, and also for its retention and recurrence when Situation X recurs.

Information Handling Requirements

1. A transcript of the effective stimulus in the situation
2. A transcript of the goal sought or intent realized in the situation
3. A transcript of the original response that was made
4. A record of the consequence of that response

5. Some record of a "corrective" response or hypothesis for a corrective response
6. An associative link between (1) a mechanism for recognizing the old stimulus in a new operational cycle and (2) the "corrected" response— i.e., a mechanism for superseding the old maladaptive response to the stimulus and goal

Process Paradigm of Structural Adaptation or Learning

1. A combination of need and environmental state elicit R_A (R_A has been previously "learned" to this situation).

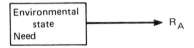

2. The consequence of R_A fails to satisfy the need.

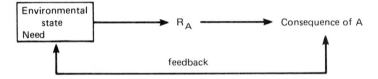

3. Response A is extinguished and Response B in the device's repertory is substituted. The consequence of Response B does reduce the need.
4. The adaptive device substitutes the linkage or Response B to this need and environmental state in its memory.
5. The environmental state and need recur on a later occasion. The device *identifies* the recurrence of the old stimulus and the old need. Assume the linkage or R_B has been effectively stored. Response B is emitted. Learned behavior is demonstrated.

GOAL IMAGE   A picture of a task well done

The operator's goal image embodies criteria for terminating a task or segment of work or mission with an experience of some degree of success or failure. The goal image is a mental picture of the conditions that should obtain when a task cycle is completed. Different goal images may apply to different levels of work activity. The goal image serves as both a steering and power reference for moving from a present state of affairs into and through a projected route of action. Goal information is meaningful operationally insofar as the behavior of the system is not rigidly programmed, that is, when the system has options for activity in mind and amount.

Behavior tendencies include the following. The student initially may be preoccupied by learning procedures and operations, rather than goals and goal variables. With increasing degrees of practice, what may once have been a clear goal image deteriorates, especially under stress and fatigue and from repetition. A high degree of routinization induces the emitting of chains of behavior in an automatic fashion.

When loss of goal image may be maladaptive, the operator can postpone deterioration by maintaining a continuously higher level of aspiration than his performance level. Training strategy obviously should emphasize and test the student's acquisition of goal variables and images of goal states that are realistic and reasonable for aspiration. The training situation also may demonstrate concrete instances of goal states that barely are acceptable (for given sets of circumstances), as well as goal states that barely are unacceptable. It is insufficient to limit these demonstrations merely to the orientation stages of training; they must be frequently reintroduced even into the mastery stages of student skill.

If the student is instructed in the tolerance ranges of goal variables, and if he is in the cognitively active mode, he can interpret task feedback and, thus instruct himself. But requires direction, opportunity, and encouragement. Ideally, the student will continue this activity after he terminates formal training.

To the extent that the operator has a clear picture of goal states, and is guided and driven by them, he has a basis for rational control over his own emotional impulses and his own tendencies for the expedience of the moment. The active control of a powerful goal image may enable the operator better to withstand the stress, including periods of boredom. The indoctrination and refurbishing of the subjective goal image, therefore, has a continuing strategic value for operator performance.

Although these comments about goal image are self-evident, generally they seem not to be put into serious practice by managers or by specialists in the training and educational arts. Mechanized training procedures especially are prone to skip adequate training in purpose, goal image, and goal criteria, perhaps because they assume that the student, as a passive mechanism, can acquire these implicitly when he learns procedures and task formats.

In conclusion, the strategic objective for training the student in goal images and goal criteria is to make him cognitively active and aggressive as an operator. Otherwise, he might be limited to passively emitting chains of responses that have been programmed into him. The operational "liability" is that he may be less docile to arbitrary external control. This liability will be counterbalanced by his more effective capability for behavioral change that will be required either because of new operational goals or because of new operational conditions.

APPENDIX B

Updated Definitions for the Ability Categories in Recent Forms of the Manual for the Ability Requirements Scales (MARS)[1]

1. *Oral Comprehension* is the ability to understand spoken English words and sentences.

2. *Written Comprehension* is the ability to understand written sentences and paragraphs.

3. *Oral Expression* is the ability to use English words or sentences in speaking so others will understand.

4. *Written Expression* is the ability to use English words or sentences in writing so others will understand.

5. *Fluency of Ideas* is the ability to produce a number of ideas about a given topic.

6. *Originality* is the ability to produce unusual or clever ideas about a given topic or situation. It is the ability to invent creative solutions to problems or to develop new procedures to situations in which standard operating procedures do not apply.

7. *Memorization* is the ability to remember information, such as words, numbers, pictures, and procedures. Pieces of information can be remembered by themselves or with other pieces of information.

8. *Problem Sensitivity* is the ability to tell when something is wrong or is likely to go wrong. It includes being able to identify the whole problem as well as the elements of the problem.

[1]Adapted with permission from (1) Fleishman, E. A. *Development of ability requirements scales for the analysis of Bell System jobs.* Bethesda, MD.: Management Research Institute, 1975; (2) Fleishman, E. A. & Hogan, J. C. A taxonomic method for assessing the physical requirements of jobs: The physical abilities analysis approach (ARRO Final Report 3012/R78-7). Washington, D.C.: Advanced Research Resources Organization, June 1978; (3) Hogan, J. C., Ogden, G. D., & Fleishman, E. A. *Assessing physical requirements for establishing medical standards in selected benchmark jobs* (ARRO Final Report 3012/R78-8). Washington, D.C.: Advanced Research Resources Organization, June 1978; and (4) Schemmer, F. M. *Development of rating scales for selected visual, auditory and speech abilities* (ARRO Final Report 3064). Washington, D.C.: Advanced Research Resources Organization, June 1982.

9. *Mathematical Reasoning* is the ability to understand and organize a problem and then to select a mathematical method or formula to solve the problem. It encompasses reasoning through mathematical problems to determine appropriate operations that can be performed to solve problems. It also includes the understanding or structuring of mathematical problems. The actual manipulation of numbers is not included in this ability.

10. *Number Facility* involves the degree to which adding, subtracting, multiplying, and dividing can be done quickly and correctly. These can be steps in other operations like finding percentages and taking square roots.

11. *Deductive Reasoning* is the ability to apply general rules to specific problems to come up with logical answers. It involves deciding if an answer makes sense.

12. *Inductive Reasoning* is the ability to combine separate pieces of information, or specific answers to problems, to form general rules or conclusions. It involves the ability to think of possible reasons for why things go together.

13. *Information Ordering* is the ability to follow correctly a rule or set of rules to arrange things or actions in a certain order. The rule or set of rules used must be given. The things or actions to be put in order can include numbers, letters, words, pictures, procedures, sentences, and mathematical or logical operations.

14. *Category Flexibility* is the ability to produce many rules so that each rule tells how to group a set of things in a different way. Each different group must contain at least two things from the original set of things.

15. *Speed of Closure* involves the degree to which different pieces of information can be combined and organized into one meaningful pattern quickly. It is not known beforehand what the pattern will be. The material may be visual or auditory.

16. *Flexibility of Closure* is the ability to identify or detect a known pattern (like a figure, word, or object) that is hidden in other material. The task is to pick out the disguised pattern from the background material.

17. *Spatial Orientation* is the ability to tell where you are in relation to the location of some object or to tell where the object is in relation to you.

18. *Visualization* is the ability to imagine how something will look when it is moved around or when its parts are moved or rearranged. It requires the forming of mental images of how patterns or objects would look after certain changes, such as unfolding or rotation. One has to predict how an object, set of objects, or pattern will appear after the changes are carried out.

19. *Perceptual Speed* involves the degree to which one can compare letters, numbers, objects, pictures, or patterns, quickly and accurately. The things to be compared may be presented at the same time or one after the other. This ability also includes comparing a presented object with a remembered object.

20. *Control Precision* is the ability to move controls of a machine or vehicle. This involves the degree to which these controls can be moved quickly and repeatedly to exact positions.

21. *Multilimb Coordination* is the ability to coordinate movements of two or more limbs (for example, two arms, two legs, or one leg and one arm), such

as in moving equipment controls. Two or more limbs are in motion while the individual is sitting, standing, or lying down.

22. *Response Orientation* is the ability to choose between two or more movements quickly and accurately when two or more different signals (lights, sounds, pictures) are given. The ability is concerned with the speed with which the right response can be started with the hand, foot, or other parts of the body.

23. *Rate Control* is the ability to adjust an equipment control in response to changes in the speed and/or directions of a continuously moving object or scene. The ability involves timing these adjustments in anticipating these changes. This ability does not extend to situations in which both the speed and direction of the object are perfectly predictable.

24. *Reaction Time* is the ability to give one fast response to one signal (sound, light, picture) when it appears. This ability is concerned with the speed with which the movement can be started with the hand, foot, or other parts of the body.

25. *Arm–Hand Steadiness* is the ability to keep the hand and arm steady. It includes steadiness while making an arm movement as well as while holding the arm and hand in one position. This ability does not involve strength or speed.

26. *Manual Dexterity* is the ability to make skillful coordinated movements of one hand, a hand together with its arm, or two hands to grasp, place, move, or assemble objects like hand tools or blocks. This ability involves the degree to which these arm–hand movements can be carried out quickly. It does not involve moving machine or equipment controls like levers.

27. *Finger Dexterity* is the ability to make skillful, coordinated movements of the fingers of one or both hands and to grasp, place, or move small objects. This ability involves the degree to which these finger movements can be carried out quickly.

28. *Wrist–Finger Speed* is the ability to make fast, simple repeated movements of the fingers, hands, and wrists. It involves little, if any, accuracy or eye–hand coordination.

29. *Speed of Limb Movement* involves the speed with which a single movement of the arms or legs can be made. This ability does not include accuracy, careful control, or coordination of movement.

30. *Selective Attention* is the ability to concentrate on a task one is doing. This ability involves concentrating while performing a boring task and not being distracted.

31. *Time Sharing* is the ability to shift back and forth between two or more sources of information.

32. *Static Strength* is the ability to use muscle force in order to lift, push, pull, or carry objects. It is the maximum force that one can exert for a brief period of time.

33. *Explosive Strength* is the ability to use short bursts of muscle force to propel oneself or an object. It requires gathering energy for bursts of muscle effort over a very short time period.

34. *Dynamic Strength* is the ability of the muscles to exert force repeatedly

or continuously over a long time period. This is the ability to support, hold up, or move the body's own weight and/or objects repeatedly over time. It represents muscular endurance and emphasizes the resistance of the muscles to fatigue.

35. *Trunk Strength* involves the degree to which one's stomach and lower back muscles can support part of the body repeatedly or continuously over time. The ability involves the degree to which these trunk muscles do not fatigue when they are put under such repeated or continuous strain.

36. *Extent Flexibility* is the ability to bend, stretch, twist, or reach out with the body, arms, or legs.

37. *Dynamic Flexibility* is the ability to bend, stretch, twist, or reach out with the body, arms and/or legs, both quickly and repeatedly.

38. *Gross Body Coordination* is the ability to coordinate the movement of the arms, legs, and torso together in activities in which the whole body is in motion.

39. *Gross Body Equilibrium* is the ability to keep or regain one's body balance or to stay upright when in an unstable position. This ability includes maintaining one's balance when changing direction while moving or standing motionless.

40. *Stamina* is the ability of the lungs and circulatory systems of the body to perform efficiently over long time periods. This is the ability to exert oneself physically without getting out of breath.

41. *Near Vision* is the capacity to see close environmental surroundings.

42. *Far Vision* is the capacity to see distant environmental surroundings.

43. *Visual Color Discrimination* is the capacity to match or discriminate between colors. This capacity also includes detecting differences in color purity (saturation) and brightness (brilliance).

44. *Night Vision* is the ability to see under low light conditions.

45. *Peripheral Vision* is the ability to perceive objects or movement towards the edges of the visual field.

46. *Depth Perception* is the ability to distinguish which of several objects is more distant from or nearer to the observer, or to judge the distance of an object from the observer.

47. *Glare Sensitivity* is the ability to see objects in the presence of glare or bright ambient lighting.

48. *General Hearing* is the ability to detect and to discriminate among sounds that vary over broad ranges of pitch and/or loudness.

49. *Auditory Attention* is the ability to focus on a single source of auditory information in the presence of other distracting and irrelevant auditory stimuli.

50. *Sound Localization* is the ability to identify the direction from which an auditory stimulus originated relative to the observer.

51. *Speech Hearing* is the ability to learn and understand the speech of another person.

52. *Speech Clarity* is the ability to communicate orally in a clear fashion understandable to a listener.

Tasks Representing Different Ability Categories[1]

Selected ability–task items	Mean	Standard deviation
1. Oral Comprehension		
Understand a lecture on navigating in space.	6.28	.75
Understand instructions for a sport.	3.48	1.09
Understand a McDonald's hamburger commercial.	1.17	.60
2. Written Comprehension		
Understand an instruction book on repairing a missile guidance system.	6.68	.77
Understand an apartment lease.	4.14	1.43
Read a road map.	1.21	1.50
3. Oral Expression		
Give a talk on a technical subject before a professional society using new concepts.	6.24	.91
Give directions to a motorist so that he can reach his destination.	3.72	.99
Cancel newspaper delivery by phone.	1.69	1.34
4. Written Expression		
Write an instruction book for computer systems.	6.84	1.18
Write a job recommendation for a subordinate.	3.76	1.18
Write a note to remind someone to take something out of the freezer to thaw.	1.13	.35
5. Fluency of Ideas		
Name all the possible problems that might occur with a space launch.	6.59	1.02
Think of as many new ideas as possible for the name of a new research firm.	3.59	1.38
Name four brands of toothpaste.	1.66	1.26

(continued)

APPENDIX C *Continued*

Selected ability–task items	Mean	Standard deviation
6. *Originality*		
Invent a new synthetic fiber.	6.28	.84
Make job tasks more interesting for subordinates.	4.41	1.27
Use a credit card to open a locked door.	1.97	1.02
7. *Memorization*		
Memorize the Gettysburg address after studying it for 15 minutes.	5.86	1.25
Memorize the pledge to the flag.	2.55	1.35
Memorize the number on your bus to be sure you get back on the right one.	1.18	.81
8. *Problem Sensitivity*		
Recognize an illness at an early stage of a disease when there are only a few symptoms.	5.62	1.50
Recognize from the mood of prisoners that a riot is likely to occur.	3.86	1.60
Recognize that an unplugged lamp won't work.	1.31	.97
9. *Mathematical Reasoning*		
Determine mathematics for simulating a lunar approach and landing.	6.83	.60
Decide how to calculate profits to determine size of Christmas bonuses.	4.17	1.31
Decide how much 10 oranges will cost when they are 2 for 29¢.	1.41	.63
10. *Number Facility*		
Compute interest payment which should be generated from investment.	4.59	1.57
Reconcile checking account monthly statement.	2.72	.88
Add 2 and 7.	1.03	.19
11. *Deductive Reasoning*		
Design an aircraft wing using the principles of aerodynamics.	6.21	.98
Decide what factors to consider in selecting stocks.	4.86	1.16

APPENDIX C *Continued*

Selected ability–task items	Mean	Standard deviation
Know that you can coast down the hill due to the law of gravity when you've run out of gas.	1.55	.87
12. *Inductive Reasoning*		
Diagnose a disease utilizing knowledge from many lab tests.	5.03	1.74
Interpret a weather chart.	3.52	1.57
Order a seafood platter at a restaurant to determine whether or not you like seafood.	1.79	.90
13. *Information Ordering*		
Determine the appropriate sequence of checkout procedures for the Apollo rocket.	6.75	.52
Arrange five sentences into a paragraph that makes sense.	3.21	1.26
Put things in numerical order.	1.32	1.16
14. *Category Flexibility*		
Classify synthetic fibers in terms of their strength, cost, elasticity, melting points, etc.	5.86	1.18
Classify flowers according to size, color, odor, and uses.	3.43	1.67
Sort nails in a tool box on the basis of length.	1.71	1.15
15. *Speed of Closure*		
Interpret the patterns on the weather radar to decide if the weather is changing.	5.14	1.41
Find five camouflaged birds in a picture.	4.41	1.50
While listening to the radio, recognize and start to hum an old song after hearing only the first few lines.	2.69	1.61
16. *Flexibility of Closure*		
Receive high speed Morse code in presence of similar background signals.	6.14	1.03
Look for a golf ball in the rough.	4.03	1.27
Find a steak knife in a utensil drawer.	1.83	.93

(*continued*)

APPENDIX C *Continued*

Selected ability–task items	Mean	Standard deviation
17. *Spatial Orientation*		
Be aware of your orientation upon awakening in a gravity-free environment, like a spacecraft.	5.71	1.12
While lost in a rural area, locate your position on a road map.	4.32	1.49
Find your way through a familiar room when lights are out without bumping into anything.	3.36	1.37
18. *Visualization*		
Anticipate your opponent's as well as your own future moves in a chess game.	6.00	.94
Know how to cut and fold a piece of paper to make a cube.	4.21	1.50
Imagine how to put paper in the typewriter so the letterhead comes out at the top.	1.46	.69
19. *Perceptual Speed*		
Inspect assembled electrical components for defects as they flow by on a fast-moving assembly line.	5.31	1.19
Read 5 temperature gauges in 30 seconds to insure temperature is within safe limits.	4.04	1.64
Scan the list of batting records in Sunday sports section to see who scored the most runs.	2.35	.89
20. *Control Precision*		
Drill a tooth.	5.96	1.07
Manipulate farm tractor controls.	3.71	1.08
Throw a light switch.	1.25	.52
21. *Multilimb Coordination*		
Play drum set in a jazz band.	5.74	1.10
Operate a forklift truck in the warehouse.	4.07	1.36
Operate a sewing machine with a foot treadle.	2.86	1.46

APPENDIX C *Continued*

Selected ability–task items	Mean	Standard deviation
22. *Response Orientation*		
In a spacecraft out of control, quickly choose one of 5 possible corrections in 0.7 seconds.	6.52	.74
Operate a busy switchboard where you must plug calls in and out quickly and accurately every few seconds.	4.83	1.31
When a doorbell and telephone ring simultaneously, select one to answer first in one second.	2.93	1.22
23. *Rate Control*		
Operate aircraft controls to land a jet on aircraft carrier in turbulent weather.	6.46	.92
Keep up with a car you are following where the speed of the first car may vary.	3.64	1.22
Ride a bicycle alongside a runner.	2.39	1.23
24. *Reaction Time*		
Hit back the ball which has been slammed at you in a ping-pong game.	5.48	1.18
Duck to miss being hit by a snowball thrown from across the street.	3.62	1.37
Start to apply brakes on your car 1 second after the light turns red.	2.28	1.13
25. *Arm–Hand Steadiness*		
Cut facets in diamonds.	6.32	.77
Thread a needle.	4.14	1.24
Light a cigarette.	1.71	.85
26. *Manual Dexterity*		
Perform open heart surgery.	6.75	.52
Package oranges in crates as rapidly as possible.	4.07	1.39
Tie a necktie.	2.43	.96
27. *Finger Dexterity*		
Play a classical flamenco piece on the guitar.	5.79	1.60

(*continued*)

APPENDIX C *Continued*

Selected ability–task items	Mean	Standard deviation
Untie a knot in a long-awaited package.	3.54	1.37
Put coins in a parking meter.	1.46	.79
28. *Wrist–Finger Speed*		
Send Morse code messages using a manual telegraph key at 25 words per minute.	5.34	1.14
Scramble eggs with a fork.	3.00	1.36
Use a pencil sharpener.	1.97	1.18
29. *Speed of Limb Movement*		
Play bongo drums in a band.	5.52	1.33
Swat a fly with a fly swatter.	4.21	1.78
Saw through a thin piece of wood.	2.28	.96
30. *Selective Attention*		
Study for a math exam in a house of noisy, young children.	5.45	1.50
Listen to a news broadcast during a dinner conversation.	4.10	1.32
Have a conversation with a friend at a noisy cocktail party.	2.69	1.37
31. *Time Sharing*		
As air traffic controller, monitor a radar scope to keep track of all inbound and outbound planes during a period of heavy, congested traffic.	6.07	.98
Monitor several teletypes at the same time in a newsroom.	4.76	1.18
Watch street signs and road while driving 30 miles per hour.	3.31	1.54
32. *Static Strength*		
Lift up the front end of a V.W.	6.15	1.26
Push open a stuck door.	3.30	1.10
Lift a dining room chair.	1.48	.70
33. *Explosive Strength*		
Win the shot-put event in the Olympics.	6.39	.92
Drive a golf ball 200 yards.	3.96	1.53
Shoot a marble.	1.00	.0

APPENDIX C *Continued*

Selected ability–task items	Mean	Standard deviation
34. *Dynamic Strength*		
Win the rings event in the U.S. gymnastic finals.	6.81	.80
Do 25 push-ups.	4.43	1.53
Squeeze fresh oranges to make orange juice.	1.57	.74
35. *Trunk Strength*		
Do 100 sit-ups.	6.46	.92
While lying on one's back, raise the legs off the floor for 5 seconds; repeat 10 times.	4.57	1.35
Sit up in a reclining chair.	2.32	1.66
36. *Extent Flexibility*		
Win a limbo championship.	6.04	1.40
Reach for something on the top shelf.	3.46	1.20
Reach for a soda in the back of a refrigerator.	2.0	1.25
37. *Dynamic Flexibility*		
Do the butterfly stroke in a championship swim competition at the Olympics.	6.11	1.26
Shovel coal in a furnace.	3.93	1.59
Fill a bag with shells at the seashore.	2.21	1.23
38. *Gross Body Coordination*		
Perform a skilled ballet dance like Swan Lake.	6.29	1.05
Jump rope for 5 minutes without tripping or stopping.	4.54	1.20
Get around an obstacle course with no time limit.	2.54	1.48
39. *Gross Body Equilibrium*		
Ride a surfboard when waves average 10 feet.	6.32	.82
Walk on ice across a 25 foot pond.	4.11	1.59
Stand on a ladder.	2.0	1.39
40. *Stamina*		
Bicycle 20 miles to work.	6.07	.96

(*continued*)

APPENDIX C *Continued*

Selected ability–task items	Mean	Standard deviation
Mow a small yard.	2.43	.84
Walk around the block.	1.18	.39
41. *Near Vision*		
Read the fine print of legal journals.	5.89	.90
Cut and mount color film transparencies.	4.67	.97
Plug in a TV set.	1.44	.62
42. *Far Vision*		
Detect differences in ocean vessels on the horizon.	6.50	.62
Drive a moving van across country.	4.33	1.03
Mop a long, wide hallway.	1.44	.70
43. *Visual Color Discrimination*		
Paint a portrait from a living subject.	6.00	.91
Match wood grains in a lumber yard.	3.72	1.18
Wash soiled sheets and linens.	1.50	.71
44. *Night Vision*		
Catch lightning bugs on a summer evening.	5.41	1.47
Take notes during a slide presentation.	4.33	1.64
Examine the positions of pieces on a chessboard.	2.89	1.40
45. *Peripheral Vision*		
Monitor the instrument panel of a jet aircraft.	4.44	1.95
Monitor opponent's position while returning tennis serve.	3.89	1.74
Transcribe handwritten notes onto formal record sheets.	3.15	1.94
46. *Depth Perception*		
Thread a needle.	5.37	2.00
Operate a construction crane.	4.15	1.35
Judge which of two distant buildings is closer.	3.04	1.74
47. *Glare Sensitivity*		
Snow ski in bright sunlight.	5.89	1.12
See boats on the horizon when sailing.	4.63	1.60
Drive nails with a hammer.	3.41	1.42

APPENDIX C *Continued*

Selected ability–task items	Mean	Standard deviation
48. *General Hearing*		
Identify a bird species by its call.	5.93	1.36
Monitor electronic equipment at a nurses' station.	4.11	1.87
Notice the carriage return bell while typing.	2.11	1.22
49. *Auditory Attention*		
Receive Morse code in a noisy radio room.	6.04	1.09
Listen for your flight announcement at an airport.	4.70	1.44
Locate someone calling you in a heavily wooded area.	2.30	1.54
50. *Sound Localization*		
Locate someone calling your name in the midst of a crowd.	5.15	1.61
Find a ringing telephone in an unfamiliar apartment.	3.70	1.73
Take legal dictation.	2.74	1.58
51. *Speech Hearing*		
Understand instructions regarding the statistical analysis of a very complex data set.	5.67	1.44
Locate someone calling you in a heavily wooded area.	3.74	1.68
Have a friendly telephone conversation.	1.56	1.19
52. *Speech Clarity*		
Present a financial status report to an executive board.	5.52	1.22
Discuss a news item with a friend.	3.59	1.12
Call the numbers in a bingo game.	1.56	1.25

[1]Adapted with permission from (1) Fleishman, E. A. *Development of ability requirements scales for the analysis of Bell System jobs.* Bethesda, MD.: Management Research Institute, 1975; (2) Fleishman, E. A. & Hogan, J. C. A taxonomic method for assessing the physical requirements of jobs: The physical abilities analysis approach (ARRO Final Report 3012/R78-7). Washington, D.C.: Advanced Research Resources Organization, June 1978; (3) Hogan, J. C., Ogden, G. D., & Fleishman, E. A. *Assessing physical requirements for establishing medical standards in selected benchmark jobs* (ARRO Final Report 3012/R78-8). Washington, D.C.: Advanced Research Resources Organization, June 1978; and (4) Schemmer, F. M. *Development of rating scales for selected visual, auditory and speech abilities* (ARRO Final Report 3064). Washington, D.C.: Advanced Research Resources Organization, June 1982.

APPENDIX D

Task Characteristic Rating Scales[1]

1. Scale for NUMBER OF OUTPUT UNITS

The entire purpose of the task is to create output units. *An output unit is the end produce resulting from the task.* Output units can take different forms. For example, sometimes the output unit is a physical *object* assembled from several parts. It may also take the form of a *relationship* between two or more things, e.g., drive three car-lengths behind the car in front of you. An output unit might also be a *destination*, e.g., run from here to the corner, with the corner being the destination.

First, identify what the output unit(s) is in the present task. Now, judge the *number* of such output units that someone performing this task is supposed to produce.

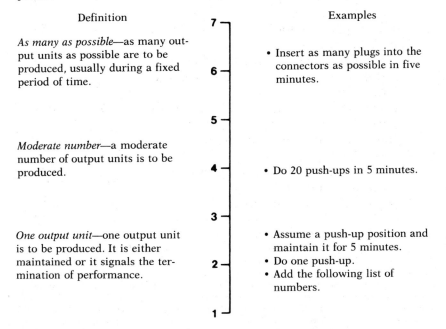

Definition		Examples

As many as possible—as many output units as possible are to be produced, usually during a fixed period of time.
— 7
— 6
• Insert as many plugs into the connectors as possible in five minutes.
— 5

Moderate number—a moderate number of output units is to be produced.
— 4
• Do 20 push-ups in 5 minutes.
— 3

One output unit—one output unit is to be produced. It is either maintained or it signals the termination of performance.
— 2
• Assume a push-up position and maintain it for 5 minutes.
• Do one push-up.
• Add the following list of numbers.
— 1

[1]Adapted with permission from (1) Farina, A. J., & Wheaton, G. R. *Development of a taxonomy of human performance: The task characteristics approach to performance pre-*

2. Scale for DURATION FOR WHICH AN OUTPUT UNIT IS MAINTAINED

Once the operator has produced an output unit he may be required to maintain or continue it for one of several time periods. For example, it can be maintained for as long as possible. Another alternative is that completing one output unit is a signal to leave it and go on to produce the next output unit. Or, having produced the output unit, performance ends.

Decide where the present output units belong on the below scale.

Definition

Maintenance for as long as possible—an output unit (body position, stimulus–control relationship, etc.) is to be maintained for as long as possible.

Moderate maintenance—relative to other possible periods of maintenance, an output unit is to be maintained for a moderate period of time.

Short maintenance—production of an output unit signals the end of performance or the production of additional units. Maintenance, therefore, is minimal time.

Examples

7 —

• Hang in a bent-arm position for as long as possible.

6 —

• Maintain a stimulus–control relationship for 20 minutes.

5 —

• Maintain a stimulus–control relationship for 5 minutes.

4 —

• Do as many push-ups as possible in 10 minutes, holding each "down" position for 30 seconds.

3 —

2 —

• Solve the following trigonometric problems.

1 —

diction (Tech. Rep. AIR-726/2035-2/71-TR7). Silver Spring, M.D., American Institutes for Research, February 1971; (2) Wheaton, G. R., & Mirabella, A. *Effects of task index variations on training effectiveness criteria* (NAVTRAEQUIPCEN 71-L-0059-1). Orlando, FL: Naval Training Equipment Center, October 1972; and (3) Wheaton, G. R., Mirabella, A., & Farina, A. J., Jr. *Trainee and instructor Task quantification: Development of quantitative indices and a predictive methodology* (NAVTRADEVCEN 69-C-0278-1). Orlando, FL: U.S. Naval Training Device Center, January 1971.

3. Scale for NUMBER OF ELEMENTS PER OUTPUT UNIT

One way of describing an output unit is in terms of the number of elements involved in its production. By elements we mean the parts or components which comprise the output unit. In an addition problem, for example, the numbers to be added are the elements which comprise the output unit. In a more physical task, the elements could be parts to be assembled or apparatus to be manipulated.

Rate the present task on the scale below in terms of the number of elements entering into a single output unit.

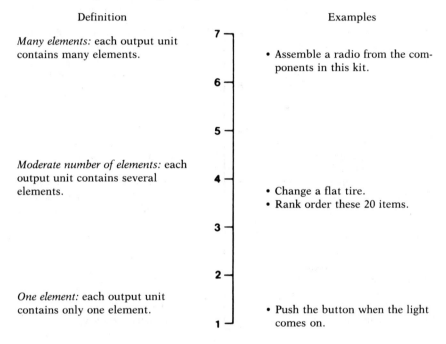

Definition		Examples
Many elements: each output unit contains many elements.	7	• Assemble a radio from the components in this kit.
	6	
	5	
Moderate number of elements: each output unit contains several elements.	4	• Change a flat tire. • Rank order these 20 items.
	3	
	2	
One element: each output unit contains only one element.	1	• Push the button when the light comes on.

4. Scale for WORK LOAD

Word load refers to the number of output units to be produced relative to the time allowed for their production. We are interested in the ratio of the number of output units per unit time. For example, make 5 widgets in 10 minutes = 1 widget produced every two minutes.

However, there are tasks in which the goal is to *maintain* a situation rather than to produce multiple output units. For example, a driving task where you are to stay within 40 feet of the vehicle ahead of you. For these types of tasks, work load refers to the length of time for which maintenance is required. The longer the maintenance period, the higher the work load.

Therefore, rating a task in terms of work load resolves to answering one of two questions:

1. How much has to be produced in what amount of time; or
2. How long does this situation have to be maintained or continued?

Definitions		Examples

High word load—as many output units as possible are to be produced in a fixed period of time; a relatively large number of output units is to be produced in a relatively short period of time; an output unit is to be maintained for a relatively long time or for as long as possible.

7 —
6 —
5 —

• Drive as many nails as possible in five minutes.
• Maintain a stimulus–control relationship as long as possible.

Moderate word load—a moderate number of output units is to be produced in a reasonable period of time; an output unit is to be maintained for a moderate period of time relative to other possible periods.

4 —
3 —

• Drive 10 nails in 5 minutes.
• Maintain a stimulus–control relationship for 3 minutes.

Low work load—a small number of output units is to be produced in a relatively long period of time; an output unit is to be maintained for a relatively short period of time.

2 —
1 —

• Drive these two nails in the next five minutes.
• Sum the following five numbers.
• Maintain a stimulus–control relationship for 30 seconds.

5. Scale for DIFFICULTY OF GOAL ATTAINMENT

Difficulty of goal attainment is a function of two things: (1) the number of elements in an output unit, and (2) the degree of work load (both these terms have been previously defined). The greater the work load and the higher the number of elements, the more difficult is the goal.

Definition   Examples

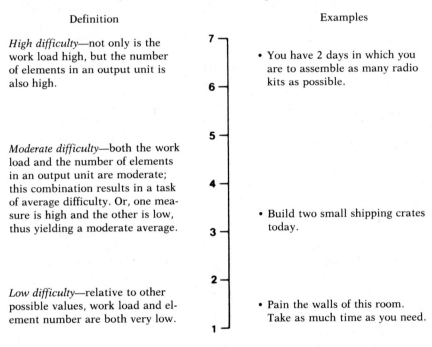

High difficulty—not only is the work load high, but the number of elements in an output unit is also high.

7

• You have 2 days in which you are to assemble as many radio kits as possible.

6

5

Moderate difficulty—both the work load and the number of elements in an output unit are moderate; this combination results in a task of average difficulty. Or, one measure is high and the other is low, thus yielding a moderate average.

4

3

• Build two small shipping crates today.

2

Low difficulty—relative to other possible values, work load and element number are both very low.

• Pain the walls of this room. Take as much time as you need.

1

6. Scale for **PRECISION OF RESPONSES**

Tasks may differ in terms of how precise or exact the operator's responses must be. Judge the degree of precision involved in the present task by considering the *most* precise response made in producing an output unit.

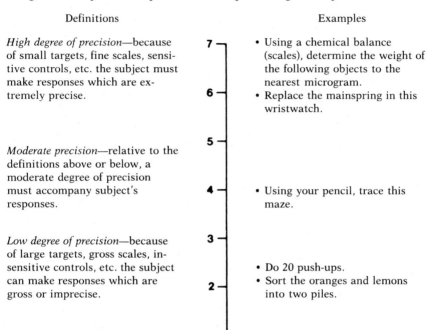

Definitions

Examples

High degree of precision—because of small targets, fine scales, sensitive controls, etc. the subject must make responses which are extremely precise.

7 — 6 —

• Using a chemical balance (scales), determine the weight of the following objects to the nearest microgram.
• Replace the mainspring in this wristwatch.

Moderate precision—relative to the definitions above or below, a moderate degree of precision must accompany subject's responses.

5 — 4 —

• Using your pencil, trace this maze.

Low degree of precision—because of large targets, gross scales, insensitive controls, etc. the subject can make responses which are gross or imprecise.

3 — 2 — 1 —

• Do 20 push-ups.
• Sort the oranges and lemons into two piles.

7. Scale for **RESPONSE RATE**

Responses can be made at different rates. That is, the frequency with which responses must be made can vary from task to task. For example, you would have a higher rate of responding if you were playing a singles game of tennis than if you were playing chess. The responses would come more frequently in the first case than in the second. You are to judge what rate of responding is called for in producing *one* output unit in the task being judged.

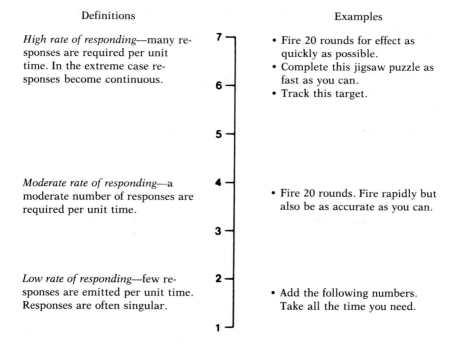

Definitions

High rate of responding—many responses are required per unit time. In the extreme case responses become continuous.

Moderate rate of responding—a moderate number of responses are required per unit time.

Low rate of responding—few responses are emitted per unit time. Responses are often singular.

Examples

- Fire 20 rounds for effect as quickly as possible.
- Complete this jigsaw puzzle as fast as you can.
- Track this target.

- Fire 20 rounds. Fire rapidly but also be as accurate as you can.

- Add the following numbers. Take all the time you need.

8. Scale for SIMULTANEITY OF RESPONSES

The responses which the operator makes in producing an output may involve one of more effectors (e.g., hand, foot, arm, voice, etc.). Depending upon the task, these effectors may or may not be used *simulatneously*. For example, both hands (two effectors) are used simultaneously in playing a piano.

You are to rate the degree of simultaneity involved in using the effectors needed for the response(s).

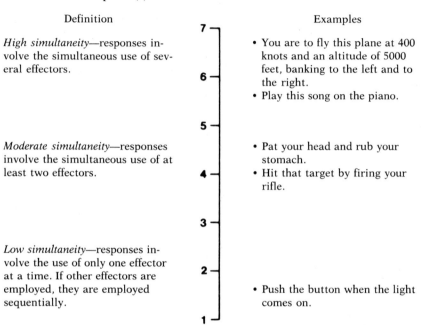

		Examples

Definition

7

High simultaneity—responses involve the simultaneous use of several effectors.

6

• You are to fly this plane at 400 knots and an altitude of 5000 feet, banking to the left and to the right.
• Play this song on the piano.

5

Moderate simultaneity—responses involve the simultaneous use of at least two effectors.

4

• Pat your head and rub your stomach.
• Hit that target by firing your rifle.

3

Low simultaneity—responses involve the use of only one effector at a time. If other effectors are employed, they are employed sequentially.

2

• Push the button when the light comes on.

1

9. Scale for **DEGREE OF MUSCULAR EFFORT INVOLVED**

This dimension considers the amount of muscular effort required to perform the task. Examine the task and identify the most physically strenuous part of it. Rate this part on the scale below.

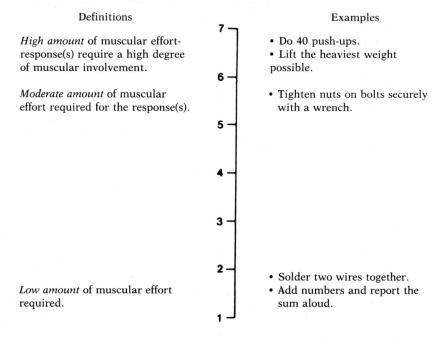

Definitions

High amount of muscular effort-response(s) require a high degree of muscular involvement.

Moderate amount of muscular effort required for the response(s).

Low amount of muscular effort required.

Examples

7
• Do 40 push-ups.
• Lift the heaviest weight possible.
6
• Tighten nuts on bolts securely with a wrench.
5

4

3

2
• Solder two wires together.
• Add numbers and report the sum aloud.
1

10. Scale for NUMBER OF PROCEDURAL STEPS

Earlier we were concerned about the number of elements, i.e., objects or components, involved in the production of one output unit. Now we want to consider the number of procedural steps (responses) needed to produce one output unit. There isn't a necessary one-to-one relationship between objects and responses.

Consider the number of responses or steps involved in producing one output unit for the present task. Rate this task on the scale below.

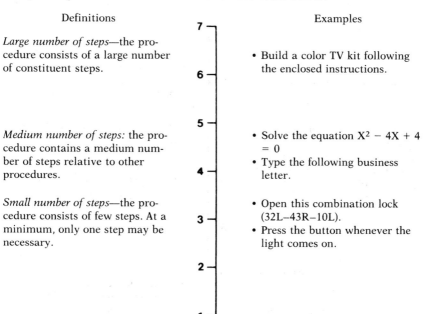

Definitions

Large number of steps—the procedure consists of a large number of constituent steps.

Medium number of steps: the procedure contains a medium number of steps relative to other procedures.

Small number of steps—the procedure consists of few steps. At a minimum, only one step may be necessary.

Examples

• Build a color TV kit following the enclosed instructions.

• Solve the equation $X^2 - 4X + 4 = 0$
• Type the following business letter.

• Open this combination lock (32L–43R–10L).
• Press the button whenever the light comes on.

11. Scale for DEPENDENCY OF PROCEDURAL STEPS

Consider again the number of steps (responses) involved in producing one output unit. The steps may be described in terms of the dependency among them; *dependency concerns the extent to which the steps must be done in some specified order.* For example, dependency exists between steps A and B if step B cannot be accomplished without step A being done first. *Note:* Procedures which have only one step are automatically low in dependency.

Definition		Examples

High dependency among steps— each step in the procedure is completely dependent upon the preceding procedural step. Systematic ordering of steps is at a maximum.

7 —

6 —

- Using the combination you've been given, open the safe.
- Dial this telephone number.

Moderate dependency among steps—in the total number of steps comprising the procedure, approximately 50% are dependent upon preceding steps.

5 —

4 —

- Using colored blocks, stack them into columns four blocks high. Do this in the order red and green for the first two blocks. The remaining blocks may be of any color.

3 —

Low dependency among steps—procedural steps are not organized in any particular sequence. Step "A" may precede "B" or "B" may precede "A". Procedures having one step are low in dependency.

2 —

1 —

- Using colored blocks, stack them into columns four blocks high. Order of color is unimportant.

12. Scale for ADHERENCE TO PROCEDURES

Tasks may vary in the extent to which the operator must faithfully adhere to the procedures set forth. In some types of tasks strict adherence is critical; in others, the operator may depart somewhat from stated procedures without jeopardy to the performance.

Judge the degree of adherence to stated procedures for the present task.

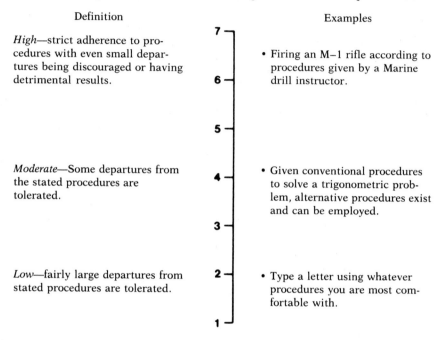

Definition

High—strict adherence to procedures with even small departures being discouraged or having detrimental results.

Moderate—Some departures from the stated procedures are tolerated.

Low—fairly large departures from stated procedures are tolerated.

Examples

• Firing an M–1 rifle according to procedures given by a Marine drill instructor.

• Given conventional procedures to solve a trigonometric problem, alternative procedures exist and can be employed.

• Type a letter using whatever procedures you are most comfortable with.

13. Scale for **PROCEDURAL COMPLEXITY**

Procedural complexity is a function of the number of steps or responses
leading to an output unit and the degree of dependency among these steps.
Rate the present task in terms of its procedural complexity.

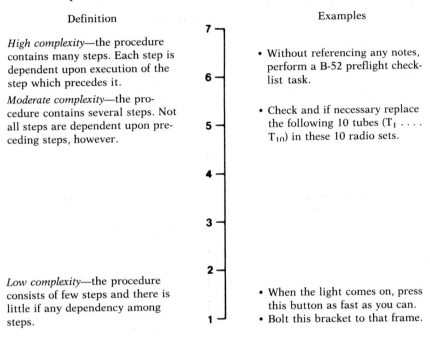

Definition

High complexity—the procedure
contains many steps. Each step is
dependent upon execution of the
step which precedes it.

Moderate complexity—the procedure contains several steps. Not
all steps are dependent upon preceding steps, however.

Low complexity—the procedure
consists of few steps and there is
little if any dependency among
steps.

Examples

• Without referencing any notes,
  perform a B-52 preflight checklist task.

• Check and if necessary replace
  the following 10 tubes (T_1 . . . .
  T_{10}) in these 10 radio sets.

• When the light comes on, press
  this button as fast as you can.
• Bolt this bracket to that frame.

14. Scale for VARIABILITY OF STIMULUS LOCATION

Judge the degree to which the physical location of the stimulus or stimulus complex is predictable over task time.

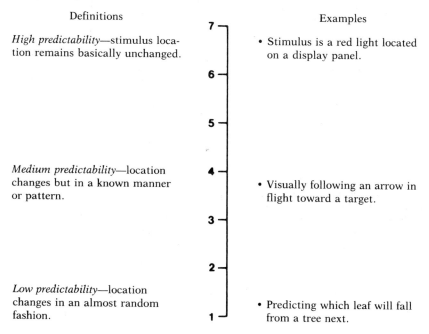

Definitions

High predictability—stimulus location remains basically unchanged.

Medium predictability—location changes but in a known manner or pattern.

Low predictability—location changes in an almost random fashion.

Examples

• Stimulus is a red light located on a display panel.

• Visually following an arrow in flight toward a target.

• Predicting which leaf will fall from a tree next.

7

6

5

4

3

2

1

15. Scale for STIMULUS OR STIMULUS-COMPLEX DURATION

Consider the critical stimulus or stimulus-complex to which the operator must attend in performing the task. Relative to the total task time, for how long a duration is the stimulus or stimulus complex present during the task?

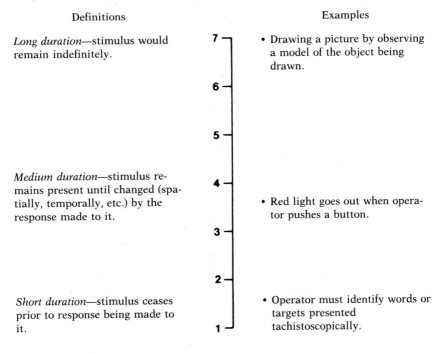

Definitions

Long duration—stimulus would remain indefinitely.

Medium duration—stimulus remains present until changed (spatially, temporally, etc.) by the response made to it.

Short duration—stimulus ceases prior to response being made to it.

Examples

• Drawing a picture by observing a model of the object being drawn.

• Red light goes out when operator pushes a button.

• Operator must identify words or targets presented tachistoscopically.

16.   Scale for REGULARITY OF STIMULUS OCCURRENCE

Consider the critical stimulus or stimulus complex to which the operator must attend. Does it occur at regular (i.e., equal) intervals or at irregular intervals? Treat regular intervals and constant presence of the stimulus as equivalent conditions.

Rate the present task on this dimension.

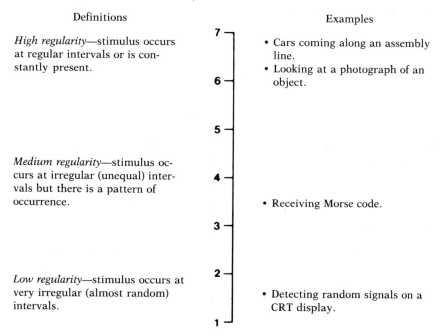

Definitions

High regularity—stimulus occurs at regular intervals or is constantly present.

Medium regularity—stimulus occurs at irregular (unequal) intervals but there is a pattern of occurrence.

Low regularity—stimulus occurs at very irregular (almost random) intervals.

Examples

7

6

5

4

3

2

1

• Cars coming along an assembly line.
• Looking at a photograph of an object.

• Receiving Morse code.

• Detecting random signals on a CRT display.

17. Scale for OPERATOR CONTROL OF THE STIMULUS

What degree of control does the operator have over either the occurrence or relevance of the stimulus?

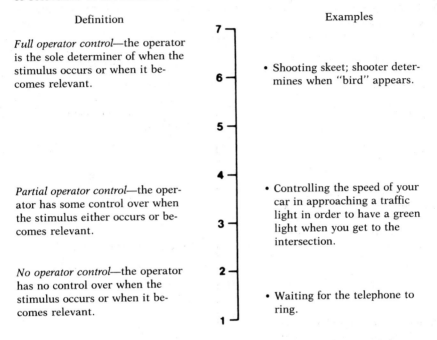

Definition		Examples
Full operator control—the operator is the sole determiner of when the stimulus occurs or when it becomes relevant.	7 6 5	• Shooting skeet; shooter determines when "bird" appears.
Partial operator control—the operator has some control over when the stimulus either occurs or becomes relevant.	4 3	• Controlling the speed of your car in approaching a traffic light in order to have a green light when you get to the intersection.
No operator control—the operator has no control over when the stimulus occurs or when it becomes relevant.	2 1	• Waiting for the telephone to ring.

18. Scale for **OPERATOR CONTROL OF THE RESPONSE**

Given the occurrence of the stimulus, what degree of control does the operator have over when he must initiate response?

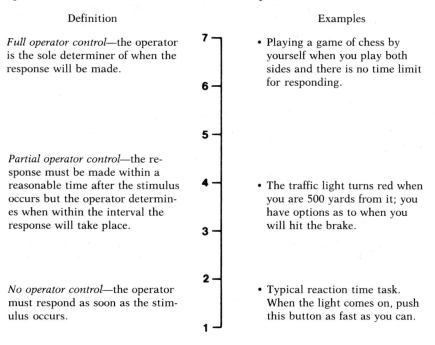

| | Definition | Examples |

Definition

Full operator control—the operator is the sole determiner of when the response will be made.

Partial operator control—the response must be made within a reasonable time after the stimulus occurs but the operator determines when within the interval the response will take place.

No operator control—the operator must respond as soon as the stimulus occurs.

Examples

• Playing a game of chess by yourself when you play both sides and there is no time limit for responding.

• The traffic light turns red when you are 500 yards from it; you have options as to when you will hit the brake.

• Typical reaction time task. When the light comes on, push this button as fast as you can.

19. Scale for REACTION TIME/FEEDBACK LAG RELATIONSHIP

What relationship exists between the operator's reaction time interval (i.e., the time between stimulus appearance and initiation of the operator's response) and the time lag interval occurring before feedback (i.e., knowledge of the effects of the response) begins? Note carefully that the two intervals of interest are formed by the *initiation* of the stimulus, response, and feedback, as in the following diagram:

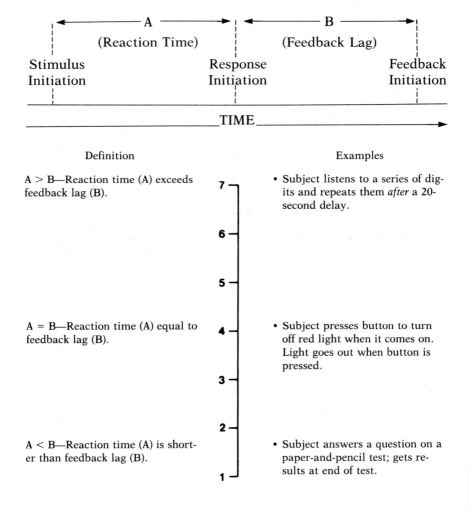

Definition	Examples
A > B—Reaction time (A) exceeds feedback lag (B).	• Subject listens to a series of digits and repeats them *after* a 20-second delay.
A = B—Reaction time (A) equal to feedback lag (B).	• Subject presses button to turn off red light when it comes on. Light goes out when button is pressed.
A < B—Reaction time (A) is shorter than feedback lag (B).	• Subject answers a question on a paper-and-pencil test; gets results at end of test.

20. Scale for FEEDBACK

For present purposes the term FEEDBACK refers to information which an operator may get about the correctness of a response. In this scale we are interested in *how quickly feedback occurs* once the response is made.

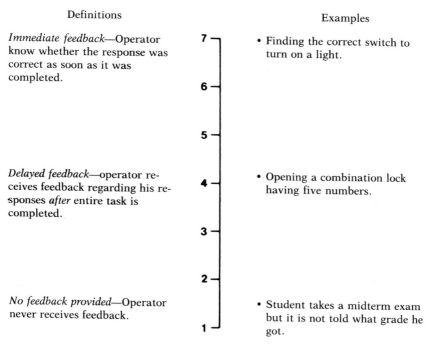

Definitions

Immediate feedback—Operator know whether the response was correct as soon as it was completed.

Delayed feedback—operator receives feedback regarding his responses *after* entire task is completed.

No feedback provided—Operator never receives feedback.

Examples

7

• Finding the correct switch to turn on a light.

6

5

4

• Opening a combination lock having five numbers.

3

2

1

• Student takes a midterm exam but it is not told what grade he got.

21. Scale for DECISION MAKING

The task instructions guide the operator in producing an output unit. Frequently, the steps leading to the output unit are not of an "A–B–C" nature, but instead they involve choice-points where the operator must decide which of several potential steps should be done next. He bases his choice on the outcome of the last step. For example, the instructions might say, "Press button A and observe the outcome; if a red light comes on, throw the red switch. If the blue light comes on, throw the blue switch." The key feature of this situation is that the operator must decide what to do next on the basis of the feedback or outcome of his last response.

Rate the present task on the extent to which it contains choice-points in the steps leading to an output unit.

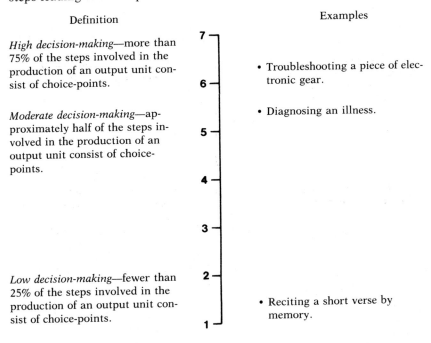

Definition

High decision-making—more than 75% of the steps involved in the production of an output unit consist of choice-points.

Moderate decision-making—approximately half of the steps involved in the production of an output unit consist of choice-points.

Low decision-making—fewer than 25% of the steps involved in the production of an output unit consist of choice-points.

Examples

7

6   • Troubleshooting a piece of electronic gear.

5   • Diagnosing an illness.

4

3

2

1   • Reciting a short verse by memory.

Author Index

Numbers in italics show the page on which the complete reference is cited.

Subject Index

A

Abilities
  derivation of, 138–146, 149, 153–169, 306–314
  identified, 163–167, 322–325, 329, 461–464
  measurement system, 312–327
  task examples of, 465–473
Abilities Analysis, *see* Ability Requirements Scales
Ability
  defined, 153, 162
Ability Rating Procedures, *see* Ability Requirements Scales
Ability Requirements/Ability Requirements Approach, 11, 14, 53–55, 73, 82, 92, 153–169, 178, 179, 205, 221, 238, 264, 266, 306–353, 425
  conceptual basis, 306–308
  effects of drugs, 340–342
  effects of noise, 342–346
  evaluation of, 332–350, 428–429
  in job analysis, 344–345
  in laboratory task development, 340–344
  measurement systems, 312–327
  in predicting learning, 336–340, 346
  in predicting performance levels, 336–340, 346
  relation to task requirements, 430–436
  reliability studies, 315–317
  in setting medical standards, 345–346
  in setting performance standards, 345

  in test development, 344–345
  use in integrating research data, 332–336
  validity, 321, 326–327
Ability Requirements Scales
  definitions, 322–325, 461–469
  development of, 317–330
  evaluation of, 332–344
  use in classifying jobs and tasks, 344–349
Adjustment–Emotionality
  defined, 398
Advanced Research Resources Organization (ARRO), 346
Aerobic Capacity, *see* Stamina
Affective Domain, 397–398, 407
Aging, 154
Aiming
  defined, 165
Alcohol
  effects on performance, 190, 203, 205, 335–336
Alderfer's ERG Theory, 412–415
Alertness, 161
Alluisi's Critical Functions, 102, 133–135
American Psychiatric Association's Diagnostic and Statistical Manual (DSM III), 387–388
Anoxia, 167
Anxiety, 387
Aptitude, *see* Abilities
Arm–Hand Steadiness, 165, 314, 326
  defined, 325, 463
  tasks representing, 469